'This text is a timely contribution to the field of sustainable entreprene of increasing importance to our global society. The book offers novel e conceptually-derived insights into the motivations and challenges of sustai neurship, and proposes potential solutions for leading and inspiring real e action toward a more sustainable economy. With an impressive collection c scholars, the chapters explore contemporary sustainable entrepreneurship i graphical, cultural, and industry contexts, applying a range of theoretic book will be of value to academics, researchers, policy makers, and practiti

Prof. Colette Henry, Dundalk Institute of Technol

'Sustainable entrepreneurship can help to resolve the environmental and so that our postmodern society is facing. Thinking about sustainability when creating, and seizing entrepreneurial opportunities and being prepared to act able entrepreneur become more and more important in a globalised world. I book, Adam Lindgreen and his colleagues address a number of key issues in sustainable entrepreneurship, identifying, for example, the intentions and behind sustainable entrepreneurship, or examining the role of entrepreneuri fostering and enacting sustainability. For the editors and authors of the book, entrepreneurship is mainly a matter of education, training, and leadership and the way to show how to develop sustainable entrepreneurial action. I heart mend this book to both academics and practitioners.'

Distinguished prof. Alain Fayolle, Direct
Entrepreneurship Research Centre, emlyon busine

'The real work of sustainable entrepreneurship is just now starting. This anth great place to begin in grasping the depth and breadth of this new inspiring of research. You will find a focused and clearly articulated coverage of the key sustainable entrepreneurship. It encourages your personal critical reflections an exploration of how sustainable entrepreneurs can save planet earth for future gen A must-read for everyone.'

Gjalt de Jong, Prof. of Sustainable Entrepren
in a Circular Economy, University of Gro

'This book focuses on the relatively unexplored research field of sustainable preneurship. It addresses a variety of questions such as: What are the intentio motivations of sustainable entrepreneurs? What are their actual practices in differe of the world? And why can they be considered future-oriented leaders? The broac of contributions makes this book worth reading.'

Jacqueline Cramer, Prof. of Sustai
Innovation, Utrecht Univ

Sustainable Entrepreneurship

The way organizations manage entrepreneurship has changed dramatically over the past decade. Today, organizations take account of economic issues, but they also adopt a broader perspective of their purpose including social and environmental issues (i.e. sustainability). Yet, despite its global spread, sustainable entrepreneurship remains an uncertain and poorly defined ambition with few absolutes.

This book reaffirms the important need to improve comprehension and explore the subtleties of how individuals, groups, and organizations can discover, create, and seize opportunities for blended value generation, by designing and operating sustainable ventures. It examines, in an interdisciplinary fashion and across sectoral and geographical boundaries, how entrepreneurial activities can be developed to be generally consistent with sustainable development goals, as well as by whom, for what reasons, and with what implications. The Editors comprehensively review key dimensions of the sustainable entrepreneurship phenomenon to establish an essential definition and up-to-date picture of the field. The 19 chapters cover 4 main topics:

- Understanding the intentions and motivations for sustainable entrepreneurship
- Fostering and enacting sustainability through entrepreneurial action
- Leading and inspiring sustainable entrepreneurial action
- Contextually grounded implications and challenges for sustainable entrepreneurship and blended value generation

This book is an important resource for entrepreneurs and policy makers, as well as students in the fields of entrepreneurship, innovation, and sustainability.

Dr. Adam Lindgreen is Professor at Copenhagen Business School where he heads the Department of Marketing. He is also Extra Ordinary Professor with University of Pretoria's Gordon Institute of Business Science. Dr. Lindgreen received his PhD from Cranfield University. He has published in *California Management Review*, *Journal of Business Ethics*, *Journal of Product and Innovation Management*, *Journal of the Academy of Marketing Science*, and *Journal of World Business*, among others.

Dr. François Maon is Associate Professor at IESEG School of Management. He received his PhD from Université catholique de Louvain, Belgium. Dr. Maon has published in *California Management Review*, *Journal of Business Ethics*, and *International Journal of Management Reviews*, among others.

Dr. Christine Vallaster is Professor at the University of Applied Sciences in Salzburg. Dr. Vallaster received her post-doctoral qualification from the University of Innsbruck, Austria. She has published in *California Management Review, Journal of Business Research, European Journal of Marketing*, and *Journal of World Business*, among others.

Dr. Shumaila Yousafzai is Associate Professor at Cardiff University, UK. Her research focuses on the contextual embeddedness of entrepreneurship, institutional theory, and entrepreneurial orientation. She is the Associate Editor of *Journal of Small Business Management* and has extensively published in various international journals. She has also co-edited a special issue on Women's entrepreneurship for *Entrepreneurship & Regional Development* and edited volumes on women's entrepreneurship with Edward Elgar and Routledge.

Dr. Beatriz Palacios Florencio is Associate Professor at Pablo de Olavide University at Seville. Her main research is corporate social responsibility and tourism. She has published in *Journal of Business Research, Total Quality Management & Business Excellence, Management Decision, and Environmental Engineering and Management Journal*, among others.

Sustainable Entrepreneurship

Discovering, Creating and Seizing Opportunities for Blended Value Generation

Edited by Adam Lindgreen, François Maon, Christine Vallaster, Shumaila Yousafzai and Beatriz Palacios Florencio

Routledge
Taylor & Francis Group
LONDON AND NEW YORK

First published 2019
by Routledge
2 Park Square, Milton Park, Abingdon, Oxon OX14 4RN

and by Routledge
711 Third Avenue, New York, NY 10017

Routledge is an imprint of the Taylor & Francis Group, an informa business

British Library Cataloguing-in-Publication Data
A catalogue record for this book is available from the British Library

Library of Congress Cataloging-in-Publication Data
A catalog record has been requested for this book

ISBN: 9781472483591 (hbk)
ISBN: 9781315611495 (ebk)

Typeset in Bembo
by Swales & Willis Ltd, Exeter, Devon, UK

MIX
Paper from responsible sources
FSC www.fsc.org FSC® C013056

Printed and bound in Great Britain by
TJ International Ltd, Padstow, Cornwall

For Christine, François, Joëlle, Martin, and Michael, collaborating with you over the years has been great fun—Adam

For my family—Christine

For my grandfathers Eugene and Emile—François

For Ferhat, a loving friend and a wonderful father to the four little people in our life—Shumaila

For my sisters Gema and Raquel—Beatriz

Contents

Figures

Tables

Editors

Adam Lindgreen

After studies in chemistry (Copenhagen University), engineering (the Engineering Academy of Denmark), and physics (Copenhagen University), Adam Lindgreen completed an MSc in food science and technology at the Technical University of Denmark. He also finished an MBA at the University of Leicester, UK. Professor Lindgreen received his PhD in marketing from Cranfield University, UK. His first appointments were with the Catholique University of Louvain (2000–2001), Belgium, and Eindhoven University of Technology (2002–2007), the Netherlands. Subsequently, he served as Professor of Marketing at Hull University's Business School (2007–2010); University of Birmingham's Business School (2010), where he also was the research director in the Department of Marketing; and University of Cardiff's Business School (2011–2016), all in the UK. Under his leadership, the Department of Marketing and Strategy at Cardiff Business School ranked first among all marketing departments in Australia, Canada, New Zealand, the UK, and the United States, based upon the hg indices of senior faculty. Since 2016, he has been Professor of Marketing at Copenhagen Business School, where he also heads the Department of Marketing. Since 2018, he is also Extra Ordinary Professor with University of Pretoria's Gordon Institute of Business Science, South Africa, as well as Visiting Professor with University of Northumbria's Newcastle Business School, UK.

Professor Lindgreen has been a visiting professor with various institutions, including Georgia State University, USA, Groupe HEC in France, and Melbourne University, Australia. His publications have appeared in *Business Horizons, California Management Review, Entrepreneurship and Regional Development, Industrial Marketing Management, International Journal of Management Reviews, Journal of Advertising, Journal of Business Ethics, European Journal of Marketing, Journal of Business and Industrial Marketing, Journal of Marketing Management, Journal of the Academy of Marketing Science, Journal of Product Innovation Management, Journal of World Business, Psychology & Marketing*, and *Supply Chain Management: An International Journal*, among others.

Professor Lindgreen's books include *A Stakeholder Approach to Corporate Social Responsibility* (with Kotler, Vanhamme, and Maon), *Managing Market Relationships, Memorable Customer Experiences* (with Vanhamme and Beverland), *Not All Claps and Cheers* (with Maon, Vanhamme, Angell, and Memery), *Sustainable Value Chain Management* (with Maon, Vanhamme, and Sen), and *Women Entrepreneurs and the Myth of 'Underperformance'* (with Yousafzai, Fayolle, Henry, Saeed, and Sheikh).

The recipient of the "Outstanding Article 2005" award from *Industrial Marketing Management* and the runner-up for the same award in 2016, Professor Lindgreen serves on the board of several scientific journals; he is co-editor-in-chief of *Industrial Marketing*

Management and previously was the joint editor of the *Journal of Business Ethics*' section on corporate responsibility. His research interests include business and industrial marketing management, corporate social responsibility, and sustainability. Professor Lindgreen has been awarded the Dean's Award for Excellence in Executive Teaching. Furthermore, he has served as an examiner (for dissertations, modules, and programs) at a wide variety of institutions, including the Australian National University, Unitec, University of Amsterdam, University of Bath's Management School, University of Lethbridge, and University of Mauritius.

Professor Lindgreen is a member of the International Scientific Advisory Panel of the New Zealand Food Safety Science and Research Centre (a partnership among government, industry organizations, and research institutions), as well as of the Chartered Association of Business Schools' Academic Journal Guide Scientific Committee in the field of marketing.

Beyond these academic contributions to marketing, Professor Lindgreen has discovered and excavated settlements from the Stone Age in Denmark, including the only major kitchen midden – Sparregård – in the south-east of Denmark; because of its importance, the kitchen midden was later excavated by the National Museum and then protected as a historical monument for future generations. He is also an avid genealogist, having traced his family back to 1390 and published widely in scientific journals (*Personalhistorisk Tidsskrift*, *The Genealogist*, and *Slægt & Data*) related to methodological issues in genealogy, accounts of population development, and particular family lineages.

Christine Vallaster

Christine Vallaster studied international business and management at University of Innsbruck, Austria, where she also received her post-doctoral qualification (habilitation) in 2009. Her research was supported by DFG Deutsche Forschungsgemeinschaft and Humboldt Stiftung, among others. During her academic career, Professor Vallaster has held permanent full- or part-time jobs in Austria and Liechtenstein. In addition, she has held or currently holds visiting professorships at University of Bolzano, Italy; University of Würzburg, Germany; and IAE Buenos Aires, Argentina. She is a Professor at the University of Applied Sciences, Salzburg, Austria, where she heads the department of Marketing and Relationship Management. Her qualitative research broadly pertains to strategic corporate brand management and social responsibility/sustainability in an entrepreneurial context. Professor Vallaster examines these two research topics mainly from an internal perspective, reflecting her continued focus on aligning internal processes. She has published in *Journal of World Business*, *Journal of Business Research*, *California Management Review*, *European Journal of Marketing*, *Industrial Marketing Management*, and *Journal of Marketing Management*, among others. She serves on the editorial board of *Corporate Social Responsibility and Environmental Management*. Her book on *Connective Branding* has been endorsed by leading academics in this field (David Aaker and Majken Schultz), as well as by notable businesspeople working for companies such as Patagonia and Hilti. Her latest research revolves around efforts to measure the impact of sustainability practices. In this role, Professor Vallaster is a Research Associate at the University of the Armed Forces in Munich, Germany. She also works as a Consultant for corporate brand management and has helped companies in China, Austria, and Germany develop and implement marketing and brand strategies. She started her consulting career with Bain & Co. in Hong Kong and China.

François Maon

François Maon received his PhD in 2010 from Catholic University of Louvain's Louvain School of Management, Belgium. After a visiting scholarship at the University of California, USA, he is now an Associate Professor at IESEG School of Management, France, where he teaches strategy, business ethics, and corporate social responsibility. In his research, Dr. Maon focuses mainly on topics linked to corporate social responsibility, learning, implementation, and change-related processes; cross-sector social partnerships; and stakeholder influence strategies. He has published articles in various international journals such as *California Management Review, European Journal of Marketing, European Management Review, International Journal of Management Reviews, Journal of Business Ethics,* and *Supply Chain Management: An International Journal*. Dr. Maon has co-edited several special issues of academic journals and books, including *A Stakeholder Approach to Corporate Social Responsibility* and *Not All Claps and Cheers*. He serves on the editorial boards of *Business and Society* and *M@n@gement* and is the founder of the IESEG Center for Organizational Responsibility (ICOR).

Shumaila Yousafzai

Shumaila Yousafzai is an Associate Professor (Reader) at Cardiff University's Business School, UK, where she teaches entrepreneurship, marketing, and consumer behaviour. After her undergraduate studies in physics and mathematics at the University of Balochistan, Pakistan, and earning an MSc in electronic commerce from Coventry University, UK, Dr. Yousafzai finished her PG diploma in research methods and then her PhD in 2005, both from Cardiff University, UK. In her research, Dr. Yousafzai focuses mainly on topics linked to the contextual embeddedness of entrepreneurship, firm performance, institutional theory, and entrepreneurial orientation. She has published articles in various international journals such as *Entrepreneurship Theory and Practice, Journal of Small Business Management, Industrial Marketing Management, Technovation, Journal of Business Ethics, Psychology & Marketing, Journal of Applied Social Psychology*, and *Computers in Human Behavior*. She is the associate editor of *Journal of Small Business Management* and has co-edited a special issue of *Entrepreneurship & Regional Development* on women's entrepreneurship.

Beatriz Palacios Florencio

Beatriz Palacios Florencio is an Associate Professor at the University Pablo de Olavide, Spain. She has been a visiting professor at the University Facsul Uniao Metropolitana-Unime, Spain, and Cardiff University's Business School, UK. Dr. Florencio is a member of the research group Red Hispano-Lusa de Investigadores en Turismo and serves as the area coordinator of social corporate responsibility for the European Academia of Firm Management and Economics. Her research spans two principal lines: corporate social responsibility and tourism. She has published in journals such as *Journal of Business Research, Internet Research, Management Decision, Total Quality Management & Business Excellence*, and *Environmental Engineering and Management Journal*. Dr. Florencio has also taken part in national projects, as well as being an assessor for contracts with private firms.

Contributors

Martin Angerer is Assistant Professor of Finance at the University of Liechtenstein. He received his PhD from the University of Innsbruck, Austria. He has published in *Experimental Economics, Schmalenbach's Business Review, Journal of Risk Finance*, and *Journal of Entrepreneurial Finance and Sustainability*, among others. His research interests include experimental finance, behavioural finance, crowdfunding, blockchain technology, pension finance, and entrepreneurial finance. Dr. Angerer teaches finance courses in several European countries, as well as in Bangkok, Thailand.

Tamsin Angus-Leppan completed a PhD in corporate social responsibility in 2010. She currently works part time as the project coordinator for the OLT-funded Learning & Teaching Sustainability website and as a senior researcher in the School of Management at the University of Technology Sydney, working on circular economy and sustainability education research. Dr. Tamsin previously served as an Associate Lecturer and Research Associate in the School of Marketing and Management at the University of Technology Sydney and as project leader on several projects for ARIES.

Suzanne Benn is Professor of Sustainable Enterprise in the University of Technology Sydney's Business School. She was previously Professor of Education for Sustainability, Director of ARIES, and Head of the Graduate School of the Environment at Macquarie University, Australia. Dr. Benn has backgrounds in both the sciences and the social sciences. She has wide experience working across the range of educational sectors and as a research and industrial scientist. Her current research interests include corporate sustainability and corporate social responsibility, business education for sustainability, and organizational change and development for sustainability. Her interdisciplinary academic publications include 4 books and more than 100 refereed journal articles, book chapters, and conference papers.

Nancy M.P. Bocken is Professor of Sustainable Business Management and Practice at the International Institute for Industrial Environmental Economics at Lund University, Denmark. She is also Associate Professor at Delft University of Technology, the Netherlands, and a fellow with the Cambridge Institute for Sustainability Leadership, UK. Dr. Bocken's main sustainability-related research interests involve business models, business experimentation, innovation for sustainability, scaling up sustainable businesses, and closing the idea–action gap. Interwoven with her academic work, Dr. Bocken regularly advises a range of organizations across sectors and continents, as well as various sustainability start-up initiatives. She co-founded HOMIE, which develops and tests circular business models, starting with pay-per-use home appliances. Before entering academia, Dr. Bocken held positions in the logistics, banking, and consulting sectors. Originally from the Netherlands, she has lived and worked in France, the UK, the United States, and now Sweden. Dr. Bocken holds a PhD in Engineering from the University of Cambridge, UK.

René Bohnsack is Assistant Professor of Strategy and Innovation at Católica-Lisbon, Portugal. Before joining Católica-Lisbon, Dr. Bohnsack was an Assistant Professor at the University of Amsterdam Business School and a research fellow with the University of St. Gallen, Switzerland. He earned his PhD from University of Amsterdam. Dr. Bohnsack researches the diffusion of sustainable innovations and has published in *Research Policy, Journal of Business Venturing, Journal of Product Innovation Management, California Management Review*, and *Technological Forecasting & Social Change*, among others. Dr. Bohnsack also is the founder and director of the Smart City Innovation Lab (www.smartcityinnovationlab.com), a multi-disciplinary research unit developing cutting-edge knowledge about how to create well-being in urban areas through sustainable technologies and digital transformations.

Juan D. Borrero is Associate Professor of Management in the Department of Management & Marketing, Huelva University, Spain. He obtained his PhD in economics from Huelva University in 2002, and he is now Director of the Social Entrepreneurship Laboratory (SimpleLab) and Director of the Agricultural Economics Research Group at Huelva University. He also earned an MBA, has degrees in agronomics engineering (Cordoba University, Spain) and law (Huelva University), and is a founder of the spin-off Bo True Activities. His current research interests include entrepreneurship, social entrepreneurship, digital social networks, big data, and the Internet of Things.

Rob Boyle is Assistant Professor of Management and a member of the Entrepreneurship Teaching Team in the John Cook School of Business at Saint Louis University, USA. Dr. Boyle received his PhD from Saint Louis University and earned a Certificate in Social Entrepreneurship from the United States Association for Small Business and Entrepreneurship. He has published in *Journal of Applied Management and Entrepreneurship, Verbum Incarnatum*, and *International Journal of Business and Management Studies*. His research interests include servant leadership, employee transitions, and entrepreneurial service excellence. He is on the board of directors for multiple non-profit organizations and is a member of the Board of Advisors for 4Pure, Inc.

Janina Burtscher currently is a business administration student at the University of Liechtenstein, majoring in entrepreneurship and international management. During her studies and research, she has focused on sustainable entrepreneurship. Her work has been published in *Sustainability*.

David Coldwell is Professor of Management and HRM in the School of Economic and Business Sciences at University of the Witwatersrand in Johannesburg, South Africa. He is a Fellow of the Chartered Institute of Personnel and Development (London) and an accredited National Research Foundation researcher. He has published in *Journal of Business Ethics, Journal for the Theory of Social Behavior, International Journal of Cross Cultural Management*, and *Entropy*. He has co-edited *Business Research Methods* (Juta, 2004); contributed chapters to *Handbook of Research on Knowledge Management* (Edward Elgar, 2014), *Corporate Social Responsibility and Sustainability* (Emerald, 2014), and *Encyclopedia of Business and Professional Ethics* (Springer, 2017); and is an associate editor of *Personnel Review*.

Edwin B.P. de Jong is an Assistant Professor in the Department of Anthropology and Development Studies at Radboud University, the Netherlands. His research focuses on nature and natural resource politics, corporate social responsibility, sustainability, and livelihoods. He heads the interdisciplinary research program "New Indonesian Frontiers: Stuck between market, state, civil society and the contest over natural resources". He has published on these topics in *Journal of Business Ethics, Wetlands, Critical Asian Studies*, and *Journal of Southeast Asian Studies*, among others.

Mara Del Baldo is Associate Professor of Financial Accounting, Entrepreneurship and Small Business Management, and Economics of Sustainability and Accountability at University of Urbino, Italy. She is a member of the European Council for Small Business, Centre for Social and Environmental Accounting Research, SPES Forum, Global Corporate Governance Institute, and European Business Ethics Network, among others. She is an editorial board member and reviewer for various international scientific journals. She has published in *Accounting History, Meditari Accountancy Research, European Journal of International Management, International Journal of Social Ecology and Sustainable Development, International Journal of Society Systems Science, Journal of Management and Governance*, and *International Journal of Corporate Social Responsibility*, among others.

Lori DiVito is an Associate Professor at Amsterdam School of International Business and has teaching affiliations with Amsterdam Business School, University of Amsterdam, and Manchester Business School, UK. She received her PhD from Manchester Business School with a dissertation that performed a comparative analysis of innovation systems and institutional entrepreneurship among pharmaceutical biotechnology start-ups in the UK and the Netherlands. Dr. DiVito's research focuses on interfirm relations in contexts marked by the emergence and growth of high-tech/biotech firms and collective action in sustainable entrepreneurship. She is currently engaged in a project, the Alliance for Responsible Denim, funded by the Dutch government, in which she studies in real time how competitors collaborate to improve sustainability and realize systemic change. Her work has been published in *Journal of Business Venturing, Research Policy, Long Range Planning*, and *Academy of Management Proceedings*.

Shuili Du is Associate Professor of Marketing at the Peter T. Paul College of Business and Economics, USA. She received her PhD in Marketing from the Questrom School of Business, Boston University, USA. Dr. Du's research expertise lies in understanding the various ways corporate social responsibility and sustainability initiatives create business value. Her research has appeared in many premier journals, including *Journal of Consumer Research, Management Science, Harvard Business Review, International Journal of Research in Marketing, International Journal of Management Review, Journal of Product Innovation Management*, and others.

Melissa Edwards is a senior Lecturer in the Business School at University of Technology Sydney. She researches and teaches in the areas of sustainable enterprise, the circular economy, social impact, and complexity. Her work is transdisciplinary and directed toward understanding how people organize, learn, and adapt to sustainable transitions. Her current research focuses on the circular economy, the professionalization of corporate sustainability, systemic approaches to social impact, the development of proactive stakeholder relationships, and learning for sustainability. Her work has been published in various books and journal articles, and she led the development of an online sharing community of practice, through the platform www.sustainability.edu.au.

Martin Hingley is Professor of Strategic Marketing at Lincoln University's International Business School, UK. His current research interests focus on corporate social responsibility reporting, marketing and supply chain management, power in interfirm and network relations, the interface of marketing and purchasing, and local and regional network marketing. He has published widely in journals including *Industrial Marketing Management, Journal of Marketing Management, Supply Chain Management: An International Journal*, and *Entrepreneurship and Regional Development*, as well as four joint edited books in the Food and Agricultural Marketing series (Gower-Routledge).

Jessica J. Jones is a PhD candidate at the University of Colorado, USA, studying entrepreneurship and management. Her research interests include topics related to entrepreneurial knowledge, entrepreneurial identity, and social entrepreneurship. She focuses on understanding how entrepreneurial solutions promote the sustainability and scalability of new products and services that promote social and environmental impact. Prior to beginning at University of Colorado, Ms. Jones was the Assistant Director for the Page Center for Entrepreneurship at Miami University, USA. She also has worked in a variety of global and local entrepreneurial contexts focused on entrepreneurial solutions to poverty.

Rita Klapper is Senior Assistant Professor at the Copernicus Institute of Sustainable Development at Utrecht University, the Netherlands. Prior to this she was a Senior Lecturer in entrepreneurship and small business at Liverpool John Moore University, UK. She specializes in insider perspectives on entrepreneurship and sustainable enterprise, sustainable enterprise education and responsible management education, and the roles of values and leadership in non-secular contexts.

Luuk Knippenberg is an Assistant Professor at the Institute for Science, Innovation and Society at Radboud University, the Netherlands. His research focuses on the social, political, and economic aspects of corporate social responsibility, sustainable development, nature and biodiversity, ecosystem services, and social-ecological transformations. Dr. Knippenberg has co-headed and chaired the EU FP7 research project Biomot, investigating motivations to act for biodiversity, and he has published on these subjects in *Environmental Conservation, Journal of Environmental Management*, and *Journal of Business Ethics*, among others.

Jonas Kolenberg is a recent graduate of the Master's Program in Anthropology and Development Studies at Radboud University, the Netherlands. His research focuses on sustainable governance arrangements through intersectoral collaborations in global value chains. He has been working in the field of agricultural and community development in Southeast Asia for Oxfam. He currently works as a consultant, specializing in circular business design and corporate sustainability in the Dutch building sector.

Sacha Kraus is a Research Professor for Innovation & Entrepreneurship at ESCE International Business School, France. Prior to that, he was a Full Professor and Chair in Strategic Management and Entrepreneurship at the University of Liechtenstein, and, parallel to that, Visiting Professor at Copenhagen Business School, Denmark, in 2015, and at the University of St. Gallen, Switzerland. He holds a doctorate in Social and Economic Sciences from Klagenfurt University, Austria; a PhD degree in Industrial Engineering and Management from Helsinki University of Technology; and a Habilitation (Venia Docendi) from Laapeenranta University of Technology, both in Finland.

J. Howard Kucher is an Assistant Professor in the Brown School of Business and Leadership at Stevenson University, USA, where he teaches social and commercial entrepreneurship, marketing, management, sales, project management, and product development. Previously, Dr. Kucher was the Founding Executive Director of Entrepreneurship Programs at the University of Baltimore, USA, where he led the Baltimore Social Enterprise Collaborative. Dr. Kucher has successfully secured over $70 million in working capital on behalf of mission-oriented enterprises and assisted more than 100 nonprofits and social enterprises in developing new models to meet the needs of their constituents while increasing the sustainability of their organizations.

Fernando Lourenço is an Assistant Professor at the Institute for Tourism Studies in Macao. In 2009, he was awarded the National Enterprise Educators Award (UK). He has published in *International Small Business Journal, Business Ethics: A European Review, International Journal of Social Research Methodology, International Journal of Entrepreneurial Behaviour and Research, Journal of Small Business and Enterprise Development,* and *International Journal of Entrepreneurship and Innovation*, among others. Dr. Lourenço's research interests include entrepreneurship, opportunity identification, creativity, sustainability, ethics, corporate social responsibility, education, creative industries, tourism, and hospitality. He also is involved in a range of entrepreneurial activities in Macao.

Chris I. Martin is Research Fellow at the Earth Surface Science Institute at the University of Leeds, UK. Prior to this he was a Research Associate in the Department of Geography at Durham University, UK. His research explores the processes and politics of environmental innovation in cities. Dr. Martin's work has focused on innovations including the sharing economy, the development of smart-sustainable urban districts, and the development of novel forms of green-blue infrastructure in cities.

Rosario Michel-Villarreal is an Associate Lecturer and PhD student at University of Lincoln's International Business School, UK. Her research focus is on the organization and its relationship to the sustainability of rural farmers, resilience, and small enterprises in sustainable supply chain arrangements. She received a BSc (with distinction) in industrial and systems engineering and an MEng in quality systems and productivity from Tecnológico de Monterrey, Mexico.

Moreno Muffatto is Professor of Entrepreneurship and Coordinator of the Management and Entrepreneurship Research Group in the Department of Industrial Engineering, University of Padova, Italy. He currently supervises one post- and two PhD students. He is the team leader of Global Entrepreneurship Monitor Italy and the founder and director of the School of Entrepreneurship, Research Innovation and Entrepreneurship Forum, as well as the International Summer School on Entrepreneurship and Innovation. His research focuses on cross-cultural entrepreneurship, institutional conditions, and entrepreneurial ecosystems and has been published in a range of quality outlets.

Andrew Ngawenja Mzembe is a Lecturer in sustainable business models at NHTV Breda University of Applied Sciences, the Netherlands. Dr. Mzembe received his PhD from University of Huddersfield, UK. His research interests include sustainable business models and corporate social responsibility. Some of his work on corporate social responsibility and sustainable business models has appeared in edited books and journals in the field of business and management.

Robert Perey is a Research Associate with the Centre for Business and Social Innovation in the Management Discipline group at University of Technology Sydney. Previously, he was a program manager in the Australian Research Institute in Education for Sustainability at Macquarie University. Dr. Perey's work is transdisciplinary, focusing on organizational and societal change. He has worked on projects ranging from biodiversity awareness in culturally and linguistically diverse communities (CALD); sustainability case study development for inclusion in MBA programs; and investigating emerging business models, which promote circular flows of resources that include waste as a valuable product. Dr. Perey's work has been published in books and journal articles, and his research interests centre on ecological sustainability, complexity, social imaginaries, aesthetics, and the degrowth economy.

Saadat Saeed is Associate Professor of Entrepreneurship in the Durham University Business School, UK. His research focuses on cross-cultural entrepreneurship, adversity, and innovative outcomes and has been published in a range of journals including *Entrepreneurship Theory and Practice*, *Journal of Small Business Management*, and *Industrial Marketing Management*. He also guest edited a special issue of *Entrepreneurship & Regional Development* and has edited books on entrepreneurship. He is part of the Global Entrepreneurship Monitor Team.

Michael T. Schaper is currently Deputy Chairman of the Australian Competition & Consumer Commission, as well as the author of numerous books including *Making Ecopreneurs: Developing Sustainable Entrepreneurship*. Dr. Schaper previously managed a community small business centre; served as an adviser to both state and federal governments; and held lecturing, professorial, and dean roles at multiple business schools in Australian universities. He is also a previous president of the Small Enterprise Association of Australia & New Zealand, served as Small Business Commissioner for the Australian Capital Territory government, and in 2009 was named the "national champion" by the Council of Small Business Organisations of Australia. Dr. Schaper is currently an Adjunct Professor with Curtin University and Western Sydney University in Australia.

Sankar Sen is the Lawrence and Carol Zicklin Chair in Corporate Integrity and Governance at Baruch College/City University of New York. Dr. Sen's research interests lie at the intersection of sustainability and consumer behaviour. His book, *Leveraging Corporate Responsibility: The Stakeholder Route to Maximizing Business and Social Value*, was published by Cambridge University Press. Dr. Sen's research has appeared in both academic (e.g. *Journal of Business Ethics*, *Journal of Consumer Research*, *Journal of Economic Theory*, *Journal of Marketing Research*, *Journal of Marketing*, and *Management Science*) and practitioner (e.g. *California Management Review*, *Sloan Management Review*, *McKinsey Quarterly*, and *Business Horizons*) journals, and he serves as an associate editor of the *Journal of Consumer Research* and on the editorial boards of *Journal of Marketing*, *Journal of Public Policy & Marketing*, *Journal of Consumer Psychology*, *Academy of Marketing Science Review*, and *Corporate Reputation Review*.

Valérie Swaen is Professor of Marketing and Corporate Social Responsibility at the Louvain School of Management, Belgium, and at IESEG School of Management, France. She studied corporate social responsibility in different management fields (marketing, organizational behaviour, strategy, leadership, and accounting), but her main research interest pertains to stakeholders' reactions to corporate social responsibility communication. She has published in journals such as *Journal of Management, Journal of Management Studies, Marketing Letters, Journal of Business Ethics*, and *International Journal of Management Reviews*, among others. She is the co-editor of *Journal of Business Ethics*' section on corporate social responsibility–quantitative issues.

Paul Upham is Chair of Human Behaviour and Sustainable Development at Leuphana University, Germany, and Visiting Professor at the Copernicus Institute of Sustainable Development at Utrecht University, the Netherlands. He is also affiliated with the Sustainability Research Institute at University of Leeds, UK, and has been visiting Professor in governance of energy systems and climate change at the Finnish Environment Institute. Dr. Upham works on energy technology governance, particularly public opinion and engagement.

Robert Venter is a senior lecturer in the School of Economic and Business Sciences, University of the Witwatersrand Johannesburg, South Africa, and holds a sessional lectureship at the Wits Business School, South Africa. He received his PhD from the same university. His major research interest is development entrepreneurship, with a particular emphasis on the intersection of economic inclusivity and sustainability, as well as enterprise development and entrepreneurial ethics. He has published mainly on entrepreneurship in the informal economy and has co-edited three books for Oxford University Press: *Entrepreneurship Theory in Practice, Labour Relations in South Africa*, and *Project Management in Perspective*.

Eliseo Vilalta-Perdomo is a Senior Lecturer in operations and logistics management at University of Lincoln's International Business School, UK. His current research focuses on how to improve individual and collective performance simultaneously. His research approach involves the exploration of human and technological interfaces across different supply arrangements, with the aim of developing sustainable, resilient communities of micro-producers. He has extensive international professional experience, in both government and private sectors. He has published in *Journal of the Operational Research Society*.

Zhifang Wu is a research fellow at the University of South Australia's Business School. She received her PhD from University of South Australia. She has published in *Australasian Journal of Environmental Management, Journal of Water Reuse and Desalination*, the MDPI open access journal *Water, Water Resources Management*, and *Water Policy*, among others. Dr. Wu also has published book chapters with Springer Nature, Taylor & Francis Group, Edward Elgar, and others. She serves as an editorial board member for *Modern Management Forum*. Her research interests include community attitudes and behaviours; water policies, laws, and institutions; water entrepreneurs; governance of "new" waters including treated storm water, recycled wastewater, and desalinated water; and water taxes, levies, and pricing.

Mirella Yani-de-Soriano is a senior lecturer in marketing at Cardiff University, UK. She had managerial and consultancy experience, gained with international corporations such as The Gillette Company, before joining academia. Her research focuses on consumer behaviour, particularly in the areas of cross-cultural consumer research, emotions in consumption and retail environments, online consumer behaviour, anti-consumption, and addiction behaviour. Her work has been published in international journals such as *Journal of Business Research, Journal of Business Ethics, Psychology & Marketing, Journal of Small Business Management*, and *Computers in Human Behavior.*

Jeffrey G. York is Associate Professor of Strategy and Entrepreneurship and Shane Faculty Scholar at the University of Colorado, USA. He received his PhD from the Darden School of Business at University of Virginia, USA. Dr. York's teaching and research focus on environmental entrepreneurship, as well as the simultaneous creation of ecological and economic goods. He is interested in how and why entrepreneurs create new products, services, and industries that reduce environmental degradation. Dr. York has published in *Academy of Management Journal, Academy of Management Review, Journal of Business Venturing, Organization Science*, and *Strategic Management Journal.* He serves as a field editor for the *Journal of Business Venturing* and sits on the editorial boards of *Academy of Management Journal, Entrepreneurship Theory & Practice*, and *Strategic Entrepreneurship Journal.*

Foreword and acknowledgments

Business organizations in many sectors face increasing environmental and social challenges. Despite extensive economic growth and wide-ranging improvements to the overall quality of life in the past century or so, this era also has imposed detrimental, adverse effects on the natural environment, and the benefits are not shared equally by everyone. Thus, issues involving climate change, plummeting biodiversity, resource scarcity, food insecurity, rising inequality, and poverty rank high on the global agenda.

In this context, the growing importance of sustainable development concerns and ideas—emerging as perhaps the most prominent topic of our time—generates not only new risks and responsibilities for business but also new opportunities. Stakeholders expect businesses to meet a triple bottom line, of economic, environmental, and social value creation (Elkington, 1997). Scholars claim that entrepreneurial action can contribute constructively to enhanced global development (Dean and McMullen, 2007; Hart and Milstein, 2003; Schaltegger, Lüdeke-Freund and Hansen, 2016) that can meet "the needs of the present without compromising the ability of future generations to meet their own needs" (WECD, 1987). In this sense, entrepreneurship mechanisms and processes that explicitly revolve around ideas and issues related to sustainable development may offer a central mechanism to help address deep, complex social and environmental challenges.

Sustainable entrepreneurship in this perspective represents a vital, growing area of entrepreneurship and management studies. In a broad sense, the relatively recent notion of sustainable entrepreneurship relates to the innovative behaviors of business actors in sustainability contexts, such that it can be linked to various other notions and phenomena, including corporate sustainability, corporate social responsibility, corporate citizenship, the creation of shared value, or social entrepreneurship. From a more detailed perspective, though the definitions vary, sustainable entrepreneurship is essentially a proactive and innovation-oriented business approach, aimed at "generating competitive advantage by identifying sustainability as new business opportunities, resulting in new and sustainable products, methods of production or ways of organizing business processes in a sustainable way" (Lans, Blok, and Wesselink, 2014: 37).

To create ventures that are commercially viable but also purposefully advance the causes of environmental protection and social justice (Munoz and Dimov, 2015), such that they create value that is simultaneously economic, social, and environmental (Emerson, 2003; Kickul, Janssen-Selvadurai, and Griffiths, 2012), entrepreneurs first must recognize the existence of a sustainability-related entrepreneurial opportunity, then determine that this opportunity is one they want to pursue (Shepherd, McMullen, and Jennings, 2008). Beyond the discovery dimension, sustainable entrepreneurship relates to the "creation, and exploitation of opportunities to create future goods and services that sustain the natural and/or communal environment and provide development gain for others" (Patzelt and Shepherd, 2011: 632). It pertains to a holistic integration, by individuals and teams, of the blended goals of economic, social, and environmental entrepreneurship into an organization that is sustainable in its objectives, operations, and wealth generation methods (Munoz and Cohen, 2018; Tilley and Young, 2009).

Sustainable entrepreneurship research in turn is concerned with "how opportunities to bring into existence future goods and services are discovered, created, and exploited, by whom, and with what economic, psychological, social, and environmental consequences" (Cohen and Winn, 2007: 35). In recent decades, this research field progressively has emerged as a dynamic perspective on the upwelling of potential business-driven solutions to social and environmental problems. Despite this substantial increase in academic interest though, the call "to explore the role of entrepreneurial action as a mechanism for sustaining nature and ecosystems while providing economic and non-economic gains for investors, entrepreneurs and societies" (Shepherd and Patzelt, 2011: 138) remains vivid and forceful. Empirical research into sustainable entrepreneurship is lacking; extensive calls cite the need to design and adopt methodological approaches that can deal with the relevant phenomena in a more holistic fashion, so that scholars can advance empirically informed, robust theoretical developments. That is, "aside from its aspirational appeal, there remains a lack of understanding of the nature of the [sustainable entrepreneurship] phenomenon and the future of sustainable entrepreneurship in theory and practice" (Munoz and Cohen, 2018: 300).

With this research anthology, we reaffirm the important need to improve comprehension and explore the subtleties of how individuals, groups, and organizations can discover, create, and seize opportunities for blended value generation, by designing and operating sustainable ventures. This anthology examines, in an interdisciplinary fashion and across sectoral and geographical boundaries, how entrepreneurial activities can be developed to be generally consistent with sustainable development goals (Pacheco, Dean, and Payne, 2010), as well as by whom, for what reasons, and with what implications. In the 19 chapters that constitute it, this anthology comprehensively reviews key dimensions of the sustainable entrepreneurship phenomenon to establish an essential definition and up-to-date picture of the field. In particular, the 19 chapters cover four main topics:

- Understanding the intentions and motivations for sustainable entrepreneurship
- Fostering and enacting sustainability through entrepreneurial action
- Leading and inspiring sustainable entrepreneurial action
- Contextually grounded implications and challenges for sustainable entrepreneurship and blended value generation

Understanding the intentions and motivations for sustainable entrepreneurship

In the first part of this research anthology, four chapters address central questions: What drives and what impedes efforts by "entrepreneurs who start a business to serve both self-interests and collective interests by addressing unmet social and environmental needs" (Hoogendoorn, van der Zwan, and Thurik, 2017: 1)? Sustainable entrepreneurs respond to specific motivators and require distinct abilities and skill sets, related to delivering the sustainability-oriented business and organizational outcomes; they also likely encounter specific challenges and opportunities (Bacq, Hartog, and Hoogendoorn, 2016; Kirkwood and Walton, 2010; Parrish, 2010).

For example, educational support may be critical to entrepreneurs' emergence, so in "The role of perceived university support in the formation of students' entrepreneurial intention," Saadat Saeed, Shumaila Y. Yousafzai, Mirella Yani-de-Soriano, and Moreno Muffatto propose an integrative, multi-perspective framework in which three dimensions of university support—perceived educational support, concept development support, and business development support—together with institutional support, shape students' entrepreneurial self-efficacy. This self-efficacy, along with individual motivations, then should drive intentions to start a business. They find that perceived educational support exerts the strongest influence on entrepreneurial self-efficacy, followed by concept development support, business development support, and institutional support. Self-efficacy then has a significant effect on entrepreneurial intentions, together with individual motivations such as self-realization, recognition, and roles. Yet these intentions are not related to financial success, innovation, or independence. Still, this holistic perspective provides a more meaningful sense of how perceived university support can encourage students' entrepreneurial intentions.

Once they have decided to start their business, sustainable entrepreneurs need to determine how to balance social, environmental, and economic goals. The way they establish that balance might define different types of sustainable entrepreneurs. The authors study sustainable entrepreneur archetypes based on their motivations to start a venture and on their entrepreneurial orientation. To determine the "Motivations and entrepreneurial orientation of sustainable entrepreneurs: an exploratory study of sustainable entrepreneurship archetypes in the fashion industry," René Bohnsack and Lori DiVito undertake an exploratory study of 24 sustainable fashion firms that suggest four sustainable entrepreneurship archetypes: idealists, evangelists, realists, and opportunists. They differ in both their motivation and entrepreneurial orientations, signaling the need to consider what type of entrepreneur is in focus, in both research and practice.

Another typology emerges from the "Gender analysis of social entrepreneurial intention: a case of Morocco and Spain." Juan D. Borrero considers whether women and men from two regions (southern Spain and northern Morocco) express similar perceptions of social entrepreneurship. He examines their perceptions of social self-efficacy, passion, and intentions to start new social businesses, as well as the influences of these variables on entrepreneurial intentions. The comparative findings, obtained from university students from Spain and Morocco, reveal that social entrepreneurial self-efficacy and passion constitute antecedents of social entrepreneurial intention for both women and men, though the links are weaker for women. The gender differences also are greater in Spain, which is more developed and has a higher equality index than Morocco.

Finally, Chris I. Martin, Paul Upham, and Rita Klapper examine the UK nonprofit social enterprise Freegle, which is a sharing economy offshoot of Freecycle. This case study, offering a value-based characterization of sustainable entrepreneurship, draws on Schwartz's quantitative approach to the psychology of values, as well as interview data. In "Non-profit entrepreneurial activism: values, behaviour and sociotechnical dimensions of social entrepreneurship in the case of Freegle," these authors demonstrate that universalist and benevolent values are more strongly adopted among Freegle activists than the wider UK population; Freegle activists also exhibit stronger self-directive values, reflecting the need for autonomy and self-expression commonly associated with commercial entrepreneurs. These findings are particularly interesting in view of entrepreneurship perspectives that do not require profit maximization to be the primary motive. This chapter also can inform literature that applies sociotechnical transitions thinking to grassroots innovations.

Fostering and enacting sustainability through entrepreneurial action

In this part, five chapters focus on the development of entrepreneurial action, organizational capabilities, and business models that can ensure the emergence of ventures that are able to tackle sustainability-oriented challenges through commercial activities.

Noting the vast increase in research into the investor's perspective on sustainable investments since the global financial crisis, Sacha Kraus, Janina Burtscher, Christine Vallaster, and Martin Angerer start this part with a structure review of entrepreneurial and financial literature, "Sustainable entrepreneurship orientation: a reflection on status-quo research on factors facilitating responsible managerial practices." They identify three relevant levels that determine the successful implementation of sustainable practices. On an individual level, sustainable entrepreneurs derive a motive to act more sustainably from their personal values and traits. On an organizational level, small enterprises' internal cultures and resource reconfigurations determine whether they adopt a sustainable entrepreneurial orientation. On the contextual level, extant research provides insights into how entrepreneurs can help society and the environment through their sustainable entrepreneurship, acting as role models or change agents for the nascent practice of investing or financing on a sustainability basis. This overview of research findings thus offers a clearer understanding of how to implement and facilitate sustainable practices across various levels.

Calling for "Sustainable consumption through new business models: the role of sustainable entrepreneurship," Nancy M.P. Bocken argues that companies can drive sustainable consumption patterns with new business models. Using illustrative cases of car sharing and clothing reuse, she analyzes individual, social, and broader influence tactics, as well as the implemented business model strategies and their potential for mass-market success. These strategies include sharing instead of ownership, moderated sales and promotion, extended product life cycles, direct reuse, and full life cycle sufficiency. The new business models diffuse due to their scalability, replicability, integrability, and imitability, as well as their synergies, co-existence, and compatibility. Furthermore, value propositions that include multiple customer benefits can appeal to a wider customer group than just green consumers.

Another business activity that represents sustainable entrepreneurial action is the notion of the circular economy, which pursues opportunities related to limited resources and waste minimization. In an exploratory study, "Enacting sustainable entrepreneurial action for a circular economy," Melissa Edwards, Suzanne Benn, Tamsin Angus-Leppan, and Robert Perey interview businesspeople adopting circular economy approaches, then apply semantic analysis to determine how this model enables them to conceive of and enact entrepreneurial action, even in juxtaposition to a dominant linear economy. The challenges they encounter span two main categories: tensions, which they accept as insurmountable, and interesting, which appear implicit to their stewardship approach. Entrepreneurs in smaller organizations are more likely than intraprenuers within multinationals to leverage tensions to enact opportunities to design waste out of systems.

Another set of in-depth interviews provides the input for the chapter, "Policy entrepreneurs and sustainable water resources management in Australia: some empirical findings." Zhifang Wu seeks to explore the challenges to integrated urban water management in South Australia and thus interviewed 55 key actors, including senior urban water managers and planners from various public- and private-sector stakeholder groups. These informants cite institutional fragmentation, unclear ownership and access rights, unclear roles and responsibilities, and a lack of an integrated framework as critical barriers. Most of these identified challenges pertain to "new" water sources, such as treated stormwater, recycled wastewater, or desalinated water. The author also suggests some general recommendations for potential solutions to help urban water managers and strategists develop well-targeted legal, policy, and institutional programs.

In the last chapter in this part, David Coldwell and Robert Venter argue that sustainable entrepreneurship must be ethically imbued and driven by sustainability, such that it maintains natural capital even as it develops manufactured capital. Studying the case of South Africa, they describe "Integrated sustainable entrepreneurship: a view from the South" with examples of entrepreneurship in that part of the world, according to a heuristic in which ethically valid, integrated, sustainable entrepreneurship consists of balances among environmental, social, and economic aspects. With an integrated model of sustainable entrepreneurship, they offer a means for current generations to meet their triple bottom line needs without jeopardizing future generations' abilities to meet theirs.

Leading and inspiring sustainable entrepreneurial action

The third part of this research anthology addresses leadership questions associated with sustainable entrepreneurial action, considering how the actors involved in sustainable entrepreneurship can drive sustainable ventures and inspire others to challenge traditional business processes, confront the status quo, and leverage the creation of blended value. The four chapters in this part focus on how individuals and organizations can foster sustainable entrepreneurial action and potentially act as role models by "[shaping] markets and society substantially" (Schaltegger and Wagner, 2011: 223).

First, Jessica J. Jones and Jeffrey G. York turn to identity theory, which explains how role and social identity relate, and apply it to processes of sustainable entrepreneurship. In "Fitting in and standing out: an identity approach for sustainable entrepreneurs," the authors theorize about the social and role identities of sustainable entrepreneurs who focus on economic, social, and environmental goals, within an entrepreneurial accelerator setting. In particular, sustainable entrepreneurs might benefit from joining traditional, economically focused accelerators, but those benefits depend on entrepreneurs' ability to manage their various identities. With a process model, the authors propose that the relative salience or dissonance of role and social identities determines the emergence of sustainable ventures, positively or negatively.

Second, with the assertion that leadership has been insufficiently addressed as a key component of effective corporate social responsibility strategies or a means to explain the success of sustainable entrepreneurship, the chapter "The ethical and moral-based dimension of leadership in corporate social responsibility-oriented strategies and sustainable entrepreneurship" addresses leadership and its influences. Mara Del Baldo uses a deductive, literature-based approach to answer two central questions: How does leadership enhance CSR? Are ethical and virtue-based models of leadership effective for developing CSR and fostering sustainable entrepreneurship? With a critical review of different leadership approaches, the author links ethically and morally based leadership to both CRS and sustainable entrepreneurship discourses, thus deriving propositions about the relevance of an authentic orientation and moral- and virtues-based leadership.

Third, the next chapter investigates the interplay of leadership styles and institutional corporate social responsibility practices. In "The roles of leadership styles in corporate social responsibility," Shuili Du, Valérie Swaen, Adam Lindgreen, and Sankar Sen present the results of a large-scale field survey of managers, including the finding that firms with greater transformational leadership engage more in institutional corporate social responsibility practices, whereas transactional leadership is not associated with such practices. They also find that stakeholder-oriented marketing reinforces the positive link between transformational leadership and institutional corporate social responsibility. Transactional leadership enhances, whereas transformational leadership diminishes, the positive relationship between institutional corporate social responsibility practices and organizational outcomes. Thus, transformational and transactional leadership styles have notably distinct influences on a firm's institutional corporate social responsibility practices.

Fourth, Fernando Lourenço builds on the idea that entrepreneurship relies on sustainability challenges as sources of inspiration and opportunities to innovate new businesses. The goal of "Teaching sustainability via entrepreneurship education in tourism and hospitality school" is to highlight entrepreneurship courses integrated into tourism and hospitality degree programs at the Institute for Tourism Studies in Macau. The shared experiences and best practices can guide educators in ways to instill positive, opportunistic, and sustainability-driven mindsets toward sustainability in entrepreneurship courses.

Contextually grounded implications and challenges for sustainable entrepreneurship and blended value generation

In the last part of this research anthology, six chapters delineate specific contextual challenges and opportunities faced by individuals and their organizations in their efforts to design, deploy, and assess sustainable entrepreneurial action and its outcomes. These chapters together highlight the influence of contextual factors on the sustainability-driven entrepreneurial process and the generation of blended value across different geographical, institutional, and sectoral environments.

Michael T. Schaper starts this part by asking: What green business practices do firms undertake, and what factors encourage or discourage them from seizing new entrepreneurial opportunities by improving their environmental performance? This chapter, "Motivations and barriers to going green amongst Australian businesses: identifying the on and off switches in small, medium, and large firms," relies on evidence from a large-scale survey of 21,000 firms by the Australian Bureau of Statistics, in which few firms report undertaking any environmental management activities, and pronounced differences emerge according to firm size. That is, approximately 37 percent of small firms undertook such work; almost 80 percent of large firms did so. Firms that pursued green-friendly business practices did so for various reasons, though ethical considerations were the single greatest motivator for firms all sizes. Other motives reflected the 4Cs (compliance with regulatory requirements, cost considerations, customers and reputational issues, and cautionary risk management). Impeding these efforts were cost considerations, insufficient resources, a lack of internal expertise, and regulatory barriers.

In exploring "Independent coffee shops in the U.S.: a closer look at sustainable social entrepreneurship," Rob Boyle investigates Crave Coffeehouse in St. Louis, Urban Abbey in Omaha, and Rohs Street Café in Cincinnati, as representative nonprofit coffee shops. Reflecting their strategic goals and outcomes, these small businesses demonstrate how sustainability, as it relates to social entrepreneurship, can evoke various connotations related to the buildings that house the businesses, the places where clients and customers gather, and the neighborhoods in which businesses locate.

Among the options for better ways to fund a social enterprise, J. Howard "Jim" Kucher highlights the notion of social venture capital in his chapter "The SBA 7(A) Loan Program and the American social entrepreneur." That is, a proposed solution would expand the SBA 7(A) Loan Program to nonprofit enterprises. To address the potential success of this proposal, this chapter reviews the history and performance of the SBA in general and the 7(A) Program in particular, then proposes specific changes to the SBA's general operations that could help it meet the growing need for capital to build social enterprises.

Edwin B.P. de Jong, Jonas Kolenberg, and Luuk Knippenberg recognize that, due to radical transformations in the Indonesian cacao sector, international firms increasingly seek sustainable, long-term solutions and adaptations to context-specific measures, through dialogue, negotiation, and collaboration with various stakeholders, to secure production by smallholder farmers. At first sight, this effort seems paradoxical: The firms are working to upgrade their corporate social responsibility activities but avoid labeling it this way. In detailing "The corporate social responsibility paradox: present-day firm challenges in the cacao sector of Indonesia," the authors examine the policies and practices of the leading firms, as well as their collaborations with other stakeholders, to propose that the corporate social responsibility debate should be reframed and moved, from a consumer-informed to a producer-informed approach. Doing so would shift the focus from downstream consumption to upstream sustainable production and entrepreneurship.

Rather than cacao, Andrew Ngawenja Mzembe and Adam Lindgreen study tea. In their chapter, "Reconciling managerial and stakeholders' perceptions: corporate social responsibility in Malawi," they acknowledge that corporate social responsibility concepts thus far have focused too much on developed countries, despite the crucial need for it in developing countries. Their exploratory case study of Eastern Produce Malawi Limited, a subsidiary of a UK-based multinational, includes both managerial and stakeholder perceptions. Management's understanding of corporate social responsibility largely reflects the firm's efforts to reconcile global expectations of a multinational subsidiary with the ever changing expectations of Malawian society. The stakeholders also exhibit a broad understanding of corporate social responsibility, though tensions still emerge of course. These insights also challenge the application of existing models of corporate social responsibility to all African countries, because contextual elements have fundamental influences on the priorities adopted. For example, social and ethical responsibilities are more highly regarded than legal responsibilities among managers and most stakeholders, which has critical managerial and public policy implications.

The last chapter in this anthology emphasizes "The value of public data for assessing sustainability: the case of Mexican entrepreneurs and the rural census." Noting the variety of frameworks available to evaluate sustainable food systems, Eliseo Vilalta-Perdomo, Rosario Michel-Villarreal, and Martin Hingley describe how their different coverage, assessment levels, and precision create barriers to benchmarking and comparisons of sustainability performance. In response, the FAO has issued the Sustainability Assessment of Food and Agriculture systems (SAFA) framework. But can the SAFA framework accurately evaluate sustainable food systems? Testing its ability to evaluate rural Mexican entrepreneurs' sustainability, the authors find that public data from a rural census cannot provide a comprehensive evaluation of sustainability, yet these data also facilitate evaluations of nearly two-thirds of SAFA's indicators, so they can further the quest to overcome sustainability evaluation limits.

Closing remarks

We extend a special thanks to Routledge and its staff, who have been most helpful throughout this entire process. Equally, we warmly thank all of the authors who submitted their manuscripts for consideration for this book. They have exhibited the desire to share their knowledge and experience with the book's readers—and a willingness to put forward their views for possible challenge by their peers. We also thank the reviewers, who provided excellent, independent, and incisive consideration of the anonymous submissions.

We hope that this compendium of chapters and themes stimulates and contributes to the ongoing debate surrounding sustainable entrepreneurship. The chapters in this book can help fill some knowledge gaps, while also stimulating further thought and action pertaining to the multiple aspects surrounding sustainable entrepreneurship.

Adam Lindgreen, PhD
Copenhagen, Denmark and Pretoria, South Africa
François Maon, PhD
Lille, France
Christine Vallaster, PhD
Salzburg, Austria
Shumaila Yousofzai, PhD
Cardiff, Wales
Beatriz Palacios Florencio, PhD
Seville, Spain
1 August, 2018

References

Bacq, S., Hartog, C., & Hoogendoorn, B. (2016). Beyond the moral portrayal of social entrepreneurs: An empirical approach to who they are and what drives them. *Journal of Business Ethics*, 133(4), 703–718.

Cohen, B., & Winn, M. I. (2007). Market imperfections, opportunity and sustainable entrepreneurship. *Journal of Business Venturing*, 22(1), 29–49.

Dean, T. J., & McMullen, J. S. (2007). Toward a theory of sustainable entrepreneurship: Reducing environmental degradation through entrepreneurial action. *Journal of Business Venturing*, 22(1), 50–76.

Elkington, J. (1997). *Cannibals With Forks: The Triple Bottom Line of 21st Century Business*. Oxford, UK: Capstone.

Emerson, J. (2003). The blended value proposition: Integrating social and financial returns. *California Management Review*, 45(4), 35–51.

Hart, S. L., & Milstein, M. B. (2003). Creating sustainable value. *Academy of Management Executive*, 17(2), 56–67.

Hoogendoorn, B., van der Zwan, P., & Thurik, R. (2017). Sustainable entrepreneurship: The role of perceived barriers and risk. *Journal of Business Ethics*, in press, 1–22.

Kickul, J., Janssen-Selvadurai, C. & Griffiths, M. D. (2012). A blended value framework for educating the next cadre of social entrepreneurs. *Academy of Management Learning and Education* 11(3), 479–493.

Kirkwood, J., & Walton, S. (2010). What motivates ecopreneurs to start businesses? *International Journal of Entrepreneurial Behavior & Research*, 16(3), 204–228.

Lans, T., Blok, V., & Wesselink, R. (2014). Learning apart and together: Towards an integrated competence framework for sustainable entrepreneurship in higher education. *Journal of Cleaner Production*, 62(1), 37–47.

Munoz, P., & Cohen, B. (2018). Sustainable entrepreneurship research: Taking stock and looking ahead. *Business Strategy and the Environment*, 27(3), 300–322.

Munoz, P., & Dimov, D. (2015). The call of the whole in understanding the development of sustainable ventures. *Journal of Business Venturing*, 30(4), 632–654.

Pacheco, D. F., Dean, T. J., & Payne, D. S. (2010). Escaping the green prison: Entrepreneurship and the creation of opportunities for sustainable development. *Journal of Business Venturing*, 25(5), 464–480.

Parrish, B. D. (2010). Sustainability-driven entrepreneurship: Principles of organization design. *Journal of Business Venturing*, 25(5), 510–523.

Patzelt, H., & Shepherd, D. A. (2011). Recognizing opportunities for sustainable development. *Entrepreneurship Theory and Practice*, 35(4), 631–652.

Schaltegger, S., Lüdeke-Freund, F., & Hansen, E. G. (2016). Business models for sustainability: A co-evolutionary analysis of sustainable entrepreneurship, innovation, and transformation. *Organization & Environment*, 29(3), 264–289.

Schaltegger, S., & Wagner, M. (2011). Sustainable entrepreneurship and sustainability innovation: Categories and interactions. *Business Strategy and the Environment*, 20(4), 222–237.

Shepherd, D. A., McMullen, J. S., & Jennings, P. D. (2008). The formation of opportunity beliefs: Overcoming ignorance and reducing doubt. *Strategic Entrepreneurship Journal*, 1(1), 75–95.

Shepherd D. A. & Patzelt, H. (2011). The new field of sustainable entrepreneurship: Studying entrepreneurial action linking 'what is to be sustained' with 'what is to be developed'. *Entrepreneurship Theory and Practice*, 35(1), 135–163.

Tilley, F. & Young, W. (2009) Sustainability entrepreneurs: Could they be the true wealth generators of the future? *Greener Management International*, 55(1), 79–92.

WECD (1987). *From One Earth to One World: An Overview*. Oxford, UK: Oxford University Press.

Part I

Understanding intentions and motivations behind sustainable entrepreneurship

1.1 The role of perceived university support in the formation of students' entrepreneurial intention

Saadat Saeed, Shumaila Yousafzai, Mirella Yani-de-Soriano, and Moreno Muffatto

Introduction

The impact of entrepreneurship education (EE), training and support has been recognized as one of the crucial factors in developing positive perceptions of competence for start-up firms (Hartshorn and Hannon 2005; Zhao, Seibert, and Hills 2005), the development of favorable attitudes toward self-employment (Krueger and Brazeal 1994), and related entrepreneurship preferences and intentions (Chen, Greene, and Crick 1998). Despite the increasing interest in academic entrepreneurship and new venture creation by students, very little empirical research has identified EE and the support factors that can foster entrepreneurship among university students (Walter, Auer, and Ritter 2006). Furthermore, in spite of the growth in the number of entrepreneurship courses and curricula and the link between EE and entrepreneurial behavior (Galloway and Brown 2002; Lüthje and Franke 2003), student entrepreneurship figures still remain low (Kraaijenbrink, Groen, and Bos 2010).

Previous studies which have attempted to examine the effectiveness of formal EE have been inconclusive, perhaps due to the outcome measures they have used, including student satisfaction and performance in the course, which may be insufficient indicators of educational effectiveness (Cox, Mueller, and Moss 2002). Although self-efficacy has been rarely used as an outcome measure, one study by Peterman and Kennedy (2003) found that participation in an entrepreneurship program significantly increased the perceived feasibility of starting a business, which implies that EE can enhance entrepreneurial intention (EI). Kraaijenbrink et al. (2010) suggested that although universities can support entrepreneurship in many objectively measured ways, in order to understand the effect of such measures it was crucial to gauge the extent to which they could have an impact on students. This can be achieved by measuring students' perceptions of the university support that they receive or "perceived university support" (PUS).

Although EE can increase EI, it is not the only influence affecting it. Therefore, it is important to understand the process that underlies the emergence of EI. Some scholars have focused primarily on individual factors as the potential determinants of EI. These factors include: demographic characteristics, the status of parents and grandparents, role models, entrepreneurial self-efficacy (ESE), locus of control, self-realization, independence, recognition, entrepreneurial experience, personality traits, and subjective norms. Other researchers have focused on organizational factors, such as organizational culture and organizational norms (Louis, Blumenthal, Gluck, and Stoto 1989), university quality (Di Gregorio and Shane 2003), and the impact of EE on students' EI (Souitaris, Zerbinati, and Allaham 2007). Finally, when looking at some of the institutional factors affecting entrepreneurial development, researchers have focused on economic stability (McMillan and Woodruff 2002), capital availability (de Bettignies and Brander 2007), and reduced personal income taxes (Gentry and Hubbard 2000)

These multi-level factors may interact with each other to synergize EI, but most researchers have treated them independently rather than considering the effects of their potential inter-relations and inter-dependency. However, social science research expects a more holistic view to explain phenomena by taking into account the inter-connections of various factors. Research has emphasized that although individual-level factors have some impact on EI, it may be better to consider the impact of some contextual factors as well (Turker and Selcuk 2009). Following the argument of Ireland and Webb (2007) that a single perspective in behavioral studies offers an incomplete account of phenomena, our study takes a multi-perspective approach to assess the impact of EE on EI.

This chapter proposes the following research questions: (1) How do students perceive EE and the support they receive from their universities? (2) Does PUS have an impact on students' ESE? (3) How important is PUS in influencing students' EI within the context of other factors, such as institutional support (IS) and individual motivations? (4) How can universities be more effective in their provision of EE and support to their students? To answer these questions, we have developed a conceptual framework that reflects the role of EE within the context of other influences such as IS and individual motivations, rather than studying it in an isolated manner. This should permit a deeper and more meaningful analysis and understanding of the topic.

In our conceptual framework, EI represents a university student's intention to start a new business (Krueger and Brazeal 1994). Such intention is a conscious state of mind that precedes action and directs attention toward the goal of establishing a new business (Bird 1988). In order to understand how this intention is formed, we have followed Shapero and Sokol (1982) by examining the impact of perceived desirability and perceived feasibility on EI. Perceived desirability constitutes our individual-level perspective, comprising six individual motivation factors used by Carter, Gartner, Shaver, and Gatewood (2003): self-realization, financial success, role, innovation, recognition, and independence. These factors differentiate individuals on the basis of how they discover, evaluate, and exploit entrepreneurial opportunities. Perceived feasibility has been conceptualized as ESE (Chen et al. 1998). We propose that individuals with a sense of ESE may be drawn to the desirable opportunities and benefits of self-employment, and thus they are likely to form intentions and goals for self-employment. Previous research indicates that self-efficacy is not a static trait, but that it can be changed (Hollenbeck and Hall 2004). Considering that changes may come from targeted educational and institutional efforts, we examine the possible link between EE, IS, and ESE.

Entrepreneurship education is the focus of our chapter and constitutes our organizational-level perspective. Following Kraaijenbrink et al. (2010), we have conceptualized PUS by means of three separate but related constructs: perceived educational support (ES), perceived concept development support (CDS), and perceived business development support (BDS). In our framework we have integrated an institutional-level perspective by conceptualizing students' perception of the support they receive from the government as perceived IS. This refers to the policies, regulations, and programs that the country has undertaken to support entrepreneurship (Turker and Selcuk 2009). We have hypothesized that the three constructs of PUS and perceived IS would increase perceived feasibility, as measured by ESE.

The main contribution of the chapter is to provide a better understanding of the role of EE and support and its impact on EI. The aim of the study is to assess the extent of students' PUS and whether it affects their ESE. In turn, ESE may have an impact on EI. We examine this within the context of other influences, such as IS and individual motivations, which allow us to assess the relative importance of EE. Considering that there are few studies measuring the impact of EE, our research fills a gap in the literature by measuring the impact of EE within an integrative, multi-perspective framework, thus providing a broader view of this topic. The findings will help university managers and policy-makers to understand the effectiveness of current practices and initiatives, particularly in developing economies such as Pakistan. Since the late 2000s, Pakistan has been trying to build its economic growth on the basis of educational policies. The Higher Education Commission (HEC) of Pakistan has recently developed the National Business Education Accreditation Council (NBEAC) to promote business education, particularly with the aim of stimulating EE and culture in Pakistani universities. Entrepreneurship has been selected by students as an elective subject during the final semester of their undergraduate programs. Nevertheless, the NBEAC seeks to promote entrepreneurship as a major field of study in higher education, thus making Pakistan a model context for our study. Our proposed research framework is presented in Figure 1.1.1

Entrepreneurial intention

Entrepreneurship is the process of venture creation and EI is crucial in this process. EI identifies the link between ideas and action which is critical for understanding the entrepreneurial process (Bird 1988; Krueger and Carsrud 1993). According to Ajzen

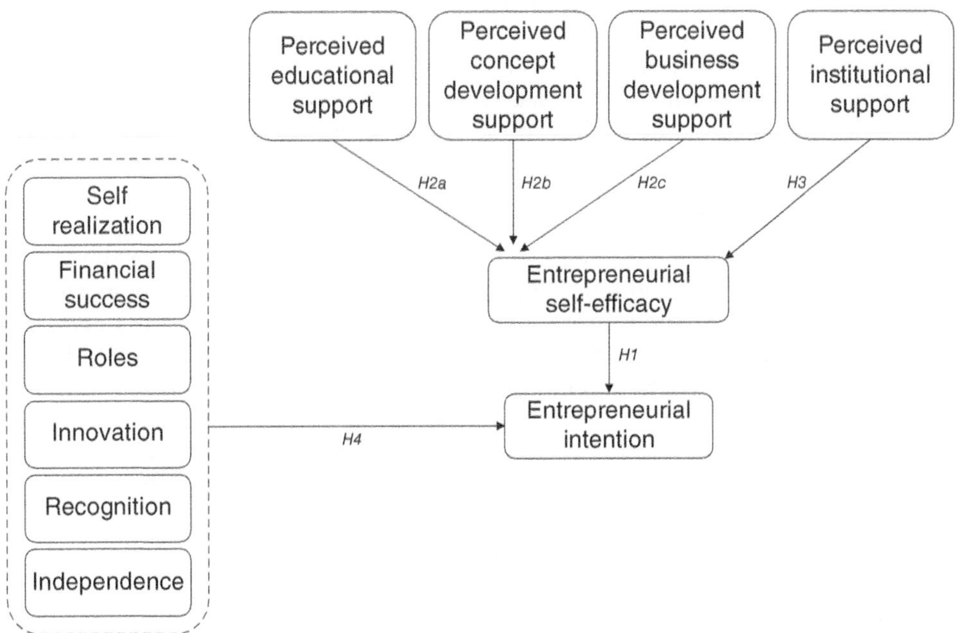

Figure 1.1.1 Proposed research framework

(1991), intention captures the degree to which people show their motivation and willingness to execute the desired behavior. Intention has also been defined as a state of mind that directs a person's attention (and therefore experience and actions) toward a specific object (goal) or path in order to achieve something (for example, becoming an entrepreneur) (Bird 1988). Intention has been shown to be the best predictor of planned behavior (Bagozzi, Baumgartner, and Yi 1989), particularly when that behavior is rare, hard to observe, or involves unpredictable time lags (Bird 1988; Krueger and Brazeal 1994). A new business emerges over time and involves considerable planning, and thus entrepreneurship is exactly the type of planned behavior (Bird 1988) for which intention models are ideally suited.

Previous research has proposed several conceptual models for understanding EI, including the Entrepreneurial Event Model (Shapero and Sokol 1982); the Intentional Basic Model (Krueger and Carsrud 1993); the Entrepreneurial Potential Model (Krueger and Brazeal 1994); and the Davidsson Model (Davidsson 1995). However, research has shown that there is little difference in the approaches taken by these models (Krueger et al. 2000). In the current study, our understanding of EI has been guided primarily by two models: (1) Azjen's (1991) Theory of Planned Behavior (TPB) and (2) Shapero and Sokol's (1982) model of Entrepreneurial Event (SEE). While these models vary in terms of their underlying concepts, they provide comparable interpretations of EI (Krueger et al. 2000).

Ajzen (1991) argues that intentions in general depend on the attitude toward the act, social norms, and perceived behavioral control. The attitude toward the act reflects individuals' assessment of the personal desirability of creating a new business. Subjective norms reflect individuals' perceptions of what important people in their lives think about business creation. Finally, perceived behavioral control reflects individuals' perception of their ability to initiate a new business successfully. Interestingly, the domain of entrepreneurship had already provided a model quite similar to the TPB well before Ajzen formulated it. Shapero (1975) proposed that the entrepreneurial event (defined as initiating entrepreneurial behavior) depends on the presence of a salient, personally credible opportunity, which in turn depends on perceptions of desirability and feasibility. Shapero (1975) defined perceived desirability as the attractiveness (both personal and social) of starting a business, and perceived feasibility (both personal and social) as the degree to which an individual feels capable of starting a business.

The fact that two scholars in two different academic areas produced highly similar models attests to the value of intention models. Krueger, Reilly, and Carsrud (2000) tested the TPB and SEE and found support for both models. They demonstrated that attitudes and subjective norms in the TPB model are conceptually related to perceived desirability in the SEE, while perceived behavioral control in the TPB corresponds with perceived feasibility in the SEE model. Considering that perceived behavioral control is largely synonymous with ESE (Boyd and Vozikis 1994), ESE would be the main indicator of perceived feasibility. Essentially, it can be concluded that perceived desirability and perceived feasibility are the fundamental elements of EI (Douglas and Shepherd 2002).

Perceived feasibility: entrepreneurial self-efficacy

If the perception that a new venture is feasible is a predictor of the intention to launch it, then it is critical to examine the key indicator of perceived feasibility: ESE. Self-efficacy is the academic term for the belief that one can execute a target behavior. It is firmly based in individuals' self-perceptions of their skills and abilities (Bandura 1986). It reflects individuals' innermost thoughts on whether they have what is needed to perform a certain task successfully. Actual abilities only matter if individuals have self-confidence in those abilities, and also the self-confidence that they will be able to convert those skills effectively into a chosen outcome (Bandura 1989). Evidence suggests that general self-efficacy is central to most human functioning and is based more on what people believe than on what is objectively true (Markham, Balkin, and Baron 2002). Research in this area has consistently emphasized the importance of perceived self-efficacy as a key factor in determining human agency (Bandura 1989) and has shown that those with high perceptions of self-efficacy for a certain task are more likely to pursue and persist in that task (Bandura 1992).

In the field of entrepreneurship, ESE has proved to be a remarkable predictor of EI (Chen et al. 1998; Krueger et al. 2000). Boyd and Vozikis (1994, p. 66) defined ESE as "an important explanatory variable in determining both the strength of entrepreneurship intentions and the likelihood that those intentions will result in entrepreneurial actions". Similarly, Krueger and Brazeal (1994) proposed that ESE constitutes one of the key prerequisites for the potential entrepreneur. Therefore, we hypothesize that:

> ***H1.*** *Entrepreneurial self-efficacy positively influences entrepreneurial intention.*

In turn, ESE can be influenced by experience, vicarious learning, social persuasion, and support and personal judgments or physiological states, such as arousal (Boyd and Vozikis 1994; Krueger and Brazeal 1994). Peterman and Kennedy (2003) showed that exposure to EE programs increases ESE. Subsequently, we discuss the role of PUS and perceived IS in shaping ESE.

Perceived university support and entrepreneurial self-efficacy

The development of entrepreneurial universities constitutes a widespread phenomenon across the world, which has attracted the attention of policy-makers. Entrepreneurial universities are valued because of their economic outputs (such as patents, licenses, and start-up firms) and technology transfer mechanisms (Tijssen 2006). Furthermore, a significant amount of scholarship has considered universities as seedbeds for fostering entrepreneurial spirit and culture. Universities can play an important role in identifying and developing entrepreneurial traits and inclinations among students and making them capable of starting their own venture, thus effectively contributing to economic prosperity and job creation (Debackere and Veugelers 2005). It is, therefore, important for universities to position themselves as a hub of new venture creation by nurturing an entrepreneurial environment and contributing substantially to the economy and society (Gnyawali and Fogel 1994).

Previous research has recognized the value of EE and support in the development of favorable perceptions of competence for start-up firms (Hartshorn and Hannon 2005; Zhao et al. 2005). EE has been associated with enhanced attitudes and intentions toward starting a new business (Chen et al. 1998; Krueger and Brazeal, 1994). In fact, university students who took entrepreneurship courses had a greater interest in becoming entrepreneurs compared with those who did not take it (Kolvereid and Moen 1997). Upton, Sexton, and Moore (1995) reported that 40 percent of those who attended entrepreneurship courses had started their own businesses. Previous research has suggested that certain university support policies and practices can foster entrepreneurial activities among students, for example, technology transfer offices and faculty consultants (Mian 1996), university incubators and physical resources (Mian 1997), and university venture funds (Lerner 2005). It is clear that an effective EE program and the entrepreneurial support provided by universities are efficient ways of obtaining the necessary knowledge about entrepreneurship and motivating young people to seek an entrepreneurial career (Henderson and Robertson 2000).

However, despite the increasing number of entrepreneurship courses and the link between EE and entrepreneurial behavior (Galloway and Brown 2002; Lüthje and Franke 2003), student entrepreneurship figures still remain low (Kraaijenbrink et al. 2010). Wang and Wong (2004, p. 170) pointed out the fact that the entrepreneurial dreams of many students are hindered by inadequate preparation: "their business knowledge is insufficient, and more importantly, they are not prepared to take risks to realize their dreams". Timmons and Spinelli (2004) suggested that EE is effective when it enables participants to develop a higher capacity for imagination, flexibility, and creativity, as well as developing the ability to think conceptually and perceive change as opportunity.

One way for an EE program to increase the ESE of students is to provide mastery experiences or "learning by doing". This includes the opportunity to conduct feasibility studies, develop business plans, and to benefit from business simulation, case studies, guest speakers, and meaningful apprenticeships (Cox et al. 2002). Another way is to have a supportive environment, for example, by offering resources such as a network of individuals to provide specific expertise in areas such as marketing or accounting, the inclusion of role models, and the provision of one-to-one support. This support may give some people the confidence to initiate their own business venture (Kraaijenbrink et al. 2010). Previous studies have suggested that the attitude model of entrepreneurship has implications for EE programs, as attitudes are open to change and, therefore, can be influenced by educators and practitioners (Souitaris et al. 2007; Wang and Wong 2004). However, empirical research attempting to identify university support factors that can foster entrepreneurship among university students have remained limited (Walter et al. 2006).

Kraaijenbrink et al. (2010) suggested that although universities can support entrepreneurship in many objectively measured ways, in order to understand the effect of such measures, it was crucial to gauge the extent to which they could have an impact on students. This can be achieved by measuring students' perceptions of the university support that they receive. They proposed three aspects of PUS: perceived educational support (ES), perceived concept development support (CDS), and perceived business development support (BDS). First, as part of their traditional teaching role, universities can provide ES by teaching students the general knowledge and skills that are needed to initiate a new venture. Second, considering their commercialization role, universities can also provide individual students or groups of students with a more targeted and specific support for starting their own firm. This targeted support can be of two types: CDS and BDS. CDS can provide awareness, motivation, and business ideas in the early stages of the entrepreneurial process, in which opportunity recognition and development take place (Shane and Venkataraman 2000). BDS is typically given to the start-up firm rather than to individual students in the later stages of the entrepreneurial process.

Krueger and Brazeal (1994) suggested that EE should improve perceived feasibility of entrepreneurship by increasing the knowledge of students, building confidence, and promoting self-efficacy. Thus, it can be inferred that the entrepreneurship programs and related support provided by academic institutions can play an important role in fostering ESE among their students. We propose:

> ***H2a.*** *Perceived educational support positively influences entrepreneurial self-efficacy.*
>
> ***H2b.*** *Perceived concept development support positively influences entrepreneurial self-efficacy.*
>
> ***H2c.*** *Perceived business development support positively influences entrepreneurial self-efficacy.*

Perceived institutional support and entrepreneurial self-efficacy

Entrepreneurs do not exist in isolation and many social, cultural, economic, and political factors may affect their entrepreneurial behavior. A country's public and private institutional structures establish the rules of the game for organizations and determine which specific skills and knowledge result in the maximum payoff (North 2005). While public institutions create laws, regulations, and policies regarding government assistance for the promotion of entrepreneurship, private institutions define the culture, norms, beliefs, and expectations of this activity (Ingram and Silverman 2002). A recent study by Bosma, Wennekers, and Amoros (2011) found a correlation between a country's GDP per capita, national economic growth rate, and the level and type of entrepreneurial activity in the country. Previous research has also found that some key factors for entrepreneurial development include: economic stability (McMillan and Woodruff 2002), capital availability (de Bettignies and Brander 2007), and reduced personal income taxes (Gentry and Hubbard 2000). These studies suggest that individuals' EI is a reflection of the institutional structure and the economic and political stability of their country. This means that productive entrepreneurship would be at low levels where the incentives supporting it are weak (Baumol 1993). Some of these incentives include access to capital and markets and the availability of information (Basu 1998). Studies on students have revealed that the lack of funds is a major barrier to entrepreneurship (Henderson and Robertson 2000; Li 2007; Robertson et al. 2003).

An institutional environment can use both tangible and intangible measures to support entrepreneurship activities. Tangible measures include flexible and friendly credit conditions, venture capital availability, physical infrastructure, corporate physical assets, R&D laboratories, training opportunities, and business plan competition. Intangible measures include making human capital available and providing sufficient legitimacy for entrepreneurship. If individuals perceive that the institutional environment is supportive, they will be more confident in their ability to become entrepreneurs and thus their ESE would increase (Luthje and Franke 2003; Schwarz, Wdowiak, Almer-Jarz, and Breitenecker 2009; Turker and Selcuk 2009). Therefore, we propose:

> ***H3.*** *Perceived institutional support positively influences entrepreneurial self-efficacy.*

Perceived desirability: individual motivations

Schumpeter (1934) defined entrepreneurs as those individuals who attempt to reform or revolutionize the pattern of production by exploiting an invention or untried technical possibility for producing a new commodity or producing an old one in a new way. He further mentioned that these efforts require aptitudes that are present in only a small fraction of the population. It can be inferred from Schumpeter's definition that, in addition to a supportive organizational and institutional environment, the success of entrepreneurial activity depends upon the attitudes, interests, and values of the individuals who are likely to form a new venture (Bird 1988). Thus, the reasons that these potential entrepreneurs give for starting a business should have a significant influence on whether they would actually engage in entrepreneurial activity, that is, their EI (Ajzen 1991; Kolvereid 1996; Krueger and Brazeal 1994; Krueger and Carsrud 1993). In the TPB, these reasons are salient beliefs which determine individuals' attitudes toward self-employment. Similarly, within the SEE framework, they can be seen as perceived desirability factors leading to the formation of EI.

Although a number of researchers have attempted to identify relevant reasons for new business formation, the specific individual motives that are consistently related to EI have shown mixed results. For example, Scheinberg and MacMillan (1988) reported that the need for approval, the perceived instrumentality of wealth, the degree of community, the need for personal development, the need for independence, and the need for escape are factors which have led individuals toward new firm formation. However, these motivational factors were not always supported in other studies (Stewart et al. 1999). Following a thorough review of the entrepreneurship literature and after careful consideration, we decided to represent perceived desirability by means of the six factors identified by Carter et al. (2003) as major reasons or motivations for starting a new venture, namely: self-realization, financial success, role, innovation, recognition, and independence.

Self-realization refers to the motivations involved in pursuing self-directed goals (Carter et al. 2003). This measure corresponds to Birley and Westhead's (1994) need for personal development and McClelland's (1961) need for achievement. Individuals with a high level of self-realization are expected to show a greater willingness to engage in entrepreneurial activity because this provides them with challenges that are associated with goal achievement and personal development (Carree and Thurik 2005). Selecting an entrepreneurial career is no longer under-employment or a "mom and pop" establishment; it is a way to achieve a variety of personal goals (Kirchhoff 1996). Higher self-realization will result in a higher level of EI.

Financial success is described as an individual's desire to earn more money and achieve financial security (Carter et al. 2003). Previous research has shown mixed results for this construct. On the one hand, McQueen and Wallmark (1991) found that most of the founders of new ventures did not establish their companies to generate wealth, but rather to fulfill their goal of commercializing their technologies. On the other, Scheinberg and MacMillan (1988) and Birley and Westhead (1994) all labeled financial success as a perceived instrumentality of wealth and found it to be related to EI. We have included financial success to clarify these findings.

Role is the individual's desire to follow family tradition and emulate the example of others (Birley and Westhead 1994; Carter et al. 2003; Shane, Kolvereid, and Westhead 1991). Research has shown that individuals are attracted to role models who can help them to develop themselves further by learning new tasks and skills (Gibson 2004). It has long been acknowledged that role models may have a profound influence on career decisions (Kolvereid 1996; Krueger et al. 2000).

Innovation relates to an individual's desire to accomplish something new (McClelland 1961). It is often referred to as a primary motive behind EI (Mueller and Thomas 2001) and has been shown to have a significant effect on venture performance (Utsch and Rauch 2000). Feldman and Bolino (2000) found that individuals with a strong desire for innovation were motivated to become self-employed because of the opportunity to use their skills and be creative as well as to capitalize on a good business idea.

Recognition describes an individual's desire to gain status, approval, and recognition from family, friends, and the community (Carter et al. 2003). Manolova, Brush, and

Edelman (2008) defined recognition as an individual's position relative to others in a given social situation. According to Gatewood (1993), recognition is a second-level outcome or reason for desiring to start a new venture. In our proposed framework, recognition corresponds to the measures "recognition" in Shane et al.'s (1991) new firm formation typology, and "need for approval" in the studies of Birley and Westhead (1994) and Scheinberg and MacMillan (1988).

Independence describes an individual's desirability for freedom, control, and flexibility in the use of time (Birley and Westhead 1994; Carter et al. 2003; Scheinberg and MacMillan 1988). As a general rule, individuals requiring a strong need for independence seek careers with more freedom. They choose an entrepreneurial career because they prefer to make decisions independently, set their own goals, develop their own plans of actions, and control goal achievement themselves (Wilson, Marlino, and Kickul 2004). Thus we propose:

> ***H4.*** *Perceived desirability (measured by self-realization, financial success, role, innovation, recognition, and independence) positively influences entrepreneurial intention.*

Method

Sample and procedure

To ensure the variability and representativity of respondents, we selected universities in the largest province of Pakistan, Punjab. In Punjab we targeted Lahore, Faisalabad, and Sahiwal, which are considered the educational hub in this region. First, we selected five universities on the basis of their provision of EE and whether they were registered with HEC and thus offered approved programs. Second, we contacted undergraduate students who had studied or were studying a course of entrepreneurship in those universities and had agreed to participate in our study. Some 1,000 questionnaires were distributed and 850 were returned, of which 45 were subsequently discarded. The final sample consisted of 805 participants. Of these, 547 were males (68 percent) and 258 females (32 percent). The average age was 21 years ($SD = 0.54$).

Measurement variables

Table 1.1.1 presents the scales used to measure the main variables. *EI* was measured with three statements to assess whether participants intended to start a new business. The first statement, "Have you ever seriously considered becoming an entrepreneur?" was adapted from Veciana, Aponte, and Urbano (2005) and was measured on a dichotomous scale of "yes/no". The other two statements were adapted from Liñán and Chen (2009). *Perceived feasibility* was measured through *ESE* by employing a task-specific scale from Chen et al. (1998). Respondents were asked to rate their skill level in 26 roles and tasks in 5 areas of entrepreneurship: marketing, innovation, management, risk-taking, and financial control.

Perceived ES was measured with a six-item scale rating students' perception of the traditional teaching role of universities and included statements such as "my university offers project work focused on entrepreneurship" (Kraaijenbrink et al. 2010). *Perceived CDS* was measured with a four-item scale rating students' perception of the support that the university can provide beyond teaching and included statements such as "my university provides students with ideas to start a new business" (Kraaijenbrink et al. 2010).

Perceived BDS was measured by means of a three-item scale rating students' perception of the support that the university can provide to the start-up firm and included statements such as "my university provides students with the financial means to start a business" (Kraaijenbrink et al. 2010). *Perceived IS* was measured through a four-item scale developed by Turker and Selcuk (2009). The questions were related to the opportunities provided to entrepreneurs in terms of the ease or difficulty in taking loans from banks, the legal constraints of running a business, and the economic stability in Pakistan. Finally, *Perceived desirability* was assessed by means of these six factors identified by Carter et al. (2003): *Self-realization* (four items); *Financial success* (four items); *Role* (three items); *Innovation* (two items); *Recognition* (two items); and *Independence* (two items).

Results

Assessment of measures

Exploratory factor analysis (EFA) and confirmatory factor analysis (CFA) were conducted. Structural equation modelling (SEM)(AMOS version 18.0) was employed for the CFA and to test the structural models and to conduct multi-group moderator analysis by using the maximum likelihood estimation procedure. The inter-correlations and square root of the average variance extracted (AVE) are presented in Table 1.1.2. These results suggest that each construct shared more variance with its items than with other constructs. In addition, the correlation matrix provides no evidence of multi-collinearity among the variables as all the coefficients were within an acceptable range and none of them exceeded the cut-off point of 0.85 (Fornell and Larcker 1981). These analyses provide evidence of discriminant validity. Furthermore, as shown in Table 1.1.1, all items loaded significantly on their corresponding constructs with factor loadings ranging from 0.50 to 0.95, thus meeting the threshold of 0.50 set by Hair et al. (2006), and demonstrating convergent validity at the item level. Following Fornell and Larcker (1981) we assessed the convergent validity through item reliability, composite reliability (CR) and the AVE. The Cronbach's alphas for all the constructs were well above the threshold level of 0.70 (Nunnally and Bernstein 1994), with the exception of the newly developed scales by Kraaijenbrink et al. (2010), which showed somewhat lower reliabilities: perceived ES ($\alpha = 0.60$), perceived CDS ($\alpha = 0.65$), perceived BDS ($\alpha = 0.60$). However, the authors showed reliabilities around 0.90 in their original work. To address this problem, we followed Hair et al.'s (2006) recommendation that the CR should be used in conjunction with SEM to address the tendency of the Cronbach's alpha to understate reliability. Nunnally and Bernstein (1994) recommended a value of 0.70 and higher for CR to be adequate. The CRs for the three Kraaijenbrink et al.'s (2010) variables ranged between 0.90 and 0.92, which indicates good reliability.

The final indicator of convergent validity is achieved when AVE equals or exceeds 0.50. In addition, comparisons of the AVE with its shared variance (Φ^2) and other constructs indicated that the measures exhibit discriminant validity, since, in each case, the AVE was greater than the proportion of the shared variance (Fornell and Larcker 1981). In addition, a test was performed to investigate the presence for common method variance. The initial EFA with oblique rotation of items measuring the ten constructs

Table 1.1.1 Results of confirmatory factor analysis

Construct (Items)	*Factor loading (t-values*)*
Entrepreneurial intention (α = 0.80; CR=0.90; AVE=0.93; Φ^2=0.03–0.52)	
1 Have you ever seriously considered becoming an entrepreneur? (Yes/No)	0.810 (84.163)
2 I will make every effort to start and run my own firm.[a]	0.820 (94.293)
3 I have got firm intention to start a firm someday.[a]	0.816 (86.577)
Entrepreneurial self-efficacy[c] (α = 0.92; CR=0.90; AVE=0.89; Φ^2=0.03–0.52)	
26 items were used. Respondents were asked to rate their skill level in marketing, innovation, management, risk-management, financial control.	0.835 (73.886)
Perceived educational support[a] (α = 0.6; CR=0.92; AVE=0.88; Φ^2 =0.02–0.42)	
1 My university offers elective courses on entrepreneurship.	0.812 (88.692)
2 My university offers project work focused on entrepreneurship.	0.826 (81.260)
3 My university offers internships focused on entrepreneurship.	0.830 (90.886)
4 My university offers a bachelor or master study on entrepreneurship.	0.854 (89.345)
5 My university arranges conferences / workshops on entrepreneurship.	0.621 (80.110)
6 My university brings entrepreneurial students into contact with each other.	0.652 (78.907)
Perceived concept development support[a] (α = 0.65; CR=0.90; AVE=0.89; Φ^2 =0.02–0.38)	
7 My university creates awareness of entrepreneurship as a possible career choice.	0.788 (84.849)
8 My university motivates students to start a new business.	0.609 (66.566)
9 My university provides students with ideas from which to start a new business.	0.812 (78.191)
10 My university provides students with the knowledge needed to start a new business.	0.826 (88.471)
Perceived business development support[a] (α = 0.6; CR=0.92; AVE=0.93; Φ^2 =0.02–0.32)	
11 My university provides students with the financial means to start a new business.	0.854 (69.541)
12 My university uses its reputation to support students that start a new business.	0.621 (75.540)
13 My university serves as a lead customer of students that start a new business.	0.652 (73.823)
Perceived institutional support[a] (α = 0.80; CR=0.82; AVE=0.75; Φ^2=0.04–0.45)	
1 In Pakistan, entrepreneurs are encouraged by an institutional structure.	0.605 (75.297)
2 The Pakistani economy provides many opportunities for entrepreneurs.	0.683 (84.468)
3 Taking bank loans is quite difficult for entrepreneurs in Pakistan. (R)	0.589 (92.943)
4 Pakistani state laws are averse to running a business. (R)	0.509 (92.943)
Self-realization[b] To what extent is the following reason important to you in establishing a new business: (α = 0.78; CR=0.84; AVE=0.81; Φ^2=0.03–0.38)	
1 To challenge myself.	0.835 (84.235)
2 To fulfill a personal vision.	0.720 (78.231)
3 To grow and learn as a person.	0.701 (76.325)
4 To lead and motivate others.	0.781 (81.254)

(continued)

Table 1.1.1 (continued)

Construct (Items)	*Factor loading (t-values*)*
Financial success[b] To what extent is the following reason important to you in establishing a new business: (α = 0.75; CR=0.78; AVE=0.79; Φ^2=0.15–0.25)	
1 To earn a larger personal income.	0.948 (71.258)
2 To give myself, my spouse, and children financial security.	0.731 (65.320)
3 To have a chance to build great wealth / high income.	0.746 (81.269)
4 To build a business my children can inherit.	0.680 (78.362)
Role[b] To what extent is the following reason important to you in establishing a new business: (α = 0.80; CR=0.87; AVE=0.83; Φ^2=0.07–0.30)	
1 To continue a family tradition.	0.701 (72.356)
2 To follow example of a person I admire.	0.710 (78.246)
3 To be respected by my friends.	0.670 (80.234)
Innovation[b] To what extent is the following reason important to you in establishing a new business: (α = 0.74; CR=0.80; AVE=0.80; Φ^2=0.10–0.35)	
1 To be innovative at the forefront of technology.	0.832 (87.390)
2 To develop an idea for a product.	0.726 (80.236)
Recognition[b] To what extent is the following reason important to you in establishing a new business: (α = 0.84; CR=0.87; AVE=0.76; Φ^2=0.12–0.47)	
1 To achieve something / get recognition.	0.839 (77.230)
2 To gain a higher position for myself.	0.849 (73.258)
Independence[b] To what extent is the following reason important to you in establishing a new business: (α = 0.90; CR=0.92; AVE=0.86; Φ^2=0.09–0.18)	
1 To get greater flexibility for personal life.	0.777 (75.361)
2 To be free to adapt my approach to work.	0.614 (83.697)
Model fit statistics: $\chi^2_{(94)}$= 612.50 (p=.036); RMSEA = 0.046; GFI = 0.95; NFI = 0.95; CFI = 0.98; TLI =0.85	

(R) reversed coding; α = Cronbach's alpha, *CR* = composite reliability, and *AVE* = average variance extracted.

*Significant at $p \leq .01$; [a] 5-point Likert Scale (1) strongly disagree (5) strongly agree; [b] 5-point Likert Scale (1) to no extent (5) to a very great extent; [c] 5-point Likert scale (1) = None, (2) = Basic, (3) = Competent, (4) = Advanced, (5) = Expert

of interest produced ten factors with eigen values larger than one, which collectively accounted for 65 percent of the variance. The first factor accounted for 41 percent of the variance, which suggests that common method bias may not be a major concern (Podsakoff et al. 2003).

Testing the structural model (without moderator variables)

The results of the structural model presented in Table 1.1.3 are within the recommended values, thus providing support to proceed with hypotheses testing. Our first hypothesis, H1, was supported, that is, ESE positively influenced EI (β = 0.47; p <.05). The results

Table 1.1.2 Correlations and square roots of average variance extracted

Constructs	*1*	*2*	*3*	*4*	*5*	*6*	*7*	*8*	*9*	*10*	*11*	*12*
1 Entrepreneurial intentions	0.96											
2 Entrepreneurial self-efficacy	0.49*	0.89										
3 Perceived educational support	0.43*	0.63*	0.88									
4 Perceived concept development support	0.38*	0.55*	0.63*	0.89								
5 Perceived business development support	0.35*	0.53*	0.60*	0.58*	0.93							
6 Perceived institutional support	0.16*	0.31*	0.21*	0.21*	0.21*	0.87						
7 Self-realization	0.43*	0.49*	0.35*	0.35*	0.35*	0.19*	0.90					
8 Financial success	−0.09	0.04	−0.01	−0.01	−0.01	0.17*	0.01	0.89				
9 Role	0.40*	0.59*	0.39*	0.39*	0.39*	0.26*	0.44*	0.05	0.91			
10 Innovation	0.24	0.28*	0.28*	0.28*	0.28*	0.07	0.22*	0.02	0.29*	0.89		
11 Recognition	0.73*	0.57*	0.37*	0.37*	0.37*	0.20*	0.45*	−0.10	0.45*	0.26*	0.87	
12 Independence	0.37*	0.52*	0.38*	0.38*	0.38*	0.23*	0.44*	0.04	0.48*	0.23*	0.42*	0.93
Mean	3.51	3.75	4.55	4.13	3.48	3.44	3.70	3.0	3.80	3.97	3.52	3.92
Standard deviation	1.04	0.69	1.21	1.31	1.4	0.84	0.99	1.14	0.95	0.99	0.98	1.01

*Significant at $p < .01$
Diagonal values represented in italics are square roots of AVE; off-diagonal values are correlations between constructs.

Table 1.1.3 Results of the structural model

Hypothesis	*Hypothesized path*	*Standardized estimates*	*Results*
H1	ESE → EI	0.47*	Supported
H2a	Perceived educational support → ESE	0.37**	Supported
H2b	Perceived concept development support → ESE	0.34**	Supported
H2c	Perceived business development support → ESE	0.32**	Supported
H3	Perceived institutional support → ESE	0.17**	Supported
H4a	Self-realization → EI	0.37*	Supported
H4b	Financial success → EI	−0.02	Not supported
H4c	Role → EI	0.30*	Supported
H4d	Innovativeness → EI	0.20	Not supported
H4e	Recognition → EI	0.65**	Supported
H4f	Independence → EI	0.18	Not supported
Model fit statistics: $\chi^2_{(94)}$= *612.50* (*p*=.036), RMSEA = 0.046, GFI = 0.95, NFI = 0., NNFI = 0.95, CFI = 0.98, TLI =0.85			

**Significant at $p<.01$; *Significant at $p<.05$
EI = Entrepreneurial intention; ESE = Entrepreneurial self-efficacy

showed a highly significant influence of perceived ES ($\beta = 0.37$; $p<.01$), perceived CDS ($\beta = 0.34$; $p<.01$), and perceived BDS ($\beta = 0.32$; $p<.01$), which provide support for H2a, H2b, and H2c, respectively. The results also showed a highly significant influence of perceived IS ($\beta = 0.17$; $p<.01$) on ESE, thus supporting H3. These results explained a substantial proportion of the variance in ESE (42 percent). In H4, we proposed that the six perceived desirability factors would be positively associated with EI. The results presented in Table 1.1.3 partially support this hypothesis. Out of the six variables tested, three showed no significant effect on EI: financial success, innovativeness, and independence. However, self-realization ($\beta = 0.37$; $p<.05$), role ($\beta = 0.30$; $p<.05$), and recognition ($\beta = 0.65$; $p<.01$) showed a significant positive influence on EI. These variables and ESE explained most of the variance in EI (64 percent).

Discussion and conclusions

The main aim of this study was to assess the extent of students' PUS and its impact on their ESE, which in turn would influence their EI. We examined this proposition within the context of IS and individual motivations. Overall, our results support our hypotheses. In line with previous studies, the results in Table 1.1.3 showed the important role of students' ESE in the prediction of their EI (Boyd and Vozikis 1994; Chen et al. 1998; Krueger et al. 2000) and its usefulness in representing perceived feasibility. They also reflected the importance of perceived organizational-level and institutional-level factors in influencing students' ESE. Our results revealed that perceived ES, perceived CDS, perceived BDS, and perceived IS exerted a significant positive influence on students' ESE, which characterizes perceived feasibility. This suggests that self-efficacy is not a static trait, but rather that it can be changed (Hollenbeck and Hall 2004), which has implications for targeted educational and institutional efforts.

Our findings have demonstrated the significant role of EE and entrepreneurial support as students perceived the education and support that they received from their universities as the most important influence on their ability to become entrepreneurs, which is consistent with previous research (Peterman and Kennedy 2003). However, despite the link between EE and entrepreneurial behavior (Galloway and Brown 2002; Lüthje and Franke 2003), student entrepreneurship figures are still considered to be low (Kraaijenbrink et al. 2010). More specifically, the results showed that of the three measures of PUS, perceived ES was the most important in developing students' ESE, followed by perceived CDS and perceived BDS. Although students perceived that their university was helpful in providing them with the general knowledge and skills to initiate a new venture, they needed more targeted support in terms of concept development and business development. These results are consistent with those of Kraaijenbrink et al. (2010) and help to demonstrate the usefulness of their measures to assess PUS. Therefore, universities are able to measure the impact of their provision of EE and support in order to address the specific needs of their students.

In light of our findings and considering that most researchers agree that entrepreneurial perceptions and intentions can be enhanced by EE (Chen et al. 1998; Cox et al. 2002; Hatten and Ruhland 1995; Kraaijenbrink et al. 2010; Krueger and Brazeal 1994; Peterman and Kennedy 2003; Wang and Wong 2004), we can say that the initiatives taken by the HEC of Pakistan, such as the creation of the NBEAC, seem to be effective. This implies that the institutional efforts to promote business education by focusing on stimulating EE and culture in Pakistani universities have been implemented by universities and are being well received by students in general. Perceived ES showed the highest mean scores of PUS ($M = 4.55$) indicating that students were highly satisfied with the provision of general knowledge and skills to initiate a new venture, which includes programs, electives, projects, internships, conferences, and workshops. The variety of these learning strategies is positive as it helps to build students' self-confidence (Bandura 1992; Cox et al. 2002). Additionally, universities can increase students' ESE by providing them with opportunities to conduct feasibility studies, develop business plans, perform business simulation, use case studies, listen to guest speakers, and take part in meaningful apprenticeships (Cox et al. 2002).

However, while students seemed satisfied with traditional entrepreneurship learning, they required more support from their universities regarding both concept development and business development. This considers the commercialization role of universities and translates into providing individual students or groups of students with a more targeted and specific support for starting their own firm. As shown in Table 1.1.1, perceived CDS had lower means than perceived ES ($M = 4.13$). Therefore, universities should provide awareness, motivation, and business ideas in the early stages of the entrepreneurial process, in which opportunity recognition and development take place (Shane and Venkataraman 2000). In addition, universities could provide start-up firms with BDS at the later stages of the entrepreneurial process. This support was perceived as the weakest by students ($M = 3.48$). This type of support includes providing students with the funding to start a new business, use the university's reputation to support them, and serve as a lead customer for the new venture. This is important as previous studies have shown that the lack funding is a major barrier to student entrepreneurship (Henderson and Robertson 2000; Robertson et al. 2003). Therefore, it can be inferred that the broader support provided by academic institutions, beyond their traditional teaching role, can play an important role in fostering ESE among their students.

In addition to perceived ES, IS had a highly significant effect on EI ($\beta = 0.17$), albeit it was less important to students than PUS ($\beta = 0.33$). This suggests that although the main focus of IS is on existing entrepreneurs, students are aware of it as it could affect them in the future, which again seems to confirm the effectiveness of the initiatives taken by the HEC in Pakistan. Our findings are in line with previous research which argued that institutional factors were key to the development of entrepreneurs, as a hostile institutional environment hinders individuals' willingness to engage in entrepreneurship activities (Luthje and Franke 2003; Schwarz et al. 2009; Turker and Selcuk 2009).

The strong impact of individual motivation on students' EI is an important finding. This indicates that the perceived desirability of starting a business is a fundamental element in the formation of EI. Three factors exerted a significant influence on the formation of EI: self-realization, recognition, and role. No significant impact was found for financial success, innovation, and independence. These findings are in line with previous studies which found that EI is related to self-realization (Carter et al. 2003; Kolvereid 1996), recognition (Birley and Westhead 1994; Scheinberg and MacMillan 1988; Shane et al. 1991), and role (Birley and Westhead 1994; Shane et al. 1991). However, our results do not support previous studies which have found that the intention to be an entrepreneur is stronger for those with more positive attitudes toward innovation (Birley and Westhead 1994; Carter et al. 2003; Mueller and Thomas 2001; Scheinberg and MacMillan 1988; Shane et al. 1991) and independence (Birley and Westhead 1994; Carter et al. 2003; Shane et al. 1991). Our finding that financial success is not significantly important to EI is in line with some previous studies (McQueen and Wallmark 1991), but not with others which found the opposite to be true (Birley and Westhead 1994; Carter et al. 2003).

However, the lack of support in the current study for two important influences on EI, namely, innovation and independence, needs further qualification. A possible explanation may be provided in light of the cultural context of the study. According to Hofstede's (1980) cultural dimensions theory, Pakistan ranks high on power distance (PD), masculinity (MAS), and uncertainty avoidance (UA), but low on individualism (IDV). High PD means individuals accept and expect that power in organizations and institutions will be unequally distributed, and that there would be strong hierarchies and control mechanisms. High MAS refers to traditional male values, such as income and recognition. In high UA, individuals are likely to avoid novel or unknown situations. Finally, while low IND means that collectivism is valued and individuals exhibit long-term commitment and loyalty to their families and relationships, there is less freedom and autonomy to pursue individual interests.

Considering Pakistan's low IND, high PD, and high UA, it is possible to explain the poor results for innovation and independence. This reasoning has been supported by previous research which has found that high rates of innovation were associated with high IND, low PD, and low UA (Shane et al. 1991), and entrepreneurial activity was positively associated with high IND (Gupta et al. 2010; Hofstede 1980). In addition, Pakistan, as a collectivist society, places significant importance on "face" and so the potential loss of face from failure may also discourage innovativeness. This has been demonstrated in the Global Innovation Index published by INSEAD in 2012, which ranked Pakistan 133 out of 141 countries, indicating very low levels of innovativeness. However, low IND in Pakistan can help to explain the strong influence of the role factor on EI. Considering that conformity is emphasized as social ties are important for all members of society, the decision to select a career might be influenced by the individual's family members and friends. Finally, the country's high MAS means that Pakistan is characterized by values such as income and recognition, in which people "live in order to work" and there is emphasis on competition, achievement, and success. Self-realization and recognition were shown to have strong effects on EI, thus reflecting these cultural characteristics.

On the basis of our findings, we can answer the four questions we posed in this chapter: (1) students have a positive perception of the EE and support they receive from their universities; (2) PUS has a significant impact on ESE, and students perceive ES as the most important variable influencing their ESE, followed by CDS and BDS; (3) PUS exerts a much stronger impact on EI than IS and individual motivations; and (4) students are satisfied with the traditional EE that they receive, but they need more targeted support from their universities in terms of concept development and business development. Universities should then address these needs in order to be more effective.

In conclusion, we argue that the role of EE and support is fundamental to student entrepreneurship. Therefore, to enhance student entrepreneurship, we suggest that universities should continuously assess the extent of their support and its impact on students. Our findings show that universities are perceived to be strong in their traditional teaching role, but they are falling short in their commercialization role. They can strengthen their provision with appropriate support throughout the entrepreneurial process. EE is an important influence on EI, but it is not the only one. Thus, we have proposed that the three-dimensional support of universities together with IS increases students' perceived feasibility, as measured by ESE. In turn, ESE and perceived desirability, represented by individual motivations such as self-realization, recognition, and role, shape EI to start a business. Our findings suggest that this holistic approach provides a more meaningful understanding of the role of EE and support in the formation of students' EI.

Limitations and directions for future research

Our study is subject to some limitations. First, like the vast majority of studies in the literature, our focus is on behavioral intention rather than actual behavior. Although the predictive validity of intention has been established in a general context, it has yet to be established in the entrepreneurial context. As a consequence, our study is unable to predict how many students will actually materialize their EI. A longitudinal study could reveal a better understanding of whether EI actually turns into entrepreneurial behavior. Second, we made a selection of individual, organizational, and institutional variables that were found to be most influential in predicting EI through our extensive literature review, but other variables could also be important. Finally, our study examines university students in Pakistani universities, thus our findings may be mostly generalizable to developing countries. However, our framework provides a meaningful understanding of the topic and other researchers can apply it in different contexts in the future.

References

Ajzen, I. (1991). "The Theory of Planned Behavior," *Organizational Behavior and Human Decision Processes*, 50(2), 179–211.

Bagozzi, R., H. Baumgartner, and Y. Yi (1989). "An Investigation into the Role of Intentions as Mediators of the Attitude-Behavior Relationship," *Journal of Economic Psychology*, 10(1), 35–62.

Bandura, A. (1986). *The Social Foundations of Thought and Action*. Englewood Cliffs, NJ: Prentice-Hall.

Bandura, A. (1989). "Human Agency in Social Cognitive Theory," *American Psychologist*, 44(9), 1175–1184.

Bandura, A. (1992). "Exercise of Personal Agency through the Self-Efficacy Mechanism," in *Self-Efficacy: Thought Control of Action*. Ed. R. Schwarzer. Washington, DC: Hemisphere, 3–38.

Basu, A. (1998). "An Exploration of Entrepreneurial Activity among Asian Small Businesses in Britain," *Small Business Economics*, 10(4), 313–326.

Baumol, W. (1993). *Entrepreneurship, Management and the Structure of Payoffs*. London: MIT Press.

Bird, B. (1988). "Implementing Entrepreneurial Ideas: The Case for Intention," *Academy of Management Review*, 13(3), 442–453.

Birley, S., and P. Westhead (1994). "A Taxonomy of Business Start-Up Reasons and Their Impact on Firm Growth and Size," *Journal of Business Venturing*, 9(1), 7–31.

Bosma, N., S. Wennekers, and J. E. Amoros (2011). Global Entrepreneurship Monitor 2011 Extended Report: Entrepreneurs and Entrepreneurial Employees across the Globe. Available at: http://gemconsortium.org/docs/download/2200. Last accessed: 30–10–2012.

Boyd, N., and G. Vozikis (1994). "The Influence of Self-Efficacy on the Development of Entrepreneurial Intentions and Actions," *Entrepreneurship Theory and Practice*, 18(4), 63–77.

Carree, M., and A. Thurik (2005). "The Impact of Entrepreneurship on Economic Growth," *Handbook of Entrepreneurship Research*, 1(7), 437–471.

Carter, N. M., W. B. Gartner, K. G. Shaver, and E. J. Gatewood (2003). "The Career Reasons of Nascent Entrepreneurs," *Journal of Business Venturing*, 18(1), 13–39.

Chen, C. C., P. G. Greene, and A. Crick (1998). "Does Entrepreneurial Self-Efficacy Distinguish Entrepreneurs from Managers?" *Journal of Business Venturing*, 13(4), 295–316.

Cox, L. W., S. L. Mueller, and S. E. Moss (2002). "The Impact of Entrepreneurship Education on Entrepreneurial Self-Efficacy," *International Journal of Entrepreneurship Education*, 1(2), 2–23.

Davidsson, P. (1995). "Determinants of entrepreneurial intentions." Paper prepared for the RENT IX Workshop, Piacenza, Italy, 11. 23–24.

Debackere, K., and R. Veugelers (2005). "The Role of Academic Technology Transfer Organizations in Improving Industry Science Links," *Research Policy*, 34(3), 321–342.

De Bettignies, J.-E., and J. Brander (2007). "Financing Entrepreneurship: Bank Finance versus Venture Capital," *Journal of Business Venturing*, 22(6), 808–832.

Di Gregorio, D., and S. Shane (2003). "Why Do Some Universities Generate More Start-Ups Than Others?" *Research Policy*, 32(2), 209–227.

Douglas, E., and D. Shepherd (2002). "Self-employment as a Career Choice: Attitudes, Entrepreneurial Intentions, and Utility Maximization," *Entrepreneurial Theory and Practice*, 26(3), 81–90.

Feldman, D. C., and M. C. Bolino (2000). "Career Patterns of the Self-Employed: Career Motivations and Career Outcomes," *Journal of Small Business Management*, 38(3), 53–67.

Fornell, C., and D. F. Larcker (1981). "Evaluating Structural Equation Models with Unobservable Variables and Measurement Error," *Journal of Marketing Research*, 18(2), 39–50.

Galloway, L., and W. Brown (2002). "Entrepreneurship Education at University: A Driver in the Creation of High Growth Firms," *Education + Training*, 44(8/9), 398–405.

Gatewood, E. J. (1993). "The Expectancies in Public Sector Venture Assistance," *Entrepreneurship: Theory Practice*, 17(2), 91–95.

Gentry, W., and R. Hubbard (2000). "Tax Policy and Entrepreneurial Entry," *American Economic Review*, 90(2), 283–287.

Gibson, D. E. (2004). "Role Models in Career Development: New Directions for Theory and Research," *Journal of Vocational Behavior*, 65(1), 134–156.

Gnyawali, R., and D. S. Fogel (1994). "Environments for Entrepreneurship Development: Key Dimension," *Entrepreneurship: Theory and Practice*, 18(4), 43–62.

Gupta, V., G. Chun Guo, M. Duarte Canever, H. R. Yim, G. K. Sraw, and M. Liu (2010). *Assessing the Institutional Environment for Entrepreneurship in Rapidly Emerging Major Economies: The Case of Brazil, China, India and South Korea*. Paper presented at the 2010 Southern Management Association meeting in St. Pete Beach, FL.

Hair, J., W. Black, B. Babin, R. Anderson, and R. Tatham (2006). *Multivariate Data Analysis*, 6th ed. Upper Saddle River, NJ: Pearson Prentice Hall.

Hartshorn, C., and P.D. Hannon (2005). "Paradoxes in Entrepreneurship Education: Chalk and Talk or Chalk and Cheese? A Case Approach," *Education + Training*, 47(8/9), 616–627.

Hatten, T., and S. Ruhland (1995). "Student Attitude toward Entrepreneurship as Predicted by Participation in an SBI Program," *Journal of Education for Business*, 70(4), 224–228.

Henderson, R., and M. Robertson (2000). "Who Wants to Be an Entrepreneur? Young Adult Attitudes to Entrepreneurship as a Career," *Career Development International*, 5(6), 279–287.

Hofstede, G. (1980). *Culture's Consequences: International Differences in Work Related Values*. Beverly Hills, CA: Sage.

Hollenbeck, G. P., and D. T. Hall (2004). "Self-Confidence and Leader Performance," *Organizational Dynamics*, 33(3), 254–269.

Ingram, P. L., and B. S. Silverman (2002). "The New Institutionalism in Strategic Management," in *Advances in Strategic Management*. Ed. P. Ingram, and B. S. Silverman. Greenwich, CT: JAI, 1–32.

Ireland R. D., and J. W. Webb (2007). "Strategic Entrepreneurship: Creating Competitive Advantage through Streams of Innovation," *Business Horizons*, 50(1), 49–59.

Kirchhoff, B. A. (1996). "Self-Employment and Dynamic Capitalism," *Journal of Labor Research*, 17(4), 627–643.

Kolvereid, L. (1996). "Prediction of Employment Status Choice Intentions," *Entrepreneurship Theory & Practice*, 21(1), 47–57.

Kolvereid, L., and O. Moen (1997). "Entrepreneurship among Business Graduates: Does a Major in Entrepreneurship Make a Difference?" *Journal of European Industrial Training*, 21(4), 154–60.

Kraaijenbrink, J., A. Groen, and G. Bos (2010). "What Do Students Think of The Entrepreneurial Support Given by Their Universities?" *International Journal of Entrepreneurship and Small Business*, 9(1), 110–125.

Krueger, N. F., and D. V. Brazeal (1994). "Entrepreneurial Potential and Potential Entrepreneurs," *Entrepreneurship Theory and Practice*, 18(3), 91–104.

Krueger, N. F., and A. L. Carsrud (1993). "Entrepreneurial Intentions: Applying the Theory of Planned Behavior," *Entrepreneurship Regional Development*, 5(4), 315–330.

Krueger, N. F., M. D. Reilly, and A. L. Carsrud (2000). "Competing Models of Entrepreneurial Intentions," *Journal of Business Venturing*, 15(5–6), 411–432.

Lerner, J. (2005). "The University and the Start-Up: Lessons from the Past Two Decades," *Journal of Technology Transfer*, 30(1–2), 49–56.

Li, W. (2007). "Ethnic Entrepreneurship: Studying Chinese and Indian Students in the United States," *Journal of Developmental Entrepreneurship*, 12(4), 449–466.

Liñán, F., and Y. W. Chen (2009). "Development and Cross-Cultural Application of a Specific Instrument to Measure Entrepreneurial Intentions," *Entrepreneurship Theory and Practice*, 33(3), 593–617.

Louis, K. S., D. Blumenthal, M. E. Gluck, and M. A. Stoto (1989). "Entrepreneurs in Academe: An Exploration of Behaviors among Life Scientists," *Administrative Science Quarterly*, 34(1), 110–131.

Lüthje, C., and N. Franke (2003). "The 'Making' of an Entrepreneur: Testing a Model of Entrepreneurial Intent among Engineering Students at MIT," *R&D Management*, 33(2), 135–147.

Manolova, T. S., C. G. Brush, and L. F. Edelman (2008). "What Do Women Entrepreneurs Want?" *Strategic Change Journal*, 17(3–4), 69–82.

Markham G., D. Balkin, and R. Baron (2002). "Inventors and New Venture Formation: The Effects of General Self-Efficacy and Regretful Thinking," *Entrepreneurship Theory and Practice*, 27(2), 149–165.

McClelland, D. C. (1961). *The Achieving Society*. New York: Free Press.

McMillan, J., and C. Woodruff (2002). "The Central Role of Entrepreneurs in Transition Economies," *The Journal of Economic Perspectives*, 16(3), 153–170.

McQueen, D. H., and J. T. Wallmark (1991). "University Technical Innovation: Spin-Offs and Patents, in Goteborg, Sweden," in *University Spin-off Companies: Economic Development, Faculty Entrepreneurs, and Technology Transfers*. Ed. Brett, A. M., Gibson, D. V., and Smilor, R. W. Savage, MD: Rowman and Littlefield Publishers, 103–115.

Mian, S. A. (1996). "Assessing Value-Added Contributions of University Technology Business Incubators to Tenant Firms," *Research Policy*, 25(3), 325–335.

Mian, S. A. (1997). "Assessing and Managing the University Technology Business Incubator: An Integrative Framework," *Journal of Business Venturing*, 12(4), 251–285.

Mueller, S., and A. Thomas (2001). "Culture and Entrepreneurial Potential: A Nine Country Study of Locus of Control and Innovativeness," *Journal of Business Venturing*, 16(1), 51–75.

North, D. (2005). *Understanding the Process of Economic Change*. Princeton, NJ: Princeton University Press.

Nunnally, J. C., and I. H. Bernstein (1994). *Psychometric Theory*. New York: McGraw-Hill.

Peterman, N. E., and J. Kennedy (2003). "Enterprise Education: Influencing Students Perceptions of Entrepreneurship," *Entrepreneurship: Theory and Practice*, 28(2), 129–144.

Podsakoff, P. M., S. B. MacKenzie, J. Y. Lee, and N. P. Podsakoff (2003). "Common Method Biases in Behavioral Research: A Critical Review of the Literature and Recommended Remedies," *Journal of Applied Psychology*, 88(5), 879–903.

Robertson, M., A. Collins, N. Madeira, and J. Slater (2003). "Barriers to Start-Up and Their Effects on Aspirant Entrepreneurs," *Education + Training*, 45(6), 308–316.

Scheinberg, S., and I. MacMillan (1988). "An 11 Country Study of Motivations to Start a Business," in *Frontiers of Entrepreneurship Research*. Ed. B. Kirchoff, Long, W., McMullan, W., Vesper, K. H., and Wetzel, W. Wellesley, MA: Babson College, 669–687.

Schumpeter, J. (1934). *The Theory of Economic Development*. Cambridge, MA: Harvard University Press.

Schwarz, E.J., M. A. Wdowiak, D. A. Almer-Jarz, and R. J. Breitenecker (2009). "The Effects of Attitudes and Perceived Environment Conditions on Students' Entrepreneurial Intent," *Education + Training*, 51(4), 272–291.

Shane, S., and S. Venkataraman (2000). "The Promise of Entrepreneurship as a Field of Research," *Academy of Management Review*, 25(1), 217–226.

Shane, S., L. Kolvereid, and P. Westhead (1991). "An Exploratory Examination of the Reasons Leading to New Firm Formation Across Country and Gender," *Journal of Business Venturing*, 6(6), 431–446.

Shapero, A. (1975). "The Displaced, Uncomfortable Entrepreneur," *Psychology Today*, 9(6), 83–88.

Shapero, A., and L. Sokol (1982). "The Social Dimensions of Entrepreneurship," in *Encyclopedia of Entrepreneurship*. Ed. C. A. Kent, D. L. Sexton., and K. H. Vesper. Englewood Cliffs, NJ: Prentice Hall, 72–90.

Souitaris, V., S. Zerbinati, and A. Allaham (2007). "Do Entrepreneurship Programmes Raise Entrepreneurial Intention of Science and Engineering Students? The Effect of Learning, Inspiration and Resources," *Journal of Business Venturing*, 22(4), 566–591.

Stewart, W. H., W. E. Watson, J. C. Carland, and J. W. Carland (1999). "A Proclivity for Entrepreneurship: A Comparison of Entrepreneurs, Small Business Owners, and Corporate Managers," *Journal of Business Venturing*, 14(2), 189–214.

Tijssen, R. J. W. (2006). "Universities and Industrially Relevant Science: Toward Measurement Models and Indicators of Entrepreneurial Orientation," *Research Policy*, 35(10), 1569–1585.

Timmons, J. A., and S. Spinelli (2004). *New Venture Creation: Entrepreneurship for the 21st Century*. New York: McGraw Hill

Turker, D., and S. Selcuk (2009). "Which Factors Affect Entrepreneurial Intention of University Students?" *Journal of European Industrial Training*, 33(2), 142–159.

Upton, N., D. Sexton, and C. Moore (1995). "Have We Made a Difference? An Examination of Career Activity of Entrepreneurship Major Since 1981," *Frontiers of Entrepreneurship Research*, Proceedings of the 15th Annual Entrepreneurship Research Conference, Babson College, Wellesley, MA.

Utsch, A., and A. Rauch (2000). "Innovativeness and Initiative as Mediators between Achievement Orientation and Venture Performance," *European Journal of Work and Organizational Psychology*, 9(1), 45–62.

Veciana, J. M., M. Aponte, and D. Urbano (2005). "University Students' Attitudes towards Entrepreneurship: A Two Countries Comparison," *International Entrepreneurship and Management Journal*, 1, 165–182.

Walter, A., M. Auer, and T. Ritter (2006). "The impact of Network Capabilities and Entrepreneurial Orientation on University Spin-Off Performance," *Journal of Business Venturing*, 21(4), 541–567.

Wang, C. K., and P. K. Wong (2004). "Entrepreneurial Interest of University Students in Singapore," *Technovation*, 24(2), 163–172.

Wilson, F., D. Marlino, and J. Kickul (2004). "Our Entrepreneurial Future: Examining the Diverse Attitudes and Motivations of Teens across Gender and Ethnic Identity," *Journal of Developmental Entrepreneurship*, 9(3), 177–197.

Zhao, H., S. E. Seibert, and G. E. Hills (2005). "The Mediating Role of Self-Efficacy in the Development of Entrepreneurial Intentions," *The Journal of Applied Psychology*, 90(6), 1265–1272.

1.2 Motivations and entrepreneurial orientation of sustainable entrepreneurs

An exploratory study of sustainable entrepreneurship archetypes in the fashion industry

René Bohnsack and Lori Di Vito

Introduction

Sustainable entrepreneurs, i.e. entrepreneurs that "obtain entrepreneurial rents while simultaneously improving local and global social and environmental conditions" (Cohen & Winn, 2007: 29) frequently tackle market imperfections in a niche to challenge the unsustainable status quo (Hockerts & Wüstenhagen, 2010). It has been argued that these entrepreneurs are often motivated by internal convictions and at the same time are also profit-driven (Dixon & Clifford, 2007; Kirkwood & Walton 2010). Thus, sustainable entrepreneurs need to balance social, environmental and economic goals (Elkington, 1994). In doing so, it appears that some sustainable entrepreneurs put sustainable goals first whereas others prioritize economic outcomes, influenced by their entrepreneurial orientation (EO) (DiVito & Bohnsack, 2017). This suggests differences in types of sustainable entrepreneurs.

In this chapter we study sustainable entrepreneur archetypes based on their motivations to start a venture and on their EO. This is important to understand since the degrees of EO and motivations determine not only the sustainability of a venture but also its success and activities of sustainable entrepreneurs. In combining motivations of sustainable entrepreneurs with EO we seek to increase the explanatory power of sustainable entrepreneurship, its drivers and motivations.

For this chapter we study sustainable fashion entrepreneurs in the Netherlands and find different types of sustainable entrepreneurship. However, before moving to our empirical results we will review the theoretical basis of sustainable entrepreneurship and conceptualize the link between the motivations of sustainable entrepreneurs and EO.

Theoretical background: sustainable entrepreneurship

According to Parrish (2010), entrepreneurs are characterized as profit-oriented, opportunistic and business minded. To that end, entrepreneurship itself is "a process of identifying, evaluating and pursuing opportunities through creativity, innovativeness and transformation to produce new products, processes and values that are beneficial" (Stokes et al., 2010). It creates jobs, business opportunities and product innovation, which might help to improve the economic condition of a country. However, while entrepreneurship has created many opportunities for society and the economy, it can also exert negative impacts on the environment (Pacheco, Dean, & Payne, 2010). Thus, there is a call for 'sustainability transformation'.

A specific breed of entrepreneurs tackles these social and/or environmental problems. These have been called social entrepreneurs, ecopreneurs or sustainable entrepreneurs. While social entrepreneurs incorporate societal goals into their company and are not necessarily profit-driven, ecopreneurs focus on preserving natural resources and embed these values while creating economic development (Keogh & Polonsky, 1998; Pastakia, 1998). Finally, sustainable entrepreneurs combine these two perspectives (see Table 1.2.1 for an overview).

Sustainable entrepreneurship is about "the process of discovering, evaluating, and exploiting economic opportunities that are present in market failure which detract from sustainability, including those that are environmentally relevant" (Dean & McMullen, 2007). More specifically, Patzelt and Shepherd (2011) claim that sustainable entrepreneurship is about:

> [t]he preservation of nature, life support, and community in the pursuit of perceived opportunities to bring into existence future products, processes, and services for gain, where gain is broadly construed to include economic and non-economic gains to individuals, the economy and society.

An overview of definitions of sustainable entrepreneurship is given in Table 1.2.2.

Despite the general agreement of motivations of sustainable entrepreneurs, there is still significant heterogeneity. Vega and Kidwell (2007) studied 80 ventures and found that entrepreneurs differed in terms of traits, goals, tendencies and sources of motivation. Studies suggest that sustainable entrepreneurs are largely driven by their personal values to improve environmental and social aspects (Schaltegger & Wagner, 2011). Schick et al. (2002) equally find that sustainable entrepreneurs are in general more internally motivated, namely driven by environmental and societal concerns. In fact, according to Choi and Gray (2008), sustainable entrepreneurs are often little focused on their own personal wealth but rather are more interested in contributing to make a difference in the world. Surprising is, however, that sustainable entrepreneurs often have little or no relevant business experience (Choi & Gray, 2008) and that the more business experience increases,

Table 1.2.1 Different types of entrepreneurs

Type of entrepreneurship	*Ecopreneurship*	*Social entrepreneurship*	*Sustainable entrepreneurship*
Core motivation	Contributes to solving environmental problems and creates economic value	Contributes to solving societal problems and creates value for the society	Contributes to solving environmental and societal problems through the realization of a successful business
Main goal	Earns money by solving environmental problems	Achieves societal goal and secures funding to achieve this	Creates sustainable development through entrepreneurial corporate activities
Role of non-market goals	Environmental issues as integrated core element	Societal goals as ends	Core element of integrated end to contribute to sustainable development

Source: Adapted from Schaltegger & Wagner (2011).

Table 1.2.2 General overview of definitions of 'sustainable entrepreneurship'

Author	*Definition*
Dean & McMullen (2007: 58)	"The process of discovering, evaluating, and exploiting economic opportunities that are present in market failures which detract from sustainability, including those that are environmentally relevant".
Cohen & Winn (2007: 35)	"The examination of how opportunities to bring into existence future goods and services are discovered, created, and exploited, by whom, and with what economic, psychological, social, and environmental consequences".
Choi & Gray (2008: 559)	"Create profitable enterprises and achieve certain environmental and/or social objectives, pursue and achieve what is often referred to as the double bottom-line or triple bottom-line".
Hockerts & Wüstenhagen (2010: 482)	"The discovery and exploitation of economic opportunities through the generation of market disequilibria that initiate the transformation of a sector towards an environmentally and socially more sustainable state".
Schaltegger & Wagner (2011: 224)	"An innovative, market-oriented and personality driven form of creating economic and societal value by means of a breakthrough environmentally or socially beneficial market or institutional innovations".
Patzelt & Shepherd (2011: 142)	"Sustainable Entrepreneurship is focused on the preservation of nature, life support, and community in the pursuit of perceived opportunities to bring into existence future products, processes, and services for gain, where gain is broadly construed to include economic and non-economic gains to individuals, the economy, and society".

the more sustainability orientation (SO) is actually decreasing (Kuckertz & Wagner, 2010). Thus, with increasing experience, firms, such as sustainable SMEs, become actually less sustainable. Also, Masurel (2007) finds that SMEs, i.e. on average more established firms compared to the starting sustainable entrepreneur, are more motivated by external influences, such as government regulation or opportunities, to invest in environmental concerns rather than internal motivations. DiVito and Bohnsack (2017) shed light on this phenomenon and link SO with EO. The study shows that EO influences the decision-making of sustainable entrepreneurs, hence showing that EO is an important concept to consider for sustainable entrepreneurs.

EO is an established concept in the entrepreneurship literature and has been used to study the performance of entrepreneurial firms, decision-making styles of entrepreneurs, or internationalization in entrepreneurship to name a few (Covin & Slevin, 1989; Lumpkin & Dess, 2001). Entrepreneurial orientation is a multi-dimensional measure of innovativeness (the tendency to experiment and depart from established practice), pro-activeness (the propensity to act aggressively towards rivals and take initiative) and risk taking (the willingness to assume high risks for high rewards or losses) (Lumpkin & Dess, 1996, 2001). A high EO has been associated with higher firm performance and a low EO with lower performance.

Given the potentially different degrees (i.e. high vs. low) of sustainable motivation and EO respectively, we argue in this chapter that sustainable entrepreneurs can be allocated into four archetypes. Figure 1.2.1 illustrates that sustainable entrepreneurs can have either a low or high sustainability motivation and could have low or high EO. Sustainable

		Entrepreneurial orientation	
		Low	**High**
Sustainability motivation	**High**	1 Idealists *Make the world a better place*	2 Evangelists *Change the rules of the game*
	Low	3 Realists *There is only so much one can do*	4 Opportunists *In it for the money*

Figure 1.2.1 Sustainable entrepreneur archetypes based on sustainability motivation and entrepreneurial orientation

entrepreneurs with high sustainability motivation but low EO are likely to be inexperienced (Kuckertz & Wagner, 2010), driven by the wish to change unsustainable practices, which we coin the 'Idealist'. Sustainable entrepreneurs with more experience, e.g. from prior ventures, with high EO and sustainability motivation are probably the most desired form since they can change the rules of the game; thus we call them 'Evangelist'. On the contrary, entrepreneurs with a low EO but also somewhat lowered sustainability motivation could potentially have different characteristics. They might either have realized that a successful venture based on sustainable premises is a challenge or they want to start small and see how the venture develops; thus we call these the 'Realists'. Last, entrepreneurs with low sustainability motivation but with high EO are likely to be experienced, aware of market or regulatory opportunities based on sustainability. Clearly, for them the economic goal is more important than sustainability; thus we call them 'Opportunists'.

Thus, types of sustainable entrepreneurs are likely to be diverse and nuanced. Some want to do good while doing well and others want to do well while doing good, which has implications for the performance and longevity of ventures. In the following we set out to explore these types in an empirical setting.

Research design

In order to explore *motivations and entrepreneurial orientations of sustainable entrepreneurs*, we conducted an exploratory multiple case study of sustainable entrepreneurs. Sustainable entrepreneurs position their business models on sustainability principles or values and publicly communicate this position to various stakeholder groups (customers, employees, suppliers). In this way, sustainability concerns are part of the firms' so-called 'DNA' and integral to the firms' strategic decision-making in the fashion industry. We draw our sample of firms from the fashion industry, which faces sustainability issues throughout their value chains. On the production side, examples include water and waste management in growing cotton and dyeing fabric, along with hazardous chemical discharge and worker safety. On the consumer side, examples include overconsumption and excess waste due to short product lifecycles, along with a lack of industry infrastructure to recycle and reuse discarded textiles. Fashion brands are under increasing public scrutiny and pressure to reduce ecological and social impact of textile production, which is highly fragmented and outsourced to foreign suppliers exacerbating control and transparency issues. Additionally, small- and medium-sized firms have weak leverage over suppliers due to their lower volumes. Thus, this industry is a fertile ground for sustainable entrepreneurs.

Our study of sustainable entrepreneurs comprised several stages, namely identification and construction of cases, telephone follow-up, cluster-analysis, in-depth interviews and overall analysis (cf. Loane et al., 2006). First, we compiled a list of sustainable fashion firms by conducting web searches with the key words 'sustainable fashion' and complemented the search exhibitors at the Green Orange Fashion Fair, held annually in Amsterdam. We screened firms based on the visibility and communication of their sustainability values as part of their business model. This yielded a list of 67 firms. We first gathered information via the internet and subsequently held structured telephone interviews with 24 firms and semi-structured in-depth interviews with a subsample of 6 firms. In the interviews we gathered missing information about the firm (founding date, size, turnover), the entrepreneur (age, education and previous employment) and their motivations.

In order to measure the different aspects of sustainability motivations and EOs we applied different Likert scales. In order to measure sustainability motivations we adapted Kirkwood and Walton's (2010) scale of motivational drivers. Kirkwood and Walton (2010) found the following motivational factors for ecopreneurs to start a business: their green values, the gap in the market, making a living, being your own boss, and passion. We added social values and regulatory changes to the scale. These had to be assessed by the sustainable entrepreneurs on a scale from 1 to 5. To measure EO, we followed Tan (2007) and measured innovativeness, pro-activeness, aggressiveness, futurity and riskiness based on scales from 1 to 5. Moreover, we conducted detailed interviews subsequent to the telephone interviews in order to understand in more depth the orientations of the entrepreneurs. The data was analysed for descriptive statistics and correlations. We enriched our findings through in-depth interviews that were recorded, transcribed, coded and analysed within and across cases for patterns and emergent themes (Figure 1.2.2).

Results

In the following we report the results that emerged from our research. First, we report the general characteristics of the sample, then we present the sustainability motivations and EO and last, we explore how the ventures can be allocated into the conceptual clusters.

The majority of the firms were established recently, and in most cases, they only had one founder (70.8%). Many had entrepreneurial or business experience. Since most of the companies were in their start-up phase, they did not employ employees or only very few. The firms that had employees hired them usually after two or more years. In order to start the company, entrepreneurs need financial resources; from the results of the survey it became clear that more than half used their own private capital to finance it. The majority of the sustainable entrepreneurs reported that they were profitable. The products that were offered can be divided into five categories: clothing, women's wear, baby wear, accessories and everything. The largest group (25%) is operating in the (women's) clothing sector. For a summary, please refer to Table 1.2.3.

The sustainable entrepreneurs in the sample followed different motives to start their venture. Following Kirkwood and Walton's (2010) adapted scales, we report the sustainable motivations of the sample; the first five aspects of Table 1.2.4 are intrinsic motivations whereas the last two are extrinsic influences.

Earning a living is not the primary reason for many sustainable fashion entrepreneurs to start a business. In fact, this item had the lowest score on average (2.9) compared to

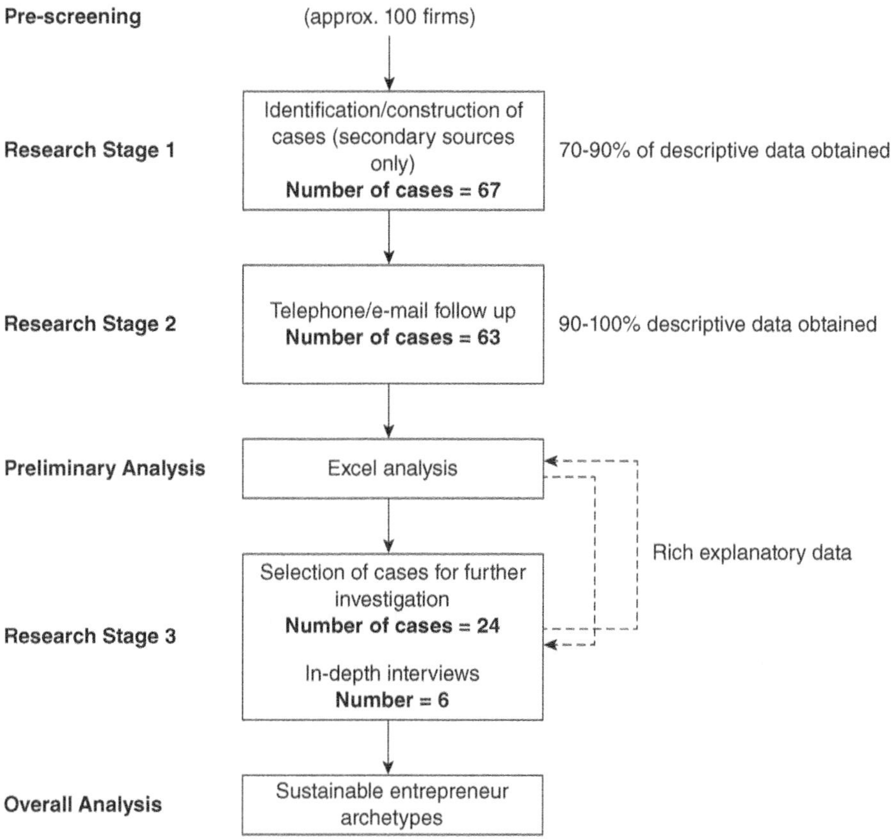

Figure 1.2.2 Research design

the other motivations. Nevertheless the majority (10 out of 22) agree that money is important to survive. The highest motivator mentioned by more than half of the entrepreneurs is that it had always been a dream for them to achieve this (4.6). The quote from company 18 indicates this:

> *Case 18: The motivation to start my own company was because making clothing is a hobby and a passion, and being free from a boss. Doing something back for society and the environment comes on the second place. Money is important because you need to have money to keep on existing, but it is not the main goal. Start with yourself, I cannot change who I am.*

However, we also found that sustainable entrepreneurs struggle to make money and thus cannot always work full time on their venture:

> *Company 1: I am planning to make this my full time job if that is possible, now it is more a hobby. I do need to pay my rent every month. Although, it is sort of a hobby I do not treat it as a hobby, I take every action really serious and it is a serious project. I spend 3,5 day on my company and besides that I work 3 days somewhere else as well.*

Table 1.2.3 General data in the base year 2014

Foundation year	*Before 2000* *3 (12.5%)*	*2000–2004* *1 (4.2%)*		*2005–2009* *9 (37.5%)*		*2010–2013* *11 (45.8%)*
Number of founders	*One founder* 17 (70.8%)			*Two founders* 7 (29.2%)		
Background	*Entrepreneurial* 8 (33.3%)	*Business* 4 (16.7%) *Marketing* 1 (4.2%) *Finance* 1 (4.2%) *Communication* 2 (8.3%)	*Fashion* 6 (25%)	*Design* 3 (12.5%)	*Sustainability* 1 (4.2%)	*Art Academy* 2 (8.3%)
Number of employees	*0* 9 (37.5%)	*1–2* 3 (12.5%)	*3–5* 3 (12.5%)	*6–10* 1 (4.2%)	*11–25* 2 (8.3%)	*N/A* 6 (25%)
Starting capital	*Private capital* 13 (54.2%)	*Public funds* 1 (4.2%)	*Multiple* 3 (12.5%) *Private and loan* 1 (4.2%) *Private loan and Venture Capital* 1 (4.2%) *Private, loan and public* 1 (4.2%)	*Other* 2 (8.3%)	*N/A* 5 (20.8%)	
Profitable	*Yes* 16 (66.7%)		*No* 6 (25%)		*N/A* 2 (8.3%)	
Product category	*Clothing* 6 (25%) *Jeans* 3 (12.5%) *T-shirts* 1 (4.2%) *All* 2 (8.3%)	*Women's wear* 8 (33.3%)	*Baby wear* 2 (8.3%)	*Accessories* 5 (20.8%) *Bags* 2 (8.3%) *Other* 3 (12.5)	*Everything* 1 (4.2%)	

Table 1.2.4 Sustainability motivations of the sample

1 = not important / 5 = very important	*1*	*2*	*3*	*4*	*5*	*N/A*	*Total**	*Average*
Intrinsic								
Earning a living	6	2	4	10	1	1	24	2.9
Green values	1	0	1	10	12	1	25	4.3
Social values	0	0	0	10	14	1	25	4.6
Entrepreneur's passion / dream	0	0	1	8	15	1	25	4.6
Being own boss	0	2	2	9	10	1	24	4.2
Extrinsic								
Gap in the market	4	3	6	10	0	1	24	3.0
Change of regulation	6	3	5	4	5	1	24	3.0

* *Total is the number of firms*

Equally high scored was social values as a motivation (4.6). Sustainable entrepreneurs are aware of the problems that exist within the supply chain of the fashion industry. Almost as high are green values (4.3), which reflects the urge to stop the lifestyle that will have a negative impact on the earth. They want to preserve the planet for their children and see the necessity to do this through a sustainable venture. Some 14 and 12 firms respectively confirm this by the highest score on both the social and green values. Nevertheless, they also often face difficulties due to their values.

> *Case 15: The most difficult situation is our actual one; we do not sell a lot of products since we started, mainly because of price. Since the beginning people tell us to stop organic and recycled fabric or to produce in foreign countries and get lower cost. But we do not want to change our DNA, we really want to produce our collections in French factories and use eco-friendly fabrics. The more difficult is to find good suppliers who can do what we want, and sometimes we prefer to drop an idea, because we cannot do it in France. But maybe one day we will have to move our production, because French factories are closing one by one . . . We sometimes lose our confidence into our values.*

On the other hand, there is also a group of entrepreneurs who did not start the business out of sustainability values, as the quote below shows:

> *Case 19: I did not start this company because I missed a sustainable label. I wanted to do something that I liked and had affinity with. Also be conscious about the process and even in the very beginning, we developed clothing that is still sold in our shop, or sold second hand because the quality is still really good.*

Our literature review revealed that extrinsic factors also motivate sustainable entrepreneurs. However, the two items 'opportunities in the market' and 'government regulation' score rather low (3.0 each), however, with a high standard deviation. Thus it seems to be important to some but less to others. This might also be due to the fact that government activities are seen with caution due to bureaucracy as the following quotes illustrate:

> *Case 9: The government writes a public tender. In which you have to declare that you do your best to prevent child labour. No results commitment but a declaration of commitment. This*

> *action will stimulate that sustainable initiatives will become useless. The same goes for signing a statement in which you declare that you won't allow structural overhours and no forced labour. On the other hand, production has to take place within two months. This means, weaving yarns, confection and doing some work in the Netherlands. Everything needs to be done within two months. This is the difference between theory and how it works in practice, this de-motivates, there are no real changes practiced.*
>
> *Company 18: There is a lot of information available about sustainability, and regulations seem to work counterproductive. You need to be able to change quickly and adjust to the environment.*

In summary, our sample seems to be largely intrinsically motivated and the firms specifically started their venture due to social and green values as well as the desire to follow their own dream.

Next to motivations for the venture, we studied the EO of the sample on the following dimensions: innovativeness, pro-activeness, aggressiveness, futurity and riskiness. Table 1.2.5 provides an overview of the results. The first three statements refer to the future orientation of the entrepreneurs. The greater part of the entrepreneurs think about the future while making strategic decisions. They also strive for long-term profitability above short-term profitability as the following quote reflects:

> *Company 2: We think long term, if you pull out a product out of the closet in 4 years time, we want you to think "I still like this jacket". It has to be durable and timeless. All our products are focused on design and the future.*

However, entrepreneurs are a bit restrained when it comes to investments that will eventually provide a competitive advantage; they are more cautious with investments. The second dimension was *innovativeness*. The majority of entrepreneurs think they are quite innovative, and when linked to sustainability, it becomes clear that innovation is very important as the following quotes illustrate:

> *Company 8: It is embedded into our company values with a circular economy as business model, we innovate every time.*
>
> *Company 2: We want the consumers to think "wow that is something I must have". So yes being innovative is very important to us.*

The next dimension reflects the proactiveness of an entrepreneur. The following statement was given "when making strategic decisions we respond to opportunities quickly". When new opportunities arise it is important for entrepreneurs to be fast, and 11 out of 23 entrepreneurs agree with this. Most of the ventures have one or two founders and therefore decision-making does not involve a long procedure. The fourth dimension is about 'aggressiveness', which refers to the propensity of an entrepreneur to challenge its competitors. The statement "we always strive to improve the position in the market and simultaneously challenge the competitors" was given, for which four entrepreneurs agreed with it. On the other hand, the nine entrepreneurs' views differ from totally agree to totally disagree. The last dimension is 'riskiness', for which two items were asked. The first one is "we always look for big opportunities regardless of the uncertainty of the outcome". Some 5 out of 12 entrepreneurs neither agreed nor disagreed. From this a conclusion can be made that, on the one hand, they do want to take risks, but on the other, they are also cautious. The other question was "the strategic decisions we made with a focus on investment include high risk and high return". One group of entrepreneurs totally agreed with this statement whereas others totally disagreed. Therefore views vary by individual.

Based on the results of the survey it can be stated that sustainable fashion entrepreneurs have three important traits: the first one is they are future-oriented when making decisions but are careful with investments; the second one is that they are innovative. This is essential because financial resources are limited and therefore new ideas need to be established. The last one is proactiveness; Sustainable entrepreneurs tend to react quickly to new opportunities and want to gain a competitive advantage.

Based on the sustainability motivations and EO data reported here, we allocated the sample according to the conceptual SE archetypes. The sum of sustainability motivation and EO respectively yielded their sustainability motivation (SM) and EO scores (see Table 1.2.6). Firms were considered to have high SM or EO respectively if their score was above the sample median. A score lower than the sample median was considered 'low'. While this approach bears the limitation that the authors may force labels upon the cases, a cross check with some of the cases confirmed the associated characteristics. The characteristics are also reflected in the quotes. Case 1 and 18 are categorized as Realists. They have a comparatively lower score on motivation and EO, which is reflected in their statements. Case 2 is an Idealist, has high sustainable motivation but lower EO, which also resonates from the quoted statement. Case 19 is clustered as an Opportunist; the quote also reflects a lower sustainable motivation but higher EO. Last, case 9 is an Evangelist with high EO and high sustainability motivation. This is reflected in the quote as being independent and caring about the changes they stand for. Thus the respective motivations and EO fit with the respective archetypes. Table 1.2.6 and Figure 1.2.3 below report the clustered sample and SE archetypes.

Table 1.2.5 Entrepreneurial orientation of the sample

1 = strongly disagree / 5 = strongly agree	*1*	*2*	*3*	*4*	*5*	*N/A*	*Total*
We think about the future when making strategic decisions	0	0	1	8	14	1	243
Long-term profitability goes above short-term profitability	0	1	3	8	11	1	243
Investments that will provide us with a competitive advantage are emphasized	0	2	12	6	3	1	243
When making strategic decisions we respond to opportunities quickly	0	2	5	11	5	1	24
We always look for new opportunities and introduce new products to the market	1	4	2	8	8	1	24
We always look for big opportunities regardless of the uncertainty of the outcome	5	3	7	7	1	1	24
The strategic decisions we made with a focus on investment include high risk and high return	5	3	10	3	2	1	24
New projects are approved with 'blanket approval' and not through various stages	4	3	12	2	2	1	24
We always strive to improve the position in the market and simultaneously challenge our competitors	3	4	4	7	4	1	23

Table 1.2.6 Sustainable entrepreneur archetype matrix

Company	*Sustainability motivation*	*Entrepreneurial orientation*	*Sustainability motivation (high = above sample median)*	*Entrepreneurial orientation (high = above sample median)*	*Type*
Case 6	22.5	33.0	high	high	Evangelist
Case 9	24.0	33.0	high	high	Evangelist
Case 14	27.0	33.0	high	high	Evangelist
Case 16	25.0	34.0	high	high	Evangelist
Case 17	24.0	33.0	high	high	Evangelist
Case 21	25.5	36.0	high	high	Evangelist
Case 24	25.0	33.0	high	high	Evangelist
Case 2	22.5	31.5	high	low	Idealist
Case 5	23.0	31.0	high	low	Idealist
Case 8	25.0	25.0	high	low	Idealist
Case 10	25.0	32.0	high	low	Idealist
Case 22	26.0	23.0	high	low	Idealist
Case 23	24.0	24.0	high	low	Idealist
Case 4	20.0	33.0	low	high	Opportunist
Case 7	22.0	37.0	low	high	Opportunist
Case 15	19.0	34.0	low	high	Opportunist
Case 19	18.0	41.0	low	high	Opportunist
Case 20	17.0	35.0	low	high	Opportunist
Case 1	21.5	18.5	low	low	Realist
Case 3	21.5	29.5	low	low	Realist
Case 11	18.0	27.0	low	low	Realist
Case 12	20.0	28.0	low	low	Realist
Case 13	22.0	30.0	low	low	Realist
Case 18	20.0	29.0	low	low	Realist
Median	**22.5**	**32.5**			

Figure 1.2.3 and Table 1.2.6 suggest an even distribution of types across the archetypes; however, this is a result of the chosen clustering approach. Future research needs to confirm the traits and thresholds of the archetypes. Due to the exploratory nature of the study, the archetypes can only give indications.

Discussion and conclusions

In this study we set out to explore different SE types based on their motivations and EO. We suggest that sustainable entrepreneurs differ in their motivations and EO, which we reflect in the four suggested archetypes: Idealists, Evangelists, Realists and Opportunists. Following a theoretical conceptualization we studied sustainable fashion entrepreneurs and clustered them into the different archetypes. While only exploratory, the results suggest a neat fit between the clusters and respective characteristics.

This study contributes to the literature on sustainable entrepreneurship by providing archetypes that reflect the differences and nuances among sustainable entrepreneurs (Schaltegger & Wagner, 2011). While some may be driven by values – such as social

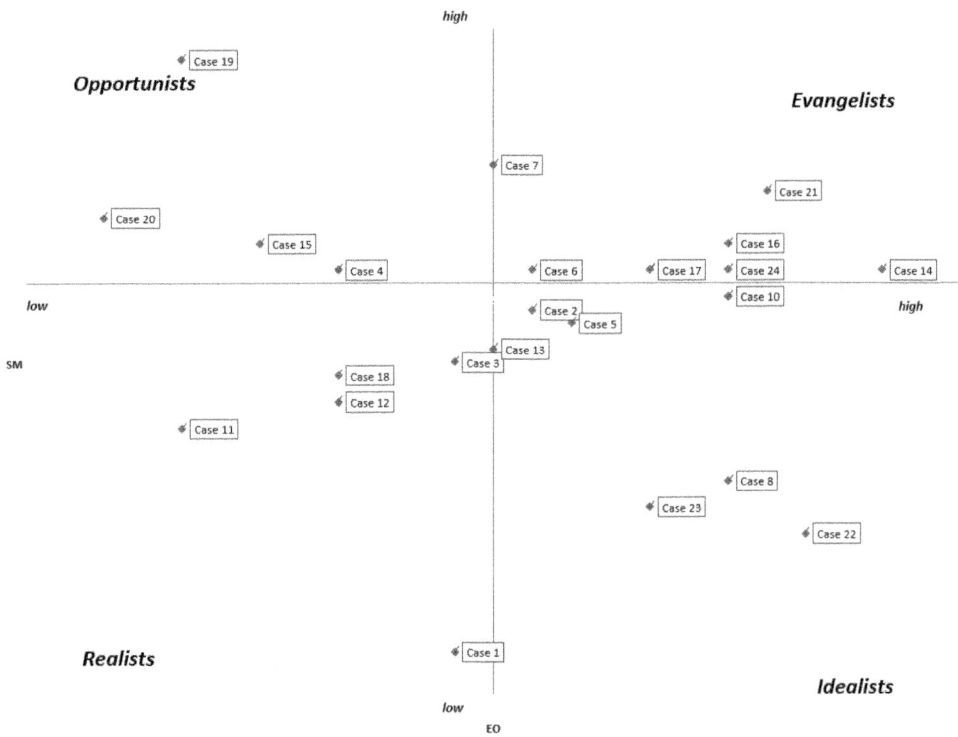

Figure 1.2.3 SE archetypes based on entrepreneurial orientation and sustainability motivation

entrepreneurs (Dacin et al., 2010; Zahra et al., 2009) – others may be driven by market opportunities and see sustainability as a means to an (profitable) end and exploit economic and non-economic rents (Dean & McMullen, 2007). The suggested archetypes are also complementary to existing typologies in the field of entrepreneurship (e.g. Fauchart & Gruber, 2011) and sustainable entrepreneurship (e.g. Zahra et al., 2009). Last, our study makes a contribution to the sustainable investment literature. As we show, entrepreneurial traits may differ substantially, and given their proven influence on performance, may help to predict success or failure. This could be relevant for sustainability investors who could better match sustainable entrepreneurs' archetypes with their respective investment motives. Also, they could develop a more holistic strategy and invest in evangelists, provide business education for idealists, avoid investment in realists, and monitor the sustainability performance of opportunists (Jansson & Biel, 2011).

Due to its exploratory nature the results of this study can only serve as a first step to understand SE archetypes. The sustainable entrepreneur archetypes can help us to think about sustainable entrepreneurs from a different perspective and inspire future research on the different archetypes as well as on the intersection of SO and EO. Next to a larger sample size in a quantitative study, more in-depth qualitative research is needed in this nascent field. There is much more to uncover about sustainable entrepreneurs and the relation between sustainability motivations and entrepreneurial processes, such as growth rates or capability development. Also, we suggest that future research takes a dynamic perspective, for instance in a longitudinal study to explore how archetypes evolve. Next to the sample size, this study was designed to study a group of entrepreneurs in a specific setting, namely the fashion industry, which may pose additional limitations to the generalization of the findings to a broader group of firms and entrepreneurs. Despite this, we believe that the findings may also be applicable to manufacturing industries that have complex, fragmented or outsourced value and production chains. This is the case for instance in various agriculture industries (e.g. cacao or coffee), durable goods products (e.g. automobiles or computer hardware) and other high technology industries (e.g. renewable energy, nanotechnology).

Acknowledgments

We gratefully acknowledge research assistance from Tuanh Lam and Carlijn van Drenth.

References

Choi, D. Y., & Gray, E. R. (2008). The venture development processes of "sustainable" entrepreneurs. *Management Research News*, 31(8), 558–569.

Cohen, B., & Winn, M. I. (2007). Market imperfections, opportunity and sustainable entrepreneurship. *Journal of Business Venturing*, 22(1), 29–49.

Covin, J. G., & Slevin, D. P. (1989). Strategic management of small firms in hostile and benign environments. *Strategic Management Journal*, 10(1), 75–87.

Dacin, P. A., Dacin, M. T., & Matear, M. (2010). Social entrepreneurship: Why we don't need a new theory and how we move forward from here. *The Academy of Management Perspectives*, 24(3), 37–57.

Dean, T. J., & McMullen, J. S. (2007). Toward a theory of sustainable entrepreneurship: Reducing environmental degradation through entrepreneurial action. *Journal of Business Venturing*, 22(1), 50–76.

DiVito, L., & Bohnsack, R. (2017). Entrepreneurial orientation and its effect on sustainability decision tradeoffs: The case of sustainable fashion firms. *Journal of Business Venturing*, 32, 569–587.

Dixon, S. E., & Clifford, A. (2007). Ecopreneurship: A new approach to managing the triple bottom line. *Journal of Organizational Change Management*, 20(3), 326–345.

Elkington, J. (1994). Towards the suitable corporation: Win-win-win business strategies for sustainable development. *California Management Review*, 36(2), 90–100.

Fauchart, E., & Gruber, M. (2011). Darwinians, communitarians, and missionaries: The role of founder identity in entrepreneurship. *Academy of Management Journal*, 54(5), 935–957.

Hockerts, K., & Wüstenhagen, R. (2010). Greening Goliaths versus emerging Davids: Theorizing about the role of incumbents and new entrants in sustainable entrepreneurship. *Journal of Business Venturing*, 25(5), 481–492.

Jansson, M., & Biel, A. (2011). Motives to engage in sustainable investment: A comparison between institutional and private investors. *Sustainable Development*, 19(2), 135–142.

Keogh, P. D., & Polonsky, M. J. (1998). Environmental commitment: A basis for environmental entrepreneurship? *Journal of Organizational Change Management*, 11(1), 38–49.

Kirkwood, J., & Walton, S. (2010). What motivates ecopreneurs to start businesses? *International Journal of Entrepreneurial Behavior & Research*, 16(3), 204–228.

Kuckertz, A., & Wagner, M. (2010). The influence of sustainability orientation on entrepreneurial intentions: Investigating the role of business experience. *Journal of Business Venturing*, 25(5), 524–539.

Loane, S., Bell, J., & McNaughton, R. (2006). Employing information communication technologies to enhance qualitative international marketing enquiry. *International Marketing Review*, 23(4), 438–455.

Lumpkin, G. T., & Dess, G. G. (1996). Clarifying the entrepreneurial orientation construct and linking it to performance. *Academy of Management Review*, 21(1), 135–172.

Lumpkin, G. T., & Dess, G. G. (2001). Linking two dimensions of entrepreneurial orientation to firm performance: The moderating role of environment and industry life cycle. *Journal of Business Venturing*, 16(5), 429–451.

Masurel, E. (2007). Why SMEs invest in environmental measures: Sustainability evidence from small and medium-sized printing firms. *Business Strategy and the Environment*, 16(3), 190–201.

Pacheco, D. F., Dean, T. J., & Payne, D. S. (2010). Escaping the green prison: Entrepreneurship and the creation of opportunities for sustainable development. *Journal of Business Venturing*, 25(5), 464–480.

Parrish, B. D. (2010). Sustainability-driven entrepreneurship: Principles of organization design. *Journal of Business Venturing*, 25(5), 510–523.

Pastakia, A. (1998). Grassroots ecopreneurs: Change agents for a sustainable society. *Journal of Organizational Change Management*, 11(2), 157–173.

Patzelt, H., & Shepherd, D. A. (2011). Recognizing opportunities for sustainable development. *Entrepreneurship Theory and Practice*, 35(4), 631–652.

Schaltegger, S., & Wagner, M. (2011). Sustainable entrepreneurship and sustainability innovation: Categories and interactions. *Business Strategy and the Environment*, 20(4), 222–237.

Schick, H., Marxen, S., & Freimann, J. (2002). Sustainability issues for start-up entrepreneurs. *Greener Management International*, 38, 59–70.

Stokes, D., Wilson, N., & Wilson, N. (2010). *Small Business Management and Entrepreneurship*. Cengage Learning EMEA: Hampshire.

Tan, J. (2007). Phase transitions and emergence of entrepreneurship: The transformation of Chinese SOEs over time. *Journal of Business Venturing*, 22(1), 77–96.

Vega, G., & Kidwell, R. E. (2007). Toward a typology of new venture creators: Similarities and contrasts between business and social entrepreneurs. *New England Journal of Entrepreneurship*, 10(2), Article 4.

Zahra, S. A., Gedajlovic, E., Neubaum, D. O., & Shulman, J. M. (2009). A typology of social entrepreneurs: Motives, search processes and ethical challenges. *Journal of Business Venturing*, 24(5), 519–532.

1.3 Gender analysis of social entrepreneurial intention

A case of Morocco and Spain

Juan D. Borrero

Introduction

This chapter seeks to consider new ideas about whether women and men from two different regions (southern Spain and northern Morocco) have the same perceptions in the context of social entrepreneurship. The focus is on the interesting comparative gender analysis about social entrepreneurship from people who live in countries with different incomes and culture. This chapter will detail an enquiry, based on personal questionnaires with university students from Morocco and Spain, into the perceptions of social self-efficacy, passion and intention toward the start of new social business. Specifically:

1 Are passion (PAS) and social entrepreneurial self-efficacy (SESE) antecedents of social entrepreneurial intention (SEI)?
2 Are there differences between women and men in SEI across different contexts and regions as southern Spain and northern Morocco?

Social entrepreneurship and gender

The existence of differences between women and men in entrepreneurship has been the subject of much debate and has been studied from many different angles, including psychology, sociology and economics (Hughes et al., 2012). In recent years, social entrepreneurship has also been gaining research interest (Defourny and Nyssens, 2008; Haugh, 2007; Hockerts, 2006; Mair and Martí, 2006; Short, Moss and Lumpkin, 2009; Spear, 2006).

In a broad definition of social entrepreneurship, it refers to innovative activity with a social objective that can occur within for profit or nonprofit organizations (e.g. Dees and Anderson, 2006). Under a narrow definition, social entrepreneurship typically refers to the phenomenon of applying business expertise and market-based skills in the nonprofit sector (Thompson, 2002). We will use this broader conceptualization of social entrepreneurship to offer a comparative gender analysis across two different countries, because the "social" concept is better suited to the entrepreneur than to the categories of organizations.

Following this conceptualization, social enterprises could be considered as organizations that aim to achieve social goals or create social value such as the integration into the labor market of disadvantaged social groups, and/or environmental sustainability (Corner and Ho, 2010; Sanchis-Palacio, Campos-Climent and Mohedano-Suanes, 2013; Yunus, Moingeon and Lehmann-Ortega, 2010).

However, although the term social entrepreneur has been widely used in academic and business circles (Witkamp, Royakkers and Raven, 2011), some authors (Dacin and Dacin, 2011; Harding, 2004; Mair and Martí, 2006; Weerawardena and Mort, 2006) consider there is no clear definition for the concept, partly due to the fact that it has been used in different areas and consequently is dealt with from different perspectives (Zahra et al., 2008). To contextualize our analysis and following the line of certain authors, we will consider the social entrepreneurs as people whose primary motivation for starting enterprises is to solve social problems such as illiteracy, the integration of minorities, environmental pollution, and so on (Austin et al., 2006; Cukier et al., 2011; Martin and Osberg, 2007; Renko, 2013; Zahra et al., 2009).

Related to gender, it is often stated that the gender gap for social entrepreneurship is smaller than that of traditional entrepreneurship (European Institute for Gender Equality [EIGE], 2015). Research shows women are more active as entrepreneurs in social ventures than men (GEM, 2012), firstly, because women have a higher level of altruism than men, and secondly, women are more averse to competition and hence are more attracted to the newer market of social enterprises (Huysentruyt, 2014). However, although other studies also show that women have a greater tendency toward social orientation in projects than men (Cukier et al., 2011; Van Ryzin et al., 2009; Witkamp et al., 2011), the conclusions are still not definitive (GEM 2012; Sastre-Castillo et al., 2015).

Social entrepreneurship in two different contexts: Spain and Morocco

In terms of entrepreneurial intention (EI), Morocco has a higher rate (35.80%) compared to developed countries such as Spain (6.10%), although, as indicated in Figure 1.3.1, the entrepreneurial activity is different. The total entrepreneurship activity (TEA) is higher in Spain than in Morocco.

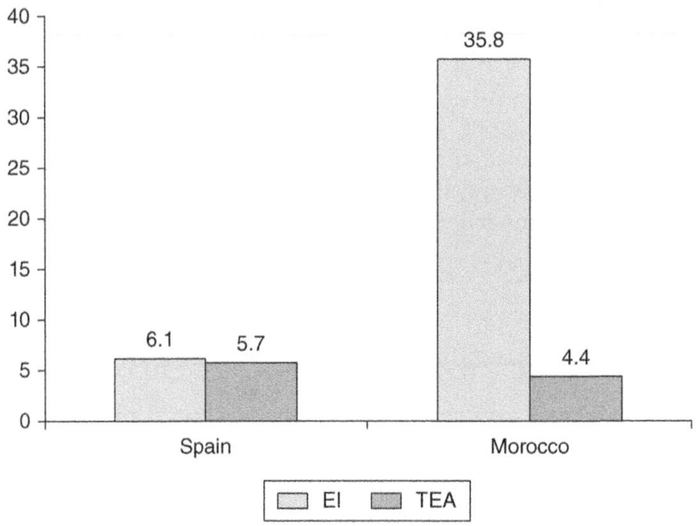

Figure 1.3.1 Entrepreneurship intention (EI) and total entrepreneurship activity (TEA). Spain and Morocco (% of adult population)

Source: GEM 2015a, 2015b.

The survey data in 2015 (GEM 2015a, 2015b) also show that entrepreneurial activity is still dominated by men in both countries, even though women have experienced significant growth in recent years. The Flash Eurobarometer of 2012 found that European women are effectively less likely than men (17% to 29%) to have either started a business or planned to start their own company (European Commission, 2012). Similarly, Moroccan women seem less confident in their ability to create a business in comparison with men (35% against 60%) (GEM, 2015b).

Results show that social entrepreneurship activity (SEA) rates are much lower than TEA rates in both countries. An explanation for this could be that regular entrepreneurs do not recognize themselves as social entrepreneurs since they do not know how to interpret what is considered a "social activity" and what is not.

We analyzed the data concerning these people by the demographic characteristics of gender. Just as with TEA, women are generally less likely to start a social venture than men (see Table 1.3.1).

We also found low levels of SEA in both genders and in both countries in comparison with other countries. It seems that these countries (Spain and Morocco) are less inclined to create social enterprises than others like Iceland, Argentina or the United States (GEM, 2012).

However, the male/female SEA ratio varies tremendously across countries. Morocco has the lowest level of female participation (0.00%). The low level of participation may be related to women's lack of participation in the labor market in this country.

Theoretical framework and methodology

The phenomenon of entrepreneurship understood as a process that occurs over time begins a long time before the individual actually starts up a firm. Thus, like any behavior, entrepreneurship requires a certain amount of planning until EI is produced. This intention, prior to the creation of a firm, might be considered the single and best predictor that it will actually be carried out (Ajzen, 2002).

Previous research has proposed several conceptual models for understanding EI, including Ajzen's (1991) Theory of Planned Behavior (TPB) and the Entrepreneurial Event Model (SEE) (Shapero and Sokol, 1982).

Krueger, Reilly, and Carsrud (2000) tested TPB and SEE, and found support for both models. They demonstrated that attitudes and subjective norms in the TPB model were conceptually related to perceived desirability in the SEE, whereas perceived behavioral control in the TPB corresponded with perceived feasibility in the SEE model.

Table 1.3.1 Social entrepreneurship activity (SEA) in Spain and Morocco (% of the working population).

	Spain	*Morocco*
Nascent social entrepreneurship	0.37	0.26
Early-stage social entrepreneurship	0.55	0.39
Total social entrepreneurship activity (SEA)	0.91	0.79
Female SEA participation	0.40	0.00
Male SEA participation	0.70	0.81

Source: GEM 2009 Adult Population Survey (GEM, 2012).

Essentially, it can be concluded that perceived desirability and perceived feasibility could be fundamental elements of EI.

Much research into social entrepreneurship has looked at issues of recognition, exploitation, and growth of social opportunities as well as the measurement of their impact on society (Bloom and Chatterji, 2009; Bugg-Levine and Emerson, 2011) but few studies try to analyze what elements would actually impact the likelihood of SEI. Mair and Noboa's (2006) and Hockerts' (2015) research adapted these models and they inferred that PAS and SESE were SEI antecedents; the first one equates to perceived desirability and the second to perceived feasibility. This conclusion makes sense because the idea of social entrepreneurship combines passion (Bornstein, 1998; Boschee, 1995) with an image of business-like discipline (Dees, 1998; Mair and Noboa, 2006).

Self-efficacy describes an individual's perceptions of his or her ability to carry out an intended action (Bandura, 1977). In business ethics research self-efficacy has been found to predict the likelihood of entrepreneurial behavior (Chen, Greene, and Crick, 1998) as well as the likelihood that an individual will engage in civic activities (Weber, Weber, Sleeper, and Scheider, 2004). So, in the context of social entrepreneurship, a high level of self-efficacy allows a person to perceive the creation of a social venture as feasible, which positively affects the formation of the corresponding behavioral intention (Mair and Noboa, 2006; Smith and Woodworth, 2012). This study proposes SESE as a measure of an individual's belief of whether he or she can generate significant social impact within the context of solving social problems that are appropriate to his or her needs (Radin and Zaidatol, 2014).

Any discussion of the EI process, also requires rigorous attention to the important aspect of how decision making is thoroughly intertwined with emotional appraisal (Bagozzi et al., 2003; Dholakia and Bagozzi, 2002). In this way, several social entrepreneurship scholars posit that empathy is a major driver of social entrepreneurial behavior. Empathy is a well-specified construct in psychology (Jolliffe and Farrington, 2006). In management studies empathy has been used in research on stakeholders (Strong, Ringer, and Taylor, 2001), leadership (Holt and Marques, 2012), and business ethics education (Cohen, 2012). Within the context of social entrepreneurship, this study is interested not so much in a person's general empathy but rather empathic concern (Zahn-Waxler and Radke-Yarrow, 1990), empathy with a very specific group of people or with a social cause (Mair and Noboa, 2006; Niezink et al., 2012). By adopting the Mair and Noboa (2006) perspective, it uses PAS as representative of empathy, which in turn creates an altruistic motivation in the social entrepreneur to reduce the pain of others. Hence, this study defines PAS as the passion they feel about a cause and undertaking a business-like activity that earns money (or provides other resources) to support that cause.

To achieve the aims proposed and taking the approach of Shapero and Sokol's (1982) and Ajzen's (1991) models as reference points, a model is put forward in which SEI is conceptualized as a latent variable depending on two others: the perception of the SESE and PAS in starting up a social firm (see Figure 1.3.2). Gender (GEN) and nationality (NAT) are included as control variables that can have some influence on the factors that predict SEI.

SEI was measured by a single-item from Battilana and Lee (2014). To measure the scales of SESE, the proposals of Urban (2013) were used which consisted of 14 items. Finally, the questionnaire included six items for measuring PAS related to intense positive feelings (Cardon et al., 2013).

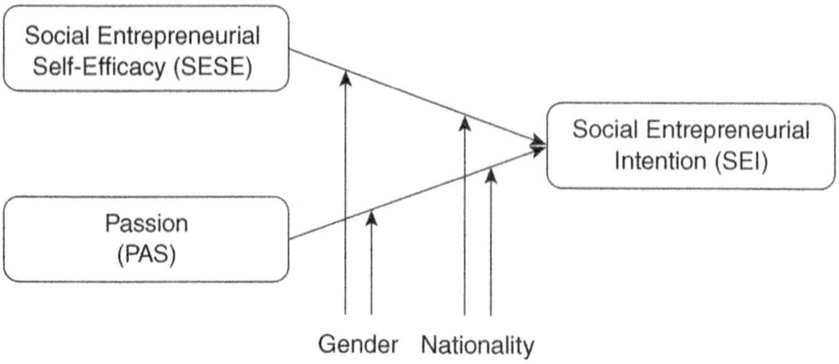

Figure 1.3.2 Research model

Following the research model depicted in Figure 1.3.2, and taking into account that the influence of basic perceptions on intention-model elements should be similar for both genders (Arenius and Minniti, 2005; Minniti and Nardone, 2007), two hypotheses will be tested:

> ***H1a:*** *SESE has a positive impact on SEI, and it is weaker for women.*
>
> ***H1b:*** *PAS has a positive impact on SEI, and it is weaker for women.*

However, the literature also points out that culture and context exert a different influence on women's and men's perceptions and intentions regarding entrepreneurship (Eddleston and Powell, 2008). Although this influence tends to be weaker for women (Verheul, Uhlaner, and Thurik, 2005; Watson and Newby, 2005), these differences in environmental influences have been found to be stronger in less developed regions or countries (Bertaux and Crable, 2007; Roomi and Parrot, 2008), and they seem to depend on the level of economic and social development (Iakovleva, Kolvereid, and Stephan, 2011; Liñán and Chen, 2009). This therefore leads to the following hypotheses being proposed:

> ***H2a:*** *There are gender differences (stronger in Morocco than in Spain) in the relationship between SESE and SEI.*
>
> ***H2b:*** *There are gender differences (stronger in Morocco than in Spain) in the relationship between PAS and SEI.*

With regard to the collection of information, five-point Likert surveys were carried out among university students because this group was majoring in business and were likely to start a business (see Genescà and Veciana 1984). Various studies have examined the sociodemographic profile of social entrepreneurs, which found the prototype of social entrepreneur to be young and highly educated (Chung, 2014; Cukier et al., 2011; GEM, 2012; Harding, 2004; Van Ryzin et al., 2009; Witkamp et al., 2011). Likewise, social entrepreneurship is a rapidly growing movement within higher education (Pache and Chowdhury, 2012).

A total of 752 valid questionnaires were collected, 320 from Spain and 432 from Morocco. Of the full sample, 63.03% were female (62.50%/63.43%), and 36.97% male (37.50%/36.57%). The principal methodological details from the research are summarized in Table 1.3.2.

Table 1.3.2 Summary of characteristics of the subsamples.

Region, country	Andalusia, Spain	Tangier, Morocco
Population	8,424,102	3,157,075
Sample	University students	University students
Geographic area	Huelva (University of Huelva)	Tangier (Université Abdemalek Essaadi)
Sample design	A stratified random systematic sample of the university	A stratified random systematic sample of the university
Sample size	320 questionnaires	432 questionnaires
Male	37.50%	36.57%
Female	62.50%	63.43%
Collection of information	Personal questionnaires	Personal questionnaires

Given the relationships between different perceptions and SEI, structural equation modeling (SEM) was chosen for the analysis. In particular, partial least squares (PLS) was applied (Sanchez, 2013) using R v.3.1.1 software for the data analysis (R Core Team, 2016) and the PLS-PM package (Sanchez, Trinchera, and Russolillo, 2015).

To test H1, a confirmatory factor analysis (CFA) was conducted using data from the full sample (Tangier and Huelva together). Then, to compare gender differences, with the resulting constructs (SEI, SESE, and PAS), we performed two PLS models: one for men and one for women.

Regarding H2, a dichotomous control variable (NAT) was included in the two previous PLS models (for men and women) to reflect the influence of the regional environment. Then, a multigroup analysis was performed to look for statistically significant differences in path coefficients (Chin, 1998; Chin and Dibbern, 2010).

Results

The analysis of the measurement model for the full sample found low loadings for a small number of items. They were removed, and the model was run again. Scores regarding item reliability, construct reliability, and convergent and discriminant validity were then satisfactory (see Tables 1.3.3 and 1.3.4).

The models were tested separately on the subsample for all men and the subsample for all women for both locations. The values reached after running the bootstrapping test (with 5,000 samples) confirm the statistical significance for both constructs, SESE and PAS. The model explained 20.4% (for women) and 40.9% (for men) of the variance in SEI (see Figure 1.3.3). Results showed that the relationship between SESE and SEI was significant and positive for both women and men. We found similar results with PAS. In all cases the relationships were weaker for women than for men, supporting H1a and H1b hypotheses, as some literature point out (Arenius and Minniti, 2005; Minniti and Nardone, 2007).

This study also found out that PAS is more relevant than SESE as an antecedent of SEI for women (0.377/0.131) and for men (0.436/0.317). This means that positive feelings toward social entrepreneurship prevail over the individual's belief to handle particular social problems. These results are in line with other researchers (Bornstein, 1998; Cardon et al., 2009; Kelley et al., 2011).

Table 1.3.3 Reliability and convergent validity analysis for the full sample (Tangier and Huelva, N=752).

Construct	*Items*	*Loadings*	*Communalities*	*Cronbach*	*AVE*
SESE	SESE2	0.7543	0.5690	0.931	0.6140
		SESE5	0.7738		0.5987
		SESE6	0.8500		0.7219
		SESE7	0.8393		0.7045
		SESE8	0.8126		0.6004
		SESE9	0.7750		0.6007
		SESE10	0.7014		0.4920
		SESE11	0.8242		0.6793
		SESE12	0.7316		0.5352
		SESE13	0.7615		0.5999
PAS	PAS1	0.7724	0.5966	0.8530	0.6310
		PAS2	0.8259		0.6820
		PAS3	0.8274		0.6845
		PAS5	0.8188		0.6750
		PAS6	0.7218		0.5211
SEI	SEI1	1.0000	1.0000	1.0000	1.0000

Table 1.3.4 Discriminant validity for the full sample: cross loadings (Tangier and Huelva, N=752).

Items	*SESE*	*PAS*	*SEI*
SESE2	0.7542979	0.3197971	0.2674553
SESE5	0.7737600	0.2873878	0.2675073
SESE6	0.8496664	0.3678897	0.3485417
SESE7	0.8393326	0.4072382	0.3550269
SESE8	0.8126308	0.4125334	0.2860031
SESE9	0.7750272	0.3202086	0.2979001
SESE10	0.7014378	0.3564603	0.2263428
SESE11	0.8241957	0.3039680	0.2031505
SESE12	0.7315876	0.2533343	0.1194965
SESE13	0.7615180	0.2998011	0.2375468
PAS1	0.3728114	0.7723928	0.3899395
PAS2	0.3104555	0.8258503	0.3256761
PAS3	0.3647368	0.8273611	0.4021926
PAS5	0.3949986	0.8188444	0.4332104
PAS6	0.2533762	0.7218472	0.3305092
SEI	0.3515208	0.4790654	1.0000000

To statistically test H2, a permutation test for multigroup analysis (Chin and Dibbern, 2010) was carried out. As may be seen in Table 1.3.5, there are no significant differences between women and men in any path in Morocco. However, we found gender differences in the relationship between SESE and SEI in Spain. In any case, the differences are stronger in Spain than in Morocco, a less developed country. Therefore, this result leads to the rejection of H2a and H2b, contradicting previous research about EI (Iakovleva,

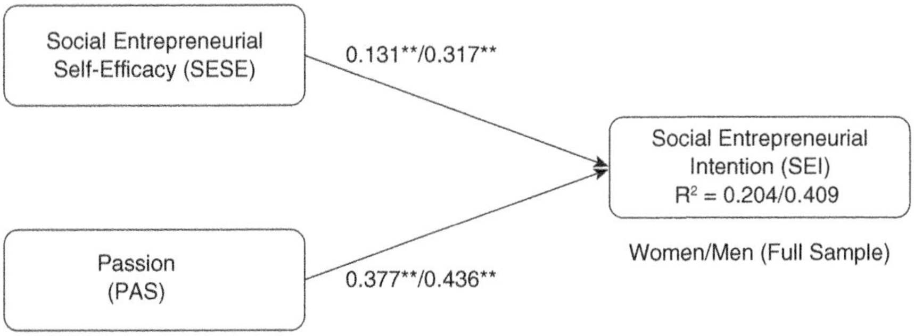

Figure 1.3.3 Structural model for women and men in the two regions (N_{women} = 474 and N_{men} = 278)

Kolvereid, and Stephan, 2011; Liñán and Chen, 2009) and the GEM data report (2012) in which the SEA gender gap increases in developing economies (GEM, 2012).

Discussion

Following Mair and Noboa's work (2006), this study has validated two new constructs for SEI, concluding that SESE and PAS fit as antecedents of SEI. Relationships are positive for both constructs, both for women and men, although weaker for women as the literature exposes for the case of IE. In this context, it is also true for SEI. It was also found that PAS is a more relevant antecedent than SESE. Hence, this research confirms the applicability of the Theory of Planned Behavior and the Entrepreneurial Event model to social entrepreneurship, irrespective of gender.

On the other hand, in a similar manner, the gender differences detected are greater in Spain (a more developed country and with a higher equality index) than in Morocco, as opposed to the literature.

The SESE perception is significantly different for men than for women in Spain. This weakness found for Spanish women is a strength for Moroccan women. Although possibly Spanish women are best at working with social causes than men, in terms of SEI, confidence in their abilities is still lower than that of men (Kickul et al., 2008).

Even though our results detect some weakness in the perceptions of women, such as scholars have pointed out (see Hughes et al., 2012), these are not conclusive.

Table 1.3.5 t-Tests for multi group analysis: gender differences

Links	*Path: men*	*Path: women*	*Path difference*	p *value*	*sig. 05*
Morocco (Tangier)					
SESE→SEI	0.08	0.17	−0.09	0.43	no
PAS→SEI	0.49	0.47	0.02	0.78	no
Spain (Huelva)					
SESE→SEI	0.31	0.13	0.18	0.02	yes
PAS→SEI	0.50	0.41	0.09	0.31	no

Conclusions

Living with a gender difference is part of the business world in general and the social business world in particular. On the whole, a positive relationship between PAS and SESE is the norm. Previous studies offer similar findings about the link between PAS and SESE in terms of entrepreneurship intent. This chapter emphasizes gender in the increasingly important role of the social entrepreneurship field.

Extensive studies detail gender and country differences in EI, but less research has investigated the effect of these differences jointly in the field of social entrepreneurship.

Finally, this chapter has demonstrated that bridging the SEI gender gap requires both desire (PAS) and feasibility (SESE). Furthermore, government and universities should provide social entrepreneurial education, and course programs should be provided to Spanish women as incentives to improve their SESE for social entrepreneurship.

References

Ajzen, I. (1991). The theory of planned behavior. *Organizational Behavior and Human Decision Processes*, 50(2), 179–211.

Ajzen, I. (2002). Perceived behavioral control, self-efficacy, locus of control, and the theory of planned behavior. *Journal of Applied Social Psychology*, 32(4), 665–683.

Arenius, P., and Minniti, M. (2005). Perceptual variables and nascent entrepreneurship. *Small Business Economics*, 24(3), 233–247.

Austin, J., Stevenson, H., and Wei-Skillern, J. (2006). social and commercial entrepreneurship: Same, different or both? *Entrepreneurship Theory and Practice*, 30(1), 1–22.

Bagozzi, R. P., Dholakia, U., and Basuron, S. (2003). How effortful decisions get enacted: The motivating role of decision processes, desires and anticipated emotions. *Journal of Behavioral Decision Making*, 16, 273–295.

Bandura, A. (1977). Self-efficacy: towards a unifying theory of behavioural change. *Psychological Review*, 84, 191–215.

Battilana, J., and Lee, M. (2014). Advancing research on hybrid organizing: Insights from the study of social enterprises. *The Academy of Management Annals*, 8(1), 397–441.

Bertaux, N., and Crable, E. (2007). Learning about women, economic development, entrepreneurship and the environment in India: A case study. *Journal of Developmental Entrepreneurship*, 12(4), 467–478.

Bloom, P. N., and Chatterji, A. K. (2009). Scaling social entrepreneurial impact. *California Management Review*, 51(3), 114–133.

Bornstein, D. (1998). Changing the world on a shoestring. *Atlantic Monthly*, 281(1), 34–39.

Boschee, J. (1995). Social entrepreneurship. *Across the Board*, 32(3), 20–25.

Bugg-Levine, A., and Emerson, J. (2011). Impact investing: Transforming how we make money while making a difference. *Innovations: Technology, Governance, Globalization*, 6(3), 9–18.

Cardon, M. S., Gregoire, D. A., Stevens, C. E., and Patel, P. C. (2013). Measuring entrepreneurial passion: Conceptual foundations and scale validation. *Journal of Business Venturing*, 28, 373–396.

Cardon, M. S., Wincent, J., Singh, J., and Drnovsek, M. (2009). The nature and experience of entrepreneurial passion. *Academy of Management Review*, 34(3), 511–532.

Chen, C. C., Greene, P. G., and Crick, A. (1998). Does entrepreneurial self-efficacy distinguish entrepreneurs from managers? *Journal of Business Venturing*, 13(4), 295–316.

Chin, W. W. (1998). The partial least squares approach to structural equation modelling. In G. A. Marcoulides (ed.), *Modern Methods for Business Research*. (pp. 295–336). Mahwah, NJ: Lawrence Erlbaum Associates.

Chin, W. W., and Dibbern, J. (2010). An introduction to a permutation based procedures for multi-group PLS analysis: Results tests of differences on simulated data and cross cultural analysis of the sourcing of information system services between Germany and the USA.

In E. Vinzi, W. W. Chin, J. Henseler, and H. Wang (eds.), *Handbook of Partial Least Square: Concepts, Methods and Applications* (pp. 171–193). Springer Handbooks of Computational Statistics Series, Vol. II V. Heidelberg, Germany; Dordrecht, the Netherlands; London; New York: Springer.

Chung, C. (2014). *A Report on the Social Enterprise Landscape in Morocco*. Social Enterprise UK: British Council. www.britishcouncil.org/sites/default/files/morocco_report.pdf.

Cohen, M. A. (2012). Empathy in business ethics education. *Journal of Business Ethics Education*, 9, 359–375.

Corner, P. D., and Ho, M. (2010). How opportunities develop in social entrepreneurship. *Entrepreneurship Theory and Practice*, 34(4), 635–659.

Cukier, W., Trenholm, S., Carl, D., and Gekas, G. (2011). Social entrepreneurship: A content analysis. *Journal of Strategic Innovation and Sustainability*, 7(1), 99–119.

Dacin, M. T., and Dacin, P. A. (2011). Social entrepreneurship: A critique and future directions. *Organization Science*, 22(5), 1203–1213.

Dees, J. G. (1998). *The Meaning of "Social Entrepreneurship"*. Kauffman Foundation and Stanford University. https://entrepreneurship.duke.edu/news-item/the-meaning-of-social-entrepreneurship/.

Dees, J. G., and Anderson, B. (2006). Framing a theory of social entrepreneurship: Building on two schools of practice and thought. Research on social entrepreneurship. *ARNOVA Occasional Paper Series*, 1(3), 39–66.

Defourny, J., and Nyssens, M. (2008). Social enterprise in Europe: Recent trends and developments. *Social Enterprise Journal*, 4(3), 202–228.

Dholakia, U., and Bagozzi, R. (2002). Mustering motivation to enact decisions: How decision process characteristics influence goal realizations. *Journal of Behavioral Decision Making*, 15, 167–188.

Eddleston, K. A., and Powell, G. N. (2008). The role of gender identity in explaining sex differences in business owners' career satisfier preferences. *Journal of Business Venturing*, 23(2), 244–256.

European Commission (2012). *Entrepreneurship in the EU and Beyond*. Flash Eurobarometer 354. http://ec.europa.eu/public_opinion/flash/fl_354_en.pdf.

European Institute for Gender Equality [EIGE] (2015). *Promoting Women's Economic Independence and Entrepreneurship: Good Practices*. http://eige.europa.eu/rdc/eige-publications/promoting-womens-economic-independence-and-entrepreneurship-good-practices.

GEM Consortium (2012). 2009 Report on social entrepreneurship. *Global Entrepreneurship Monitor*. www.gemconsortium.org/report/48437.

GEM Consortium (2015a). Informe GEM España 2015. *Global Entrepreneurship Monitor*. www.gem-spain.com/wp-content/uploads/2015/03/Informe-GEM-2015-esafp.pdf.

GEM Consortium (2015b). La Dynamique Entrepreneuriale au Maroc 2015. *Global Entrepreneurship Monitor*. www.entrepreneurship.univcasa.ma/wp-content/uploads/2016/08/Maroc-RAPPORT-GEM-2015.pdf.

Genescà, E., and Veciana, J. M. (1984). Actitudes hacia la creación de empresas. *Información Comercial Española*, 611, 147–155.

Harding, R. (2004). Social enterprise: The new economic engine? *Business Strategy Review, Winter*, 39–43.

Haugh, H. (2007). Community-led social venture creation. *Entrepreneurship Theory and Practice*, 31(2), 161–182.

Hockerts, K. (2006). Entrepreneurial opportunity in social purpose business ventures. In J. Mair, J. Robinson, and K. Hockerts (eds.), *Social Entrepreneurship* (pp. 142–154). Cheltenham, UK: Edward Elgar

Hockerts, K. (2015). The social entrepreneurial antecedents scale (SEAS): A validation study. *Social Enterprise Journal*, 11(3), 260–280.

Holt, S., and Marques, J. (2012). Empathy in leadership: Appropriate or misplaced? An empirical study on a topic that is asking for attention. *Journal of Business Ethics*, 105(1), 95–105.

Hughes, K. D., Jennings, J. E., Brush, C. G., Carter, S., and Welter, F. (2012). Extending women's entrepreneurship research in new directions. *Entrepreneurship Theory and Practice*, 36(3), 429–442.

Huysentruyt, M. (2014). Women's social entrepreneurship and innovation. *OECD Local Economic and Employment Development (LEED)* Working Papers, 2014/01, OECD Publishing. http://dx.doi.org/10.1787/5jxzkq2sr7d4-en.

Iakovleva, T., Kolvereid, L., and Stephan, U. (2011). Entrepreneurial intentions in developing and developed countries. *Education and Training*, 53(5), 353–370.

Jolliffe, D., and Farrington, D. P. (2006). Development and validation of the basic empathy scale. *Journal of Adolescence*, 29(4), 589–611.

Kelley, D., Bosma, N., and Amorós, J.E. (2011). *Global Entrepreneurship Monitor 2010 Global Report*. Wellesley, MA and Santiago, Chile: Babson College & Universidad del Desarrollo.

Kickul, J., Wilson, F., Marlino, D., and Barbosa, S. D. (2008). Are misalignments of perceptions and self-efficacy causing gender gaps in entrepreneurial intentions among our nation's teens? *Journal of Small Business and Enterprise Development*, 15(2), 321–335.

Krueger, N. F., Reilly, M. D., and Carsrud, A. L. (2000). Competing models of entrepreneurial intentions. *Journal of Business Venturing*, 15(5), 411–432.

Liñán, F., and Chen, Y. W. (2009). Development and cross-cultural application of a specific instrument to measure entrepreneurial intentions. *Entrepreneurship Theory and Practice*, 33(3), 593–617.

Mair, J., and Martí, I. (2006). Social entrepreneurship research: A source of explanation, prediction, and delight. *Journal of World Business*, 41(1), 36–44.

Mair, J., and Noboa, E. (2006). Social entrepreneurship: How intentions to create a social venture are formed. In J. Mair, J. Robinson and K. Hockerts (eds.), *Social Entrepreneurship* (pp. 121–136). New York: Palgrave MacMillan.

Martin, R. L., and Osberg, S. (2007). Social entrepreneurship: The case for definition. *Stanford Social Innovation Review, Spring*, 29–39.

Minniti, M., and Nardone, C. (2007). Being in someone else's shoes: Gender and nascent entrepreneurship. *Small Business Economics Journal*, 28(2–3), 223–239.

Niezink, L. W., Siero, F. W., Dijkstra, P., Buunk, A. P., and Barelds, D. P. H. (2012). Empathic concern: Distinguishing between tenderness and sympathy. *Motivation and Emotion*, 36(4), 544–549.

Pache, A. C., and Chowdhury, I. (2012). Social entrepreneurs as institutionally embedded entrepreneurs: Toward a new model of social entrepreneurship education. *Academy of Management Learning and Education*, 11(3), 494–510.

Radin, S., and Zaidatol, A. (2014). Validation of a social entrepreneurial self-efficacy. *IOSR Journal of Business and Management*, 16(11), 133–141.

R Core Team. (2016). *R: A Language and Environment for Statistical Computing. R Foundation for Statistical Computing*, Vienna, Austria. R version 3.3.1. www.r-project.org.

Renko, M. (2013). Early challenges of nascent social entrepreneurs. *Entrepreneurship Theory and Practice*, 37(5), 1045–1069.

Roomi, M. A., and Parrot, G. (2008). Barriers to progression of women entrepreneurs in Pakistan. *Journal of Entrepreneurship*, 17(1), 59–72.

Sanchez, G. (2013). *PLS Path Modeling with R*. Berkeley, CA: Trowchez Editions.

Sanchez, G., Trinchera, L., and Russolillo, G. (2015). *Partial Least Squares Path Modeling (PLS-PM) Analysis for Both Metric and Non-Metric Data, as Well as REBUS Analysis*. R package version 0.4.7. https://cran.r-project.org.

Sanchis-Palacio, J. R., Campos-Climent, V., and Mohedano-Suanes, A. (2013). Management in social enterprises: The influence of the use of strategic tools in business performance. *International Entrepreneurship and Management Journal*, 9, 541–555.

Sastre-Castillo, M. A., Peris-Ortiz, M., and Danvila-Del Valle, I. (2015). What is different about the profile of the social entrepreneur? *Non Profit Management and Leadership*, 25(4), 349–370.

Shapero, A., and Sokol, L. (1982). The social dimensions of entrepreneurship. *Encyclopedia of Entrepreneurship* (pp. 72–90). Englewood Cliffs, NJ: Prentice Hall.

Short, J. C., Moss, T. W., and Lumpkin, G. T. (2009). Research in social entrepreneurship: Past contributions and future opportunities. *Strategic Entrepreneurship Journal*, 3(2), 161–194.

Smith, I. H., and Woodworth, W. (2012). Developing social entrepreneurs and social innovators: A social identity and self-efficacy approach. *Academy of Management Learning and Education*, 11, 390–407.

Spear, R. (2006). Social entrepreneurship: A different model? *International Journal of Social Economics*, 33(5/6), 399–410.

Strong, K. C., Ringer, R. C., and Taylor, S. A. (2001). The rules of stakeholders satisfaction (timeliness, honesty, empathy). *Journal of Business Ethics*, 32(3), 219–230.

Thompson, J. (2002). The world of the social entrepreneur. *The International Journal of Public Sector Management*, 15(5), 412–431.

Urban, B. (2013). Social entrepreneurship in an emerging economy: A focus on the institutional environment and social entrepreneurial self-efficacy. *Managing Global Transitions*, 11(1), 3–25.

Van Ryzin, G. G., Grossman, S., DiPadova-Stocks, L., and Bergrud. E. (2009). Portrait of the social entrepreneur: Statistical evidence from a US panel. *Voluntas*, 20, 129–140.

Verheul, I., Uhlaner, L., and Thurik, R. (2005). Business accomplishments, gender and entrepreneurial self-image. *Journal of Business Venturing*, 20(4), 483–518.

Watson, J., and Newby, R. (2005). Biological sex, stereotypical sex-roles and some owner characteristics. *International Journal of Entrepreneurial Behavior and Research*, 11(2), 129–143.

Weber, P. S., Weber, J. E., Sleeper, B. R., and Scheider, K. L. (2004). Self-efficacy toward service, civic participation and the business student: Scale development and validation. *Journal of Business Ethics*, 49(4), 359–369.

Weerawardena, J., and Mort, G. S. (2006). Investigating social entrepreneurship: A multidimensional model. *Journal of World Business*, 41(1), 21–35.

Witkamp, M. J., Royakkers, L. M., and Raven, R. P. (2011). From cowboys to diplomats: Challenges for social entrepreneurship in the Netherlands. *Voluntas*, 22, 283–310.

Yunus, M., Moingeon, B., and Lehmann-Ortega, L. (2010). Building social business models: Lessons from the Grameen experience. *Long Range Planning*, 43(2–3), 308–325.

Zahn-Waxler, C., and Radke-Yarrow, M. (1990). The origins of empathic concern. *Motivation and Emotion*, 14(2), 107–130.

Zahra, S. A., Gedajlovic, E., Neubaum, D. O., and Shulman, J. M. (2009). A typology of social entrepreneurs: Motives, search processes and ethical challenges. *Journal of Business Venturing*, 24(5), 519–532.

Zahra, S.A., Rawhouser, H. N., Bhawe, N., Neubaum, D. O., and Hayton, J. C. (2008). Globalization of social entrepreneurship opportunities. *Strategic Entrepreneurship Journal*, 2(2), 117–131.

1.4 Non-profit entrepreneurial activism

Values, behaviour, and sociotechnical dimensions of social entrepreneurship in the case of Freegle

Chris I. Martin, Paul Upham, and Rita Klapper

Introduction

It has long been recognised that the entrepreneurship literature has relevance for the non-profit sector (Badelt, 1997), though historically much of the associated discussion has been in the German-speaking countries as part of *Betriebswirtschaflslehre*, which is management science or business administration, rather than as part of *Volkwirtschaftslehre*, which is economics (*ibid.*). In other words, in the German tradition, entrepreneurship has been viewed as a management or business practice that need not necessarily involve a profit-seeking motive. Similarly, Badelt (*ibid.*) reminds us of Schumpeter's (1934) definition of entrepreneurs as individuals who are driven from within to creatively exercise their power, ingenuity and initiative in the material world, but who do not necessarily do this as business owners or for material benefit (Badelt, 1997). Entrepreneurs may also be regarded as demand-driven, without the nature of that demand being viewed as important definitionally (*ibid.*).

With this in mind, there is growing interest in the potential of what has been described as *the sharing economy*[1] to enable sustainable consumption practices and peer-to-peer economic activity. Not only are the origins of this term unclear, but there is arguably "no 'shared' consensus on what activities comprise the 'sharing economy'" (Codagnone and Martens, 2016). Nonetheless, advocates argue that online, peer-to-peer sharing economy platforms enable citizens to share, lend, gift, sell and rent resources at an unprecedented scale; hence, promoting more efficient use of underutilised resources (Botsman and Rogers, 2010). The sharing economy is also often framed as a digital or business model innovation and a considerable commercial opportunity. PwC (2014) speculatively estimates that the global revenues generated by the sharing economy were \$15 billion in 2014 (potentially growing to \$335 billion by 2025). Grassroots and social economy actors (e.g. Freecycle, Couchsurfing, Streetbank) also play an important role in driving innovation (Botsman and Rogers, 2010).

Given that our context is the sharing economy, specifically the non-profit sector, and our interest here is in the values pursued by those involved in the Freegle venture, we take the broader context of the chapter as *social entrepreneurship*. As Austin, Stevenson and Wei-Skillern (2006) highlight, definitions of social entrepreneurship range from broad to narrow, yet common to both approaches is the underlying motivation of the social entrepreneur to create social value, rather than personal and shareholder wealth. The activity is characterised by innovation or the creation of something new. Harding (2007: 74), for instance, defined social entrepreneurship as:

> [a]ny attempt at new social enterprise activity or new enterprise creation, such as self-employment, a new enterprise, or the expansion of an existing social enterprise by an individual, team of individuals or established social enterprise, with social or community goals as its base and where the profit is invested in the activity or venture itself rather than returned to investors.

Austin et al. (2006: 3), on the other hand, define social entrepreneurship as an "innovative, social value creating activity that can occur within or across the non-profit, business or government sectors". This brief selection of definitions highlights: a) the entrepreneurial motivation to create social value, b) that something new/innovative is created, c) that social/community goals are pursued, d) that profits (if made at all) are reinvested in the venture and e) that social entrepreneurship can occur across a range of non-profit and for profit activities.

We focus on a notable example within the sharing economy of what has been termed 'grassroots innovations' (Seyfang and Smith, 2007), exploring the case study of Freegle. Freegle is a UK-based platform, established following the fragmentation of the Freecycle network, that claims to have mobilised millions of people (Freegle, 2015). Freegle participants work to promote reuse and reduce waste, developing and maintaining an online peer-to-peer platform that enables citizens to gift unwanted items (typically consumer goods) to other members of their local community (rather than sending these items to the waste management system).[2] These participants may be considered simultaneously volunteers, activists and entrepreneurial and enterprising in their behaviour, competences and skills. They promote a cause, driven by a vision and (as we show) both pro-social and pro-environmental values; and they do so largely through the medium of a platform dedicated to non-monetarised but nonetheless valuable transactions. It may even be suggested that the non-monetarised, values-driven character of the transactions and the associated entrepreneurial venture (i.e. Freegle) which acts as an enabling platform to make such transactions possible, constitutes the uniqueness of this business model as part of the sharing economy. In fact, it is argued that Freegle creates other types of value for its members. Drawing on the literatures of sociotechnical transitions, values psychology and Alain Gibb's (2005) work on entrepreneurial competences, skills and behaviour, we view Freegle as a form of grassroots innovation within a sociotechnical niche of production and consumption that deploys and is distinguished by a combination of entrepreneurial, pro-social, pro-environmental and non-monetarised value transactions.

The concept of grassroots innovation has recently emerged within the interdisciplinary field of sustainability transitions (Markard et al., 2012; Smith et al., 2010) and is defined by Seyfang and Smith (2007: 585) as "networks of activists and organisations generating novel bottom-up solutions for sustainable development; solutions that respond to the local situation and the interests and values of the communities involved". Here we use the sustainability (sociotechnical) transitions literature as a specific perspective within the broader frame of social entrepreneurship, consistent with our research focus being on the application of digital technology by particular members of society (i.e. Freegle founders), with the aim of offering solutions for sustainability (here recycling and waste management). This interaction of society and (in this case digital) technology also has, as suggested earlier, links with entrepreneurship and associated behaviour, skills, competences and values of a non-profit nature.[3]

Studies of grassroots innovations include community energy projects (Hargreaves et al., 2013), community currencies (Seyfang and Longhurst, 2013a), co-housing (Boyer, 2014), and community-based renewable energy transitions (Süsser et al., 2016). However, to date, research focussed on grassroots innovation within the sharing economy remains limited, with the notable exceptions of Martin and Upham (2015) and Martin et al. (2015). Some researchers have turned to sociotechnical niche theory (Smith and Raven, 2012) to understand the processes by which grassroots innovations might grow and transform the prevailing sociotechnical structures of society (Seyfang and Longhurst, 2013a; Seyfang et al., 2014). From this perspective grassroots innovations are framed as potentially transformative niches; networks of related grassroots projects, each rooted in a specific geographic location, and the associated innovation intermediaries who seek to empower these projects (e.g. investors, funders and national associations).

This chapter thus centres specifically on the values that motivate the efforts and initiatives of individuals acting within this particular niche of the sharing economy: founders and users of the platform. Within the wider framework of values' exploration we address three broader themes: firstly, at the most general macro level, the case study explores the nature of the relationship between individual actors and the systemic, structural changes, such as in this case the ways we produce and consume, with which sociotechnical transition discussions are concerned.

Secondly, in doing this, we examine some of the micro, i.e. psychological dimensions of actors in the niche. The concept of the niche is prominent in entrepreneurship and strategic management literatures; in the sociotechnical transitions literature it is understood as a protective space (Smith and Raven, 2012) within which: a) entrepreneurs can experiment with their innovative ideas, with an emphasis on sociotechnical innovation and b) where there is potential for path-breaking innovations to emerge and develop. These innovations are considered to be in part the outcome of entrepreneurial activity that mobilises a network of people and resources.

Thirdly, our work explores to what extent those involved in these niches may also be described as entrepreneurial, pursuing pro-social and pro-environmental ends in contexts that involve the distribution of goods, but without the motive of profit. It is posited that what we see in the case of Freegle exemplifies a form of activist-entrepreneurship. To make this case, we contrast the values of those involved in Freegle with those of the general population. We also discuss the implications of these values in terms of what it means to be 'entrepreneurial' in the sharing economy, particularly for the scale-up of niche activities by actors who, while motivated to engage broader publics, are unwilling to do so at the cost of compromising particular values.

To this end, we draw selectively on the literatures concerned with values in both pro-environmental behaviour and entrepreneurial behaviour, competences and skills applied within a sociotechnical transition context. Finally, we connect to enduring sociological debate, discussing the connections between agency and structure in the context of social entrepreneurship, specifically the relationship between values and the structural capacity of niche values to propagate more widely. As said, we position the overall chapter within the developing field of sustainable entrepreneurship (e.g. Klapper and Upham 2016; Kyrö, 2015; Schaltegger and Wagner, 2011).

In the next section of the chapter, we outline the theoretical contexts selected to reflect the premise that activists' work on niche development and maintenance – particularly in the sharing economy – which has simultaneous pro-environmental, pro-social and entrepreneurial dimensions. We then describe the case study background, outlining the nature and development of Freegle. The case study methods are then set out, followed by research results relating to the values of those involved, including comparison with the wider population. Overall this enables us to characterise: a) at a macro level, the relationship between the actors and the system within the sharing economy against the framework of sociotechnical transitions literature, b) at a micro level, we identify notable psychological aspects of the niche and c) we suggest possible implications for grassroots innovation theory and practice within the sharing economy, with recourse to entrepreneurial competences, skills, behaviours and values as employed in the case of Freegle, an example of the sharing economy.

Theory

Grassroots innovations as niche activity

Several authors have viewed grassroots innovations through the lens of sociotechnical transitions theory (see Figure 1.4.1) and have identified where the approach both helps and is limited as an explanatory account (e.g. Seyfang and Longhurst, 2013a, 2015; Seyfang et al., 2014). The value of doing so lies in the (assumed) motivations underlying such innovations, namely that they are formed in response to the perception that mainstream systems are unsustainable, with the aim of promoting alternative systems of provision (Seyfang and Longhurst, 2016: 1). Those systems of provision are the chosen analytic foci of the sustainability transitions literature, which commonly incorporates the sociotechnical assumption of co-evolving social and technological components.

The local level of the niche is from this perspective viewed as a network of related projects, each of which is shaped by the grassroots practices and values of local activists. The global level of the niche consists of actors – including funders, activist networks and national associations – who seek to nurture and protect the local projects (Smith and Raven, 2012). Inferring from Seyfang and Smith's (2007: 585) definition of grassroots innovation referred to earlier, three key characteristics of grassroots innovation projects can be identified:

1. Grassroots innovation projects *generate solutions for sustainable development*, hence challenging the unsustainable practices and sociotechnical structures of the prevailing regime (Seyfang and Smith, 2007). For example, activists might generate solutions for reducing carbon emissions by deploying micro-renewable energy generation technologies within communities.
2. Grassroots innovation projects *mobilise the voluntary efforts of activists motivated by pro-environmental and pro-social values* (Martin and Upham, 2015). These values are theorised to be in conflict with the values enacted and propagated by the prevailing regimes (Seyfang and Smith, 2007). For example, community energy projects might be run by volunteers motivated by marginalised environmental and communitarian values (Seyfang et al., 2014).
3. Grassroots innovation projects adopt a *local community focus*, seeking to develop "social structures and . . . build resilience at a community level" and "respond to locally identified problems" (Kirwan et al., 2013: 831). For example, community currencies seek to promote economic activity within a specific locality (Seyfang and Longhurst, 2013b), while local food systems seek to connect communities to the food produce of their locality (Kirwan et al., 2013).

Theory relating to sociotechnical niches has been applied to analyse the dynamics and transformative potential of grassroots innovations (e.g. Seyfang and Longhurst, 2013a, 2015; Seyfang et al., 2014). Such studies have found that grassroots innovations face considerable challenges establishing both niche development processes and a robust network of global niche actors. Furthermore, the sociotechnical transitions literature aims inter alia to provide an account of the dynamics of sociotechnological innovation, as enacted through entrepreneurs, in the niche within the bigger framework of the market economy. Our work suggests that the sociotechnical transition literature is directly transferable to provide an account of the dynamics of grassroots social innovation emerging from civil society. While market-based innovations often enact values and institutional logics (e.g. efficiency and the market respectively) that are aligned with the values of the regime, grassroots innovations enact values and institutional logics (e.g. social justice and community respectively) which are in conflict with those of the regime (Witkamp et al., 2011). Given these differences Smith and Seyfang (2013: 829) suggest that "more managerial thinking in the niche analysis literature is . . . perhaps unsurprisingly . . . less appropriate amidst the messier pluralities and voluntary associations of grassroots innovation".

Nonetheless, while sociotechnical niche theory is admittedly somewhat strained when applied to grassroots innovations, arguably part of its enduring value lies in its identification of the functional roles of a range of key actors, plus the need for their alignment, as conditions for successful niche development. Arguably many of the Freegle activists and their activities bear a resemblance to entrepreneurial behaviours, competences, skills and values. Hence the next section will discuss the relevant literature.

Entrepreneurial behaviours, competences, skills and values

Arguably, sharing economy activists do not simply hold particular values: they enact them in entrepreneurial ways, by initiating organisational forms, typically involving transactions that may or may not be monetarised. Much of the literature dealing with the nature of commercial entrepreneurship has been focussed on individual characteristics and intentions (Fayolle et al., 2014), although the importance of social context and signals in catalysing entrepreneurship has been increasingly acknowledged (Chell, 2007). Indeed, despite the increasing level of attention given to entrepreneurial competences, skills, behaviours and values in a variety of contexts, and, more recently in the sharing economy, research in these fields is still in its early stages.[4] Attention has historically focussed on traits such as the need for achievement, locus of control, desire for autonomy, deviancy, creativity and opportunism, risk-taking ability and intuition (Kirby, 2004). Others have added, for example, traits of tolerance for ambiguity, self-efficacy, goal setting, independence, drive and egoistic passion (Shane et al., 2003). Only relatively recently has closer attention been paid to values rather than traits as antecedents of the intention to establish a business (Fayolle et al., 2014). Klapper and Farber (2016) explored entrepreneurial behaviours, competences, skills and values (Gibb 2005) in a CSR context at a Peruvian HEI, and Klapper and Upham (2015) focussed on the role of pro-environmental and pro-social values as motivators in driving small businesses in Cheshire towards economic, social and environmental sustainability in their transactions, which is similar to Saatci et al. (2014).

Here we draw in particular on Gibb's (2005) taxonomy of entrepreneurial behaviours, values, competences and outcomes, which was later adopted and modified by the UK Quality Assurance Agency (QAA Guidance 2012) as a foundation for the creation of guidelines for a curriculum in enterprise education. In his work, Gibb (2005) defined a range of behaviours, values and competences that are most commonly associated with the entrepreneur in the literature. As *behaviours* Gibb included, e.g. seeking opportunities, taking the initiative, commitment to look beyond, controlling one's own destiny, making intuitive decisions in situations of little information, etc., all of which are amenable to development. Arguably some individuals may be more or less endowed with any one or more of these. Gibb argued that these behaviours support an individual or team wanting to achieve and be capable of driving change through new ideas and innovations rather than sitting back and responding to events.

Entrepreneurial competences covered aspects such as, for example, being good at finding and evaluating an idea, being good at seeing problems as opportunities, being good at identifying key people influential for the entrepreneurial venture, good at learning from relationships, good at knowing where to find answers. *Entrepreneurial values*, as defined by Gibb (2005), include, for example, a strong sense of independence, a strong sense of belonging, being self-sufficient, hard work bringing rewards, being convinced that anything is possible with confidence.

Pro-environmental and pro-social values and behaviour

In seeking psychological predictors for behaviour, the literature on pro-environmental and pro-social values has arguably been dominated by empirical models that connect the posited psychological constructs of values, norms (personal and social) and attitudes (Rhead et al., 2015). The strength and mediated nature of the relationships among these constructs and between the constructs and actual or self-reported behaviour, vary across contexts. Generally, though, studies find that values play a role in explaining environmental attitudes, behaviours and concerns, alongside personal and social norms (for a short review, see Poortinga et al., 2004). Here we focus on values, for which analysts have developed several question sets and measurement scales. Those relevant here can be categorised as those that are intentionally 'universal' and cross-cultural (e.g. Rokeach, 1973; Schwartz, 1994), the latter of which we use here due to the availability of population-scale studies for comparison; those focussed on pro-environmental and pro-social values (e.g. Stern and Dietz, 1994); and those specific to sustainable consumption (e.g. Poortinga et al., 2004). Schwartz (1992) identifies ten basic values (see Table 1.4.1) which are theorised to form a circular motivational continuum (see Figure 1.4.1) where the distinction between adjacent values is blurred (Schwartz, 1992; Schwartz et al., 2012) and the proximity or distance between a given pair of values suggests the degree of compatibility or conflict between them. Each basic value is theorised to be connected to one of four more abstract values: openness to change, conservation, self-transcendence and self-enhancement (Schwartz, 1992).

In this research the questionnaire survey instrument was Schwartz's Portrait Value Questionnaire (PVQ) (Schwartz, 2006; Schwartz et al., 2012); its basis and its use in this work on sharing economy values are described in more detail elsewhere (Martin and Upham, 2015). Schwartz's value survey scales are among the most commonly used scales in contemporary value research (Lindeman and Verkasalo, 2005) and has been applied in an entrepreneurship context by Liñán et al. 2015.

Table 1.4.1 Conceptual definitions of ten basic values according to their motivational goals (Schwartz et al., 2012)

Basic value	*Definitions of basic values according to their motivational goals*
Self-direction	Independent thought and action
Stimulation	Choosing, creating, exploring excitement, novelty and challenge in life
Hedonism	Pleasure and sensuous gratification for oneself
Achievement	Personal success through demonstrating competence according to social standards
Power	Social status and prestige, control or dominance over people and resources
Security	Safety, harmony, and stability of society, of relationships and of self
Conformity	Restraint of actions, inclinations, and impulses likely to upset or harm others and violate social expectations or norms
Tradition	Respect, commitment and acceptance of the customs and ideas that traditional culture or religion provides
Benevolence	Preservation and enhancement of the welfare of people with whom one is in frequent personal contact
Universalism	Understanding, appreciation, tolerance and protection for the welfare of all people and for nature

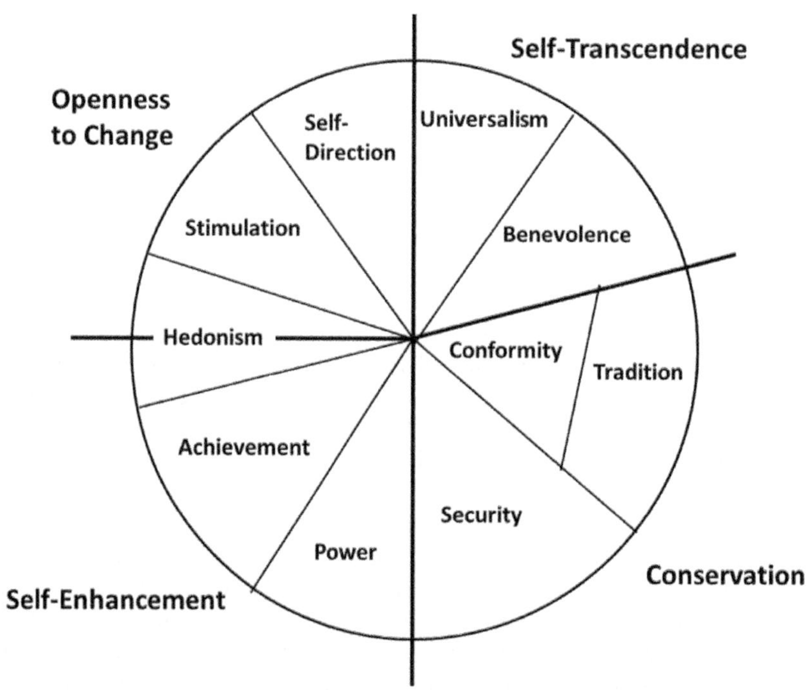

Figure 1.4.1 Theoretical model of relations between ten basic values

Source: Schwartz (1992) and Schwartz et al. (2012).

Material and methods

Case study background: Freegle and the online free reuse niche

Our empirical focus is Freegle, a grassroots network of activists who run online groups which promote the reuse of durable goods within local communities. These *free reuse groups* take the form of online message boards and enable their members[5] to post OFFERS – offering an item that other members of the group might want or need and WANTEDS – requesting an item that members of the group might be willing to give. Members reply directly by email to the individual making an offer or request, and arrangements are then made for the item to be gifted. Where a member receives multiple replies to an offer post they can freely choose, on whatever basis they prefer, who to give the item to. Anyone interested in participating in the groups can join and all items are given freely; payment for items or delivery is prohibited. The groups themselves in principle serve a specific geographic area, e.g. a city or a rural district, to limit the distance members need to travel to collect items (Botsman and Rogers, 2010). Furthermore, each group is run by one or more activists, who support group members, enforce group rules and promote participation.

Most of the academic literature relevant to the Freegle case study focusses on the motivations of the members participating in free reuse groups. A diverse range of motivations have been identified including: enjoying the experience of gifting an item (Nelson et al., 2007), engaging in an ethical or sustainable form of consumption (Foden, 2012), engaging in a form of anti-consumption (Harvey et al., 2014), saving money (Foden, 2012) and avoiding the inconveniences of other forms of waste disposal or gift-giving practices (Guillard and Bucchia, 2012). However, little research has explored the types of items gifted. The limited evidence available (Groomes and Seyfang, 2012) suggests that durable household and consumer goods (e.g. furniture and electronics) may be prominent. Furthermore, it is unclear if free reuse groups compete within other forms of reuse – such as giving items to friends, family or charity – or promote additional reuse (Demailly and Novel, 2014). Freegle's history is intertwined with that of Freecycle, and we now turn to outline these histories.

Freecycle's story and relationship with Freegle

Freecycle was founded in May 2003 by Derron Beal (Freecycle, 2015) as an online group to promote reuse in Tucson, USA. The idea spread rapidly, and between 2004 and 2010 thousands of free reuse groups were established across the USA, Canada, the UK and beyond. By late 2014 the Freecycle network claimed to have more than 5000 groups, across 85 countries (Freecycle, 2015), with approaching 9 million members (Freecycle, 2014). As the Freecycle network grew, it received considerable media coverage[6] particularly in the USA and the UK. In 2007 *Fortune Magazine* heralded Freecycle as "an amazing Internet phenomenon . . . In four years, it's become one of the most effective environmental groups around" (Gunther, 2007).

Freecycle itself consists of a network of activists and a small professional management team (Freecycle, 2015). Throughout Freecycle's development tensions emerged within the movement, the most contentious being the increasingly commercial orientation of the professional management team, which led to collaborations within for-profit companies and trademark disputes (Freecycle Forever, 2015). These tensions led to the fragmentation of the movement with some activists leaving Freecycle to establish independent free reuse groups or to develop parallel networks (Freecycle Forever, 2015). The notable instance of fragmentation came in early autumn 2009, when hundreds of UK activists left Freecycle to form Freegle (Freegle, 2014), a UK network which now incorporates 403 free reuse groups with approximately 2 million members (Freegle, 2015). Furthermore, since 2009, Freegle has developed distinctively online, democratic governance processes and resisted considerable pressures to become more commercially orientated (Martin et al., 2015). These governance processes and interactions between Freegle activists take place almost exclusively online, using semi-public online message boards. Furthermore, free reuse groups within the Freegle network have retained the same basic rules used by Freecycle groups. A detailed account of Freegle's development can be found in Martin et al. (2015).

As stated, online free reuse groups can be conceptualised as a grassroots niche (see Figure 1.4.2). From this perspective, these groups enable their members to enact alternative waste disposal and consumption practices. Hence the niche can be conceptualised as responding to both dominant waste and consumption regimes. At the global level, the niche can be viewed as consisting of both the Freecycle and Freegle umbrella organisations, which seek to mobilise resources within, and sustain and grow, their respective networks. These umbrella organisations also govern the local level of the niche, setting the basic rules by which groups operate, e.g. mandating all items offered must be legal and given freely. However, beyond these basic rules, activists have significant autonomy to run free reuse groups in a manner that aligns with their personal values and ideologies. At the local level the niche consists of an international network of free reuse groups (i.e. grassroots projects), each run by activists and participated in by group members. These groups are either associated with Freecycle or Freegle or other smaller networks or are independent (i.e. not affiliated with a network). Figure 1.4.2 summarises this configuration.

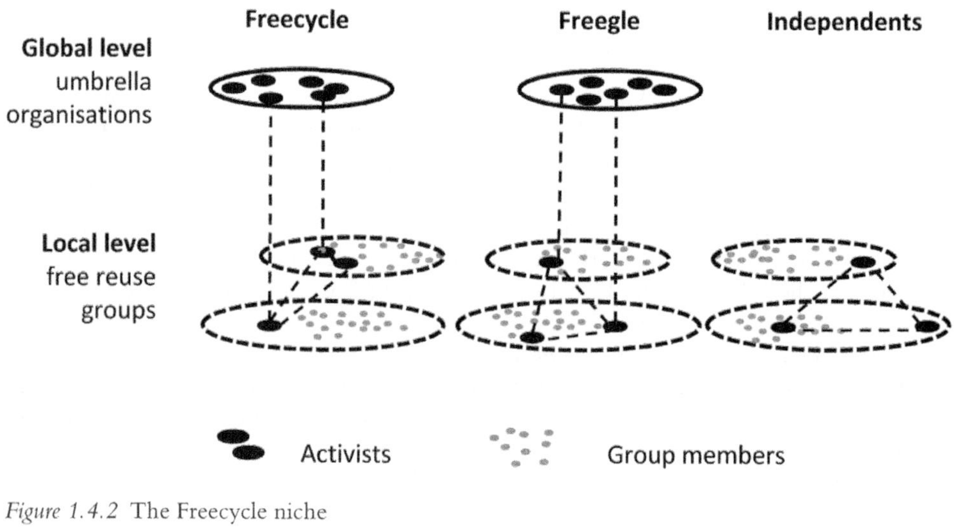

Figure 1.4.2 The Freecycle niche
Source: Adapted from Martin and Upham (2015).

Research methods

Research design

In this research we focussed on the Freegle network. The research design was case study based (Yin, 2014) and data were gathered using five different strands:

1 In-depth semi-structured interviews with 13 Freegle members and leaders, 12 of whom were formerly members of Freecycle
2 Participant observation by one of the authors who worked as an activist from June–December 2014
3 Online interaction data collection
4 A questionnaire survey using Schwartz's Portrait Value Questionnaire (PVQ) (Schwartz, 2006), responded to by 187 Freegle members
5 Publicly available online data relating to Freegle such as blogs, newspapers articles, message board postings, wikis and 198 reports, produced by Freegle members.

The Freegle reports proved a particularly rich source of data, as they summarised the online discussions of the leadership of Freegle, and activist groups focussed on developing Freegle's impact, technological infrastructure and media profile. In the next section we bring together quantitative and qualitative data with which we reflect on the values of Freegle activists and the implications of these for sharing economy and sociotechnical transition processes.

Results and discussion

In this section we evidence and discuss the implications of the values of the Freegle activists for both the sharing economy and the grassroots niche of which this is comprised. We divide the section into key themes grounded in the data.

The core values of Freegle activists

A small majority of the 89 Freegle activists participating in the values survey were female (57%) and many were highly educated (46% had studied at undergraduate degree level or above). The age range of participants was broad (from 18 to 89 years old), though most were aged between 43 and 69 years old (mean age – 56 years, standard deviation of 13 years). The participants tended to live in households with relatively low incomes: 67% – household income under £25,000; 25% – £25,000 to £49,999; 8% – and £50,000 or over. The Freegle activists who took part in the survey tended to emphasise the values of benevolence, universalism and self-direction, as shown by the negative mean value scores in Table 1.4.2. Furthermore, for these three values the activists' mean scores are significantly higher than the mean values scores of the general population (see Table 1.4.2 and Figure 1.4.3). Hence, the respondents have stronger self-transcendence and self-direction values than the average member of the UK population. The strength of self-transcendence is unsurprising, insofar as value theory implies that reuse behaviours are motivated by – and are an expression of – pro-social values (i.e. self-transcendence values) (Cecere et al., 2014; Gregson et al., 2013). Furthermore, in this regard, Freegle activists display a value profile that contrasts with a profile that would arguably be expected for a for-profit entrepreneur, i.e. an emphasis on self-enhancement (power and achievement) and openness to change values (stimulation and self-direction) (Holland and Shepherd, 2013; Liñán et al., 2015; Moriano et al., 2011). Hence, while a 'typical' Freegle activist and a 'typical' for-profit entrepreneur are arguably likely to share strong self-direction values, they are also likely to hold, respectively, the conflicting values of self-transcendence and self-enhancement.

Table 1.4.2 The mean basic values scores of survey respondents and the general population

		Survey participants		*General population*	
		Mean value score	*Std. deviation*	*Mean value score*	*Std. deviation*
Conservation	Security	−0.16	1.07	−0.51	0.76
	Conformity	0.18	1.00	0.12	0.97
	Tradition	−0.06	1.01	−0.05	0.88
Self-transcendence	Benevolence	−0.98	0.69	−0.81	0.63
	Universalism	−1.01	0.72	−0.56	0.63
Openness to change	Self-direction	−0.64	0.79	−0.40	0.76
	Stimulation	0.45	0.98	0.64	0.99
	Hedonism	0.76	0.88	0.44	0.94
Self-enhancement	Achievement	0.65	0.98	0.42	0.94
	Power	1.32	0.85	1.00	0.88

Notes: Highlighted in bold are survey participant value scores where participants tend to emphasise a value to a greater, statistically significant, degree relative to members of the UK population. The statistical tests are t-tests for equality of means and the probabilities of significant difference are all reported by SPSS as p>0.000. As recommended by Schwartz et al. (2015), the mean values are 'centred' (the mean is subtracted) to account for individual differences in scale use: hence the narrow range and negative values. Benevolence values relate to helping those with whom we interact directly; Universalism relates to a wider, geographically global ethic of unity, equality etc; Self-direction relates to creativity and independence.

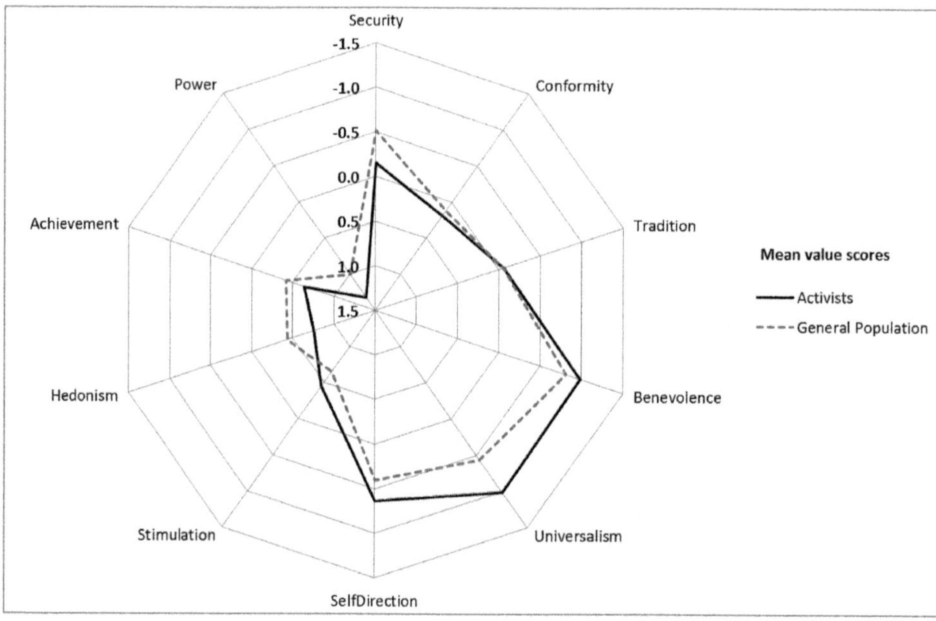

Figure 1.4.3 Mean basic values scores: Freegle activists and UK population

Source: Martin and Upham (2015).

The activists seek to propagate their self-transcendence values through the defining and central rule of the free reuse group: mandating that all items must be offered and given freely to others (Martin and Upham, 2015). Furthermore, these self-transcendence values shape the collaborative practices and organisational structures of the Freegle organisation. In particular, the welfare and contributions of each activist are valued through the democratic decision-making processes of the Freegle umbrella organisation (which rely on online discussions between activists and voting) (Martin et al., 2015). The strong self-direction values of Freegle activists (−0.64 in Table 1.4.2) are reflected in the loosely coupled nature of the Freegle network, whereby activists have significant local autonomy to choose how they run, promote and develop their free reuse group. In this regard, we would suggest that they exhibit entrepreneurial traits such as initiative and independence, but for non-profit motives.

Grounded by these core values, Freegle has developed a shared vision and a strong collective identity around the goal of promoting reuse and reducing waste. Furthermore, the Freegle leadership (i.e. global niche actors) actively fosters respect for, and tolerance of, diverse values and motivations within the network. As described by a current director of Freegle, activists with diverse and potentially conflicting values, interests and ideologies are welcomed (hence in Table 1.4.2 a significantly stronger Benevolence value of −0.98, relative to the wider UK population).

> So we think reuse is a good thing . . . But there might be, for example, a lot of people within Freegle who think wind farms are brilliant; there might be people who think wind farms are terrible – we would not agree on that, nor do we need to for the purposes of what we're doing.
>
> (Activist 3)

In this way, Freegle seeks to mobilise a diverse network of activists ranging from deep green environmentalists participating in Freegle alongside other forms of environmental activism (e.g. the Transitions Town movement) to (micro-) volunteers participating as a minor form of active citizenship.

Values and their expression at the local level of the Freegle niche

Most of the interviewees spoke about how they had become involved as activists following positive experiences of using their local free reuse group. Furthermore, many of these activists framed their participation in a way that resonated with multiple social and environmental values including local community, environmental protection, sociability and generosity (hence strong benevolence values). Nonetheless, more pragmatic motivations were also evident, expressed in terms of helping people 'de-clutter' and free reuse groups providing a convenient way to dispose of unwanted items.

> So I wanted to help . . . for usual reasons . . . to save resources, to help people out who haven't got items and to help people clear clutter and reduce the amount going to landfills.
>
> (Activist 6)

> The idea of throwing something out because you don't know what else to do with it resonates with everyone. It's wasteful, even if you don't care about the planet. The feeling of giving to someone who wants your stuff is a lovely one; . . . Making new

> connections with people in one's own community and meeting decent people who you wouldn't otherwise have met is very special and worthwhile. The convenience of having particularly large items taken away instead of having to arrange . . . for their disposal is marvellous.
>
> (Activist 10; also reflects strong benevolence values)

Perhaps surprisingly, given that the values of local community were often reflected upon by the interviewees, there was also some evidence of activists engaging in grassroots innovation beyond their immediate locality. For instance, activists running groups for geographic areas and communities they do not live in (in some cases hundreds of miles away from their homes); having taken responsibility for groups that had been 'abandoned' (Activist 9) by their previous owner. These connections outside of actors' usual, immediate contexts are indicative of their strong universalist values (Table 1.4.2).

Promoting social inclusion

The almost exclusively online nature of the Freegle network reduces the barriers faced by activists seeking to enact pro-social or environmental values. The majority of activists participate through the practice of online micro-activism (Marichal, 2013; Nekmat et al., 2015), i.e. participating in online grassroots action for short periods of time (minutes) on a regular (daily) basis. This practice of micro-activism was described by one activist as follows.

> There's not an awful lot of work to do, and we've got very simple rules . . . so, generally, I have ten minutes work to do a day . . . on actual day-to-day running, and [then] I can concentrate on promotion.
>
> (Activist 2; reflects self-directive values)

Hence, Freegle seeks to be inclusive to people who might be excluded from offline forms of activism which require a greater, or different form of, time commitment; for example, those with family and caring commitments. Furthermore, the online nature of the movement enables people with health conditions that impact upon their mobility to participate in grassroots innovation, as noted by one activist:

> We have quite a lot of volunteers who are agoraphobic, and it's brilliant that they can volunteer and make their community a better place without going outside.
>
> (Activist 3; also reflects strong benevolence values)

Values at the global level of the Freegle niche

For those activists contributing a predominately voluntary effort to run the Freegle umbrella organisation (i.e. working at the global niche level), there was evidence of rather different values and motivations being enacted. For several members of the leadership team, Freegle represents an opportunity to employ their professional skills, capabilities and resources (developing in either the ICT or communications sector) to create social or environmental value:

> [t]he motivation for me there was that this [Freegle] was a good thing happening through technology . . . so I found that very satisfying that that was an example of technology doing good stuff, because I come from an IT technical background.
>
> (Activist 3)

> [m]y area of skill, or what I could volunteer to do really easily was promotion and publicity.
>
> (Activist 4; reflects self-directive values)

> We went out, got some funding to write a [new] system designed around what we perceived the ideal needs of a Freegle system were, which, because I run an IT business I said I would largely subsidise; I couldn't afford to do it completely free because . . . it was too big a project for me to do myself so I had to pay my staff to do some of it, so we probably covered about 50% of the costs [from external funding] which still meant I've put quite a lot of funding into it.
>
> (Activist 8)

Furthermore, in contrast to the locally oriented values and motivations of the activists running free reuse groups, members of the leadership valued the potential of Freegle to influence prevailing sociotechnical systems (e.g. the waste regime) and prevailing social practices (e.g. consumption and waste disposal) through an all-inclusive approach. Hence, demonstrating an ambition to mobilise and connect local grassroots action as a means of promoting systemic change through an all-inclusive movement:

> Ideally, we'd want everyone in Britain to be a member and never throw away a reusable item – that's the aim. It's rather a lofty aim, and probably unrealistic . . . But that's what we'd hope for.
>
> (Activist 2; universalist values)

> [t]here are just loads of different layers and levels, that Freegle is relevant [to], . . . it is relevant just in local communities, just to individual people, it is relevant to local authorities, it actually connects with national policy and strategy, it connects with EU ambitions and targets and directives.
>
> (Activist 4)

> So we decided that we didn't want to have a general political agenda, because, actually, that would fragment the [Freegle] movement, and also fragments the appeal. We're not thinking of reuse as something that can only be done by people of a particular political persuasion – we want it to be something that everybody does.
>
> (Activist 3; universalist values)

Tensions between local and global values and interests

The structure of the Freegle niche creates tensions between the interests of the network of local activists (focussed on providing a service to a local community) and the interests of the leadership of the movement (focussed on sustaining and growing a national network). This tension is described, in general terms, by one of the directors of Freegle:

> So within the reuse movement . . . there had always been a tension between the grassroots . . . we've just set this thing up, it's local to our city, it's run by volunteers, it's ours. Versus the top-down, no, you're a branch of a national thing and you need to do things the way that the national organisation says.
>
> (Activist 3)

We suggest that this tension arises due to a degree of misalignment of the core and local-level values of Freegle and the values of the global niche, which in turn acts to limit the potential of the Freegle niche to grow and influence the regime. In particular, the values that shape Freegle's organisational structure – democracy, self-direction, voluntarism and local community – are not the same as the goals of the global level of the niche, which aim at system change via the professionalisation and income generation that the leadership view as prerequisites to further growth and impact (Martin et al., 2015). This misalignment of values is illustrated by the experience of one activist, who unsuccessfully explored the potential to monetise Freegle's user-base, by sending promotional advertisements to members of local free reuse groups:

> I've got my own business which could potentially help Freegle loads . . . I distribute . . . [an *environmental-friendly consumer product]* . . . and I was willing to give a percentage back of my sales to Freegle . . . If every group promoted this [product] to their users, it could bring income back and it's saving people money.

A couple of people responded and said, "Well does that meet with our ethos?" (Activist 1; self-direction values).

This misalignment is also illustrated by a limited degree of development of the global niche. In particular, development has been limited by a reliance on micro-activism as a means of mobilising voluntary effort. However, many global niche activities – including fundraising, developing technological services for local groups and advocacy – require volunteers to commit days of effort and are not compatible with the practices of micro-activism and voluntarism. Hence, the movement has become over-reliant on a very small number of highly committed activists with specialist skills and knowledge who face unsustainable demands on their time:

> [i]t seems like if you're involved with [organising] Freegle . . . you've got to keep your eye on the ball 24 hours a day and if you go away or don't look for a week [at the message boards used by activists], then . . . a different decision has been made or discussions been had.
>
> (Activist 6)

Implications for grassroots innovation theory

The degree of inclusivity of a grassroots innovation has implications for its degree of uptake or spread, and this inclusivity may be considered at the level of both users and 'producers' of the innovation. In terms of its values, we would suggest that Freegle is a relatively inclusive form of grassroots innovation at the user level (Martin and Upham, 2015) and the producer level. The Freegle activists (i.e. producers) interviewed tended to think of themselves as offering and maintaining a service for members of a wider community, rather than as generating solutions for sustainable development per se, in the sense posited by grassroots innovation theory (Seyfang and Smith, 2007; Smith and Seyfang, 2013). The innovative nature of the Freegle network itself is clear: as an online, democratic community of environmental activists that has achieved considerable scale and success. However, to date, grassroots innovation research has focussed on activities that are viewed by both insiders and outsiders as 'radical' at the local scale (e.g. Ornetzeder and Rohracher, 2013; White and Stirling, 2013). Less attention has been paid to the potential of grassroots innovations in which novelty emerges through the interactions of local projects that aim for incremental system change.

At the 'producer' level, Freegle's inclusivity is also reflected through the form of micro-activism that enables people who might otherwise be excluded from grassroots innovations to participate. However it should be noted that this inclusion is limited: the digital nature of the work will likely exclude those who lack the skills and equipment to engage in supporting online activity. This potential of grassroots innovations to include some and exclude others has also been noted by Seyfang and Smith (2007). Nonetheless, given that transitions research focusses on the potential for increasing participation in grassroots innovations, the issue of inclusivity and exclusivity merits further research.

Also notable is the spatial dimension of inclusivity. Given that activists predominately participate in Freegle online, it is perhaps surprising that the movement has retained a strong, local community focus. Nonetheless, the digitally mediated nature of the movement has enabled some activists to establish and maintain free reuse groups that lie beyond their immediate geographic locality, contrary to the generally accepted assumption that grassroots innovations should by definition be based within and focussed upon communities within specific localities (Seyfang and Smith, 2007). Future research might further explore this spatial dimension of both digital mediated grassroots innovations and the sharing economy in general, connecting to the emerging body of work on the spatial dimensions of transitions (Murphy, 2015) and the importance of place as well as networked social movements (Castells, 2013).

Implications for grassroots innovation within the sharing economy

In the case of Freegle, we have argued that the values of activists potentially constrain the potential for the niche to grow. In particular, we suggest that the reliance on voluntary effort and resistance to monetising the platform could be limiting growth. Here, we observe a contrast with the rapid growth of the sharing economy's most prominent success stories, Airbnb and Uber, which has been driven by monetisation of the platform's user-base. This raises the question of whether grassroots values can or should be compromised in the hope of destabilising prevailing regimes and wider impacts. As discussed earlier, Freegle is far from a radical form of grassroots innovation, but appears to remain committed to prioritising grassroots values over the potential for growing impact. Perhaps this is unsurprising given that the activists' values are strongly held, as evidenced by the survey results. So, we suggest these results raise concerns that more radical forms of grassroots innovation – presumably motivated by more radical values than those prominent in the case of Freegle – within and beyond the sharing economy may also be self-limiting. However, from an alternative perspective, we might celebrate the fact that Freegle has maintained a focus on its core objective of increasing reuse by enabling people to gift unwanted items to strangers, and, in doing so, the network has resisted considerable pressure to become more commercially orientated. So, while the corporate co-option of sharing economy platforms, including Airbnb and Couchsurfing, is a considerable concern (Schor, 2014), the case of Freegle demonstrates that grassroots platforms can operate at considerable scale without significantly compromising on core values and objectives.

Finally, we observe that activists appear to have played, and continue to play, an important role in promoting and sustaining user activity within Freegle reuse groups. However, other grassroots actors within the sharing economy (e.g. Streetbank) have not yet developed networks of local activists to promote user activity on their platforms.

Furthermore, with the exception of Couchsurfing and Freecycle, these grassroots platforms appear to have struggled to mobilise large numbers of users. Hence, grassroots platforms seeking to grow their user communities might benefit from considering how a similar network of local activists might be developed.

Implications for conceptions of entrepreneurship in the sharing economy

We stated near the beginning of this chapter that we were not going to engage in detailed definitional discussion, much as this may have its own merits. At the same time, the case of Freegle does have implications for the nature of entrepreneurship in the context of the sharing economy. The latter, however, exactly defined, is patently heterogeneous. Just as Freegle bears only a superficial resemblance to eBay, so is it a also world apart from Uber, the multi-billion dollar, often controversial, taxi service and ride sharing platform that makes a profit by taking a 20% commission from drivers. While financially successful, Uber is dogged by controversy internationally for its avoidance of licensing, insurance and other (often labour protection-related) laws that regular taxi firms and drivers are subject to. Indeed, this divergence in values in turn illustrates the case for using values and motivations as a way of characterising and distinguishing actors involved in activities that have economic but not necessarily for-profit dimensions.

Freegle participants subsidise and materially maintain the organisation and its practices through the free donation of participants' time and to some extent resources. Through these inputs, which have value, they conserve the value of the goods that are passed on to new users, for at least one more use cycle. However, entrepreneurship at the most basic level is generally viewed as a process of value creation (Bruyat, 1993; Bruyat and Julien, 2001). Bruyat's (1993) concept is in turn based on Gartner's (1985) four-variable model for entrepreneurship, comprising: a) the individual, b) the process, c) the environment in a general sense and d) the enterprise. This approach views value as created in terms of more or less intense change in the environment directly as a function of the entrepreneurial process (Verstraete and Fayolle, 2005), though, notably, this intensity is not usually conceived of in relation to environmental sustainability (i.e. in terms of materials or energy intensity).

Can the conservation of value be considered a form of entrepreneurship? In one sense this conservation is materially little different to any resale market where used goods are resold, with the obvious difference being the lack of monetary exchange and the lack of profit levered in return for brokering. In this respect we have already referred to the parallels with eBay. Again, it is the motives and values of the participants – the non-profit intent – that constitutes a key part of the difference. This therefore raises a further question: need entrepreneurship be for-profit? or, a related but somewhat different question: how important need the profit motive be to a definition of entrepreneurship? There are two main possibilities here: either we can restrict our understanding or definition of entrepreneurship to for-profit activities, or we can expand that definition to include a wider range of activities relating to the organisation of goods and services provision. While expanding the breadth of activities in which we view entrepreneurship or entrepreneurialism as inherent risks losing definitional focus and seeing entrepreneurship everywhere, does this not have merit? Why should entrepreneurship be inherently associated with a profit motive? Arguably, entrepreneurship captures as a term a broad range of human attributes, while profit-seeking is in part a product of the economic systems in which entrepreneurial individuals find themselves.

In sustainability circles there is arguably a lack of trust in the capacity of entrepreneurs to transform society in ways consistent with non-economic values, despite an increasing interest in the function of the social entrepreneur and in social entrepreneurship in general. Entrepreneurs tend to be viewed as part of the problem rather than a solution. Moreover, notwithstanding the emergence of sustainable entrepreneurship as a sub-field in entrepreneurship research, particularly in relation to new business models (Schaltegger and Wagner, 2011; Schaltegger et al., 2017), the observation by Hall et al. (2010) that the academic discourse on sustainable development within the entrepreneurship literature and in entrepreneurship education (Wyness et al., 2015) has been sparse, still has resonance. Here we have sought to broaden the focus of what entrepreneurialism is and what it might be, by exploring the values of those deploying ingenuity, initiative and drive to provide goods to others, but without a profit motive.

Conclusions

There is growing interest in the sharing economy, a digitally mediated innovation with the potential to play a role in the transition to a sustainable society. The sharing economy is primarily framed as a digital or business model innovation; however, grassroots social innovations including Freegle could also play an important role. Here we have employed sociotechnical transitions theory to conceptualise Freegle as part of a niche of grassroots innovation, and through an empirical case study have analysed the characteristics of this niche activity, focussing particularly on participant values and the enactment of these.

Our research results suggest that the free reuse groups run by the Freegle network are an incremental and inclusive form of grassroots innovation that we would suggest involves many of the traits of entrepreneurship. More specifically, these groups are run by micro-activists, motivated by a diverse range of values, who use initiative and drive to offer and maintain a service for members of a wider community. Furthermore, we have observed a misalignment between the values and motivations of Freegle activists operating at the local and global levels of the niche. We have argued that the consequences of this misalignment are mixed: both limiting the potential for Freegle to grow, but at the same time enabling Freegle to resist corporate co-option. Accordingly, we suggest that the psychological dimensions of grassroots and sharing economy niches, such as activists' values, might create a self-limiting niche dynamic.

We are not convinced that a definition of entrepreneurship need involve profit-seeking as a high priority. With a wide range of traits held to be involved in entrepreneurship, including the drive to autonomy or self-directedness, and with a high level of the latter also being found in our sample of Freegle participants relative to a relevant general population, we suggest that there is merit in viewing profit-seeking, particularly profit-maximising, entrepreneurship as one form among multiple forms. We might also point out that there are many different approaches to thinking about values. We have used an approach from the psychological literature, but values per se are obviously a key theme in the ethics literature, with attempts to define the nature of good living dating at least to Aristotle's *Nicomachean Ethics*. Values thus provide another point of entry into a discussion of the distinguishing features of different forms of entrepreneurialism in different economic contexts. Indeed, we might also observe that what is niche and what is mainstream (in the dominant regime) reflects which and whose values dominate in a social setting. The extent to which dominant values need to change for sustainability are a matter of debate, but we think that most would agree that some rapprochement of social, economic and environmental values is required.

Notes

1 We make few assumptions about the nature of the sharing economy, with the exception that peer-to-peer digital platforms are prevalent in the modus operandi of the companies and organisations that are often deemed to be a part of, and arguably to a significant extent constitute, what is typically described as the sharing economy.
2 While it is arguable that Freegle does reduce the environmental impact of the recipients of used goods through a substitution effect (i.e. marginal demand for new versions of such goods is at least postponed), the sustainability credentials of the sharing economy in general should not be assumed (Martin, 2016). Assessing this raises issues of analytic boundaries and baselines, spatial, temporal and functional, all of which inform the choice of comparator.
3 Markard et al. (2012) provide a detailed account of the nature and history of the sociotechnical, sustainability transitions literature. The term sociotechnical was coined in the 1960s in relation to coal-mining (Emery et al., 1960) and the core meaning remains the same: the social and the technical are seen as interconnected. The contemporary sustainability transitions literature has brought the term together with processual ideas of system change and has taken it in normative directions (i.e. oriented to sustainability).
4 One might also wonder whether this in part reflects the publishing practices of elite social science journals, which have been very late in acknowledging climate change (Goodall, 2008).
5 Freegle refers to the individuals who use their free reuse groups as members (and hence we use this terminology). However, we note that these individuals might be better characterised as users of the Freegle platform.
6 A search of the LexisNexis database on 29 March 2015 for 'freecycle network' returned 994 English language media articles.

References

Austin, J., Stevenson, H. and Wei-Skillern, J. (2006). Social and commercial entrepreneurship: Same, different, or both? *Entrepreneurship theory and practice*, 30(1): 1–22.

Badelt, C. (1997). Entrepreneurship theories of the non-profit sector. *VOLUNTAS: International Journal of Voluntary and Nonprofit Organizations*, 8/2: 162–178.

Botsman, R. and Rogers, R. (2010). What's mine is yours: how collaborative consumption is changing the way we live. London: Collins.

Boyer, R. (2014). Sociotechnical transitions and urban planning: A case study of eco-cohousing in Tompkins County, New York. *Journal of Planning Education and Research*, 34: 451–464.

Bruyat, C. (1993) Création d'entreprise: contributions épistémologiques et modélisation. Thèse pour le Doctorat de Sciences de Gestion, ESA. PhD dissertation. Grenoble, France: Université Grenoble II.

Bruyat, C. and Julien, P.A. (2001). Defining the field of entrepreneurship. *Journal of Business Venturing*, 16(2): 165–180.

Castells, M. (2013). Networks of outrage and hope: Social movements in the Internet age. Cambridge, UK: John Wiley & Sons.

Cecere, G., Mancinelli, S. and Mazzanti, M. (2014). Waste prevention and social preferences: The role of intrinsic and extrinsic motivations. *Ecological Economics*, 107: 163–176.

Chell, E. (2007). Social enterprise and entrepreneurship: Towards a convergent theory of the entrepreneurial process. *International Small Business Journal*, 25: 5–26.

Codagnone, C. and Martens, B. (2016). Scoping the sharing economy: Origins, definitions, impact and regulatory issues, JRC Technical Reports, European Union. *Brussels*. Available at: https://ec.europa.eu/jrc/sites/jrcsh/files/JRC100369.pdf (accessed 4 January 2018).

Demailly, D. and Novel, A. (2014). *The sharing economy: Make it sustainable.* Available at: www.iddri.org/Evenements/Interventions/ST0314_DD%20ASN_sharing%20economy.pdf (accessed 22 July 2015).

Emery, F.E. and Trist, E.L. (1960). Socio-technical systems. In C.W. Churchman and M. Verhulst (eds.) *Management Science Models and Techniques*, vol. 2. Oxford, UK, Pergamon, pp. 83–97.

Fayolle, A., Liñán, F. and Moriano, J. (2014). Beyond entrepreneurial intentions: Values and motivations in entrepreneurship. *International Entrepreneurship and Management Journal*, 10: 679–689.

Foden, M. (2012). Everyday consumption practices as a site for activism? Exploring the motivations of grassroots reuse groups. *People, Place & Policy Online*, 6: 148–163.

Freecycle. (2014). *The Freecycle Network* (Online). Available at: www.freecycle.org/ (accessed 11 November 2014).

Freecycle. (2015). *History & Background Information* (Online). Available at: www.freecycle.org/about/background (accessed 22 July 2015).

Freecycle Forever. (2015). *History* (Online). Available at: www.freecycleforever.org/history (accessed 22 July 2015).

Freegle (2014). *About Freegle* (Online). Available at: www.ilovefreegle.org/about/ (accessed 19 November 2014).

Freegle (2015). *Freegle: Don't throw it away – Give it away!* (Online). Available: www.ilovefreegle.org/ (accessed 3 November 2015).

Gartner, WB. (1985). A conceptual framework for describing the phenomenon of new venture creation. *Academy of Management Review*, 10(4): 696–706.

Gibb, A.A. (2005). Towards the entrepreneurial university entrepreneurship education as a lever for change. National Council for Graduate Entrepreneurship (NCGE), Policy Paper No. 003, Birmingham. http://ncee.org.uk/wp-content/uploads/2018/01/towards_the_entrepreneurial_university.pdf (accessed 16 July 2018).

Goodall, A.H. (2008). Why have the leading journals in management (and other social sciences) failed to respond to climate change? *Journal of Management Inquiry*, 17: 408–420.

Gregson, N., Crang, M., Laws, J., Fleetwood, T. and Holmes, H. (2013). Moving up the waste hierarchy: Car boot sales, reuse exchange and the challenges of consumer culture to waste prevention. *Resources, Conservation and Recycling*, 77: 97–107.

Groomes, L. and Seyfang, G. (2012). *Secondhand spaces and sustainable consumption: Examining Freecycle's environmental impacts and user motivations.* Available at: www.3s.uea.ac.uk/publications/secondhand-spaces-and-sustainable-consumption-examining-freecycle%E2%80%99s-environmental-impac (accessed 19 November 2014).

Guillard, V. and Bucchia, C.D. (2012). How about giving my things away over the internet? When internet makes it easier to give things away. In: Gürhan-Canli, Z., Otnes, C. and Zhu, R. J. (eds.) *Advances in Consumer Research*. Duluth, MN: Association for Consumer Research.

Gunther, M. (2007). *The amazing Freecycle story* (Online). *Fortune*. Available: http://archive.fortune.com/2007/07/13/magazines/fortune/pluggedin_gunther_freecycle.fortune/index.htm (accessed 22 July 2015).

Hall, J.K., Daneke, G.A. and Lenox, M.J. (2010). Sustainable development and entrepreneurship: Past contributions and future directions. *Journal of Business Venturing*, 25(5): 439–448.

Harding, R. (2007). Understanding social entrepreneurship. *Industry & Higher Education*, 21(1): 74.

Hargreaves, T., Hielscher, S., Seyfang, G. and Smith, A. (2013). Grassroots innovations in community energy: The role of intermediaries in niche development. *Global Environmental Change*, 23: 868–880.

Harvey, J., Smith, A. and Golightly, D. (2014). Giving and sharing in the computer-mediated economy. *Journal of Consumer Behaviour*, 16: 363–371.

Holland, D.V. and Shepherd, D.A. (2013). Deciding to persist: Adversity, values, and entrepreneurs' decision policies. *Entrepreneurship Theory and Practice*, 37: 331–358.

Kirby, D.A. (2004). Entrepreneurship education: Can business schools meet the challenge? *Education + Training*, 46: 510–519.

Kirwan, J., Ilbery, B., Maye, D. and Carey, J. (2013). Grassroots social innovations and food localisation: An investigation of the Local Food programme in England. *Global Environmental Change*, 23: 830–837.

Klapper, R.G. and Farber, V.A. (2016). In Alain Gibb's footsteps: Evaluating alternative approaches to sustainable enterprise education (SEE). *The International Journal of Management Education*, 14: 422–439.

Klapper, R. and Upham, P. (2015). A model of small business and sustainable development: Values, value creation and the limits to codified knowledge tools. In: Kyro, P. and Fayolle, A. (eds.) *Sustainable Entrepreneurship*. Cheltenham, UK: Edward Elgar, pp. 275–296.

Kyrö, P. (2015). Handbook of entrepreneurship and sustainable development research. Cheltenham, UK: Edward Elgar.

Liñán, F., Moriano, J.A. and Jaén, I. (2015). Individualism and entrepreneurship: Does the pattern depend on the social context? *International Small Business Journal*, 34(6): 760–776.

Lindeman, M. and Verkasalo, M. (2005). Measuring values with the Short Schwartz's Value Survey. *Journal of Personality Assessment*, 85(2): 170–178,

Marichal, J. (2013). Political Facebook groups: Micro-activism and the digital front stage. *First Monday*, 18. http://dx.doi.org/10.5210/fm.v18i12.4653.

Markard, J., Raven, R. and Truffer, B. (2012). Sustainability transitions: An emerging field of research and its prospects. *Research Policy*, 41: 955–967.

Martin, C.J. (2016). The sharing economy: A pathway to sustainability or a nightmarish form of neoliberal capitalism? *Ecological Economics*, 121: 149–159.

Martin, C.J. and Upham, P. (2015). Grassroots social innovation and the mobilisation of values in collaborative consumption: A conceptual model. *The Journal of Cleaner Production*, 134, Part A: 204–213.

Martin, C.J., Upham, P. and Budd, L. (2015). Commercial orientation in grassroots social innovation: Insights from the sharing economy. *Ecological Economics*, 118: 240–251.

Moriano, J.A., Gorgievski, M., Laguna, M., Stephan, U. and Zarafshani, K. (2011). A cross-cultural approach to understanding entrepreneurial intention. *Journal of Career Development*, 39(2): 162–185.

Murphy, J.T. (2015). Human geography and socio-technical transition studies: Promising intersections. *Environmental Innovation and Societal Transitions*, 17: 73–91.

Nekmat, E., Gower, K.K., Gonzenbach, W.J. and Flanagin, A.J. (2015). Source effects in the micro-mobilization of collective action via social media. *Information Communication and Society*, 18(9): 1076–1091.

Nelson, M.R., Rademacher, M.A. and Paek, H.-J. (2007). Downshifting consumer = upshifting citizen? An examination of a local Freecycle community. *The ANNALS of the American Academy of Political and Social Science*, 611: 141–156.

Ornetzeder, M. and Rohracher, H. (2013). Of solar collectors, wind power, and car sharing: Comparing and understanding successful cases of grassroots innovations. Global Environmental Change, 23: 856–867.

Poortinga, W., Steg, L. and Vlek, C. (2004). Values, environmental concern, and environmental behavior: A study into household energy use. *Environment and Behavior*, 36: 70–93.

PwC. (2014). *The sharing economy: How will it disrupt your business? Megatrends: the collisions*. Available at: http://pwc.blogs.com/files/sharing-economy-final_0814.pdf (accessed 22 April 2015).

QAA Guidance (2012) *Enterprise and Entrepreneurship Education: Guidance for Higher Education Providers*. www.qaa.ac.uk/# (accessed 16 July 2018).

Rhead, R., Elliot, M. and Upham, P. (2015). Assessing the structure of UK environmental concern and its association with pro-environmental behaviour. *Journal of Environmental Psychology*, 43: 175–183.

Rokeach, M. (1973). Rokeach Values Survey. The nature of human values. New York: Free Press.

Saatci, E.Y., Arikan, S. and Çal, B.T. (2014). Values? How social entrepreneurs' portrait values differ from commercial entrepreneurs? *International Journal of Education and Research*, 2: 143–160.

Schaltegger, S., Hörisch, J. and Freeman, R.E. (2017). Business cases for sustainability: A stakeholder theory perspective. *Organization & Environment* 108602661772288. doi:10.1177/1086026617722882.

Schaltegger, S. and Wagner, M. (2011). Sustainable entrepreneurship and sustainability innovation: Categories and interactions. *Business Strategy and the Environment*, 20(4): 222–237.

Schor, J. (2014). Debating the sharing economy. Available at: http://greattransition.org/publication/debating-the-sharing-economy (accessed 19 January 2015).

Schumpeter, J.A. (1934). *The Theory of Economic Development*. Cambridge, MA: Harvard University Press.

Schwartz, S.H. (1992). Universals in the content and structure of values: Theoretical advances and empirical tests in 20 countries. *Advances in Experimental Social Psychology*, 25: 1–65.

Schwartz, S.H. (1994). Are there universal aspects in the structure and contents of human values? *Journal of Social Issues*, 50: 19–45.

Schwartz, S.H. (2006). Les valeurs de base de la personne: théorie, mesures et applications. *Revue française de sociologie*, 47: 929–968.

Schwartz, S.H., Breyer, B. and Danner, D. (2015). Human Values Scale (ESS). *Zusammenstellung sozialwissenschaftlicher Items und Skalen*. doi:10.6102/zis234.

Schwartz, S.H., Cieciuch, J., Vecchione, M., Davidov, E., Fischer, R., Beierlein, C., Ramos, A., Verkasalo, M., Lönnqvist, J.-E., Demirutku, K., Dirilen-Gumus, O. and Konty, M. (2012). Refining the theory of basic individual values. *Journal of Personality and Social Psychology*, 103: 663–688.

Seyfang, G., Hielscher, S., Hargreaves, T., Martiskainen, M. and Smith, A. (2014). A grassroots sustainable energy niche? Reflections on community energy in the UK. *Environmental Innovation and Societal Transitions*, 13: 21–44.

Seyfang, G. and Longhurst, N. (2013a). Desperately seeking niches: Grassroots innovations and niche development in the community currency field. *Global Environmental Change*, 23: 881–891.

Seyfang, G. and Longhurst, N. (2013b). Growing green money? Mapping community currencies for sustainable development. *Ecological Economics*, 86: 65–77.

Seyfang, G. and Longhurst, N. (2016). What influences the diffusion of grassroots innovations for sustainability? Investigating community currency niches. *Technology Analysis & Strategic Management*, 28(1): 1–23.

Seyfang, G. and Smith, A. (2007). Grassroots innovations for sustainable development: Towards a new research and policy agenda. *Environmental Politics*, 16: 584–603.

Shane, S., Locke, E.A. and Collins, C.J. (2003). Entrepreneurial motivation. *Human Resource Management Review*, 13: 257–279.

Smith, A. and Raven, R. (2012). What is protective space? Reconsidering niches in transitions to sustainability. *Research Policy*, 41: 1025–1036.

Smith, A. and Seyfang, G. (2013). Constructing grassroots innovations for sustainability. *Global Environmental Change*, 23: 827–829.

Smith, A., Voß, J.-P. and Grin, J. (2010). Innovation studies and sustainability transitions: The allure of the multi-level perspective and its challenges. *Research Policy*, 39: 435–448.

Stern, P.C. and Dietz, T. (1994). The value basis of environmental concern. *Journal of Social Issues*, 50: 65–84.

Süsser, D., Ratter, B. and Scheffran, J. (2016). People-powered local energy transition: Mitigating climate change with commuity-based renewable energy in North Frisia. Doctoral dissertation, Universität Hamburg Hamburg, Germany.

Verstraete, T. and Fayolle, A. (2005) *Revue de l'Entrepreneuriat*, 4(1): 33–52. Available from: www.researchgate.net/publication/242749974_Paradigmes_et_entrepreneuriat (accessed 16 July 2018).

White, R. and Stirling, A. (2013). Sustaining trajectories towards sustainability: Dynamics and diversity in UK communal growing activities. *Global Environmental Change*, 23: 838–846.

Witkamp, M.J., Raven, R.P.J.M. and Royakkers, L.M.M. (2011). Strategic niche management of social innovations: The case of social entrepreneurship. *Technology Analysis & Strategic Management*, 23: 667–681.

Wyness, L., Jones, P. and Klapper, R. (2015). Sustainability: What the entrepreneurship educators think. *Education + Training*, 57(8/9): 834–852.

Yin, R.K. (2014). *Case study research: Design and methods*. Thousand Oaks, CA: Sage.

Part II

Fostering and enacting sustainability through entrepreneurial action

2.1 Sustainable entrepreneurship orientation

Reflection on status-quo research on factors facilitating responsible managerial practices*

Sacha Kraus, Janina Burtscher, Christine Vallaster, and Martin Angerer

Introduction

The global financial system has undergone a huge transformation process since the financial crisis of 2007 and the subsequent crises. One main driver of the turbulences was the dominating objective of securing fast profits with high leverage, neglecting sustainability and other social aspects [1]. The financial (investor-side-based) academic literature has immediately responded and already offers a huge amount of studies on the development and performance of companies that do business in a sustainable way. Friede et al. contribute a literature review of over 2000 studies just on the topic of financial performance of ESG (environmental, sustainable and green) investments [2]. Others look at more specific cases, e.g. [3], which use a database on eco-efficiency scores and find that companies that have good scores also have better financial performance. They also show that financial performance is time-lagged with better scores. However, the financial system consists not only of investors but also of entrepreneurs that choose how to run their companies. While the investor's point of view on sustainable investments and a sustainable system is already heavily researched, there is a lack of research on the side of entrepreneurs. In this chapter we develop this side to contribute to the understanding of sustainable financial markets by bringing together entrepreneurial and financial research.

Although the importance of sustainable entrepreneurship has increased in academia as well as in the global societal discourse, the concept itself is still developing [4–6]. While common entrepreneurship theories are based on discovering and exploiting economic opportunities through entrepreneurial orientation (EO) [7], sustainable entrepreneurship deals with the transformation of society towards a more environmental, social and economic equilibrium through sustainable entrepreneurial orientation (SEO) [8]. Research on this field has evolved and includes the "green entrepreneur", the "social entrepreneur" and the "sustainable entrepreneur" [9], following the same ESG structure as the financial literature does.

First introduced by Berle, green entrepreneurship is widely concerned with environmental challenges [10]. Green entrepreneurs build their businesses with environmental values as their foundation. But taking these into account, they also seek competitive advantages [11]. The US outdoor clothing company Patagonia (www.patagonia.com) is a green enterprise, and its business model blends entrepreneurial goals with a successful economic (profit, market share, etc.) return, while minimizing its negative impact on the environment wherever possible. Patagonia's mission statement is "Build the best product. Cause no unnecessary harm. Use business to inspire and implement solutions to the environmental crisis". Ecological entrepreneurship can here be defined as a process where opportunities are identified, analysed and taken on with the aim of minimizing a firms' exploitation of the natural environment, generating benefits for future societal and economic needs in the process.

Social entrepreneurs assign the utmost priority to the creation of social value, with economic value creation only being a necessary condition for financial viability [12,13]. Magda's hotel in Vienna, Austria (www.magdas-hotel.at) is an example of this kind of "hybrid organization" in how it combines features from both the non-profit and for-profit sectors [14]. The hotel is run completely by refugees (who are legally permitted to work in Austria). A profit orientation characterizes their work approach. The identity of Magda's hotel is thus formed by both social ambitions and utilitarian economics [15].

Researchers like Isaak [16] or Schaltegger and Wagner [17] have linked green entrepreneurship and social entrepreneurship to sustainable entrepreneurship, as all three categories share the common goal of positive environmental impacts. Sustainable entrepreneurship in existing firms, especially SMEs, is led by an entrepreneur who carries out managerial sustainable practices (MSP) through innovation and creating value [6]. SEO is crucial for the implementation of sustainable entrepreneurship within an organization, making corporate social responsibility (CSR) a strategic issue [18]. While strong research has evolved around strategic CSR, e.g. [19–23], a lack of structured review remains for understanding both the investors' and the entrepreneurs' side to establish a sustainable financial system. Particularly, there is a lack of consensus when it comes to identifying entrepreneurial sustainability practices [24].

In this chapter, we aim to close this gap by providing a structured literature review drawing on the structure that Spence et al. introduced [25]. Here the authors identify three relevant levels which they believe have an effect on the successful implementation of managerial sustainable practices: the individual, the firm and contextual levels.

The remaining part of this chapter is structured as follows. The first part of the literature review sets the stage for and defines the influence of CSR on entrepreneurship orientation (EO), followed by a discussion that shifts the perspective from EO to sustainable entrepreneurship orientation (SEO). The second part introduces the methodology used for this structured review process. Finally, the reviewed research highlights foundational factors thought to influence sustainable entrepreneurial managerial practices. We conclude with a look at further paths for future research.

Setting the stage

Sustainable entrepreneurship in this chapter is defined as the need to integrate environmental, social, sustainable and economic activities. The environmental aspect typically attempts to reduce the exploitation of valuable resources and the environment, decrease the creation and use of harmful substances, and curb environmental pollution and waste production [26–28]. Sustainability in the social realm can involve promoting social integration; nurturing societies that are characterized by safety, stability and justice; advancing and protecting human rights, diversity and equality; and securing livelihoods [29]. A possible definition here (and that is balanced with the more long-term view of sustainable development) is provided by Choi and Gray who conceive sustainable entrepreneurs as "individuals who are creating and building profitable companies that also pursue environmental or social causes" [30].

The influence of CSR on EO

With the above understanding in mind, sustainable entrepreneurship is strongly linked to the recent discussions revolving around CSR. Not only within the academic world is CSR gaining a significant amount of relevance. It is also becoming an increasingly pressing item for the agendas of corporations as well. While the traditional focus of corporations should be to conduct their activities in a profitable manner, studies regarding CSR argue that a socially responsible corporation should, besides making a profit, strive to obey all applicable laws, behave in an ethical and responsible way, and be a "good corporate citizen" [31–33].

A growing amount of research has delivered numerous definitions of CSR to address what exactly is meant by companies being socially and ecologically responsible. The most widely adopted definition of CSR has been the result of the work by Carroll [34], who designed a model consisting of four major pillars of responsibilities including economic, legal, ethical as well as philanthropic responsibilities. As the traditional main objective of business is to conduct them in a profitable manner, a major topic within the literature is whether companies should be concerned with other responsibilities besides their own, often sole responsibility of simply achieving a profit [35].

Multiple studies in business literature have recently focused on CSR and the EO of businesses. As studies have shown, CSR is an important and even central priority for companies and their management within their daily business activities due to CSR's ability to create shared value [36]; it is also a key factor in increasing greater social cohesion. This in turn leads to a higher degree of sustainable economic growth, encompassing economic, social and environmental goals [37].

The EO of businesses is regarded as a predictor of the success of corporations [38]. After all, the EO of enterprises has a significant influence on business performance as well as its ability to create value [39–42]. Looking at the financial performance of stock companies classified as ESG investments, Auer et al. [43] find that overall their performance is comparable to the broad market and only worse in some sub-regions and sub-ESG classes. Furthermore, an EO has an even more rigorous effect on a more general level because it is deemed capable of improving the economy on a macroeconomic scale through the creation of wealth. It can therefore be of essential help on the way to a more sustainable financial system as a whole. It also encourages and facilitates the degree of competition within today's global employment environment [44], making it one of the top priorities of many governments [45].

The action a firm takes in response to environmental pressure can be shaped by the entrepreneurial strategies it adopts, enabling a firm to improve its sustainability activities [46]. Based on the traditional literature on entrepreneurship, the sole focus has been this topic's relationship to economic development, merely observing the economic impact of enterprises, e.g. Schumpeter [7]. The link between entrepreneurship and sustainable development has gained academic interest only very recently [47,6]. To effectively be able to compete within a market, companies must develop new and innovative ways to secure their long-term existence [48]. So fostering the positive factors and actively curbing the negative factors within the market makes analyses of what affects business performance necessary. Not until the emergence of the stakeholder theory formally introduced by Freeman [49] had CSR attracted much academic attention, even though its origins date back to the beginning of the 20th century [50]. Now a priority for companies and managers in today's world [36], CSR has been strategically integrated into the core of many firms' activities [18] thanks to its ability to create shared value for businesses and society alike [37].

Moving from EO to SEO

More researchers have recently devoted their attention to SEO, an idea formed out of the concepts of EO [39,41] as well as sustainability orientation [51].

First introduced by Miller [41], EO has become a much-researched topic in business science [52]. Today it is one of the most prominent research topics within entrepreneurship research [53]. While this growing research led to an establishment of comprehensive knowledge [44,54–56], it also resulted in multiple reformulations of its original conception. Miller's original notion of EO is based on the three dimensions of proactiveness, innovativeness and risk-taking [41]. The innovativeness of a firm can be measured by observing the actions taken towards engaging and backing new ideas, advocating creative measures, and encouraging experiment and testing processes. Actions like these are linked to product service and/or process innovation [57]. A popular indicator of the proactiveness of a company is its willingness to anticipate and react to changes in the future, a behaviour often resulting in proactive enterprises being the "first movers" and forerunners in the market [57,58], while reactive companies respond and follow.

Acting entrepreneurially requires enduring a certain amount of risk, uncertainty and high probability of loss. This is often used synonymously with a willingness towards risk-taking [59]. However, this readiness to invest in opportunities that go along with this uncertainty about the prospect of succeeding often does not include blindly investing in high-risk and uncontrollable ventures, but rather taking calculated risks after an extensive examination of possible outcomes [60]. Miller and Friesen [61] clearly understand EO as a decision-making process affecting not only the enterprise's willingness to innovate but to outshine the competition with regard to proactiveness and taking risks as well. Enterprises implementing EO as their strategic orientation are able to discover, evaluate and exploit new opportunities to create new products, services and/or processes [54,62,63]. Gasser et al. [64] provide evidence from financial stock markets that stock returns of ESG-rated companies are slightly lower but not riskier than others when considering standard deviation as a measure. Running a sustainable and competitive business is therefore also not expected to be riskier by the financial markets.

Just like EO, SEO is a strategic orientation formed in the context of a competitive culture [65]. While EO is a popular research topic, SEO is a rather novel research issue that has only recently grabbed the attention of researchers such as Bos-Brouwers [51] and Kuckertz and Wagner [66]. Although in most cases SEO is conceptualized on the individual level [67], in the context of forming a definition for SEO, Bos-Brouwers defined it as a unidimensional system which displays itself in three different schemes that build upon the firms' perception of sustainability: as a cost, obligation or opportunity [51]. Moreover, SEO also consists of two underlying factors enabling the implementation and integration of sustainability into the enterprise: consciousness and motivation [51,68]. By integrating sustainability into their business strategy, enterprises enable themselves to respond to the uncertainty of their environment and therefore adapt their strategic orientation correspondingly [69].

Current research shows that in order to be able to respond to market changes, rather than focusing on one strategic orientation, companies have to build their strategy based on multiple ones [63,65]. These numerous strategic orientations then build an overall strategic orientation of the company [70]. One of these overall strategic orientations emerging out of two different strategic orientations includes SEO. Criado-Gomis et al. suggest that the difficulty of implementing measures regarding sustainable development can be reduced by incorporating SEO as a strategic resource [71], which enables companies to implement triple-bottom-line objectives into their corporate culture. The combination of the decision-making and behavioural aspects of EO, with innovativeness, proactiveness and risk-taking [41], on the one hand, and SO with consciousness and awareness of sustainable development on the other [51], build a unique strategic opportunity for the sustainable enterprise to be on the market's cutting edge, grow and remain in business for the long haul [71].

Although research has been on the rise, there is a lack of a structured research review identifying sustainable entrepreneurial managerial practices on an individual, organizational and contextual/market level. We contribute to the literature by closing this gap and outline in the following paragraphs the methodology for our literature review.

Literature review approach

The procedure for this literature review was based on Tranfield et al. [72]. This review method was chosen because of its tenacity. It enables the reviewers to minimize bias by researching and reviewing a distinct topic with autonomous reviewers debating the overall method as well as the incorporation and elimination of articles [72]. Furthermore, by outlining the steps taken, the method provides transparency, as the steps could potentially be reproduced by other researchers [72]. The steps that were taken in this research are described in the following paragraphs and illustrated in Figure 2.1.1.

In a first step, the electronic databases Web of Science, ScienceDirect, ABI-Inform/ProQuest, JSTOR and Google Scholar were systematically searched. In order to ensure a widespread search, the keywords used were "sustainable entrepreneurship" or "corporate sustainability". The scan was applied to the respective title, abstract and keywords. The main focus was on journal articles published in ranked journals. The time frame of the search was limited to 1990–2017 (which also marks the end of the literature search for this chapter). The search generated 2990 results, which were assessed in four ensuing steps. Second, duplicates and entries that were not journal articles were eliminated, leaving 2300 results for further review.

Third, the titles of the journals were examined, resulting in the elimination of papers published in journals that were not relevant for the purpose of this study (e.g. Conservation Biology), following our goal of providing purely the entrepreneur's point of view. Conducting this second step left 407 research articles for consideration. In a fourth step the titles of the journal articles were screened, resulting in the exclusion of articles that did not fit the matter of this research. The fifth step involved reading the abstracts of the remaining 213 articles and analysing them regarding their research question and study approach. As the aim of this chapter is to provide an overview of factors facilitating responsible managerial practices, the criteria for the papers chosen for the final review was that the research was focused on or included the investigation of factors influencing SEO. Within the fifth step, journal articles whose foci did not fit the focus of this thesis were eliminated, resulting in a final set of 53 articles.

Next, the remaining 53 were further analysed and clustered based on the aforementioned analysis. In this chapter, we adopt Spence et al.'s [25] analytical structure to review literature and cluster articles according to their level of analysis. Namely, the individual level

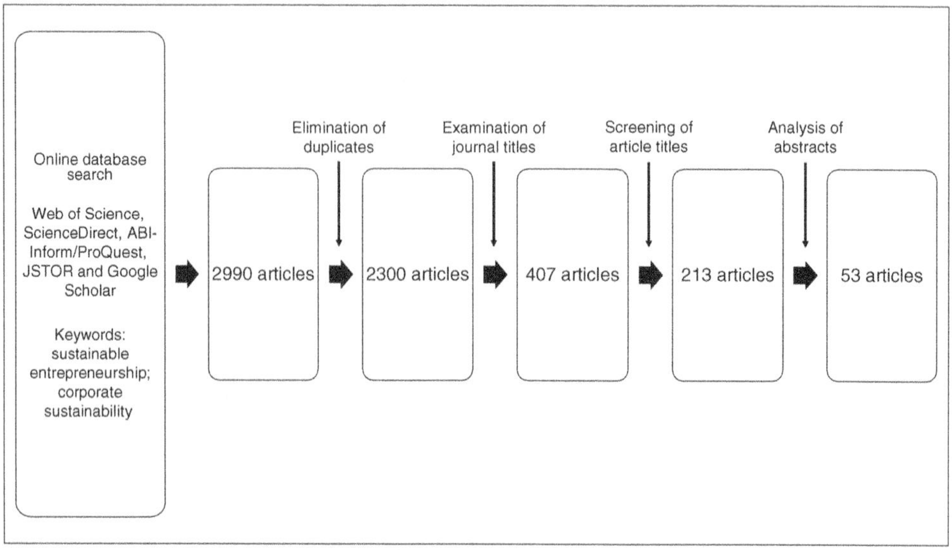

Figure 2.1.1 Systematic review process

(including personality traits/characteristics, belief systems, values, and personal capabilities and skills), the organizational level (degree of formalization of sustainable development, strategic orientation, relationship with stakeholders and company culture), and the contextual level (that is isolating factors influencing the company to act sustainably).

In order to present a transparent and consistent method of reviewing, the final set of articles is listed in the appendix in Table 2.1.1 to highlight the selection of the independent variables. Regarding the distribution of the reviewed articles, over time it can be said

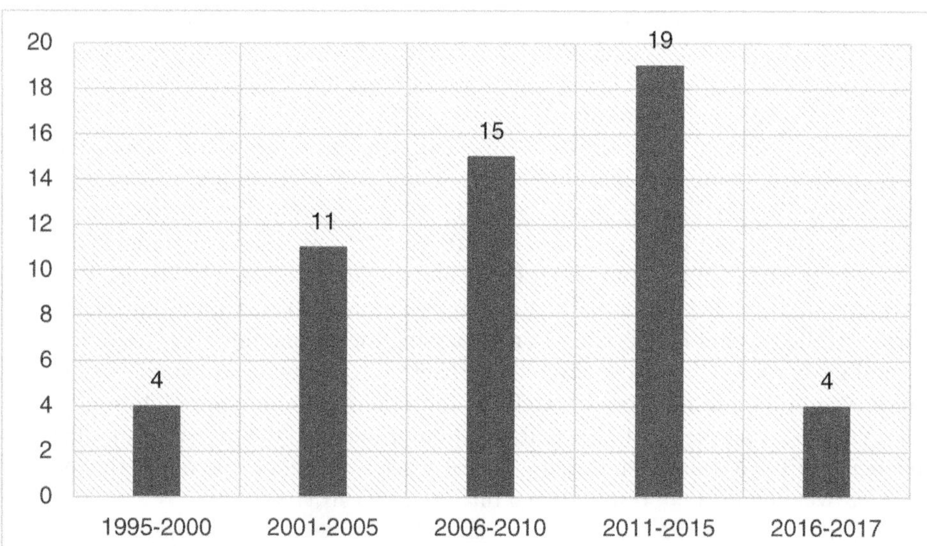

Figure 2.1.2 Reviewed articles per period of publication

that 7.55% of them were published between 1996–2000, 20.75% between 2001–2005, 28.30% between 2006–2010, 35.85% between 2011–2015 and 7.55% between 2016–2017 (Figure 2.1.2). This indicates that recent years have seen an increased interest in the research field examined.

After an extensive analysis of the articles, important concepts shaping the SEO could be extracted. To present a comprehensive understanding of the concepts introduced in the literature review of this research, the information extracted from the final set of the literature review is supported by additional sources. First, the closed-circle system was applied, for which relevant references cited in the remaining set of articles were also examined and important findings used to refine the final argumentation. Second, other relevant research papers were used to introduce more general entrepreneurship concepts such as EO.

Results: SEO – identifying the factors that facilitate responsible managerial practices

Sustainable entrepreneurship in existing firms, especially SMEs, is led by an entrepreneur who carries out MSP through innovation and by creating value [6]. These entrepreneurially sustainable practices manifest sustainable entrepreneurship within an organization [17,36,68,71,73–76]. While research has strongly developed over the past years, there remains a lack of consensus when it comes to classifying these sustainable EO practices.

As mentioned, the clustering of the articles was based on Spence et al.'s [25] analytical structure of dividing the influencing factors into individual, organizational and contextual factors. The final set of clusters is illustrated in Figure 2.1.3, showing the reviewed

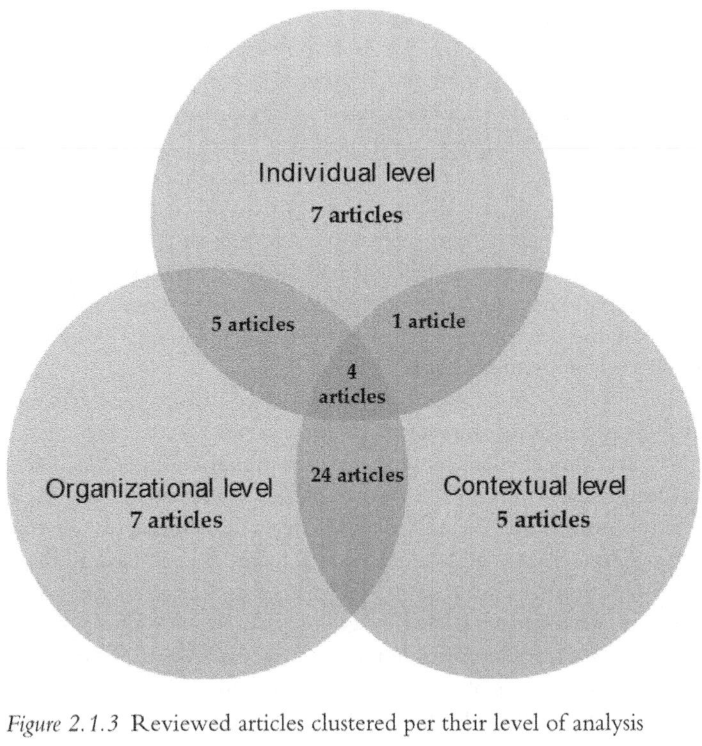

Figure 2.1.3 Reviewed articles clustered per their level of analysis

articles clustered according to their level of analysis. The summarized findings of this literature review are presented in the following paragraphs.

Individual level

Brem et al. highlight how entrepreneurs show a more sustainably oriented set of entrepreneurial actions when their belief in a just world is strong [77]. Managers who possess a strong belief in a just world tend to avoid unethical behaviour when it directly influences other people at their workplace and therefore prefer a more ethical style of decision-making, as shown by previous studies [78]. When it comes to the individual level of the single entrepreneur, the existing literature suggests that sustainable entrepreneurs are value-driven, while enterprises that are established and run based on particular individual values include but are not limited to sustainability [79,80]. Based on the above-mentioned values, sustainable entrepreneurs commit themselves and their firms to an effort towards a unique, outstanding competitive position. They also want to reach a certain level of efficiency in the three areas of sustainability. The common characteristic(s) typically held by social and environmental entrepreneurs can also be applied to sustainable entrepreneurs, who can be described as "change agents", implying a certain disagreement with prevailing existing paradigms. They also communicate a desire to implement a more long-term focus, limiting themselves to doing more with fewer inputs [12,81]. Personality characteristics also contribute to the likelihood of effective leadership. With these, it has been found that environmental leaders working for both non-profit and for-profit organizations achieve more favourable outcomes than their conventional counterparts at other organizations when it comes to the "need for achievement", "need for affiliation", "self-confidence", as well as "emotional maturity" [79]. Furthermore, when taking an even closer, more finite look at the differences between social and conventional entrepreneurs, social entrepreneurs are more likely to be described as charismatic, highly skilled and showing a high degree of initiative. This stands in contrast to the conventional entrepreneur who can be characterized as "pragmatic", "opportunistic" and "imitating". All of this indicates the potential competitive advantages of non-conventional entrepreneurs [82]. An additional potential competitive advantage of sustainable entrepreneurs is the increased level of persistence they display when compared to conventional entrepreneurs. This allows them to maintain an overview and "stay in the loop" at all times despite the minor and major obstacles they face as part of their business operations [82]. The contingency characteristic of sustainable entrepreneurs furthermore enables them to successfully adapt to changing environmental parameters, acclimatizing to new circumstances and exploiting new opportunities as they do so [12].

The personality characteristics thus described form a theoretically solid starting point for an analysis of the distinguishing characteristics of sustainable entrepreneurs and the effect of these traits on the expected success of these entrepreneurs [25,66,83]. However, the puzzle of success consists of additional elements when it comes to successfully engaging in sustainable entrepreneurship. As Tilley and Young conclude, owner-managers are required to have personal values and beliefs that find their motivation, align with, and are an extension of, sustainable principles [84]. These include (but are not limited to) the values of social and environmental entrepreneurs that are based on altruism. This distinguishes them from conventional entrepreneurs, where the needs of others (including nature) are put ahead of the needs of the entrepreneurs themselves [81,85]. However, the principles mentioned do not exclude the common components found in traditional entrepreneurial processes. In the case of environmental leaders [79], an optimal mix of leadership styles is required, thus necessitating not only well-argued values but rational inputs as well, not to mention the taken-for-granted rules and norms as the motives of sustainable entrepreneurship on the individual level.

To sum up, research has shown that sustainable entrepreneurs tend to derive their will to act more sustainably from their personal values or traits. These findings are consistent with the "upper echelons theory" which states that the strategic actions of entrepreneurs inherently reflect their values, beliefs and orientations [86,87]. While there is great merit to this research, we argue that more research is needed to better understand the nature of practices that founders or leaders of sustainable enterprises adopt in order to ensure SEO throughout their enterprises.

Organizational level

Sustainable enterprises ensure SEO on a voluntary, albeit formalized and integrated basis. The formalized aspect of the sustainable enterprise can be concretized by the implementation of certain types of control systems, reporting procedures, as well as the formal style of tracking the progress of the entity's sustainable practices [75]. However, the formal aspects of the sustainable enterprise tend to be counterintuitive and potentially disadvantageous to how SMEs are normally observed and assessed [88], as they tend to practise sustainability in a "blind" manner, not knowing how their actions could theoretically and practically contribute to a generally sustainable outcome [25]. According to the literature, an SEO in firms, or even making sustainability the core foundation of enterprises, could potentially be hazardous. In other words, the formalized aspect of sustainable firms goes against the widespread assumption of SMEs being characterized by a small degree of formalization as well as the intuitive management style these firms are likely to display [25]. With this being said, the formalization aspect of SMEs has in fact undergone a transformation regarding the reporting standards and management practices applied within organizations. New SME research shows that enterprises have adopted more formalized management approaches as well as the implementation of quality standards [89].

In addition to the degree of formalization, the corporate behaviour of firms is deemed a critical component in SMEs with its sustainable behaviour specifically constituting the relevant foundation on which sustainable entrepreneurship can be carried out successfully. According to Covin and Slevin [39] and Knight [90], the sustainable behavioural aspect of entrepreneurship theory can be defined as the pro-activeness, innovativeness and risk-taking ability of enterprises. The idea that sustainable enterprises need to be proactive, innovative and risk-taking [17,41,91], while being aware of and conscious about the environment [51], was formerly seen as the combination of sustainable and entrepreneurial orientation, as well as the overall strategic orientation of a sustainable entrepreneurial approach [71]. At the core of SMEs lies the driving force to move forward and excel in markets, constituting the willingness and pro-activeness to go beyond borders and discover and conquer new markets. Here, innovation is the outcome of this pro-activity, which in turn is a driving force for the establishment and integration of formalized sustainable practices [81,92]. As mentioned, sustainable entrepreneurship is a long-term, relatively risky endeavour. Its scope tends to look further down the road, therefore requiring a relatively large degree of patience and a longer-than-conventional waiting period until a healthy return on investments can be achieved. As the sustainability market is still in a relatively young stage of development, with customers not translating their sustainable desires into purchases frequently enough, entrepreneurs are required to and are taking moderate or calculated risks, despite sustainable entrepreneurs being long-term oriented and risk-averse due to their volatile stream of revenues [93]. This implies the need for risk-limiting techniques and processes.

Firms vary in age and size. This means they also vary in their resource combinations [94,95]. Katz and Gartner argue that when founding and growing a new enterprise, a crucial factor is identifying and acquiring resources [96]. The entrepreneurship literature emphasizes how liabilities of smallness and resource constraints in firms can be mitigated through social capital [97]. This makes social and financial networks particularly important for access to a diverse set of both tangible and intangible resources [98]. Access to these kinds of networks is especially crucial due to how they can take on several important functions such as the connection of entrepreneurs to information services. This is why they are so important for sustainable entrepreneurs and the companies they are managing. A connection to these services provides access to capital, low-cost support services, infrastructure that enables entrepreneurs to share ideas and resources among each other, not to mention the opportunity to strengthen local entrepreneurial culture [99,100]. Current literature on ecologically sustainable entrepreneurship stresses how sustainable entrepreneurs need to create and alter relationships with external stakeholders. As mentioned earlier, entrepreneurs have to be able to influence opinion leaders and key actors to get the most out of their capability of establishing [101] and modifying powerful relationships among different actors [102]. This need helps make clear the critical nature of ecologically sustainable entrepreneurs with their external environment [73,103–105]. Here, there is no recognizable further distinction or separation between formal and informal institutions [106–108]; neither is there cooperation and mutual support in networks [109–111]. Research shows that entrepreneurs leading sustainable enterprises maintain sustainable growth in pursuit of their long-term survival by being more inclined towards successful networking within and across industries [81,112].

This kind of relationship development between internal and external partners tends to help sustainable entrepreneurs be on the cutting edge of their market. They are among the first to identify new, sustainable business opportunities which are most likely to lead to a reliable source of income and the potential to earn a higher profit than other firms [113]. Because it involves a certain degree of risk that is specifically caused by the unexplored direction a firm is planning on exploring, this strategy of defining front-line opportunities and tackling them as "first movers" in the general market economy has to be defined as "proactive" [114,115].

Summarizing, we can conclude that an SME's internal culture and the reconfiguration of resources [116] are critical determinants for adopting an SEO. A potential lack of acceptance of sustainable development principles can lead to institutional isolation, as the resources needed for sustainable development may not be adequately mobilized [117], thus requiring a supportive internal culture and external support in the form of networks or agents to enable an SEO. While there is research emerging because of increasing transparency, there is still a need to understand ethical dimensions when it comes to developing close relations with external, supportive partners. For example, who owns the intellectual property rights of the jointly created outputs? Where does responsibility lie when things go wrong? What is the proper division of labour? How does SEO impact company performance?

Contextual/market level

In addition to the organizational and individual factors, contextual factors are deemed to have an important influence on the success of firms. After all, the environment from which it operates is of critical importance for the overall degree of success when implementing an entrepreneur's project [118]. Traditional theories of the competitive dimension of a firm emphasize the significance of the owner-manager construction in strategic decision-making [49,119], underestimating the importance of the wider context on a firm; this is a "gap" that neo-institutional theory is filling. The context a firm operates in, even when assumed to be unfavourable at first glance, could in fact possess new opportunities for firms when being approached actively, as is the case with citizens' trust towards public policies, specifically regarding environmental laws [120]. As Gast et al. point out, there are four dominant impulses for enterprises to implement sustainable entrepreneurship: "regulation, public concern, expected competitive advantage, and top management commitment" [6: p. 46].

We live in a global setting where growth through entrepreneurship as well as the striving for and achievement of sustainable development are fostered by (supra-) national as well as local governments [71]. Attaining opportunities at the intersection of sustainable development and entrepreneurship is a major challenge for organizations throughout all levels on the global, regional and local scales [121]. To avoid the complete loss of the numerous economic, social and natural resources society currently possesses, steps have to be taken to reverse their depletion.

Another powerful external motive for conducting business more sustainably includes the public concern expressed, e.g. by consumer behaviour. As Prothero et al. point out, participating in CSR generally is very socially and ecologically sustainable [122]. This makes the perceived value of sustainability as regards CSR issues a potentially key factor in the willingness of people to consume more consciously. An increase in perceived value is an important factor companies consider when making the decision to act more sustainably [123]. In their paper, Wang and Ho introduce the idea that true sustainability solutions are to be found within the emerging domain of the sharing economy, where access to rather than owning an asset contributes and becomes the key to economic growth, scale advantages and profits [123]. The authors base this idea on Brahme who concludes in his article that the true solution to sustainability is actually not found within CSR and its practitioners [124]. Important here is that this does not imply that CSR should be dismissed as such. According to Tian et al., on the other hand, companies are "obliged" to a certain extent to facilitate and achieve a fundamental level of economic and legal CSR and should therefore not neglect their importance, because the sharing economy model enables a two-way avenue to higher levels of CSR practice and ethical and philanthropic responsibilities [100]. Moreover, an increase in customer perception can be linked to an improvement in terms of reputation. Considering reputation as a strategic asset, Pineiro-Chousa et al. introduced the concept of using the implementation of sustainable practices as a suitable risk hedging strategy [125,126].

The rise in the perceived value of the product can also be considered a competitive advantage. As Lordkipanidze et al. point out, a competitive advantage in terms of cost reduction or the perceived value of the product which raises the likelihood of the consumer to buy the product is likely to be achieved by a focus on environmental sustainability [127]. This rise in perceived value or cost reduction of the product can be accomplished by implementing more sustainable measures in terms of sourcing, production, etc. towards innovative changes facilitating more ecological sustainability.

The profit-generating potential for the enterprise and its stakeholders justifies the risks involved in creating societal value. This contribution to socio-economic development [128], is seen as being enabled by a potential change in the environmental- and sustainability-oriented thinking of sustainable firms [76,83,129–132]. These kinds of firms are understood as promoting a greener future by acting as role models [30,128,133]. Or put differently, and as Tilley and Young describe them, as "wealth generators of the future" [84: p. 79]. Being a role model is reflected in these firms' solution-providing orientation. They deliver solutions to environmental challenges and ecological decay [74,134] via eco-innovations [6,91]. In doing this, they advocate a transition towards more sustainable methods of production and consumption [68,92]. Activating and mobilizing key actors within a community can also dramatically contribute to a change in consumer mindsets, not to mention enterprises and their surrounding environments [131]. An example of this would be the organization of a special community event such as waste recycling training with the objective of creating and increasing awareness of consumer habits and consumption patterns; developing an interest in local products; and promoting the use of sustainable design and consumption [130].

We can finally state that researchers have focused on a better understanding of how entrepreneurs can help society and the environment through sustainable entrepreneurship, and how they can act as role models or change agents in light of the fact that sustainable consumption or investing/financing based on sustainability is still in its infancy. To really understand the role of entrepreneurs in driving social change, we need more research that identifies the links between organizational and contextual levels. How do these different levels interact? What practices can be derived? How do external partners and sustainable enterprises need to interact in order to create eco-systems, facilitating social or ecological change?

Limitations

Evidently, this review has limitations that need to be acknowledged. First, while this chapter is comprehensive in its kind, the literature review approach applied could be criticized for taking a reduced selection of publications as a base for further analysis and therefore not including all the relevant work on sustainable entrepreneurship; namely, focusing too much on the managerial aspect of SEO. Nevertheless, the systematic literature review procedure applied enables us to form a literature base representing the status-quo research on facilitating factors of responsible managerial practices as completely as possible within the sustainable entrepreneurship research. Thus, the probability of having excluded critical studies with findings that would have strongly altered this chapter's conclusion is restricted.

Another limitation is the missing segregation of papers investigating enterprises founded based on the premises of sustainability as such, e.g. start-ups with eco-innovations and articles researching companies implementing sustainable managerial practices. This missing differentiation is also reflected in the chosen key words of "sustainable entrepreneurship" and "corporate sustainability". This can be justified with the intention of providing an extensive overview over the status-quo research on influencing factors of SEO and therefore making it necessary to broaden the initial search. However, investigating whether there is a difference in factors influencing SEO could potentially be an interesting topic for further research.

Moreover, we acknowledge the limitations regarding the objectivity of the analysis results. Evidently, the allocation of the main focus, the selection of data and the interpretation of the results are subjective. In order to minimize the bias, the multiple assessor method was applied.

Conclusions: relevance for theory and practice and recommendations for further research

In this chapter we contribute to existing literature by providing a structured literature review of identifying factors that facilitate responsible managerial practices. This is relevant to understand and develop a more sustainable financial system. Financial academic literature has shown that ESG investments are equally profitable or only slightly underperforming depending on the researched area. While there are no official selling numbers, the pure increase of offered products and indices shows that ESG investments are well sold by the financial industry and therefore that the demand for ESG products is significant. With the rising importance for society and companies alike to act sustainably in terms of social, economic and ecological capital [9], this chapter contributes to both theory and practice by introducing factors that facilitate sustainable, responsible practices on the entrepreneur's side and connecting the findings with existing financial research.

These responsible managerial practices were located on the individual, organizational and contextual level. Figure 2.1.3 indicates that some research exclusively puts its focus on one level, whereas other research considers the relation between two levels more extensively. On each level, we identified the following possible research avenues:

From an individual perspective, this research has great value. This is why we argue that more of it is needed to better understand the antecedents of practices (e.g. training as put forward by Azeez Olugbola [135]) or the nature of practices that founders or leaders of sustainable enterprises adopt in order to ensure SEO throughout their enterprises.

On the organizational level, investigations towards fully understanding the ethical dimensions when it comes to developing close relations with external, supportive partners are evidently needed. While there is research emerging due to greater transparency, there is still a need to achieve a deeper understanding of the ethical dimensions when it comes to developing close relations with external, supportive partners. Some examples here include: who owns the intellectual property rights of the jointly created outputs? Where does responsibility lie when things don't run as planned? What is the proper division of labour? Another research stream is to investigate closer the relationship between corporate ethical practices and corporate financial performance as put forward by Cuomo et al. [136]. These are just a few of the questions that would allow deeper, better insight.

Finally, we also propose providing a joint analysis of entrepreneurs and investors concerning environmental, social and sustainable business. It is important to analyse and compare their respective expectations with each other, joint goals and the drivers of perceived risk on the way to develop a more sustainable financial system. Furthermore, to really understand the role of entrepreneurs in driving social change, research will have to identify the links between organizational and contextual levels. How do these different levels interact? What practices can be derived? How do external partners and sustainable enterprises need to interact to create the ecosystems that facilitate social or ecological change?

Appendix

Table 2.1.1 Overview of reviewed articles

Title	*Author*	*Year*	*Journal/medium*	*Level of analysis*
Who takes more sustainability-oriented entrepreneurial actions? The role of entrepreneurs' values, beliefs and orientations	Brem, A., Bhattacharjee, A., & Jahanshahi, A. A.	2017	*Sustainability*	Individual
Bad apples in bad barrels revisited: Cognitive moral development, just world beliefs, rewards, and ethical decision-making	Ashkanasy, N. M., Windsor, C. A., & Treviño, L. K.	2006	*Business Ethics Quarterly*	Individual
Toward a typology of new venture creators: Similarities and contrasts between business and social entrepreneurs	Vega, G., & Kidwell, R. E.	2007	*New England Journal of Entrepreneurship*	Individual
What motivates ecopreneurs to start businesses?	Kirkwood, J., & Walton, S.	2010	*International Journal of Entrepreneurial Behavior & Research*	Individual
The Meaning of "Social Entrepreneurship"	Dees, J. G.	2001	Book	Individual / organizational / contextual
Strategic entrepreneurship and managerial activities in SMEs	Messeghem, K.	2003	*International Small Business Journal*	Individual / organizational
Investigating social entrepreneurship: A multidimensional model	Weerawardena, J., & Mort, G. S.	2006	*Journal of World Business*	Individual / organizational
Sustainable entrepreneurship: Is entrepreneurial will enough? a north-south comparison	Spence, M., Gherib, J. B., & Biwolé, V. O.	2011	*Journal of Business Ethics*	Individual / organizational
Corporate sustainability and innovation in SMEs: Evidence of themes and activities in practice	Bos-Brouwers, H. E. J.	2010	*Business Strategy and the Environment*	Individual / organizational
Ecological entrepreneurship support networks: Roles and functions for conversation organizations	Kimmel, C. E., & Hull, R. B.	2012	*Geoform*	Organizational
Seeing ecology and "green" innovations as a source of change	Azzone, G., & Noci, G.	1998	*Journal of Organizational Change Management*	Organizational / contextual
Nascent green-technology ventures: A study assessing the role of partnership diversity in firm success	Meysen, M., & Carsrud, A. L	2013	*Small Business Economics*	Organizational / contextual
Beyond green niches? Growth strategies of environmentally-motivated social enterprises	Vickers, I., & Lyon, F.	2012	*International Small Business Journal*	Organizational / contextual
Corporate social responsibility and corporate performance: The case of Italian SMEs	Longo, M., Mura, M., & Bonoli, A.	2005	*Corporate Governance*	Individual / organizational
Green Goliaths versus emerging Davids: Theorizing about the role of incumbents and entrants in sustainable entrepreneurship	Hockerts, K., & Wüstenhagen, R.	2010	*Journal of Business Venturing*	Organizational

Sustainable entrepreneurship and sustainability innovation: Categories and interactions	Schaltegger, S., & Wagner, M.	2010	*Business Strategy and the Environment*	Organizational
Doing business in a green way: A systematic review of the ecological sustainability entrepreneurship literature and future research directions	Gast, J., Gundolf, K., & Cesinger, B.	2017	*Journal of Cleaner Production*	Individual / organizational / contextual
The sustainability balanced scorecard: Linking sustainability management to business strategy	Figge, F., Hahn, T., Schaltegger, S., & Wagner, M.	2002	*Business Strategy and the Environment*	Organizational
The influence of sustainability orientation on entrepreneurial intentions: Investigating the role of business experience	Kuckertz, A., & Wagner, M.	2010	*Journal of Business Venturing*	Individual
Social entrepreneurship: A new look at the people and the potential	Thompson, J., Alvy, G., & Lees, A.	2000	*Management Decision*	Individual
The venture development processes of "sustainable" entrepreneurs	Choi, D. Y., & Gray, E. R.	2008	*Management Research News*	Organizational / contextual
The environmental–social interface of sustainable development: Capabilities, social capital, institutions	Lehtonen, M.	2004	*Ecological Economies*	Organizational / contextual
Achieving sustainability through environmental innovation: The role of SMEs	Biondi, V., Iraldo, F., & Meredith, S.	2002	*International Journal of Technology Management*	Organizational / Contextual
Family and territory values for a sustainable entrepreneurship: The experience of Loccioni Group and Varnelli Distillery in Italy	Del Baldo, M.	2012	*Journal of Marketing Development and Competitiveness*	Individual
Sustainability through food and conversation: The role of an entrepreneurial restaurateur in fostering engagement with sustainable development issues	Moskwa, E., Higgins-Desbiolles, F., & Gifford, S.	2015	*Journal of Sustainable Tourism*	Organizational / contextual
Ecological entrepreneurship: Sustainable development in local communities through quality food production and local branding	Marsden, T., & Smith, E.	2005	*Geoform*	Organizational / contextual
Business strategies for effective entrepreneurship: A panacea for sustainable development and livelihood in the family	Oguonu, C.	2015	*International Journal of Management and Sustainability*	Organizational / contextual
Sustainability entrepreneurship and equitable transitions to a low-carbon economy	Parrish, B. D., & Foxon, T. J.	2006	*Greener Management International*	Organizational / contextual
Supporting green entrepreneurship in Romania: Imperative of sustainable development	Zamfir, P. B.	2014	*Romanian Economic and Business Review*	Organizational / contextual
Sustainability entrepreneurs: Could they be the true wealth generators of the future?	Tilley, F., & Young, W.	2006	*Greener Management International*	Individual / contextual

(continued)

Table 2.1.1 (continued)

Title	*Author*	*Year*	*Journal/medium*	*Level of analysis*
Toward a theory of sustainable entrepreneurship: Reducing environmental degradation through entrepreneurial action	Dean, T. J., & McMullen, J. S.	2007	*Journal of Business Venturing*	Individual / organizational / contextual
Shaping the future: Sustainable innovation and entrepreneurship	Belz, F. M.	2013	*Social Business*	Organizational / contextual
The transition to the sustainable enterprise	Keijzers, G.	2002	*Journal of Cleaner Production*	Organizational / contextual
Sustainable innovation through an entrepreneurship lens	Larson, A. L.	2000	*Business Strategy and the Environment*	Organizational
Environmental entrepreneurship in organic agriculture in Järna, Sweden	Larson, A. L.	2012	*Journal of Sustainable Agriculture*	Organizational / contextual
Urban development projects catalyst for sustainable transformations: The need for entrepreneurial political leadership	Block, T., & Paredis, E.	2013	*Journal of Cleaner Production*	Organizational / contextual
Entrepreneurship, management, and sustainable development	Ahmed, A., & McQuaid, R. W.	2005	*World Review of Entrepreneurship, Management and Sustainable Development*	Organizational / contextual
Place attachment and social legitimacy: Revisiting the sustainable entrepreneurship journey	Kibler, E., Fink, M., Lang, R., & Munoz, P.	2015	*Journal of Business Venturing Insights*	Organizational / contextual
Escaping the green prison: Entrepreneurship and the creation of opportunities for sustainable development	Pacheco, D. F., Dean, T. J., & Payne, D. S.	2010	*Journal of Business Venturing*	Organizational / contextual
Institutional entrepreneurship capabilities for interorganizational sustainable supply chain strategies	Peters, N. J., Hofstetter, J. S., & Hoffmann, V. H.	2011	*The International Journal of Logistics Management*	Organizational / contextual
Sustainable entrepreneurship and corporate political activity: Overcoming market barriers in the clean energy sector	Pinkse, J., & Groot, K.	2015	*Entrepreneurship Theory and Practice*	Organizational / contextual
Greening regions: The effect of social entrepreneurship, co-decision and co-creation on the embrace of good sustainable development practices	Barrutia, J. M., & Echebarria, C.	2012	*Journal of Environmental Planning and Management*	Organizational / contextual
Sustainable valley entrepreneurial ecosystems	Cohen, B.	2005	*Business Strategy and the Environment*	Organizational / contextual

Redefining innovation: Eco-innovation research and the contribution from ecological economies	Rennings, K.	2000	*Ecological Economies*	Organizational
Entrepreneurial orientation: A business strategic approach for sustainable development	Criado-Gomis, A., Cervera-Taulet, A., & Iniesta-Bonillo, M. A.	2017	*Sustainability*	Organizational
Sustainable corporate entrepreneurship	Miles, M. P., Munilla, L. S., & Darroch, J.	2009	*International Entrepreneurship and Management Journal*	Contextual
Sustainable consumption: Opportunities for consumer research and public policy	Prothero, A., Dobscha, S., Freung, J., Kilbourne, W. E., Luchs, M. G., Qzanne, L. K., & Thogersen, J.	2011	*Journal of Public Policy & Marketing*	Contextual
No money? No problem! The value of sustainability: Social capital drives the relationship among customer identification and citizenship behavior in sharing economy	Wang, Y. B., & Ho, C. W.	2017	*Sustainability*	Organizational / contextual
Consumer responses to corporate social responsibility in China	Tian, Z., Wang, R., & Yang, W.	2011	*Journal of Business Ethics*	Contextual
The entrepreneurship factor in sustainable tourism development	Lordkipanidze, M., Brezet, H., & Backman, M.	2005	*Journal of Cleaner Production*	Contextual
The entrepreneur-environment nexus: Uncertainty, innovation and allocation	York, J. G., & Venkataraman, S.	2010	*Journal of Business Venturing*	Organizational / contextual
The rationality and irrationality of financing green start-ups	Bergset, L.	2015	*Administrative Sciences*	Contextual

Reprint

Kraus, S.; Burtscher, J.; Vallaster, C.; Angerer, M. (2018): Sustainable Entrepreneurship Orientation: A Reflection on Status-Quo Research on Factors Facilitating Responsible Managerial Practices. *Sustainability*, 10, 444. doi:10.3390/su10020444, Link: www.mdpi.com/2071-1050/10/2/444.

Note

* This chapter is an update of an article of the same name that appeared in *Sustainability*, 2017, 9, 1828; doi:10.3390/su9101828.

References

1 Archarya, V. V.; Richardson, M. Causes of the financial crisis. *Journal of Politics and Society* 2009, 21, 195–210.
2 Friede, G.; Busch, T.; Bassen, A. ESG and financial performance: Aggregated evidence from more than 2000 empirical studies. *Journal of Sustainable Finance & Investment* 2014, 5, 210–233.
3 Guenster, N.; Bauer, R.; Derwall, J.; Koedijk, K. The economy value of corporate eco-efficiency. *European Financial Management* 2011, 17, 679–704.
4 Hall, J.; Daneke, G.; Lenox, M. Sustainable development and entrepreneurship: Past contributions and future directions. *Journal of Business Venturing* 2010, 25, 439–448.
5 Fellnhofer, K.; Kraus, S.; Bouncken, R. B. The current state of research on sustainable entrepreneurship. *International Journal of Business Research* 2014, 14, 163–172.
6 Gast, J.; Gundolf, K.; Cesinger, B. Doing business in a green way: A systematic review of the ecological sustainability entrepreneurship literature and future research directions. *Journal of Cleaner Production* 2017, 147, 44–56.
7 Schumpeter, J. A. *The Theory of Economic Development*; Harvard University Press: Cambridge, MA, 1934.
8 Cohen, B.; Winn, M. I. Market imperfections, opportunity and sustainable entrepreneurship. *Journal of Business Venturing* 2007, 22, 29–49.
9 Melay, I.; Kraus, S. Green entrepreneurship: Definition of related concepts. *International Journal of Strategic Management* 2012, 12, 1–12.
10 Berle, G. *The Green Entrepreneur: Business Opportunities That Can Save the Earth and Make You Money*; Blue Ridge, PA, 1991.
11 Allen, J. C.; Malin, S. Green entrepreneurship: A method for managing natural resources? *Society and Natural Resources* 2008, 21, 828–844.
12 Dees, J. G. *The Meaning of "Social Entrepreneurship"*; Stanford University: Stanford, CA, 2001.
13 Mair, J.; Marti, I. Social entrepreneurship research: A source of explanation, prediction, and delight. *Journal of World Business* 2006, 41, 36–44.
14 Smith, W. K.; Gonin, M.; Besharov, M. L. Managing social-business tensions. *Business Ethics Quarterly* 2013, 23, 407–442.
15 Moss, T. W.; Short, J. C.; Payne, G. T.; Lumpkin, G. T. Dual identities in social ventures: An exploratory study. *Entrepreneurship Theory and Practice* 2011, 35, 805–830.
16 Isaak, R. *Green Logic: Ecopreneurship, Theory and Ethics*; Routledge: West Hartford, CT, 1998.
17 Schaltegger, S.; Wagner, M. Sustainable entrepreneurship and sustainability innovation: Categories and interactions. *Business Strategy and the Environment* 2010, 20, 222–237.
18 Vallaster, C. Managing a company crisis through strategic corporate social responsibility: A practice-based analysis. *Corporate Social Responsibility and Environmental Management* 2017, 24, 509–523.
19 McWilliams, A.; Siegel. D.; Wright, P. M. Corporate social responsibility: Strategic implications. *Journal of Management Studies* 2006, 43, 1–18.
20 Orlitzky, M.; Siegel, D. S.; Waldman, D. A. Strategic corporate social responsibility and environmental sustainability. *Business & Society* 2011, 50, 6–27.
21 Peloza, J.; Shang, J. How can corporate social responsibility activities create value for stakeholders? A systematic review. *Journal of the Academy of Marketing Science* 2011, 39, 117–135.
22 Bruyaka, O.; Zeitzmann, H.; Chalamon, I.; Wokutch, R.; Thakur, P. Strategic corporate social responsibility and orphan drug development: Insights from the US and the EU biopharmaceutical industry. *Journal of Business Ethics* 2013, 117, 45–56.

23 Acquier, A.; Valiorgue, B.; Daudigeos, T. Sharing the shared value: A transaction cost perspective on strategic CSR policies in global value chains. *Journal of Business Ethics* 2017, 144, 139–152..

24 Kolk, A.; Mauser, A. The evolution of environmental management: From stage models to performance evaluation. *Business Strategy and the Environment* 2002, 11, 14–31.

25 Spence, M.; Gherib, J. B.; Biwolé, V. O. Sustainable entrepreneurship: Is entrepreneurial will enough? A north-south comparison. *Journal of Business Ethics* 2011, 99, 335–367.

26 Brown, S.; Lugo, A.E. Rehabilitation of tropical lands: A key to sustaining development. *Restoring Energy* 1994, 2, 97–111.

27 Daly, H. E.; Cobb, J. B.; Cobb, C. W. *For the Common Good: Redirecting the Economy toward Community, the Environment, and a Sustainable Future*; Beacon Press: Boston, MA, 1994.

28 Littig, B.; Griessler, E. Social sustainability: A catchword between political pragmatism and social theory. *International Journal of Sustainable Development* 2005, 8, 65–79.

29 International Labour Office. *Report VI: The Promotion of Sustainable Enterprises, International Labour Conference – 96th Session*; International Labour Office: Geneva, Switzerland, 2007.

30 Choi, D. Y.; Gray, E. R. The venture development processes of "sustainable" entrepreneurs. *Management Research News* 2008, 31, 558–569.

31 Harrison, J.; Freeman, R. Stakeholders, social responsibility, and performance: Empirical evidence and theoretical perspectives. *Academy of Management Journal* 1999, 42, 479–485.

32 Waddock, S.; Smith, N. Corporate social responsibility audits: Doing well by doing good. *Sloan Management Review* 2000, 41, 75–83.

33 Carroll, A. B. The pyramid of corporate social responsibility: Toward the moral management of organizational stakeholders. *Business Horizons* 1991, 34, 39–48.

34 Carroll, A. B. A three-dimensional conceptual model of corporate performance. *The Academy of Management Review* 1979, 4, 497–505.

35 Mohr, L. A.; Webb, D. J.; Harris, K. E. Do consumers expect companies to be socially responsible? The impact of corporate social responsibility on buying behavior. *Journal of Consumer Affairs* 2001, 35, 45–72.

36 Lozano, R.; Carpenter, A.; Huisingh, D. A review of "theories of the firm" and their contributions to corporate sustainability. *Journal of Cleaner Production* 2015, 106, 430–442.

37 Kramer, M. R.; Porter, M. E. Creating shared value. *Harvard Business Review* 2011, 89, 62–77.

38 Kraus, S.; Rigtering, J. C.; Hughes, M.; Hosman, V. Entrepreneurial orientation and the business performance of SMEs: A quantitative study from the Netherlands. *Review of Managerial Science* 2012, 6, 161–182.

39 Covin, J. G.; Slevin, D. P. Strategic management of small firms in hostile and benign environments. *Strategic Management Journal* 1989, 10, 75–87.

40 Huarng, K. H.; Hui-Kuang Yu, T. Entrepreneurship, process innovation and value creation by a non-profit SME. *Management Decision* 2011, 49, 284–296.

41 Miller, D. The correlates of entrepreneurship in three types of firms. *Management Science* 1983, 29, 770–791.

42 Zahra, S. A. Predictors and financial outcomes of corporate entrepreneurship: An exploratory study. *Journal of Business Venturing* 1991, 6, 259–285.

43 Auer, B.R.; Schuhmacher, F. Do socially (ir)responsible investments pay? New evidence from international ESG data. *The Quarterly Review of Economics and Finance* 2016, 59, 51–62.

44 Huarng, K. H.; Ribeiro-Soriano, D. E. Developmental management: Theories, methods, and applications in entrepreneurship, innovation, and sensemaking. *Journal of Business Research* 2014, 67, 657–662.

45 Mas-Tur, A.; Ribeiro-Soriano, D. The level of innovation among young innovative companies: The impacts of knowledge-intensive services use, firm characteristics and the entrepreneur attributes. *Service Business* 2014, 8, 51–63.

46 Klein Woolthuis, R. J. Sustainable entrepreneurship in the Dutch construction industry. *Sustainability* 2010, 2, 505–523.
47 Dean, T. J.; McMullen, J. S. Toward a theory of sustainable entrepreneurship: Reducing environmental degradation through entrepreneurial action. *Journal of Business Venturing* 2007, 22, 50–76.
48 Kirzner, I. M. *Competition and Entrepreneurship*; University of Chicago Press: Chicago, IL, 1973.
49 Freeman, R. E. *Strategic Management: A Stakeholders Approach*; Pitman: Boston, MA, 1984
50 Barnard, C. *The Functions of the Executive*; Harvard University Press: Cambridge, MA, 1938.
51 Bos-Brouwers, H. E. J. Corporate sustainability and innovation in SMEs: Evidence of themes and activities in practice. *Business Strategy and the Environment* 2010, 19, 417–435.
52 Urbano, D.; Toledano, N.; Ribeiro-Soriano, D. Socio-cultural factors and transnational entrepreneurship: A multiple case study in Spain. *International Small Business Journal* 2011, 29, 119–134.
53 Covin, J. G.; Lumpkin, G. T. Entrepreneurial orientation theory and research: Reflections on a needed construct. *Entrepreneurship Theory and Practice* 2011, 35, 855–872.
54 Covin, J. G.; Slevin, D. P. A conceptual model of entrepreneurship as firm behavior. *Entrepreneurship: Critical Perspectives on Business and Management* 1991, 3, 5–28.
55 Covin, J. G.; Miller, D. International entrepreneurial orientation: Conceptual considerations, research themes, measurement issues, and future research directions. *Entrepreneurship Theory and Practice* 2014, 38, 11–44.
56 Rauch, A.; Wiklund, J.; Lumpkin, G. T.; Frese, M. Entrepreneurial orientation and business performance: An assessment of past research and suggestions for the future. *Entrepreneurship Theory and Practice* 2009, 33, 761–787.
57 Lumpkin, G. T.; Dess, G. G. Clarifying the entrepreneurial orientation construct and linking it to performance. *Academy of Management Review* 1996, 21, 135–172.
58 Eggers, F.; Kraus, S.; Jensen, S. H.; Rigtering, J. P. C. A comparative analysis of the entrepreneurial orientation/growth relationship in service firms and manufacturing firms. *The Service Industries Journal* 2014, 34, 275–294.
59 Low, M. B.; MacMillan, I. C. Entrepreneurship: Past research and future challenges. *Journal of Management* 1988, 14, 139–161.
60 Morris, M. H.; Kuratko, D. F.; Covin, J. G. *Corporate Entrepreneurship & Innovation*; Thomson Higher Education: Mason, OH, 2008.
61 Miller, D.; Friesen, P. H. Strategy making and environment: The third link. *Strategic Management Journal* 1983, 4, 221–235.
62 Engelen, A.; Kubea, H.; Schmidt, S.; Flatten, C. Entrepreneurial orientation in turbulent environments: The moderating role of absorptive capacity. *Research Policy* 2014, 43, 1353–1369.
63 Matsuno, K.; Mentzer, J. T.; Ozsomer, A. The effects of entrepreneurial proclivity and market orientation on business performance. *Journal of Marketing* 2002, 66, 18–32.
64 Gasser, S. M; Rammerstorfer, M.; Weinmayer, K. Markowitz revisited: Social portfolio engineering. *European Journal of Operational Research* 2017, 258, 1181–1190.
65 Noble, C.; Sinha, R. K.; Kumar, A. Market orientation and alternative strategic orientations: A longitudinal assessment of performance implications. *Journal of Marketing* 2002, 66, 25–39.
66 Kuckertz, A.; Wagner, M. The influence of sustainability orientation on entrepreneurial intentions: Investigating the role of business experience. *Journal of Business Venturing* 2010, 25, 524–539.
67 Parboteeah, K. P.; Addae, H. M.; Cullen, J. B. Propensity to support sustainability initiatives: A cross-national model. *Journal of Business Ethics* 2012, 105, 408–413.
68 Keijzers, G. The transition to the sustainable enterprise. *Journal of Cleaner Production* 2002, 10, 349–359.

69 Hakala, H. Strategic orientations in management literature: Three approaches to understanding the interaction between market, technology, entrepreneurial and learning orientations. *International Journal of Management Reviews* 2011, 13, 199–217.
70 Kwak, H.; Jaju, A.; Puzakova, M.; Rocereto, J. F. The connubial relationship between market orientation and entrepreneurial orientation. *Journal of Marketing Theory and Practice* 2013, 21, 141–162.
71 Criado-Gomis, A.; Cervera-Taulet, A.; Iniesta-Bonillo, M. A. Sustainable entrepreneurial orientation: A business strategic approach for sustainable development. *Sustainability* 2017, 9, 1667; doi:10.3390/su9091667.
72 Tranfield, D.; Denyer, D.; Smart, P. Towards a methodology for developing evidence-informed management knowledge by means of systematic review. *British Journal of Management* 2003, 14, 207–222.
73 Ahmed, A.; McQuaid, R. W. Entrepreneurship, management, and sustainable development. *World Review of Entrepreneurship, Management and Sustainable Development* 2005, 1, 6–30.
74 Dyllick, T.; Hockerts, K. Beyond the business case for corporate sustainability. *Business Strategy and the Environment* 2002, 11, 130–141.
75 Figge, F.; Hahn, T.; Schaltegger, S.; Wagner, M. The sustainability balanced scorecard: Linking sustainability management to business strategy. *Business Strategy and the Environment* 2002, 11, 269–284.
76 Oguonu, C. Business strategies for effective entrepreneurship: A panacea for sustainable development and livelihood in the family. *International Journal of Management and Sustainability* 2015, 4, 10–19.
77 Jahanshahi, A. A.; Brem, A.; Bhattacharjee, A. Who takes more sustainability-oriented entrepreneurial actions? The role of entrepreneurs' values, beliefs and orientations. *Sustainability* 2017, 9, 1636.
78 Ashkanasy, N. M.; Windsor, C. A.; Treviño, L. K. Bad apples in bad barrels revisited: Cognitive moral development, just world beliefs, rewards, and ethical decision-making. *Business Ethics Quarterly* 2006, 16, 449–473.
79 Egri, C. P.; Herman, S. Leadership in the North American environmental sector: Values, leadership styles, and contexts of environmental leaders and their organizations. *Academy of Management Journal* 2000, 43, 571–604.
80 Kirkwood, J.; Walton, S. What motivates ecopreneurs to start businesses? *International Journal of Entrepreneurial Behavior & Research* 2010, 16, 204–228.
81 Larson, A. L. Sustainable innovation through an entrepreneurship lens. *Business Strategy and the Environment* 2000, 9, 304–317.
82 Vega, G.; Kidwell, R. E. Toward a typology of new venture creators: Similarities and contrasts between business and social entrepreneurs. *New England Journal of Entrepreneurship* 2007, 10, 15–28.
83 Del Baldo, M. Family and territory values for a sustainable entrepreneurship: The experience of Loccioni Group and Varnelli Distillery in Italy. *Journal of Marketing Development and Competitiveness* 2012, 6, 120–139.
84 Tilley, F.; Young, W. Sustainability entrepreneurs: Could they be the true wealth generators of the future? *Greener Management International* 2006, 55, 79–92.
85 Thompson, J.; Alvy, G.; Lees, A. Social entrepreneurship: A new look at the people and the potential. *Management Decision* 2000, 38, 328–228.
86 Hambrick, D. C. Upper echelons theory: An update. *The Academy of Management Review* 2007, 32, 334–343.
87 Hambrick, D. C.; Mason, P. A. Upper echelons: The organization as a reflection of its top managers. *Academy of Management Review* 1984, 9, 193–206.
88 Jenkins, H. Corporate social responsibility and the mining industry: Conflicts and constructs. *Corporate Social Responsibility and Environmental Management* 2004, 11, 23–34.

89 Messeghem, K. Strategic entrepreneurship and managerial activities in SMEs. *International Small Business Journal* 2003, 21, 197–212.
90 Knight, G. A. Cross-cultural reliability and validity of a scale to measure firm entrepreneurial orientation. *Journal of Business Venturing* 1997, 12, 213–225.
91 Rennings, K. Redefining innovation: Eco-innovation research and the contribution from ecological economies. *Ecological Economies* 2000, 32, 319–332.
92 Belz, F. M. Shaping the future: Sustainable innovation and entrepreneurship. *Social Business* 2013, 3, 311–324.
93 Weerawardena, J.; Mort, G. S. Investigating social entrepreneurship: A multidimensional model. *Journal of World Business* 2006, 41, 21–35.
94 Brush, C. G.; Chaganti, R. Businesses without glamour? An analysis of resources on performance by size and age in small service and retail firms. *Journal of Business Venturing* 1999, 14, 233–257.
95 Mosakowski, E. A. Resource-based perspective on the dynamic strategy-performance relationship: An empirical examination of the focus and differentiation strategies in entrepreneurial firms. *Journal of Management* 1993, 19, 819–839.
96 Katz, J.; Gartner, W. B. Properties of emerging organizations. *The Academy of Management Review* 1988, 13, 429–441.
97 Chollet, B.; Geraudel, M.; Mothe, C. Generating business referrals for SMEs: The contingent value of CEOs social capital. *Journal of Small Business Management* 2013, 52, 79–101.
98 Greve, A.; Salaff, J. W. Social networks and entrepreneurship. *Entrepreneurship Theory and Practice* 2003, 28, 1–22.
99 Kimmel, C. E.; Hull, R. B. Ecological entrepreneurship support networks: Roles and functions for conversation organizations. *Geoforum* 2012, 43, 58–67.
100 Tian, Z.; Wang, R.; Yang, W. Consumer responses to corporate social responsibility in China. *Journal of Business Ethics* 2011, 101, 197–212.
101 Block, T.; Paredis, E. Urban development projects catalyst for sustainable transformations: The need for entrepreneurial political leadership. *Journal of Cleaner Production* 2013, 50, 181–188.
102 Azzone, G.; Noci, G. Seeing ecology and "green" innovations as a source of change. *Journal of Organizational Change Management* 1998, 11, 94–111.
103 Kibler, E.; Fink, M.; Lang, R.; Munoz, P. Place attachment and social legitimacy: Revisiting the sustainable entrepreneurship journey. *Journal of Business Venturing Insights* 2015, 3, 24–29.
104 Meysen, M.; Carsrud, A. L. Nascent green-technology ventures: A study assessing the role of partnership diversity in firm success. *Small Business Economics* 2013, 40, 739–759.
105 Vickers, I.; Lyon, F. Beyond green niches? Growth strategies of environmentally-motivated social enterprises. *International Small Business Journal* 2012, 32, 449–470.
106 Pacheco, D. F.; Dean, T. J.; Payne, D. S. Escaping the green prison: Entrepreneurship and the creation of opportunities for sustainable development. *Journal of Business Venturing* 2010, 25, 464–480.
107 Peters, N. J.; Hofstetter, J. S.; Hoffmann, V. H. Institutional entrepreneurship capabilities for interorganizational sustainable supply chain strategies. *The International Journal of Logistics Management* 2011, 22, 52–86.
108 Pinkse, J.; Groot, K. Sustainable entrepreneurship and corporate political activity: Overcoming market barriers in the clean energy sector. *Entrepreneurship Theory and Practice* 2015, 39, 633–654.
109 Barrutia, J. M.; Echebarria, C. Greening regions: The effect of social entrepreneurship, co-decision and co-creation on the embrace of good sustainable development practices. *Journal of Environmental Planning and Management* 2012, 55, 1348–1368.
110 Cohen, B. Sustainable valley entrepreneurial ecosystems. *Business Strategy and the Environment* 2005, 15, 1–14.

111 Larsson, M. Environmental entrepreneurship in organic agriculture in Järna, Sweden. *Journal of Sustainable Agriculture* 2012, 36, 153–179.
112 Carson, D.; Gilmore, A.; Rocks, S. SME marketing networking: A strategic approach. *Strategic Change* 2004, 13, 369–382.
113 Biondi, V.; Iraldo, F.; Meredith, S. Achieving sustainability through environmental innovation: The role of SMEs. *International Journal of Technology Management* 2002, 24, 612–626.
114 Longo, M.; Mura, M.; Bonoli, A. Corporate social responsibility and corporate performance: The case of Italian SMEs. *Corporate Governance* 2005, 5, 28–42.
115 Hockerts, K.; Wüstenhagen, R. Green Goliaths versus emerging Davids: Theorizing about the role of incumbents and entrants in sustainable entrepreneurship. *Journal of Business Venturing* 2010, 25, 481–492.
116 Lehtonen, M. The environmental–social interface of sustainable development: Capabilities, social capital, institutions. *Ecological Economies* 2004, 49, 199–214.
117 Oliver, C. Sustainable competitive advantage: Combining institutional and resource-based views. *Strategic Management Journal* 1997, 18, 697–713.
118 Molina-Azorín, J. F.; Tarí, J. J.; Pereira-Moliner, J.; López-Gamero, M. D.; Pertusa-Ortega, E. M. The effects of quality and environmental management on competitive advantage: A mixed methods study in the hotel industry. *Tourism Management* 2015, 50, 41–54.
119 Porter, M. E. *Competitive Advantage: Creating and Sustaining Superior Performance*; The Free Press: New York, 1985.
120 Rice, G. Pro-environmental behavior in Egypt: Is there a role for Islamic environmental ethics? *Journal of Business Ethics* 2006, 65, 373–390.
121 Miles, M. P.; Munilla, L. S.; Darroch, J. Sustainable corporate entrepreneurship. *International Entrepreneurship and Management Journal* 2009, 5, 65–76.
122 Prothero, A.; Dobscha, S.; Freung, J.; Kilbourne, W. E.; Luchs, M. G.; Qzanne, L. K.; Thogersen, J. Sustainable consumption: Opportunities for consumer research and public policy. *Journal of Public Policy & Marketing* 2011, 30, 31–38.
123 Wang, Y. B.; Ho, C. W. No money? No problem! The value of sustainability: Social capital drives the relationship among customer identification and citizenship behavior in sharing economy. *Sustainability* 2017, 9, 1400.
124 Brahme, U. Sharing economy, CSR and sustainability: Making the connection – I. Retrieved 30 October 2017, from www.linkedin.com/pulse/sharing-economy-csr-sustainability-making-connection-i-unmesh-brahme; 2017.
125 Pineiro-Chousa, J.; Vizcaíno-González, M.; López-Cabarcos, M. Á. Reputation, game theory and entrepreneurial sustainability. *Sustainability* 2016, 8, 1196.
126 Pineiro-Chousa, J.; Vizcaíno-González, M.; López-Cabarcos, M. Á; Romero-Castro, N. Managing reputational risk through environmental management and reporting: An options theory approach. *Sustainability* 2017, 9, 376.
127 Lordkipanidze, M.; Brezet, H.; Backman, M. The entrepreneurship factor in sustainable tourism development. *Journal of Cleaner Production* 2005, 13, 787–798.
128 Pastakia, A. Grassroots ecopreneurs: Change agents for a sustainable society. *Journal of Organizational Change Management* 1998, 11, 153–173.
129 Bergset, L. The rationality and irrationality of financing green start-ups. *Administrative Sciences* 2015, 5, 260–285.
130 Moskwa, E.; Higgins-Desbiolles, F.; Gifford, S. Sustainability through food and conversation: The role of an entrepreneurial restaurateur in fostering engagement with sustainable development issues. *Journal of Sustainable Tourism* 2015, 23, 125–145.
131 Marsden, T.; Smith, E. Ecological entrepreneurship: Sustainable development in local communities through quality food production and local branding. *Geoforum* 2005, 36, 440–451.
132 Parrish, B. D.; Foxon, T. J. Sustainability entrepreneurship and equitable transitions to a low-carbon economy. *Greener Management International* 2006, 55, 47–52.

133 Zamfir, P. B. Supporting green entrepreneurship in Romania: Imperative of sustainable development. *Romanian Economic and Business Review* 2014, 9, 35–44.
134 York, J. G.; Venkataraman, S. The entrepreneur-environment nexus: Uncertainty, innovation and allocation. *Journal of Business Venturing* 2010, 25, 449–463.
135 Azeez Olugbola, S. Exploring entrepreneurial readiness of youth and startup success components: Entrepreneurship training as a moderator. *Journal of Innovation and Knowledge* 2017, 2, 155–171.
136 Cuomo, M. T.; Tortora, D.; Mazzucchelli, A.; Festa, G.; Di Gregorio, A.; Metallo, G. Impacts of code of ethics on financial performance in the Italian listed companies of bank sector. *Journal of Business Accounting and Finance Perspectives* 2018, 1 (in press).

2.2 Sustainable consumption through new business models

The role of sustainable entrepreneurship[1]

Nancy M.P. Bocken

Introduction

Globally, consumption and production patterns need to radically transform to tackle the looming sustainability crisis.[2] A large part of the world needs significant further development to build infrastructures and tackle poverty, health and sanitation issues, whereas in the developed world the negative side effects of over-consumption, from health to well-being, need to be targeted.[3] Growth needs to be decoupled from environmental impact and different forms of production and consumption are required. Change will need to be significant – the EU low carbon economy roadmap recommends cutting carbon emissions to 80 per cent below 1990 levels by 2050.[4] Significant cuts are required for transport, buildings, industry and agriculture.[5] While challenging, this stepwise transformation is not impossible. Indeed, the International Energy Agency (IEA) reported that since 2015 the global economy has grown by 6.5 per cent, while carbon emissions from energy generation and transport have not grown,[6] indicating early evidence for the ability to decouple economic growth from environmental impact. However, as (EU) product lifetimes are decreasing[7] and people are found to replace products like smartphones faster than T-shirts,[8] significant work is still to be done.

Companies drive consumption patterns through marketing, branding and business models. The current 'linear economy' is focused on a 'take-make-dispose' model where planned product obsolescence typically drives sales.[9] Unsustainable consumption patterns, more often than not, are fuelled by such unsustainable business practices, which are at the heart of the current unsustainability crisis. Alternative business models would incorporate longer product lifetimes, as well as product reparability, refurbishment and remanufacturing,[10] and encouraging slower forms of consumption. However, to date, such business models are the exception rather than the norm.[11] Moreover, consumption patterns are difficult to influence, being embedded in social, cultural and institutional contexts.[12] Consumption patterns are linked to individual factors (e.g. personality, knowledge), social factors (e.g. norms, social environment) and wider contextual factors (e.g. political, economic, environmental, societal, technical and infrastructural).[13] Even though consumers may have good intentions and know how to behave and consume sustainably, their actual behaviour falls behind, which is referred to as the values-action gap.[14]

This research investigates the role of sustainable entrepreneurship in driving sustainable consumption through new business models: businesses can drive sustainable consumption patterns through the way business is done.[15] Sustainable entrepreneurship has been recognised as a key driver for sustainable products, processes and business models. New ventures are being positioned as an answer to societal and environmental problems.[16]

Sustainable entrepreneurship is about entrepreneurial activities that contribute positively to sustainable development and the objectives derived from it.[17] Sustainable entrepreneurs balance economic health (economy), social equity (people) and environmental resilience (planet) through their entrepreneurial behaviour.[18] They discover and exploit economic opportunities to create change in markets and initiate transformation of sectors towards an environmentally and socially more sustainable state[19] by developing business opportunities from sustainability issues and trying to resolve those while creating superior customer value.[20] They may develop sustainable business models, which drive sustainable business and consumption patterns.[21] As such, sustainable entrepreneurs may kick off a sustainability transformation, if successful cases are followed by market incumbents.[22] Evidently, it is a promising view that sustainable entrepreneurs can succeed and trigger new business models that encourage sustainable consumption and production.

There is decent knowledge of the traits of sustainable entrepreneurs,[23] the barriers and opportunities of growing sustainable ventures[24] and specific examples of sustainable ventures and business models.[25] However, the role of sustainable entrepreneurs in driving sustainable consumption through new business models is as yet underexplored. Through the use of illustrative cases, this chapter investigates the following question: How are entrepreneurs stimulating sustainable consumption through new business models?

Sustainable consumption

Sustainable consumption is concerned with the use of goods and services that respond to basic needs and bring a better quality of life, while minimising the use of natural resources, toxic materials and emissions across the life cycle, without jeopardising the needs of future generation.[26] Sustainable consumption is about promoting inclusive societies, building supportive communities, providing meaningful work and encouraging purposeful lives.[27] Key authors and institutes argue that economic growth should be questioned: the economy needs to be aligned with sustainable development, which requires new forms of consumption.[28]

Traditionally, sustainable consumption in literature and practice has focused on product buying choices (e.g. ethical, organic), but it is increasingly framed around 'changing consumer behaviour'.[29] The way we view sustainable consumption needs to move away from a product focus to a focus on transforming consumer behaviour. Perhaps paradoxically, marketing techniques could be used to influence (consumer) behaviours towards reduced consumption or 'anti-consumption' to the benefit of individuals and society as a whole.[30] This indicates the need for a 'systems view' on consumption, moving away from single products or services to a holistic view on how business is done. To create systemic impact, strategies will need to focus on influencing the individual context (influencing individual choices), social context (normalising through the social environment) and wider context (political, economic, societal, technological and environmental).[31]

Sustainable business models

The business model is a way of looking at businesses and the way business is done in a systemic way. *Sustainable* business models seek to incorporate a wider range of stakeholders' concerns than just the firm and its customers in key business practices. Disparate stakeholders such as 'the Environment' and 'Society' are deliberately considered.[32] This systemic view is needed to make the significant changes required to transform global consumption patterns. As such, sustainable business models are focused on as a key driver for sustainable consumption that could be pushed by entrepreneurs. Sustainable business models have the promise to contribute to competitive advantage while delivering positive societal and environmental impact.[33] Typically, they are depicted by a value proposition (product/ service offering – what value is provided and to whom), value creation and delivery (how value is provided) and value captured (how the company makes money and captures other forms of value).[34]

Sustainable business models can take different forms, ranging from more technical (e.g. move to renewables), social (e.g. moving from products to services) or organisational (e.g. repurposing the business for social impact) innovations.[35] Sufficiency-driven business models as a more social type of innovation focus on curbing consumption as part of the business model.[36] They deliver sustainability by reducing absolute material throughput and energy use associated with provision of goods and services by moderating end-user consumption encouraging consumers to make do with less.[37] Sufficiency-driven business model strategies can take different forms (Table 2.2.1).

There has been a keen interest in the links and co-emergence of sustainable business models across sustainable start-ups and large business.[40] Schaltegger and colleagues[41] identify strategies to describe how sustainable business model innovations may diffuse to the mass market. These include: (1) Scalability – business models that can be scaled without rebound effects; (2) Replicability – business models that can be replicated without cannibalisation; (3) Integrability – business models that can be merged with existing organisations; and (4) Imitability – business models that can be imitated and adapted by others. This suggests that there are emerging strategies that support the diffusion of sustainable business models that can be followed by others, or can be integrated in existing businesses.

Sustainable entrepreneurship

Sustainable entrepreneurs create opportunities from social and environmental challenges and could initiate transformations of sectors towards an environmentally and socially more sustainable state.[42] Sustainable entrepreneurs differ from 'conventional' entrepreneurs in the sense that they focus on an organisational purpose, which maximises the value of human and natural resources. They seek to create synergies and pursue 'benefits stacking' (multiple forms of value/benefits), focus on satisfying multiple stakeholder needs (not only the firm and its customers) and manage the quality of outcomes and allocation of benefits across stakeholders who contributed positively to the enterprise (not just to those with most power).[43] These entrepreneurs typically have a pronounced value-based approach and intention to create social and environmental change in society.[44] However, innovations pursued without any sustainability intentions may also create environmental benefits, such as the move to digital music delivery and media sales creating the potential for dematerialisation.[45] Of course, such innovations may also lead to additional energy use from devices and data centres. On the other hand, companies who start off with a sustainability purpose need to continuously track progress towards sustainability goals to fulfil this purpose. In this research, the aim is to include examples of entrepreneurial efforts with a sustainability purpose since initiation.

Sustainable entrepreneurs and sustainable consumption: case approach

While there is a clear view about the potential of sustainable entrepreneurs in driving a sustainable transformation,[46] it is less clear how they might contribute to a transformation

Table 2.2.1 Strategies to encourage sufficiency[38]

Business model initiative	*Value creation logic*	*Examples*
Sharing, no ownership Sharing the same product across multiple customers.	Companies are paid for services rather than product ownership. The customer benefits from convenience and transparency.	Car sharing companies, e.g. Zipcar, BlaBla Car; Home sharing, e.g. Couchsurfing, Airbnb; Product sharing platforms, e.g. Peerby and Yerdle; Pay per use, e.g. launderettes, HOMIE pay per use[39])
Demand reduction services Solutions that mitigate energy use and resources by individuals and businesses.	The firm is paid for the services, while the consumer makes savings greater than the fees so consumers and firms benefit. A better business case for the company could be established for instance through paid systems that reduce energy use.	ESCOs; Subsidies for home insulation and double-glazing; Energy management devices (e.g. NEST).
Moderating sales and promotion Conscious action to moderate sales and focus on needs based selling.	Long-term customer relations and trust in mutual benefits through customer loyalty, reputation and service. Revenue models focused on premium pricing.	Slow fashion brands; Vitsœ only selling what is needed; Patagonia focusing on conscious purchasing.
Extending product life Provide products to last a lifetime, be reparable, upgradable and not subject to fashion.	Long-term customer relations and trust in mutual benefits through reputation and service. Price premiums or follow on services may justify slower sales. Customers save in through-life cost savings.	Companies Cucinelli, Vitsœ; Customer pledges to repair more and buy less enabled by better design (e.g. Patagonia and eBay Common Threads).
Direct reuse Creating markets for used goods to reduce waste to landfill and idle assets	Buying high quality gets rewarded: products retain value. Others will be able to access quality more cheaply. Companies benefit from the brand value and value through the platform.	Antiques markets; Organised clothing swaps; Director barter; Clothes reuse: Patagonia and eBay; M&S and Oxfam.
Full life cycle sufficiency Design and product use focused on fully reduced resource use, such as 'frugal innovations'. Unfortunately these are often limited to low-income countries.	Customers benefit from cost reduction in the use phase. For frugal innovation, lower pricing or leasing may be adopted, while premium pricing might apply in developed markets	Company Kyocera's full life cycle approach; MittiCool no-electricity fridge and solar cooker; Advocacy – Unilever Sustainable Living Plan

in sustainable *consumption* patterns. This research discusses forms of sustainable consumption pursued by sustainable entrepreneurs and some of the responses from incumbents using illustrative cases. While the focus is on the actions by sustainable entrepreneurs, (re)actions by incumbents are also included. The two illustrative cases are car sharing and clothing consumption. They represent two important industries: transport contributes to 23 per cent of energy-related CO_2 emissions worldwide[47] whereas fashion is the third largest industry in the world and assumed to be the second most polluting industry after oil.[48] For each of the industries, multiple illustrative case examples of business model innovations potentially contributing to sustainable consumption are presented. The business models, sustainable consumption influencing techniques and diffusion potential of the examples are analysed using the framework in Table 2.2.2, based on the literature.

Two illustrative cases

This section introduces a range of illustrative case examples within the emergent industries of car sharing and clothing reuse to demonstrate the types of business model strategies to encourage sustainable consumption.

Case 1: car sharing

Passenger road transport continues to be responsible for the highest emissions share within the transport sector.[53] Impacts could be mitigated through (1) increased efficiency of existing transport; (2) shifting from fossil fuels to electric vehicles; and (3) slowing demand growth, e.g. through behavioural and infrastructural changes.[54] The combined mitigation potential in urban transport via such options amounts to 20 to 50 per cent between 2010 and 2050.[55] Car sharing as an example of slowing demand growth could help reduce the carbon footprint associated with transport by reducing car sales and usage and replacement with more efficient and electric cars. The car sharing model taps into the sustainability opportunity that most cars in Europe are only used 10 per cent of the time and by on average one or two people at a time, so sharing would make better use of vehicles.[56]

Car sharing models can encourage car companies to enhance reparability, fuel efficiency and cost-savings, because these strategies would reduce the product life cycle cost.[57] It could also help customers reduce car usage because it makes them more aware of how much they drive. Car sharing can take different forms, e.g. using monthly fees for shared cars in urban areas (e.g. Zipcar, DriveNow), peer-to-peer car rental (e.g. Drivy) and empty car seat sharing (e.g. BlablaCar). Other companies might optimise the design of cars for new 'performance type' business models. Riversimple's car for instance is only

Table 2.2.2 Framework to analyse the cases

Sustainable business models identified[49]	*Sustainable business model elements*[50]	*Sustainable consumption influencing mechanisms*[51]	*Potential diffusion of business models*[52]
- Sharing, no ownership - Demand reduction services - Moderating sales and promotion - Extending product life - Direct reuse - Full life cycle sufficiency	- Value proposition (customer, society, environment) - Value creation and delivery - Value capture (business, society, environment)	- Individual context - Social context - Wider context	- Scalability - Replicability - Integrability - Imitability

one-tenth of the typical weight of a car, uses hydrogen fuel technology and is compact,[58] presenting an example of full life cycle sufficiency (Table 2.2.3).

Several types of start-ups have emerged and incumbents have followed with their own models or mergers and acquisitions. Zipcar was founded in 2000, while BlaBlaCar was founded in 2006, Drivy in 2010 and DriveNow in 2011. In a relatively short-term period, these have grown in size, value and usership and have established partnerships. Zipcar as one of the more established international car sharing businesses was created based on the belief that people desired an easy cost-effective way to share cars, which would reduce emissions.[59] The company estimates that each Zipcar takes six personally owned vehicles off the road and that 40 per cent of users sold their car or did not buy a new one.[60] BlaBlaCar connects travellers with drivers who have empty seats and estimates that it saved 1,000,000 tons of CO_2 in 2016 and increased car occupancy to about 2.8 people.[61] French peer-to-peer car sharing start-up Drivy lets people hire out their cars.[62] It acquired start-up Buzzcar in 2015. Zipcar has been acquired by incumbent car rental company Avis. Incumbents BMW and car rental company Sixt have jointly established DriveNow (using the BMWi). Incumbent Daimler AG established Car2Go in 2008. Both Car2Go and DriveNow focus on inner city car sharing. In contrast to the other companies, cars can be parked anywhere within the inner city area instead of a designated parking space. Country Manager of Drivy, Gero Graf, in an interview describes these services as highly complementary rather than competing: the average trip on DriveNow or Car2Go is only half an hour, and in France Drivy's average rental is 3.5 days.[63] This shows the compatibility of different models, but also consolidation through mergers and acquisitions, where incumbent car manufacturers (e.g. BMW, Daimler AG) services employ their own cars for car sharing, and incumbent car rental services (e.g. Sixt, Avis) expand their services to short-term 'rental' or sharing. Moreover, quickly growing 'start-ups' (e.g. Drivy) are acquiring other start-ups.

Table 2.2.3 summarises the car sharing case to investigate how sustainable entrepreneurs have contributed to sustainable consumption in the car industry. In the *individual context* they contributed to demonstrating the benefits of car sharing. For instance, Zipcar on its website quotes financial, practical and also environmental benefits rather than targeting just 'green consumers'.[64] BlaBlaCar emphasises comfort, cost savings and trust.[65] However, an overemphasis on 'other benefits' might detract from a focus on the potential environmental benefits that such business models could deliver. In the *social context*, the plethora of car sharing companies helps normalise this type of business model to make it more accessible for incumbents. It is clear from the examples that car sharing in different forms has gained traction with start-ups and incumbents. In the *wider context* start-ups are helping to change laws and regulations. Robin Chase, co-founder of Zipcar, for example, is pushing for regulatory change to pave the way for new start-ups.[66] Furthermore, it seems that the innovations in the car industry are quite complementary, where established businesses fill 'competitive gaps' through city-centred sharing models.[67]

Several sharing types of models (e.g. long vs. short distance) co-exist (Table 2.2.3). The value proposition goes beyond 'sustainability', and new business models pursued by entrepreneurs appear to co-exist in a synergistic way with initiatives by incumbents. Incumbents who have a stake in sustaining and expanding their own business (car manufacturing and rental) are adopting car sharing. Whereas business models are being imitated, the long-term effects on sustainability are difficult to predict. To illustrate, it is projected that the global vehicle stock will be 2.5 times greater in 2030 than in 2002 – also new car registrations globally are on the rise.[68] Moreover, wider accessibility of cars,

Table 2.2.3 Case analysis framework for car sharing

Sustainable business models identified[70]	*Sustainable business model elements*[71]	*Sustainable consumption influencing mechanisms*[72]	*Potential diffusion of business models*[73]
- Sharing, no ownership (e.g. Zipcar, BlaBlaCar) - Full life cycle sufficiency (e.g. Riversimple)	- Value proposition: mobility with flexibility, convenience, cost savings and environmental benefit - Value creation and delivery: smaller efficient, renewable energy cars, in convenient locations and enabled by apps for payment and access - Value capture: pay per performance; environmental benefits of driving less, societal benefits of clean air in urban areas when using fewer cleaner cars	- Individual context: demonstrating the benefits of car sharing - Social context: normalising car sharing; sharing with others (e.g. BlaBlaCar) - Wider context: start-ups pushing laws and regulations for new business models. Improving the infrastructure for car sharing (e.g. parking); supporting co-existence of business models	- Scalability: potential rebound effects of driving more and greater access to cars - Replicability: could generate additional revenue streams for incumbents and sustain existing business (e.g. more car manufacturing or extending rental to very short-term services) - Integrability: can be merged within existing organisations, e.g. Zipcar has been acquired by car rental company Avis - Imitability: since Zipcar, many sharing models have emerged - Synergies/ compatibility / co-existence – business models can be compatible with each other (e.g. city-scale sharing of DriveNow vs. long distance sharing of Drivy)

also through taxi services such as Uber and Lyft, might lead to greater car usage. In order to close the 'values-action gap' in sustainability values and action for consumers, 'slowing demand growth' as a strategy[69] is still a big gap. This could be targeted by emphasising the environmental benefits of driving less and sharing more, which would require even more advanced business models less dependent on numbers of trips or miles driven but focusing on innovative services for instance.

Case 2: clothing reuse

The major environmental impacts of clothing originate from fossil fuels used in washing and cleaning and material processing along the value chain; the use of toxic chemicals in cotton agriculture and various manufacturing stages; water use for cotton crop cultivation and laundry; and clothing waste.[74] Each phase across the product life cycle from materials extraction to processing, use and disposal has notable environmental impacts. Moreover, over a quarter of the (UK) population (28 per cent) say they buy more clothes than they need[75] and throw away about 30 kg of clothing per annum.[76] This unsustainable trend, generating significant waste streams, is prevalent in other developed countries.[77] The benefits of directly reusing clothing are clear. Providing 1 tonne of cotton T-shirts for direct reuse (e.g. a charity shop) can result in a net saving of about 3 kg CO_2-eq. per T-shirt, and preparation for a reuse network can still result in a net saving of about 2.5 kg CO_2-eq. per T-shirt.[78] In parallel, there is a reduction in waste, water, toxic chemical use and extra revenue from the same material.

Clothing sharing focuses on reducing the number of clothes being manufactured and sold thus contributing to reducing total clothing consumption. There are different business models, including a 'library type of contract' with a monthly number of items that can be rented (e.g. LENA Fashion library), rental pay per item (e.g. Rentez-Vous, Girl Meets Dress), subscription services (e.g. for socks and underwear), leasing (e.g. MUD Jeans leasing jeans), deposit systems (incentives to return clothing), second hand clothing sales (e.g. Patagonia and eBay; Tradesey; Filippa K) and clothing swap platforms (e.g. Swap style, The Clothing Exchange). Often, there are collaborations with emerging fashion designers (e.g. LENA Fashion library, Rentez-Vous). Girl Meets Dress, for example, was founded in 2009 capitalising on the growing preference for experience over ownership, and similar to LENA Fashion Library and Rentez-Vous makes available (upcoming) designer clothes.[79]

In contrast, established clothing retailers such as H&M and M&S developed clothing take-back systems, where they collect used clothing from consumers (launched in 2013 and 2012 respectively). Others such as Marimekko[80] and Filipa K sell second hand in their stores and online. Since H&M started their garment collecting initiative in 2013, they have gathered over 22,000 tonnes of garments – the equivalent of 100 million T-shirts in terms of fabric[81] and estimates that 95 per cent of these clothes could be reworn or recycled (2016 data). M&S has collected 7.8 million items generating £5.5 million in value (2016 data).[82] Other more premium-priced incumbents such as Filippa K and Patagonia have started second-hand initiatives.[83] For example, in Filippa K's quest to encourage reuse, they opened their first second hand store in Stockholm in 2008 in collaboration with a local entrepreneur.[84] An internal study among Filippa K customers shows that 74 per cent of their customers keep their products more than four years and that 70 per cent of their existing customers would sell in the second hand store and 87 per cent would buy second hand Filippa K clothes.[85] Patagonia through its Common Threads Platform encourages reuse and repair, and through collaborations with eBay it wants to encourage a second hand market.[86] Whereas until recently, fashion companies' focus was on creating and capturing value from the sale of new products, which, once they left the shop were out of the business's control, this model is now changing in start-up and incumbent environments.[87] Continued clothing reuse is becoming a business opportunity.

Table 2.2.4 summarises the case about the role of sustainable entrepreneurs in triggering sustainable consumption in the clothing and fashion industry. In the *individual context*, start-ups have provided innovative alternatives for clothing *sales*, often through rental and subscription type of services. These services can provide convenience (e.g. delivered to your doorstep; monthly subscription) and innovativeness (e.g. access to designer or vintage clothes). Incumbent companies such as H&M and Filipa K are investing in, or are collaborating with, 'sustainable start-ups' in the areas of new services and quality online second hand retailing.[88] Patagonia's Worn Wear program, along with provocative messaging around 'not buying' clothes can encourage a rethink of consumer buying choices.[89] Stimulating repair and reuse through good design and extensive customer service can enable this. In the *social context*, start-ups help normalise the second hand (second hand shops, swapping) and reuse market (rental, subscription) and improve these markets through new value propositions around innovative design or 'vintage' and digitalisation. In the *wider context* technical and social advancements (digitalisation and social networks) can enable new types of consuming, creating global online communities. Start-up TredUP[90] for instance allows customers to browse high quality certified second hand clothes. Similar to car sharing, multiple business model strategies are pursued.

From the examples, it appears that incumbents are closely following start-up actions and are even starting to invest in these directly (e.g. H&M's recycling start-up competition led to investments in start-ups).[91] Multiple benefits are created for customers beyond 'sustainability' (e.g. access to more clothes, special vintage collections, or 'try before buy' options).[92] Business model innovations such as take-back systems pursued by companies like H&M and M&S are compatible with incumbents' current business models. The actual sustainability impacts are hard to predict. To illustrate, global textile fibre consumption is estimated to grow by 3 per cent annually.[93] Hence, companies truly aiming to pursue sustainability strategies need to find ways to measure their real impact, for example, the amount of *new* clothing sales prevented (for second hand models) or clothing collected (for take-back models). Incumbents with co-existing business models, such as Patagonia and its Worn Wear initiative, or Filipa K and Marimekko pursuing second hand sales, could set targets to increase second hand sales and track whether these cannibalise new clothing sales.[94] Similarly, start-ups like LENA who have 'try before buy' options and MUD Jeans who have a 'buy and deposit' system in addition to leasing will need to remain aware of the sustainability implications of their co-existing business models and track their aspired impacts.[95] To close the values-action gap, new business models should thus further reduce the dependency on continuous new clothing sales through new propositions focused on long-lasting products that customers will want to reuse, thus reducing virgin material use and unnecessary waste.

Discussion and conclusions

How are sustainable entrepreneurs stimulating sustainable consumption through new business models? It was found that sustainable entrepreneurs could kick off sustainability transformations, which are followed by synergistic business models by incumbents.[104]

Across two industries – personal mobility and clothing – innovative new business models were identified that have the potential to transform consumption patterns. The framework in Table 2.2.5 was developed to analyse the cases and summarises the key findings. An additional potential diffusion strategy of 'synergies, compatibility and co-existence' was identified. This is an evolutionary business model strategy for incumbents not able (or willing) to radically transform their entire business model fast. Because of the rapid growth and emergence of new business models – both in car sharing and clothing reuse – it seems that these practices have become normalised (social context) and that the new required infrastructure is slowly maturing (wider context). Furthermore, individual incentives have extended beyond sustainability and satisfying 'green customers' to more mainstream customer groups, seeking convenience, transparency, novelty and new experiences rather than product ownership and innovation.

Table 2.2.4 Case analysis framework for clothing reuse

Sustainable business models identified[96]	*Sustainable business model elements*[97]	*Sustainable consumption influencing mechanisms*[98]	*Potential diffusion of business models*[99]
- Sharing, no ownership - Moderating sales and promotion (e.g. Patagonia) - Extending product life (e.g. Patagonia) - Direct reuse (e.g. Filipa K, Tradesey) - Full life cycle sufficiency (other innovations, such as 'waterless jeans',[100] iron free shirts or stain or odour repellent fabrics and recycled and reclaimed materials)[101]	- Value proposition: experience rather than ownership, 'less is more', access to quality, special items - Value creation and delivery: online sharing (e.g. Tradesey, eBay) or physical sharing spaces (e.g. Rentez-Vous, LENA) - Value capture: Fee per garment or use period; transaction fees for using the platform; incentives for product take-back (e.g. deposit or discount vouchers with MUD Jeans)	- Individual context: sharing is fun; 'Don't Buy This Jacket' by Patagonia - Social context: start-ups normalising reuse; making reuse more available. Incumbents (e.g. H&M, M&S) also encouraging recycling - Wider context: fashion is still cheap and would need to take into account the full price of clothing (e.g. Environmental P&L – Puma being a start)[102]	- Scalability: collaborations with existing platforms (e.g. eBay) can help create scale - Possible 'unsustainable copycats' leading to more consumption - Replicability/ integrability: Patagonia, Marimekko and Filipa K have co-existing business models promoting second hand in addition to new clothing sales; companies such as M&S and H&M have take-back systems combined with their 'fast fashion' model - Imitability: several start-ups have emerged in the clothing reuse space, and incumbents are following suit with second hand initiatives next to existing business models[103] - Synergies / compatibility / co-existence: fast fashion, leasing/ rental and second hand markets co-exist with multiple business models; sometimes co-existing within one company (e.g. Patagonia)

Although an organisation may not project all essential characteristics of a sustainable enterprise to influence sustainable consumption patterns, emergent business model strategies indicate an important shift in business models. By nature, business model innovation is an evolving process, and gradual change might indicate the start of a more fundamental shift in business models towards sustainability. Within the diversity of emergent business models, it appears that incumbents are developing business models that fit well with current trends and models (e.g. city car sharing, clothing take back) but will also largely sustain their existing business models (car manufacturing and rental, and clothing retailing respectively). However, to make a real sustainability impact, novel impact measures (e.g. increased second hand to new clothing sales ratios or prevented new car sales) need to

Table 2.2.5 Cross case summary

	Sustainable business models identified[105]	*Sustainable business model elements*[106]	*Sustainable consumption influencing mechanisms*[107]	*Potential diffusion of business models*[108]
Framework	– Sharing, no ownership – Demand reduction services – Moderating sales and promotion – Extending product life – Direct reuse – Full life cycle sufficiency	– Value proposition (customer, society, environment) – Value creation and delivery – Value capture (business, society, environment)	– Individual context – Social context – Wider context	– Scalability – Replicability – Integrability – Imitability – Synergies/ compatibility / co-existence
Cases	Multiple business models are pursued: sustainable start-ups experiment with multiple business model innovations, balancing sustainability and customer preference; incumbents retain their own models while adding innovative models	Focus on multiple benefits for customers (e.g. convenience, experience, innovation)	Sustainable start-ups help normalise new behaviour and help change the individual, social and wider context	Sustainable start-ups create a new space for incumbents who can enter the market with synergistic co-existing business models

be developed and targeted if incumbents continue to pursue co-existing business models. Moreover, the business model innovation process will need to be framed and tracked against such sustainability goals[109] (e.g. waste reduction, avoid new clothing sales, reduced car usage or sales).

Consumers also have a key role to play. The rising number of 'sharing start-ups' indicates a positive consumer trend. However, a clear 'values-action' gap has been identified in earlier work on behaviour science.[110] Consumers may have good sustainability values, intentions and knowledge, but don't always act upon them.[111] The co-existence of business models might halt a rapid radical transformation. While fashion generally is still cheap, not internalising cost for environmental (and social) degradation, it will be difficult to compete with second hand products. Greater access to cars through car sharing might lead to greater car usage. Moreover, while these new business models appear promising, it is essential to mitigate rebound effects where an improvement in consumption patterns (e.g. reduced total mobility and clothing cost) is offset by spending money on unsustainable products or services (e.g. flights).[112] While clothing sharing business models emerge, these co-exist with the fast fashion model by incumbents and take-back systems might encourage even faster consumption. Hence, sustainable business model innovation pursued by entrepreneurs and incumbents, while rightly emphasising novel customer benefits associated with such business models, should more clearly build in sustainability benefits and steer away from adverse incentives (e.g. buying more, driving more), but rather build in new revenue models to generate the desired sustainability impacts.

To conclude, new sharing models pursued by sustainable start-ups are promising and spark a shift in the industry. However, fundamental changes to the way clothing and fashion are provided to the customer, revenue models, as well as true pricing of goods and performance measures are essential.[113] To mitigate environmental impact associated with consumption, Clift and colleagues[114] describe the importance of spending money on 'luxury and quality' at a higher price and lower environmental impact (i.e. quality above quantity), originating from equitable supply chains where value added and environmental impact are fairly distributed. While sustainable entrepreneurs are essential to drive sustainable consumption, and indeed global de-growth has been identified the past years,[115] future business strategies and government policies will need to focus on encouraging *absolute* reductions in resource consumption. Sustainable entrepreneurs, by pushing new sustainable business models, have a key role to play in incentivising, normalising and even establishing the infrastructures to transform consumption patterns for sustainability. Incumbents will need to respond with synergistic collaborations and truly transformational business models with a measurable improved environmental and societal impact compared to the status quo.

Notes

1 Some examples draw on Bocken, N.M.P. 2017. Business-led sustainable consumption initiatives: Impacts and lessons learned. *Journal of Management Development*, 36(1), 81–96.
2 IPCC. 2014. *Climate Change 2014 Synthesis Report. Summary for Policy Makers*. Available at: www.ipcc.ch/pdf/assessment-report/ar5/syr/AR5_SYR_FINAL_SPM.pdf (accessed 28 July 2016).
3 Bocken, N., Short, S. 2016. Towards a sufficiency-driven business model: Experiences and opportunities. *Environmental Innovation and Societal Transitions*, 18, 41–61; Bocken, N., Fil, A., Prabhu, J. 2016. Scaling up social businesses in developing markets. *Journal of Cleaner Production*, 139, 295–308
4 European Commission. 2016. *2050 Low-Carbon Economy*. Available at: http://ec.europa.eu/clima/policies/strategies/2050/index_en.htm (accessed 28 July 2016).
5 European Commission. 2016. *2050 Low-Carbon Economy*. Available at: http://ec.europa.eu/clima/policies/strategies/2050/index_en.htm (accessed 28 July 2016).
6 IEA. 2016. *Decoupling of Global Emissions and Economic Growth Confirmed*. Available at: www.iea.org/newsroomandevents/pressreleases/2016/march/decoupling-of-global-emissions-and-economic-growth-confirmed.html (accessed 28 July 2016).
7 Bakker, C., Wang, F., Huisman, J., den Hollander, M. 2014. Products that go round: exploring product life extension through design. *Journal of Cleaner Production*, 69, 10–16.
8 Tröger, N., Wieser, H., Hübner, R. 2017. *Smartphones are Replaced More Frequently Than T-shirts. Patterns of Consumer Use and Reasons for Replacing Durable Goods*. AK Wien, Vienna, February 2017. Available at: www.akeuropa.eu/_includes/mods/akeu/docs/main_report_en_457.pdf (accessed 26 April 2017).
9 Bakker, C., Wang, F., Huisman, J., den Hollander, M. 2014. Products that go round: exploring product life extension through design. *Journal of Cleaner Production*, 69, 10–16.
10 Bakker, C., Wang, F., Huisman, J., den Hollander, M. 2014. Products that go round: exploring product life extension through design. *Journal of Cleaner Production*, 69, 10–16.
11 Bocken, N.M.P. 2017. Business-led sustainable consumption initiatives: Impacts and lessons learned. *Journal of Management Development*, 36(1), 81–96

12 Jackson, T. 2009. *Prosperity Without Growth. Prosperity Without Growth: Economics for a Finite Planet*. Earthscan, London; Bocken, N., Allwood, J. 2012. Strategies to reduce the carbon footprint of consumer goods by influencing stakeholders. *Journal of Cleaner Production*, 35, 118–129.

13 Kollmuss, A., Agyeman, J. 2002. Mind the gap: Why do people act environmentally and what are the barriers to pro-environmental behaviour? *Environmental Education Research*, 8(3), 239–260; Bocken, N.M.P. 2017. Business-led sustainable consumption initiatives: Impacts and lessons learned. *Journal of Management Development*, 36(1), 81–96.

14 Young, W., Hwang, K., McDonald, S., Oates, C. 2010. Sustainable consumption: Green consumer behavior when purchasing products. *Sustainable Development*, 18, 20–31.

15 Bocken, N.M.P. 2017. Business-led sustainable consumption initiatives: Impacts and lessons learned. *Journal of Management Development*, 36(1), 81–96.

16 Pacheco, D., Dean, T., Payne, D. 2010. Escaping the green prison: Entrepreneurship and the creation of opportunities for sustainable development. *Journal of Bus. Venturing*, 25(5), 464–480; Hall, J., Daneke, J., Lenox, M. 2010. Sustainable development and entrepreneurship: Past contributions and future directions. *Journal of Bus. Venturing*, 25, 439–448; Bocken, N. 2015. Sustainable venture capital: Catalyst for sustainable start-up success? *Journal of Cleaner Production*, 108, Part A, 647–658; Schaltegger, S., Hansen, E.G., Lüdeke-Freund, F. 2016. A co-evolutionary analysis of sustainable entrepreneurship, innovation, and transformation. *Organization and the Environment*, 29, 1–26.

17 Kuckertz, A., Wagner, B. 2010. The influence of sustainability orientation on entrepreneurial intentions: Investigating the role of business experience. sustainable development and entrepreneurship. *Journal of Business Venturing*, 25(5), 524–539.

18 Hockerts, K., Wüstenhagen, R. 2010. Greening Goliaths versus emerging Davids: Theorizing about the role of incumbents and new entrants in sustainable entrepreneurship. *Journal of Business Venturing*, 25(5), 481–492.

19 Hockerts, K., Wüstenhagen, R. 2010. Greening Goliaths versus emerging Davids: Theorizing about the role of incumbents and new entrants in sustainable entrepreneurship. *Journal of Business Venturing*, 25(5), 481–492.

20 Bocken, N. 2015. Sustainable venture capital: Catalyst for sustainable start-up success? *Journal of Cleaner Production*, 108, Part A, 647–658

21 Boons, F., Lüdeke-Freund, F. 2013. Business models for sustainable innovation: State-of-the-art and steps towards a research agenda. *Journal of Cleaner Production*, 45, 9–19.

22 Hockerts, K., Wüstenhagen, R. 2010. Greening Goliaths versus emerging Davids: Theorizing about the role of incumbents and new entrants in sustainable entrepreneurship. *Journal of Business Venturing*, 25(5), 481–492.

23 Kirkwood, J., Walton, S. 2010. What motivates ecopreneurs to start businesses? *The International Journal of Entrepreneurial Behavior & Research*, 16(3), 204–228; Kuckertz, A., Wagner, B. 2010. The influence of sustainability orientation on entrepreneurial intentions: Investigating the role of business experience. sustainable development and entrepreneurship. *Journal of Business Venturing*, 5, 524–539.

24 Bocken, N. 2015. Sustainable venture capital – catalyst for sustainable start-up success? *Journal of Cleaner Production*, 108, Part A, 647–658

25 Boehnke, J., Wüstenhagen, R. 2007. *Business Models for Distributed Energy Technologies: Evidence from German Cleantech Firms*. 2007 Academy of Management Annual Meeting, Philadelphia, PA, USA.
Wüstenhagen, R., Boehnke, J. 2006. Business models for sustainable energy. In: M. Andersen, A. Tukker (Eds.), *Proceedings of the Workshop of the Sustainable Consumption Research Exchange (SCORE!) Network: Perspectives on Radical Changes to Sustainable Consumption and Production*, 20–21 April 2006, Copenhagen, Denmark (2006), pp. 253–258.

26 UNEP. 2016. *What is SCP?* Available at: www.unep.org/resourceefficiency/Home/WhatisSCP/tabid/105574/Default.aspx (accessed 21 July 2016).

27 Sustainable Development Commission. 2016. *SDC Challenge Paper: Measuring What Matters in Light of the Stiglitz Report*. SDC 2011. Available at: www.sd-commission.org.uk/data/files/publications/SDC_Indicators_Challenge_Paper_2011.pdf (accessed 21 July 2016).

28 Seyfang, G. 2005. Shopping for sustainability: Can sustainable consumption promote ecological citizenship? *Environmental Politics*, 14(2), 290–306; Jackson, T. 2009. *Prosperity without Growth: Economics for a Finite Planet*. Earthscan, London; nef (The new economics foundation). 2012. *The Happy Planet Index: 2012 Report*. A global index of sustainable wellbeing. Available at: http://b.3cdn.net/nefoundation/d8879619b64bae461f_opm6ixqee.pdf (accessed 21 July 2016); CISL. 2016. *Rewiring the Economy. Ten Tasks, ten Years*. Available at: www.cisl.cam.ac.uk/publications/publication-pdfs/rewiring-the-economy-report.pdf (accessed 21 July 2016).

29 Seyfang, G. 2005. Shopping for sustainability: Can sustainable consumption promote ecological citizenship? *Environmental Politics*, 14(2), 290–306; Blowfield, M. 2013. *Business and Sustainability*. Oxford University Press, Oxford, UK (p. 270); Bocken, N.M.P. 2017. Business-led sustainable consumption initiatives – impacts and lessons learned. *Journal of Management Development*, 36(1), 81–96.

30 Social Marketing Quarterly. 2016. *Social Marketing Defined*. Available at: www.socialmarketingquarterly.com/learn/ (accessed 21 July 2016); Peattie, K., Peattie, S. 2009. Social marketing: A pathway to consumption reduction? *Journal of Business Research*, 62, 260–268.

31 Bocken, N.M.P. 2017. Business-led sustainable consumption initiatives: Impacts and lessons learned. *Journal of Management Development*, 36(1), 81–96.

32 Stubbs, W., Cocklin, C., 2008. Conceptualizing a sustainability business model. *Organization & Environment*, 21, 103–127; Bocken, N.M.P., Short, S.W., Rana, P., Evans, S., 2013. A value mapping tool for sustainable business modelling. *Corporate Governance*, 13, 482–497.

33 Boons, F., Lüdeke-Freund, F. 2013. Business models for sustainable innovation. State-of-the-art and steps towards a research agenda. *Journal of Cleaner Production*, 45, 9–19.

34 Richardson, J., 2008. The business model: An integrative framework for strategy execution. *Strategic Change*, 17, 133–144; Bocken, N., Short, S. 2016. Towards a sufficiency-driven business model: Experiences and opportunities. *Environmental Innovation and Societal Transitions*, 18, 41–61.

35 Boons, F., Lüdeke-Freund, F. 2013. Business models for sustainable innovation. State-of-the-art and steps towards a research agenda. *Journal of Cleaner Production*, 45, 9–19; Bocken, N., Short, S., Rana, P., Evans, S. 2014. A literature and practice review to develop sustainable business model archetypes. *Journal of Cleaner Production*, 65, 42–56.

36 Bocken, N., Short, S. 2016. Towards a sufficiency-driven business model: Experiences and opportunities. *Environmental Innovation and Societal Transitions*, 18, 41–61.

37 Bocken, N., Short, S. 2016. Towards a sufficiency-driven business model: Experiences and opportunities. *Environmental Innovation and Societal Transitions*, 18, 41–61.

38 Bocken, N.M.P. 2014. *Sufficiency Based Sustainable Business Model Innovation*. Sustainability Science Congress, 22–23 October 2014. Copenhagen; Bocken, N., Short, S. 2016. Towards a sufficiency-driven business model: Experiences and opportunities. *Environmental Innovation and Societal Transitions*, 18, 41–61.

39 HOMIE. 2016. www.homiepayperuse.com/ (accessed 13 April 2017).

40 Hockerts, K., Wüstenhagen, R. 2010. Greening Goliaths versus emerging Davids: Theorizing about the role of incumbents and new entrants in sustainable entrepreneurship. *Journal of Business Venturing*, 25(5), 481–492.

41 Schaltegger, S., Hansen, E.G., Lüdeke-Freund, F. 2016. A co-evolutionary analysis of sustainable entrepreneurship, innovation, and transformation. *Organization and the Environment*, 29, 1–26.

42 Hockerts, K., Wüstenhagen, R. 2010. Greening Goliaths versus emerging Davids: Theorizing about the role of incumbents and new entrants in sustainable entrepreneurship. *Journal of Business Venturing*, 25(5), 481–492.

43 Parrish, B. 2010. Sustainability-driven entrepreneurship: Principles of organization design. *Journal of Business Venturing*, 25, 510–523.

44 Hockerts, K., Wüstenhagen, R. 2010. Greening Goliaths versus emerging Davids: Theorizing about the role of incumbents and new entrants in sustainable entrepreneurship. *Journal of Business Venturing*, 25(5), 481–492; Pacheco, D., Dean, T., Payne, D. 2010. Escaping the green prison: Entrepreneurship and the creation of opportunities for sustainable development. *Journal of Business Venturing*, 25(5), 464–480.

45 Hogg, N., Jackson, T. 2009. Digital media and dematerialization: An exploration of the potential for reduced material intensity in music delivery. *Journal of Industrial Ecology*, 13(1), 127–146.

46 Hockerts, K., Wüstenhagen, R. 2010. Greening Goliaths versus emerging Davids: Theorizing about the role of incumbents and new entrants in sustainable entrepreneurship. *Journal of Business Venturing*, 25(5), 481–492.

47 Creutzig, F., Jochem, P., Edelenbosch, O., Mattauch, L., van Vuuren, D., McCollum, D., Minx, J. 2015. Transport: A roadblock to climate change mitigation? *Science* 350(6263), 911–912.

48 Nordic Fashion Association. 2016. *About*. Available at: http://nordicfashionassociation.com/codeofconduct/about (accessed 29 July 2016); European Year for Development. 2015. *Europe in the World: The Garment, Textiles & Fashion Industry*. Available at: https://europa.eu/eyd2015/en/fashion-revolution/posts/europe-world-garment-textiles-and-fashion-industry (accessed 29 July 2016).

49 Bocken, N., Short, S. 2016. Towards a sufficiency-driven business model: Experiences and opportunities. *Environmental Innovation and Societal Transitions*, 18, 41–61.

50 Bocken, N., Short, S. 2016. Towards a sufficiency-driven business model: Experiences and opportunities. *Environmental Innovation and Societal Transitions*, 18, 41–61.

51 Bocken, N.M.P. 2017. Business-led sustainable consumption initiatives: Impacts and lessons learned. *Journal of Management Development*, 36(1), 81–96; Kollmuss, A., Agyeman, J. 2002. Mind the gap: Why do people act environmentally and what are the barriers to pro-environmental behaviour? *Environmental Education Research*, 8(3), 239–260.

52 Schaltegger, S., Hansen, E.G., Lüdeke-Freund, F. 2016. A co-evolutionary analysis of sustainable entrepreneurship, innovation, and transformation. *Organization and the Environment*, 29, 1–26.

53 Creutzig, F., Jochem, P., Edelenbosch, O., Mattauch, L., van Vuuren, D., McCollum, D., Minx, J. 2015. Transport: A roadblock to climate change mitigation? *Science* 350 (6263), 911–912.

54 Creutzig, F., Jochem, P., Edelenbosch, O., Mattauch, L., van Vuuren, D., McCollum, D., Minx, J. 2015. Transport: A roadblock to climate change mitigation? *Science* 350 (6263), 911–912.

55 Creutzig, F., Jochem, P., Edelenbosch, O., Mattauch, L., van Vuuren, D., McCollum, D., Minx, J. 2015. Transport: A roadblock to climate change mitigation? *Science* 350 (6263), 911–912.

56 Kraaijenhagen, C., Van Oppen, C., Bocken. N., 2016. *Circular Business. Collaborate & Circulate. Circular Collaboration*. Amersfoort, The Netherlands. Available at: circularcollaboration.com (accessed 18 July 2018).

57 Bocken, N.M.P. 2017. Business-led sustainable consumption initiatives: Impacts and lessons learned. *Journal of Management Development*, 36(1), 81–96.

58 Kraaijenhagen, C., Van Oppen, C., Bocken. N., 2016. *Circular Business. Collaborate & Circulate. Circular Collaboration*. Amersfoort, The Netherlands. Available at circularcollaboration.com (accessed).

59 MIT Sloan School of Management. 2013. *Robin Chase*. Available at: http://mitsloan.mit.edu/sustainability/profile/robin-chase (accessed 25 July 2016).

60 Chase, R. 2012. *How Technology Enables the Shared Economy*. Available at: www.greenbiz.com/video/2012/05/02/how-technology-enables-shared-economy (accessed 28 July 2016); Bocken, N.M.P. 2017. Business-led sustainable consumption initiatives: Impacts and lessons learned. *Journal of Management Development*, 36(1), 81–96.

61 BlaBla Car (2016a). www.blablacar.com/ (accessed 20 July 2016); BlaBla Car (2016b). *About Us*. Available at: www.blablacar.co.uk/about-us (accessed 20 July 2016); BlaBla Car (2016c). *Reinventing Travel*. Available at: www.blablacar.co.uk/blablalife/reinventing-travel/european-economic-and-social-committee-supports-ridesharing (accessed 25 July 2016).

62 Kahn, J. 2016. *'Airbnb for Cars'. Startup Drivy Gets $35 Million to Expand*. Bloomberg Technology, 28 April 2016. Available at: www.bloomberg.com/news/articles/2016–04–28/-airbnb-for-cars-startup-drivy-gets-35-million-to-expand (accessed 25 July 2016).

63 Tobias Schwarz's Logbook. 2016. Drivy Founder Paulin Dementhon: "Berlin is Quite Unique Worldwide". 4 December 2014. Available at: http://isarmatrose.com/?p=4126 (accessed 25 July 2016).

64 ZipCar. 2016. Car Hire Made Simple. Available at: www.zipcar.co.uk/what-is-zipcar (accessed 25 July 2016).

65 BlaBlaCar. 2017. www.blablacar.nl/ (accessed 30 April 2017).
66 MIT Sloan School of Management. 2013. *Robin Chase*. Available at: http://mitsloan.mit.edu/sustainability/profile/robin-chase (accessed 25 July 2016).
67 Tobias Schwarz's Logbook. 2016. Drivy Founder Paulin Dementhon: "Berlin is Quite Unique Worldwide". 4 December 2014. Available at: http://isarmatrose.com/?p=4126 (accessed 25 July 2016).
68 Dargay, J., Gately, D., Sommer, M. 2007. Vehicle ownership and income growth, worldwide: 1960–2030. *The Energy Journal*, 28(4), 143–170.
69 Creutzig, F., Jochem, P., Edelenbosch, O., Mattauch, L., van Vuuren, D., McCollum, D., Minx, J. 2015. Transport: A roadblock to climate change mitigation? *Science* 350 (6263), 911–912.
70 Bocken, N., Short, S. 2016. Towards a sufficiency-driven business model: Experiences and opportunities. *Environmental Innovation and Societal Transitions*, 18, 41–61.
71 Bocken, N., Short, S. 2016. Towards a sufficiency-driven business model: Experiences and opportunities. *Environmental Innovation and Societal Transitions*, 18, 41–61.
72 Bocken, N.M.P. 2017. Business-led sustainable consumption initiatives: Impacts and lessons learned. *Journal of Management Development*, 36(1), 81–96; Kollmuss, A., Agyeman, J. 2002. Mind the gap: Why do people act environmentally and what are the barriers to pro-environmental behaviour? *Environmental Education Research*, 8(3), 239–260.
73 Schaltegger, S., Hansen, E.G., Lüdeke-Freund, F. 2016. A co-evolutionary analysis of sustainable entrepreneurship, innovation, and transformation. *Organization and the Environment*, 29, 1–26.
74 Allwood, J., Ellebæk Laursen, S., Malvido de Rodríguez, C., Bocken, N. 2006. *Well Dressed? The Present and Future Sustainability of Clothing and Textiles in the United Kingdom*. University of Cambridge, Institute for Manufacturing, Cambridge, UK.
75 WRAP. 2012. *Valuing Our Clothes*. Available at: www.wrap.org.uk/sites/files/wrap/VoC%20FINAL%20online%202012%2007%2011.pdf (accessed 24 May 2016).
76 Allwood, J., Ellebæk Laursen, S., Malvido de Rodríguez, C., Bocken, N. 2006. *Well Dressed? The Present and Future Sustainability of Clothing and Textiles in the United Kingdom*. University of Cambridge, Institute for Manufacturing, Cambridge, UK.
77 Kant Hvass, K. 2014. Post-retail responsibility of garments – a fashion industry perspective. *Journal of Fashion Marketing and Management*, 18(4), 413–430.
78 WRAP. 2016. *Benefits of Reuse Case Study: Clothing*. Available at: www.wrap.org.uk/sites/files/wrap/Clothing%20reuse_final.pdf (accessed 26 July 2016).
79 Davidi, A. 2014. *How Girl Meets Dress is Capitalising on the Demise of Ownership*. Available at: www.theguardian.com/media-network/media-network-blog/2014/jun/11/girl-meets-dress-anna-bance (accessed 2 August 2016).
80 We Started This. 2017. *We Started This / Second Hand Online*. Available at: http://wst.fi/ (accessed 24 April 2017).
81 H&M. 2016. *Garment Collecting*. Available at: http://about.hm.com/en/About/sustainability/commitments/reduce-waste/garment-collecting.html (accessed 25 July 2016).
82 Marks and Spencer plc. 2015. *Shwopping*. Available at: https://corporate.marksandspencer.com/plan-a/our-stories/about-our-initiatives/shwopping (accessed 2 August 2016).
83 Hvass, K. 2015. Business model innovation through second hand retailing: A fashion industry case. *Journal of Corporate Citizenship*, 57(22), 11–32; Bocken, N., Short, S. 2016. Towards a sufficiency-driven business model: Experiences and opportunities. *Environmental Innovation and Societal Transitions*, 18, 41–61.
84 Kant Hvass, K. 2015. Business model innovation through second hand retailing: A fashion industry case. *Journal of Corporate Citizenship*, 57(22), 11–32.
85 Kant Hvass, K. 2015. Business model innovation through second hand retailing: A fashion industry case. *Journal of Corporate Citizenship*, 57(22), 11–32.
86 Patagonia. 2016. *Environmental and Social Responsibility*. Available at: http://eu.patagonia.com/enGB/common-threads/ (accessed 25 July 2016); Bocken, N., Short, S. 2016. Towards a sufficiency-driven business model: Experiences and opportunities. *Environmental Innovation and Societal Transitions*, 18, 41–61.
87 Kant Hvass, K. 2015. Business model innovation through second hand retailing: A fashion industry case. *Journal of Corporate Citizenship*, 57(22), 11–32.

88 Turula, T. 2016. *These Startups Are Helping H&M to Envision a Circular Fashion Industry.* Available at: http://nordic.businessinsider.com/this-is-how-hm-relies-on-startups-to-build-a-smarter-future-for-the-dirtiest-industry-in-the-world-after-oil-2016-11/ (accessed 26 April 2017).
89 Bocken, N., Short, S. 2016. Towards a sufficiency-driven business model: Experiences and opportunities. *Environmental Innovation and Societal Transitions*, 18, 41–61.
90 thredUP. 2016. *About thredUP.* Available at: www.thredup.com/about (accessed 26 July 2016).
91 Turula, T. 2016. These Startups Are Helping H&M to Envision a Circular Fashion Industry. Available at: http://nordic.businessinsider.com/this-is-how-hm-relies-on-startups-to-build-a-smarter-future-for-the-dirtiest-industry-in-the-world-after-oil-2016-11/ (accessed 26 April 2017).
92 LENA Fashion Library. Available at: www.lena-library.com/ (accessed 23 April 2017).
93 Jänecke, M. 2017. *Technical Textiles & Nonwovens: A Global Market Overview.* Available at: https://techtextil-russia.ru.messefrankfurt.com/content/dam/techtextilrussia/ttr_2016_files/presentations2016/World%20Techtextil%20Market%20Michael%20Janecke.pdf (accessed 23 April 2017).
94 Patagonia. 2017. Worn Wear website. Available at: http://www.patagonia.com/worn-wear.html (accessed 24 April 2017).
95 Bocken, N.M.P., Weissbrod, I., Tennant, M. 2016. *Business Model Experimentation for Sustainability.* Sustainable Design & Manufacturing Conference, Crete, Greece, 4–6 April 2016.
96 Bocken, N., Short, S. 2016. Towards a sufficiency-driven business model: Experiences and opportunities. *Environmental Innovation and Societal Transitions*, 18, 41–61.
97 Bocken, N., Short, S. 2016. Towards a sufficiency-driven business model: Experiences and opportunities. *Environmental Innovation and Societal Transitions*, 18, 41–61.
98 Bocken, N.M.P. 2017. Business-led sustainable consumption initiatives: Impacts and lessons learned. *Journal of Management Development*, 36(1), 81–96; Kollmuss, A., Agyeman, J. 2002. Mind the gap: Why do people act environmentally and what are the barriers to pro-environmental behaviour? *Environmental Education Research*, 8(3), 239–260.
99 Schaltegger, S., Hansen, E.G., Lüdeke-Freund, F. 2016. A co-evolutionary analysis of sustainable entrepreneurship, innovation, and transformation. *Organization and the Environment*, 29, 1–26.
100 Levi Strauss & Co. 2012. Available at: http://store.levi.com/waterless/ (accessed 2 August 2016).
101 Patagionia. 2016. *Recycled Polyester.* Available at: www.patagonia.com/recycled-polyester.html (accessed 2 August 2016); ReBlend. 2016. *About Us.* Available at: www.reblend.nl/about-us/ (accessed 2 August 2016).
102 PUMA. 2010. *PUMA's Environmental Profit and Loss Account for the Year Ended 31 December 2010.* Available at: http://about.puma.com/damfiles/default/sustainability/environment/e-p-l/EPL080212final-3cdfc1bdca0821c6ec1cf4b89935bb5f.pdf (accessed 2 August 2016).
103 Kant Hvass, K. 2015. Business model innovation through second hand retailing: A fashion industry case. *Journal of Corporate Citizenship*, 57 (22), 11–32.
104 Hockerts, K., Wüstenhagen, R. 2010. Greening Goliaths versus emerging Davids: Theorizing about the role of incumbents and new entrants in sustainable entrepreneurship. *Journal of Business Venturing*, 25(5), 481–492.
105 Bocken, N., Short, S. 2016. Towards a sufficiency-driven business model: Experiences and opportunities. *Environmental Innovation and Societal Transitions*, 18, 41–61.
106 Bocken, N., Short, S. 2016. Towards a sufficiency-driven business model: Experiences and opportunities. *Environmental Innovation and Societal Transitions*, 18, 41–61.
107 Bocken, N.M.P. 2017. Business-led sustainable consumption initiatives: Impacts and lessons learned. *Journal of Management Development*, 36 (1), 81–96; Kollmuss, A., Agyeman, J. 2002. Mind the gap: Why do people act environmentally and what are the barriers to pro-environmental behaviour? *Environmental Education Research*, 8 (3), 239–260.
108 Schaltegger, S., Hansen, E.G., Lüdeke-Freund, F. 2016. A co-evolutionary analysis of sustainable entrepreneurship, innovation, and transformation. *Organization and the Environment*, 29, 1–26.
109 Weissbrod, I., Bocken, N. 2017. Developing sustainable business experimentation capability: A case study. *Journal of Cleaner Production*, 142, Part 4, 2663–2676.

110 Kollmuss, A., Agyeman, J. 2002. Mind the gap: Why do people act environmentally and what are the barriers to pro-environmental behaviour? *Environmental Education Research*, 8(3), 239–260.

111 Young, W., Hwang, K., McDonald, S., Oates, C. 2010. Sustainable consumption: Green consumer behavior when purchasing products. *Sustainable Development*, 18, 20–31.

112 Druckman, A., Chitnis, M., Sorrell, S., Jackson, T. 2011. Missing carbon reductions? Exploring rebound and backfire effects in UK households. *Energy Policy*, 39, 3572–3581.

113 PUMA. 2010. *PUMA's Environmental Profit and Loss Account for the Year Ended 31 December 2010*. Available at: http://about.puma.com/damfiles/default/sustainability/environment/e-p-l/EPL080212final-3cdfc1bdca0821c6ec1cf4b89935bb5f.pdf (accessed 2 August 2016).

114 Clift, R., Sim, S., Sinclair, P. 2013. Sustainable consumption and production: quality, luxury and supply chain equity. In: *Treatise in Sustainability Science and Engineering*. (Ed. I.S. Jawahir, S. Sikhdar and Y. Huang). Dordrecht, the Netherlands, Springer Publishers.

115 IEA. 2016. *Decoupling of Global Emissions and Economic Growth Confirmed*. Available at: www.iea.org/newsroomandevents/pressreleases/2016/march/decoupling-of-global-emissions-and-economic-growth-confirmed.html (accessed 28 July 2016).

2.3 Enacting sustainable entrepreneurial action for a circular economy

Melissa Edwards, Suzanne Benn, Tamsin Angus-Leppan, and Robert Perey

Introduction

In recent times, there have been increasing pressures on businesses arising from resource scarcity, commodity insecurities and waste (Lieder and Rashid, 2016). There is evidence that industrial processes have already breached several planetary boundaries (Steffen et al., 2015) and that this poses a challenge for business leaders to consider their impacts through adoption of systems thinking (Whiteman et al., 2013; Perey et al., forthcoming). Simultaneously, a projected further three billion middle-class consumers will enter the market by 2030 (Nguyen et al., 2014). Trends project upward material consumption growth per capita (Fridolin et al., 1989), and even moderate United Nations scenarios indicate that such continued upward population and consumption trends means that the equivalent of two Earths will be needed to support the human resource demand and absorption of its wastes (Footprint, 2014). In addition to these growth trends, as global supply chains become more complex and dispersed, material leakages, whereby materials are wasted in the supply chain, persist. Consequently, waste is being produced at a rate far beyond what can be absorbed or recycled by the Earth's ecological systems (WWF, 2015).

As tensions between rising consumption demands and resource usage intensify, innovative resource management approaches will become more significant for business. One such model is the Circular Economy (CE), which proposes a systemic redesign of production and consumption systems and a reconceptualization of waste as a resource to fulfil growing consumption demands within biospheric bounds. Blomsma and Brennan (2017) highlight how the CE acts as an 'umbrella concept' that synthesizes previous schools of thought to provide a new cognitive unit and discursive space to reimagine waste and resource management. Bocken and colleagues (2016) define the CE as slowing, closing and narrowing resource loops, and it therefore provides one archetype among other sustainable business models (Bocken, 2014). Such systemic approaches extend beyond the action of individuals and organizations. According to a recent EU communiqué, transition to a CE requires 'innovation not only in technologies, but also in organization, society, finance methods and policies' (EU, 2014). Systemic change of this magnitude may provoke opportunities for sustainable entrepreneurial action to create and take up business activities that incorporate CE principles.

Entrepreneurial action takes an evolutionary, process-based perspective to determine how opportunities emerge and are enacted between humans coordinating action within economic systems (Alvarez and Barney, 2013 [2007]). Such an approach has been under-examined in the context of sustainable entrepreneurship where the dominant focus has been on the characteristics of the entrepreneur or their enterprise. Sustainable entrepreneurial action extends this evolutionary approach to understand how novel and innovative actions emerge that are economically feasible, while also being regenerative of Earth and social systems. The CE provides one such systems-level model that could create opportunities to provoke sustainable entrepreneurial action. At the same time, the CE is an 'idealized' sustainable model, not yet materialized, that provides a novel framework through which an entrepreneur may envision, catalyze and enact sustainable business opportunities. It is juxtaposed against the dominant linear economy that overly frames entrepreneurial action through an economic viability approach. The research gap here is to discover how sustainable entrepreneurial actions may enable emergence of a CE.

In this chapter, findings of an exploratory qualitative study[1] are synthesized. We take an interpretative approach to analyze how sustainable entrepreneurial actions enable the emergence and enactment of a CE model. Creating and enacting a CE model is catalyzed by individuals harnessing systemic CE principles as a form of sustainable entrepreneurial action. These individuals may be catalysts as intrapreneurs (Pinchot, 1985), creating business development in large multi-national enterprises (MNCs) or as entrepreneurs, creating new ventures in existing or as new small- and medium-sized enterprises (SMEs). While the structural conditions may be different, and entrepreneurs may possess a greater proclivity toward risk (Stewart et al., 1999), in the nascent CE context, we view such individuals as similar types of ecopreneurs (Schaper, 2010) and seek to understand how they envision and catalyze sustainable entrepreneurial action by adopting systemic CE principles in their business activities. The chapter commences by unpacking how an 'idealized' CE model is enacted through sustainable entrepreneurial action to answer the research question: how do individuals envision and enact opportunities for sustainable entrepreneurial action using systemic CE principles, when the systemic conditions for a CE model are not the dominant economic model? Firstly, we synthesize the sustainable entrepreneurship and entrepreneurial action literature to conceptualize sustainable entrepreneurial action. Secondly, key systemic principles of the CE model are highlighted as setting the opportunity context in which sustainable entrepreneurial actions emerge. Key insights from the qualitative study are discussed to explore how sustainable entrepreneurial action is being catalyzed and enacted to enable the emergence of the CE model.

Sustainable entrepreneurial action and the CE

Sustainable entrepreneurship is a form of action to address market failures and enable market opportunities that generate net positive benefits for environment, society and the economy (Cohen and Winn, 2007; Dean and McMullen, 2007). At least two prominent lines of research have emerged in this nascent field: one which emphasizes attainment of sustainable development and the triple bottom line (TBL) through entrepreneurial activities, and another which focuses on sustainability in the process of entrepreneurship at the nexus of individuals and opportunities (Beltz and Binder, 2017). We build on the latter view which defines sustainable entrepreneurship as: 'the recognition, development and exploitation of opportunities by individuals to bring into existence future goods and services with economic, social and ecological gains' (Beltz and Binder, 2017). Therefore, sustainable entrepreneurial action is the evolutionary process occurring when individuals enact opportunities to create 'win-win' solutions through the attainment of a TBL (Elkington, 1997; Cohen and Winn, 2007). Sustainable entrepreneurial action addresses complex sustainability issues through the creation of viable business opportunities which may be conducted in either SME entrepreneurial ventures or within larger organizations.

Some theorists have developed broader, systems-level conceptualizations of sustainable entrepreneurial action (Patzelt and Shepherd, 2011). One such approach specifically focuses on corporate entrepreneurial activities directed toward addressing sustainable development goals (Schaltegger and Wagner, 2011). These approaches extend the definition of sustainable entrepreneurial action as that which is realized through 'the discovery, creation, and exploitation of opportunities to create future goods and services opportunities that sustain the natural and/or communal environment as well as provide development gain for others benefit' (Patzelt and Shepherd, 2011: 632). Through this perspective sustainable entrepreneurial action is directed toward attainment of broader sustainable development aims motivated by altruism for others and a perception that the natural/communal environment is threatened. As an 'ideal' model, the CE is an approach that sets the systems conditions to enable the emergence of opportunities in this broader form of sustainable entrepreneurial action.

An ongoing debate in entrepreneurship studies concerns how entrepreneurial opportunities emerge or are created. Some focus on the entrepreneurs as individuals who uncover opportunities (Shane and Venkataraman, 2000), while others frame opportunities as emerging from complex interactions within production and consumption systems (Sarasvathy, 2001; Lichtenstein, 2011). Regardless, it is widely agreed that in process-based models, opportunities represent the initiation of entrepreneurial action (Alvarez and Barney, 2007; Moroz and Hindle, 2012). Entrepreneurial action through an evolutionary perspective focuses on the emergent processes occurring when individuals interact within production and consumption systems. Therefore, of significance is how an individual perceives and relates to the mechanisms, structural characteristics and interactions between other individuals, as they act as the catalyst for enabling entrepreneurial action within systems.

Evolutionary perspectives therefore encompass the social constructivist view of creation, such as those outlined in the effectuation perspective (Sarasvathy, 2001) where action is contingent upon the individual's cognitive logic of perceiving and acting on opportunities despite knowing the certainty of outcomes. Alvarez and Barney (2013) describe evolutionary entrepreneurial action processes as complex, messy and non-linear that are both path-dependent (structurally conditioned) and emergent. Adopting this evolutionary perspective in the sustainable entrepreneurship field opens the analytical lens to consider how entrepreneurial action enables the emergence of the CE model. CE principles provide opportunities, but the CE model is an 'ideal type' that is not structurally present. Just as the idealized CE model inspires opportunities for sustainable entrepreneurial action, such action iteratively creates the emergence of a CE. Such an evolutionary process-based view therefore allows consideration of the 'lived experiences' of those enabling the emergence of the CE model.

CE as context for entrepreneurial opportunities

A CE model is a 'restorative' alternative to the dominant linear 'take, make, consume and dispose' logic embedded in neoclassical economics. Andersen (2007) outlines how neoclassical economics values the utility of the environment in terms of human welfare. In this linear model, the environment is considered in amenity terms, as being a resource base for the economy, or as a sink for residual flows, or as a life support system. The environment has been undervalued as being a sink or life support system as these amenities are framed as externalities. As a resource base, a linear approach assumes infinite extraction. The CE model reveals opportunities to revalue the environment through the creation of products and services that optimize the entire value chain on the logic of 'take, make and re-create' (EMF 2013/2014; EU 2014; Webster 2013). Production and consumption systems should have a net positive effect on the environment (Murray et al., 2017), and certain resources and materials are valued as being limited and/or finite. CE opportunities arise beyond a recycling logic, to reduce, reuse and recirculate, and where appropriate, redesign processes and materials for renewability (Ghisellini et al., 2016). The CE model is 'a regenerative system in which resource input and waste, emission, and energy leakage are minimized by slowing, closing, and narrowing material and energy loops' (Geissdoerfer et al., 2017). The challenge for entrepreneurship is profound as opportunities arise 'throughout value chains, from product design to new business and market models, from new ways of turning waste into a resource to new modes of consumer behaviour' (EU, 2014).

Conceptually, the CE model is interpreted as an 'ideal type', a hypothetical, abstract construction that provides a vision for new economic systems, new opportunities for entrepreneurial action that can be business driven. This business-driven approach is especially important in economies where CE initiatives are largely producer-led. In some countries, the drive for a CE model has been facilitated by policy-driven initiatives, for example in Europe (see, EC, 2015) and China (see Yuan et al., 2006; Mathews and Tan, 2011). Policy is in a nascent form in countries such as Australia, and therefore adoption of a CE model is principle driven, providing impetus for the design of innovative business practices. Design plays a critical role both in product design (through design for disassembly) and in redesigning business models (Giurco et al., 2014) but also in designing systems to optimize flows. In this section, we focus on the latter two and the potential opportunities they provide for sustainable entrepreneurial action.

Optimizing systems flows as opportunities for entrepreneurial action

Rather than providing a cohesive or formulaic model, CE principles related to systems flows prompt revitalized thinking about consumption and production systems as a series of restorative and regenerative industrial and biological systems (Hobson, 2016) designed to optimize material, information, human and energy flows (Webster, 2013). Material flows are separated into technical and ecological nutrients, or otherwise termed as durable and consumable (Nguyen et al., 2014). A guiding rationale of the CE model is that ecological nutrients should return to the biosphere with a net restorative impact, and technical nutrients should be used such that they are circulated for longer (i.e. products that are built to last) or designed into products in such a way that they can be repaired, reused, remanufactured or recycled at the end of life. Wherever possible, sustainable materials such as those which are compostable, biodegradable, renewable or non-toxic are introduced or substituted into supply chains.

Another key systems flow principle is borrowed from industrial ecology whereby waste from one organization may be considered an input for another (Frosch and Gallopoulos, 1989). Such revaluing of waste demands materials be valued across their lifespan as flows rather than stocks, and this requires cooperation between entities across an entire supply chain (Spekman et al., 1998), which is known as responsible supply chain management (Giurco et al., 2014). In open supply chains, a circular waste flow can be valued as a resource, but this requires greater alignment, integration and coordination of business practices and fostering of more sophisticated relationships with key stakeholders, particularly customers, suppliers and partners (Tsvetkova and Gustafsson, 2012).

For example, the dynamic between customer value creation and business value creation shifts as products may now be offered as services (Stahel, 2006) with the nexus being governed by service contracts rather than sales and guarantees. Thereby, a CE model provides opportunities for entrepreneurial action to generate new forms of value creation that move away 'from generating profits from selling artefacts, to generating profits from the flow of materials and products over time' (Bocken et al., 2016: 3), which in turn impact their interaction with stakeholders across their supply chains.

Opportunities for redesigning business models

Redesigning business models to enable transition to a CE is a key opportunity. Lacy and Rutqvist (2015) have identified at least five different business models to transition to a CE. These have been categorized as circular supply chain, recovery and recycling, product life-extension, sharing platform and product as service. In each of these models, actions are required beyond the individual business model.

Conceptualizing entrepreneurial opportunities as action directed toward enacting a CE beyond the bounds of any one organization, is mirrored in the sustainable business literature. There have been calls to move beyond *business sustainability* to *business for sustainability* (Schaltegger et al., 2012), Business 3.0 (Dyllick and Muff, 2015) or the 'ideal corporation' (Benn et al., 2014). Sustainable business models are often conceptualized as continuums, typologies, archetypes or developmental frameworks (Hunt and Auster, 1990; Roome, 1992; Winn and Angell, 2000; Maon et al., 2009; Schaltegger et al., 2012; Benn et al., 2014; Bocken et al., 2014). According to these approaches, sustainable enterprises are directed toward outcomes, guided by the intention to contribute to the solution of societal and environmental problems. A number of these models differentiate between 'efficiency' and 'proactive' or 'strategic sustainability' approaches where the former is focused on cost minimization while the latter integrates sustainability into core business logic. Innovation and entrepreneurship are key characteristics required for strategic approaches such that business models can be redesigned.

A recent addition to phase and stage models has been proposed by Bocken and colleagues (2016) to capture business model strategies along a continuum spanning two broad categories from slowing loops (pursuing efficiency approaches such as reuse and restoration) through to closing loops (designing processes to enable circular flows such as recycling and remanufacturing). Ghisellini and colleagues (2016) demonstrate how the CE is generative of new business models strongly connected to sustainable development, and Sauvé and colleagues (2016) note the CE offers a set of tools to operationalize the promise of sustainable development. Similarly, sustainable entrepreneurial action for enacting a CE may incorporate a variety of different approaches.

Following the broader approaches taken by Patzelt and Shepherd (2011) and Schaltegger and Wagner (2011), we propose the CE model enables opportunities for sustainable entrepreneurial action directed toward addressing systemic-level concerns particularly related to materials scarcity. Examples of such opportunities include addressing market failures (Andersen, 2007) by valuing waste as a resource or internalizing the true costs of externalities, or by educating or advocating for the introduction of new materials or processes across a value chain. Innovative materials management and new business models that rely on collaboration between stakeholders are foundational to the CE model and could extend 'win-win' outcomes beyond the TBL of any one business.

Methodology

Because this work was exploratory, a qualitative and grounded research design (Strauss and Corbin, 1994) was adopted. A sample of ten business owners or sustainability officers was selected taking the broad view of sustainable entrepreneurial action. This view encompasses systemic approaches to addressing complex issues (Schaltegger and Wagner, 2011) and considers how catalysts envision and enact action as being both intrapreneurs in MNCs and entrepreneurs associated with SMEs. Sampled individuals were known to the research team as being responsible for the implementation and design of CE businesses practices. They typified individuals who had envisioned and enacted CE opportunities through sustainable entrepreneurial action that involved taking action beyond the bounds of their individual enterprise. Questions were designed to discover how they enacted CE principles, through the recycling, remanufacturing, reuse, redistribution or maintaining of the longevity of material resources in the production and/or consumption cycles (we termed this 'circularity practices'). One hour-long semi-structured interviews were recorded and transcribed verbatim, allowing the interviewers to concentrate on questioning and listening, to provide an accurate record (Saunders et al., 2003). We also sought secondary data for each business in the form of reports, newsletters and other forms of publicly available information. Table 2.3.1 contains a list of the pseudonyms used to represent these businesses, their industry sector and company size, and the main ways in which we identified that 'circularity practices' were being enacted.

We analyzed the interview transcripts through computer-aided textual analysis using the standard 'discovery' mode in Leximancer (Leximancer, 2005). The transcripts were analyzed using conceptual and relational content analysis. Content analysis is a research technique for breaking down text into categories based on explicit rules of coding (Krippendorff, 2004). Conceptual analysis, the most common form of content analysis, involves the detection of explicit and implicit concepts in the text. Relational analysis considers the relationships between concepts. Leximancer was used to add reliability by using machine learning to automatically and entirely code the text rather than using the researcher's interpretations to do so (Gephart, 2004; Smith and Humphries, 2006). Leximancer provides an overview of the cognitive structure of the interview data, thereby revealing how CE entrepreneurs were developing actions in relation to the CE opportunities. The discovery mode Leximancer map is an overview of the cognitive structure and content of the data. Figure 2.3.1 shows the discovery mode Leximancer map for the transcripts for all ten interviews.

Themes are groupings of concepts. The theme is named according to the most frequently occurring concept within the theme. Ten theme circles are visible. The more predominant the theme, the 'hotter' is the colour of the theme circle. The ten themes, in ranked order, are: 'tension', 'money', 'recycled', 'interesting', 'change', 'design', 'packaging', 'competitors', 'research' and 'paradox'. The themes are sprinkled with 'concepts' and speaker tags. There is an especially large spatial separation and hence diversity between speaker tags belonging to interviews with large MNCs in the top half of the map (e.g. 'Logistics' and 'Recycler 1') and entrepreneurial SMEs in the bottom half of the map (e.g. 'Nappies', 'Sharers' and 'Makers').

Looking next at the overall content of the map, two streams of discussion can be seen: the highly-populated stream at the top half of the Leximancer map that centres on the 'tension' around making stewardship work in the current system, particularly around recycling, and the less populated stream on the bottom half of the map centered on

Table 2.3.1 Company list by company type, participant, purpose in the CE and key circularity practices

Name	*Type*	*Interviewee*	*Business Purpose*	*Circularity practice*
Makers	SME	Co-Founder	Digital fabrication and design. Shared makers space, reuse and recycle materials.	Adopts 3D printing for prototyping to reduce waste. Reuses wasted materials.
Nappies	SME	CEO	Children's wear, non-durable consumer goods. Compostable materials and recirculate materials.	Evaluated the life cycle of their product. Developed a closed loop system to compost nappy inserts. Outer layer of the nappy is durable and can be recirculated. Has B Corp certification and is a member of the EMF CE100.
Sharers	SME	Co-Founder	Sharing platform and logistics. Recirculation of materials, extending product life, using idle capacity in logistics value chain.	The sharing platform enables goods to be recirculated. The logistics component provides cost effective transport by using smart technology to freight products in the idle capacity of courier vans. Has B Corp certification.
Remanufacturers	MNC	Eco Manufacturing Ops Manager	Office equipment production and distribution – multinational. Provider/supplier of printers and photocopiers	Industrial symbiosis strategy implemented has successfully created a new and highly collaborative supply chain designed to prioritize revaluation of waste.
Recycler 1	SME	National Sales and Marketing Manager	Waste management. Provides service eliminating waste from restaurant food packaging including all food and packaging from restaurant and cafeteria practices to zero.	Life cycle processes from ordering products and services, to the disposal of wastes from their client operations. Solutions include: installation of bio-digesters to create compost, then given or sold; and reducing excess and inappropriate food packaging and providing biodegradable alternatives.

(continued)

Table 2.3.1 (continued)

Name	*Type*	*Interviewee*	*Business Purpose*	*Circularity practice*
Recycler 2	SME	Managing Director	Waste management – national. Collects and processes used toner cartridges for reuse or repurposing.	Evaluated product life cycle (toner cartridges) and created new waste collector relationships between their manufacturer and customers. Used cartridges collected and recycled or remanufactured. When degraded at end of life, it is shredded into constituent parts and sold as raw materials.
Logistics	MNC	General Manager	Logistics – management and delivery – multinational. Provides warehousing and logistics services.	Outsources operations of organizations to manage the warehousing of products at a cheaper and more convenient rate through leveraging their logistics operations and expertise. Advise better waste management practices such as reduced packaging. Coordination of government sponsored product stewardship scheme for e-waste.
Designers	SME	Managing Director	Office – national. Textile manufacturer.	Business model is to set up a green value chain that starts with the producers of their raw materials. Involves agreements with farmers to provide organic wool, which is then spun and processed according to an ethical and organic standard. Green value chain involved changing wool broking and processing practices.
Waste	MNC	Senior Business Development Manager	Waste management – multinational. Waste recycler.	Assembles e-waste into raw material streams – sent offshore for remanufacture. Rescues metals and materials for recycling from household and industry waste streams. Coordination of government sponsored product stewardship scheme for e-waste.
Dairy	SME	Managing Director	Dairy products manufacturer.	Organic farm collaborating with organizations such as Recycler 1 to obtain compost to replace urea, an industrially produced fertilizer. Experimenting with their own nutrient production and returning some of their farmland back to pre-colonial bushland. Production process involves recycled packaging, the use of renewable energy and the diversion of waste heat from their machinery to sterilize milk.

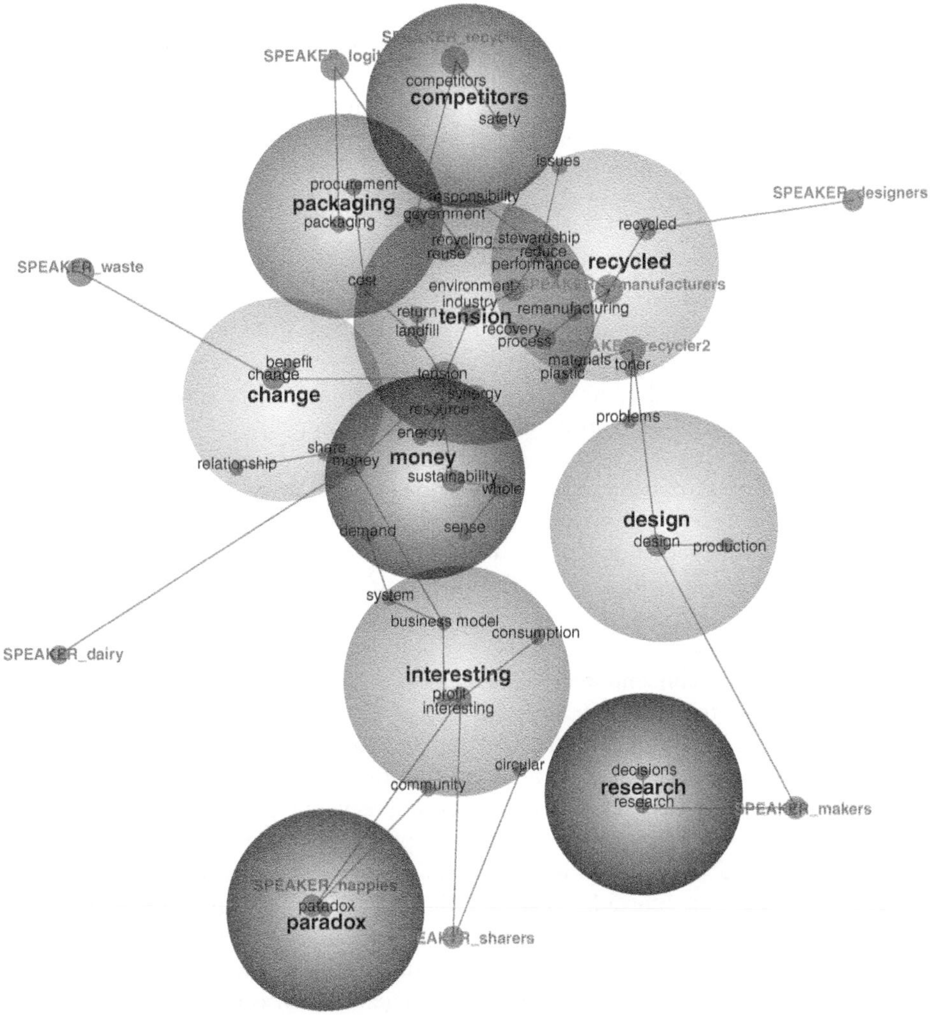

Figure 2.3.1 Leximancer map of interview transcripts (the map is set at default theme size 33%)

'interesting' and 'paradox'. The overall picture presented in Figure 2.3.1 is that organizational leaders perceive the relationship between the CE approach and the linear economy as either beset with issues that are a source of 'tension' or paradoxical challenges that are considered 'interesting'. In the next section, we provide an overview of the further analysis which dived deeper into these themes.

Findings

Turning challenges into opportunities

A key finding of the content analysis related to how entrepreneurs perceived their own abilities to enact opportunities in the CE. The content analysis demonstrated how the entrepreneurs perceived challenges they encountered in 'the system' when seeking CE opportunities. Some had been seeking to implement such initiatives consistent with CE principles while using different terminology. Interviewees discuss seemingly intractable problems, where they sought to implement their CE practices in the linear economy as either beset with issues that are a source of insurmountable 'tension', or challenges that are considered 'interesting'. They either feel stuck in a problem or intrigued by the possibilities presented. Predominantly these concepts co-occurred alongside 'stewardship', 'synergy', 'money' and 'recycling', meaning these were the major sources of either tension or challenge.

'Tension' was the most prevalent reoccurring theme and concept. It arose when entrepreneurs were discussing how they encountered a barrier in the system. Keywords that comprised the 'tension' concept were trying, problem, issue, challenge, challenges, problems, control, political, negative and cynical. These words were used in phrases especially when they described how they were attempting to make stewardship work in the current system, particularly around recycling. For example:

> Weak enforcement of rules and regulations around the processing of waste . . . that's probably one of the biggest issues of the business and it's an external issue that we need to work really hard on. It's not an internal issue that we can control . . . there's days I don't want to do this, it's really difficult. It's very political.
>
> ('Recycler 1')

Additionally, there is concentrated overlap between themes within the concept, for example the theme 'tension' overlaps with five of the nine themes: 'recycled', 'competitors', 'packaging', 'change' and 'money', indicating that these themes are frequently spoken about in the same context as 'tension'. In summary, our data analysis reveals that 'tension' is mostly experienced when implementing recycling practices, that stewardship of products and packaging is complex because responsibility for and distribution of costs and benefits between stakeholders is contested, and that traditional lines of competition and cooperation become blurred. Those working in MNCs were more likely to see the 'tensions' as insurmountable barriers, but SMEs also mentioned them to a lesser extent.

'Tension' is also perceived to come from pressure to make their CE initiatives financially viable. This 'tension' sometimes manifests as a generalized assumption. For example, 'Remanufacturers' remarks that 'everyone wants to be able to recycle things for nothing'. It may arise as the entrepreneurs felt they needed to convince other stakeholders of the likely feasibility of their CE initiatives. As 'Dairy' states:

> [w]e've got a whole section on renewable energy in Sydney . . . I know this project is cash flow positive . . . But it's just – you know, feeling confident and making sure my bankers are comfortable with it.

At other times, this financial pressure is associated with the perception (and assumption) that the government prioritizes the economic over environmental considerations. For example, 'I lost business to competitors that were supported by the state government because they didn't budget to dispose of their glass and I did' ('Recycler 1'). Furthermore, the tension is increased when there is a perceived lack of government support for sustainable businesses: 'I'm sick of dealing with government and especially councils . . . they weren't prepared to share those financial benefits with the businesses that are making the change' ('Waste').

Essentially the perceptions of 'tension' reflected pessimistic views of the problems faced. These quotes talk about 'frustration', feeling 'stuck', 'political', 'really hard'. They are largely 'external issues', 'political', where things are stuck at 'status quo', demonstrating that where tension is perceived, it usually involves external stakeholders, and often government is associated with inertia.

Contrastingly, we found that those SMEs were more likely to see challenges as being 'interesting' and therefore they continued to find ways to implement their work. The concept 'interesting' is used semantically, as in 'the interesting thing is . . .' and 'there's a really interesting piece'. The 'interesting' theme is closely related to the themes 'research' and 'design', all concepts used to describe future opportunity, profits and innovation. Noteworthy is the proximity of the theme 'interesting' to the 'paradox' theme. A challenge viewed as 'interesting' can be perceived paradoxically as one that can be kept open and 'lived with'. Our data indicates that entrepreneurs in these SMEs cope with some challenges encountered when enacting CE opportunities within a linear economy by viewing them as 'interesting'.

What is 'interesting' to interviewees is also sometimes about systemic barriers in their immediate operating environment, but the language used is 'interesting', 'paradox', 'perverse', 'ironically', 'creative', 'disruptive' and 'changes the game'. The quotes reveal creative solutions, breakthroughs in innovation and cooperation, essentially reflecting optimistic views of the problems faced. For example, when 'Nappies' talk about their board being unsupportive of them becoming a 'B Corp', they frame this set back as 'an interesting journey' which led them to recreate their business model. Interviewees express acceptance of the 'interesting' challenges, by finding solutions or 'synergy' demonstrating the creative innovation that results from interesting challenges. For example, 'Sharers' discuss their 'postage solution': they wanted to prioritize the environment and realized this could be achieved through making use of the idle capacity of local courier vans. But they encountered an 'interesting thing' when the postal service was uninterested in the solution because they were stuck in linear thinking. They found an alternate approach by directly approaching couriers and using smart technology to enable the solution, avoiding the barrier of the linear postal service system.

'Interesting' challenges are closely linked in the minds of these entrepreneurs as 'perverse' and 'ironic', leading them to question assumptions they had about how stakeholders would respond and thereby earning their attention and prompting innovation. For example, 'Nappies' talks about how they assumed their board would approve changes in line with being a B Corp and were surprised when the board refused. They fired the board and began looking for alternative funding sources that understood their mission expressed as:

> We are really interested in . . . how do you create products that . . . are regenerative . . . and the paradox is there are some massive financial rewards in innovation.
>
> ('Nappies')

Also, 'interesting' points to instances where entrepreneurs overturn assumptions themselves by, for example, creating unprecedented cooperation between competitors: 'It was interesting, I was able to convince competitors, printer and copier companies who were competitors to cooperate' ('Recycler 2'). Likewise, 'Makers' discusses how competitors helped one another establish new enterprises and initiatives, 'so it's hard for it to be competitive. It's very much about sharing that information. Yeah, because if you don't then we'll all have a hard time. So, it's a joint effort I think'.

Other entrepreneurs ('Recycler 1' and 'Recycler 2') talked about 'changing the game', 'taking a voluntary approach' and 'disrupting the model', when they were describing something as 'interesting'. They created ways to collaborate with MNCs to recycle waste through inventing 'value added reuse for these non-renewable resources (such as plastics)' despite challenges and despite an absence of regulation completing such practices. 'Recycler 1' stated that their predominate aim when working with large MNCs 'is about challenging the status quo to inspire behavioural change. That's our business. That's what we do'. Furthermore, this goal carries through to influence other small stakeholders (such as cleaning contractors, waste contractors and catering contractors) when they are collaborating on large events. They purposefully seek authority from the MNC upper management contracting their services to allow 'Recycler 1' to enforce practices related to waste handling and packaging to all the other contractors.

Essentially, these interviewees creatively developed solutions in order to enact their circularity practices by working with their stakeholders. For example, 'Logistics' tried to exert influence despite a contradiction between their environmental goals and a client's low costs emphasis as regards packaging decisions. The shared meaning between the logistics company and their client is product quality, so the logistics company used the fact that their client's money-saving around packaging was causing 'handling issues and those handling issues are causing issues to your product' to influence the client's packaging decisions. An initial tension between cost and environmental benefits was resolved when a new shared meaning was established that accommodated the supposed trade-off. Across these SME entrepreneurs, embracing the tensions between the economic, social and environmental sustainability dimensions did not imply inaction as waste was built as a resource into their business model.

Another example of this opportunity enactment is evident where entrepreneurs sought to decouple the 'usual' value and meaning attributed to resources and reattach it in different ways. For example, 'Sharers' sought to establish a form of social value creation in the act of giving that might compel consumers to freely share their used and under-utilized material stocks to maintain and recirculate products for longer. This circularity practice came into direct conflict with the linear logic of the dominant economy where materials are valued in monetary terms. In their business model, they purposefully decoupled materials from their monetary valuation and instead attached a social value that could be obtained in the act of giving, rather than trading. Thereby, 'Sharers' collaborated with consumers and facilitated collaboration between consumers to dislocate the value of products from being attributed to ownership to being attributed to sharing.

Essentially, 'interesting' challenges represented instances where entrepreneurial action was directed toward overcoming potential systemic barriers, for innovating their immediate stakeholder relationships to enact new shared means of valuing waste as a resource.

Discussion and future directions

A spectrum of entrepreneurial business models

Insights regarding how individuals made sense of challenges and how they conceptualized waste reveal diverse ways that CE opportunities are enacted through sustainable entrepreneurial action. Similar to the existing categorizations of various sustainable business models, these insights allude to different sustainable entrepreneurship approaches. As outlined earlier, such approaches are common in the sustainable business literature.

Benn et al. (2014), for example, suggest a six phase or progressive sustainable business model, ranging from rejection, through non-responsiveness, through to compliance, efficiency, strategic proactivity and the final phase of the 'ideal' sustainable organization. Such a categorization is useful to discern the different ways that sustainable entrepreneurship is enacted. In particular, three latter phases (efficiency, strategic proactivity and transformation or 'ideal') align with the different ways we found waste valued and allow categorization of the different ways CE opportunities are enacted as insurmountable tensions or interesting challenges (see Table 2.3.2).

Considering waste as a cost typifies an 'efficiency' approach to a sustainable entrepreneurship where the purpose of the action might be directed toward minimizing energy consumption or material waste, but the business driver is to minimize costs and capture more value. This rationale underpins many of the current efficiency frameworks businesses follow, for example, TQM and Lean approaches (Schaltegger et al., 2012; Benn et. al., 2014) and also reflects business practices such as extending product value or encouraging sufficiency that characterize business model strategies for closing loops (Bocken et al., 2016). All of the entrepreneurs interviewed in our study identified a cost saving benefit that came from their CE entrepreneurial action. Perversely, some of the MNCs highlighted that cost was a barrier for them in being able to develop more radical practices for addressing waste.

This was not typical of the SMEs, who were more likely to engage in forms of action to reconceptualize waste as being a resource within their close supply network relationships. Their capacity to intentionally design new practices to make productive use of 'waste' was a key feature of their business. When waste was reconceptualized as a resource, incorporating CE (Andersen, 2007) influences on their business practices aligned the organization with the 'strategic proactivity' sustainable business phase (Benn et al., 2014), or Bocken and colleagues' (2016) business model strategies for closing and slowing loops. Such sustainable entrepreneurship is more likely to be driven by a purpose to address resource scarcity, often seen in moral terms.

In several instances, we found radical forms of entrepreneurial action akin to the systems approach to sustainable entrepreneurship (Patzelt and Shepherd, 2011). Both SMEs and MNCs were engaged in such forms of entrepreneurial action where they envisioned and enacted approaches to design waste out of consumption and production systems.

Table 2.3.2 Categorization of CE sustainable business models

Sustainable business category	*Entrepreneurial approach*	*Concept of waste*
Efficiency	Circularity as a means for more effective usage of materials or secure supply.	Waste as a burden. Cost reduction sought through waste management.
Strategic proactivity	Circularity as core purpose for value capture and creation in a set of close stakeholder relationships.	Waste as a resource. Revalue waste streams.
Sustainable transformation	Create positive feedback loops in the system of stakeholder relationships to optimize circular flows.	Design waste out of the system.

Such approaches entail a more radical reconceptualization of value creation, which is similar to the 'sustainable transformation' or 'ideal organization' phase (Benn et al., 2014). For example, some forms of action were enacted to decouple economic value from material value, such that new forms of social value could be attached to products so they might remain in productive use through being restored and recirculated in the system, or where production and consumption systems were designed with regenerative loops such that waste was food. Such approaches were associated with a heightened sense of the importance of collaboration with a series of stakeholders within the value network.

Sustainable entrepreneurship and systems business models

Cohen and colleagues (2008) encouraged the focus of entrepreneurial studies to go beyond the focus on economic outcomes. Their inclusive typology highlights the various different forms of value creation enabled through entrepreneurial action. In support of this work, we found environmental value creation was most significant in relation to the CE opportunities especially in relation to reconceptualizing waste and reconsidering waste and material flows in supply networks. Specifically, entrepreneurs created opportunities through sustainable innovation, eco-efficiency (innovative materials usages, renewable energy and green procurement), perpetuity (life cycle analysis and product design, waste management), and stewardship (recycling, reuse and remanufacture of materials, designing out waste). The latter were more challenging for MNEs than SMEs who were more likely to see challenges as opportunities to change the game.

When entrepreneurs seek sustainable transformation through CE opportunities, they encounter challenges arising between their business activities and their operating systems, particularly in relation to establishing financial viability and clashes with government policy that were designed to incentivize a linear economy. Sustainable entrepreneurial action was more likely to occur when such challenges were viewed as 'interesting', being instances where the 'rules of the game' could be changed and new collaborative arrangements for shared meaning making could be enacted. Entrepreneurial action was enacted when systems thinking led to collaboration between stakeholders to reconceptualize or design out waste and to revalue materials so that a regenerative logic might prevail. In this way, the CE model could be understood as a 'break-through' innovation (Schaltegger and Wagner, 2011) that enabled sustainable entrepreneurial opportunities to be enacted.

Significant break-through innovation occurred when the entrepreneurial action process was directed toward reinventing stakeholder relationships guided by systems thinking. This was carried by implementing CE principles aimed at optimizing material flows within systems, thereby considering optimization of the system over and above the component parts, or their individual business outcomes. Recent studies have begun to develop business models for sustainability from a systems dynamic perspective (Abdelkafi and Täuscher, 2016) in which the values, beliefs and norms of the people in the system are a dynamic antecedent. We found evidence of positive reinforcing feedback loops in the entrepreneurial action enacted by the SMEs in particular. This occurred when tensions were framed as 'interesting' challenges to be overcome through developing favourable relationships with their stakeholders to change consumer behaviour, or co-create ways to circulate materials flows, or intentionally design waste out of the system. In these instances, the enacted entrepreneurial action to 'change the game' was driven by the positive feedback loops between the business, customers and suppliers to preserve material flows or restore the natural environment. In several cases, a new form of certification that signified their 'purpose-driven' approach (the B Corp certification) was a fundamental signifier. While the values may be specifically environmental, they are only realized through innovative social interactions where entrepreneurs challenge the status quo of a 'business as usual' approach.

Conclusions

As an idealized economic model premised on restorative design and circular flows, the CE promises opportunities for sustainable entrepreneurial action to address the conflicting demands of a growing consumer base and increasingly restricted resources. Where there is a deficit of policy or economic incentives, the entrepreneurial action process may encounter tensions when seeking to develop new business models that rely on a system of circular material, information and energy flows. This is especially challenging in relation to attaining financial viability and aligning with stakeholders who understand the value of a CE such that stewardship approaches can be realized. Moving the economy to operate on circular flows requires business models, design innovations (Bocken et al., 2016) and application of systems thinking. Entrepreneurial action processes to enable these are most likely facilitated when entrepreneurs overcome tensions that are encountered when business activities challenge the status quo of the dominant linear economy.

Such opportunities are more likely to be enacted when sustainable entrepreneurial action operates to drive innovation in between organizations and their stakeholders with a collaborative aim to optimize material flows and design waste out of production and consumption systems. This chapter uncovered that entrepreneurs acting as catalysts were inspired by CE principles and when encountering barriers, opportunistically reframed these as interesting challenges. Synergistic relationships between individuals in SMEs and MNCs catalyzed sustainable entrepreneurial action to enable the emergence of a CE. Such sustainable entrepreneurship is most likely enacted through CE practices in SMEs, and a shift to a CE may be highly dependent upon the actions of purpose-based business models, such as B Corps, underpinned by a transformative mission toward a sustainable society. However, intrapreneurs working in MNCs should not be forgotten, as their actions to collaborate with SMEs and embed break-through innovations within MNCs may possibly expedite the transition to a CE. The characteristics of the relationships between SMEs and MNCs as either working collaboratively with or seeking to disrupt the business models of the larger MNCs deserves further investigation. This area is somewhat contested in the literature and could be clarified by further research.

Note

1 This research was undertaken as part of the Wealth from Waste Cluster, a collaborative research program between the Australian Commonwealth Scientific and Industrial Research Organization (CSIRO); University of Technology Sydney; The University of Queensland, Swinburne University of Technology, Monash University and Yale University. The authors gratefully acknowledge the contribution from each partner and the CSIRO Flagship Collaboration Fund. The Wealth from Waste Cluster is a part of the Mineral Resources National Research Flagship and is supported by the Manufacturing National Research Flagship.

References

Abdelkafi, N. and Täuscher, K. (2016). Business models for sustainability from a systems dynamics perspective. *Organization and Environment*, 29(1), 74–96.

Alvarez, S. A. and Barney, J. B. (2007). Discovery and creation: Alternative theories of entrepreneurial action. *Strategic Entrepreneurship Journal*, 1(1–2), 11–26.

Alvarez, S. A. and Barney, J. B. (2013). Epistemology, opportunities, and entrepreneurship: Comments on Venkataraman et al. (2012) and Shane (2012). *Academy of Management Review*, 38(1), 154–157.

Andersen, M. S. (2007). An introductory note on the environmental economics of the circular economy. *Sustainability Science*, 2(1), 133–140.

Belz, F. M. and Binder, J. K. (2017). Sustainable entrepreneurship: A convergent process model. *Business Strategy and the Environment*, 26(1), 1–17.

Benn, S., Dunphy, D. and Griffiths, A. (2014). *Organisational Change for Corporate Sustainability*, 3rd edition. London and New York: Routledge.

Blomsma, F. and Brennan, G. (2017). The emergence of circular economy: A new framing around prolonging resource productivity. *Journal of Industrial Ecology*, 21(3), 603–614.

Bocken, N. M. P., de Pauw, I., van der Grinten, B. and Bakker, C. (2016). Product design and business model strategies for a circular economy. *Journal of Industrial and Production Engineering*, 33(5), 308–320.

Bocken, N. M. P., Short, S. W., Rana, P. and Evans, S. (2014). A literature and practice review to develop sustainable business model archetypes. *Journal of Cleaner Production*, 65, 42–56.

Cohen, B., Smith, B. and Mitchell, R. (2008). Toward a sustainable conceptualization of dependent variables in entrepreneurship research. *Business Strategy and the Environment*, 17(2), 107–119.

Cohen, B. and Winn, M. (2007). Market imperfections, opportunity and sustainable entrepreneurship. *Journal of Business Venturing*, 22(1), 29–49.

Dean, T. J. and McMullen, J. S. (2007). Toward a theory of sustainable entrepreneurship: Reducing environmental degradation through entrepreneurial action. *Journal of Business Venturing*, 27(1), 50–76.

Dyllick, T. and Muff, K. (2015). Clarifying the meaning of sustainable business introducing a typology from business-as-usual to true business sustainability. *Organization & Environment*, 29(2), 156–174.

EC (2015). *Circular Economy Strategy: Roadmap*. Available at: http://ec.europa.eu/environment/circular-economy/index_en.htm (accessed 18 July 2018).

Elkington, J. (1997). *Cannibals with Forks: The Triple Bottom Line of 21st Century Business*. Gabriola Island, Canada: New Society Publishers.

EMF (2013). *Towards the Circular Economy: Economic and Business Rationale for an Accelerated Transition*. Oxford, UK: Seacourt, The Ellen McArthur Foundation.

EU (2014). *Communication from the Commission to the European Parliament, the Council, the European economic and social committee and the committee of the regions. Towards a circular economy: A zero waste programme for Europe*. Available at: http://eur-lex.europa.eu/legal-content/EN/TXT/?uri=CELEX:52014DC0398R%2801%29 (accessed 30 November 2016).

Footprint (2014). The World Footprint. Available at: www.footprintnetwork.org/en/index.php/GFN/page/world_footprint/ (accessed 15 November 2016).

Fridolin, K., Gingrich, S., Eisenmenger, N., Erb, K., Haberl, H., Fischer-Frosch, R. A. and Gallopoulos, N. E. (1989). Strategies for manufacturing. *Scientific American*, 261(3), 144–152.

Frosch, R. A. and Gallopoulos, N. E. (1989). Strategies for manufacturing: Waste from one industrial process can serve as the raw materials for another, thereby reducing the impact of industry on the environment. *Scientific American*, 261(3), 144–152.

Geissdoerfer, M., Savaget, P., Bocken, N. M. P. and Hultink, E. J. (2017). The circular economy: A new sustainability paradigm? *Journal of Cleaner Production*, 143, 757–768.

Gephart R. P. (2004). From the editors: Qualitative research and the *Academy of Management Journal*. *Academy of Management Journal*, 47(4), 454–462.

Ghisellini, P., Cialani, C. and Ulgiati, S. (2016). A review on circular economy: The expected transition to a balanced interplay of environmental and economic systems. *Journal of Cleaner Production*, 114, 11–32.

Giurco, D., Littleboy, A., Boyle, T., Fyfe, J. and White, S. (2014). Circular economy: Questions for responsible minerals, additive manufacturing and recycling of metals. *Resources*, 3(2), 432–453.

Hobson, K. (2016). Closing the loop or squaring the circle? Locating generative spaces for the circular economy. *Progress in Human Geography*, 40(1), 88–104.

Hunt, C. and Auster, E. (1990). Proactive environmental management: Avoiding the toxic trap. *MIT Sloan Management Review*, 31(2), 7–18.

Krippendorff, K. (2004). Reliability in content analysis: Some common misconceptions and recommendations. *Human Communication Research*, 30(3), 411–433.

Lacy, P. and Rutqvist, J. (2015). *Waste to Wealth: The Circular Economy Advantage*. Dordrecht, the Netherlands: Springer.

Leximancer. (2005). *Leximancer Manual Version 2.2*. Available at: www.leximancer.com/documents/Leximancer2_Manual.pdf (accessed 6 June 2008).

Lichtenstein, B. B (2011). Complexity science contributions to the field of entrepreneurship, in Allen, P., Maguire, S. and McKelvey, B. (Eds.), *The Sage Handbook of Complexity and Management*. Thousand Oaks, CA: Sage, 471–493.

Lieder, M. and Rashid, A. (2016). Towards circular economy implementation: A comprehensive view in context of manufacturing industry. *Journal of Cleaner Production*, 115, 36–51.

Maon, F., Lindgreen, A. and Swaen, V. (2009). Designing and implementing corporate social responsibility: An integrative framework grounded in theory and practice. *Journal of Business Ethics*, 87(1), 71–89.

Mathews, J. A. and Tan, H. (2011). Progress toward a circular economy in China. *Journal of Industrial Ecology*, 15(3), 435–457.

Moroz, P. W. and Hindle, K. (2012). Entrepreneurship as a process: Toward harmonizing multiple perspectives. *Entrepreneurship Theory and Practice*, 36(4), 781–818.

Murray, A., Skene, K. and Haynes, K. (2017). The circular economy: An interdisciplinary exploration of the concept and application in a global context. *Journal of Business Ethics*, 140(3), 369–380.

Nguyen, H., Stuchtey, M. and Zils, M. (2014). Remaking the industrial economy, *McKinsey Quarterly*. Available at: www.mckinsey.com/business-functions/sustainability-and-resource-productivity/our-insights/remaking-the-industrial-economy (accessed February 2014).

Patzelt, H. and Shepherd, D. A. (2011). Recognizing opportunities for sustainable development. *Entrepreneurship Theory and Practice*, 35(4), 631–652.

Perey, R., Agarwal, R., Benn, S. and Edwards, M. (forthcoming). The place of waste: Changing business value for the circular economy. *Business Strategy and the Environment*, Special issue.

Pinchot, G. (1985). *Intrapreneuring: Why You Do Not Have to Leave the Corporation to Become an Entrepreneur*. New York: Harper & Row.

Roome, N. (1992). Developing environmental management strategies. *Business Strategy and the Environment*, 1(1), 1–23.

Sarasvathy, S. D. (2001). Causation and effectuation: Toward a theoretical shift from economic inevitability to entrepreneurial contingency. *Academy of Management Review*, 26(2), 243–263.

Saunders, M., Lewis, P. and Thornhill, A. (2003). *Research Methods for Business Students*, 3rd edition. London: Prentice-Hall.

Sauvé, S., Bernard, S., and Sloan, P. (2016). Environmental sciences, sustainable development and circular economy: Alternative concepts for trans-disciplinary research. *Environmental Development*, 17, 48–56.

Schaltegger, S., Ludekefreund, F. and Hansen, E. G. (2012). Business cases for sustainability: The role of business model innovation for corporate sustainability. *International Journal of Innovation and Sustainable Development*, 6(2), 95–119.

Schaltegger, S. and Wagner, M. (2011). Sustainable entrepreneurship and sustainability innovation: categories and interactions. *Business Strategy and the Environment*, 20(4), 222–237.

Schaper, M. (2010). Understanding the green entrepreneur, in Schaper, M. (Ed.), *Making Ecopreneurs: Developing Sustainable Entrepreneurship*. London: CRC Press, 7–20.

Shane, S. and Venkataraman, S. (2000). The promise of entrepreneurship as a field of research. *Academy of Management Review*, 25(1), 217–226.

Smith, A. and Humphries, M. (2006). Evaluation of unsupervised semantic mapping of natural language with Leximancer concept mapping. *Behavior Research Methods*, 38(2), 262–279.

Spekman, R. E., Kamauff , J. W. Jr. and Myhr, N. (1998). An empirical investigation into supply chain management: A perspective on partnerships. *Supply Chain Management: An International Journal*, 3(2), 53–67.

Stahel W. R. (2006). *The Performance Economy*. London: Palgrave Macmillan.

Steffen, W., Richardson, K., Rockström, J., Cornell, S. E., Fetzer, I., Bennett, E. M., Biggs, R., Carpenter, S. R., de Vries, W., de Wit, C. A., Folke, C., Gerten, D., Heinke, J., Mace, G. M., Persson, L. M., Ramanathan, V., Reyers, B. and Sörlin, S. (2015). Planetary boundaries: Guiding human development on a changing planet. *Science*, 347(6223), 736–746.

Stewart, W. H., Watson, W. E., Carland, J. C. and Carland, J.W. (1999). A proclivity for entrepreneurship: A comparison of entrepreneurs, small business owners, and corporate managers. *Journal of Business Venturing*, 14(2), 189–214.

Strauss, A. and Corbin, J. (1994). Grounded theory methodology. *Handbook of Qualitative Research*, 17, 273–285.

Tsvetkova, A. and Gustafsson, M. (2012). Business models for industrial ecosystems: A modular approach. *Journal of Cleaner Production*, 29, 246–254.

Webster, K. (2013). What might we say about a circular economy? Some temptations to avoid if possible. *World Futures*, 69(7–8), 542–554.

Whiteman, G., Walker, B. and Perego, P. M. (2013). Planetary boundaries: Ecological foundations for corporate sustainability. *Journal of Management Studies*, 50, 307–336.

Winn, M. L. and Angell, L. (2000). Towards a process model of corporate greening. *Organization Studies*, 21(6), 1119–1147.

WWF (2015). Living Planet Report 2014. Available at: http://wwf.panda.org/about_our_earth/all_publications/living_planet_report/ (accessed 20 May 2015).

Yuan, Z., Bi, J. and Moriguichi, Y. (2006). The circular economy: A new development strategy in China. *Journal of Industrial Ecology*, 10(1–2), 4–8.

2.4 Policy entrepreneurs and sustainable water resources management in Australia

Some empirical findings

Zhifang Wu

Introduction

Water management in Australia is a complex process that falls within the power of the states; the governance arrangements are complex, with over 14 different types of legal forms of water supply businesses.[1] Furthermore, the Council of Australian Government (COAG) reforms in 1994 and the National Water Initiative (NWI) in 2004 have resulted in notable transformation of the water governance structures. As a result, all Australian States have been directed to achieve Ecologically Sustainable Development (ESD). Consequently, all State governments in Australia have enacted comprehensive water legislation to ensure sustainable use of the limited water resources. Similarly, in an urban context, the objectives of the National Water Initiative (NWI) have been agreed to by the Australian States and Territories; however, implementation of Integrated Urban Water Management (IUWM) remains a challenge for each individual State/Territory. The main challenge is the presence of different institutional models for the management of urban water supplies.[2] The situation has become more complex with the inclusion of 'new sources' of water, such as treated stormwater and recycled wastewater into the supply mix. The addition of these new sources has resulted in a complex entitlements regime together with related issues around access rights, because the current entitlement arrangements governing these sources of water within the urban water supply are not clearly defined.[2] Given this situation, 'policy entrepreneurs' have an important role to play in achieving ESD objectives as well as implementing IUWM.

Therefore, to better understand the role of policy entrepreneurs in the implementation of IUWM this chapter draws heavily from an in-depth interview with key actors which was conducted in Adelaide, South Australia. The study highlights the uncertainties, challenges and barriers in implementing the IUWM strategy as perceived by the key actors.

Concept of water policy entrepreneur

The way in which water is managed has changed considerably over time and the changes reflect the evolving technological achievements, people's understandings of water, changing lifestyles and locations, and economic development.[3]

Since changes in water management are often preceded by changes in government policy and regulations, it is necessary for us to understand water policy changes.[3]

That explains why the issue of policy changes has attracted considerable academic attention. This chapter is specifically interested in what role the key actors play in the process of preparing, instigating and implementing water policy changes. This question is particularly interesting because the work of such actors is underappreciated in common understandings of policy change.[3]

The theories from the policy sciences suggest that policy transitions are related to the emergence of new ideas which challenge the existing paradigm.[3,4] Such ideas must be outputs of the key actors who carry ample work experience in the area and prepare them until they are ready for consideration.[5] Those key actors are called 'policy entrepreneurs'.[5] Water policy entrepreneurs are those key actors who have been particularly active in influencing and connecting water management and policy changes in order to challenge the traditional water agenda and influence water policy in more sustainable terms.[4,6] In Huitema and Meijerink's study,[3] each of the models they examined suggests that certain individuals and organisations (key actors) can affect water policy changes and they may succeed in doing so through a set of skills and strategies.

How do policy entrepreneurs affect policy changes? As Bachrach and Baratz show,[7] changes can be instigated both from within and from outside of government. Within government, the key actors seeking changes may be politicians or bureaucrats. Outside of government, they can be representatives of non-governmental organisations (NGOs), academics or individual citizens.[5] The type of key actors under the examination of this chapter is recognised in the policy sciences and other literatures as a change agent, which is sometimes described as a 'boundary spanner', a 'policy advocate' or a 'visionary leader'.[5,8] Working to achieve policy changes obviously involves different challenges for different types of policy entrepreneurs.[5] Throughout the transition period, water policy entrepreneurs are persistent in attaining recognition that the traditional supply-based approach to water management is unsustainable, and they manage to put forward alternative ideas on water management by employing a wide range of strategies.[6]

According to Howard,[9] in Australian public policy literature the focus has largely been on the entrepreneurial activity in areas of government, and policy entrepreneurs are often identified as elected representatives or high-profile appointed officials. The author describes them as 'administrative entrepreneurs' who are non-elected officials, who work inside government to move policy solutions and at times attempt to compensate for a lack of interest in a policy issue on the part of elected representatives.[9]

This chapter draws attention to the institutional arrangements in Adelaide's water management and adjacent policy fields. Regardless of the wider institutional context, the chapter proposes that water policy entrepreneurs may employ a set of strategies which are closely connected to the way policy change is achieved according to the policy sciences.[3] The focus of this chapter is on the role of key actors who work to pursue sustainable water management in South Australia. Generally speaking, these key actors are public agency administrators[10] and/or high-profile appointed officials promoting a particular public policy.[9] They promote policy change and influence the policy process effectively[11] in South Australia. In the water sector these key actors can affect shifts in water resource management through a set of strategies, such as advocating new ideas, defining and reframing problems, coalition building, mobilising public opinion, network management and specifying policy alternatives.[4,8] Furthermore, they invest their time, knowledge and skills into instigating and implementing a policy change[5] and have energies and talents that could influence alternative spheres of political activity.[12]

Methodology

As Connor[13] suggests, in solving water-related problems, a valuable source of knowledge is the experience gained by local water professionals from their participation in 'hands-on management'. Importantly, local managers are aware of the many risks and uncertainties related to the water system in which they operate, and they are often the first to identify new issues and problems, as well as solutions.[13] Local solutions are often workable as they reflect local and indigenous practices and knowledge and are aimed at meeting local priorities.[13] Local knowledge should be captured and communicated to decision-makers at higher levels, to inform policy formulation.[13] Based on these considerations, the key actors that this chapter targets are the local water professionals in South Australia. Hence, the people that were interviewed for this study were made water policy entrepreneurs by statute.

The development phase of the survey involved a number of pilot processes to test its design and 'usability'. It was important that the survey made sense to the user and did not take too long to complete, but at the same time, it needed to elicit the necessary data for a receptivity analysis. The draft survey was sent to five senior policy/strategy officers and scientists for content test and the survey was amended in accordance with received comments.

The questionnaire contained 29 questions focused on capturing the views of professionals working in the urban water management area across Metropolitan Adelaide. The survey started with a few general questions exploring how water professionals perceive the IUWM strategy to a sustainable Adelaide. It then continued with questions about participants' perception of how 'committed' they considered each stakeholder was to diversifying water supply sources across Adelaide. It also asked participants to classify stakeholders in relation to their power and the extent to which they were likely to show interest in the implementation of an IUWM strategy.

Participants' perceptions of policy and legal challenges to implementing an integrated urban water management strategy in Adelaide and potential solutions for overcoming the challenges were explored afterwards. Participants were also asked to describe the degree of (policy, climate, financial and other) uncertainties (at degree of high, medium, low and no) associated with each of Adelaide's seven potential sources of water supply.

To make it user-friendly, the survey provided some statements generated from the scoping study conducted as part of the Optimal Water Resources Mix for Metropolitan Adelaide for participants to rate on the Likert Scale. Meanwhile, participants were encouraged to write down their additional suggestions/answers to avoid missing information.

The following questions were posed with regards to resource ownership and responsibility. Participants were asked to state in both their opinion and their organisation's opinion: (1) who should control the access to Adelaide's new sources of water (e.g. desalinated water, recycled stormwater/wastewater, rainwater; and (2) who should be responsible for governing these sources of water. Again the survey provided options for participants to rate and they were also able to make their own suggestions. Participants' perception of trust and coordination between government authorities and perceived performance of institutional network were explored as well.

The questionnaire was anonymous and was approved by University of South Australia's research ethics committee. Detailed information on how participants' confidentiality would be maintained was provided via a participant information sheet attached to the invitation email to participants.

An online questionnaire internet site called Survey Monkey was chosen because it provided efficient and effective data management capabilities. The questionnaire took around 30 minutes to complete. If the entry was interrupted, the participant was able to close this questionnaire and complete it later. When it was reopened, the participant was able to pick up from where they had left off.

To increase the survey response rate, prior to the online survey going live, heads of relevant organisations were contacted and asked to encourage their staff to participate in this survey. At the same time we contacted the reception of these organisations and requested details of who would be the most appropriate contact in the organisation for the purposes of the survey. Accordingly, an invitation email was sent to each contact. The email contained one participant information sheet and a web link. The participant information sheet explained the project aim, method and the maintenance of participation confidentiality to participants. The web link directed recipients to the online survey. The recipients were encouraged to forward the invitation to people who they considered could be of interest and relevance to the survey.

It was difficult for us as researchers to obtain a list of relevant private sectors. As an organisation which has more than 180 members across water industries, the Water Industry Alliance agreed to help circulate the survey to its members who represented the private sectors. Only those members who were relevant to this survey were selected and contacted.

Eventually there were 55 key stakeholders that participated in the survey. The participants were water managers and planners from both the public and private sectors, including local government officers, consultants, engineers, planners, policy/strategy officers, scientists, land developers and economists at a senior level.

The survey was launched in February 2014 and closed in June 2014. We aimed to have a good coverage of the identified stakeholders. However, given they were all at a senior level and had very busy schedules, it was difficult getting people to do the survey. During the four months, we sent off one invitation and three reminders. The reminders were undertaken by both email and phone call.

The representation achieved from stakeholder groups is presented in Table 2.4.1. Overall, there was a good representation from the breadth of organisations involved in urban water management. Indeed, the percentage weightings of respondents from the various organisations reflected the day-to-day operating environment in urban water management. For example, those organisations with a major responsibility for urban water management were well represented, such as the water utilities/retailers and local governments, whereas organisations with an 'interest' (stake) in urban water management (such as the health and economic regulators and researchers) were less well represented in total numbers.

All the respondents had years of experience in the public sector and held senior positions in their organisation/department, such as Director, Policy and Planning; Senior Policy Officer/Senior Water Planning Officer; Manager, Water Planning.

Findings

The uncertainties which the participants perceived in relation to implementing the IUWM in Adelaide include: climate uncertainties, policy uncertainties and other factors. The results of the survey revealed a comprehensive list of challenges and barriers to the implementation of the IUWM in Adelaide and have provided potential solutions in

Table 2.4.1 Representativeness of the respondent population

Stakeholders	*Number of entries*
SA Water	9
Department of Environment, Water and Natural Resources	5
Environment Protection Authority	3
Department of Primary Industries and Regions	2
Essential Services Commission of South Australia	1
Stormwater Management Authority	1
SA Health	1
Department of Planning, Transport and Infrastructure	1
Conservation Council of South Australia	1
Adelaide & Mount Lofty Range NRM Board	1
Local Governments (there are 17 city councils in metro Adelaide)	13
The International Centre of Excellence in Water Resources Management (ICE WaRM)	3
Water Industry Alliance	1
Private Sector	12
Unspecified	1
Total	55

overcoming these challenges and barriers. It is important to note that most of the challenges were related to the 'new' water sources. Major barriers to the implementation of IUWM in Adelaide included the organisational/corporate culture within the water sector, institutional capacity, institutional uncertainty about access rights and the ownership of water, and full compliance with environmental and public health regulations.

Uncertainties in relation to implementing an integrated urban water management strategy in Adelaide

Risk and uncertainty characterise much of what water managers and socio-economic policy-makers must deal with.[13,14] The more they understand these uncertainties and risks, the more effectively they can plan, design and manage water systems to reduce these risks and uncertainties.[13] Today, water planners and engineers are particularly concerned with the uncertainties associated with extremes that have not yet been observed and are outside the scope of variability defined by past events.[15] No matter which design is chosen, there is always the risk of failure. The decision-making process should encourage active participation from interested stakeholder groups. This will ensure that differences in the perception of risks and values are fully explored within the risk-assessment and decision-appraisal processes.[13]

As well, climate change may have an impact on water resource management conditions in unpredictable ways. A key challenge for water managers is how to incorporate highly uncertain information about potential climate change from global models into local- and regional-scale water management models and tools to support local planning.[16] Water planners also face other important uncertainties about future conditions, and the derived climate sequences can also be combined with other assumptions about uncertain planning conditions to develop numerous scenarios.[16]

The key actors surveyed in this study had significant experience in planning and operating their systems in the face of uncertainties associated with future hydrology, weather, available water supply and projected water demand (which was a key selection criterion for participation). The project aimed to explore these professionals' perceptions of the uncertainties involved in implementing the IUWM in Adelaide. The participants' perceived degrees of climate and policy change uncertainties associated with each of Adelaide's seven potential sources of water supply are illustrated in Figures 2.4.1 and 2.4.2.

None of the eight sources of water (seven sources of supply, plus demand management measures) are perceived as having no uncertainties. Not surprisingly, given their climate-dependent nature, catchment water, Murray River water, stormwater and rainwater/roof water are perceived as having a medium to high degree of climate

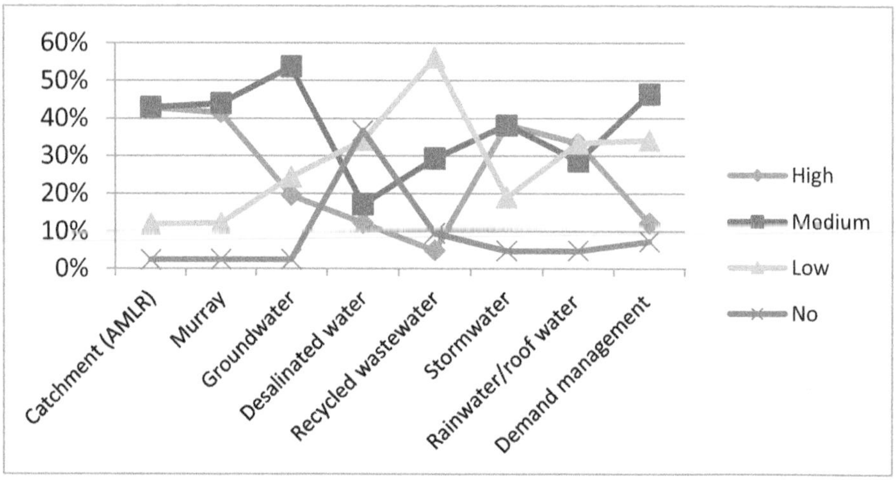

Figure 2.4.1 Perceived degrees of climate change uncertainty (high, medium, low, and no) associated with each of Adelaide's seven potential sources of water supply

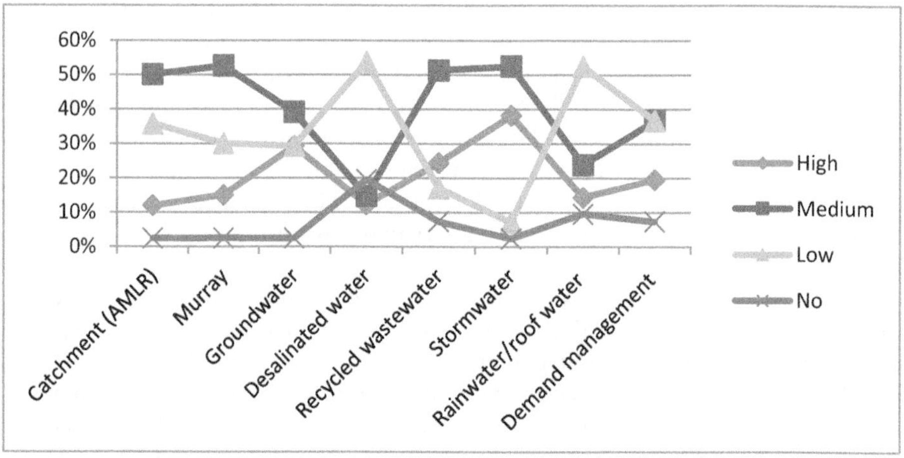

Figure 2.4.2 Perceived degrees of policy change uncertainty (high, medium, low, and no) associated with each of Adelaide's seven potential sources of water supply

change uncertainty. Desalinated water, recycled wastewater, groundwater and demand management are perceived as having low to high climate change uncertainty, as they are not climate-dependent sources.

Water has been under the control of the states in Australia for over 100 years.[16] Nevertheless, Section 100 of the Australian Constitution remains unchanged and states:

> The Commonwealth shall not, by any law or regulation of trade or commerce, abridge the rights of the States or of the residents therein to the reasonable use of waters of rivers from conservation or irrigation.

However, this has been questioned by Crase[17] as a result of the release of the National Plan for Water Security (the Plan) in 2007. The Plan has seen the federal government taking more control over water resource management, particularly in the Murray-Darling Basin. One study found that the federal governance of water has achieved significant public acceptance.[18]

Many of the significant policy modifications in the industry began towards the end of the 20th century. Crase[17] commented that some of the reforms have achieved progress but others have failed. The policy failures have been addressed by subsequent reforms, but only to a relatively minor extent. Crase[17] argued that the future environment is unlikely to resemble the present, particularly given the predictions of climate change and the evident economic and social trends. Importantly, policy-makers need to take care when formulating policy in this environment and should resist the temptation to 'pick winners' on the basis of values formed in a different time period.

In this chapter, all the listed sources of water, except stormwater, were perceived as having low to medium levels of policy-change uncertainty. Stormwater was perceived as having medium to high levels of policy change uncertainty, because this source of water is comparatively new compared to others. The policy environment for stormwater management is still in its infancy and is experiencing rapid change.

In addition to 'policy change' and 'climate change', 'energy policy and cost' was considered by the participants as being uncertain. For example, one participant argued that:

> Already the oversized ADP (Adelaide Desalination Plant) is too expensive to run in comparison with water conservation and other sources. It was sized to prevent water restrictions, but then was extravagant. The cost increases to water bills have effectively created a permanent water restriction, but the extra 50GL size of the plant was not needed to put the price of water bills up. Electricity is a key input to all recycled water, so the uncertainty over whether renewables can be incorporated into water policy and the impact of electricity pricing make energy a key uncertainty.

There were other uncertainties which the participants described, including:

- Price and affordability – it is difficult to ascertain how much consumers are willing to pay.
- Future interstate access to the Murray River is uncertain.
- Variable application of science-based policy continues to threaten some stormwater schemes in the region.
- Waste-water recycling has resulted in public resistance.
- Stormwater requires land planning.
- Insufficient knowledge about groundwater.

Challenges to implementing integrated urban water management strategy in Adelaide

The challenges and potential solutions to facilitating the implementation of the IUWM in Adelaide were identified through the interviews which were conducted in the previous scoping study. The responses were then organised into two categories – policy challenges and legal challenges. In the study, the participants were first asked to rate the specified challenges by using 'agree and disagree' scales and were then encouraged to make additional recommendations in relation to overcoming these challenges. The results are presented in Table 2.4.2.

Giordano and Shah[19] argued that, in essence, integrated water resources management is a call to stop fragmentary approaches to water management. Fragmentation occurs where responsibility for water governance is allocated among multiple actors and/or agencies with relatively little, or no, coordination and a lack of clarity around how final decisions are made.[20]

Water management in Australia is characterised by a lack of inter-governmental coordination, as indicated by the study participants in the following comments: 'Too many different regulations and licenses are administered by a large number of different government agencies', and 'Lack of [an] integrated framework to draw policy perspectives together' (see Table 2.4.2). One participant even argued that:

> After nearly a decade of NWI, management of environmental externalities is more disintegrated from water policy than ever before. The Water Proofing Adelaide/4-Way Water Security Strategy never led to carbon neutral approaches for desalination or any integration of emissions reduction/renewable energy with water policy.

The relationships among key players were considered to be complex, and 'SA[1] Water is too influential in its non-integrated water roles and under-used in its engineering capacity'. 'Lack of clarity on rights and responsibilities for all aspects of water management and use' was considered as a very real concern to implementing the IUWM in Adelaide for operators, as was the long processing time for licensing.

To some extent these issues are universal given that water is a multipurpose flow resource that constantly transgresses political boundaries, authority over which is continually negotiated between different users, sectors and scales of governance. This raises the issue of how best to address the fragmentation that is so characteristic of water governance.[2] The setting 'up [of] a process to work more collaboratively' and the 'develop[ment] of an integrated water management plan' were strongly recommended by the participants. 'A clear lead role for one agency' or 'coordinat[ion] through one state agency' were other suggestions put forward by key actors (see Table 2.4.2). However, the participants pointed out that 'there is a danger that this would add one more layer to the complexity' and that the 'lead agency will be crucial for ownership but must be careful not to only have one perspective (e.g. environmental and not industry)'.

'Cross-boundary disputes' and 'unclear property rights/ownership rights for non-prescribed water sources' were considered as important legal challenges to the implementation of an integrated urban water management strategy in Adelaide. 'Unclear access rights to water sources on private land' and 'unclear private ownership of water courses' were not, however, viewed as major challenges. The participants argued that 'ownership is clear but not well understood, and expensive for individual landowners, e.g. First

Table 2.4.2 Challenges to implementing the IUWM and potential solutions

	Strongly disagree	*Disagree*	*Neutral*	*Agree*	*Strongly agree*	*Unsure*
1 Policy challenges						
Too many different regulations and licenses are administered by a large number of different government agencies	0%	8.70%	6.52%	41.30%	39.13%	4.35%
Lack of clarity on rights and responsibilities for all aspects of water management and use	0%	6.52%	13.04%	36.96%	36.96%	6.52%
Lack of integrated framework to draw policy perspectives together	0%	4.35%	17.39%	30.43%	47.83%	0%
Processing of licensing takes far too long	2.17%	6.52%	30.43%	30.43%	19.57%	10.87%
• **Suggested solutions**						
✓ Set up a process to work more collaboratively	0%	0%	9.09%	45.45%	43.18%	2.27%
✓ Developed an integrated water management plan	0%	6.82%	25.00%	29.55%	36.36%	2.27%
✓ A clear lead role for one agency	2.27%	4.55%	20.45%	36.36%	36.36%	0%
✓ Recommend to coordinate through one state-based agency	6.82%	2.27%	22.73%	38.64%	29.55%	0%
2 Legal challenges						
Cross-boundary disputes	0%	10.87%	10.87%	56.52%	15.22%	6.52%
Unclear property rights/ownership rights for non-prescribed water sources	0%	13.04%	17.39%	39.13%	21.74%	8.70%
Unclear access rights to water sources on private land	0%	23.91%	21.74%	30.43%	17.39%	6.52%
Unclear private ownership of water courses	0%	26.09%	21.74%	30.43%	17.39%	4.35%
• **Suggested solutions**						
✓ There should be certainty and a collaborative effort for best policy instrument	0%	0%	10.87%	41.30%	43.38%	4.35%
✓ Clarify the ownership of stormwater and water in the creek, and if they need to be part of the optimal mix in case of aquifer recharge-injected water entitlements	2.17%	4.35%	13.04%	54.35%	21.74%	4.35%
✓ Political solution – NRM Code of Conduct for maintaining water sources	2.22%	6.67%	35.56%	35.56%	8.89%	11.11%

Creek/Waterfall Gully', and 'according to legislation, watercourse ownership is clear. What's not clear are the obligations attached to this'. In addition, the fact that 'the economic regulation of water virtually prevents [the establishment of] environmental and sustainability initiatives [by] SA Water', was also considered to be a major challenge. The participants argued that:

> [t]his extends throughout the water, wastewater, and recycled water markets, whether by local government or the private sector. Unless sustainability can be re-integrated into water policy, there will be a disintegrated approach that simply drives water sources to be least cost.

'Certainty, collaborative effort for best policy instrument' was strongly recommended for overcoming the challenges by the participants. 'Clarify[ing] the ownership of stormwater and water in the creek if they need to be part of the optimal mix and in case of aquifer recharge-injected water entitlements' and 'political solution – NRM Code of Conduct for maintaining water sources' were considered to be required. The participants further indicated that 'the code of conduct must incorporate environmental objectives, including for biodiversity opportunities, greenhouse mitigation and green power procurement'. Meanwhile, 'a clear Act for a multipurpose sustainable IUWM strategy/plan' was considered to be important; however, the participants perceived that it may take a considerable amount of time to achieve a certain, collaborative effort for best policy instrument and a clear ownership from the perspective of practical work.

Barriers to implementing the IUWM strategy in Adelaide

In the literature, there is agreement about the hurdles faced in implementing an IUWM strategy, and two factors – organisational culture and institutional capacity – emerge as important elements that influence this change, particularly with respect to the diversification of water sources.[21] Organisational culture is defined in many different ways in the culture literature. However, the most commonly understood definition of organisational culture is 'the way we do things around here' (p. 168).[22] Another important issue related to implementing the 'new' water projects is institutional capacity. The building of institutional capacity is important for encouraging institutional change.[23] Also, as Wakely[24] argues, institutional capacity determines the ability of an institution to perform effectively at its own tasks and to coordinate with others in its field. Within the water industry, as Mukheibir et al. (p. 71)[25] argued, 'the rigid cultural norms of organisations, professionals and academics . . . and capacity development, are barriers to integrated and innovative water management'. In this regard, the project team explored the perceptions of the key stakeholders in the South Australian urban water sector about these barriers. Results are shown in Figure 2.4.3.

The organisational culture of government departments and SA Water (which, although it is a utility company, is government-owned and operated) was considered as a major barrier to the implementation of IUWM in Adelaide:

> In SA Water and Government, the culture is one where mistakes are never acknowledged. The organisations do not hold themselves accountable for their failings and broken promises. Until the Government and SA Water can change, the entire sector will be uncertain.

> SA Water and pockets of un-thinking regulators, especially in Health, EPA, are main barriers.
>
> Narrow focus on legislative requirements, inevitable in a resource-constrained situation, or due to certain organisational cultures, is a barrier to integration and lateral thinking (e.g. DEWNR & SA Water).
>
> There is no clear perceived need for this by the public. Now that the desalination plant is in operation, the perception is that the water supply is 'secure'. Any other initiative is perceived as 'green politics' that are only likely to drive up the cost of water.

In terms of the significance of the impact of these barriers, the above issue of organisational culture was followed by institutional capacity, institutional uncertainty about access rights and institutional uncertainty about the ownership of water. Full compliance with environmental regulations and public health regulations were not considered to be major barriers.

In fact, 'institutional capacity' was not considered to be an issue by the participants, only that it was considered to be too dispersed/unfocused at present. This was primarily considered to be a financial issue about the resourcing of SA Water and the Department of Environment, Water, and Natural Resources (DEWNR). The participants further indicated that 'institutional uncertainty about the ownership of water' and 'institutional uncertainty about access rights' depended on the source and were related to non-prescribed sources only. These were primarily related to stormwater reuse and managed aquifer recharge (MAR) schemes. 'Full compliance with public health regulations' was not considered as a major barrier to the implementation of IUWM in Adelaide; however, 'compliance' was perceived as being necessary.

The participants agreed that 'IUWM must be established to be environmentally-sustainable'. Rather than a barrier, 'full compliance with environmental regulations' was considered to be a driver because more wastewater and stormwater reuse results in less environmental impact on marine waters. In addition, 'environmental regulation' was

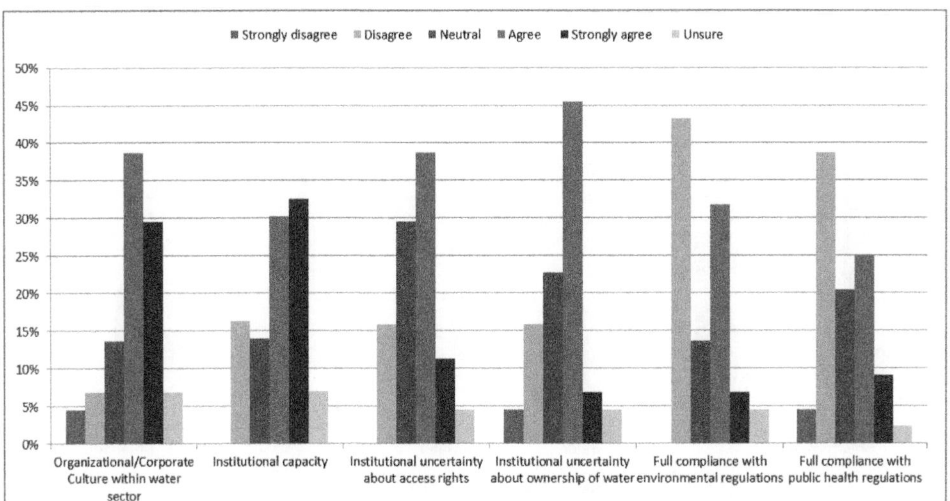

Figure 2.4.3 Barriers to implementing an integrated urban water management strategy in Adelaide

criticised as being 'a rubber stamping exercise', and 'the real barrier is that organisational players cannot make clear commitments towards how they will protect and enhance biodiversity, or how they will transition towards truly sustainable management practices'.

Ownership and governance structures

Literature shows much progress has been made on the scientific and technical aspects of IUWM, but there are significant institutional aspects that require equal attention. Studies[18,26–30] have identified a wide range of social and institutional barriers to the adoption of such arrangements, including insufficient practitioner skills and knowledge, organisational resistance, lack of political will, limited regulatory incentives and unskilled institutional capacity. Thus, the impediments to implementing an integrated approach are not generally technological but are, instead, socio-institutional. In the Australian context, while the water reforms have led to the State governments and their agencies better aligning planning and development requirements with an integrated approach for the management of the urban water cycle, there are a range of governance factors, including regulatory conditions, management systems and institutional arrangements, that are impeding new practices. This case study explored the perceptions of stakeholder groups in the South Australian urban water sector in relation to the governance challenges to the implementation of an integrated approach, particularly with respect to source diversification.

Participants were asked for their opinions about demand management and the existing governance arrangements related to different water sources available in Adelaide. The results are illustrated in Figure 2.4.4. Responses showed it was clear that DEWNR was responsible for the management of the catchments and groundwater, while SA Water played a larger role in governing desalinated water and recycled wastewater. When it comes to stormwater and rainwater, local governments had a major role to play.

However, in terms of the effectiveness of existing arrangements, approximately half of participants perceived them as being poor or very poor (see Figure 2.4.5). Participants

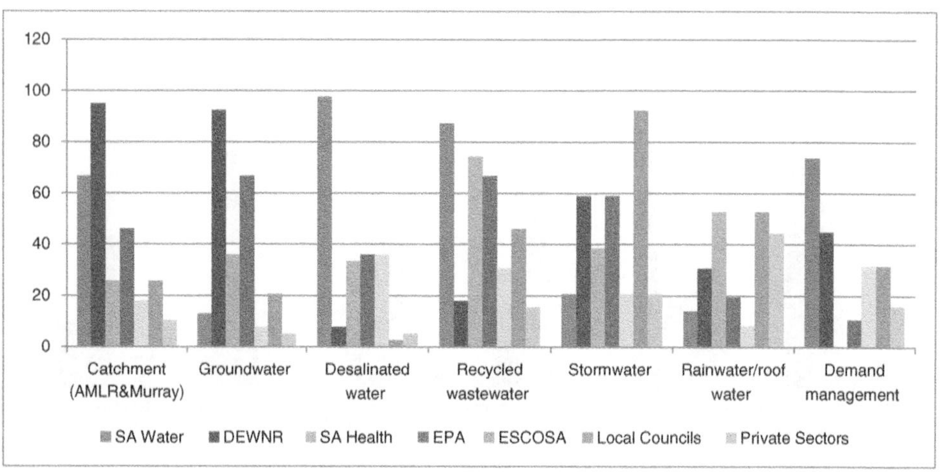

Figure 2.4.4 Stakeholders' perceptions about existing governance arrangements related to different water sources

substantiated their responses with further description of why they perceived the existing arrangements to be poor:

> SA Water have little true interest in conserving water when they need to sell more to pay for the desal plant and south north interconnector. DEWNR are under-resourced to manage catchments and groundwater systems, The Adelaide Desalination Plant demonstrates a systemic extravagance, wasting huge amounts of state financial resources, whilst failing to be carbon neutral for its construction and operations, bringing the whole planning system into disrepute. Stormwater, recycled water and rainwater have led successfully, project by project but could be better integrated with sustainability outcomes. Water Conservation should be led by a structure that is independent of the financial needs of SA Water and Government.
>
> Unclear who is responsible or the driver for what . . . Near impossible to get diverse water supply projects being undertaken. State Gov. has no funding, staff or capacity to implement or administer/approve others to implement.
>
> Too many BODIES trying to apply too many POLICIES for such a complex and life-critical resource.
>
> Emphasis is still on traditional sources of water. Whilst excellent progress on using recycled water sources (inc. stormwater) has been made, this is not matched at a State Gov. level and so governance arrangements remain unclear and forgotten.
>
> Highly fragmented with differing responsibilities with established cultures.
>
> Still too little influence held by regulator ESCOSA, too much by SA Water/Treasury.

As well, 26% responded that the arrangements were good and said that 'Governance arrangement only need fine tuning – no perceived need by the public means no leadership by the political class'. There were no respondents that stated the existing arrangements were very good while 16% were neutral (Figure 2.4.5).

Participants were further asked to indicate who, according to them, should be governing these water resources. Results are illustrated in Figure 2.4.6. DEWNR was expected to play an enhanced role in the management of all types of water resources except for 'desalinated water' and 'recycled wastewater', which were perceived as private sectors'

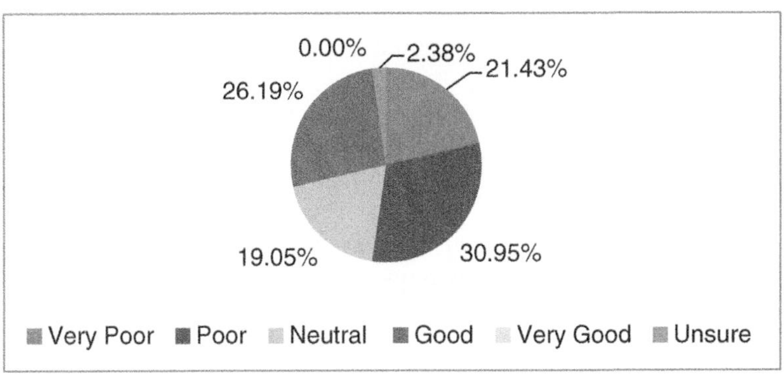

Figure 2.4.5 Effectiveness of existing arrangements

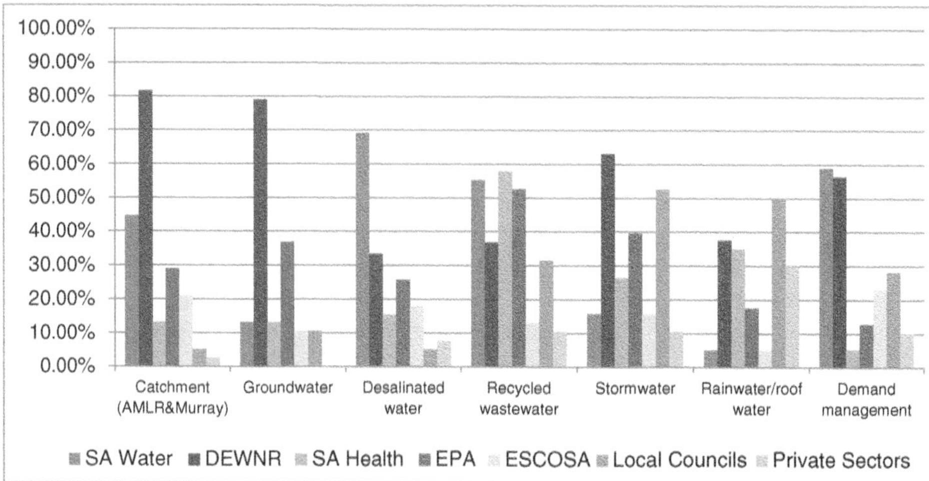

Figure 2.4.6 Stakeholders' perceptions on who should be responsible for governing the water sources

leading role. 'Demand management' was perceived to be governed by DEWNR and private sectors almost equally.

To improve the existing arrangements, participants recommended:

> We could consider a high-level small Adelaide Water Authority reporting direct to / or chaired by the Minister with sole responsibility for Adelaide's source water supplies. This Authority could consist of a rep from each of these existing orgs.
>
> DEWNR/ESCOSA to draw up strategy for legalising IUWM after Goyder has set up the principles.
>
> I've indicated DEWNR from the list however consideration of a multi-stakeholder supported entity possibly lead by DEWNR may also be considered.

The majority of participants considered that SA Water should control access to desalinated water (80%) and recycled water (>60%). In relation to stormwater, the majority of the stakeholders (>70%) thought that DEWNR should control access, followed by local councils (around 60%). As for roof-top water/rainwater, more than 60% of the stakeholders perceived that local councils should control access, followed by DEWNR at around 37% (see Figure 2.4.7).

In controlling the access to Adelaide's new water sources, participants also recommended:

> Adelaide needs a respected body strong enough to oversee the management of Adelaide's Total Water Sources.
>
> Stormwater control via mandated WSUD provisions in Development Regs should be instituted by DPTI but they refuse to say 'Must' for anything & gave it to DEWNR who also stopped short of mandating.
>
> Under IUWM access will be centralised, with input from areas involved with the various water sources and interests.
>
> Under current governance arrangements there is no one body that should be in control of access to stormwater. Would need to change the governance arrangements.

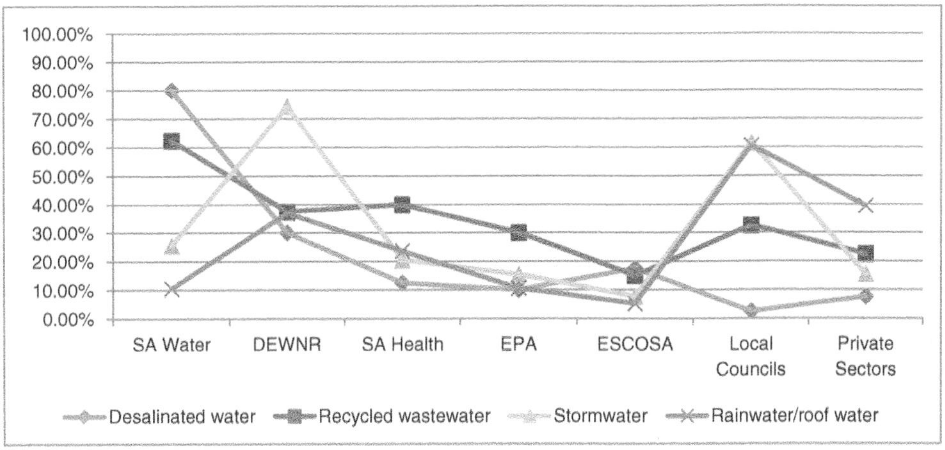

Figure 2.4.7 Stakeholders' perceptions on who should control access to Adelaide's new sources of water

Trust and coordination

Previous studies on water governance in Australia[18,31] indicated that water management in Australia is criticised as a lack of inter-governmental coordination. There are too many different regulations and licenses that are administered by a large number of different government departments. 'Cross-boundary disputes' was found to be one of the important legal challenges. This case study explored the stakeholders' opinions about these issues. Results are presented in Figure 2.4.8.

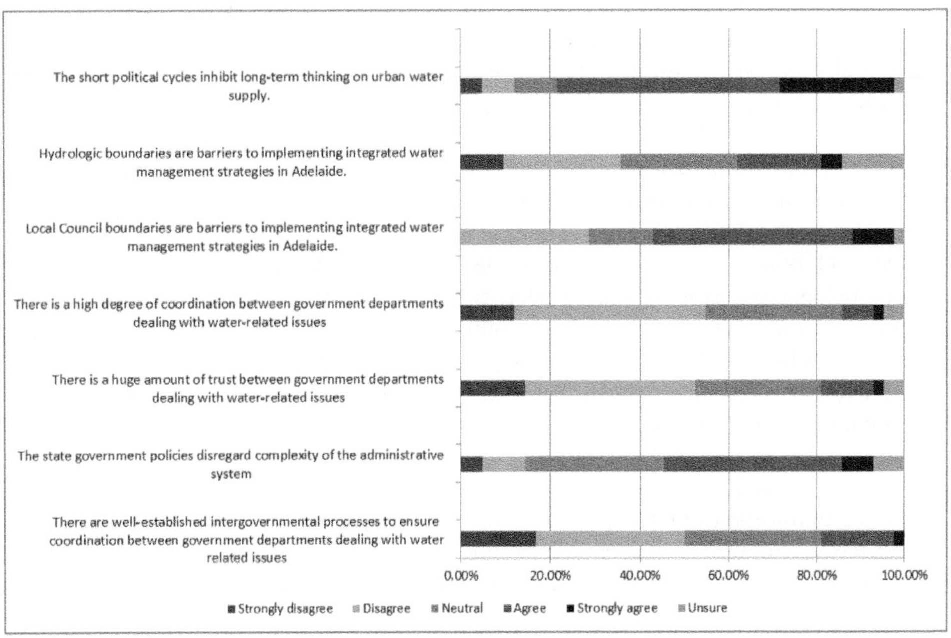

Figure 2.4.8 Stakeholders' perceptions on trust and coordination issues

More than 50% of the respondents disagreed with the statements about trust and coordination between government departments dealing with water-related issues. An equal percentage of respondents (around 50%) disagreed with the statement about intergovernmental processes being in place to ensure good coordination between the departments dealing with water issues. With respect to the statements about boundary disputes, administrative boundaries was perceived to be a major barrier compared to the hydrologic boundaries, with around 55% of the respondents agreeing that local council boundaries were a barrier to implementing the IUWM strategy in Adelaide. This was an issue more with the non-traditional or the 'new' sources of water. Another major barrier to implementing the IUWM strategy in Adelaide, as perceived by stakeholders, was the 'short political cycles' as more than 75% of the respondents agreed that short political cycles inhibit long-term thinking on urban water supply including the implementation of the IUWM strategy.

Conclusions

The learnings from this case study establish that engaging stakeholders effectively facilitates the decision-making process, with stakeholders providing useful and relevant knowledge and, more importantly, the likelihood of greater stakeholder acceptance. Also, it is useful for understanding any potential conflicts and forms the basis for developing coalitions of support at different stages of a project and/or policy development and implementation.

Urbanisation, growing population, economic growth and climate change all have placed increasing pressure on the existing water supplies and raised concerns about environmental impacts. It is an imperative to diverse urban water supplies to include new sources of water, e.g. stormwater, recycled wastewater and desalinated water. While there is growing support for implementing a portfolio of water supply sources, it is also true there are impediments to implementing this approach. These impediments are not generally technological, but are, instead, socio-institutional and in policy and legal areas.[2,26,32,33] Also, most of the challenges are related to the 'new' water sources – stormwater and recycled wastewater. The findings of this study concur with this in that the major policy and legal challenges highlighted by key stakeholders were related to treated stormwater and recycled wastewater. The most commonly identified impediment was the lack of a coordinated institutional framework, revealing poor inter-organisational collaboration and coordination. In particular, the issues included the lack of an integrated water management plan, fragmented roles and responsibilities, unclear property rights and the lack of one leading agency to implement the IUWM, often resulting in organisations being more reactive rather than reinforcing a proactive operational culture.[23] Fragmented and unclear roles and responsibilities relate to not only internal issues within organisations but also between and among other organisations.

Addressing these issues and achieving sustainable urban water management may require institutional change and extensive redesign of organisations and their basic operating practices.[34] This implies that two factors – organisational culture and institutional capacity – are important to achieving organisational transformation. But, achieving (cultural) transformations to encourage institutional change for implementation of an integrated urban water management approach may take several years, and therefore planners and policy-makers must have a long-term framework for addressing these issues.

While it is beyond the remit of this chapter to specify tangible strategies to overcome the challenges and barriers, it touches upon the concerns raised by the sustainability policy entrepreneurs in that it shows how a transparent and enhanced consultation process can tackle the challenges highlighted by the water planners. The findings also elucidate the role of sustainability policy entrepreneurs in shaping policy outcomes. At the same time, policy entrepreneurs single-handedly cannot influence a policy; it has to be a combination of the personal attributes of the individuals, the contextual factors such as legislative environment, policy and social networks, and last but not the least strategies adopted by the key policy actors in influencing the change process. As evidenced from this study, the most influential strategy was developing trust, building long-term relationships with key stakeholders and having continuous interactions with the stakeholders and, most importantly, maintaining transparency throughout the process. This implies there is no 'one size fits all' strategy to achieve sustainable water management. What is required is a new paradigm to address the challenges, specifically engaging the governments, corporations and community in a three-way collaborative effort.[35,36]

Acknowledgments

The author is grateful for the sponsorship provided by the Goyder Institute for Water Research, South Australia and to Dr Ganesh Keremane for comments and also thanks the participants for their time and effort.

Note

1 SA Water is a government business enterprise wholly owned by the government of South Australia, which provides water and wastewater services to a population of approximately 1.5 million people across South Australia.

References

1 McKay, J.M. (2007). Groundwater as the Cinderella of water laws, policies and institutions in Australia, in S Ragone (ed.), *The Global Importance of Groundwater in the 21st Century: Proceedings of the International Symposium on Groundwater Sustainability*, Westerville, OH: National Groundwater Association, pp. 321–327.

2 Keremane, G., Wu, Z. and McKay, J. (2014). *Institutional Arrangements for Implementing Diverse Water Supply Portfolio in Metropolitan Adelaide* – Scoping Study, Goyder Institute for Water Research Technical Report Series No. XX/x, Adelaide, South Australia.

3 Huitema, D. and Meijerink, S. (2010). 'Realizing water transitions: the role of policy entrepreneurs in water policy change', *Ecology and Society*, 15(2), available at www.ecologyandsociety.org, accessed 10 August 2014.

4 Roberts, N.C. and King, P.J. (1991). 'Policy entrepreneurs: Their activity structure and function in the policy process', *Journal of Public Administration Research and Theory*, 2, 147–175.

5 Huitema, D., Lebel, L. and Meijerink, S. (2011). 'The strategies of policy entrepreneurs in water transitions around the world', *Water Policy*, 13(5), 717–733.

6 Font, N. and Subirats, J. (2010). 'Water Management in Spain: The Role of Policy Entrepreneurs in Change', *Ecology and Society*, 15(2), 15.

7 Bachrach, P. and Baratz, M.S. (1970). *Power and Poverty; Theory and Practice*. New York.

8 Huitema, D. and Meijerink, S. (eds) (2009). *Water Policy Entrepreneurs: A Research Companion to Water Transitions around the Globe*. Cheltenham, UK and Northampton, MA: Edward Elgar Publishing.

9 Howard, C. (2001). 'Bureaucrats in the social policy process: Administrative policy entrepreneurs and the case of working nation', *Australian Journal of Public Administration*, 60(3), 56–65.

10 Teodoro, M.P. (2009). 'Bureaucratic job mobility and the diffusion of innovations', *American Journal of Political Science*, 53(1), 175–189.
11 Crow, D.A. (2010). 'Policy entrepreneurs, issue experts, and water rights policy change in Colorado', *Review of Policy Research*, 27(3), 299–315.
12 Schneider, M. and Teske, P. (1992). 'Toward a theory of the political entrepreneur: Evidence from local government', *American Political Science Review*, 86(3), 737–747.
13 Connor, R. (2012). *Managing Water under Uncertainty and Risk*, The United Nations World Water Development Report 4, Executive Summary, Published in 2012 by the United Nations Educational, Scientific and Cultural Organization organizations: 7, place de Fontenoy, 75352 Paris 07 SP, France.
14 Baroang, K.M., Hellmuth, M. and Block, P. (2014). *Identifying Uncertainty and Defining Risk in the Context of the WWDR-4*. Discussion paper prepared for the World Water Assessment Programme, International Research Institute for Climate and Society, Earth Institute, Columbia University, accessed on 15 September 2014 via www.unesco.org/new/fileadmin/MULTIMEDIA/HQ/SC/temp/wwap_pdf/WWAP%20WWDR4_Risk_and_Uncertainty_Paper.pdf.
15 Enhealth (2014). *Environmental Health Risk Assessment: Guidelines for Assessing Human Health Risks from Environmental Hazards*, © Commonwealth of Australia 2012, accessed on 18 August 2014 via www.health.gov.au/internet/main/publishing.nsf/Content/A12B57E41EC9F326CA257BF0001F9E7D/$File/DoHA-EHRA-120910.pdf.
16 Groves, D.G., Yates, D. and Tebaldi, C. (2008). 'Developing and applying uncertain global climate change projections for regional water management planning', *Water Resources Research*, vol. 44, W12413, doi:10.1029/2008WR006964.
17 Crase, L. (ed.) (2011). *Water Policy in Australia: The Impact of Change and Uncertainty*. Washington, DC: RFF Press.
18 Wu, Z., McKay, J. and Keremane, G.B. (2012). 'Governance of urban freshwater: Some views of three urban communities in Australia', *Water*, 39(1), 88–92.
19 Giordano, M. and Shah, T. (2014). 'From IWRM back to integrated water resources management', *International Journal of Water Resources Development*, 30(3), 364–376.
20 Bakker, K. and Cook, C. (2011). 'Water governance in Canada: Innovation and fragmentation', *International Journal of Water Resources Development*, 27(2), 275–289.
21 Wallington, T., Robinson, C.J. and Head, B. (2010). *Institutional Capacity for Sustainable and Integrated Water Management: Interview Results*. Urban Water Security Research Alliance Technical Report No. 22.
22 Lundy, O. and Cowling, A. (1996). *Strategic Human Resource Management*. London: Routledge.
23 Brown, R.R. and Farrelly, M.A. (2009). 'Delivering sustainable urban water management: A review of the hurdles we face', *Water Science & Technology*, 59(5), 839–846.
24 Wakely, P. (1997). 'Capacity building for better cities', *Journal of the Development Planning Unit, University College London*. www.gdrc.org/uem/capacity-build.html (accessed 7 November 2014).
25 Mukheibir, P., Howe, C. and Gallet, D. (2014). 'What's getting in the way of a "one water" approach to water services planning and management? An analysis of the challenges and barriers to an integrated approach to water', *AWA Water Journal*, 41(3), 67–73.
26 Uhlendahla, T., Salianb, P., Casarottoc, C. and Doetschd, J. (2011). 'Good water governance and IWRM in Zambia: challenges and chances', *Water Policy*, 13, 845–862.
27 McKay, J.M. (2005). 'Water institutional reform in Australia', *Water Policy*, 7(2), 35–52.
28 Brown, R., Mouritz, M. and Taylor, A. (2006). 'Institutional capacity', in T. Wong (Ed.), *Australian Runoff Quality: A Guide to Water Sensitive Urban Design* (pp. 5–20). Melbourne, Victoria: Engineers Australia.
29 Mitchell, V.G. (2006). 'Applying integrated urban water management concepts: A review of Australian experience', *Environmental Management*, 37(5), 589–605.

30 Keremane, G.B. and McKay, J.M. (2011). 'Using Photostory to capture irrigators' motions about water policy and sustainable development objectives: A case study in rural Australia', *Action Research*, 9(4), 405–425.
31 Wu, Z., McKay, J.M. and Keremane, G. (2014). 'Stormwater reuse for sustainable cities: The South Australian experience', in B. Maheshawari, R. Purohit, H. Malano, V.P. Singh and P. Amerasinghe (eds), *The Security of Water, Food, Energy and Liveability of Cities*, pp. 137–150. New York: Springer.
32 Keeley, J. and Scoones, I. (2003). *Understanding Environmental Policy Processes: Cases from Africa.* London: Earthscan.
33 Gupta, J. (2007). *'Glocal' Water Governance: Controversies and Choices.* Discussion Paper on Governance. UNESCO-IHE, Institute for Water Education, Delft.
34 Brown, R. (2008). 'Local institutional development and organizational change for advancing sustainable urban water futures', *Environmental Management*, 41, 221–233.
35 Chiplunkar, A., Seetharam, K. and Tan, C. (eds). (2012). *Good Practices in Urban Water Management: Decoding Good Practices for a Successful Future.* Mandaluyong City, Philippines: Asian Development Bank.
36 Brown, R. (2005). 'Impediments to integrated stormwater management: The need for institutional reform', *Environmental Management*, 36(3), 455–468.

2.5 Integrated sustainable entrepreneurship

A view from the South

David Coldwell and Robert Venter

Introduction

The chapter aims to indicate how *sustainable* entrepreneurship must ultimately be ethically imbued, 'strong sustainability', which maintains 'natural capital' while developing 'manufactured capital'. The chapter gives a view from the South (in this case South Africa) by indicating examples of forms that entrepreneurship takes in this part of the world and in terms of a heuristic that considers ethically valid integrated sustainable entrepreneurship as consisting of a balance between environmental, social and economic concerns which, in effect, allow the current generation to meet its needs without jeopardising the ability of future generations to meet theirs.

The chapter takes the following structure. First, the concepts of strong and weak sustainability are defined and discussed. This is followed by an outline description of strong and weak sustainability, with a separate section on the ethical aspects of these approaches. A description of the methodology follows, after which a reconceptualisation of sustainable entrepreneurship is proposed using an integrative model. The integrative model is illustrated using secondary data and eclectic case studies of South African entrepreneurship, which indicate some of the various non-integrative, partially and fully integrative forms these take. The conclusion outlines limitations and practical implications of the study and briefly makes recommendations for further research.

Dimensions of sustainability

Strong and weak sustainability

The literature on strong and weak sustainability is used in two distinct ways. The environmental disciplinary perspective refers to sustainability in terms of environmental 'natural capital'. In contrast, the economic disciplinary perspective refers to economic 'manufactured capital' of goods and services. The concept of capital is defined by Neumayer (2003: 8) as, "stock that provides current and future utility" and *natural* capital as capital that endows human beings with "material and nonmaterial utility" (*ibid.*). Man-made capital includes: technology, factories, railways and roads. Human capital encompasses human knowledge as a whole (Neumayer, 2003).

Davies (2013) suggests that natural capital consists of *critical, constant* and *tradeable* aspects. *Critical capital* is capital that is required to sustain human life. It includes the earth's atmosphere, the protective ozone layer and rare species under threat of extinction. Once destroyed or irreversibly damaged, critical capital cannot be replenished. *Constant capital* is natural capital that is important but can be substituted fairly easily as in the case of, for example, the substitution of a forest by a nature park. Finally, *tradeable capital* is capital not highly valued in its own right but which can be readily substituted or replaced.

Combining the environmental and economic disciplinary perspectives reveals that the core issue of concern between the two approaches is the substitutability between the economic and the environmental factors. As Ayres et al. (1998: 12) put it:

> Much of the confusion in the discussion of strong sustainability arises from a failure to distinguish between the two assumptions dividing weak and strong sustainability. The first is the assumption of substitutability between natural and manufactured capital. The second is that economic well-being "covers" all other concerns. If the second assumption is accepted (as it sometimes is by advocates of strong sustainability) then the argument about substitutability boils down to a purely economic debate about elasticities of substitution, technological advance and so on. If, on the other hand, substituting financial capital for natural resources is incompatible with maintaining a suitable physical environment for the human species, then strong sustainability implies that we must step outside the conventional market framework in order to establish the conditions for maintaining human happiness.

Ayres et al. (1998) maintain that strong sustainability considers maintenance of the natural environment suitable for human existence as non-negotiable in any proposed manufactured economic capital substitution. Perspectives on sustainability that focus purely or largely on economic capital are regarded by Ayres et al. (1998) as 'weak sustainability'. This is because such a perspective incorporates an overriding concern to increase manufactured capital even in situations where this results in the destruction of natural environmental capital, including those essential for human survival.

In this regard, Gray and Bebbington's (2000) study, commissioned by the United Nations, investigated to what extent large corporations understood environmental accounting and sustainability and what impediments they saw in adopting the idea and practices of 'accountability' more fully. The study used multilingual questionnaires, interviews and mini-case studies with some of the largest companies in the world in 19 different countries. The study shows what Gray (2008: 12–13) regards as a self-evident truth:

> [n]amely that social justice and environmental stewardship (sustainability in other words) are anything but "safe in the hands of business". And yet this is exactly what business – typically through organs such as WBCSD, ICC, WTO, Davos – does indeed claim. And these claims have influenced governments and pan-national bodies and persuaded them not to legislate nor to exercise any form of control over (particularly) MNC activity. This conclusion of self-delusion or deliberate deceit in the face of increasingly desperate social and environmental disaster has forced me to develop yet further, my increasingly radical orientation.

Long-term implications of weak sustainability which advocates unbridled growth in economic capital are provided by the catastrophic effects it produced on the tiny Pacific island of Nauru (Gowdy and McDaniel, 1999). In 1900 it was found that the island contained one of the richest deposits of phosphate worldwide. Over 90 years of continuous heavy mining had left the island almost derelict of 'natural capital'. Nauru islanders have benefited from high per capita income for several decades which allowed them to establish a trust fund of around US$1 billion that offered some kind of material 'substitution' for their loss of 'natural capital'. Unfortunately, the Asian financial crisis destroyed the trust fund and, as a result, Nauru islanders have nothing to show for the loss of their natural environment. Nauru islanders' experience illustrates the central problem that a 'weak sustainability' approach embodies, which in its extreme forms can lead to the destruction of 'natural capital' and the exhaustion of non-renewable natural resources. In such circumstances a substitution of natural for economic capital generates a one-way, irreversible course with no possible return.

In stark contrast, 'strong sustainability' aims at attaining a non-diminishing pool of natural, social and environmental capital and the prospect of further accumulation of these. There is also the recognition in the 'strong sustainability' approach that 'natural capital' is essential for both accumulation and development of 'manufactured capital' and the preservation of human life and welfare. Both sources of capital cannot be fully substituted by manufactured capital alone, even on purely economic grounds. Thus the argument for 'weak sustainability' becomes untenable.

Furthermore, on ethical grounds, 'weak sustainability' is problematical. Perhaps the most fundamental human moral motive and behavioural rationale underpinning human morality is that of altruism, or the concern and awareness of others' needs. It is this ethical perspective that differentiates human life from all other forms and constitutes the apex of evolutionary development in that species, which suggests that the destruction of natural resources and diminishing or eradicating entirely their use for future generations is contrary to human moral sentiment, depriving them of the opportunity for sustained economic development and eliminating the propensity for manufactured capital production and, ultimately, human life altogether.

In fact, as Baldarelli (2013) suggests, the numbers accountants report should be regarded as representing stories and accounting statements as the expression of human relationships. Baldarelli (2013) indicates there is a close link between culture, ethical relativism and account reporting, especially corporate social responsibility (CSR) reporting, and such cultural influences are often the result of values deposited by charismatic figures which have solidified over time. For Baldarelli (2013), seeing reality in a new light is a 'gift of charisma' "which highlights the relational nature of human beings, those who participate (accountants and economists) and see things which seem invisible, raise new questions and suggest solutions" (Bruni and Sena, 2013: 5). For Baldarelli (2013), a charismatic economy is one where, "Economic life is the setting of passions, ideals suffering and love; not just the search for interests, envy, meanness, speculations and profits" (Bruni and Smerilli, 2008: 15). Thus Baldarelli (2013) maintains, a charismatic economy is an ideal one built on new ways of seeing economic reality and measuring it, derived from the insights of charismatic thinkers.

However, having said this, 'ultra-strong sustainability', which promotes the intrinsic right of nature to exist unmolested by human intervention and which is advocated by the Deep Ecology group, is also untenable. Ayres et al. (1998) point out the idea of an unmolested natural environment is impossible for at least two fundamental reasons. The first is that the sustainability of current global economic structures and the quality of human life itself depend on natural resources. The second is that ecosystems themselves are continuously in a state of flux of being born, maturating and dying off, even without human intervention. A third reason and one not apparently recognised by the Deep Ecology movement, is that humans themselves are an integral part of nature and that their actions and motives to 'molest' other natural capital derives from natural evolutionary development. Thus, Ayres et al. (1998) advocate a 'compromise' approach that recognises the intrinsic need to preserve natural resources necessary for life-support and is also required for efficient economic production and resources that are of a unique and irreplaceable natural value.

In the accounting field, Baldarelli and Del Baldo (2017) indicate that charismatic leadership in the business context can aid in generating innovative kinds of CSR through an *accountability* approach that promotes dialogue, trust, reciprocity and universal fraternity. This approach is apparent in the mission and governance of industrial parks that are part of the Economy of Communion project (EoC), which are distinguished, when compared with other companies, by the CSR goals that they have set themselves. The *accountability* approach adopted in the Italian Incisa Valdarno EoC is used to illustrate and analyse the advantages and disadvantages of combining traditional accounting instruments with new tools that have yet to be fully articulated, to create innovative and better business combinations.

Baker (2006) views the concepts of weak and strong sustainability as incorporating dynamics that change over time and lead to the development of the Environmental Kuznets Curve (EKC) described as an inverted U-shaped curve with pollution on the vertical axis and per-capita income on the horizontal axis. The EKC indicates that a direct positive relationship between pollution and economic development has reached a 'turning point' through greater environmental education and awareness of people and organisations in reducing pollution while allowing economic development to proceed. This 'enlightenment' in public attitude towards pollution mainstreamed in the West after the Second World War from apocalyptical publications such as Carson's (1962) *Silent Spring* on the effects of pollution on fauna and Shute's (1957) *On the Beach* novel about the effects of nuclear fallout. The EKC curve plots the progression over time from strong to weak sustainability and from the 'turning point' post Second World War, from weak to strong sustainability. Certainly in the West, societal values have shifted towards greater environmental awareness; however, this has not generally led to across-the-board changes in business behaviour, and the drive for manufactured capital still takes precedence in many instances over the careful use of natural capital.

In sum, the concept of 'weak sustainability' that regards natural and man-made capital as freely substitutable is based on the work by Solow (1974, 1986, 1993) and Hartwick (1977, 1978, 1990). 'Weak sustainability' maintains that man-made, manufactured capital is of greater importance than natural capital and can easily substitute it. 'Strong sustainability' recognises that natural capital is often not substitutable by man-made capital and in certain instances such as those concerning critical capital, can never be substituted by it. The concept of strong sustainability is used in the current chapter as its conceptual point of departure.

The ethics of strong and weak sustainability: a brief overview

An extreme anthropocentric (human-centred) approach to environmental resources entails an exploitive use of natural resources which adopts a drive for economic growth with no consideration for ethical and natural capital issues of intergenerational equity. This approach directly or indirectly to the position we are faced with today where critical natural capital, essential for human survival, has been depleted. What are the effects of critical capital depletion and how can they be contained? Antal and Van den Bergh (2014: 3) indicate:

> Under different income and population scenarios and a policy target of 450 ppm for atmospheric CO_2 in 2050, carbon intensity – the average amount of carbon emitted to produce a unit of economic output – has to be reduced by 82–97% between 2010 and 2050. The lower-end value of 82% is calculated for 1.5% per capita economic growth. In view of historical trends of average energy efficiency improvements in most countries, the feasibility of such dramatic reductions over the course of 3 to 5 decades through efficiency improvements and structural change while preserving growth (i.e. decoupling) is highly uncertain.

From an ethical theoretical point of view the extreme anthropocentric approach can be regarded as a form of 'act utilitarianism' aimed at the maximisation of current individual utilities without consideration of the effects on future individual utilities or concern for intergenerational equity. The anthropocentric approach advocates unbridled economic growth without natural capital 'impediments', or other than short-term ethical considerations. Ethical justifications for the unbridled economic growth and strongly anthropocentric approach to natural resource utilisation are equivocal. The full-on economic growth using conventional direct (i.e. without consideration of externalities) cost-benefit analyses with no allowance for intergenerational equity is the most ethically untenable. On utilitarian grounds (Mill, 1972) it might be justified in that it produces the greatest utility to the greatest number of current members in the short term, but it has no notion of intergenerational equity in which future generations could be expected to inherit at least the same stock of natural resources as the generations before them (in line with the Constant Natural Assets, CNA rule, Pearce, 1993). Future provision of the CNA rule can, however, be justified on deontological grounds. Kant's (1991) categorical imperative criterion: "do to others as you would they do to you" appears to offer support for the intergenerational equity sustainability criterion of the Bruntland Commission.

A *resource conservationist approach* gives provision for intergenerational equity and managed economic growth. With this approach, a 'balance' between the anthropocentric and ecocentric (natural capital centred) approaches adopts a modified cost-benefit analysis that incorporates full-cost accounting (Schmidtz, 2001). Full- cost accounting in cost-benefit analysis tries to take account of all known external and internal costs. Full-cost accounting cost-benefit analysis is not anthropocentric and can take into account cost benefits to non-human animals and the environment in general (Schmidtz, 2001). Ethically speaking, the conservationist approach can be justified by deontological theory and, more specifically, Rawls' (1971) theory of justice. By allowing for intergenerational equity and the CNA rule, the conservationist approach fulfils an essential criterion of Rawls' theory: equal opportunity for future generations. Rawls' (1971) theory of justice embodies several principles. The first principle is *liberty*, which he defines as each person having an equal right to the most extensive basic liberties that do not encroach on similar equal liberties for all. A given person's liberty can only be restricted for the sake of liberty in general. The second principle is *wealth*, which is defined as wealth which should be for the greatest benefit to the least advantaged in society consistent with the principle of just savings and attached to offices and positions open to everyone. Any inequality of opportunity must be aimed to enhance the opportunities of those with lesser opportunities. Rawls' *difference* principle states that unless there is a wealth distribution that makes both persons better off (in a dyad) an equal distribution is preferred. Rawls' theory has guidelines for ensuring intergenerational equity in his idea of a 'veil of ignorance'.

The 'veil of ignorance' was derived from the premise that rational people will accept his equality – laden with justice principles if they operate behind a veil of ignorance which expunges their knowledge about their actual current personal circumstances. A 'veil of ignorance' of our current circumstances is necessary if we are not to introduce biases into our judgements that give us unfair advantages in life. Thus the resource conservationist seems to afford a powerful and coherent ethically imbued strong sustainability approach to entrepreneurship.

The *preservationist* approaches incorporate a more ecocentric (nature-centred) environmental mix. Turner (1991) suggests the preservationist approach involves: a nature-centred bias towards natural capital, criteria for the preservation of natural capital based on non-economic factors (e.g. history, culture and aesthetics), and a radically modified full-cost accounting process which puts greater weight on natural capital value and promotes its preservation.

The *ultra-preservationist* perspective occupies the opposite polarised position of the anthropocentric approach where economic development is considered the only aspect of legitimate focus and replaces it with a 'nature is all' perspective of the Deep Ecology movement and involves a complete abandonment of cost-benefit analysis, with natural capital being regarded as having an intrinsic non-economic value. Ecocentric ethics' central concern is:

> [t]he ecological system or biotic community and its subsystems, rather [than] the individual members it contains. Ecocentrism is based on the claim that ecology has revealed human beings and the rest of nature to be related both diachronically (through time) and synchronically (at one time) and to be part of the web of life.
>
> (Bunnin and Yu, 2004: 197)

Callicot (1989) maintains that although original ecocentric ideas can be found in the natural sympathy ethics of Hume (2011) and Adam Smith (Macfie, 1967), they do not propose that *basic* human needs must be sacrificed for the pristine preservation of natural capital. Ecocentricism regards humans and ecosystems as of equal intrinsic value. The ecocentric approach cannot be advocated since its approach would lead to economic growth being severely constrained or ceasing altogether and would thus undermine future generations' ability to meet their needs. In short, the extreme ecocentric position undermines the prospect of current needs being satisfied, and anthropocentricism is unlikely to allow the needs' satisfaction of future generations. Rees (1988: 608) warns against the unbridled use of natural capital when he writes:

> Clearly, any human activity dependent on the consumptive use of ecological resources (forestry, fisheries, agriculture, waste disposal, urban sprawl onto agricultural land) cannot be sustained indefinitely if it consumes not only the animal production from that resource (the "interest"), but also cuts into our capital base.

The upshot is that of the various approaches to natural capital utilisation and economic capital development outlined, the conservationist approach, combining as it does a concern for economic, social and ecological factors with intergenerational equity sensitivity and awareness, offers the most favourable prospect of entrepreneurial organisations' sustainability.

Methodology

The study adopts a secondary research approach based on case and field study research.

Leedy (1993: 123) defines the case and field study methodology as, "A type of descriptive research in which data are gathered directly from individuals (individual cases) or social or community groups in their natural environment for the purpose of studying interactions, attitudes, or characteristics of individuals or groups". Secondary data and eclectic case studies of South African field study research are used to illustrate dimensions of an integrated taxonomic heuristic device.

An integrative approach to sustainable entrepreneurship

Having discussed the notion of weak vs strong sustainability and indeed, the ethics of sustainability, an integrative approach to conceptualising sustainable entrepreneurship will now be explored. For the purposes of this chapter, and as illustrated in Figure 2.5.1, sustainable entrepreneurship, which is explored in more depth later in this chapter, exists at the nexus between economic, social and environmental motives of entrepreneurs. It is precisely this conceptualisation which finds a fit with broader notions of what constitutes sustainable development, such that economic, environmental and social concerns are considered interrelated and intertwined rather than being treated as separate and distinct (Giddings et al., 2002). To this end, Del Baldo (2014: 136) suggests that sustainable entrepreneurship is "a combination of creating sustainable development – on the one hand – and entrepreneurship on the other". Thus, using social entrepreneurship discourse (as discussed later), sustainable entrepreneurs are seen to run mission-driven enterprises which attempt to integrate and navigate both societal and environmental concerns through the adoption of profit-driven business models. Although such a conceptualisation of sustainable entrepreneurship is relatively common place (see, for instance, Hamann et al., 2014; Hockerts and Wüstenhagen, 2010), we propose that sustainable entrepreneurship should be further ethically strengthened by a sensitivity towards intergenerational equity, and for this purpose we have developed a taxonomic tool for indicating degrees to which particular entrepreneurial organisations have embraced strong sustainability foci.

Figure 2.5.1 indicates a model of integrated sustainable entrepreneurship consisting of a Venn diagram with People, Profits and Planet circles. The People and Profit circles intermesh as social entrepreneurship, Profit and Planet circles intermesh as Environmental entrepreneurship, and the Planet and People circles intermesh as 'Non-market-driven alternatives'. In each of these cases only two of the three criteria (economic, social and environmental) of strong sustainability are met, and thus none of these types of entrepreneurship is sensitive to intergenerational equity. Sustainable entrepreneurship is attained only when the three criteria for sustainability are met and the enterprise is ethically sensitive to intergenerational equity aspects of its functioning. This is shown in Figure 2.5.1 as the core point where all three circles enmesh together. The points in the triangle that envelop the Venn diagram displayed in Figure 2.5.1 refer to various mainstream outcomes of Profit-, People- and Planet-oriented entrepreneurial approaches. The People-oriented approach to entrepreneurship generates non-sustainable, anthropocentric human-centred business which tends to focus on 'satisficing' economic growth and thus makes it vulnerable to sudden economic downturns. A Profit-oriented entrepreneurial approach emphasises an econocentric, unbridled economic growth to the detriment of social and natural capital. It tends to be exploitive both of human beings and the environment and

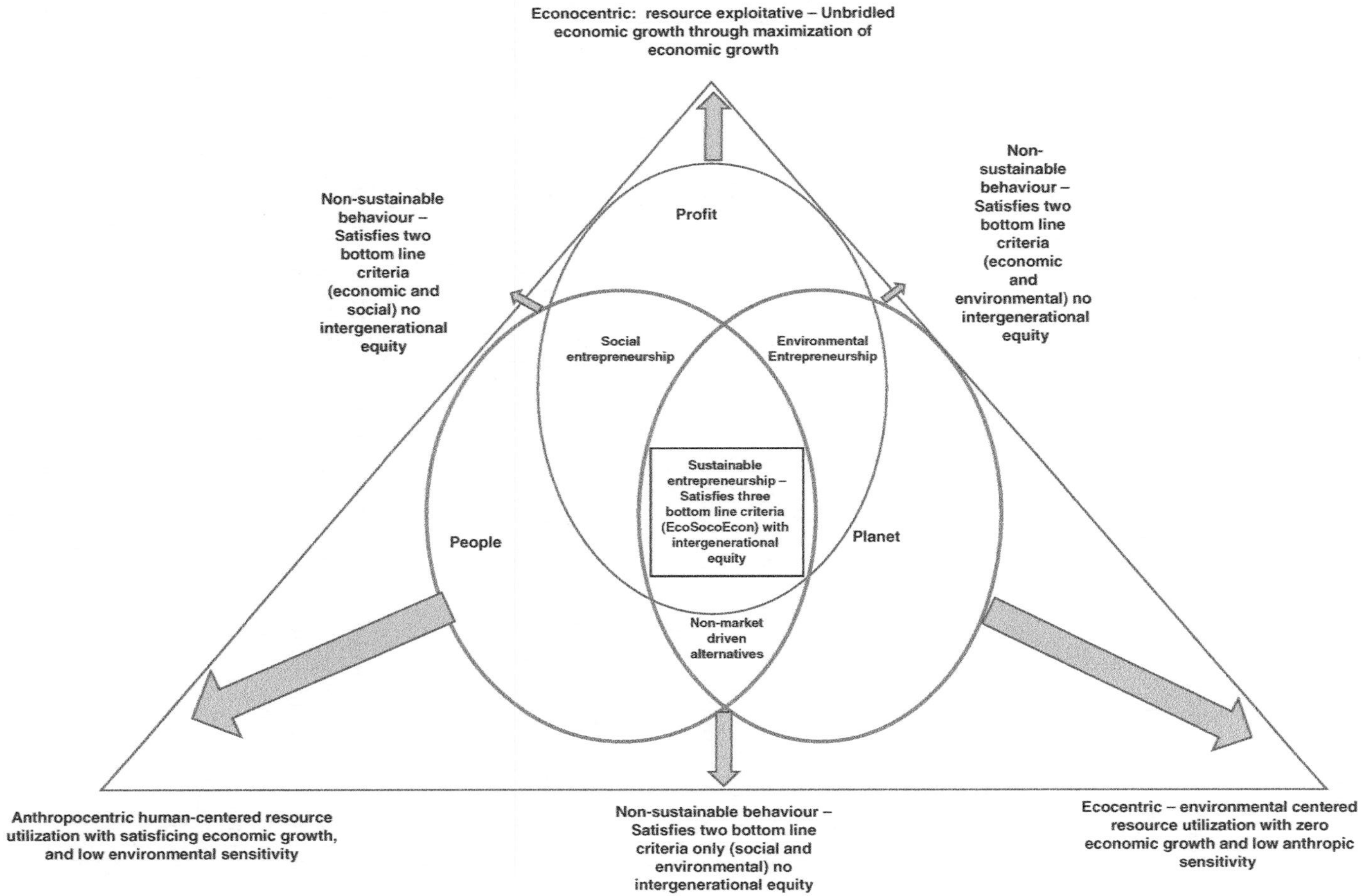

Figure 2.5.1 An integrated model of sustainable entrepreneurship

is therefore unsustainable. Finally, the Planet approach to entrepreneurship advocates an unsustainable ecocentric, Deep Ecology perspective that prioritises natural capital to the detriment of economic and social capital. Pure mainstream People, Profit and Planet entrepreneurial forms are rare and tend to be unworkable. The case study examples presented later thus focus on the more viable forms of entrepreneurship that satisfy at least two of the criteria of strong sustainability. These are discussed in the following sections.

Social entrepreneurship: dualism of people and profit motives

The people-profit duality suggests a double bottom-line focus on addressing social ills through the adoption of for-profit business models, as exemplified by social entrepreneurs (Dees, 1998; Townsend and Hart, 2008; Wilburn and Wilburn, 2014). Social entrepreneurs are not dissimilar to commercial entrepreneurs to the extent that they engage in opportunity identification and exploitation through the development of innovative responses and harnessing of resources. However, where commercial entrepreneurs see social good as a by-product of their efforts, for social entrepreneurs, it is precisely the generation of social value which is their raison d'être. Social entrepreneurs thus recognise a so-called 'wicked problem' and in response, formulate a mission, identify and pursue opportunities, and introduce social innovations, to best serve the mission and thus redress the problem (Dees, 1998, 2001; Venter, 2015). In so doing, they seek to shift societies away from unjust, exclusionary yet stable equilibriums to states of greater equality which are inherently more inclusive (Martin and Osberg, 2007). Central to the attainment of the social mission (and hence this new equilibrium through the redress of the wicked problem) is how to best generate scalability through identifying ways to achieve greatest spread of their innovation and thus increase social impact. For many social entrepreneurs this then further implies the need for viable and profitable business models to achieve their objectives.

It is necessary, however, to qualify what is meant by 'profitable business models' within the context of social entrepreneurship. For social entrepreneurs, profits are arguably not seen as an 'end' per se, but rather a means to an 'end' (with the end, here, being the creation of social value) (Martin and Osberg, 2007). Chell (2007: 18) alternatively, and usefully, refers to "not-for-personal-profit enterprises [that] comprise business activities that generate value for social ends and wealth to enable reinvestment and sustainability of the business". The focus, then, for social entrepreneurs (unlike their commercial counterparts) is less on personal wealth accumulation through profit generation, but rather on achieving maximum social benefit and impact through for-profit models. The United Kingdom's Community Interest Company, as a venture form for social enterprises, is particularly illustrative of this, through its focus on use of profits for public good, rather than for the benefit of shareholders.

If, however, profit is merely a means, then what might the incentive be for social entrepreneurs to engage in the pursuit of social opportunities? The answer to this potentially lies in understanding drivers of social entrepreneurial intent. Mair and Noboa's (2006) model of social entrepreneurship intent formation is particularly useful in this regard. Their model proposes moral judgement and empathy as two possible antecedents of intent. Here, the social entrepreneur's ability to identify with the suffering of others, together with their innate sense of social justice, compels them to identify and redress social ills. Therefore, social entrepreneurs will likely pursue those opportunities which provide non-financial incentives underscored by the creation of social value, which in turn is realised at the expense of pure financial return (McMullen, 2011; Zahra et al., 2008, 2009).

Social value for social entrepreneurs is, for the most part, realised through the identification and redress of wicked problems. By definition, these are not considered 'wicked' because they are ethically deplorable, but rather because of their relative complexity and lack of ready solution (Rittel and Webber, 1973). Thus, such problems are "social or cultural problems that are difficult or impossible to solve because of incomplete or contradictory knowledge, the number of people and opinions involved, the large economic burden, and the interconnected nature of these problems with other problems" (Kolko, 2012: para. 1). A prime example here, with particular reference to the South African context, is that of HIV/AIDS. Contested opinions around the linkages between HIV and AIDS, as experienced under the Mbeki administration, led to a misdirection of funding, poor problem solving and a spiralling social impact through increasing incidents of HIV/AIDs, rising health care costs, as well as the emergence of child-headed households (Venter, 2015). For the most, and political eccentricities notwithstanding, state intervention in the form of public expenditure and policy is largely considered insufficient to deal with the sheer magnitude of 'wicked problems', which by and large require a multitude of different responses if they are to be effectively solved (Hamann et al., 2014). Here, market-led, social entrepreneurship is one such alternative.

The mission, or social value proposition as it is sometimes known (Austin et al., 2006), provides critical direction to the social entrepreneur. The mission in essence brings the social change that the social entrepreneur wishes to bring about into sharp relief and, in so doing, informs the nature of opportunities pursued as well as the ensuing social innovations. As such, the mission (or social value proposition) is located within a broader framework which underscores its feasibility and sustainability. Through this framework, alignment is sought between the external environment, the opportunity itself, human and financial resources, as well as market potential (Austin et al., 2006; National Centre for Social Entrepreneurs, 2001). Here, therefore, there is a dynamic interplay between the environment for the social entrepreneur and his/her mission. The sustainability of the mission, in turn, is simultaneously determined by the availability of people and other resources, financial capital as well as a market for the social innovation (Austin et al., 2006; Chell, 2007).

Social opportunities and associated social innovations are, as suggested, shaped by the mission. The opportunity represents the chance to redress a social ill through the introduction of social innovation (which, in turn, might be something entirely new, or alternatively an improvement on what already exists) (Venter, 2015). Social innovation is envisaged as "the carrying out of a combination of new capabilities" and as such involves "doings and beings" (Ziegler, 2010: 265). This conceptualisation builds on the Schumpeterian conceptualisation of 'creative destruction', such that entrepreneurial actions result in the creation of a new equilibrium through the destruction of existing order. In the context of social entrepreneurship, as suggested previously, such creative destruction implies the introduction of a just, inclusive equilibrium. But what, then, is meant by 'combinations of new capabilities'? Here, there is an enactment of capabilities as envisaged by Nussbaum (2003) and Sen (1999). Such capabilities are fundamental rights which enable the enactment of a full and dignified life, such that each and every human is treated as an end and not merely as a tangential means to another's end (Nussbaum, 2003). Such capabilities include life, bodily health and integrity, use of senses and emotions and the like. Importantly, there is a complementarity and mutuality among such capabilities such that one is required for, and indeed, strengthens, another (Sen, 1999; Ziegler, 2010).

An alternative approach to the enactment of social innovation is provided through a consideration of Max-Neef's (1991) conceptualisation of human needs and concomitant satisfiers as well as economic goods. For Max-Neef (1991), "the relations established between needs and their satisfiers make it possible to develop a philosophy and a policy for development which are genuinely humanistic" (23). Human needs, here, are nine-fold and include subsistence, protection, affection, understanding, participation, idleness, creation, identity and freedom. Satisfiers, on the other hand, allow for the actualisation of different needs, through "being, having, doing and interacting" (*ibid.*, 30). Economic goods lead to the 'enhancement' of satisfiers. Thus, by way of example, if one were to consider the different ways one might enact 'having' as a satisfier to enable the need for creativity, these might include abilities, skills and method. Economic goods such as books, training programmes, software and the like might then enhance these satisfiers. Social innovation might accordingly, therefore, be enacted indirectly through different satisfiers and directly through the provision of relevant economic goods.

Scalability through the spread of social innovation is achieved, in turn, through a combination of various enablers, which include issues as diverse as staffing of the social venture, stakeholder communication and alliance building, lobbying and advocacy, replication of initiatives, as well as the creation of markets for different offerings (Bloom and Smith, 2010). A further key element of successful scalability is that of income generation (*ibid.*). This implies the adoption of various alternatives in order to fund not only the operations of the venture but, in turn, various scaling activities. Such income generation is largely dependent on which one of the three enterprise models is adopted, which are non-profit, for-profit or hybrid. Social entrepreneurs adopting non-profit alternatives, which would focus only on social returns and thus the beneficiary, might source funding from diverse sources such as grants and philanthropy (Nicholls, 2010). For-profit ventures would look only to market returns and thus would look to solely benefit the investor. They might include sources such as social venture capital, banks, as well as other mainstream investors. A blended or hybrid model looks ultimately at derived benefit for both the investor and beneficiary as a form of social impact investment. This includes blended approaches to funding often associated with a hybrid structure, which includes both a for- and non-profit entity (such as a foundation) which is cross-subsidised in turn by profit-generating activities.

Social entrepreneurship, as the overlap between profit and people, represents non-sustainable behaviour, as conceptualised in the model, to the extent that only two bottom-line criteria are satisfied. As such, then, no intergenerational equity is delivered.

Ecopreneurship: dualism of environmental and profit motives

While social entrepreneurship is primarily concerned with a 'people/profit' focus, ecopreneurship (alternatively ecological, green or environmental entrepreneurship) considers a different double bottom line, namely, the interface between environmental and economic sustainability (Allen and Malin, 2008). Entrepreneurs engaged in this space therefore seek to achieve positive environmental impact through profitable business practices (Hendrickson and Tuttle, 1997). As such, ecopreneurs are distinguishable from other types of actors in the environmental/business interface to the extent that "environmental issues [are] central to their core business because their economic success is strongly linked to their environmental performance" (Schaltegger, 2002: 49). Such an approach might be juxtaposed with businesses that are merely compliant with different laws regulating environmental protection, or those that demonstrate environmental sensitivity by managing environmental issues, proactively through environmental policies, but in a supplementary fashion (*ibid.*). Isaak (2002) further distinguishes ideal-typical ecopreneurs as those who start 'green-green' as opposed to 'green' businesses. By definition:

> [a] "green-green business" is one that is designed to be green in its processes and products from scratch, as a start-up, and, furthermore, is intended to transform socially the industrial sector in which it is located towards a model of sustainable development.
>
> (Isaak, 2002: 82)

By contrast, 'green' businesses are those who green their existing operations (rather than from the outset). Taylor and Walley (2003) further extend Isaak's (2002) dichotomy of green entrepreneurs by suggesting that a more expansive and inclusive approach to defining ecopreneurs is required such that all entrepreneurs who engage in green business, regardless of their underlying motives, should be incorporated within the boarder understanding of what green entrepreneurship entails. In other words, entrepreneurs who happen to identify a green opportunity but pursue this to maximise profits from the outset rather than purely from a perspective of building a sustainable business, might also be termed 'green'.

The rise in ecopreneurship is attributed to different factors. Prime among these is the rise in environmentalism and the increased awareness of the global effects of environmental degradation together with the concomitant sensitisation to the opportunities presented to businesses by adopting a 'green agenda' (Hall et al., 2010; Hamann et al, 2012; Taylor and Walley, 2003). This free-market approach to environmentalism, which, when introduced in the 1970s was simply a school of thought on addressing environmental issues, has subsequently become part of mainstream economic discourse through its focus on presenting free-market alternatives to addressing the tragedy of the commons (Anderson and Shaw, 1999). Here, there is an acknowledgment therefore that "that the well-accepted principles that explain market behaviour and underlie prosperity also explain environmental problems and offer ways to solve them" (*ibid.*: 1). This is arguably best evidenced by the growth, globally, in the market for environmentally friendly products such as alternative energy, organic produce and the like. At the same time, it is further contended that environmentally responsive behaviour on the part of a business might well enhance economic performance through operational efficiencies and cost savings, as well as increased sales, rather than being seen as costly and unprofitable (Schaltegger and Synnestvedt, 2002). Here, then, ecopreneurs, through demonstrating the environmental benefits of greening their businesses, serve as role models to other businesses who then follow suit (Schaper, 2002).

Environmental problems might, moreover, be easily categorised as 'wicked problems', as conceptualised previously, such that they are often seen as largely insoluble, but giving rise, nonetheless, to both the opportunity for and innovation of the ecopreneur. Here, environmental and social concerns become less distinguishable to the extent that they are interconnected and mutually reinforcing. Here, for instance, Taylor and Walley (2003) contend that ecopreneurs might well have mixed motives which go beyond being purely green to incorporate social considerations too. Issues of food security, for instance, extend beyond a narrow focus on agricultural production to include other factors such as poverty and the unaffordability of food, as well as concerns related to the impact of poor nutrition on the performance of learners, the efficacy of treatment for HIV/AIDS and the like (see, for instance, Hamann et al., 2011; Misselhorn, 2005).

This interrelatedness between social and environmental concerns serves to underscore, precisely, the nature of the sustainable entrepreneur such that s/he will really limit him/herself to just one category of concern, but will likely seek solutions which are cross-cutting (Hamann et al., 2012). It is precisely through this juncture between the social and environmental motives underscoring different classes of entrepreneurs that alternative conceptualisations of ecopreneurship have emerged. Isaak (1997: 80), for example, defines ecopreneurship as "system-transforming, socially committed environmental businesses characterised by breakthrough innovation". By extending definitions of ecopreneurship to include a social-commitment on the part of the ecopreneur, the dynamic interplay between the social and environmental concerns is acknowledged. This is further echoed by Dixon and Clifford (2007) who use the term 'social ecopreneurship' in much the same way that we have defined sustainable entrepreneurship, as the nexus between commercial, social and environmental motives. However, while there might well be interrelatedness between social and environmental concerns, it is rare for either type of entrepreneur to give equal priority to both simultaneously, with trade-offs occurring between social and environmental motives depending on the orientation of the particular entrepreneur as well as, indeed, the nature of the opportunity (Hamann et al., 2012).

Therefore, the notion of 'socio-ecopreneurship' notwithstanding, ecopreneurship in its absolute form, as conceptualised through the overlap between environmental and profit motives only provides little intergenerational equity. Through its limited focus on social concerns, it is thus not considered to be sustainable in the long term.

Non-market driven alternatives: dualism between social and environmental motives

While this chapter represents a market-driven solution to sustainability, non- and anti-market alternatives are represented in the model at the intersection between purely social and environmental motives to the exclusion of profit generation. While these aspects fall outside of what we propose to represent as sustainable entrepreneurship, a brief consideration of government-centric (non-market) as well eco-socialist and eco-feminist approaches (anti-market) will be provided in the interests of fully explaining and clarifying the model.

Government-centric environmentalism, which is derived from a Keynesian perspective, suggests that the state is better than the market at regulating common goods, largely because the state machinery is perceived to have less of a self-interested orientation than those engaging in market-driven transactions, or alternatively, is better positioned to make decisions for the greater good (Anderson and Shaw, 1999). As such, government intervention is required to compensate for the failure of the market. Of course, proponents of market-led environmentalism would argue that the state is every bit as susceptible to self-interested behaviours, through mechanisms such as state capture and, in turn, suggest that deregulation of the commons is more desirable since private ownership leads to heightened accountability (*ibid.*). Here, the market compensates, in turn, for the failure of the state. Of course, it must be acknowledged that these are diametric positions, as there are few if any cases of completely unfettered markets, particularly vis-à-vis the commons.

Anti-market sentiments pertaining to environmentalism are more directly expressed through eco-socialist as well as eco-feminist ideologies. At the heart of eco-socialism (alternatively, eco-Marxism) is the assumption that "sustainable, ecologically sound capitalist development is a contradiction in terms that never can be realized" (Mebratu, 1998: 507). Capitalism is thus blamed for the current environmental crisis through its creation of value without any apparent regard to the environment in so doing (Kovel, 2008; Löwy, 2005). Eco-feminism, on the other hand, adopts an androcentric perspective on the current environmental crisis such that there is a relationship between the domination of women and the environment (Mebratu, 1998). Plumwood (2003: 25) states it thus:

> [c]haracteristics traditionally associated with dominant masculinism are also those used to define what is distinctively human: for example, rationality (and selected mental characteristics and skills); transcendence and intervention in and domination and control of nature, as opposed to passive immersion in it. The only likely solution is gynocentric in nature through the removal, by women, of this male domination.

Such ideological positions are, however, for the purposes of our model, considered to be largely unsustainable, not least because only two bottom-line criteria are satisfied. As such, therefore, no intergenerational equity is apparent. It is our contention, in keeping with the logic of free-market environmentalism, that market forces are necessary to deliver true sustainability, through their nexus between social and environmental motives. It is only at this juncture that real intergenerational equity is realised. A fuller consideration of non-market alternatives is thus considered to fall outside the scope of this chapter.

Sustainable entrepreneurship: the transformative EcoSocoEcon nexus

The EcoSocoEcon nexus has already been established, earlier in this chapter, as the basis for our understanding of sustainable entrepreneurship, such that, through market-driven business models, entrepreneurs seek to achieve both environmental and social impact. Here, therefore, true sustainability is realised through the creation of intergenerational equity. What bears further consideration is the 'transformative' nature of this critical nexus between motives. By this, what is meant is transformation through the introduction of disruptive sustainable innovation. Such transformation might either be seen within the context of an industry (Hockerts and Wüstenhagen, 2010), or at a more systemic level (McMullen, 2011; Zahra et al., 2009).

Hockerts and Wüstenhagen (2010) propose that sustainable industrial transformation is a dynamic interaction between start-ups (or, so-called 'Davids') and incumbents ('Greening Goliaths') such that sustainable start-ups introduce new disruptive, green innovation into an industry which is then taken up by established firms. Here, parallels might be drawn between Isaak's (2002) notion of green-green entrepreneurs and 'Davids' with ideal-typical ecopreneurs, through a focus on and commitment to environmental and social concerns, 'greening' their business at the outset. Similarly, Goliaths, much like green entrepreneurs, are early adopters of green innovations and tend to prioritise economic motives over environmental and social objectives. Critically, each category is necessary for the successful sustainable transformation of an industry, with small enterprises introducing an innovation which is either taken up and spread through incumbents, or potentially further honed and developed by start-ups as they in turn grow and mature (Hockerts and Wüstenhagen, 2010).

A more systemic approach to transformational change extends the analysis beyond the meso-(industrial) level. Here, change happens at a more fundamental level such that sustainable entrepreneurs challenge and shift prevailing institutional machinery that serves as a barrier to transformation (McMullen, 2011; Zahra et al., 2009). Such action, which is seen to be radically transformative, is epitomised by Zahra et al.'s (2009) notion of the 'social engineer' or alternatively through conceptualisations of institutional entrepreneurship. The 'social engineer' constitutes one of three types of social entrepreneur. 'Social Bricoleurs' enact change at a localised level through the adoption of resources and knowledges which are locally sourced and which they readily have at their disposal. Hockerts and Wüstenhagen (2010) liken Social Bricoleurs to their notion of 'Davids' to the extent that certain start-ups might be more engaged in a localised socio-environmental space without any real desire to impact a wider market. The second category, beyond Social Bricoleurs, is that of the Social Constructionist (Zahra et al., 2009). Such social entrepreneurs are engaged in pursuing social opportunities which arise as a result of problems which are inadequately addressed by the state, as well as other institutions.

It is, however, the social engineer, in his/her role as institutional entrepreneur, which, as suggested earlier, generates significant, revolutionary transformation, through bringing about institutional change. Institutional entrepreneurs thus "whether organisations or individuals, are agents who initiate, and actively participate in the implementation of changes that diverge from existing institutions" (Battilana et al., 2009: 72). Such changes, within the context of sustainable entrepreneurship, are likely to be more long-lasting and enduring as new institutional orders are introduced. As such, they are best likened to Schumpeter's notion of creative destruction through the creation of new equilibria that are epitomised by fundamentally different, empowering institutions which are more inclusive (Zahra et al., 2009). Since these new institutions are seen to run against the 'established order', social engineers are often seen as divisive (*ibid.*). This, notwithstanding, however, the systemic change they do introduce might be seen to address fundamental causes rather than symptoms by "interrogating institutional arrangements that produce perverse outcomes" (Cho, 2006: 51), rather than simply responding to the inefficiencies of the state.

Sustainable entrepreneurship in the South African context

South Africa's challenges to sustainability might be viewed using two particular indicators. The first is the Gini coefficient, as a measure of income inequality and hence poverty. South Africa's coefficient of 0.63, making it the fourth most unequal country in the world (and certainly the least equal of the BRICS countries) (Chitiga et al., 2014). The second is South Africa's carbon footprint, as determined by its greenhouse gas (GHG) emissions. The most recent data from 2010 suggested that South Africa's emissions increased by 21.1% over a ten-year period to 544 314 kt CO_2 eq. (excluding carbon sinks) (Witi and Stevens, 2010). This decline in South Africa's environmental performance over time, together with its poor Gini coefficient, suggests a need for interventions which are both social and environmental in nature.

The 2008 Framework for National Sustainability Development in South Africa, much like this chapter, envisages sustainability as an overlap between social, economic and environmental systems, such that each is embedded within one another and, indeed, are mutually reinforcing. This sentiment is further echoed by Blignaut et al. (2008) who maintain the need to acknowledge "the interconnectedness among socio-ecological systems" in mitigation of climate change. These authors further point to the market potential of eco-system services in South Africa, having estimated these to be in the region of ZAR17 billion per annum with a potential to create 350,000 person-years of employment opportunities (Blignaut et al., 2008).

With the overall support lent to our conceptualisation of the EcoSocoEcon nexus at the policy level, and indeed bearing in mind the need as well as the relative size of the market for sustainable entrepreneurship in South Africa, two particular cases are discussed in order to contextualise our proposed framework. Because of their focus on addressing both environmental and social challenges through market-driven solutions, both cases are seen to best epitomise sustainable entrepreneurship within the South African context.

Rethaka: repurpose backpacks

Rethaka, a for-profit women-owned social purpose company, which operates out of Rustenberg in the North-West province of South Africa, is best known for its green/social innovation called the 'Repurpose' school bag (Venter, 2015). The bag, which is made out of plastic textile manufactured from recycled plastic, incorporates retroreflective material and a solar light. The intention of the innovation is thus to reduce the extent of plastic pollution while providing a school bag which not only affords dignity to school children from impoverished areas but indeed makes them more visible. At the same time it provides a safe alternative to kerosene lamps (www.repurposeschoolbags.com/anatomyofaschoolbag/). The business model that Retaka relies on is for so-called 'giving partners' to purchase bags on behalf of children. Such partners are largely corporates who sponsor bags through their CSR spend.

Retaka, through its market-driven commitment to both environmental and social impact, demonstrates a useful example of sustainable entrepreneurship. Their mission statement underscores this: "Through our green innovations, we redefine societal problems into solutions. We make it our business to uncover sustainable opportunities that create a far-reaching impact for low-income communities, with a particular focus on children and women" (www.repurposeschoolbags.com/whoweare/). As a self-defined 'purpose-driven' business, they distinguish themselves from charities.

Reel Gardening: the 'miraculous' seed strip

Through its patented seed strip, Reel Gardening and its subsidiary, Reel Life, seeks to redress food security in South Africa. These pre-fertilised strips made of biodegradable paper make the planting of vegetables and herbs simpler, more cost-effective and, indeed, water-efficient (Truscott et al., 2014). Seeds within the strip are correctly spaced and at the correct depth, with clear illustrated instructions provided to account for high levels of illiteracy among potential beneficiaries.

The innovation was first conceived of by Claire Reed, the founder of Reel Gardening, in 2002, as part of a high school project, in response to the difficulties she experienced in starting a vegetable garden. She found seeds and fertiliser to be expensive, and seed packs were impractical given the amount of seed sold versus the actual amount required. At the same time, having brought in her domestic helper to assist in the process, she realised that instructions written in English and which required basic mathematical knowledge were inaccessible to many South Africans (www.reelgardening.co.za/pages/how-it-all-began). Finally, the seeded patch was vulnerable to heavy rains which washed the seeds away as well as birds who ate the seed. At the same time, she realised that access to water was particularly problematic in many parts of South Africa and, thus, water-intensive gardens would not be feasible. She thus went about creating a more viable solution to growing vegetables which would be easy to use and generate a high yield with minimal water.

This initial iteration of the strip, which was made out of newspaper, went on to win the Eskom Expo for Young Scientists in 2002, and was the winner of the South African Youth Water Prize as well as the Stockholm Junior Water Prize 2003 based on the water saving capacity of the strip being 80% in the germination phase (Truscott et al., 2014). It was only later, however, that the innovation was commercialised. Claire went on to become an architect and, while working on a sustainable development housing project, mentioned her concept to the client, Anglo American. They were impressed by the idea, and Claire was given a ZAR1 million loan through Anglo Zimele (the enterprise development arm of Anglo American). In 2013, Claire was the runner up in the prestigious Hult Prize to solve the global food crisis, which was hosted by the previous president of America, Bill Clinton. The competition attracted over 11,000 applicants from 150 countries around the globe (www.reelgardening.co.za/pages/awards).

Today, Reel Gardening might be seen to adopt a hybrid business model consisting of two parts: the for-profit company, which sells strips to the public either through stores or online, as well as selling branded strips to corporates. Reel Life is a non-profit organisation which is at the heart of addressing issues of food security throughout the country, through the establishment of vegetable gardens using the Reel Strip technology (www.reellife.org.za/about-us.html).

Discussion

Both Rethaka and Reel Gardening exemplify sustainable entrepreneurship through their clear foci on the EcoSocoEnviron nexus. As such, both exhibit a propensity for the provision and maintenance of intergenerational equity, a necessary indicator of sustainability from an ethical perspective as per the model presented in this chapter. Reel Gardening, through its patented Seed Strip, demonstrates a concern for both water and food security, while simultaneously adopting a hybrid venture form in order to financially sustain its operations. Reel Gardening might, through its evolution, be seen to be akin to a 'social constructionist', given its focus on redressing problems which receive inadequate focus from the state. Through its disruptive innovation, it might also be seen as a 'David' in an early growth phase with its dual focus on both environmental and social impact (Hockerts and Wüstenhagen, 2010).

Rethaka, on the other hand, through its 'Repurpose Backpack' addresses the multiple environmental and social challenges of both plastic pollution, alternative energy, as well as visibility of learners while at the same time affording dignity to school goers in impoverished areas. Once again, the organisation is able to maintain a for-profit model to sustain its operations. However, in this instance, this is achieved by tapping into the CSR spend of corporates. Rethaka might best be positioned as a 'Social Bricoleur' to the extent that the founding entrepreneurs used "existing resources to solve problems and leverage new opportunities" (Zahra et al., 2009: 524). Through their innovation, they address a multiplicity of different needs which, while apparent, often fall 'below the radar'.

Conclusions

The chapter suggests that ethically imbued strong sustainability approaches to entrepreneurship in South Africa are sparse. There are few enterprises that satisfy the full criteria of sustainable entrepreneurship consisting of the economic, social and environmental triple bottom line and embrace 'strong sustainability' in their emphasis on intergenerational equity. The heuristic device shown in Figure 2.5.1 has indicated the necessary ingredients to achieve this, and although South African entrepreneurial enterprises fall short of attaining the standards required for strong sustainability and intergenerational equity, the same could be said for many other developing countries throughout the world. The South African situation is further complicated by the fact that large inequalities exist between the rich minority and the poor majority, which have only marginally improved since the democratically elected ANC government took over the reins of power. This means that the kind of rigorous, strong sustainability expressed in the model may not yet be fully appropriate in the South African context and indeed in other similar contexts, where wide socio-economic disparities exist. The depth of this aspect in the South African context has been clearly emphasised recently by Mashele (2017), a prominent South African political analyst, who recently pointed out that poverty is largely a black issue and that sustainability issues such as the elimination of rhino poaching to ensure the survival of the animal for future generations is considered of very little significance when confronted with their own personal struggle for economic survival. However, despite this South African contextual feature, it remains evident that truly sustainable entrepreneurs must drive enterprises which integrate other societal and environmental concerns through the adoption of profit-driven business models and, as we propose in the chapter, sustainable entrepreneurship should be further ethically strengthened by sensitivity towards intergenerational equity.

The study has various limitations. The case studies offer 'a view from the South' which are restricted in scope and therefore are not necessarily fully representative of South African entrepreneurial undertakings in general, or of those existing in other parts of the world. The model's comprehensiveness as a taxonomic instrument in measuring entrepreneurial sustainability also requires further verification. As indicated earlier, the model propounded in this chapter is an 'ideal type' model that may not as yet be fully appropriate for implementation in developing countries such as South Africa, where high levels of poverty exist in large sections of the population. Further research could usefully apply itself to testing the model using the case study methodology to assess sustainability in entrepreneurial enterprises in both developed and developing countries. For example, a comparative analysis of sustainability approaches in entrepreneurial enterprises and how closely they meet the criteria in the model could be conducted and would present a measure of comparative levels of international sustainability in such organisations.

It is the authors' contention that the model presented in this chapter provides a useful analytic taxonomic tool that has the potential to be practically applied by management to position existing entrepreneurial organisations and to offer entrepreneurs themselves a useable 'sustainability compass' to guide them in the future *socially conscious* development of their organisations.

References

Allen, J.C. and Malin, S. (2008). Green entrepreneurship: A method for managing natural resources? *Society and Natural Resources*, 21(9), 828–844.

Anderson, T. and Shaw, J. (1999). Is free-market environmentalism 'mainstream'? in Shaw, J. (ed.) *A Blue Print for Environmental Education*. Bozeman, MT: PERC (the Property and Environment Research Centre).

Antal, M. and Van den Bergh, J. (2014). 'Macroeconomics, financial crisis and the environment: Strategies for a sustainability transition. *Policy Paper no 10 WWW for Europe project*. Accessed 11 August 2016 at: www.wifo.ac.at/jart/prj3/wifo/resources/person_dokument/person_dokument.jart?publikationsid=47013&mime_type=application/pdf.

Austin, J., Stevenson, H. and Wei-Skillern, J. (2006). Social and commercial entrepreneurship: Same, different or both? *Entrepreneurship: Theory and Practise*, 30(1), 1–22.

Ayres R.U., van den Bergh, J. and Gowdy, J.M. (1998). Viewpoint: Weak versus strong sustainability. *Center for the Management of Environmental Resources*. Accessed 11 August 2016 at: http://dspace.ubvu.vu.nl/bitstream/handle/1871/9295/98103.pdf?sequence=1.

Baker, S. (2006). *Sustainable Development*. Abingdon, UK: Routledge.

Baldarelli, M.G. (2013). Accounting: Ability and 'charisma' – conceptual network and implementation. *Ekonomska istraživanja: Economic Research Special Issue 2013*.

Baldarelli, M.G. and Del Baldo, M. (2017). From weak to strong CSR: The contribution of new categories in the account(ing) ability of EoC industrial parks, in Vertigans, S. and Idowu, S.O (eds) *Corporate Social Responsibility. Academic Insights and Impacts*. Cham, Switzerland: Springer, 45–65.

Battilana, J., Leca, B. and Boxenbaum, E. (2009). How actors change institutions: Towards a theory of institutional entrepreneurship. *The Academy of Management Annals*, 3(1), 65–107.

Blignaut, J., Marais, C., Rouget, M., Mander, M., Turpie, J., Klaasen., T. and Preston, G. (2008). *Making Markets Work for People and the Environment: Employment Creation from Payment for Eco-Systems Services*. Accessed 17 June 2017 at: www.tips.org.za/files/EGS_report_-_18_Nov.pdf.

Bloom, P. and Smith, B. (2010). Identifying the drivers of social entrepreneurial impact: Theoretical development and an exploratory empirical test of SCALERS. *Journal of Social Entrepreneurship*, 1(1), 126–145.

Bruni, L. and Sena, B. (2013). *The Charismatic Principle in Social life*. New York: Routledge.

Bruni, L. and Smerilli, A. (2008). *Benedetta Economica*. Rome: Citta Nouva.

Bunnin, N. and Yu, J. (2004). *The Blackwell Dictionary of Western Philosophy*. Oxford, UK: Blackwell Publishing.

Callicot, J.B. (1989). *In Defence of the Land Ethic: Essays in Environmental Philosophy*. New York: SUNY Press.

Carson, R. (1962). *Silent Spring*. Harmondsworth, UK: Penguin Books.

Chell, E. (2007). Social enterprise and entrepreneurship: Towards a convergent theory of the entrepreneurial process. *International Small Business Journal*, 25(5), 5–26.

Chitiga, M., Sekyere, E. and Tsoanamatsie, N. (2014). Income inequality and limitations of the Gini index: The case of South Africa. Accessed 8 October 2016 at: www.hsrc.ac.za/en/review/hsrc-review-november-2014/limitations-of-gini-index.

Cho, A. (2006). Politics, values and social entrepreneurship: A critical appraisal, in Mair, J., Robinson, J. and Hockerts, K. (eds) *Social Entrepreneurship*. New York: Palgrave Macmillan.

Davies, G.R. (2013). Appraising weak and strong sustainability: Searching for a middle ground. *Consilience: The Journal of Sustainable Development*, 10, 111–124.

Dees, G. (2001 [1998]). *The Meaning of Social Entrepreneurship*. Accessed 25 September 2016 at: https://entrepreneurship.duke.edu/news-item/the-meaning-of-social-entrepreneurship/.

Del Baldo, M. (2014). Sustainable entrepreneurship: Next stage of responsible business, in Weidinger, C., Fischler, F. and Schmidpeter, R. (eds) *Sustainable Entrepreneurship. Business Success through Sustainability*. Berlin Heidelberg: Springer-Verlag, 135–153.

Dixon, S. and Clifford, A. (2007). Ecopreneurship: A new approach to managing the triple bottom line. *Journal of Organizational Change Management*, 20(3), 326–345.

Giddings, B., Hopwood, B. and O'Brien, G. (2002). Environment, economy and society: Fitting them together into sustainable development. *Sustainable Development*, 10(4), 187–196.

Gowdy, J.M. and McDaniel, C. (1999). The physical destruction of Nauru: An example of weak sustainability. *Land Economics*, 75(2), 33–38.

Gray, R.H. (2008). Social and environmental accounting and reporting: From ridicule to revolution? From hope to hubris? A personal review of the field. *Issues in Social and Environmental Accounting*, 2(1), 3–18.

Gray, R.H. and Bebbington, K.J. (2000). Environmental accounting, managerialism and sustainability: Is the planet safe in the hands of business and accounting? *Advances in Environmental Accounting and Management*, 1, 1–44.

Hall, J., Daneke, G. and Lenox, M. (2010). Sustainable development and entrepreneurship: Past contributions and future directions. *Journal of Business Venturing*, 25(5), 439–448.

Hamann, R., Giamporcaro, S., Johnston, D. and Yachkaschi, S. (2011). The role of business and cross-sector collaboration in addressing the 'wicked problem' of food insecurity. *Development Southern Africa*, 28(4), 579–594.

Hamann, H., Bonnnici, F., Nwosu, E. and Holt, D. (2014). Sustainability entrepreneurship, in Urban, B (ed.) *Entrepreneurship and Society*. Cape Town: Pearson.

Hartwick, J. (1977). Intergenerational equity and the investing of rents from exhaustible resources. *American Economic Review*, 67, 972–974.

Hartwick, J. (1978). Substitution among exhaustible resources and intergenerational Equity. *Review of Economic Studies*, 45, 347–354.

Hartwick, J. (1990). Natural resource accounting and economic depreciation. *Journal of Public Economics*, 43, 291–304.

Hendrickson, L.U. and Tuttle, D.B. (1997). Dynamic management of the environmental enterprise: A qualitative analysis. *Journal of Organizational Change Management*, 10(4), 363–382.

Hockerts, K. and Wüstenhagen, R. (2010). Greening Goliaths versus emerging Davids: Theorizing about the role of incumbents and new entrants in sustainable entrepreneurship. *Journal of Business Venturing*, 25(5), 481–492.

Hume, D. (2011). *New Letters of David Hume*, Kilbansky, R. and Mossner, E.C. (eds). Oxford, UK: Oxford University Press.

Isaak, R. (1997). Globalisation and green entrepreneurship. *Greener Management International*, 18, 80–90.

Isaak, R. (2002). The making of the ecopreneur. *Greener Management International*, 38, 81–91.

Kant, I. (1991). *Groundwork of the Metaphysic of Morals*, trans. Paton, H.J. London: Routledge.

Kolko, J. (2012). *Wicked Problems: Problems Worth Solving – A Handbook & A Call to Action*. Austin, TX: Austin Centre for Design. Accessed 29 September 2016 at: www.wickedproblems.com/1_wicked_problems.php.

Kovel, J. (2008). Ecosocialism, global justice, and climate change. *Capitalism Nature Socialism*, 19(2), 4–14.

Leedy. P.D. (1993). *Practical Research Planning and Design*, 5th ed. New York: Macmillan.

Löwy, M. (2005). What is ecosocialism? *Capitalism Nature Socialism*, 16(2), 15–24.

Macfie, A.L. (1967). *The Individual in Society: Papers on Adam Smith*. London: Allen & Unwin.

Mair, J. and Noboa, E. (2006). Social entrepreneurship: How intentions to create a social venture are formed, in Mair, J., Robinson, J. and Hockerts, K. (eds) *Social Entrepreneurship*. New York: Palgrave Macmillan.

Martin, R. and Osberg, S. (2007). Social entrepreneurship: The case for definition. *Stanford Social Innovation Review*, Spring, 28–39.

Mashele, P. (2017). Zuma's radical economic transformation ideas are a 'looting mechanism'. *Accessed* 19 May 2017 at: www.huffingtonpost.co.za.

Max-Neef, M.A. (1991). *Human Scale Development: Conception, Application and Further Reflections*. New York: The Apex Press.

McMullen, J.S. (2011). Delineating the domain of development entrepreneurship: A market-based approach to facilitating inclusive economic growth. *Entrepreneurship Theory and Practice*, 35(1), 185–193.

Mebratu, D. (1998). Sustainability and sustainable development: Historical and conceptual review. *Environmental Impact Assessment Review*, 18(6), 493–520.

Mill, J.S. (1972). *Utilitarianism*. Acton, H.B. (ed.). London: Dent.

Misselhorn, A. (2005). What drives food insecurity in southern Africa? A meta-analysis of household economy studies. *Global Environmental Change*, 15(1), 33–43.

National Centre for Social Entrepreneurs. (2001). *Merging Mission, Market and Money: A Nonprofit's Guide to Social Entrepreneurship*. Minnesota, MN: National Centre For Social Entrepreneurs.

Neumayer, E. (2003). *Weak versus Strong Sustainability: Exploring the Limits of Two Opposing Paradigms*. London: Edward Elgar.

Nicholls, A. (2010). The institutionalization of social investment: The interplay of investment logics and investor rationalities. *Journal of Social Entrepreneurship*, 1(1), 70–100.

Nussbaum, M. (2003). Capabilities as fundamental entitlements: Sen and social justice. *Feminist Economics*, 9(2–3), 33–59.

Pearce, D. (1993). *Blueprint 3: Measuring Sustainable Development*. London: Earthscan.

People – Planet – Prosperity: A National Framework for Sustainable Development in South Africa. (n.d.) Accessed 8 October 2016 at: www.gov.za/sites/www.gov.za/files/nationalf rameworkfor_sustainabledevelopment_a_0.pdf.

Plumwood, V. (2003). *Feminism and the Mastery of Nature*. London: Routledge.

Rawls, J. (1971). *A Theory of Justice*. Cambridge, MA: Harvard University Press.

Rees, W.E. (1988). Sustainable development, economic myths and global realities, in Pojman, L.P. and Polman, P. (eds) *Environmental Ethics: Readings in Theory and Application*. Belmont, CA: Thomson.

Rittel, H.W. and Webber, M.M. (1973). Dilemmas in a general theory of planning. *Policy Sciences*, 4(2), 155–169.

Schaltegger, S. (2002). A framework for ecopreneurship. *Greener Management International*, 38(1), 45–59.

Schaltegger, S. and Synnestvedt, T. (2002). The link between 'green' and economic success: Environmental management as the crucial trigger between environmental and economic performance. *Journal of Environmental Management*, 65(4), 339–346.

Schaper, M. (2002). The essence of ecopreneurship. *Greener Management International*, 38(1), 26–30.

Schmidtz, D. (2001). A place for cost-benefit analysis. *Philosophical Issues*, 11, 148–171.

Sen, A. (1999). *Development as Freedom*. Oxford, UK: Oxford University Press.

Shute, N. (1957). *On the Beach*. Sydney, Australia: Heinemann.

Solow, R. (1974). The economics of resources and the resources of economics. *American Economic Review*, 64, 1–14.

Solow, R. (1986). On the intergenerational allocation of natural resources. *Scandinavian Journal of Economics*, 88(1), 141–149.

Solow, R. (1993). An almost practical step toward sustainability. *Resources Policy*, 2, 162–172.

Taylor, D. and Walley, E. (2003). The green entrepreneur: Visionary, maverick or opportunist? Manchester Metropolitan University Business School Working Paper Series. Accessed 17 June 2017 at: http://econwpa.repec.org/eps/mic/papers/0307/0307002.pdf.

Townsend, D. and Hart, T. (2008). Perceived institutional ambiguity and the choice of organizational form in social entrepreneurial ventures. *Entrepreneurship Theory and Practice*, 32(4), 685–700.

Truscott, A., Urban, B. and Venter, R. (2014). *Reel Gardening: Making a Profit to Fight Poverty*. Case Study. Graduate School of Business Administration, University of the Witwatersrand, South Africa.

Turner R.K. (1991). Environment, economics and ethics, in Pearce, D. (ed.) *Blueprint 2: Greening the World Economy*. London: Earthscan.

Venter, R. (2015). Social entrepreneurship, in Venter, R. and Urban, B. (eds) *Entrepreneurship Theory in Practice*. Cape Town, South Africa: Oxford University Press.

Wilburn, K. and Wilburn, R. (2014). The double bottom line: Profit and social benefit. *Business Horizons*, 57(1), 11–20.

Witi, J., and Stevens, L. (2010). *GHG Inventory for South Africa*. Accessed 8 October 2016 at: www.environment.gov.za/sites/default/files/docs/greenhousegas_inventorysouthafrica.pdf.

Zahra, S., Gedajlovic, E., Neubaum, O. and Shulman, J. (2009). A typology of social entrepreneurs: Motives, search processes and ethical challenges. *Journal of Business Venturing*, 24(5), 519–532.

Zahra, S., Rawhouser, H., Bhawe, N., Neubaum, D. and Hayton, J. (2008). Globalization of social entrepreneurship opportunities. *Strategic Entrepreneurship Journal*, 2(2), 117–131.

Ziegler, R. (2010). Innovations in doing and being: Capability innovations at the intersection of Schumpeterian political economy and human development. *Journal of Social Entrepreneurship*, 1(2), 255–272.

Part III

Leading and inspiring sustainable entrepreneurial action

3.1 Fitting in and standing out

An identity approach for sustainable entrepreneurs

Jessica J. Jones and Jeffrey G. York

Introduction

Scholars have long theorized how entrepreneurs address societal problems through venture creation (Dacin, Dacin, & Tracey, 2011; Short, Moss, & Lumpkin, 2009; Venkataraman, 1997). Sustainable entrepreneurs focus simultaneously on social welfare, reducing environmental degradation and maximizing profit through entrepreneurial action (Thompson, Kiefer, & York, 2011). Prior research suggests that sustainable entrepreneurs see market failure as an opportunity for creating new ventures (Dean & McMullen, 2007; York & Venkataraman, 2010) and often develop institutions to address such problems (Pacheco, Dean & Payne, 2010). How and why entrepreneurs choose to pursue different types of ventures, including those focused on sustainability, may be rooted in identity (Fauchart & Gruber, 2011; Shepherd & Haynie, 2009; York, O'Neil, & Sarasvathy, 2016). Understanding an entrepreneur's concept of self is important to consider as entrepreneurial activities are often an expression of identity (Fauchart & Gruber, 2011).

However, sustainable entrepreneurs pursuing environmental, social, and economic goals, likely hold multiple, often competing, identities. For example, identities linked to a profit-maximizing and a community benefit logic may directly conflict (Moss et al., 2011). Nascent research has emerged to better understand how sustainable entrepreneurs' identity strategies can shape organizations (O'Neil & Ucbasaran, 2016), how greater identity awareness can overcome gaps in business models and social relationships (Wry & York, 2017) and also how venture goals depend on the strength or priority of identity coupling (York, O'Neil, & Sarasvathy, 2016). For sustainable entrepreneurs, the motivation to gain support from others derives from a need to belong, while the motivation to pursue societal change comes from the need to be distinct (Ashforth, 2001; Brewer, 1991; O'Neil & Ucbasaran, 2016).

Yet, there is very little known about the interaction of the *role identity* (Burke, 2006; Burke & Stets, 2009; Stryker & Burke, 2000) of sustainable entrepreneurs and *social identity* (Tajfel & Turner, 1979) of the collective organizations they join. One example is accelerators, organizations designed to assist new ventures in achieving emergence (Cohen, 2013; Hochberg, 2015). In this chapter, we explore the specific context of sustainable entrepreneurs who join accelerators to theorize how the social identity of accelerators influences the role identity of sustainable entrepreneurs.

Our research question asks: how does an entrepreneur' s role identity and an accelerator's social identity influence sustainable venture emergence? We propose the relationship between the entrepreneurs' role identity and venture emergence is moderated by the social identity of the accelerator; counter intuitively, we theorize that joining an accelerator with conflicting social identity than the entrepreneur's may lead to faster venture emergence. Our theory has implications for the literature on sustainable entrepreneurship, identity, and entrepreneurial accelerators.

Sustainable entrepreneurship and identity

There is growing interest in studying the impact of entrepreneurship beyond economic growth, using the nomenclature of social, environmental, and sustainable entrepreneurship. While the definition of an entrepreneur is generally referred to as one who engages in the process of discovery, evaluation, and exploitation of opportunities (Venkataraman, 1997), ambiguous definitions abound for social, environmental, and sustainable entrepreneurs (Christie & Honig, 2006; Dacin, Dacin, & Matear, 2010; Weerawardena & Mort, 2006). Some suggest that the intent of all social, environmental, and sustainable entrepreneurs is for their actions to contribute positively to society, but that distinctions remain between each (Thompson et al., 2011).

Social entrepreneurs tend to focus primarily on opportunities to create positive social value (Alvarez & Barney, 2007; Dees, 1998), prioritizing social benefits over economic goals. Social entrepreneurs are regularly characterized as a passionate group of socially aware actors whose heroic efforts are "changing the world" (Bornstein, 2004). The mission and purpose of social entrepreneurs often align with the nonprofit and public sectors and can include other types of organizations such as nongovernmental organizations, community-based enterprises, social enterprises, hybrid organizations, and nonprofits (Battilana & Lee, 2014; Peredo & McLean, 2006; Weerawardena & Mort, 2006). Regardless of form, social entrepreneurs focus on social value creation outcomes (Dacin et al., 2010). Social value is critical to not just the venture, but also to the entrepreneur pursuing her or his venture as social value creation can be identity-driven (Weerawardena & Mort, 2006). Although "social" encompasses a broad scope and is often criticized for its wide conceptualizations, there is a unique and growing amount of scholarly work focused on how alternative forms of organizations with a similar social value focus have individual-level similarities, such as identity (Dacin, Dacin & Tracey, 2011; Dey, 2006; Thompson et al., 2011).

Environmental entrepreneurs prioritize economically profitable ventures to environmental degradation (Dean & McMullen, 2007; Lenox & York, 2011; Sine & Lee, 2009; York et al., 2016). Using business solutions, environmental entrepreneurs focus on making an impact on environmental issues, often at the institutional level (Isaak, 2002; Lenox & York, 2011; Pacheco, York, Dean & Sarasvathy 2010). Environmental entrepreneurs may be characterized as a subset of sustainable entrepreneurs (Dean & McMullen, 2007) or as eco-preneurs (Beveridge & Guy, 2005; Gibbs, 2009). Studies of environmental entrepreneurs examine how individuals simultaneously create economic growth and environmental benefits (Dean & McMullen, 2007; Meek, Pacheco, & York, 2010; York & Venkataraman, 2010).

Few studies have explicitly examined sustainable entrepreneurs (Hall, Daneke & Lenox, 2010), but interest in the topic is growing (Thompson et al., 2011; York, 2009). Rooted in the goals of sustainable development (Gibbs, 1996; Jacobs, 1995; Tilley & Young, 2006), sustainable entrepreneurs focus on social welfare, reducing environmental degradation and maximizing profit through entrepreneurial action (Dean & McMullen, 2007). Scholars suggest that sustainable entrepreneurs can be interdisciplinary and integrate the preservation and growth of individuals, economy, and society from a variety of domains (Dean & McMullen, 2007; Shepherd & Patzelt 2011; Thompson et al., 2011). Other scholars (Shepherd & Patzelt, 2011) categorize sustainable entrepreneurs as an umbrella term, incorporating both environmental and social entrepreneurs, regardless of their differences. In this chapter, we build on Thompson et al. (2011) to define sustainable entrepreneurship as *blending social welfare, economic, and ecological logics into the form of a hybrid organization* (Battilana & Lee, 2014; Haigh & Hoffman, 2012).

Sustainable entrepreneurs endure many challenges as they pursue multiple, often competing logics to grow their organizations and contribute to sustainable livelihoods (Pierre et al., 2015). For example, they can face competitive disadvantages when pursuing costly sustainable actions (Pacheco, York et al., 2010), but they can also make tradeoffs in short-term decision-making for long-term results (Parrish, 2010). Sustainable entrepreneurs must identify how to prioritize different dimensions of their hybrid organizations (Battilana & Lee, 2014) and understand how to balance their own beliefs as they establish legitimacy from diverse audiences (O'Neil & Ucbasaran, 2016).

While this nascent literature identifies the challenges sustainable entrepreneurs face, scholars are beginning to ask how, and why, entrepreneurs endure such challenges. As entrepreneurs remain closely associated to their organizations, the identity of such entrepreneurs may play a pivotal role (Wry & York, 2017) in the growth of their organizations. For example, Fauchart and Gruber's (2011) typology of founder identity illustrates how a "missionary founder" may create products intended to change the consumption patterns of customers that include environmental or social benefits. We argue that the growing literature stream on identity and entrepreneurship provides a useful lens for understanding sustainable entrepreneurship.

Identity and entrepreneurship

Identity research seeks to explain how society shapes social behavior and the self (Mead, 1934; Stryker, 1980) by placing relationships and roles into meaningful categories (Tajfel & Turner, 1979). Two theories comprise the majority of identity scholarship (Hogg, Terry, & White, 1995) that each take differing, yet interrelated, lenses to describe how individuals make sense of themselves (Burke & Stets, 2009; Tajfel & Turner, 1979). Identity theory (IDT) focuses on role identities as the meanings people attribute to themselves while in various roles and are based on the social positions individuals hold (Burke & Stets, 2009; Burke & Reitzes, 1981; McCall & Simmons, 1978; Stryker, 1980; Thoits, 1983), such as a researcher, a mother, or an athlete. Social identity theory (SIT), on the other hand, focuses on identities across social groups, such as organizational memberships, religious affiliations, teams, or gender represent social identities. Thus, social identities are based on individuals' memberships in certain groups and are assumed when individuals view themselves within a particular group (Burke & Stets, 2009; Oakes, Haslam, & Turner, 1994).

We begin with IDT and role identity. IDT is concerned with how people ascribe definitions for each role they occupy and the subsequent behavior associated with those roles (Stryker & Burke, 2000). Each role carries a specific behavioral standard (Burke & Stets, 2009; Hogg & Abrams, 1990; Stryker & Burke, 2000) which helps provide structure, organization, and meaning to situations. Individuals then establish expectations tied to a role that guide their attitudes and behaviors (Burke & Stets, 2009; Hogg & Abrams, 1990). Role identity is internalized partly from culture (McCall & Simmons, 1978) and partly from the individuals' distinctive interpretation of the role (Burke & Stets, 2009). When role identities are more salient in a given situation, they carry important self-meanings and are enacted with specific sets of social relations, which carry both internal and external accountability pressures (Wry & York, 2017).

Entrepreneurs, like all individuals, have multiple roles that may, or may not, be salient based on the entrepreneurs' current situation. Founders use different lines of reasoning in their attention to risk when assuming the role identity of entrepreneur, manager, or investor (Mathias & Williams, 2014). Decisions may also depend on the level of one's entrepreneurial passion, also linked to identity-relevant tasks (Cardon et al., 2009). In addition to professional roles related to economic growth, sustainable entrepreneurs likely also integrate role identities related to creating positive social and environmental outcomes.

In contrast to IDT, SIT focuses on intergroup relations within social categories (e.g., gender, nationality, sports team), and the cognitive processes associated with belonging to those groups (Hogg et al., 1995). For SIT a sense of self is derived from group membership (Burke & Stets, 2009; Tajfel & Turner, 1979). The social identities that the organization and its members ascribe to can help explain intergroup behavior, their network of relationships, and the ways in which people perceive and distinguish the organization (Shepherd & Haynie, 2009). Fauchart and Gruber (2011) showed that entrepreneurs behave and act in ways consistent with their social identities and therefore imprint their self-concepts on key dimensions of their emerging firm. In some ventures, founders ascribe to a missionary social identity, in which the entrepreneur desires to be a powerful change agent in society (Fauchart & Gruber, 2011). For sustainable entrepreneurs, SIT would suggest that entrepreneurial actions focus on distinguishing the entrepreneur and his or her organization from others and enhances the concept of self as being unique and different (Oyserman, Coon, & Kemmelmeier, 2002). The more differentiated a sustainable entrepreneur is from a traditional entrepreneur, the more likely their social identity will ascribe to environmental and social welfare logics (Wry & York, 2017). However, the need for belongingness with others is also a component of social identity necessary to maximize an entrepreneur's psychological well-being (Shepherd & Haynie, 2009). Prior work has shown social identity affects identity verification and self-efficacy at the individual level (Burke & Stets, 2009). However, there is little known about how social identities of individuals, such as entrepreneurs, impact performance outcomes of new ventures.

In the entrepreneurship literature, individual-level entrepreneurial identities influence organizational level entrepreneurial resilience. For example, Powell and Baker (2014) show how entrepreneurs' role identities influence the level of resilience utilized when creating and building a new organization. Murnieks and Mosakowski (2007) extend SIT (Stryker, 1989; Stryker & Burke, 2000) to propose that certain individuals hold salient entrepreneurial identities which motivate them to act as entrepreneurs. Other recent studies have expanded on the notion of entrepreneurial identity and its influence on entrepreneurial passion (Cardon et al., 2009), identity aspiration (Farmer, Yao, & Kung-Mcintyre, 2011), investor perceptions (Navis & Glynn, 2011), and commitment to entrepreneurial behavior (Murnieks, Mosakowski, & Cardon, 2014). Similarly, founder identity has been used to better understand role transitions (Hoang & Gimeno, 2010) and how a founder's identity shapes organizational identity (Fauchart & Gruber, 2011). At a more general level, individual identity has been a context for understanding identity conflicts in family business (Shepherd & Haynie, 2009), different roles entrepreneurs take on as they grow their ventures (Mathias & Williams, 2014; Teoh & Foo, 1997), organizational identity (Fauchart & Gruber, 2011; Moss et al., 2011; Powell & Baker, 2014), and social venture creation (Wry & York, 2017). Despite these studies, there is still little known about how social and role identity interact in the sustainable entrepreneurship context. To address this gap, we propose the relationship between sustainable entrepreneurs and entrepreneurial accelerators provides a robust context for developing theory. Sustainable entrepreneurs likely enter accelerator environments with different identities, and the ventures formed may be influenced by these identities.

Sustainable entrepreneurs and accelerators

Accelerators are a recently developed method for supporting the development of entrepreneurs (Hallen, Bingham, & Cohen, 2014). These programs help entrepreneurs with the new venture process by providing formal training and mentorship in a full-time, short-term cohort model (Cohen, 2013; Hochberg, 2015). Scholars suggest that accelerators emphasize expanding entrepreneurs' networks through mentoring, education (Cohen, 2013; Radojevich-Kelley & Hoffman, 2012), and improving opportunities for future investor relationships and capital investments (Fehder & Hochberg, 2014; Miller & Bound, 2011). Despite exponential growth since the first accelerator program in 2006 (Miller & Bound, 2011), little is known regarding the value of these programs, how they are defined and distinguished from other network/investment groups, and how micro processes create value for entrepreneurs (Hallen et al., 2014, Hochberg, 2015; Lall, Bowles, & Baird, 2013; Radojevich-Kelley & Hoffman, 2012).

We know even less about the relationship between sustainable entrepreneurs and accelerators. Two preliminary studies aim to understand how incubators and accelerators aid in the development of the social entrepreneurship sector (Casasnovas & Bruno, 2013; Levinsohn, 2014), but have limited findings. Levinsohn classified differences between social incubators and social accelerators, while Casasnovas and Bruno found three accelerators strengthened their financial sustainability and ability to communicate their social impact but had difficulty in attracting investment. Because accelerators are less than ten years old, data on the survival and performance of such organizations, and their respective portfolio companies, are limited. There is an opportunity to better understand how and why sustainable entrepreneurs join accelerator groups and navigate those relationships to grow and scale their ventures. First, we distinguish between an economically-driven accelerator and a sustainability-driven accelerator. We define *traditional accelerators* as economically-driven, whose primary focus is to find the most efficient way to scale new ventures and maximize profits; we define *impact accelerators* as sustainability-driven and primarily focus on building scalable ventures that provide positive social, environmental, and economic impact.

By using sustainable entrepreneurship and identity as theoretical lenses, we examine the effects of joining different types of accelerators. In accelerators, organized programs, and groups, sustainable entrepreneurs inherently take on social and role identities that become more, or less, salient depending on the type of accelerator joined. We next theorize how accelerator membership and interaction of social identities with specific role identities of the sustainable entrepreneur can be utilized to understand the impact the group membership has on entrepreneurs and their ventures.

Theoretical development

As discussed, previous research in identity and entrepreneurship has looked at the influence of role identity (Wry & York, 2017) and social identity (Fauchart & Gruber, 2011) independently. In this chapter, we integrate both role and social identity in the context of sustainable entrepreneurs (Powell & Baker, 2014). We theorize that sustainable entrepreneurs have salient role identities based on their previous professional and personal experiences; however, reasons vary as to what has brought them to start a sustainable venture. For example, one individual may have worked for a solar-energy nongovernmental organization, while another formerly worked for a tech-based company. Both individuals may decide to start a sustainable venture, but for different reasons rooted in their previous role identities (York et al., 2016). Entrepreneurship research suggests individuals who start sustainable enterprises have a salient economic *and* social/ecological welfare identity (Rindova, Barry, & Ketchen, 2009). However, the entrepreneurs who balance this tension equitably are quite rare, as most individuals will tilt towards one logic over the other (Wry & York, 2017). The challenge, then, is that sustainable entrepreneurs may experience internal conflict as they pursue their venture, but may not be fully aware of the source of tension. We know very little about the individual's awareness and proactive management of such tensions. Identity control theory (ICT) can help explain this relationship.

ICT (Burke 2003, 2006) seeks to understand the emotions and behaviors that result from mitigating identity discrepancies and preserving the relationships that help define the identity of an individual (Stets & Burke, 2005). Essentially, ICT argues that identities within the self are potentially *malleable* based on feedback received from others. Thus, the extent to which individuals form a more salient and confident perception of identity depends on the feedback they receive and how they process such feedback (Burke, 2006). ICT explains how individuals manage the tensions between multiple identities.

Central to ICT are two assumptions: each identity has meaning, and each identity is viewed as a control system comprised of four parts (Brewer, 1991). First, the *identity standard* is the set of meanings or common responses associated with an identity. Second, each identity has specific *perceptions* of meanings, mostly from others, in the situation relevant to one's identity. The perceptions and identity standard are compared against a *comparator*, and the remaining *discrepancy*, or error, results in behavior change to minimize the discrepancy. This process is used to verify or confirm one's identity, and each identity works to align perceived meanings to the expected identity standard. A sustainable entrepreneur faces the challenge of having multiple, often conflicting, identity standards and perceptions with potentially large discrepancies about the social, environmental, and economic impact she or he aims to have with her or his venture. As she or he aims to minimize discrepancies others may perceive about their roles in making a social, environmental, and economic impact of her or his venture, she or he will also clarify her or his identity in those decisions. ICT can thus be a mechanism to explain how particular role identities may lead beyond opportunity recognition and into venture creation and emergence.

Wry and York (2017) illustrate how sustainable entrepreneurs at the pre-venture stage will identify and develop opportunities based on the salience of their role identity. For example, entrepreneurs may form a more commercial venture if they have a more salient economic role identity (e.g., the entrepreneur previously worked as an investment banker). Consider the following anecdotal example: a sustainable entrepreneur with a role identity as a former venture capitalist, but also a personal passion for, and thus identity linked to, social welfare, decides to pursue a venture focused on water technology in developing countries. As she pursues her new venture, ICT becomes a mechanism to monitor whether her identity standard as a sustainable entrepreneur matches the perceptions of others. Feedback from others may question who she is and what she aims to do with her venture, especially given her former experience as a venture capitalist. In order to mitigate discrepancies from others related to her role identity as a previous venture capitalist, or her passion for social welfare, she uses ICT to align her own identity standard and feedback from others by either changing the way she thinks of her role or shifts her focus.

It is important to note the entrepreneurs' desire to pursue social, economic, or ecological value also depends on the salience of such value ascribed to her identity. While the aforementioned example is based on one anecdotal informal interview, we recognize the extent to which the entrepreneur is aware of these multiple identities, and the different feedback she receives will play a role in not only the stakeholder relationships developed but the survival of the venture. Thus, the entrepreneurs' use of ICT and her ability to manage tensions within her multiple role identities illustrates our first proposition:

> ***Proposition 1. The greater the sustainable entrepreneur's awareness of, and ability to manage, role identity tensions, the more likely the entrepreneur will reach venture emergence.***

Sustainable entrepreneurs, role identity, and social identity

Sustainable entrepreneurs must not only manage multiple role identities but also social identities as the new venture and its members seek stakeholder relationships. All entrepreneurs interact with stakeholders to reduce uncertainty and build credibility (Sarasvathy, 2001). While role identities are likely more salient than social identities at the opportunity identification stage of a venture, social identities play a critical role in venture growth and building stakeholder relationships. The social relationships developed at early stages of a sustainable enterprise are crucial to the emergence of an enterprise for two reasons (Battilana & Dorado, 2010). First, sustainable entrepreneurs seek groups to belong to and achieve psychological well-being (Shepherd & Haynie, 2009). Support groups and startup meet ups have become a popular example of how entrepreneurs achieve a sense of belonging. Second, social identities help to explain the ways in which people perceive and distinguish the organization (Shepherd & Haynie, 2009), providing signals to potential customers and investors about the nature of the organization. For example, belonging to a co-working space founded by an experienced entrepreneur serves to mitigate uncertainty about the credibility of the entrepreneur (Plummer, Allison, & Connelly, 2015). Without an entrepreneur's sense of well-being and credibility, the venture risks failure.

Accelerators seek to provide a social identity for entrepreneurs to overcome this risk. Entrepreneurs join accelerators with the intention of "accelerating" their venture's emergence. Role identities held by the entrepreneurs will likely impact the type of accelerator they pursue, but entrepreneurs will also take on a new social identity once they join the accelerator. The accelerator model is built on the assumption that entrepreneurs seek groups similar to themselves to strengthen their sense of belonging in an often lonely journey (Hallen et al., 2014). Because sustainable entrepreneurs hold multiple role identities, some of which may conflict with the economic pursuit of traditional accelerators, we would expect sustainable entrepreneurs to pursue an impact accelerator over and above a traditional economic accelerator. Wry and York (2017) theorized that *balanced* entrepreneurs with role identities equally linked to commercial and social welfare logics will be more willing to work with diverse stakeholders, are better equipped to create hybrid organizations, and will join groups that hold different social identities. However, the majority of individuals pursuing sustainable ventures likely fall into the *mixed* entrepreneur category, in which role identities tilt either towards the social/ecological logic *or* the commercial logic. When the entrepreneur's role identity salience tilts more towards a commercial logic or a social welfare logic, they will then pursue accelerators that resonate with the more highly salient role identity. For example, a sustainable entrepreneur looking for advocacy support of a particular sustainable fish-farm model in rural Africa may join an accelerator that has other ventures who work in Africa and hold similar logics. Alternatively, entrepreneurs may opt for a mismatch of their role identity to the accelerator's social identity. One example may be the sustainable entrepreneur that is looking for capital support and may join a group unassociated with social welfare or the pursuit of environmental goals to create legitimacy in the eyes of investors. The question then becomes: what happens when *mixed* sustainable entrepreneurs join a traditional, rather than impact, accelerator?

Recall the aforementioned anecdote of the former venture capitalist pursuing a water technology for developing countries. Because of her network from her previous job and relative accessibility to the tech-community in her local community, she applies to a traditional accelerator with a dominant economic logic. The entrepreneur joins the accelerator and quickly realizes that the salient social identity is focused on technology and economic impact over and above social and environmental impact. Herein lies an inherent conflict, as membership in a traditional accelerator will typically not endorse a social identity focused on the social welfare or environmental aspect of the venture. The entrepreneur acquired the social identity that the accelerator holds. In order to mitigate the discrepancy from perceived identities and her identity standard, she shifts her current identities. Utilizing ICT, she must manage this shift by creating a new role identity as a result, either ignoring the ecological and social welfare logic, integrating it, or strengthening it. The more she is able to manage her own identity, the more she will be able to manage different stakeholders relevant to the growth of her venture and integrate her identities focused on social, environmental, and economic pursuits. The emergence of her sustainable venture depends on how well she can manage working with stakeholders who may not hold an environmental or social welfare identity. Thus, we theorize that the sustainable entrepreneur's venture also depends on the social identity of the accelerator:

> ***Proposition 2. The relationship between the entrepreneur's awareness of role identity tension and venture emergence is moderated by the social identity of the accelerator.***

Sustainable entrepreneurs, accelerator membership, and emergence

We propose this entrepreneur's performance in the accelerator and beyond depends on the ability to manage the identity conflicts incurring in the accelerator and with other stakeholders as proposed by ICT. Accelerator membership, whether traditional or impact focused, conveys a specific social identity the entrepreneur will adopt when they join. What then do entrepreneurs give up or gain based on alignment between their personal role identities and the social identity of the accelerators they join?

In our anecdote, the former venture capitalist turned sustainable entrepreneur involved in a traditional economic accelerator will likely face conflicting role and social identities. Conversely, the social welfare role identity of a sustainable entrepreneur will likely complement the social identity of an impact accelerator. Thus, the entrepreneur has an opportunity to choose either a conflicting or complementing social identity through their choice of accelerator membership. The misalignment of accelerator membership's social identity and role identity of the entrepreneur may have important performance implications.

Continuing our thought experiment of the water technology sustainable venture, the entrepreneur may be able to gain resources that are otherwise unattainable through joining a traditional accelerator that focuses on economic potential and growth. At the same time, the sustainable entrepreneur likely faces the tradeoff of not finding others who align with their social welfare and ecological values. For example, the venture may gain valuable performance metrics, such as a decrease in customer acquisition costs, due to attention focused on economic performance metrics in the traditional economic accelerator. In the impact accelerator, the ventures are focused on resource acquisition and growth in both social-performance metrics and economic metrics. The entrepreneurs and accelerators must manage additional metrics with limited time and bandwidth. When a role identity does not align with the social identity of the accelerator, the entrepreneur is likely to have more economic venture-performance-related benefits than when it is aligned because the focus becomes solely on metrics related to economic performance and resource acquisition. In this sense, the sustainable entrepreneur may reach venture emergence at a faster pace in a traditional accelerator than one in an impact accelerator. Conversely, a sustainable entrepreneur whose identity tips more towards salient commercially oriented roles may gain more help and feedback from an impact accelerator. In sum, we posit that accelerator membership that endorses a social identity that is in conflict with the dominant role identities of the entrepreneur may provide greater assistance and, thus, improve the speed of firm emergence. These relationships are captured in the model presented in Figure 3.1.1 and visually represented in Figure 3.1.2.

Proposition 3a. When sustainable entrepreneurs join accelerators that hold a conflicting social identity with the entrepreneurs' current role identities, their ventures will emerge more quickly.

Proposition 3b. When sustainable entrepreneurs join accelerators that hold a complementing social identity with the entrepreneurs' role identities, their ventures will emerge more slowly.

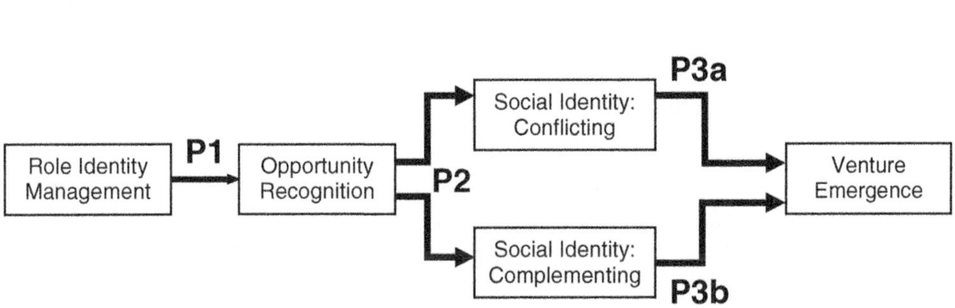

Figure 3.1.1 A process model demonstrating the interaction of role identity and social identity when sustainable entrepreneurs join accelerators

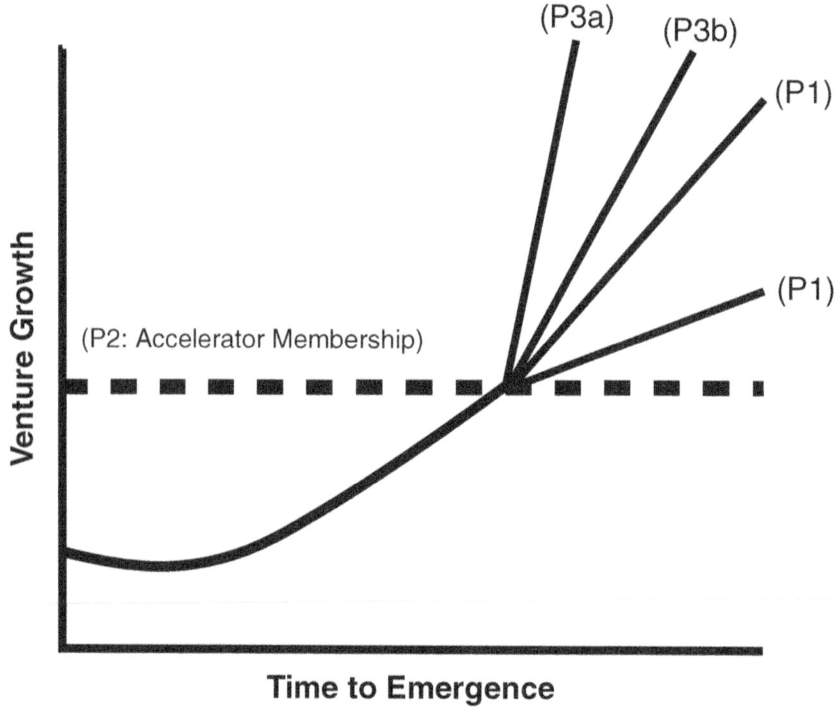

Figure 3.1.2 Sustainable entrepreneurs venture emergence relative to types of social identities

Of course, venture emergence in accelerators likely does not come without tradeoffs. For example, upon joining a traditional economic accelerator that focuses solely on economic performance, sustainable entrepreneurs find a way to grapple with the tension of prioritizing social, environmental, and economic metrics without necessarily having a guiding model to do so (O'Neil & Ucbasaran, 2016). The ability of the entrepreneur to successfully engage in an economic accelerator, emerge as a venture, and continue to pursue a sustainable mission is likely difficult. We propose that the success of the entrepreneur and the sustainable venture is dependent on ICT's notion of identity self-management. Venture emergence and growth in accelerator memberships becomes a matter of whether the sustainable entrepreneur can successfully manage her own identities and recognize the long-term goals over the short-term tradeoffs.

Discussion and conclusions

This chapter aimed to develop a theory about sustainable entrepreneurs at a critical point in venture emergence. First, we looked at how sustainable entrepreneurs manage multiple identities and how his or her awareness and self-management influence his or her venture. We then looked at how both social and role identity interact at the earliest stage of sustainable ventures to propose how and why role and social identities may impact venture emergence. In addition, we theorized the role of accelerators, as they are emerging and quickly becoming an important resource for many entrepreneurs

(Cohen & Hochberg, 2014). Current work in identity salience and identity management strategies for hybrid entrepreneurs looks only at the nascent stage of deciding to establish a venture (Fauchart & Gruber, 2011; Wry & York, 2017). We built off this work to theorize the implications on venture emergence for sustainable entrepreneurs pursuing accelerator memberships.

Our analysis raises several important implications. First, we theorize about the inherent identity tensions of sustainable entrepreneurs. A sustainable entrepreneur seeking stakeholder relationships must be aware of how belonging to various social groups may conflict with, or change the salience of, currently held role identities. Second, we suggest that the interaction of role and social identity can be understood better through the context of sustainable entrepreneurship and specifically within accelerator membership. Following ICT, sustainable entrepreneurs can either become polarized in such a conflict or be willing to internalize the tensions and grow from the conflict. Third, we theorize about accelerators specifically. We propose testable propositions to identify whether conflicting social and role identities may help accelerate the venture at a faster pace than if social and role identities were in complete alignment. While the interaction of social and role identities can be applied to a wide variety of organization contexts, our propositions provide specific insights in the literatures of sustainable entrepreneurship, identity and entrepreneurship, and the accelerator context.

Sustainable entrepreneurs focus on social welfare, reducing environmental degradation and maximizing profit through entrepreneurial action (Thompson et al., 2011). They endure significant challenges as they pursue hybrid organizations (Battilana & Lee, 2014) and understand how to balance their own beliefs as they establish legitimacy from diverse audiences (O'Neil & Ucbasaran, 2016). We theorize how identity may help sustainable entrepreneurs overcome these challenges as they pursue stakeholder groups such as accelerators. As soon as they belong to an accelerator, they have to develop a new social identity, especially if they join a group with conflicting logics. This may, in turn, lead to building stakeholder relationships they otherwise would have never had and, thus, may lead to rapid growth for the venture in the long term. However, if the entrepreneur believes these are sacrifices he or she needs to make, he or she will view economic identities as negative and be unable to manage the tension within his or her own role identity. ICT is an important mechanism that entrepreneurs may use to combat their biases and determine the most beneficial partners. Future studies can test these propositions by studying what types of accelerators sustainable entrepreneurs join and the implications of belonging to them. Further research could then be designed to understand how sustainable entrepreneurs pursue growth along with social and environmental goals.

Our testable propositions provide additional insights into the growing body of literature in identity and entrepreneurship. While Wry and York (2017) illustrated how role identities may influence stakeholder relationships, and Fauchart and Gruber (2011) showed social identity impacting typologies of entrepreneurs, there is little known about the interaction of social and role identity in the entrepreneurship context (for one exception, see Powell & Baker, 2014). We propose that role and social identity tensions occur when sustainable entrepreneurs feel as though they must lose, or give up, one identity for another. We argue that tensions do not have to lead to giving up one identity for the other but building an awareness and mechanism for managing such identities. Although there are a few identity scales related to specific role identities (i.e., Burke & Reitzes, 1981; Burke & Tilly, 1977; Callero, 1992), future research may extend such scales to entrepreneurs interacting with changes in role and social identities. This could be empirically examined by testing identity salience, especially over the time of joining groups like accelerators.

Accelerators are a promising context to study identity because of their fixed-time, cohort-based model. There is little known about how accelerators are distinct from other network/investment groups and how micro processes create value for entrepreneurs (Hallen et al., 2014, Hochberg, 2015; Lall et al., 2013, Radojevich-Kelley & Hoffman, 2012). Here, we articulate how sustainable entrepreneurs inherently take on social and role identities that become more or less salient when they join accelerators, depending on the type of accelerator. We propose that traditional accelerators with a focus on economic impact may benefit by recruiting sustainable entrepreneurs who have a willingness to pursue economically-driven social identities to gain venture emergence. Such entrepreneurs have an awareness of their role identity salience to social, environmental, and economic logics, but are willing to work around a group that holds a social identity rooted in economic goals. We also propose that impact accelerators with a focus on social and environmental impact may be most beneficial to sustainable entrepreneurs who are unable to manage such identity tensions. While these sustainable ventures may not grow as quickly, role identity salience will be strengthened towards social and environmental pursuits.

An important implication here is that accelerators, just like entrepreneurs, may not all be measured equally. The goals of an impact accelerator may be different from a traditional accelerator. However, both will benefit from understanding the previous role identities of sustainable entrepreneurs as these identities influence how the entrepreneur will integrate new social identities. This integration is also dependent on how open the accelerator is to accepting and integrating salient role identities of those entrepreneurs who join them. We know that certain salient role identities may also influence hostility towards out-group members; thus, the degree to which the accelerator views social or environmental identities as acceptable is important (Burke & Stets, 2009).

The accelerator may also play a role in encouraging the integration of role and social identity by respecting and encouraging the entrepreneur in their pursuit of social-, environmental- and economic-based logics. What we do not know is whether or not this actually happens in practice. Empirically examining the strength of entrepreneurs' salience of role and social identities throughout the accelerator could lead to further insights related to identity management. We expect that as long as both the accelerator and entrepreneur understand the needs to gain venture emergence and respects individuals' previous and current role identities, managing tensions becomes much easier. However, testing such a theory across different types of accelerators and different entrepreneurs will serve the field and catalyze further research on the impacts of such stakeholder groups for emerging organizations.

Research on identity and entrepreneurship has drawn increased attention in recent years. We see the context of sustainable entrepreneurs in accelerators as raising important implications for addressing daunting theoretical gaps. The more we understand how identities influence entrepreneurs and the groups they join, the more likely we are able to help sustainable ventures not only survive but thrive in the long term. We propose that sustainable entrepreneurs who manage multiple identity tensions may be better served in a traditional accelerator, while those unable to manage such tensions may be better served in an impact accelerator. Studying the context of sustainable entrepreneurship in accelerators has important implications for addressing pressing social and environmental problems. While empirical work is clearly required to appropriately operationalize how identity influences the emergence of sustainable ventures, our hope is that this chapter encourages research on these relationships.

References

Alvarez, S. A., & Barney, J. B. 2007. Discovery and creation: Alternative theories of entrepreneurial action. *Strategic Entrepreneurship Journal*, 1(1–2): 11–26.

Ashforth, B. E. 2001. *Role transitions in organizational life: An identity based perspective*. Mahwah: NJ: Lawrence Erlbaum Associates.

Battilana, J., & Dorado, S. 2010. Building sustainable hybrid organizations: The case of commercial microfinance organizations. *Academy of Management Journal*, 53(6): 1419–1440.

Battilana, J., & Lee, M. 2014. Advancing research on hybrid organizing: Insights from the study of social enterprises. *The Academy of Management Annals*, 8(1): 397–441.

Beveridge, R., & Guy, S. 2005. The rise of the eco-preneur and the messy world of environmental innovation. *Local Environment*, 10(6): 665–676.

Bornstein, D. 2004. *How to change the world*. New York: Oxford University Press.

Brewer, M. B. 1991. The social self: On being the same and different at the same time. *Personality and Social Psychology Bulletin*, 17: 475–482.

Burke, P. J. 2003. Relationships among multiple identities. In P.J. Burke, T.J. Ownens, R.T. Serpe, & P.A. Thoits (Eds.), *Advances in identity theory and research*. New York: Kluwer Academic/Plenum Publishers.

Burke, P. J. 2006. Identity change. *Social Psychology Quarterly*, 69(1): 81–96.

Burke, P. J., & Reitzes, D. C. 1981. The link between identity and role performance. *Social Psychology Quarterly*, 44(2): 83–92.

Burke, P. J., & Stets, J. E. 2009. *Identity theory*. Oxford, UK: Oxford University Press.

Burke, P. J., & Tilly, J. C. 1977. The measurement of role identity. *Social Forces*, 55: 881–897.

Callero, P. 1992. The meaning of self-in-role: A modified measure of role-identity. *Social Forces*, 71(2): 485–501.

Cardon, M. S., Wincent, J., Singh, J., & Drnovsek, M. 2009. The nature and experience of entrepreneurial passion. *Academy of Management Review*, 34(3): 511–532.

Casasnovas, G., & Bruno, A. V. 2013. Scaling social ventures: An exploratory study of social incubators and accelerators. *Journal of Management for Global Sustainability*, 1(2): 173–197.

Christie, M., & Honig, B. 2006. Social entrepreneurship: New research findings. *Journal of World Business*, 41(1): 1–5.

Cohen, S. 2013. What do accelerators do? Insights from incubators and angels. *Innovations*, 8(3–4): 19–25.

Cohen, S., & Hochberg, Y. V. 2014. *Accelerating startups: The seed accelerator phenomenon*. Available at SSRN 2418000.

Dacin, P., Dacin, M., & Matear, M. 2010. Social entrepreneurship: Why we don't need a new theory and how we move forward from here. *Academy of Management Perspectives*, 24(3): 37–57.

Dacin, M. T., Dacin, P. A., & Tracey, P. 2011. Social entrepreneurship: A critique and future directions. *Organization Science*, 22(5): 1203–1213.

Dean, T. J., & McMullen, J. S. 2007. Toward a theory of sustainable entrepreneurship: Reducing environmental degradation through entrepreneurial action. *Journal of Business Venturing*, 22(1): 50–76.

Dees, J. G. 1998. Enterprising nonprofits. *Harvard Business Review*, 76: 54–67.

Dey, P. 2006. The rhetoric of social entrepreneurship: Paralogy and new language games in academic discourse. In C. Steyaert & D. Hjorth (Eds.), *Entrepreneurship as social change: A third movements of entrepreneurship book*: 121–144. Cheltenham, UK: Edward Elgar.

Farmer, S. M., Yao, X., & Kung-Mcintyre, K. 2011. The behavioral impact of entrepreneur identity aspiration and prior entrepreneurial experience. *Entrepreneurship Theory and Practice*, 35(2): 245–273.

Fauchart, E., & Gruber, M. 2011. Darwinians, communitarians, and missionaries: The role of founder identity in entrepreneurship. *Academy of Management Journal*, 54(5): 935–957.

Fehder, D. C., & Hochberg, Y. V. 2014. *Accelerators and the regional supply of venture capital investment.* Available at SSRN.

Gibbs, A. A. 1996. Entrepreneurship and small business management: Can we afford to neglect them in the twenty-first century business school? *British Journal of Management*, 7(4): 309–322.

Gibbs, D. 2009. Sustainability entrepreneurs, ecopreneurs and the development of a sustainable economy. *Greener Management International*, 55: 63–78.

Haigh, N., & Hoffman, A. J. 2012. Hybrid organizations: The next chapter of sustainable business. *Organizational Dynamics*, 41: 126–134.

Hall, J. K., Daneke, G. A., & Lenox, M. J. 2010. Sustainable development and entrepreneurship: Past contributions and future directions. *Journal of Business Venturing*, 25(5): 439–448.

Hallen, B. L., Bingham, C. B., & Cohen, S. L. 2014. *Do accelerators accelerate? A study of venture accelerators as a path to success.* Available at SSRN 10.5465/AMBPP.2014.185DO.

Hoang, H., & Gimeno, J. 2010. Becoming a founder: How founder role identity affects entrepreneurial transitions and persistence in founding. *Journal of Business Venturing*, 25(1): 41–53.

Hochberg, Y. V. 2015. Accelerating entrepreneurs and ecosystems: The seed accelerator model. *Innovation Policy and the Economy*, 16: 25–51.

Hogg, M. A., & Abrams, D. 1990. Social motivation, self-esteem, and social identity. In D. Abrams & M.A. Hogg (Eds.), *Social identity theory. Constructive and critical advances*: 44–70. London: Harvester Wheatsheaf.

Hogg, M. A., Terry, D. J., & White, K. M. 1995. A tale of two theories: A critical comparison of identity theory with social identity theory. *Social Psychology Quarterly*, 58: 255–269.

Isaak, R. 2002. The making of the ecopreneur. *Greener Management International*, 38: 81–91.

Jacobs, M. 1995. Sustainable development, capital substitution and economic humility: A response to Beckerman. *Environmental Values*, 4(1): 57–68.

Lall, S., Bowles, L., & Baird, R. 2013. Bridging the "pioneer gap": The role of accelerators in launching high-impact enterprises. *Innovations*, 8(3–4): 105–137.

Lenox, M., & York, J. G. 2011. Environmental entrepreneurship. In A. J. Hoffman & T. Bansal (Eds.), *Oxford handbook of business and the environment.* Oxford, UK: Oxford University Press.

Levinsohn, D. 2014. The role of accelerators in the development of the practising social entrepreneur. In *Institute for Small Business and Entrepreneurship: The Future of Enterprise – The Innovation Revolution.* Manchester, UK. Available at: www.diva-portal.org/smash/get/diva2:762234/FULLTEXT01.pdf (accessed 16 August 2018).

Mathias, B. D., & Williams, D. W. 2014. The impact of role identities on entrepreneurs' evaluation and selection of opportunities. *Journal of Management*, 43: 1–27.

McCall, G., & Simmons, J. L. 1978. *Identities and interaction.* New York: Free Press.

Mead, G. H. 1934. *Mind, self, and society: From the stand-point of a social behaviorist.* Chicago, IL: University Chicago Press.

Meek, W. R., Pacheco, D. F., & York, J. G. 2010. The impact of social norms on entrepreneurial action: Evidence from the environmental entrepreneurship context. *Journal of Business Venturing*, 25(5): 493–509.

Miller, P., & Bound, K. 2011. *The startup factories: The rise of accelerator programmes to support new technology ventures.* London: NESTA.

Moss, T., Short, J., Payne, G. T., & Lumpkin, G. T. 2011. Dual identities in social ventures: An exploratory study. *Entrepreneurship: Theory & Practice*, 35(4): 805–830.

Murnieks, C. Y., & Mosakowski, E. 2007. Who am I? Looking inside the "entrepreneurial identity." In A. Zacharakis et al. (Eds.), *Frontiers of entrepreneurship research*, vol. 27: 5(5). Babson Park, MA: Babson College.

Murnieks, C. Y., Mosakowski, E., & Cardon, M. S. 2014. Pathways of passion identity centrality, passion, and behavior among entrepreneurs. *Journal of Management*, 40(6): 1583–1606.

Navis, C., & Glynn, M. A. 2011. Legitimate distinctiveness and the entrepreneurial identity: Influence on investor judgments of new venture plausibility. *Academy of Management Review*, 36(3): 479–499.

Oakes, P. J., Haslam, S. A., & Turner, J. C. 1994. *Stereotyping and social reality*. Malden, MA: Blackwell.

O'Neil, I., & Ucbasaran, D. 2016. Balancing "what matters to me" & "what matters to them" in entrepreneurs' legitimation efforts. *Journal of Business Venturing*, 31(2): 133–152.

Oyserman, D., Coon, H. M., & Kemmelmeier, M. 2002. Rethinking individualism and collectivism: Evaluation of theoretical assumptions and meta-analyses. *Psychological Bulletin*, 128(1): 3–72.

Pacheco, D. F., Dean, T. J., & Payne, D. S. 2010. Escaping the green prison: Entrepreneurship and the creation of opportunities for sustainable development. *Journal of Business Venturing*, 25(5): 464–480.

Pacheco, D. F., York, J. G., Dean, T. J., & Sarasvathy, S. D. 2010. The coevolution of institutional entrepreneurship: A tale of two theories. *Journal of Management*, 36(4): 974–1010.

Parrish, B. D. 2010. Sustainability-driven entrepreneurship: Principles of organization design. *Journal of Business Venturing*, 25(5): 510–523.

Peredo, A. M., & McLean, M. 2006. Social entrepreneurship: A critical review of the concept. *Journal of World Business*, 41(1): 56–65.

Pierre, K., Moss, T., & Lumpkin, G.T. 2015. An integration and extension of sustainable entrepreneurship and sustainable livelihoods. *Academy of Management Proceedings*, 1: 17806.

Plummer, L., Allison, T., & Connelly, B. 2015. Better together? Signaling interactions in new venture pursuit of initial external capital. *Academy of Management Journal*, 59(5): 1585–1604.

Powell, E. E., & Baker, T. 2014. It's what you make of it: Founder identity and enacting strategic responses to adversity. *Academy of Management Journal*, 57(5): 1406–1433.

Radojevich-Kelley, N., & Hoffman, D. L. 2012. Analysis of accelerator companies: An exploratory case study of their programs, processes, and early results. *Small Business Institute Journal*, 8(2): 54–70.

Rindova, V., Barry, D., & Ketchen, D. J. 2009. Entrepreneuring as emancipation. *Academy of Management Review*, 34(3): 477–491.

Sarasvathy, S.D. 2001. Causation and effectuation: Toward a theoretical shift from economic inevitability to entrepreneurial contingency. *Academy of Management Review*, 26: 243–263.

Shepherd, D.A., & Haynie, J. 2009. Birds of a feather don't always flock together: Identity management in entrepreneurship. *Journal of Business Venturing*, 24(4): 316–337.

Shepherd, D. A., & Patzelt, H. 2011. The new field of sustainable entrepreneurship: Studying entrepreneurial action linking "what is to be sustained" with "what is to be developed." *Entrepreneurship Theory and Practice*, 35(1): 137–163.

Short, J. C., Moss, T. W., & Lumpkin, G. T. 2009. Research in social entrepreneurship: Past contributions and future opportunities. *Strategic Entrepreneurship Journal*, 3(2): 161–194.

Sine, W. D., & Lee, B. 2009. Tilting at windmills? The environmental movement and the emergence of the U.S. wind energy sector. *Administrative Science Quarterly*, 54(1): 123–155.

Stets, J. E., & Burke, P. J. 2005. New directions in identity control theory. *Advances in Group Processes*, 22: 43–64.

Stryker, S. 1980. *Symbolic interactionism: A social structural version*. Menlo Park, CA: Benjamin/Cummings.

Stryker, S. 1989. Further developments in identity theory: Singularity versus multiplicity of self. In J. Berger, M. Zelditch & B. Anderson (Eds.), *Sociological theories in progress*. London: Sage.

Stryker, S., & Burke, P. J. 2000. The past, present, and future of an identity theory. *Social Psychology Quarterly*, 63(3): 284–297.

Tajfel, H., & Turner, J. 1979. An integrative theory of intergroup conflict. In W. Austin, & S. Worchel (Eds.), *The social psychology of intergroup relations*: 33–47. Monterey, CA: Brooks-Cole.

Teoh, H. Y., & Foo, S. L. 1997. Moderating effects of tolerance for ambiguity and risktaking propensity on the role conflict–perceived performance relationship: Evidence from Singaporean entrepreneurs. *Journal of Business Venturing*, 12: 67–81.

Thoits, P. A. 1983. Multiple identities and psychological well-being: A reformulation and test of the social isolation hypothesis. *American Sociological Review*, 48: 174–187.

Thompson, N., Kiefer, K., & York, J., 2011. Distinctions not dichotomies: Exploring social, sustainable, and environmental entrepreneurship. In G.T. Lumpkin & Jerome A. Katz (Eds.), *Social and Sustainable Entrepreneurship Advances in Entrepreneurship, Firm Emergence and Growth*: vol. 13: 201–229. Bingley, UK: Emerald Group Publishing Limited.

Tilley, F., & Young, W. 2006. Sustainability entrepreneurs: Could they be the true wealth generators of the future? *Greener Management International*, 55: 79–92.

Venkataraman, S. 1997. The distinctive domain of entrepreneurship research. In J. Katz & R. Brockhaus (Eds.), *Advances in entrepreneurship, firm emergence and growth*: 119–138. Greenwich, CT: JAI Press Inc.

Weerawardena, J., & Mort, G. S. 2006. Investigating social entrepreneurship: A multi-dimensional model. *Journal of World Business*, 41(1): 21–35.

Wry, T., & York, J. G. 2017. An identity based approach to social enterprise. *Academy of Management Review*, 42(3): 437–460.

York, J. G. 2009. Pragmatic sustainability: Translating environmental ethics into competitive advantage. *Journal of Business Ethics*, 85(Suppl. 1): 97–109.

York, J. G., O'Neil, I., & Sarasvathy, S. D. 2016. Exploring environmental entrepreneurship: Identity coupling, venture goals, and stakeholder incentives. *Journal of Management Studies*, 53(5): 695–737.

York, J. G., & Venkataraman, S. 2010. The entrepreneur–environment nexus: Uncertainty, innovation, and allocation. *Journal of Business Venturing*, 25(5): 449–463

3.2 The ethical and moral-based dimension of leadership in CSR-oriented strategies and sustainable entrepreneurship

Mara Del Baldo

Introduction

This chapter addresses the theme of leadership and its influence on corporate social responsibility (CSR) and sustainability-oriented strategies. Specifically, it aims to analyse, through a deductive and literature-based approach, the relevance of the ethical and moral leadership models with respect to the diffusion of CSR and sustainable entrepreneurship.

Raising awareness of social and environmental problems on a global scale requires more awareness for the responsible behaviour of companies. It has been noted that the best way to put sustainability into practice, both within large companies and small- and medium-sized enterprises (SMEs), is by means of CSR. The sustainability model of the Lisbon Treaty and the EU 2020 strategy – described as smart, inclusive and green growth (European Commission, 2011) – can be taken to the entrepreneurial level through various kinds of CSR activities "which include voluntary social and environmental services, private sustainability standards, transparency and stakeholder engagement, sustainable operations and relationships culminating in new business models in which sustainability constitutes the core business" (Fischler, 2014: 19).

However, the debate and implementation differ heavily (Herlyn and Radermacher, 2014; Shepherd and Patzelt, 2017b). Implementing sustainability within the business context means integrating CSR into the core business and/or reorienting enterprises with the aim of creating sustainability. On the one hand, this implies an authentic and effective CSR orientation. On the other, it implies a growth of sustainable entrepreneurship.

'Sustainable leaders' should be innovative and proactive in driving the change inside and outside the company toward sustainability. They should not be oriented to short-term financial and competitive success, or to an opportunistic use of CSR, merely aimed to increase the company's (and their own) legitimacy.

In accordance with these lines of thought, we argue that sustainable entrepreneurship requires a coherent leadership model, capable of triggering and stimulating social innovation (Vogel and Fischler-Strasak, 2014). Therefore, attention shifts to the leadership style and model adopted within an organisation, which mould the organisation's values system (starting from the vision, the norms and the employees' mindset). Thus the following questions are: How does leadership enhance CSR? Which leadership model is necessary to trigger and enhance sustainable entrepreneurship? Currently, the relationship between leadership, CSR and sustainable entrepreneurship has not been adequately investigated within both the theoretical and empirical perspectives. Nevertheless, it has been pointed out that:

> [m]any sustainability strategies still remain sidelined mostly owing to a lack of organisational will to adopt a "full monty" (that is an authentic and radical) approach to strategic roll out, despite the increase in sustainability reporting and creation of new internal functions dedicated to sustainability.
>
> (Ionescu-Somers, 2014: 180)

Linking ethical and moral-based leadership to the CSR and sustainable entrepreneurship discourse allows us to point out the relevance of an authentic orientation in supporting change and fostering sustainable entrepreneurship (Schaltegger and Wagner, 2008, 2011; Osburg, 2014; Chatterji and Zsolnai, 2017). It should be a dynamic, conceived and lived leadership, as 'a state of flux', because sustainability is a learning process and an ideal state that we are striving for (Visser, 2011).

The theoretical construct of responsible and sustainable leadership derives from the intersection of the moral-based leadership concepts with those of CSR and sustainable entrepreneurship. It is characterised by a multilevel approach that places the leader, his/her behaviour, attitudes and choices in the centre of the management of a company, division or team (Hansen, 2008; Waldman and Siegel, 2008; Magni and Pennarola, 2015). "A responsible leadership theory broadens the notion of leadership from a traditional leader-subordinate relationship to a leader-stakeholder relationship" (Du et al., 2013: 156). Responsible leadership is in fact described as "an ethical and socio-relational phenomenon that occurs in social interaction processes" (Maak and Pless, 2006: 99). The importance of approaching leadership in the context of stakeholder theory has been emphasised (Bass and Steidlmeier, 1999; Hansen, 2008; Avery and Bergsteiner, 2011). Accordingly, "building and cultivating ethically sound relations toward different stakeholders is an important responsibility of leaders in an interconnected stakeholder society" (Maak and Pless, 2006: 101). Responsible leadership requires leaders to also engage in involving stakeholders with virtue and integrity to build the best community and workplace (Jones, 2014).

Drawing from these premises, this chapter seeks to identify leadership models and attributes consistent with (and necessary to develop) an authentic CSR-oriented strategy and able to foster sustainable entrepreneurship.

Accordingly, in this chapter, we argue that leadership represents a key aspect that warrants more research within both CSR and sustainable entrepreneurship studies. The research questions that orients this study can be summarised as follows: Which leadership models favour authentic CSR practices? Are moral, ethical-based and virtues-based models of leadership effective in developing CSR and fostering sustainable entrepreneurship?

These questions guide the critical review of the different leadership approaches, bringing attention to the models that are most coherent in regard to the actual socio-economic context which requires managers and entrepreneurs to govern the internal and external complexity and actively contribute to sustainability. The methodological approach is mainly based on a literature review that surveys critical points in current literature that is relevant to the topic.

The work is structured as follows. First, we offer an analysis of the leadership theoretical framework in the context of the CSR debate. We begin with a brief methodological note, followed by an analysis of the antecedents of CSR and sustainable entrepreneurship in terms of values and virtues.

Second, a review of relevant literature on leadership approaches and models consistent with the CSR and sustainable entrepreneurship discourse is presented, emphasising the relationship between transformational, moral and virtues-based leadership and CSR-oriented strategies and sustainable entrepreneurship. Drawing from the analysis, four main propositions are introduced. The final sections illustrate the propositions and summarise the implications and limitations of the study.

Methodology

This research work is based on a literature review of scientific papers concerning leadership models and styles, focusing on ethical and moral-based leadership and virtues ethics in regard to the CSR and sustainable entrepreneurship debate. We used several databases, such as Elsevier, Essper Association, Wiley Online Library and Google Scholar. In order to identify the keywords, we considered some articles concerning leadership theories (Burns, 1978; Bass and Riggio, 2006; Brown and Treviño, 2006; Bass and Bass 2008; Melé, 2009a, 2009b; Olsen, 2010; Gardner et al., 2011). The keywords used are the following: CSR, sustainable entrepreneurship, leadership, virtues, values, ethics and morals. We checked the keywords in every part of the article: title, keywords, abstract and full article. Combining keywords, we found 230 items in the first list. Reading the abstracts, we carried out the first screening, excluding articles irrelevant to the research (59 articles). Concerning the articles, we excluded those that did not deal with the CSR, sustainable entrepreneurship and sustainability discourse (89). Moreover, we added 16 further contributions (chapters books and scientific articles) that have been suggested by experts in the field and have not previously been included among the selected ones. Finally, we obtained a list of 98 articles used as the basis of our literature review.

CSR and sustainable entrepreneurship: are they linked to leadership?

Corporate sustainability can be defined as "meeting the needs of a firm's direct and indirect stakeholders (such as shareholders, employees, clients, pressure groups, communities), without compromising its ability to meet the needs of future stakeholders as well" (Dyllick and Hockerts, 2002: 131). The concept of CSR is related to societal expectations for a business to behave ethically (York and Venkataraman, 2010).

> CSR is about how a business is run; values and beliefs become real when they are lived every day, and no amount of corporate rhetoric can substitute for direct evidence of management's sincere and meaningful dedication to a consistent set of values.
>
> (OECD, 2001: 159)

It can be appreciated as an intermediate stage (Marrewijk, 2003) through which companies try to direct themselves toward the ultimate goal of sustainability (WCED, 1987; Kaptein and Wempe, 2002; World Business Council for Sustainable Development, 2012) and voluntary incorporate social, ethical and environmental concerns in their daily business operations. Each step of this path is characterised by specific CSR activities which manifest intrinsic and extrinsic motivations (Linnanen and Panapanaan, 2002). Indeed, CSR can be either extrinsically motivated or based on intrinsic/idealistic reasons, which makes it a moral activity (Looser and Wehrmeyer, 2015: 2). Similarly, Martin (2002) identifies two types of motivation for CSR: instrumental motivations (aimed at increasing the shareholder value) and intrinsic motivations (given from the conviction that acting in a certain way is the right thing to do).

Extrinsic CSR is formalised, oriented towards increasing legitimacy by improving image and market share (Porter and Kramer, 2006) and aimed at external recognition. This opportunistic approach can render CSR a "façade" (Castelló and Lozano, 2011), giving rise to the well-known "green-washing" phenomena (Visser, 2011; Mahoney et al., 2013; Gray et al., 2014).

Intrinsic CSR is tied to a business culture consistent with responsible strategies and practices triggered by a vision promoted by the entrepreneur and/or the top management (Lamont, 2002; Jenkins, 2009) and shared within the entire organisation, making CSR a moral duty (Carroll, 1991; Campbell, 2007; Del Baldo, 2013, 2014; Looser and Wehrmeyer, 2015). It also nurtures authentic relationships with stakeholders, namely employees and customers (Graafland and Van de Ven, 2006; Story and Neves, 2015).

Extrinsic CSR is mainly diffused among large companies, while SMEs are more often intrinsically motivated and rely on their long-standing informal networks – triggered by entrepreneurs who are driven by values derived from their personal, familial and local community – rather than on formal policies (Spence and Schmidpeter, 2003; Spence et al., 2003; Matten and Moon, 2008; Fifka, 2012; Graafland and Mazereeuw-Van der Duijn Schouten, 2012; Murillo and Vallentin, 2012; Steurer et al., 2012; Del Baldo, 2013; Gunilla, 2014). Several studies in recent decades have highlighted the existence of many companies, often little known, which form a diversified universe rich of "champions" (Jenkins, 2009) that exemplifies an authentic CSR orientation and an ethical-based connotation (Hoivik von Weltzien and Melé, 2009; Hoivik von Weltzien, 2014). Notably, one can mention the community-based companies (Peredo and Chrisman, 2006), "spiritual enterprises" (Malloch, 2009; Pruzan, 2011; Capaldi, 2013), ideal-based companies (Molteni, 2009), territorial companies (Del Baldo, 2010), economy of communion companies (Del Baldo and Baldarelli, 2015), as well as family-based enterprises (Chua et al., 1999; Gallo and Cappuyns, 2004; Del Baldo, 2012; Aragón Amonarriz and Iturrioz Landart, 2016).

However, in all contexts, coherent and effective leadership approaches are required to implement sustainable entrepreneurship (Accenture, 2010; Mirvis et al., 2013) because the changing business environment has put pressure on all companies to fine-tune their business strategies and has fostered them to generate corporate social innovation (Hockerts and Wüstenhagen, 2010; Light, 2011; Osburg and Schmidpeter, 2013).

Since the late 2000s, a growing pressure due to the urgency to face economic, environmental and societal threats (see United Nations Assembly, 2015; UE Mille: 8–9) has been leading us towards the need to promote sustainable entrepreneurship. "These impellent calls signal entrepreneurs to act accordingly" (Greco and de Jong, 2017: 4), because "without sustainable organizations there is no sustainable development, thus, no future" (Weidinger, 2014: 289).

Entrepreneurship is recognised as a fundamental engine for economic and non-economic development (Schumpeter, 1934; Shane and Venkataraman, 2000; Audretsch and Thurik, 2004; Koe et al., 2014). However, as prior research has highlighted, entrepreneurs' primary objective does not necessarily imply that positive social or environmental values are being created as a result (Dean and McMullen, 2007; Pacheco et al., 2010; York and Venkataraman, 2010; Zu, 2014).

CSR is often confused with, or intended as, sustainable entrepreneurship. As a recent literature review on sustainable entrepreneurship studies points out, within the theoretical and empirical construct of sustainable entrepreneurship several concepts are involved, including CSR, the triple bottom line, social entrepreneurship, environmental entrepreneurship and mainstream entrepreneurship (Greco and de Jong, 2017). However, CSR and sustainable entrepreneurship do not exactly coincide because not only does CSR normally apply to business-oriented organisations but sustainable entrepreneurship can target different types of organisations, individuals and companies.

Sustainable entrepreneurship refers to the discovery, creation and exploitation of entrepreneurial opportunities that contribute to sustainability by generating social and environmental gains for others in society (Hockerts and Wüstenhagen, 2010; Pacheco et al., 2010; Shepherd and Patzelt, 2011; Osburg, 2014). Sustainable entrepreneurship has been widely acknowledged as the answer to the environmental (Cohen and Winn, 2007; Dean and McMullen, 2007; York and Venkataraman, 2010) and social challenges (Zahra et al., 2009). Indeed sustainable entrepreneurship is focused on the preservation of nature, life support and community in the pursuit of perceived opportunities to bring into existence future products, processes and services for gain, where gain is broadly construed to include economic and non-economic gains to individuals, the economy and society (Shepherd and Patzelt, 2011).

"Like for mainstream entrepreneurship, there have been a number of studies attempting to determine the drivers of sustainable entrepreneurship in both individuals and enterprises" (Greco and de Jong, 2017: 17). Existing literature distinguishes two classes of drivers. Internal motivations (such as inner beliefs, concerns about social and/or environmental causes) or the desire for self-employment, are internal factors, while external ones include market failures (triggering opportunity identification), network, social capital and public acceptance. However, despite the growth in sustainable entrepreneurship literature, there are still different gaps to be filled in, particularly with reference to the leadership discourse.

For instance, even if personal, environmental or social concerns have been considered individual factors that are the main predictors for sustainable entrepreneurship, how individuals are successfully balancing the economic, social and environmental dimensions in organisations is still unclear (see Greco and de Jong, 2017: 24–25). The leadership approach and the ethical and values-based dimension of leadership have not been considered as predictors of sustainable entrepreneurship success. Neither has it been considered as a driver of CSR effectiveness.

In other words, both within the prior literature on sustainable entrepreneurship and CSR, little attention has been devoted to leadership. Moreover, sustainable and responsible leadership has not been adequately investigated (Hansen, 2008).

In this regard, a question has been raised:

> Is it possible that the existing research on ethical leadership has not yet sufficiently been good enough to change practices? . . . or that the research insights are being ignored? . . . Alternatively, it may be that organizations have immense problems implementing ethical leadership and credible CSR . . . There is an ongoing discussion as to whether business ethics are just business trends with no real value.
>
> (Bachmann, 2017: 5, 6)

In fact, many executives refuse ethics programs, while some perceive business ethics and CSR as merely public relations (Crane and Matten, 2010; Blowfield and Murray, 2011). Thus the questions are *whether* and *how* leaders can translate sustainability into action. Which attributes and leadership behaviours (i.e. authenticity, honesty, integrity, fairness) are necessary to implement CSR? Are these attributes relevant in fostering sustainable entrepreneurship?

Inquiring about the nature of CSR leadership, Visser (2011) pointed out that "without bold and effective leadership – at a political, institutional and individual level – we will fail to resolve our most serious social and environmental crisis" (Visser, 2011: 1).

Given the scale and urgency of the challenges, "CSR leadership needs to be bold leadership. It also needs to be collaborative leadership – leaders acting together at all levels of organisation and society" (Visser, 2011: 9) and creative leadership. A creative response is the essential function of leaders (Herlyn and Radermacher, 2014). Moral leaders are accountable, respectful, consistent in their approach and open to communication and innovation since their behaviours rest on ethical values and virtues (Hoivik von Weltzien, 2014). Coupling management and skills with the aforementioned leadership traits helps companies to maintain a climate of social responsibility and ethics by enacting a tacit organisation-wide code of fairness and respect for others. At the same time, it requires sustainability leadership in action which in turn means that CSR leadership can only truly be seen and judged by the actions that leaders take: "CSR leadership must be judged by the success of our actions – and whether we inspire and support others to follow our vision and passion for a better world" (Visser, 2011: 9). Therefore, attention should be addressed to leadership models consistent with CSR and sustainability orientation and based on a moral and ethical construct.

At present there is still a need to develop research on how to integrate knowledge from leadership theory to render the various CSR policies more ethical (Mostovicz et al., 2009). Several recent contributions have been enriching the field of ethical leadership (Bachmann, 2017; Sison et al., 2017), and some innovative topics, such as responsible leadership, have emerged (Maak and Pless, 2006; Hansen, 2008; Pless and Maak, 2011). However, Du et al. (2013) clearly highlight the persistence of certain deficiencies in current leadership theories, particularly with regard to the interface between leadership and CSR. "Despite a growing body of research documenting the business case of CSR, our knowledge of organisational antecedents to CSR remains embryonic" (Du et al., 2013: 156). Addressing this gap, they investigate the roles of leadership styles – specifically transformational and transactional leadership – and their influence on the effectiveness of CSR (in generating positive organisational outcomes).

In light of the above, we formulate the following proposition:

> *Proposition 1*: A possible "missing link" between theory and practice of sustainability can be attributed to the lack of attention towards leadership as a key factor for concretely and effectively implementing CSR and sustainable entrepreneurship.

Leadership approaches and models for developing CSR and sustainable entrepreneurship

Leadership could be defined as "articulating visions, embodying values, and creating the environment within which things can be accomplished" (Richards and Engle, 1986: 206; Hetland, 2004). There are various theories on leadership which can be traced back to three main approaches: the trait/style school (which focuses on the characteristics or approaches of individual leaders); the situational/context school (which focuses on how the external environment shapes leadership action); and the contingency school (which is about the interaction between the individual leader and his/her framing context) (see Visser, 2011: 1). While it is not our intention to provide an exhaustive review of these approaches, among the several theoretical frameworks, we have considered the most useful ones to explain how leaders' behaviours and approaches are tied to CSR and sustainable entrepreneurship, and in particular: servant leadership, transformational/ transforming leadership and ethical and moral-based leadership, which in turn includes virtues-based leadership.

The main outlines of a servant and transformational leadership are summarised in Table 3.2.1, whereas particular emphasis is subsequently put on the ethical and moral-based construct. Finally, responsible and sustainable leadership are introduced.

As shown in Table 3.2.1, servant leadership has established a solid foundation in theory and practice (Greenleaf, 1977; Spears, 1995; Yukl, 1999; Laub; 1999; Page and Wong, 2000; Patterson, 2003; Winston, 2003; Irving, 2005), which leads us to regard it as an integrative leadership theory that stimulates responsibility. The emphasis on "the good of those led" serves as a foundation for theoretical connections between servant leadership and variables, such as commitment, organisational trust and job satisfaction, which are at the core of the CSR and sustainability discourse.

Transformational leadership has been considered an alternative research approach that investigates the moral content of already established normative leadership theories characterised by positive organisational outcomes (Olsen, 2010: 14). Transformational leaders reach high levels of moral development and articulate a vision able to "capture" the demands of different stakeholders, motivating followers to transcend their self-interest and "coupling" with the company's vision. Coherently, they are more effective at driving change than transactional leaders (Du et al., 2013). Both theoretical (Maak and Pless, 2006; Pless and Maak, 2011) and qualitative studies (Angus-Leppan et al., 2010) point out that transformational leaders are likely to exhibit ethical and responsible leadership behaviours, such as protecting and advancing the interests of secondary stakeholders, thus fostering organisational learning and CSR (Vera and Crossan, 2004; Du et al., 2013). Components of CEO transformational leadership (and in particular intellectual stimulation) have been proven as positively associated with the propensity of the company to engage in strategic CSR (Waldman et al., 2006).

Leadership ethics: ethical and moral leadership

Leadership ethics tend to emphasise leaders' behaviour and values (Sauser, 2005; Martin and Cullen, 2006; Kaptein, 2009; Lloyd and Mey, 2010). Leadership plays a crucial role in shaping ethical organisational culture through leaders' moral behaviour and values, which forges the corporate mission, the vision applying ethical values to decision-making and, therefore, affecting everyday routine and intra-organisation procedures and structures (Melé, 2012).

Ethical leadership requires personal attributes (honesty, ability to listen, allowing others autonomy of choice, openness, willingness to consult and to learn) and manifests itself in a series of executive behaviours (i.e. building ethics and values into 'hearts and minds' by means of ethics training programs, building ethical achievement into performance evaluation and creating channels of communication between the company and stakeholders) (Brown et al., 2005; Malloch, 2009; Capaldi, 2013). Leadership cannot be decoupled from ethics: "Being a moral leader and doing, acting with moral leadership are one" (Hoivik von Weltzien, 2014: 4), as shown in Table 3.2.2.

Moral behaviour and leadership are interrelated (Greenberg and Colquitt, 2005). On the one hand, moral behaviour is influenced by situational factors, such as role modelling, diffusion of responsibility, conformity, etc; on the other, individual differences

Table 3.2.1 Leadership theories 'linked to' CSR and sustainable entrepreneurship

Theoretical constructs	*Definition and characteristics*	*Effects and determinants*
Servant leadership	An understanding and practice of leadership that places the good of those led over the self-interest of the leader (Laub, 1999). Servant leadership behaviours include: *valuing people, developing people, building community*, displaying *authenticity*, providing leadership and *sharing* leadership (Laub, 1999).	Servant leadership produces a higher level of *service* by the followers (Patterson, 2003). Servant leadership results in greater *commitment* to the leader (Winston, 2003). Organisations perceived as servant-led exhibited higher levels of both *leader trust* and *organisational trust* than organisations perceived as non-servant-led (Errol and Winston, 2005). The servant leadership constructs of *service, humility and vision* contributed to *organisational commitment and job satisfaction* (West and Bocarnea, 2008). A positive relationship has been confirmed in many quantitative-based studies referred to different organisational contexts and economic sectors (Laub, 1999, 2004; Hebert, 2004; Miears, 2004; Anderson, 2005; Irving, 2005; Van Tassell, 2006).
Transformational/ transforming leadership	It refers to the process of building commitment to the organisation's goals and empowering followers in order to fulfil these goals (Burns, 1978, 2004; Bass, 1985, 1997; Bass and Avolio, 1988, 1990; Bass, 1998; Bass and Bass, 2008; Groves and LaRocca, 2011). The main dimensions include charisma and intellectual stimulation (Avolio et al., 1999; Yukl, 1999; Bass and Avolio, 2000; Parry and Proctor-Thomson, 2002; Waldman et al., 2006). The *transformational leader* is one "who articulates a vision of the future that can be shared with followers, intellectually stimulates them, and pays attention to individual differences among employees" (Du et al., 2013: 157).	It stimulates the *consciousness of followers* by appealing to *higher ideals and moral values*, such as *justice and equality* (Burns, 2004). It becomes *moral* in that "it raises the level of human conduct and ethical aspiration of both leader and led, and thus it has a transforming effect on both" (Burns, 1978: 20). Transformational leaders are *highly ethical and focused on values* (Bass and Steidlmeier, 1999). The extent to which a leader is transformational is primarily measured by the leader's effect on followers in terms of *trust, admiration, loyalty and respect*, often displayed in their motivation to do more than they thought possible (Bass and Riggio, 2006; Yukl, 2010). Transformational leadership is associated with *altruistic ethics* (Groves and LaRocca, 2011). A clear relationship between transformational leadership and the *trust, commitment*, profit and performance of positive organisational outcomes has been pointed out by a number of studies (Lowe et al., 1996; Olsen, 2010: 17–18). *Activation of moral justice and moral identity* (Aquino and Reed, 2002) is related to transformational leadership (Turner et al., 2002). Leaders with *moral integrity* (the so-called "behavioural *integrity*" (Becker, 1998)) always encourage *open and honest communication* (Gottlieb and Sanzgiri, 1996). Leaders' activation of mature justice schemas has an impact on followers' level of *justice reasoning* (Ruisi, 2010; Hoivik von Weltzien, 2014).

Table 3.2.2 The moral leader: being and doing

Being *informed by values, emotional and reasoning capability, caring. Being, visionary, proactive and innovative*	Doing *informed by relationships with all stakeholders and wanting to achieve the best for all and the common good*
• Balanced /in harmony with yourself • Reason and emotions • Integer (integrity) • Vision • Passionate • Responsible (ethical) • Trustworthy	• Relational • Affective • Supportive (always being there, included in time of crisis) • Caring • Communicating • Involving others • Responsive

Source: our adaptation of Hoivik von Weltzien (2014).

(i.e. personality and values) act as an antecedent of moral behaviour (Rest and Narvaez, 1994; Brown and Treviño, 2006). Moral leadership is inspired by constitutive moral elements: innovation, intuition and imagination (Hoivik von Weltzien, 2014). Moral imagination entails perceiving norms, social roles and relationships entwined in managerial decision-making. Moreover, it involves the ability to envision new business models that reframe problems and, in the meantime, create new solutions through economically viable and morally justifiable ways (Werhane, 1999: 93). Accordingly, the organisational culture imbued with moral leadership enjoys several benefits: understanding of the interdependence between stakeholders; learning environment; respect and trust; cooperation; responsibility and accountability. This is not an idealistic approach, given that it is possible to find companies that apply it (i.e. the Norwegian clothing company Stormberg A/S; see Hoivik von Weltzien and Melé, 2009; The Loccioni Group; see Del Baldo, 2017). Moral creativity thus fosters dynamic and innovative CSR strategies and actions and is linked to responsible and sustainable leadership (Visser, 2011; Von Ahsen, 2015). A current example of CSR leaders able to effectively implement programs and innovations through CSR is provided by the experiences of "Eco-champions" (Jones et al., 2016). Drawing from the analysis of this theoretical framework, one can formulate a second proposition:

> *Proposition 2*: A moral and virtues-based leadership consists of a set of values and behaviours that represent a key driver in implementing CSR and sustainability-driven strategies.

Virtues-based leadership

In the last few years, particularly in the light of the widespread global economic crisis, the business world and scientific community have been rediscovering the centrality of values and virtues in managing a business (Hemingway and Maclagan, 2004; Ketola, 2008) and driving CSR and sustainability-oriented strategies and actions (Vyakarnam et al., 1997). Accordingly, in regard to this orientation, business ethics literature has emphasised how the diffusion of management integrity, authenticity and virtues in the corporate context gives rise to new models of governance aimed at constructing a more civil economy and a common good (Zamagni, 1995; Carroll, 2000; Driscoll and Hoffman, 2000; Pruzan,

2001; Cortright and Naughton, 2002; Argandoña, 2003, 2011; Luthans and Avolio, 2003; Gui and Sugden, 2005; Zadek, 2006; Riggio et al., 2010; Zsolnai, 2015).

Values (from the Latin *valere*) are abstract ideals that are considered 'good', desirable and preferable. We can speak of personal values, social values, corporate values, human values and ethical values.[1] "Ethical values are based on moral qualities that contribute to human excellence: integrity, justice, gratitude, generosity, truthfulness" (Melé, 2009b: 16). Values are at the core of entrepreneurial decisions and actions, linking sustainability at the individual and community level (Stephan et al., 2016; Shepherd and Patzelt, 2017a) and are embodied in emerging models of social entrepreneurship (Seelos and Mair, 2005) and benefit corporations (André, 2012; Clark et al., 2013), which are examples of organisations driving positive social change.

Virtues (from the Latin *virtus*) are good character traits that contribute to a better perception of ethical values and reinforce the will for good behaviour. Fundamental human virtues include practical wisdom, justice, courage and self-control. "These include all other virtues (such as integrity, authenticity) necessary for human excellence" (Melé, 2009b: 97). According to Medieval philosophy, the fundamental characteristics of the human being can be traced back to the cardinal virtues: unity, truth, goodness and beauty (*unum, verum, bonum-pulchrum* and value) (Ruisi, 2010). Virtues are also conceived as spiritual values and include both the aforementioned four cardinal virtues and the three theological virtues (Faith, Hope and Charity).

By focusing on the Aristotelian and Thomistic ethics, Bastons (2008) underlines the role of cardinal virtues (Pieper, 1966) in the framing of decisions. These virtues are cardinal because they are related to the human faculties that determine the structure from which decisions are made. In this sense, fortitude (courage) is competence for operating decisions; prudence (practical wisdom) is competence for predicting; temperance (moderation) (the habit of self-control) is competence for evaluation; and justice (friendship) is integrity for action. Such virtues thus intervene in the structuring of decision-making processes and allow the integral development of a company and its stakeholders.

Cardinal virtues are relevant in the business context both at the individual and organisational level (Ruisi, 2010; Del Baldo, 2013). Bertland (2009) points out the role of organisations in developing individual abilities and enriching the setting of the virtues ethics. Virtuous managers will be able to encourage employees and strengthen their talents, enhancing dignity, promoting positive relationships with customers and involving shareholders in social commitment.

Values and virtues are also placed at the foundation of practical wisdom in European society and characterise a "maturity model of CSR" (Walker, 2015): justice has a strong relationship with respect to the values of solidarity and integrity; temperance is related to respect, appreciation and freedom; fortitude has a strong connection to the value of subsidiarity, which represents a key value for innovations; and prudence is linked to the values of responsibility, accountability and liability.

The 'ancient' roots of sustainability derive from the civic tradition of the Benedictine monasteries (Bruni and Uelmen, 2006; Inauen and Frey, 2008; Mabey et al., 2016; Chatterji and Zsolnai, 2017) that were based on perennial values applied and practised, such as moderation in everyday activity, temperance, responsibility, co-operation and coordination, respect for the environment and ability to overcome social plagues. These 'pillars' can foster a sustainable entrepreneurial spirit since the perennial values are anchored to virtues (Sedmak, 2014: 64). Proactive entrepreneurial behaviour and integrative management approaches manifest resilience through adaptability, diversity, efficiency and cohesion. All these features are the precondition for achieving sustainability (Walker and Salt, 2006) and have a common root in authenticity (Trilling, 1972), which provides the theoretical foundation for several theories of authentic leadership (Kaptein and Wempe, 2002; George, 2003; Avolio and Gardner, 2005; Gardner et al., 2005, 2011; Kernis and Goldman, 2006; Spitzmuller and Ilies, 2010).

Virtue ethics represent a developing approach within business (MacIntyre, 1985; Battaly, 2010) that attempts to ground ethics on the basis of character rather than rules (Bertland, 2009) and emphasises integrity at a personal, business and community level (Solomon 1992a, 1992b; Melé, 2009a; Hartman, 2011). Virtue ethics contribute to a business environment that fosters the best practices (Flynn, 2008) and allows us to understand the authentic 'roots' of CSR. Flores and Green (2013) used the 'Leadership Virtues Questionnaire' to measure four leader virtues (cardinal virtues): prudence, fortitude, temperance and justice, which were positively related to assessments of authentic leadership, ethical leadership and transformational leadership. A stakeholder dialogue and engagement based on virtue ethics concern the development of a virtuous corporate culture that takes on a long-term view (Alford and Signori, 2014: 6).

Virtuous leadership goes beyond effectiveness, shifting the discourse to values, attitudes and behaviours that encourage the transcendental development of leaders and followers and integrate all the features of human existence: the body (physical essence), the mind (logical/rational thought), the heart (emotions and feelings) and the spirit (Fry, 2003).

The diffusion and growth of virtues in a company, however, oppose the barriers that Martin (2002) identifies among business leaders: a lack in the ability to 'walk the talk of morals', and a charismatic approach (Liu, 2007; Olsen, 2010; Brown, 2011). Charismatic leaders are capable of turning problems into opportunities and resources thanks to their ability "to see the world" differently (Bruni and Sena, 2013) and inspire people to do their very best by creating a common sense of purpose (Shamir et al., 1993; Cardona, 2000; Jacobsen, 2001; Palshikar, 2007; Opdebeeck, 2013). Personal responsibility, vision, moral virtues, integrity, faith in personal commitment, shared social responsibility and solidarity are typical attributes of charismatic leaders (Becker, 1998) which leverage a virtuous corporate culture in organisations. The Global Leadership and Organisational Behaviour Effectiveness (GLOBE) research (2008), aimed at understanding the cultural characteristics that positively or negatively influence a leader's effectiveness, has identified several leadership dimensions: charisma and ability to motivate members of the organisation by leveraging the transmission of corporate values; ability to create and manage working groups, orienting them towards common goals; level of members involvement in the decision-making process; level of compassion and generosity and the ability to provide human support to the members of the organisation.

The aforementioned arguments have led us to formulate the following proposition:

> *Proposition 3*: A moral and virtues-based leadership supports authentic CSR and sustainable entrepreneurship.

Responsible and sustainable leadership

The theoretical construct of responsible and sustainable leadership derives from the intersection of the moral-based leadership concepts and those of social responsibility and sustainable entrepreneurship. It is characterised by a multilevel approach that places the leader, his/her behaviour, attitudes and choices in the centre of the management of a company, a division or a team (Waldman and Siegel, 2008; Magni and Pennarola, 2015). "A responsible leadership theory broadens the notion of leadership from a traditional leader-subordinate relationship to a leader-stakeholder relationship" (Du et al., 2013: 156). Responsible leadership is in fact described as "an ethical and socio-relational phenomenon that occurs in social interaction processes" (Maak and Pless, 2006: 99). The importance of approaching leadership in the context of stakeholder theory has been emphasised (Bass and Steidlmeier, 1999; Avery and Bergsteiner, 2011). Accordingly, "Building and cultivating ethically sound relations towards different stakeholders is an important responsibility of leaders in an interconnected stakeholder society" (Maak and Pless, 2006: 101). Responsible leadership requires leaders to also engage in involving stakeholders with virtue and integrity to build the best community and workplace (Jones, 2014). Therefore, it enables the integration of the leaders within the stakeholder community (Hansen, 2008).

Magni and Pennarola (2015) point out that the competencies of responsible leadership are centred on communication, involvement of people and the importance attributed to the development of a new corporate culture based on values and moral convictions. The responsible leadership model rests on five pillars: stakeholder consideration and ethical climate; integrity and climate oriented towards justice; role modelling and empowerment; climate geared towards diversity and inclusion; long-term orientation. Through this model, the responsible leader triggers a resilience path that guides the company towards sustainable development (Magni and Pennarola, 2015) and fosters sustainable entrepreneurship. Coherently, key factors of leadership style are the people strategy (the human resources management) and the culture (which enhances the basic values, such as accountability and transparency). The people strategy must be based on the enterprise conceived as a community of people. Therefore, its value is measured based on the commitment to bringing out the skills of its employees, which then leads to the virtue of humility (Seligman, 2004).

Responsible leadership may be widespread throughout businesses, affecting different levels: individual (favouring the passage from 'me to us' through collaboration and shared responsibility); team (through the development of mutual relations of trust and open communication); and organisation (structuring a coherent vision and mission). It rests on the idea that the responsible person must have flexible thinking (i.e. strategic and systematic), including the dimensions of logic (to sort, select, plan), ethics (foresight, transparency, perseverance) and aesthetic. Therefore, it requires specific cardinal virtues, such as prudence and perseverance (Sansone, 2014).

Regarding the nature of CSR leadership, Visser (2011) introduced a theoretical construct and defined a CSR leader as "someone who inspires and supports action towards a better world" (Visser, 2011: 2). He also suggested a model based on three elements: the internal/external content, the characteristics and the internal/external actions. Drawing from the results of empirical research, he observed that many characteristics (traits, styles, skills and knowledge) were associated with CSR leaders. Namely, a set of key characteristics that distinguish the leadership approach taken by individuals tackling sustainability issues. It includes:

- systemic understanding (CSR leadership results from the interaction between an organisation's social, environmental and economic context and the characteristics of individual leaders);
- emotional intelligence (the ability and the real inspiration to unlock human potential and motivate people);

- values orientation to shape culture (a values-based approach nurtured by morality and spirituality is critical);
- compelling vision (the ability to effectively communicate a compelling narrative on how their organisations can contribute to creating a better world);
- inclusive style (the leader and the followers working together to obtain certain outcomes);
- innovative approach (a willingness to innovate and be radical, stimulating lateral thinking and cross-functional, collaborative problem solving since complex problems require creative solutions);
- a long-term perspective (long-term thinking has impacts in terms of sustainability).

The theoretical constructs of sustainable leadership are closely linked to that of responsible and CSR leadership. It shares the same theoretical setting and differs from the latter only because of a greater focus on the three dimensions of sustainable development (people, planet and profits) and the creation of a social capital necessary to face times of difficulty and crisis (Avery and Bergsteiner, 2011). Namely, three main elements characterise sustainable leadership (Burns, Vaught and Bauman, 2015): 1) the need to cultivate a way of being and acting immersed in sustainability values; 2) the rootedness to the life processes; and 3) being a dynamic, inclusive and collaborative process. Therefore, the leader's role does not rest in guiding others, but in guiding with the others (Burns, Vaught and Bauman, 2015) as a result of sharing the values and the vision of sustainability inside and outside of the company.

Ultimately, the link between the theoretical framework for ethical and moral-based leadership and the CSR and sustainable entrepreneurship discourse allows one to connect the CSR authentic orientation to a coherent leadership model which is necessary to support change and foster sustainable entrepreneurship, which is responsible and sustainable leadership. Accordingly, the fourth proposition can be synthesised as follows:

> *Proposition 4*: Moral creativity fosters dynamic and innovative CSR strategies linked to responsible and sustainable leadership.

Discussion and conclusions

As already mentioned, a framework for 'CSR leadership', able to trigger change and foster sustainable entrepreneurship, includes systemic understanding, emotional intelligence and a caring attitude (towards people and the environment), values orientation, a compelling vision, inclusive style and a long-term perspective. It also requires authenticity (Hoivik von Weltzien and Melé, 2009), which emerges as a key factor, linked to intrinsic CSR and sustainable entrepreneurship (Lamont, 2002; Kernis and Goldman, 2006; Walker and Salt, 2006; Bouckaert, 2011; Walker, 2015).

A CSR leader is someone who inspires and supports actions for a better world (Goffee and Jones, 2009). However, many CSR policies have failed to render organisations more ethical because they were not authentically driven by a consistent leadership model (Mostovicz et al., 2009). An authentic CSR leader orients the company towards the common good and respects the 'golden rule' to do unto others as you would have others do unto you. The 'golden rule' translates concretely into principles that characterise purpose-led businesses: providing good and safe products and services, openly sharing knowledge and competencies, building lasting relationships, being a good citizen, nurturing a responsible and responsive employer, being a guardian for future generations, and having a purpose that delivers long-term sustainable performances (Alford, 2015). The resulting organisational culture, imbued with moral leadership, enjoys the understanding of interdependence with stakeholders, a learning environment and enhanced respect and trust, the capability to listen to the stakeholders' expectations and needs, and cooperation and active engagement (Visser, 2011; Hoivik von Weltzien, 2014).

Therefore, it can be appreciated as a possible (and necessary) challenge for businesses in a more globalised world, and many practical examples should be found and analysed. Adhering to these lines of thought, sustainable entrepreneurship can be considered as a step in the business strategy (Schmidpeter, 2014) which requires a coherent leadership model.

A challenging approach rests on the notion that business survival depends on a continuous endeavour for sustainability, and that a moral and virtues-based leadership is a key driver in implementing authentic CSR and sustainability-driven strategies, based on values such as caring, people-centredness, integrity, transparency and accountability (Oreg and Berson, 2011; Visser, 2011; Von Ahsen, 2015). The development of CSR should thus be conceived as an ongoing process, requiring both creativity and moral conviction, that is effective at building a bridge between moral leadership and economic rationality (Visser, 2011).

Throughout the literature analysis, we struggled to unite different research fields and draw insights from contributions belonging to diverse bodies of literature (CSR and sustainability, sustainable entrepreneurship and leadership) that up to now have followed separate perspectives of analysis. The possibility that there is a 'missing link' between the theory and practice of sustainability in the daily life of companies can be attributed to the lack of coherent and authentic leadership models which are consistent with sustainability orientation, based on a moral and ethical construct. Therefore, we have pointed out the importance of connecting to the theoretical framework of CSR and leadership, because the interface of organisational leadership and CSR is fundamental for assuring the effectiveness and authenticity of actions and practices oriented to sustainability.

Accordingly, we have derived the following propositions that can orient further research and should be empirically verified to validate their capability to drive change, since one of the current most important leadership responsibilities is leading change towards sustainability:

> ***Proposition 1:*** A possible "missing link" between the theory and practice of sustainability can be attributed to the lack of attention towards leadership as a key factor for concretely and effectively implementing CSR and sustainable entrepreneurship.
>
> ***Proposition 2:*** A moral and virtues-based leadership consists of a set of values and behaviours that represent a key driver in implementing CSR and sustainability-driven strategies.
>
> ***Proposition 3:*** A moral and virtues-based leadership supports authentic CSR and sustainable entrepreneurship.
>
> ***Proposition 4:*** Moral creativity fosters dynamic and innovative CSR strategies linked to responsible and sustainable leadership.

From the analysis of the different theoretical constructs on leadership models in relation to CSR and sustainable entrepreneurship, we have focused on those that form a basis for supporting responsible and sustainable leadership and among these, the ethical-based leadership theories. In other words, the virtues-ethic approach of leadership represents a powerful framework to stimulate the research on the link betweeen CSR, sustainable entrepreneurship and leadership.

We have argued that the gap between leadership and effective CSR can be attributed to the fact that CSR strategies are often driven by extrinsic motivation and are not adequately connected to an authentic ethical construct. Consequently, they cannot provide a lasting and effective contribution to sustainability, neither do they trigger sustainable entrepreneurship. It thus becomes important to distinguish between extrinsic and intrinsic (authentic and ethically-based) orientation towards CSR and sustainability, which fosters sustainable entrepreneurship. When talking about a culture of innovation – such as the sustainable innovation which is tied to forms of sustainable entrepreneurship – it is fundamental to consider the enabling factors and, among these, the organisation's value system, vision and norms on the one hand, and the employees' mindset, passion and tolerance of failure, on the other (Vogel and Fischler-Strasak, 2014).

During the last decades, an increasing number of writings have focused on the topic of moral leadership, and contemporary leadership literature emphasises moral and ethical-based leadership as a prerequisite for effective leadership (Brown, Treviño and Harrison, 2005; Rhode, 2006; Bass and Bass, 2008; Northouse, 2018). Moreover, many efforts have been devoted to identifying its content and antecedents (Brown and Treviño, 2006). Ethics literature has emphasised management integrity, authenticity and virtues, which are becoming widespread in the corporate context, giving rise to models of governance and business based on an authentic orientation towards CSR and sustainability (Becker, 1998; Garriga and Melé, 2004; Brown, 2005; Malloch, 2009; Ruisi, 2010).

The attention that has emerged from the literature is confirmed in practice since there are more and more leaders who freely admit that they are driven by an intrinsic and contagious commitment to values (Bouckaert, 2011). While some organisations do not contemplate the challenge of taking a leadership stance on CSR and sustainable entrepreneurship, there are a growing number of high performing companies, where success grows from their leaders' commitment to ethics and values (Lamont, 2002), capable of translating into successful CSR strategies (Jenkins, 2006) and sustainable entrepreneurship experiences.

Implications

This chapter provides a multidisciplinary contribution in the area of sustainable entrepreneurship and the role of leadership. It plays a part in enriching the research fields focused on leadership and CSR and amplifies the research boundaries within these different bodies of literature. Focusing on the relevance of values and virtues applied to the leadership style, it emphasises the need for coherence among leaders' behaviours and authentic CSR.

Addressing the issue of leadership and its influence on CSR and sustainability-oriented strategies, the work traces a theoretical construct useful in supporting the merging of leadership theories with CSR and sustainable entrepreneurship research.

Hence, within the scientific perspective, the value of the work is first attributable to the attention paid to transcendental virtues and values in leadership. Second, its originality is attributable to the meeting point of the interdisciplinary perspective of CSR-oriented strategies, sustainable entrepreneurship and leadership studies. Third, the chapter contributes by extending the current knowledge of the antecedents of effective leadership models in regard to responsible strategies and practices and sustainable entrepreneurship. The reflections point out the relevance of values and virtues in the entrepreneurial and business context and drive us to formulate propositions relative to the idea that these 'pillars' act as the 'hidden' driving force. This force lies at the base of CSR and sustainable orientation and fosters sustainable entrepreneurship, particularly in companies (i.e. SMEs and ideal-based companies) which attribute a central relevance to people and relationships.

This chapter also has practical implications. First, suggestions for leaders derive from the relevance attributed to values and virtues in balancing the many activities in which they are in charge of daily. Leaders (entrepreneurs and managers) are then required to exercise virtues, which are essential for the long-term success of the company founded on a multidimensional (ethical, economic, environmental and social) development. Attention then shifts towards a renewed entrepreneurial ethos in which values and virtues are the key driver in orienting leaders towards the true, the good and the beautiful, respecting people and the environment.

Finally, the propositions underline how the time for defending amoral business – business neutral to ethical norms – is over, because leaders who do not understand the core or heart of leadership, being ethics, will not be able to develop sustainable businesses in the long run or foster ethical, environmental and social innovation.

Limitations

We are aware of the fact that this work is not free of limitations. The study at its current stage is theoretically based. Consequently, further research is necessary, starting with the empirical validation of the aforementioned propositions aimed to deeply inquire and validate the assumptions made. In particular, empirical analysis could be useful to assess the relationship between individual-level behaviours and organisational outcomes and verify if and how individual-level behaviours in sustainable entrepreneurship link to corporate strategies in the lifetime of the business, providing a reply to the research questions: How can leaders translate sustainability into action? Which attributes and leadership behaviours are necessary to implement CSR effectively? Which leadership behaviours are necessary to foster sustainable entrepreneurship? To this end, a qualitative research approach could be particularly appropriate, especially if based on an action research approach and the active involvement of business leaders and scholars, in order to contribute to the implementation of the virtuous leadership models within the business context and the dissemination of concrete examples to inspire both theory and practice.

Note

1 Socio-cultural values represent one of the conditions that form the basis of the common good for each human community – family, business, religious association, sports clubs, political groups, etc. They include "full respect for human dignity and human rights, freedom, safety, order, peace and justice, which permit living together respectfully and foster a sense of tolerance and cooperation" (Melé, 2009b: 85).

References

Accenture (2010). A new era of sustainability: UN Global Compact-Accenture CEO Study. Retrieved from: www.unglobalcompact.org/library/230 (accessed 11 January 2016)

Alford, H. (2015). Against the "Hollowing-out" of Meaning. Virtue Ethics in the "Blueprint for Better Business". Lecture presented at the SPES Congress *Virtues and Vices in Economics and*

Business, Centre for Economics and Ethics of the Catholic University of Leuven in cooperation with the European SPES Institute, June 19–20, 2015, Leuven, Belgium. Retrieved from: http://eurospes.org/content/virtues-and-vices-economics-and-business#sthash.0kVF1jSz.dpuf, 1–15. (Accessed 22 December 2015].

Alford, H. and Signori, S. (2014). Brief considerations on the effectiveness of shareholder activism. A virtue ethics approach. *Impresa Progetto-Electronic Journal of Management*, 3, 1–10.

Anderson, K.P. (2005). A correlational analysis of servant leadership and job satisfaction in a religious educational organization. A dissertation presented in partial fulfillment of the requirements for the degree Doctor of Management in Organizational Leadership, University of Phoenix, USA, January 2005. Retrieved from: http://olagroup.org/Images/mmDocument/Dissertation%20-%20Kelly%20Anderson.pdf (accessed 10 September 2014).André, R. (2012). Assessing the accountability of the benefit corporation: Will this new gray sector organization enhance corporate social responsibility? *Journal of Business Ethics*, 110(1), 133–150.

Angus-Leppan, T., Metcalf, L.A. and Benn, S.H. (2010). Leadership styles and CSR practice: An examination of sensemaking, institutional drivers and CSR leadership. *Journal of BusinessEthics*, 93(2), 189–213.

Aquino, K. and Reed, A. (2002). The self-importance of moral identity. *Journal of Personality and Social Psychology*, 83, 1423–1440.

Aragón Amonarriz, C. and Iturrioz Landar, C. (2016). Responsible family ownership in small- and medium-sized family enterprises: An exploratory study. *Business Ethics: A European Review*, 25(1), 75–93.

Argandoña, A. (2003). Fostering values in organizations. *Journal of Business Ethics*, 45, 15–28.

Argandoña, A. (2011). Beyond contracts: Love in firms, *Journal of Business Ethics*, 99(1), 77–85.

Audretsch, D.B. and Thurik, A.R. (2004). A model of the entrepreneurial economy (No. 1204). *Papers on entrepreneurship, growth and public policy*. Retrieved from: https://papers.econ.mpg.de/egp/discussionpapers/2004-12.pdf (accessed 11 March 2015).

Avery, G. and Bergsteiner, H. (2011). Sustainable leadership practices for enhancing business resilience and performance. *Strategy & Leadership*, 39(3), 5–15.

Avolio, B.J., Bass, B.M. and Jung, D.I. (1999). Re-examining the components of transformational and transactional leadership using the Multifactor Leadership. *Journal of Occupational and Organizational Psychology*, 72(4), 441–462.

Avolio, B.J. and Gardner, W.L. (2005). Authentic leadership development: Getting to the root of positive forms of leadership. *The Leadership Quarterly*, 16, 315–338.

Bachmann, B. (2017). *Ethical Leadership in Organizations. Concepts and Implementation*. Cham, Switzerland: Springer.

Bass, B.M. (1985). *Leadership and Performance Beyond Expectations*. New York: Academic Press.

Bass, B.M. (1997). Does the transactional-transformational leadership paradigm transcend organizational and national borders? *American Psychologist*, 52, 130–139.

Bass, B.M. (1998). Transformational Leadership: Industrial, Military, and Educational Impact. Mahwah, NJ: Lawrence Earlbaum Associates.

Bass, M.B. and Avolio, B.J. (1988). Transformational leadership, charisma and beyond. In Hunt, J.G., Baliga, B.R., Dachler, H.P. and Schriescheim, C.A. (eds), *Emerging Leadership Vistas*. Lexington, VA: Lexington Books, pp. 29–49.

Bass, M.B. and Avolio, B.J. (1990). The implication of transactional and transformational leadership for individual, team, organizational development. *Research in Organizational Change and Development*, 4, 231–272.

Bass, B.M. and Avolio, B.J. (2000). *MLQ: Multifactor Leadership Questionnaire*, 2nd ed. Redwood City, CA: Mind Garden.

Bass, B.M. and Bass, R. (2008). *The Bass Handbook of Leadership*, 4th ed. New York: Free Press.

Bass, B.M. and Riggio, R.E. (2006). *Transformational Leadership*, 2nd ed. Mahwah, NJ: Lawrence Erlbaum Associates.

Bass, B.M. and Steidlmeier, P. (1999). Ethics, character, and authentic transformational leadership behavior. *Leadership Quarterly*, 10(2), 181–217.

Bastons, M. (2008). The role of virtues in the framing of decisions. *Journal of Business Ethics*, 78, 389–400.

Battaly, H. (2010). Introduction. virtue and vice. *Metaphilosophy*, 41(1–2), 1–21.

Becker, T. (1998). Integrity in organizations: Beyond honesty and conscientiousness. *Academy of Management Review*, 23(1), 154–161.

Bertland, A. (2009). Virtue ethics in business and the capabilities approach. *Journal of Business Ethics*, 84, 25–32.

Blowfield, M. and Murray, A. (2011). *Corporate Responsibility*. Oxford, UK: Oxford University Press.

Bouckaert, L. (2011). Spirituality and economic democracy. In L. Zsolani (eds), *Spirituality and Ethics in Management*, 2nd ed. Dordrecht, the Netherlands: Springer, pp. 41–52.

Brown, J.B. (2011). The building of a virtuous transformational leader. *The Journal of Virtues and Leadership*, 2(1), 6–14.

Brown, M.E. and Treviño, L.K. (2006). Ethical leadership: A review and future directions. *The Leadership Quarterly*, 17, 595–616.

Brown, M.E., Treviño, L.K. and Harrison, D.A. (2005). Ethical leadership: A social learning perspective for construct development and testing. *Organizational Behavior and Human Decision Processes*, 97, 117–134.

Brown, M.T. (2005). Corporate Integrity. *Rethinking Organizational Ethics and Leadership*. Cambridge, UK: Cambridge University Press.

Bruni, L. and Sena, B. (eds) (2013). *The Charismatic Principle in Social Life*. New York: Routledge.

Bruni, L. and Uelmen, A.J. (2006). Religious values and corporate decision making: The economy of communion project. *Fordham Journal of Corporate & Financial Law*, 11, 645–680.

Burns, J.M. (1978). *Leadership*. New York: Harper & Row.

Burns, J.M. (2004). Foreword. In Ciulla, J.B. (ed.), *Ethics, the Heart of Leadership*, 2nd ed. Westport, CT: Praeger.

Burns, H., Vaught, D. and Bauman, C. (2015). Leadership for sustainability: theoretical foundations and pedagogical practices that foster change. *International Journal of Leadership Studies*, 9(1), 131–143.

Campbell, J.L. (2007). Why would corporations behave in socially responsible ways? An institutional theory of corporate social responsibility. *Academy Management Review*, 32(3), 946–967.

Capaldi, N. (2013). How American spiritual capital inform business and affects the common good. In Groschl, S. (ed.), *Uncertainty, Diversity and the Common Good. Changing Norms and New Leadership Paradigms*. Farnham, UK: Gower, pp. 25–40.

Cardona, P. (2000). Transcendental leadership. *Leadership and Organization Development Journal*, 21(4), 201–206.

Carroll, A.B. (1991). The pyramid of corporate social responsibility: Toward the moral management of organisational stakeholders. *Business Horizons*, 34(4), 39–48.

Carroll, A.B. (2000). Ethical challenges for business in the new millennium: Corporate responsibility and model of management morality. *Business Ethics Quarterly*, 10(1), 33–40.

Castelló, I. and Lozano, J.M. (2011). Searching for new forms of legitimacy through corporate responsibility rhetoric. *Journal of Business Ethics*, 100(1), 11–29.

Chatterji, M. and Zsolnai, L. (2017). Ethical Leadership. *Indian and European Spiritual Approaches*. London: Palgrave.

Chua, J.H., Chrisman, J.J. and Sharma, P. (1999). Defining the family business by behavior. *Entrepreneurship Theory and Practice*, 23(4), 19–39.

Clark, W.H. Jr., Biddle, D. and Reath LLP.; Larry Vranka, Canonchet Group LLC (2013). White Paper, The need and rationale for the benefit corporation: Why it is the legal form that best addresses the needs of social entrepreneurs, investors and ultimately the public. Retrieved from www.benfitcorp.net Beneficorp.net (accessed 10 July 2014).

Cohen, B. and Winn, M.I. (2007). Market imperfections, opportunity and sustainable entrepreneurship. *Journal of Business Venturing*, 22(1), 29–49.

Cortright, S.A. and Naughton, M.J. (2002). *Rethinking the Purpose of Business. Iterdisciplinary Essays from the Catholic Social Tradition.* Notre Dame, IN: University of Notre Dame Press.

Crane, A. and Matten, D. (2010). Business Ethics: Managing Corporate Citizenship and Sustainability in the Age of Globalization. New York: Oxford University Press.

Dean, T.J. and McMullen, J.S. (2007). Toward a theory of sustainable entrepreneurship: Reducing environmental degradation through entrepreneurial action. *Journal of Business Venturing*, 22(1), 50–76.

Del Baldo, M. (2010). Corporate social responsibility and corporate governance in Italian SMEs: Toward a "territorial" model based on small "champions" of CSR. *International Journal of Sustainable Society*, 2(3), 215–247.

Del Baldo, M. (2012). Corporate social responsibility and corporate governance in Italian SMEs: The experience of some "spirited business". *Journal of Management and Governance*, 16(1), 1–36.

Del Baldo, M. (2013). CSR-oriented SMEs: A question of entrepreneurial virtues in action? Reflections in theory and practice. In J.O. Okpara, and S.O. Idowu (eds), *Corporate Social Responsibility. Challenges, Opportunities and Strategies for 21st Century Leaders.* Berlin Heidelberg: Springer-Verlag, pp. 145–170.

Del Baldo, M. (2014). Corporate social responsibility, entrepreneurial values and transcendental virtues in Italian SMEs. *International Journal of Business and Social Science*, 5(6), 25–51.

Del Baldo, M. (2017). Authentic CSR and leadership: Toward a virtues-based model of stakeholders dialogue and engagement. The Loccioni Group experience. In S.O. Idowu and S. Vertigans (eds), *Stages of Corporate Social Responsibility: From Ideas to Impacts.* Berlin Heidelberg: Springer-Verlag, pp. 179–203.

Del Baldo, M. and Baldarelli, M.G. (2015). From weak to strong CSR: The experience of the EoC (Economy of Communion) industrial parks in Germany and Italy. *UWF*, 23(4), 213–226.

Driscoll, D.M. and Hoffman, W.M. (2000). *How to Implement Values-Driven Management.* Walham, MA: Bentley College.

Du, S., Swaen, V., Lindgreen, A. and Sen, S. (2013). The roles of leadership styles in corporate social responsibility. *Journal of Business Ethics*, 114, 155–169.

Dyllick, T. and Hockerts, K. (2002). Beyond the business case for corporate sustainability. *Business Strategy and the Environment*, 11(2), 130–141.

Errol, E.J. and Winston, B.E. (2005). A correlation of servant leadership, leader trust, and organizational trust. *Leadership & Organization Development Journal*, 26(1), 6–22.

European Commission (2011). Communication to the European Parliament, the Council, the European Economic and Social Committee and the Committee of Regions, A renewed EU strategy (2011–14) for Corporate Social Responsibility (CSR), COM (2011) 681, Brussels. Retrieved from: https://publications.europa.eu/en/publication-detail/-/publication/ae5ada03-0dc3-48f8-9a32-0460e65ba7ed/language-en (accessed 10 May 2013).

Fifka, M.S. (2012). The irony of stakeholder management in Germany: The difficulty of implementing an essential concept for CSR. *UWF*, 21(1–2), 113–118.

Fischler, F. (2014). Sustainability: The concept for modern society. In C. Weidinger, F. Fischler and R. Schmidpeter (eds), *Sustainable Entrepreneurship. Business success through sustainability.* Berlin Heidelberg: Springer-Verlag, pp. 13–21.

Flores, S.L. and Green, M.T. (2013). The importance of small business leader virtues. *Small Business Institute, National Conference Proceedings*, 37(1), 252–261.

Flynn, G. (2008). The virtuous manager: A vision for leadership in business. *Journal of Business Ethics*, 78, 359–372.

Fry, L.W. (2003). Toward a theory of spiritual leadership. *The Leadership Quarterly*, 14, 693–727.

Gallo, M. and Cappuyns, K. (2004). *Characteristics of Successful Family Businesses.* WP-542, IESE Business School, University of Navarra.

Gardner, W.L., Avolio, B.J., Luthans, F., May, D.R. and Walumbwa, F.O. (2005). "Can you see the real me?" A self-based model of authentic leader and follower development. *The Leadership Quarterly*, 16, 343–372.

Gardner, W.L., Cogliser, C.C., Davis, K.M. and Dickens, M.P. (2011). Authentic leadership: A review of the literature and research agenda. *The Leadership Quarterly*, 22, 1120–1145.

Garriga, E. and Melé, D. (2004). Corporate social responsibility theories: Mapping the territory. *Journal of Business Ethics*, 53(1), 51–71.

George, W. (2003). Authentic Leadership: Rediscovering the Secrets to Creating Lasting Value. San Francisco, CA: Jossey-Bass.

GLOBE (2008). *Global Leadership and Organizational Behavior Effectiveness, Culture and Leader Effectiveness*. Retrieved from: www.ccl.org/leadership/pdf/GlobeStudy (accessed 23 July 2013).

Goffee, R. and Jones, G. (2009). Authentic leadership: Excite others to exceptional performance. *Leadership Excellence*, 26(1), 3–4.

Gottlieb, J.Z. and Sanzgiri, J. (1996). Towards an ethical dimension of decision making in organizations. *Journal of Business Ethics*, 15(12), 1275–1285.

Graafland, J.J. and Mazereeuw-Van der Duijn Schouten, C. (2012). Motives for corporate social responsibility. *De Economist*, 160(4), 377–396.

Graafland, J.J. and Van de Ven, B. (2006). Strategic and moral motivation for corporate social responsibility. *Journal of Corporate Citizenship*, 22, 111–123.

Gray, R., Adams, C.A. and Owen, D. (2014). Accountability, Social Responsibility and Sustainability. *Accounting for Society and the Environment*. Harlow, UK: Pearson.

Greco, A. and De Jong, G. (2017). *Sustainable Entrepreneurship: Definitions, Themes and Research Gaps*. Center for Sustainable Entrepreneurship Leeuwarden, The Netherlands University of Groningen/Campus Fryslân Working paper series, 1–36, June 2017. Retrieved from www.rug.nl/cf/pdfs/wps6_angela.pdf (accessed 12 June 2017).

Greenberg, J. and Colquitt, J.A. (eds) (2005). *Handbook of Organizational Justice*. Mahwah, NJ: Lawrence Erlbaum Associates.

Greenleaf, R.K. (1977). Servant Leadership: A Journey into the Nature of Legitimate Power and Greatness. New York: Paulist Press.

Groves, K.S. and LaRocca, M.A. (2011). An empirical study of leader ethical values, transformational and transactional leadership, and follower attitudes toward corporate social responsibility. *Journal of Business Ethics*, 103, 511–528.

Gui, B. and Sugden, R. (2005). *Economics and Social Interactions. Accounting for Interpersonal Relations*. Cambridge, UK: Cambridge University Press.

Gunilla, A. (2014). Sustainability and SMEs: The next steps. In C. Weidinger, F. Fischler and R. Schmidpeter (eds), *Sustainable Entrepreneurship. Business success through sustainability*. Berlin Heidelberg: Springer-Verlag, pp. 265–268.

Hansen, E.G. (2008). Responsible leadership requires responsible leadership system: The case of Merck Ltd, Thailand. *Submission to EURAM 2008 Conference in Ljubljana and Bled, Slovenia, 14–17 May 2008*. Retrived from http://ssrn.com/abstract=1440290 (accessed 12 June 2017).

Hartman, E. (2011). Virtue, profit and the separation thesis: An Aristotelian view. *Journal of Business Ethics*, 99, 5–17.

Hebert, S.C. (2004). The relationship of perceived servant leadership and job satisfaction from the follower's perspective. *Proceedings of the American Society of Business and Behavioral Sciences*, 11(1), 685–697.

Hemingway, C.A. and Maclagan, P.W. (2004). Managers' personal values as drivers of corporate social responsibility. *Journal of Business Ethics*, 50(1), 33–44.

Herlyn, E.L.A. and Radermacher, F.J. (2014). Sustainability: Challenges for the future. In C. Weidinger, F. Fischler and R. Schmidpeter (eds), *Sustainable Entrepreneurship. Business Success through Sustainability*. Berlin Heidelberg: Springer-Verlag, pp. 23–37.

Hetland, H. (2004). Leading to the Extraordinary? *Antecedents and Outcomes of Transformational Leadership*. Bergen, Norway: University of Bergen.

Hockerts, K. and Wüstenhagen, R. (2010). Greening Goliaths versus emerging Davids: Theorizing about the role of incumbents and new entrants in sustainable entrepreneurship. *Journal of Business Venturing*, 25(5), 481–492.

Hoivik von Weltzien, H. (2014). The heart of leadership is ethics. *Impresa Progetto-Electronic Journal of Management*, 11, 1–9.

Hoivik von Weltzien, H. and Melé, D. (2009). Can a SME become a global corporate citizen? Evidence from a case study. *Journal of Business Ethics*, 88, 551–562.

Inauen, E. and Frey, B.S. (2008). *The Governance of Benedictine Abbeys from an Economic Perspective*. Retrieved from: SSRN: https://ssrn.com/abstract=1268701 or http://dx.doi.org/10.2139/ssrn.1268701 (accessed 2 May 2015).

Ionescu-Somers, A. (2014). Embedding sustainable entrepreneurship in companies: The eternal internal challenge. In C. Weidinger, F. Fischler and R. Schmidpeter (eds), *Sustainable Entrepreneurship. Business Success through Sustainability*. Berlin Heidelberg: Springer-Verlag, pp. 177–189.

Irving, J. (2005). Exploring the relationship between servant leadership and team effectiveness. *Regent University Roundatble Proceedings*. Virgina Beach, VA: Regent University.

Jacobsen, C. (2001). Dynamics of charismatic leadership: A process theory, simulation model, and tests. *Leadership Quarterly*, 12(1), 75–112.

Jenkins, H. (2006). Small business champions for corporate social responsibility. *Journal of Business Ethics*, 6(3), 241–256.

Jenkins, H. (2009). A "business opportunity" model of corporate social responsibility for small- and medium-sized enterprises. *Business Ethics: A European Review*, 18(1), 21–36.

Jones, J. (2014). Leadership lessons from Levinas: Revisiting responsible leadership. *Leadership and the Humanities*, 2, 44–63.

Kaptein, M. (2009). Ethics programs and ethical culture: A next step in unravelling their multi-faceted relationship. *Journal of Business Ethics*, 89(2), 261–281.

Kaptein, M. and Wempe, G. (2002). *The Balanced Company: A Theory of Corporate Integrity*. Oxford, UK: Oxford University Press.

Kernis, M.H. and Goldman, B.M. (2006). A multicomponent conceptualization of authenticity: Theory and research. In M.P. Zanna (ed.), *Advances in Experimental Social Psychology*, vol. 38. San Diego, CA: Academic Press, pp. 283–357.

Ketola, T. (2008). A holistic corporate responsibility model: Integrating values, discourses and actions. *Journal of Business Ethics*, 80, 419–435.

Koe, W.L., Omar, R. and Juan Rizal Sa'ari, J.R. (2014). Factors associated with propensity for sustainable entrepreneurship. *Social and Behavioral Sciences*, 130, 65–74.

Lamont, G. (2002). The Spirited Business: Success Stories of Soul Friendly Companies. London: Hodder & Stoughton.

Laub, J. (1999). Assessing the servant organization: Development of the servant organizational leadership (SOLA) instrument. *Dissertation Abstracts International*, 60(02), 308. (UMI No. 9921922).

Laub, J. (2004). Defining servant leadership: A recommended typology for servant leadership studies. *Proceedings of the Servant Leadership Research Roundtable*. Retrieved from www.regent.edu/acad/global/publications/sl_proceedings/2004/ laub_defining_servant.pdf (accessed 26 March 2014).

Light, P. (2011). *Driving Social Change*. New York: Wiley.

Linnanen, L. and Panapanaan, V. (2002). *Roadmapping CSR in Finnish Companies*. Helsinki: Helsinki University of Technology.

Liu, C.H. (2007). Transactional, transformational, transcendental leadership: Motivation effectiveness and measurement of transcendental leadership. Paper presented at the Conference *Leading the Future of the Public Sector: The Third Transatlantic Dialogue*. University of Delaware, Newark, USA, May 31-June 2, 1–26.

Lloyd, H.R. and Mey, M.R. (2010). An ethics model to develop an ethical organisation. *South African Journal of Human Resource Management*, 8(1),1–12.

Looser, S. and Wehrmeyer, W. (2015). Doing well or doing good? Extrinsic and intrinsic CSR in Switzerland, *UWF*, DOI 10.1007/s00550-015-0360-9, 1–14, published on line 14 August 2015, Berlin Heidelberg: Springer-Verlag.

Lowe, K.B., Kroeck, K.G. and Sivasubramaniam, N. (1996). Effectiveness correlates of transformational and transactional leadership: A meta-analytic review of the MLD literature. *Leadership Quarterly*, 7, 385–425.

Luthans, F. and Avolio, B.J. (2003). Authentic leadership: A positive developmental approach. In K.S. Cameron, J.E. Dutton and R.E. Quinn (eds), *Positive Organizational Scholarship: Foundations of a New Discipline*. San Francisco, CA: Berrett-Koehler, pp. 241–261.

Maak, T. and Pless, N.M. (2006). Responsible leadership in a stakeholder society: A relational perspective. *Journal of Business Ethics*, 66, 99–115.

Mabey, C., Conroy, M. and Blakeley, K. (2016). Having burned the straw man of Christian spiritual leadership, what can we learn from Jesus about leading ethically? *Journal of Business Ethics*, 1–13, id 10.1007/s10551-016-3054-5, First online: 17 February 2016.

MacIntyre, A. (1985). *After Virtue. A Study in Moral Theory*, 2nd ed. London: Duckworth.

Magni, M. and Pennarola, F. (2015). Responsible Leadership: Creare benessere, sviluppo e performance a lungo termine. Milano, Italy: Egea.

Mahoney, L.S., Thorne, L., Cecil, L. and LaGore, W. (2013). A research note on standalone corporate social responsibility reports: Signaling or greenwashing? *Critical Perspectives on Accounting*, 24(4–5), 350–359.

Malloch, T.R. (2009). *Spiritual Enterprises. Doing Virtuous Business*. New York: Encounter Books.

Marrewijk, M. (2003). Concepts and definitions of CSR and corporate sustainability: Between agency and communion. *Journal of Business Ethics*, 44(2/3), 95–105.

Martin, K. and Cullen, J. (2006). Continuities and extensions of ethical climate theory: A meta-analytic review. *Journal of Business Ethics*, 69(2), 175–194.

Martin, R.L. (2002). The Virtue Matrix: Calculating the return on corporate responsibility. *Harvard Business Review*, March, 3–11.

Matten, D. and Moon, J. (2008). 'Implicit' and 'explicit' CSR: A conceptual framework for a comparative understanding of corporate social responsibility. *Academy of Management Review*, 33(2), 404–424.

Melé, D. (2009a). Integrating personalism into virtue-based business ethics: The personalist and the common good principles. *Journal of Business Ethics*, 88, 227–244.

Melé, D. (2009b). Business Ethics in Action, Seeking Human Excellence in Organizations. New York: Palgrave Macmillan.

Melé, D. (2012). Management Ethics. Placing Ethics in the Core of Good Management. New York: Palgrave Macmillan.

Miears, L.D. (2004). Servant-leadership and job satisfaction: A correlational study in Texas Education Agency Region X public schools. *DAI*, 65, (9A), 3237.

Mirvis, P., Googins, B. and Kiser, C. (2013). *Corporate Social Innovation*. Wellesley, MA: Babson College.

Molteni, M. (2009). *Aziende a movente ideale*. In L. Bruni and S. Zamagni (eds), *Dizionario di Economia Civile*. Roma: Città Nuova, pp. 65–75.

Mostovicz, I., Kakabadse, N. and Kakabadse, A. (2009). CSR: The role of leadership in driving ethical outcomes. *Corporate Governance: The International Journal of Business in Society*, 9(4), 448–460.

Murillo, D. and Vallentin, S. (2012). CSR, SMEs and social capital: An empirical study and conceptual reflection. *Journal of Applied Ethics*, 3, 17–46.

Northouse, P. (2018). *Leadership: Theory and Practice*, 10th ed. Thousand Oaks, CA: Sage Publishing.

OECD (2001). Corporate Social Responsibility, Partners for Progress. Paris: OECD.

Olsen, O.K. (2010). Are good leaders moral leaders? The relationship between effective military operational leadership and morals. Dissertation for the philosophiae doctor degree (PhD) at the University of Bergen, Norway.

Opdebeeck, H. (2013). The role of the charismatic economist E.F. Schumacher in economic and civil life: CSR and beyond. In L. Bruni and B. Sena (eds), *The Charismatic Principle in Social Life*. New York: Routledge, pp. 151–170.

Oreg, S. and Berson, Y. (2011). Leadership and employees' reactions to change: The role of leaders' personal attributes and transformational leadership style. *Personnel Psychology*, 64(3), 627–659.

Osburg, T. (2014). Sustainable entrepreneurship: A driver for social innovation. In C. Weidinger, F. Fischler and R. Schmidpeter (eds), *Sustainable Entrepreneurship. Business Success through Sustainability*. Berlin Heidelberg: Springer-Verlag, pp. 103–115.

Osburg, T. and Schmidpeter, R. (eds) (2013). *Social Innovation*. Berlin Heidelberg: Springer.

Pacheco, D.F., Dean, T.J. and Payne, D.S. (2010). Escaping the green prison: Entrepreneurship and the creation of opportunities for sustainable development. *Journal of Business Venturing*, 25(5), 464–480.

Page, D. and Wong, P.T.P. (2000). A conceptual framework for measuring servant leadership. In S. Adjibolosoo (ed.), *The Human Factor in Shaping the Course of History and Development*, chapter 5. Boston, MA: University Press of America, pp. 1–28.

Palshikar, K. (2007). *Charismatic Leadership*. Retrieved from www.unc.edu/~ketan/documents/Charismatic%20Leadership.pdf. (accessed 23 March 2014).

Parry, K.W. and Proctor-Thomson, S.B. (2002). Perceived integrity of transformational leaders in organizational settings. *Journal of Business Ethics*, 35, 75–96.

Patterson, K. (2003). Servant leadership: A theoretical model. *Dissertation Abstracts International*, 64(2), 570 (UMI No. 3082719).

Peredo, A.M. and Chrisman, J. (2006). Towards a theory of community-based enterprise. *Academy of Management Review*, 31(2), 309–328.

Pieper, J. (1966). *The Four Cardinal Virtues: Prudence, Justice, Fortitude, Temperance*. Notre Dame, IN: University of Notre Dame Press.

Pless, N.M. and Maak, T. (2011). Responsible leadership: Pathways to the future. *Journal of Business Ethics*, 98, 3–13.

Porter, M. and Kramer, M. (2006). Strategy and society: The link between competitive advantage and corporate social responsibility. *Harvard Business Review*, 84(12), 78–92.

Pruzan, P. (2001). The question of organizational consciousness: Can organizations have values, virtues and visions? *Journal of Business Ethics*, 29, 271–284.

Pruzan, P. (2011). *Spirituality as the Context for Leadership*. In Zsolani, L. (ed.) *Spirituality and Ethics in Management*, 2nd ed. Dordrecht, the Netherlands: Springer, pp. 3–22.

Rest, J. and Narvaez, D. (1994). *Moral Development in the Professions. Psychology and Applied Ethics*. Mahwah, NJ: Lawrence Erlbaum Associates.

Rhode, D.L. (2006). Introduction: Where is the leadership in moral leadership? In D.L. Rhode (ed.), *Moral Leadership. The Theory and Practice of Power, Judgment and Policy*. San Francisco, CA: John Wiley, pp. 1–53.

Richards, D. and Engle, S. (1986). After the vision: Suggestions to corporate visionaries and vision champions. In J.D. Adams (ed.), *Transforming Leadership*. Alexandria, VA: Miles River Press, pp. 199–215.

Riggio, R.E. Zhu, W., Reina, C. and Maroosis, J.A. (2010). Virtue-based measurement of ethical leadership: the *Leadership Virtues Questionnaire. Consulting Psychology Journal*, 62(4), 235–250.

Ruisi, M. (2010). Measure entrepreneurial virtues. Towards a new perspective for the indicators of corporate success. paper presented at the 23rd Eben Annual Conference *Which values for which Organisations*? Trento, Italy, 9–11 September.

Sansone, F. (2014). Leadership responsabile. *Le 10 regole per essere leader nell'economia della conoscenza*. Milano, Italy: F. Angeli.

Sauser Jr., W.I. (2005). Ethics in business: Answering the call. *Journal of Business Ethics*, 58(4), 345–357.

Schaltegger, S. and Wagner, M. (2008). Types of sustainable entrepreneurship and conditions sustainability innovation: From administration of a technical challenge to the management entrepreneurial opportunity. In R. Wustenhagen, J. Hamschmidt, S. Sharma and M. Starik (eds), *Sustainable Innovation and Entrepreneurship*. Cheltenham, UK: Edward Elgar, pp. 27–48.

Schaltegger, S. and Wagner, M. (2011). Sustainable entrepreneurship and sustainability innovation: Categories and interactions. *Business Strategy and the Environment*, 20(4), 222–237.

Schmidpeter, R. (2014). The evolution of CSR from compliance to sustainable entrepreneurship. In C. Weidinger, F. Fischler and R. Schmidpeter (eds), *Sustainable Entrepreneurship. Business Success through Sustainability*. Berlin Heidelberg: Springer-Verlag, pp. 127–134.

Schumpeter, J. (1934). *Capitalism, Socialism, and Democracy*. New York: Harper & Row.

Sedmak, C. (2014). Sustainability: Ethical perspectives. In C. Weidinger, F. Fischler and R. Schmidpeter (eds), *Sustainable Entrepreneurship. Business Success through Sustainability*. Berlin Heidelberg: Springer-Verlag, pp. 51–65.

Seelos, C. and Mair, J. (2005). Social entrepreneurship: Creating new business models to serve the poor. *Business Horizons*, 48(3), 241–246.

Seligman, M.E. (2004). *Character, Strengths and Virtues*. New York: Oxford University Press.

Shamir, B., House, R.J. and Arthur, M.B. (1993). The motivational effects of charismatic leadership: A self-concept based theory. *Organization Science*, 4(4), 577–594.

Shane, S. and Venkataraman, S. (2000). The promise of entrepreneurship as a field of research. *Academy of Management Review*, 25(1), 217–226.

Shepherd, D.A.and Patzelt, H. (2011). The new field of sustainable entrepreneurship: Studying entrepreneurial action linking "what is to be sustained" with "what is to be developed". *Entrepreneurship Theory and Practice*, 35(1), 137–163.

Shepherd, D.A. and Patzelt, H. (2017a). Researching entrepreneurships' role in sustainable development. In D.A. Shepherd and H. Patzelt (eds), *Trailblazing in Entrepreneurship: Creating New Paths for Understanding the Field*. Cham, Switzerland: Palgrave Macmillan, pp. 149–180.

Shepherd, D.A. and Patzelt, H. (2017b). Researching entrepreneurial decision making. In D.A. Shepherd and H. Patzelt (eds), *Trailblazing in entrepreneurship: Creating new paths for understanding the field*. Cham, Switzerland: Palgrave Macmillan, pp. 257–286.

Sison, A.J.G., Beabout, G.R. and Ferrero, I. (eds) (2017). *Handbook of Virtue Ethics in Business and Management*. Dordrecht, the Netherlands: Springer.

Solomon, R.C. (1992a). *Ethics and Excellence: Cooperation and Integrity in Business*. New York: Oxford University Press.

Solomon, R.C. (1992b). Corporate roles, personal virtues: An Aristotelain approach to business ethics. *Business Ethics Quarterly*, 2(3), 317–339.

Spears, L.C. (1995). Servant leadership and the Greenleaf legacy. In L.C. Spears (ed.), *Reflections on Leadership: How Robert K. Greenleaf's Theory of Servant-Leadership Influenced Today's Top Management Thinkers*. New York: John Wiley & Sons, pp. 1–14.

Spence, L.J., Habisch, A. and Schmidpeter, R. (eds) (2004). *Responsibility and Social Capital: The World of Small and Medium Sized Enterprises*. London: Palgrave Macmillan.

Spence, L.J. and Schmidpeter, R. (2003). SMEs, social capital and the common good. *Journal of Business Ethics*, 45(1–2), 93–108.

Spence, L.J., Schmidpeter, R. and Habisch, A. (2003). Assessing social capital: Small and medium sized enterprises in Germany and the UK. *Journal of Business Ethics*, 47(1), 17–29.

Spitzmuller, M. and Ilies, R. (2010). Do they [all] see my true self? Leader's relational authenticity and followers' assessments of transformational leadership. *European Journal of Work and Organizational Psychology*, 19, 304–332.

Stephan, U., Patterson, M., Kelly, C. and Mair, J. (2016). Organizations driving positive social change: A review and an integrative framework of change processes. *Journal of Management*, 42(5), 1250–1281.

Steurer, R., Martinuzzi, A. and Margula, S. (2012). Public policies on CSR in Europe: Themes, instruments, and regional differences. *Corporate Social Responsibility and Environmental Management*, 19(4), 206–227.

Story, J. and Neves, P. (2015). When corporate social responsibility (CSR) increases performance: Exploring the role of intrinsic and extrinsic CSR attribution. *Business Ethics: A European Review*, 24(2), 111–123

Trilling, L. (1972). *Sincerity and Authenticity*. Oxford, UK: Oxford University Press.

Turner, N., Barling, J., Epitropaki, O., Butcher, V. and Milner, C. (2002). Transformational leadership and moral reasoning. *Journal of Applied Psychology*, 87, 304–311.

UN (2015). *The Millennium Development Goals Report*. New York: United Nations. Retrieved from: www.un.org/millenniumgoals/2015_MDG_Report/pdf/MDG%202015%20rev%20(July%201).pdf (accessed May 13 2016).

United Nations Assembly (2015). *Transforming Our World: The 2030 Agenda for Sustainable Development*. A Report of the Secretary-General. New York: United Nations. Retrieved from www.un.org/ga/search/view_doc.asp?symbol=A/RES/70/1&Lang=E (accessed: 12 June 2017).

Van Tassell, M. (2006). Called to serve: Servant-leadership perceptions at a Franciscan sponsored university correlated with job satisfaction. *Dissertation Abstracts International* 67, No. 08A, p. 2843.

Vera, D. and Crossan, M. (2004). Strategic leadership and organizational learning. *Academy of Management Review*, 29, 222–240.

Visser, W. (2011). The nature of CSR leadership. Definitions, characteristics and paradoxes, *CSR International Paper Series*, 4, 1–10.

Vogel, P. and Fischler-Strasak, U. (2014). Fostering sustainable innovation within organizations. In C. Weidinger, F. Fischler and R. Schmidpeter (eds), *Sustainable Entrepreneurship. Business Success through Sustainability*. Berlin Heidelberg: Springer-Verlag, pp. 191–205.

Von Ahsen, A. (2015). Sustainability leadership. In S.O. Idowu, N. Capaldi, M, Fifka, L. Zu and R. Schmidpeter (eds), *Dictionary of Corporate Social Responsibility*. Berlin Heidelberg: Springer-Verlag, p. 444.

Vyakarnam, S., Bailey, A., Myers, A. and Burnett, D. (1997). Towards an understanding of ethical behaviour in small firms. *Journal of Business Ethics*, 16(15), 1625–1636.

Waldman, D.A. and Siegel, D.S. (2008). Defining the socially responsible leader. *Leadership Quarterly*, 19, 117–131.

Waldman, D.A., Siegel, D.S. and Javidan, M. (2006). Components of CEO transformational leadership and corporate social responsibility. *Journal of Management Studies*, 43, 1703–1725.

Walker, B. and Salt, D. (2006). Resilience Thinking: Sustaining Ecosystems and People in a Changing World. Washington, DC: Island Press.

Walker, T. (2015). Entrepreneurial wisdom. Paper presented at the 2nd International Conference on *CSR, Sustainability, Ethics and Governance*, Nanjing, China, July 29–31, 2015. Retrieved from 2015_01_Entrepreneurial_Wisdom_Walker_final.docm,pp 1–12. walk-on Institute for sustainable solutions. www.walk-on.co.at (accessed 18 January 2016).

WCED (World Commission on Environment and Development) (1987). *Our Common Future*. Bruntdland Report. Oxford, UK: Oxford University Press.

Weidinger, C. (2014). Business success through sustainability. In Weidinger, C., Fischler, F. and Schmidpeter, R. (eds), *Sustainable Entrepreneurship. Business Success Through Sustainability*. Berlin, Heidelberg: Springer-Verlag, pp. 287–301.

Werhane, P. (1999). *Moral Imagination and Management Decision Making*. Oxford, UK: Oxford University Press.

West, G.R.B. and Bocarnea, M. (2008). Servant leadership and organizational outcomes: Relationship in United States and Filipino higher educational settings. *Proceedings of the Servant Leadership Research Roundtable*. Retrieved from www.regent.edu/acad/global/publications/sl_proceedings/2008/West-Bocarnea.pdf (accessed 30 June 2015).

Winston, B.E. (2003). Extending Patterson's servant leadership model: Coming full circle. *Proceedings of the Servant Leadership Research Roundtable*. Retrieved from www.regent.edu/acad/global/publications/sl_proceedings/2003/winston_extending_patterson.pdf (accessed 19 August 2015).

World Business Council for Sustainable Development (2012). Retrieved from www.wbcsd.org (accessed 15 January 2015).

York, J.G. and Venkataraman, S. (2010). The entrepreneur–environment nexus: Uncertainty, innovation, and allocation. *Journal of Business Venturing*, 25(5), 449–463.

Yukl, G. (1999). An evaluation of conceptual weaknesses in transformational and charismatic leadership theories. *Leadership Quarterly*, 10, 285–305.

Yukl, G.A. (2010). *Leadership in Organizations*, 7th edn. New York: Prentice-Hall.

Zadek, S. (2006). Responsible competitiveness: Reshaping global markets through responsible business practices. *Corporate Governance*, 6(4), 334–348.

Zahra, S.A., Gedajlovic, E., Neubaum, D.O. and Shulman, J.M. (2009). A typology of social entrepreneurs: Motives, search processes and ethical challenges. *Journal of Business Venturing*, 24(5), 519–532.

Zamagni, S. (ed.) (1995). *The Economics of Altruism*. Cheltenham, UK: Edward Elgar.

Zsolnai, L. (2015). Prudence in management and economic wisdom. Lecture presented at presented at the SPES Congress *Virtues and Vices in Economics and Business*. Centre for Economics and Ethics of the Catholic University of Leuven in cooperation with the European SPES Institute, 19–20 June 2015, Leuven, Belgium.

Zu, L. (2014). International perspective on sustainable entrepreneurship. In Weidinger, C., Fischler, F. and Schmidpeter, R. (eds), *Sustainable Entrepreneurship. Business Success through Sustainability*. Berlin Heidelberg: Springer-Verlag, pp. 67–100.

3.3 The roles of leadership styles in corporate social responsibility

Shuili Du, Valérie Swaen, Adam Lindgreen, and Sankar Sen

Corporate social responsibility (CSR), defined as "the broad array of strategies and operating practices that a company develops in its efforts to deal with and create relationships with its numerous stakeholders and the natural environment" (Waddock, 2004, p. 10), has moved from ideology to reality. More than 6,000 corporations across 135 different countries have adopted the United Nation's Global Compact policy, committing to align their business operations with a set of standards of socially responsible behaviors. These widespread CSR efforts are driven not only by ideological thinking that firms can be positive forces for social change but also by the business returns that firms potentially reap from CSR engagement. Prior research has shown that CSR enables a firm to appeal to the socio-cultural norms of its institutional environment and contributes to its social legitimacy (Handelman and Arnold, 1999; Palazzo and Scherer, 2006; Scott, 1987). In turn, social legitimacy ensures the continuous flow of resources and sustained support from the firm's internal and external stakeholders (Palazzo and Scherer, 2006; Pfeffer and Salancik, 1978; Sen and Bhattacharya, 2001), which ultimately results in enhanced firm financial performance (Luo and Bhattacharya, 2006; Margolis and Walsh, 2003).

However, despite a growing body of research documenting the business case of CSR, our knowledge of organizational antecedents to CSR remains embryonic (Angus-Leppan et al., 2010). Leading scholars from various business disciplines (e.g., strategy, organizational behavior, marketing) have pointed out the dearth of research on external and internal institutional factors that might shape CSR activities in the first place and vigorously called for more research on its organizational antecedents (Campbell, 2007; Hoffman and Bazerman, 2007; Margolis and Walsh, 2003). In particular, considering the importance of leadership in shaping organizational strategies and practices, the lack of research on the interface between organizational leadership and CSR is noteworthy (Groves and LaRocca, 2011a; Waldman and Siegel, 2008).

Recent enthusiasm about the topic of responsible leadership (Maak and Pless, 2006; Pless and Maak, 2011) also highlights certain deficiencies in current leadership theories, particularly with regard to the interface between leadership and CSR. Responsible leadership theory broadens the notion of leadership from a traditional leader–subordinate relationship to leader–stakeholder relationships and contends that "building and cultivating . . . ethically sound relations toward different stakeholders is an important responsibility of leaders in an interconnected stakeholder society" (Maak and Pless, 2006, p. 101). Reflecting the urgent need to bridge leadership theories and CSR literature, Waldman et al. (2006) call specifically for research that "consider[s] a broader array of leadership components and practices" (p. 1721), such as transformational and transactional leadership styles, as drivers of CSR practices. Relatedly, although different leadership styles have been linked to organizational effectiveness measures, such as employee satisfaction and financial performance (Lowe et al., 1996), no prior research has investigated how leadership styles influence the effectiveness of CSR in generating positive organizational outcomes.

This study addresses these research gaps by investigating how the leadership styles adopted by firm managers, specifically transformational and transactional leadership, affect the firm's CSR practices and the organizational outcomes of CSR. This study contributes to the interface of organizational leadership and CSR in several significant ways. First, to the best of our knowledge, this large-scale field study is the first to investigate both transformational and transactional leadership styles exhibited by managers as potential antecedents of the firm's CSR practices. Waldman et al. (2006) find that one component of transformational leadership, intellectual stimulation, relates positively to CSR. However, they do not examine transactional leadership or other components of transformational leadership (e.g., charisma) as possible antecedents. Furthermore, they focus on CEO leadership, whereas this study considers leadership styles by management in general.

Second, going beyond a main effect model of the leadership–CSR relationship, we investigate how a firm's stakeholder-oriented marketing interacts with leadership styles to jointly influence the firm's CSR practices. We adopt a theoretical perspective that spans organizational behavior (i.e., leadership styles) and marketing (i.e., stakeholder-oriented marketing), because CSR is inherently a cross-disciplinary phenomenon (Du et al., 2011; Raghubir et al., 2010). By showing that stakeholder-oriented marketing reinforces the positive link between transformational leadership and a firm's CSR activities, this research paints a more nuanced and complex picture of organizational antecedents to CSR. Specifically, this research indicates that stakeholder-oriented marketing provides necessary cross-functional support (e.g., broader and deeper understanding of stakeholder needs) to catalyze the positive impact of transformational leadership on a firm's CSR practices. More generally, our research highlights the importance of cross-disciplinary investigations in CSR research.

Third, this study extends current knowledge about organizational factors that influence the business case of CSR. Prior literature has depicted a contingent picture of the organizational outcomes of CSR, including corporate reputation, competitive position, and the fit between CSR and core competences (Du et al., 2011; Porter and Kramer, 2011; Yoon et al., 2006). We extend this body of literature by showcasing that transformational and transactional leadership styles both moderate the organizational outcomes of CSR, but in opposite ways. Transactional leadership enhances, whereas transformational leadership diminishes, the positive relationship between CSR and organizational outcomes. This finding accentuates the unique strength of transactional leadership in deriving business benefits from CSR.

We structure the remainder of this chapter as follows. We first review relevant literature on CSR, leadership styles (transformational and transactional leadership), and stakeholder-oriented marketing to derive our conceptual framework and a set of hypotheses. We then describe our methodology and present the results of a large-scale field survey that tests these hypotheses. We end with a discussion of theoretical and managerial implications, as well as limitations of our study and avenues for further research.

Conceptual framework and hypotheses

Institutional CSR

CSR activities are manifest in organizational programs that protect and improve societal welfare, ranging from cause-related marketing, employee benefits, community outreach, to eco-friendly or sustainable business practices. According to stakeholder theory (Freeman et al., 2007), a firm interacts with both primary stakeholders who are essential to the operation of the business (i.e., customers, employees, and investors), and secondary stakeholders who can influence the firm's business operation only indirectly (i.e., community and the natural environment; Waddock, 2008).

In line with stakeholder theory, prior CSR literature has differentiated between technical CSR—activities that target the firm's primary stakeholders—and institutional CSR—activities that target the firm's secondary stakeholders (Godfrey et al., 2009). Mattingly and Berman (2006) performed an exploratory factor analysis of the Kinder Lydenburg Domini (KLD) investment firm's social rating dataset, a widely used CSR data source and perhaps one of the most authoritative ones and uncovered a pattern that differentiates between technical CSR and institutional CSR. Technical CSR mainly refers to a firm's CSR actions in product (i.e., customer), employee, and governance domains, such as actions to enhance product quality and safety, provide employee benefits (e.g., healthcare, work–life balance), and improve organizational governance (e.g., independent board members). Institutional CSR instead covers a firm's CSR activities in the community and environment domains, such as giving back to local communities (e.g., education, arts, culture) and incorporating environmental concerns in business decisions (e.g., clean technology, recycling).

We focus on institutional CSR activities for several reasons. First, they are prevalent and important. Corporate commitment to local communities is steadily increasing, despite the recent economic downturn (CorporatePhilanthropy, 2011). For example, Target Corporation, the second largest discount retailer in the United States, donates 5% of its income ($3 million per week) to communities where it operates, supporting public schools, disadvantaged children, and a wide range of programs in arts, culture, and health. More broadly, many *Fortune* 500 firms commit substantial resources to support local communities (CorporatePhilanthropy, 2011). Firms are also rapidly embracing environment-related CSR actions, as they seek to reduce their eco-footprint and engage in sustainable business practices (Waddock, 2008). Indeed, Hart (1997, p. 71) predicts, "sustainable development will constitute one of the biggest opportunities in the history of commerce."

Second, from a theoretical point of view, because primary stakeholders tend to have more power (utilitarian, coercive, or normative) in making legitimate and urgent claims on the firm, technical CSR activities are often of a reactive, "cost of doing business" nature. In contrast, because legitimate claims by secondary stakeholders often lack power or urgency (Mitchell et al., 1997), institutional CSR activities are more likely to result from discretionary decision making by organizational leaders. The linkages between leadership styles and institutional CSR thus warrant theoretical investigation.

Third, institutional CSR should generate more long-term organizational outcomes, such as positive image and stronger stakeholder relationships. Godfrey et al. (2009) argue that technical CSR activities are often perceived as self-serving and consistent with the firm's profit-making interests and therefore are more likely to produce short-term exchange capital rather than long-term moral capital or goodwill. In contrast, institutional CSR activities are likely to be viewed as voluntary acts of social beneficence, indicative of the firm's benevolent, other-regarding orientation. As such, institutional CSR is more likely to generate intangible values, such as positive corporate image.

Leadership styles and institutional CSR

Most leadership theories, such as leader–member exchange theory and individualized leadership models, focus on dyadic or small group phenomena, rather than leaders' influence over organizational processes (Waldman et al., 2006; Yukl, 1999). This research adopts the strategic leadership paradigm and focuses not on the leader–follower dyadic relationship but rather on how leaders or managers influence the firm's strategic processes, such as institutional CSR. In line with the conceptualization that leadership represents a shared or collective mental model (Bass, 1998; Basu and Palazzo, 2008), we look at leadership styles exhibited by managers throughout the firm, not just at the top level.

Burns (1978) has identified two leadership styles, transformational and transactional, that managers might exhibit. The transformational leader is one who articulates a vision of the future that can be shared with followers, intellectually stimulates followers, and pays attention to individual differences among employees. In contrast, the transactional leader motivates employees primarily through contingent-reward exchanges (Burns, 1978; Waldman et al., 1987). Although Burns (1978) originally represented transformational and transactional leadership styles as opposite ends of a continuum, subsequent research (e.g., Bass, 1985, 1998) conceptualizes them as distinct dimensions. Thus a manager may exhibit characteristics of both. Transactional leaders are more effective at operating an existing system; they set goals, articulate explicit agreements regarding expectations and rewards, and provide constructive feedback to keep everybody on task (Bass and Avolio, 1993; Vera and Crossan, 2004). Transformational leaders are more effective at driving change or transcending the status quo; they inspire followers with their vision and create excitement through use of symbolism and imagery (Bass and Avolio, 1993). By questioning the tried and true, transformational leaders seek to reframe the future (Bass and Avolio, 1993).

A firm's institutional CSR addresses the needs of its secondary stakeholders and may be capable of building social legitimacy (Handelman and Arnold, 1999), moral capital (Godfrey et al., 2009), and long-term competitive advantage (Porter and Kramer, 2011). We expect transformational (but not transactional) leadership to inspire more institutional CSR practices, for several reasons. First, transformational leadership is associated with altruistic ethics, whereas transactional leadership is associated with utilitarian ethics (e.g., use of power, rewards, and sanctions; Groves and LaRocca, 2011b). According to Bass and Steidlmeier (1999), transformational leaders are highly ethical and focused on values. Mendonca (2001) argues that transformational leaders reach higher levels of moral development than transactional leaders and articulate a vision that is both just and in sync with the demands of various stakeholders, motivating followers to transcend their self-interest for the larger vision of the firm. Recent theoretical (Maak and Pless, 2006; Pless and Maak, 2011) and qualitative (Angus-Leppan et al., 2010) studies also suggest that transformational leaders are likely to exhibit ethical or responsible leadership behaviors such as protecting and advancing the interests of secondary stakeholders.

Second, transformational leadership is intellectually stimulating and encourages followers to question old assumptions so they can approach complex problems and issues in more innovative ways (Bass, 1997). Waldman et al. (2006) argue that transformational leaders, particularly intellectually stimulating ones, scan and think broadly about the environmental context and the manner in which various organizational stakeholders may be served. These authors find that the intellectual stimulation factor of transformational leadership is positively associated with CSR practices. We argue in turn that transformational leaders are more likely to realize the complex interconnections among a firm's various stakeholders and view the firm as interdependent with, rather than isolated from, its community and natural environment. In other words, transformational leaders' broader view of the firm should stimulate organizational learning and foster institutional CSR practices that consider the needs and challenges of both primary and secondary stakeholders (Vera and Crossan, 2004). On the contrary, transactional leaders mostly focus on maintaining the status quo and only pay attention to constraints and efficiency. They likely subscribe to a narrow, predominantly shareholder-centric view of the firm and consider institutional CSR a distraction from the firm's core purpose of shareholder value maximization (Friedman, 1970). Overall, the preceding arguments indicate that firms with greater transformational leadership will have more institutional CSR practices.

> ***H1:*** Transformational (but not transactional) leadership is positively associated with a firm's institutional CSR practices.

Moderating role of stakeholder-oriented marketing

Bass (1985) states that organizational characteristics influence the overall effectiveness of transformational leadership. Similarly, the strategic view of the firm emphasizes complementarities among key capabilities or behaviors (e.g., leadership capabilities, stakeholder orientation) that can give rise to synergy among complementary activities (Stieglitz and Heine, 2007; Teece et al., 1997). In the context of the transformational leadership–institutional CSR linkage, we expect stakeholder-oriented marketing to be a key factor that impacts the process by which transformational leadership inspires the design and implementation of a firm's institutional CSR. We focus on stakeholder-oriented marketing due to its practical significance, theoretical linkage to institutional CSR, and, more importantly, its potential complementarity with transformational leadership. Theories of responsible leadership emphasize the importance of approaching leadership in the context of stakeholder theory (Bass and Steidlmeier, 1999; Pless and Maak, 2011). In the field of marketing, reflecting the paradigm shift from customer-orientation to stakeholder-orientation (Ferrell et al., 2010), more and more firms are practicing stakeholder-oriented marketing, which goes beyond a narrow customer focus to address challenges involving multiple stakeholder groups, particularly with regard to local communities and the environment (Bhattacharya and Korschun, 2008; Lindgreen et al., 2009). Stakeholder-oriented marketing, due to its more expansive perspective than the traditional customer-orientation, makes organizational members continuously aware of and willing to act on various stakeholder issues. It also stimulates a general concern for not only primary stakeholders but also secondary stakeholders, thus creating an organizational climate conducive to institutional CSR. Lindgreen et al. (2009) find that stakeholder-oriented marketing is positively associated with institutional CSR practices.

We expect that stakeholder-oriented marketing reinforces the positive impact of transformational leadership on institutional CSR. As argued previously, transformational leaders often exhibit higher levels of ethical development, are more appreciative of the interdependence between the firm and its wide range of stakeholders, and challenge followers to formulate creative solutions to address the needs of all stakeholders. These leadership characteristics favor greater institutional CSR, though complementary activities and processes, such as stakeholder-oriented marketing, will serve to catalyze the impact of transformational leadership on institutional CSR. As a critical organizational function, marketing plays an important role in facilitating CSR decision making by transformational leaders (Kotler and Lee, 2005). Consisting of both "outside-in" (e.g., environmental scanning, marketing research, understanding stakeholder needs) and "inside-out" (e.g., new product development, new service offerings introduced to the market, CSR campaigns) processes, stakeholder-oriented marketing enables a firm to better understand its environment and address its stakeholder-related challenges.

Specifically, through the broader environmental scanning necessitated by stakeholder-oriented marketing, transformational leaders acquire deeper knowledge of the firm's stakeholders (e.g., community, environment) and key issues facing them. Furthermore, by providing essential cross-functional support (e.g., R&D, public relations, community outreach), stakeholder-oriented marketing allows transformational leaders to forge strong stakeholder relationships and tap into the capabilities of secondary stakeholders (e.g., non-profit organizations) to deliver institutional CSR practices that cater to their needs (Kotler and Lee, 2005; Raghubir et al., 2010). In summary, we propose that stakeholder-oriented marketing consists of activities and processes that are complementary to transformational leadership for the design and implementation of institutional CSR practices.

> ***H2:*** Stakeholder-oriented marketing positively moderates the relationship between transformational leadership and institutional CSR practices. The relationship is more positive for firms practicing stakeholder-oriented marketing to a greater extent.

Leadership styles and the organizational outcomes of institutional CSR

In terms of the organizational outcomes of institutional CSR, prior research has shown that institutional CSR can generate various business benefits, such as stronger stakeholder relationships, a more positive corporate image, and goodwill (Bhattacharya et al., 2008; Du et al., 2011; Godfrey et al., 2009). The business impact of "doing good" hinges on a host of firm- and market-specific factors, such as firm expertise, reputation, and competitive positioning (Du et al., 2011; Godfrey et al., 2009; Luo and Bhattacharya, 2006, 2009). However, prior research has not attempted, either theoretically or empirically, to examine how leadership styles might affect the organizational outcomes of institutional CSR. We expect that transactional (but not transformational) leadership will amplify the positive impact of CSR on organizational outcomes for several reasons. First, societal impact, or the value provided to secondary stakeholders, is essential for institutional CSR to generate positive organizational outcomes (Bhattacharya et al., 2008; Du et al., 2008). Transactional leaders are more likely to apply a transactional, input–output mindset to the realm of institutional CSR and seek to maximize the societal impact at a given level of CSR commitment. These leaders, adept as they are at task implementation, set CSR-related goals, articulate explicit agreements regarding rewards to organizational members for their CSR pursuit, and provide constructive feedback to keep members on track throughout the execution of institutional CSR practices. Such active, transactional management of institutional CSR practices will likely enhance societal welfare. In turn, the greater societal impact of institutional CSR may lend credibility to the firm's CSR engagement, boosting its socially responsible image and strengthening its stakeholder relationships (Du et al., 2008; Godfrey et al., 2009).

Second, the effective implementation of institutional CSR requires a firm to capitalize on its core business competence to effect positive change (Kotler and Lee, 2005; Porter and Kramer, 2006, 2011). Leadership literature suggests that though transformational leadership is better at competence exploration (e.g., acquiring entirely new knowledge and skills), transactional leadership is better at competence exploitation (e.g., refining and extending current knowledge and skills; March, 1991; Vera and Crossan, 2004). Transactional leadership also emphasizes convergent thinking, efficiency, and continuity (Bass, 1985; Vera and Crossan, 2004). Accordingly, when implementing the firm's institutional CSR practices, transactional leaders should be more mindful of opportunities to leverage their business competence to maximize the social and business returns of institutional CSR. Close monitoring of task implementation and continuous improvement in the firm's institutional CSR practices, both characteristics of transactional leadership, also lead to more favorable organizational outcomes. We expect:

> ***H3:*** Transactional (but not transformational) leadership positively moderates the relationship between institutional CSR practices and organizational outcomes. The relationship is more positive for firms with higher transactional leadership.

Our conceptual framework is represented in Figure 3.3.1.

Method

Sample and procedures

We collected data in a nationwide, large-scale survey of managers of U.S. firms, whom we contacted through an independent marketing research firm, e-Rewards. This reputable, Dallas-based online sample provider has built its own consumer, business, and specialty panels with a total of 1.5 million members. The firm follows strict procedures

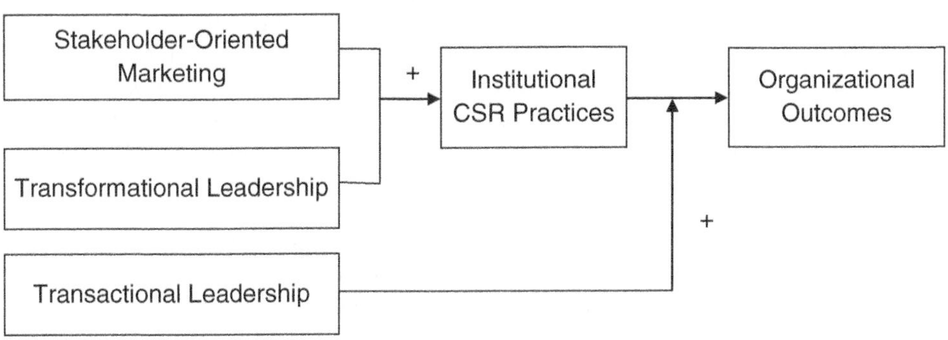

Figure 3.3.1 Conceptual framework

to ensure the quality of its panels. For example, e-Rewards fully owns and controls the panels, which have not been merged or acquired from other firms; it verifies the physical existence of all panelists; and it limits participation by the average panelist to fewer than three full surveys per year. The firm also employs different methods to exclude professional survey takers.

Our sample covered a broad range of organizations in terms of type of business activities (business-to-business or business-to-consumer, physical goods or services), amount of sales revenues (from less than US$10 million to more than US$1 billion), and number of employees (from less than 20 to more than 5,000). We screened respondents based on their functional roles to ensure that they were able to answer our survey questions as a result of their experience, knowledge of management policies, and access to organizational performance data. Most respondents held the following organizational positions: executives/owners, marketing/advertising personnel, general management, and administration. In addition, 94% of them held middle- or upper-level management positions.

Qualified respondents were contacted via e-mail with an invitation to participate in an online survey, which would feature a lengthy questionnaire that included questions for the current study as well as another related study on CSR practices. Respondents were assured that their answers would be completely confidential and anonymous and that the analysis would take place at an aggregate level. Managers from 523 different U.S. organizations completed the survey. However, because preliminary tests showed that respondents would need at least 10 minutes to answer the survey, we excluded questionnaires from respondents who spent less than 10 minutes filling out the survey. We therefore retained 440 organizations in our study. In terms of organizational demographics, business-to-business and business-to-consumer organizations were roughly equally represented (45.8% vs. 43.6%, with the remaining 10.6% engaging in both). Organizations in our sample also varied substantially in size: 37.8% had fewer than 20 employees, 14.9% had 20–100 employees, 18.1% between 100 and 1,000 employees, and 29.1% employed more than 1,000 people. In our analysis, we included organizational type (business-to-business vs. business-to-consumer) and size as covariates.

Measures

Transformational leadership. Transformational leadership was measured using items from Bass and Avolio (2000), according to three major dimensions (Bass, 1985; Waldman et al., 2006): (1) charisma (12 items) that "provides followers with a clear sense of purpose that is energizing, is a role model for ethical conduct and builds identification with the leader and his or her articulated vision" (Avolio et al., 1999, p. 444); (2) intellectual stimulation (4 items) that "gets followers to question the tried and true ways of solving problems, and encourages them to question the methods they use to improve upon them" (Avolio et al., 1999, p. 444); and (3) individualized consideration (4 items) that "focuses on understanding the needs of each follower and works continuously to get them to develop to their full potential" (Avolio et al., 1999, p. 444).

In our study, we only included items for charisma and intellectual stimulation as measures for transformational leadership. As stated previously, we adopted the strategic leadership approach and focused on how leadership influences strategic processes (i.e., institutional CSR practices); therefore, we excluded individualized consideration, which is mostly about dyadic leader–follower relationships. Because individualized consideration focuses on how a leader deals with individual followers in terms of mentoring, coaching, and individual development, it is not conceptually related to a firm's strategic decision making, such as the design and implementation of institutional CSR practices. According to Waldman et al. (2006, p. 1707), "because of the individual-level focus, a clear conceptual linkage with higher-level organizational phenomena, such as CSR, may be difficult to establish." As is evident in our conceptualization, there is theoretical support for the hypothesized linkages between the other two aspects of transformational leadership (charisma and intellectual stimulation) and institutional CSR practices (e.g., Bass and Steidlmeier, 1999; Porter and Kramer, 2011; Vera and Crossan, 2004), but not much theoretical support linking individualized consideration to institutional CSR practices. For the purpose of this study, we excluded individualized consideration from our measure of transformational leadership.

The resulting 16 items measuring charisma and intellectual stimulation are highly reliable (Cronbach's alpha = .96). We combined the two factors to form an overall measure of transformational leadership, consistent with prior research that has examined transformational leadership as a higher-order construct (e.g., Bass and Avolio, 2000; Bono and Judge, 2003; Walumbwa et al., 2008). Table 3.3.4 in the Appendix contains detailed information on the measures of transformational leadership and other key constructs.

Transactional leadership. Transactional leadership was also measured using items from Bass and Avolio (2000). Specifically, in line with prior literature (e.g., Derue et al., 2011; Lowe et al., 1996), we included (1) contingent rewards (4 items) that "clarifies what is expected from followers and what they will receive if they meet expected levels of performance" (Avolio et al., 1999, pp. 444–445) and (2) management by exception-active (MBEA, 4 items) that "focuses on monitoring task execution for any problems that might arise and correcting those problems to maintain current performance levels" (Avolio et al., 1999, p. 445). We did not include management by exception-passive (MBEP), because prior analysis has shown that MBEP does not correlate with either contingent rewards or MBEA but instead correlates highly with laissez-faire leadership, which refers to the absence of leadership behavior (Avolio et al., 1999). Thus MBEP is more frequently grouped with laissez-faire to indicate a third leadership style, passive-avoidant (Avolio et al., 1999; Derue et al., 2011).

We subsequently dropped contingent rewards from our measure of transactional leadership though. Empirically, there was a high correlation between contingent rewards and transformational leadership in our data ($r = .82$). This high correlation was consistent with prior research. In a meta-analysis of leadership literature, Derue et al. (2011) calculate an average correlation of .80 between contingent rewards and transformational leadership. Other studies (e.g., Avolio et al., 1999; Lowe et al., 1996) have found similarly high correlations, in the neighborhood of .70–.80. From a conceptual point of view, prior research (e.g., Avolio et al., 1999; Shamir, 1995; Vera and Crossan, 2004) has discussed the conceptual overlap between transformational and transactional leadership, particularly with regard to contingent rewards. For example, Shamir (1995) notes that with behaviors emphasizing contingent rewards, leaders build trust and dependability, which contribute to the high levels of trust and respect associated with transformational leadership. Similarly, Derue et al. (2011) note conceptual overlap between transformational leadership and behaviors for initiating structure, such as specifying expectations and rewards (i.e., contingent rewards). Consequently, we only included MBEA as the measure for transactional leadership. This measure is highly reliable, with a Cronbach's alpha of .87.

Stakeholder-oriented marketing. We derived the measure for stakeholder-oriented marketing from relevant literature on contemporary marketing practices (e.g., Brookes and Palmer, 2004; Coviello et al., 2002) and stakeholder orientation (Ferrell et al., 2010). Stakeholder-oriented marketing requires that marketing activities go beyond a narrow customer focus to include all relevant stakeholders, such as suppliers, service providers, and local communities. Firms practicing stakeholder-oriented marketing also commit substantial resources to cultivate networks of relationships in the wider marketing system and often involve senior management and cross-functional teams to carry out their marketing activities. Nine items were used to measure the degree to which a firm practices stakeholder-oriented marketing. The measure is highly reliable, with a Cronbach's alpha of .91.

Institutional CSR practices. In line with prior literature (e.g., Godfrey et al., 2009; Mattingly and Berman, 2006), we only included CSR activities targeting community and environment to measure institutional CSR practices. To derive the exact measurement items, we reviewed prior literature (Maignan et al., 1999; Turker, 2009) and conducted in-depth interviews with managers. This exploratory research resulted in a list of 12 items to measure institutional CSR. The measure for institutional CSR is highly reliable, with a Cronbach's alpha of .95.

Organizational outcomes. The measure for organizational outcomes came from prior literature (Brown and Dacin, 1997; Fombrun and Shanley, 1990; Freeman, 1984; Menon and Menon, 1997; Sen and Bhattacharya, 2001; Turban and Greening, 1997). We measured organizational outcomes as performance relative to expectations, rather than absolute performance, because prior research has shown that respondents not only find it easier but also are more willing to report relative performance, particularly with regard to intangible outcomes (Coviello et al., 2002; Parasuraman et al., 1994). Four items captured a firm's performance with regard to stakeholder relationship, corporate reputation, and visibility. Prior CSR literature has suggested that CSR practices have positive impacts on these organizational outcomes (Du et al., 2007; Fombrun and Shanley, 1990; Handelman and Arnold, 1999). The measure is reliable (Cronbach's alpha = .80).

Control variables. Our control variables included organizational type (business-to-business vs. business-to-consumer) and organizational size. We controlled for organizational type because research suggests that, relative to business-to-business firms, business-to-consumer firms are more likely to use CSR to build a favorable image and provide psychological benefits (i.e., identification; Drumwright, 1994; McWilliams and Siegel, 2001; Sen and Bhattacharya, 2001). Therefore, all else being equal, we expect that business-to-consumer firms engage in institutional CSR to a greater extent. We controlled for size, because research suggests that size plays a role in determining the level of a firm's CSR commitment (McWilliams and Siegel, 2001). For example, according to the resource-based view, larger firms can better afford resources to spend on institutional CSR practices and are more likely to reap benefits from institutional CSR practices (Godfrey et al., 2009).

We dummy coded these two organizational demographic variables to include them as covariates in the regression analyses. The orgtype variable equaled 1 if the organization was primarily in business-to-consumer markets, and 0 otherwise. The orgsize variable was defined by a median split of the number of people employed, equal to 1 if the organization employed more than 100 people and 0 otherwise.

Common method bias. Because we relied on a single source for our measures, common method bias in self-reported measures could be a concern. Employing the widely used

Harman's one-factor method (e.g., Carr and Kaynak, 2007; Podsakoff and Organ, 1986), we ran a factor analysis of all measures to examine the likelihood of a single or dominant factor. The unrotated solution showed no evidence of a dominant common factor (seven factors had eigenvalues greater than 1.0; the first factor accounted for only 19% of the total variance). Thus, common method bias did not seem to represent a serious issue for this study. Furthermore, prior research shows that interaction effects cannot be artifacts of common method bias; on the contrary, common method bias makes it more difficult to detect interaction effects (Siemsen et al., 2010). Therefore, at a minimum, common method bias is unlikely to account for the results relating to H2 and H3, which deal with interaction effects.

Results

We tested our hypotheses using multiple regressions with relevant interaction terms. To enhance the interpretation of the regression coefficients in moderated regression models, we mean-centered all continuous independent variables (Aiken and West, 1991). Table 3.3.1 contains the means, standard deviations, and reliability coefficients of the key variables, as well as correlations among them.

We tested H1 and H2 using a moderated regression model: institutional CSR $= f$ (transformational leadership, transactional leadership, stakeholder-oriented marketing, transformational leadership × stakeholder-oriented marketing, transactional leadership × stakeholder-oriented marketing, orgtype, orgsize). Table 3.3.2 lists the estimation results.

Table 3.3.1 Descriptive statistics and correlations

Variable		*Mean*	*SD*	*1*	*2*	*3*	*4*	*5*
1	Transformational leadership	3.68	.86	.96				
2	Transactional leadership	3.05	.99	.27	.87			
3	Stakeholder-oriented marketing	3.33	.95	.46	.28	.91		
4	Institutional CSR	4.67	1.43	.60	.19	.44	.95	
5	Organizational outcomes	3.45	.75	.42	.19	.39	.48	.80

Notes: n = 440. Reliability coefficients are reported on the diagonal. All correlations are significant at $p < .01$.

Table 3.3.2 Antecedents of institutional CSR: unstandardized regression coefficients

	Institutional CSR
Stakeholder-oriented marketing	.28**
Transformational leadership	.91**
Transactional leadership	−.01
Transformational leadership × stakeholder-oriented marketing	.16**
Transactional leadership × stakeholder-oriented marketing	−.02
Organizational type	.18+
Size	.29**
Adjusted R^2	.41
F value	43.99**

** $p < .01$, * $p < .05$, + $p < .10$.

In H1 we predicted that transformational (but not transactional) leadership is positively associated with institutional CSR. As expected, the coefficient for transformational leadership is positive and significant (b = .90, $p < .01$), whereas the coefficient for transactional leadership is not significant (b = −.01, NS), in support of H1.

Also as expected, the coefficient for stakeholder-oriented marketing is positive and significant (b = .29, $p < .01$), so stakeholder-oriented marketing relates positively to institutional CSR practices. Furthermore, in line with H2, we find a positive interaction between stakeholder-oriented marketing and transformational leadership (b = .16, $p < .01$), indicating that stakeholder-oriented marketing amplifies the positive link between transformational leadership and institutional CSR practices. To clarify the nature of this interaction, we performed a simple slope analysis (Aiken and West, 1991) by looking at the transformational leadership–institutional CSR link when the moderator variable, stakeholder-oriented marketing, was one standard deviation above and below the mean. With high stakeholder-oriented marketing (i.e., one standard deviation above the mean), the coefficient for the simple slope of transformational leadership on institutional CSR practices is b = 1.06 (t = 10.54, $p < .01$). With low stakeholder-oriented marketing (i.e., one standard deviation below the mean), the coefficient for the simple slope of transformational leadership on institutional CSR practices is b = .76 (t = 9.05, $p < .01$). These results suggest that the relationship between transformational leadership and institutional CSR practices is stronger when stakeholder-oriented marketing is high and significantly weaker when stakeholder-oriented marketing is low. Therefore, H2 is supported by our data.

Finally, H3 examines the moderating role of transactional leadership in the relationship between institutional CSR and organizational outcomes. To test H3, we ran a moderated regression: organizational outcomes = *f*(institutional CSR practices, transformational leadership, transactional leadership, transformational leadership × institutional CSR practices, transactional leadership × institutional CSR practices, stakeholder-oriented marketing, orgtype, orgsize). Stakeholder-oriented marketing is included as a covariate in this model, because research suggests that it relates positively to organizational outcomes (Bhattacharya and Korschun, 2008; Lindgreen et al., 2009). The estimation results are in Table 3.3.3.

In line with leadership literature, we find that transformational leadership is positively associated with organizational outcomes (b = .15, $p < .01$), whereas transactional

Table 3.3.3 Organizational outcomes of institutional CSR: unstandardized regression coefficients

	Organizational outcomes
Institutional CSR	.14**
Transformational leadership	.15**
Transactional leadership	.04
Institutional CSR × transformational leadership	−.04+
Institutional CSR × transactional leadership	.05*
Stakeholder-oriented marketing	.15**
Organizational type	.18**
Size	.14*
Adjusted R^2	.32
F	22.88**

** $p < .01$, * $p < .05$, + $p < .10$.

leadership is not (b = .04, NS). Stakeholder-oriented marketing is positively associated with organizational outcomes (b = .15, $p < .01$). In line with H3, we find that institutional CSR practices not only have a positive main effect (b = .14, $p < .01$) on organizational outcomes but that this positive link is greater with higher transactional leadership (i.e., positive interaction between institutional CSR practices and transactional leadership: b = .05, $p < .05$). Simple slope analysis indicates that, with transformational leadership at the mean level, when transactional leadership is high (i.e., one standard deviation above the mean), the simple slope of institutional CSR practices on organizational outcomes is b = .19 (t = 5.35, $p < .01$). Also with transformational leadership being at the mean level, when transactional leadership is low (i.e., one standard deviation below the mean), the simple slope of institutional CSR practices on organizational outcome is b = .09 (t = 2.57, $p < .05$). These results suggest that, all else being equal, transactional leadership amplifies the positive relationship between institutional CSR practices and organizational outcomes, in support of H3.

We also notice a negative interaction between institutional CSR practices and transformational leadership (b = −.04, $p < .10$), indicating that transformational leadership reduces the positive relationship between institutional CSR practices and organizational outcomes. Simple slope analysis indicates that, with transactional leadership at the mean level, when transformational leadership is high (one standard deviation above the mean), the simple slope of institutional CSR practices on organizational outcomes is b = .10 (t = 2.80, $p < .01$). With transactional leadership at the mean level, when transformational leadership is low (i.e., one standard deviation below the mean), the simple slope of institutional CSR practices on organizational outcomes is b = .18 (t = 5.04, $p < .01$). These results in turn suggest that, all else being equal, transformational leadership diminishes the positive relationship between institutional CSR practices and organizational outcomes.

Discussion

Despite the prominent place CSR has on the global corporate agenda, our understanding of micro-level organizational dynamics about CSR, such as the interface between leadership styles and CSR, remains incipient (Angus-Leppan et al., 2010; Groves and LaRocca, 2011b). This study has sought to shed light on the ways in which transformational and transactional leadership styles affect a firm's institutional CSR practices, as well as the organizational outcomes of CSR. Specifically, we developed and tested a theoretical framework pertaining to (1) how transformational (but not transactional) leadership affects institutional CSR practices, (2) how stakeholder-oriented marketing influences the transformational leadership–institutional CSR link, and (3) how leadership styles influence the relationship between institutional CSR and organizational outcomes.

Through a large-scale field survey of managers, we found that firms with greater transformational leadership are more likely to engage in institutional CSR practices, but transactional leadership is not associated with these CSR practices. Furthermore, stakeholder-oriented marketing reinforces the positive link between transformational leadership and institutional CSR practices. Finally, our results showed that transactional leadership enhances, whereas transformational leadership diminishes, the positive relationship between institutional CSR practices and organizational outcomes. Our research highlighted the differential roles that transformational and transactional leadership styles play in a firm's institutional CSR practices, which have significant implications for theory and practice.

Theoretical implications

Although much has been said about the salubrious effects of CSR on stakeholder support, loyalty, and retention (e.g., Bhattacharya et al., 2008), less is known about the driving effects of the leadership styles displayed by managers on a firm's CSR policies and outcomes (Angus-Leppan et al., 2010; Groves and LaRocca, 2011b; Waldman et al., 2006). This study has provided much needed empirical evidence concerning the differential roles of transformational and transactional leadership styles in the firm's institutional CSR practices. Our findings have implications for theories of CSR and leadership.

By documenting the positive association between transformational leadership and institutional CSR, this study advances knowledge about organizational drivers of CSR. Although prior research has conceptualized various organizational antecedents to CSR, such as managers' mental frames and sense-making processes (Basu and Palazzo, 2008), organizational culture (e.g., future or performance orientations; Berger et al., 2007), and leadership styles (Angus-Leppan et al., 2010), large-scale empirical studies of organizational drivers of CSR are lacking (cf. Waldman et al., 2006). This research bridges leadership literature and CSR literature to provide empirical evidence on the transformational leadership–institutional CSR link. Specifically, this study places transformational leadership in the context of stakeholder theory (Bass and Steidlmeier, 1999; Pless and Maak, 2011) and shows that transformational leaders are likely to exhibit responsible leadership by, among others, promoting institutional CSR that advances the welfare of secondary stakeholders. Furthermore, integrating theoretical constructs from organizational behavior and marketing, we find that the link between transformational leadership and institutional CSR is not constant across all firms but instead depends on the level of stakeholder-oriented marketing practiced by the firm. This result attests to the importance of taking a cross-disciplinary approach in CSR research (Du et al., 2011; Raghubir et al., 2010). Specifically, to fully unleash the potential of transformational leadership in promoting socially responsible business practices, complementary organizational capabilities such as stakeholder-oriented marketing are essential. This result documents, for the first time, the complementarity between a firm's leadership capabilities and marketing capabilities in driving its CSR practices. Research on organizational antecedents to CSR should continue to adopt a broad theoretical perspective that spans different business disciplines (e.g., organizational behavior, marketing, strategy, information system).

By documenting, for the first time, the moderating role of leadership styles in the organizational outcomes of CSR, this research extends prior literature on the business case of CSR. Our findings are particularly interesting in light of prior research on leadership. Specifically, prior literature has consistently found high correlations between transformational leadership and a range of effectiveness criteria, such as follower job satisfaction, percentage of goals met, and financial performance of the work unit; in contrast, transactional leadership appears less effective (Bass et al., 2003; Derue et al., 2011; Lowe et al., 1996). However, we find that transactional leadership amplifies, whereas transformational leadership diminishes, the positive link between institutional CSR and organizational outcomes. This finding accentuates the unique strength of transactional leadership in deriving business benefits from institutional CSR and suggests that, in certain circumstances, transactional leadership is effective but transformational leadership is not.

The dampening effect of transformational leadership on the organizational outcomes of CSR indicates that this leadership style is not without peril; by itself, it seems to detract from CSR's ability to create value for the firm. This unexpected finding extends prior literature, which mostly documents positive effects of transformational leadership.

Practical implications

This study highlights the importance of organizational leadership in a firm's CSR endeavors. Despite the well-accepted belief that CSR is critical to firms' ability to meet their stakeholder obligations and obtain sustained growth (Lindgreen and Swaen, 2009), many firms struggle to promote socially responsible business practices and maximize the social and business returns to their CSR (Kotler and Lee, 2005; Porter and Kramer, 2006). Our findings suggest that leadership styles play an essential role. Specifically, a transformational leadership style is best suited for initiating and designing socially responsible practices; transactional leadership is best suited for implementing and deriving business benefits from socially responsible practices. Since a "win-win" situation, by satisfying the business motives of the firm while also ensuring sustained corporate investment in CSR, feeds into a "circle of virtue," it appears that both transformational and transactional leadership styles are required for successful institutional CSR practices. Our findings thus suggest that managers should adopt a pluralistic approach to leadership and practice transformational leadership in conjunction with transactional leadership. This recommendation is consistent with Quinn's (1988) concept of a "master manager," who chooses transformational or transactional behaviors depending on the circumstances. In particular, transactional leadership behaviors, by managing the mundane, day-to-day events (e.g., monitoring, corrective actions, continuous improvement), augment transformational leadership behaviors. Collectively, both styles serve to reinforce a firm's CSR endeavors.

This study also suggests that firms should attend to the supporting role of marketing to provide the appropriate organizational context for CSR practices (Lindgreen et al., 2009). A firm's stakeholders are embedded in interconnected networks of relationships, through which the firm's marketing actions reverberate with both direct and indirect consequences (Bhattacharya and Korschun, 2008). Stakeholder-oriented marketing practices encourage organizational members to care about the welfare of all stakeholders and devise creative solutions that address stakeholder issues. Our findings confirm that by practicing stakeholder-oriented marketing, a firm can cultivate an organizational climate conducive to CSR practices. Furthermore, stakeholder-oriented marketing provides the essential cross-functional support for transformational leadership in a firm's efforts to promote CSR practices. Transformational leaders should mindfully build and leverage complementary capabilities (e.g., stakeholder-oriented marketing) that facilitate their socially responsible actions.

Limitations and further research

Several caveats should be taken into consideration when interpreting the results of this study. First, the cross-sectional design limits the degree to which we can make causal inferences and test the strength of the relationships over time. Replications and extensions of our findings using experimental and longitudinal designs are needed. Second, we employ a single-informant technique (i.e., one respondent from each firm) and measure all variables with a common method (i.e., field survey). Although our analysis indicates that common method bias is not a serious issue, additional research should employ multi-informant and multimethod designs to overcome this potential limitation. Third, this study involves only U.S. firms. Further research should examine the generalizability of our findings in countries with different cultures (e.g., individualistic vs. collectivistic) or different economic developmental stages (e.g., developing countries).

Fourth, we only use MBEA as the measure of transactional leadership. Research should examine the role of another component of transactional leadership, contingent rewards, in a firm's CSR practices. More generally, further work on how other dimensions of leadership, beyond transformational and transactional, influence CSR policies and success would help deepen understanding of this important but underexamined internal driver of CSR.

Acknowlegment

This chapter first appeared as Du, S., Swaen, V., Lindgreen, A., and Sen, S. (2013), "The roles of leadership styles in corporate social responsibility", *Journal of Business Ethics*, Vol. 114, No. 1, pp. 155–169.

Appendix

Table 3.3.4 Measurement instrument

Transformational leadership *(IS = intellectual stimulation, CHI = charisma/inspiration)*

In our firm, managers. . . (5-point scale, 1 = "never," 5 = "frequently, if not always")

1) re-examine critical assumptions to question whether these are appropriate (IS)
2) seek differing perspectives when solving problems (IS)
3) get others to look at problems from many different angles (IS)
4) suggest new ways of looking at how to complete assignments (IS)
5) talk about their most important values and beliefs (CHI)
6) specify the importance of having a strong sense of purpose (CHI)
7) consider the moral and ethical consequences of decisions (CHI)
8) emphasize the importance of having a collective sense of mission (CHI)
9) talk optimistically about the future (CHI)
10) talk enthusiastically about what needs to be accomplished (CHI)
11) articulate a compelling vision of the future (CHI)
12) express confidence that goals will be achieved (CHI)
13) instill pride in others for being associated with them (CHI)
14) go beyond self-interest for the good of the group (CHI)
15) act in ways that build others' respect for me (CHI)
16) display a sense of power and confidence (CHI)

Transactional leadership *(MBEA = management by exception-active, CR = contingent reward)*

In our firm, managers. . . (5-point scale, 1 = "never," 5 = "frequently, if not always")

1) focus attention on irregularities, mistakes, exceptions, and deviations from standards (MBEA)
2) concentrate their full attention on dealing with mistakes, complaints, and failures (MBEA)
3) keep track of all mistakes (MBEA)
4) direct their attention towards failure to meet standard (MBEA)
5) provide others with assistance in exchange for their efforts (CR)
6) discuss in specific terms who is responsible for achieving performance targets (CR)
7) make clear what one can expect to receive when performance goals are achieved (CR)
8) express satisfaction when others meet expectations (CR)

Institutional CSR practices

Our firm systematically attempts to. . . (5-point scale, 1 = "strongly disagree," 5 = "strongly agree")

1) incorporate the interests of the communities where we operate in our business decisions
2) financially support education in the communities where we operate
3) stimulate the economic development in the communities where we operate
4) help improve the quality of life in the communities where we operate
5) give money to charities in the communities where we operate
6) financially support activities (arts, culture, sports) in the communities where we operate
7) voluntarily exceed government-imposed environmental regulations
8) incorporate environmental concerns in our business decisions
9) incorporate environmental performance objectives in our organizational plans
10) financially support environmental initiatives
11) measure our organization's environmental performance
12) minimize the environmental impact of all our firm's activities

Stakeholder-oriented marketing practices

(5-point scale, 1 = "never," 5 = "always")

1) Our marketing activities are *intended* to coordinate activities between ourselves, customers, and other parties in our wider marketing system (e.g., key suppliers, service providers, and other firms with which we interact through our marketing activities).
2) Our marketing planning is *focused on* issues related to the network of relationships between individuals and organizations in our wider marketing system
3) When dealing with our market(s), our *purpose* is to form relationships with a number of firms in our market(s) or the wider marketing system
4) Our firm's *contact* with our *primary customers* is from impersonal to interpersonal (e.g., involving one-to-one interaction between people) across firms in the broader network
5) The *type of relationship* with our primary customers is characterized as contact with people in our organization and the wider marketing system that is ongoing
6) Our marketing resources (i.e., people, time, and money) are *invested in* developing our firm's network relationships within our market(s) or the wider marketing system
7) Our marketing *communication* involves senior managers networking with other managers from a variety of firms in our market(s) or the wider marketing system
8) When people from our firm *meet with* our *primary* customers it is at both a formal business level and informal social level in a wider organizational system / network
9) Overall, our firm's *general approach* to our *primary* customers involves positioning our organization in a wider organizational system / network

Organizational outcomes

This year, how has your firm performed *relative to expectations* for. . . (5-point scale, 1 = "much worse," 5 = "much better")

1) improving relations with environment (e.g., people in the community)
2) improving relations with stakeholders in general
3) improving corporate image / reputation
4) gaining national and international visibility

References

Aiken, L.S. and S.G. West, 1991, *Multiple Regression: Testing and Interpreting Interactions* (Newbury Park, CA: Sage).

Angus-Leppan, T., L. Metcalf, and S. Benn, 2010, 'Leadership styles and CSR practice: An examination of sensemaking, institutional drivers and CSR leadership', *Journal of Business Ethics* 93, 189–213.

Avolio, B.J., B.M. Bass, and D.I. Jung, 1999, 'Re-examining the components of transformational and transactional leadership using the multifactor leadership questionnaire', *Journal of Occupational and Organizational Psychology* 72, 441–462.

Bass, B.M., 1985, *Leadership and Performance Beyond Expectations* (New York: Academic Press).

Bass, B.M., 1997, 'Does the transactional-transformational leadership paradigm transcend organizational and national borders?' *American Psychologist* 52, 130–139.

Bass, B.M., 1998, *Transformational Leadership: Industrial, Military, and Educational Impact* (Mahwah, NJ: Lawrence Erlbaum Associates).

Bass, B.M. and B.J. Avolio, 1993, 'Transformational leadership and organizational culture', *Public Administration Quarterly* 17, 112–121.

Bass, B.M. and B.J. Avolio, 2000, *MLQ: Multifactor Leadership Questionnaire*, 2nd ed. (Redwood City, CA: Mind Garden).

Bass, B.M., B.J. Avolio, D.I. Jung, and Y. Berson, 2003, 'Predicting unit performance by assessing transformational and transactional leadership', *Journal of Applied Psychology* 88, 207–218.

Bass, B.M. and P. Steidlmeier, 1999, 'Ethics, character, and authentic transformational leadership behaviour', *Leadership Quarterly* 10, 181–217.

Basu, K. and G. Palazzo, 2008, 'Corporate social responsibility: A process model of sensemaking', *Academy of Management Review* 33, 122–136.

Berger, I.E., P. Cunningham, and M.E. Drumwright, 2007, 'Mainstreaming corporate social responsibility: Developing markets for virtue', *California Management Review* 49, 132–157.

Bhattacharya, C.B. and D. Korschun, 2008, 'Stakeholder marketing: Beyond the four P's and the customer', *Journal of Public Policy & Marketing* 27, 113–116.

Bhattacharya, C.B., D. Korschun, and S. Sen, 2008, 'Strengthening stakeholder-company relationships through mutually beneficial corporate social responsibility initiatives', *Journal of Business Ethics* 85, 257–272.

Bono, J.E. and T.A. Judge, 2003, 'Self-concordance at work: Toward understanding the motivational effects of transformational leaders', *Academy of Management Journal* 46, 554–571.

Brookes, R. and R. Palmer, 2004, *The New Global Marketing Reality* (London: Palgrave).

Brown, T.J. and P.A. Dacin, 1997, 'The company and the product: Corporate associations and consumer product responses', *Journal of Marketing* 61, 68–84.

Burns, J.M.G., 1978, *Leadership* (New York: Harper and Row).

Campbell, J.L., 2007, 'Why would corporations behave in socially responsible ways? An institutional theory of corporate social responsibility', *Academy of Management Review* 32, 946–967.

Carr, A. and H. Kaynak, 2007, 'Communication methods, information sharing, supplier development and performance', *International Journal of Operations and Production Management* 27, 346–370.

CorporatePhilanthropy, 2011, 'Giving in numbers: trends in corporate giving', available at: www.corporatephilanthropy.org/measurement/benchmarking-reports/giving-in-numbers.html. Accessed December 21, 2011.

Coviello, N.E., R.J. Brodie, P.J. Danaher, and W.J. Johnston, 2002, 'How firms relate to their markets: An empirical examination of contemporary marketing practices', *Journal of Marketing* 66, 33–46.

Derue, D.S., J.D. Nahrgang, N. Wellman, and S.E. Humphrey, 2011, 'Trait and behavioral theories of leadership: An integration and meta-analytic test of their relative validity', *Personnel Psychology* 64, 7–52.

Drumwright, M.E., 1994, 'Socially responsible organizational buying: Environmental concern as a noneconomic buying criterion', *Journal of Marketing* 58, 1–19.

Du, S., C.B. Bhattacharya, and S. Sen, 2007, 'Reaping relational rewards from corporate social responsibility: The role of competitive positioning', *International Journal of Research in Marketing* 24, 224–241.

Du, S., C.B. Bhattacharya, and S. Sen, 2011, 'Corporate social responsibility and competitive advantage: Overcoming the trust barrier', *Management Science* 57, 1528–1545.

Du, S., S. Sen, and C.B. Bhattacharya, 2008, 'Exploring the social and business returns of a corporate oral health initiative aimed at disadvantaged Hispanic families', *Journal of Consumer Research* 35, 483–494.

Ferrell, O.C., T.L. Gonzalez-Padron, G.T.M. Hult, and I. Maignan, 2010, 'From market orientation to stakeholder orientation', *Journal of Public Policy & Marketing* 29, 93–96.

Fombrun, C. and M. Shanley, 1990, 'What's in a name? Reputation building and corporate strategy', *Academy of Management Journal* 33, 233–258.

Freeman, R.E., 1984, *Strategic Management: A Stakeholder Approach* (Boston, MA: Pitman Publishing).

Freeman, R.E., J.S. Harrison, and A.C. Wicks, 2007, *Managing for Stakeholders: Business in the 21st Century* (New Haven, CT: Yale University Press).

Friedman, M., 1970, 'The social responsibility of business is to increase its profit', *The New York Times Magazine*, 13 September: 32–33, 122, 124, 126.

Godfrey, P.C., C.B. Merrill, and J.M. Hansen, 2009, 'The relationship between corporate social responsibility and shareholder value: An empirical test of the risk management hypothesis', *Strategic Management Journal* 30, 425–445.

Groves, K.S. and M.A. LaRocca, 2011a, 'Responsible leadership outcomes via stakeholder CSR values: Testing a values-centered model of transformational leadership', *Journal of Business Ethics* 98, 37–55.

Groves, K.S. and M.A. LaRocca, 2011b, 'An empirical study of leader ethical values, transformational and transactional leadership, and follower attitudes toward corporate social responsibility', *Journal of Business Ethics* 103, 511–528.

Handelman, J.M. and S.J. Arnold, 1999, 'The role of marketing actions with a social dimension: Appeals to the institutional environment', *Journal of Marketing* 63, 33–48.

Hart, S., 1997, 'Beyond greening: Strategies for a sustainable world', *Harvard Business Review* 75, 66–76.

Hoffman, A.J. and M.H. Bazerman, 2007, 'Changing practice on sustainability: Understanding and overcoming the organizational and psychological barriers to action', in S. Sharma, M. Starik, and B. Husted (eds.), *Organizations and the Sustainability Mosaic: Crafting Long-Term Ecological and Societal Solutions* (Northampton, MA: Edward Elgar).

Kotler, P. and N. Lee, 2005, *Corporate Social Responsibility: Doing the Most Good for Your Company and Your Cause* (Hoboken, NJ: Wiley & Sons).

Lindgreen, A. and V. Swaen, 2009, 'Corporate social responsibility', *International Journal of Management Reviews* 12, 1–7.

Lindgreen, A., V. Swaen, and W. Johnston, 2009, 'The supporting function of marketing in corporate social responsibility', *Corporate Reputation Review* 12, 120–139.

Lowe, K.B., K.G. Kroeck, and N. Sivasubramaniam, 1996, 'Effectiveness correlates of transformational and transactional leadership: A meta-analytic review of the MLD literature', *Leadership Quarterly* 7, 385–425.

Luo, X. and C.B. Bhattacharya, 2006, 'Corporate social responsibility, customer satisfaction, and market value', *Journal of Marketing* 70, 1–18.

Luo, X. and C.B. Bhattacharya, 2009, 'The debate over doing good: Corporate social performance, strategic marketing levers, and firm-idiosyncratic risk', *Journal of Marketing* 73, 198–213.

Maak, T. and N.M. Pless, 2006, 'Responsible leadership in a stakeholder society: A relational perspective', *Journal of Business Ethics* 66, 99–115.

Maignan, I., O.C. Ferrell, and G. Hult, 1999, 'Corporate citizenship: Cultural antecedents and business benefits', *Journal of the Academy of Marketing Science* 27, 455–469.

March, J., 1991, 'Exploration and exploitation in organizational learning', *Organizational Science* 2, 71–87.

Margolis, J.D. and J.P. Walsh, 2003, 'Misery loves companies: Rethinking social initiatives by business', *Administrative Science Quarterly* 48, 268–305.

Mattingly, J.E. and S. Berman, 2006, 'Measurement of corporate social action: Discovering taxonomy in the Kinder Lydenburg Domini ratings data', *Business and Society* 45, 20–46.

McWilliams, A. and D. Siegel, 2001, 'Corporate social responsibility: A theory of the firm perspective', *Academy of Management Review* 26, 117–127.

Mendonca, M., 2001, 'Preparing for ethical leadership in organizations', *Canadian Journal of Administrative Sciences* 18, 266–276.

Menon, A. and A. Menon, 1997, 'Enviropreneurial marketing strategy: The emergence of corporate environmentalism as marketing strategy', *Journal of Marketing* 61, 51–67.

Mitchell, R.K., B.R. Agle, and D.J. Wood, 1997, 'Toward a theory of stakeholder identification and salience: Defining the principle of who and what really counts', *Academy of Management Review* 22, 853–886.

Palazzo, G. and A.G. Scherer, 2006, 'Corporate legitimacy as deliberation: A communicative framework', *Journal of Business Ethics* 66, 71–88.

Parasuraman, A., V. Zeithaml, and L. Berry, 1994, 'Reassessment of expectations as a comparison standard in measuring service quality: Implications for further research', *Journal of Marketing* 58(January), 111–124.

Pfeffer, J. and G. Salancik, 1978, *The External Control of Organizations* (New York: Harper & Row).

Pless, N.M. and T. Maak, 2011, 'Responsible leadership: Pathways to the future', *Journal of Business Ethics* 98, 3–13.

Podsakoff, P.M. and D.W. Organ, 1986, 'Self-reports in organizational research: Problems and prospects', *Journal of Management* 12, 531–544.

Porter, M.E. and M.R. Kramer, 2006, 'Strategy and society: The link between competitive advantage and corporate social responsibility', *Harvard Business Review* 84, 78–92.

Porter, M.E. and M.R. Kramer, 2011, 'Creating shared value', *Harvard Business Review* 89, 62–77.

Quinn, R.E., 1988, *Beyond Rational Management: Mastering the Paradoxes and Competing Demands of High Performance* (San Francisco, CA: Jossey-Bass).

Raghubir, P., J. Roberts, K. Lemon, and R. Winer, 2010, 'Why, when, and how should the effect of marketing be measured? A stakeholder perspective for corporate social responsibility metrics', *Journal of Public Policy & Marketing* 29, 66–77.

Scott, W.R., 1987, 'The adolescence of institutional theory', *Administrative Science Quarterly* 32, 493–511.

Sen, S. and C.B. Bhattacharya, 2001, 'Does doing good always lead to doing better? Consumer reactions to corporate social responsibility', *Journal of Marketing Research* 38, 225–243.

Shamir, B., 1995, 'Social distance and charisma: Theoretical notes and an exploratory study', *Leadership Quarterly* 6, 19–47.

Siemsen, E., A. Roth, and P. Oliveira, 2010, 'Common method bias in regression models with linear, quadratic, and interactional effects', *Organizational Research Methods* 13(3), 456–476.

Stieglitz, N. and K. Heine, 2007, 'Innovation and the role of complementarities in a strategic theory of the firm', *Strategic Management Journal* 28, 1–15.

Teece, D.J., G. Pisano, and A. Shuen, 1997, 'Dynamic capabilities and strategic management', *Strategic Management Journal* 18, 509–533.

Turban, D.B. and D.W. Greening, 1997, 'Corporate social performance and organizational attractiveness to prospective employees', *Academy of Management Journal* 40, 658–672.

Turker, D., 2009, 'How corporate social responsibility influences organizational commitment', *Journal of Business Ethics* 89, 189–204.

Vera, D. and M. Crossan, 2004, 'Strategic leadership and organizational learning', *Academy of Management Review* 29, 222–240.

Waddock, S., 2004, 'Parallel universes: companies, academics, and the progress of corporate citizenship', *Business and Society Review* 109, 5–42.

Waddock, S, 2008, *Leading Corporate Citizens: Vision, Values, and Value Added*, 3rd ed. (New York: McGraw-Hill/Irwin).

Waldman, D.A., B.M. Bass, and W.O. Einstein, 1987, 'Leadership and outcomes of performance appraisal processes', *Journal of Occupational Psychology* 60, 177–186.

Waldman, D.A. and D.S. Siegel, 2008, 'Defining the socially responsible leader', *Leadership Quarterly* 19, 117–131.

Waldman, D.A., D.S. Siegel, and M. Javidan, 2006, 'Components of CEO transformational leadership and corporate social responsibility', *Journal of Management Studies* 43, 1703–1725.

Walumbwa, F.O., B.J. Avolio, and W. Zhu, 2008, 'How transformational leadership weaves its influence on individual job performance: The role of identification and efficacy beliefs', *Personnel Psychology* 61, 793–825.

Yoon, Y., Z. Gurhan-Canli, and N. Schwarz, 2006, 'The effect of corporate social responsibility: CSR activities on companies with bad reputations', *Journal of Consumer Psychology* 16, 377–390.

Yukl, G., 1999, 'An evaluation of conceptual weaknesses in transformational and charismatic leadership theories', *Leadership Quarterly* 10, 285–305.

3.4 Teaching sustainability via entrepreneurship education in tourism and hospitality school

Fernando Lourenço

Introduction

The idea that entrepreneurship perceives issues of sustainability as sources of inspiration and opportunities to build innovation and new businesses has been highlighted in recent literature. Can this perspective transform into pedagogy to support the teaching of sustainable tourism to help students taking entrepreneurship? Can this facilitate the exploration of opportunities in the tourism industry while learning sustainability? This chapter aims to showcase entrepreneurship courses integrated in a range of tourism and hospitality degree programmes at the Institute for Tourism Studies, in Macau SAR. The objectives are: (1) to discuss relevant literature that links sustainability, tourism and entrepreneurship education and (2) to describe the sustainable entrepreneurship elements found in the teaching of tourism and hospitality degrees. This chapter contributes by sharing best practice to like-minded educationalists on the approaches to instil positive attitudes that are opportunistic towards issues of sustainability within entrepreneurship courses.

Sustainable entrepreneurship

Sustainable development is a model that seeks to balance the economic, social and environmental bottom lines in order to yield positive impacts for multiple stakeholders (Elkington, 1999; UN, 2005: 11–12). The widely adopted definition follows that offered by the Brundtland Commission – led by the former Norwegian Prime Minister Gro Harlem Brundtland – which emphasises that sustainable development meets the needs of the present without compromising the ability of future generations to meet their own needs (WCED, 1987). Sustainable entrepreneurship follows the conventional for-profit perspective of entrepreneurship tempered by the triple bottom line. This direction fulfils the conventional view of wealth creation while pushing the idea of social value creation in the process (Chell, 2007; Hall, Daneke, & Lenox, 2010; Korsgaard & Anderson, 2011; Patzelt & Shepherd, 2010). The entrepreneurial approach, which emerged from the late 2000s onwards, is something of a game changer because it does not perceive issues of sustainability as a burden to businesses but instead treats the sustainability agenda as a fertile source of entrepreneurial opportunities (Cohen & Winn, 2007; Dean & McMullen, 2007; Hockerts & Wüstenhagen, 2010; Pacheco, Dean, & Payne, 2010; York & Venkataramam, 2010). It is "the discovery, creation, evaluation, and exploitation of opportunities to create future goods and services that is consistent with sustainable development goals" (Pacheco, et al., 2010: 471). For example, Cohen and Winn (2007) and Dean and McMullen (2007) suggest that entrepreneurs can use the market imperfection and market failure aspects of negative externalities to generate ideas that boost both sustainability and profitability. Such an approach can create social and environmental innovations that have the ability to disrupt the market and influence competition to follow their initiatives (Hockerts & Wüstenhagen, 2010; York & Venkataramam, 2010).

It is suggested that promoting the values and principles of sustainability to opportunistic and economic-driven and self-interest-driven individuals is also feasible in entrepreneurship education (Birnik & Billsberry, 2008). The entrepreneurial element in education for sustainable development is particularly important because "people need more than to be scolded, more than to be made to feel stupid and guilty. They need more than a vision of doom. They need a vision of the world and of themselves that inspires them" (Giacalone & Thompson, 2006: 270). This helps to move away from a reactive and incrementalism stance. This leads to a new direction to innovate and create new forms of ideas and businesses to disrupt the market and influence competitors and followers to adapt and change.

Sustainable tourism

According to a report from United Nations Environment Programme (UNEP) and World Tourism Organization (WTO), sustainable tourism is a form of tourism that is based on the principles of sustainable development that takes full account of its current and future economic, social and environmental impacts (UNEP and WTO, 2005) and addresses the needs of stakeholders (Waligo, Clarke, & Hawkins, 2013). Stakeholders can be interpreted in various forms (Donalson & Preston, 1995; Phillips, Freeman, & Wicks, 2003; Steurer, Langer, Konrad, & Martinuzzi, 2005). In business, stakeholders are parties that can affect or be affected by the actions of the business. In recent years, there has been more emphasis on the importance of managing the expectations and needs of multiple stakeholders instead of solely focusing on shareholder value creation.

It is still problematic to pinpoint what exactly is sustainable development and sustainable tourism (Macbeth, 2005; Torres-Delgado & Palomeque, 2014) because these concepts can be in many forms and philosophical positionings (Macbeth, 2005). The evolution of the tourism industry has been explained by the sequential appearance of a range of platforms or perspectives. Jafari's (1990) platform model suggests that the advocacy platform emerged during the post-war period and shows strong support for tourism for its economic benefits. The cautionary platform emerged from the 1960s to emphasise the undesirable consequences of tourism. This suggest that unregulated tourism development creates undesirable environmental, economic and socio-cultural costs for those who live in the destination. The adaptive platform emerged from the 1980s and was ideologically aligned to the cautionary platform. The adaptive platform proposes alternative forms of tourism that contrast with mass tourism and are in favour of supporting local business communities. This perspective supports the "host communities and their socio-cultural, man-made, and natural environment, and at the same time provide[s] tourists with new choices and rewarding experience" (Jafari, 1990: 35). This has given rise to many new forms of tourism, such as indigenous tourism, ecotourism, green tourism, responsible tourism, controlled tourism and small-scale tourism. This platform provides some solutions but it does not fully accommodate the mass volume of global tourism generated annually (Jafari, 1990). From the late 1980s, the knowledge-based platform emerged which recognises the complexity of the global industry and the relationship between stakeholders. This platform highlighted that even though alternative tourism is part of the solution, it may not be applicable in destinations with a strong dependency on mass tourism. This platform aims to use a systematic approach to study and apply scientific knowledge to better manage global tourism. More recently, Macbeth (2005) suggested two further platforms to accommodate the emergence of sustainable development and sustainable tourism. The fifth platform discusses the dimensions within the sustainable paradigm. The outcomes and bottom line vary based on the positioning of sustainable practice within the sustainable development spectrum. For example, on weaker forms of sustainability, it is egocentric and focuses on growth and resource exploitation. The strong form of sustainability is homecentric and focuses on the interests of the collective over the individual. And the extreme form of sustainability is ecocentric which focuses on nature's rights and is anti-economic growth and proposes a reduction of population growth. The sixth platform moves a step further by suggesting that ethical values are the main driving force that influence whatever sustainability positions and practices.

It is important to understand and to be reflexive about the ethical position that forms our sustainability paradigm, which will lead to the practice of sustainable tourism. As different forms of sustainable practice will benefit different groups of stakeholders, it is necessary to give stakeholders the chance to discuss the issues related to sustainability because it will impact their lives. All in all, implementation of sustainability is related to stakeholder involvement as much as related to priorities, resources and capabilities, and organisations (Waligo et al., 2013).

The tourism and hospitality industry

Tourism has become one of the largest and fastest growing economic sectors in the world. In 2016, travel and tourism generated US$7.6 trillion (10.2% of global GDP) and 292 million jobs in 2016, equivalent to 1 in 10 jobs in the global economy. The sector accounted for 6.6% of total global exports and almost 30% of total global service exports. International tourists are expected to increase by 3.3% a year from 2010 to 2030 to reach 1.8 billion by 2030 (United Nations World Tourism Organization, 2013; World Travel & Tourism Council, 2017).

The tourism and hospitality sector is a strong economic and social contributor across many parts of the world. Enterprises in these sectors contribute to improving the attractiveness of the community as well as supporting economic development by allowing entrepreneurs to generate their own income, generating employment opportunities, tax revenues, and stimulating other sectors of the local economy (Koh & Hatten, 2002). This fruitfulness benefits from the entrepreneurial spirit found in the hospitality, leisure and tourism sector (Ball, 2005). During the past few decades, the term entrepreneurship has been recognised as an important force behind the success in many industries (Bridge, O'Neill, & Cromie, 2003). Entrepreneurship is often associated with being a driver for change and innovation (Schumpeter, 1934) and is regarded as an essential component to drive a knowledge-based economy and an enterprising society and to maintain an economy's global competitiveness (Hartshorn & Hannon, 2005). There are constantly changing demands and expectations of hospitality, leisure and tourism consumers as well as having fierce competition within these sectors. Being entrepreneurial will support new and existing businesses to identify better ways to meet new demands, develop new concepts and new markets as well as sustain their competitiveness in their respective sectors (Ball, 2005).

Tourism business covers a wide range of tourist services in the field, such as transportation, accommodation, tour operators, travel agents, tourism promotion and advertisement, insurance and finance, food and beverage, entertainment, nature parks, zoos, event organisers (concerts, theatres and shows), gaming, conventions and meetings, translation and guiding services, retail for travel goods and so forth (Uriely, Yonay, & Simchai, 2002). With fast-changing consumer demands and expectations, entrepreneurial thinking and behaviour are critical to meet the needs of the consumers and sustain the competitiveness of each firm and the overall industry itself (Ball, 2005). Entrepreneurs are critical players in tourism development because they are those who identify, develop, market and commercialise a community's tourism resources (Koh & Hatten, 2002). The formation of enterprises in the tourism and hospitality industries will undoubtedly contribute to economic and social well-being.

Since the late 1990s in the development of tourism policy, there has been a growth of interest in small businesses. Of course, not all the characteristics associated with entrepreneurship are reflected in all types of small tourism business (Thomas, Shaw, & Page, 2011) because small businesses are heterogeneous and their behaviour is affected by a range of complex structural factors and personal agency. Nevertheless, the review of literature on tourism provided evidence of the contribution of small tourism businesses to regional development and job creation and:

> [i]ncrease the total production and the variety of products with comparatively less investment, possess greater flexibility in following technological developments, help balance the development inequalities among the regions of the country, encourage personal savings and they provide flexibility in adapting to changing economic conjuncture and keeping up with innovations . . . also offer unique benefits to the region and the community in which they operate . . . provide employment for indigenous people, encourage economic diversity and stability, speed up the development of the region and help increase the social development level, thus they deserve particular attention.
>
> (Akbaba, 2012: 33)

It is important to have entrepreneurs to support tourism development as they will serve as the catalyst for further tourism development. It is suggested that entrepreneurs are critical contributors to tourism destination development and destination competitiveness (Komppula, 2014). Their contributions relate to developing new businesses in the tourism and hospitality sector as well as supporting destination development by stimulating competition, cooperation, specialisation, innovation, investment, growth and so forth (Ritchie & Crouch, 2003). A case study conducted by Ryan, Mottiar and Quinn (2012) provided some indication of the role of the entrepreneur in the development of tourism destination competitiveness. The importance of tourism development and entrepreneurism do come with their own shortcomings as well. Mason (2003: 28) notes that:

> Tourism, as a significant form of human activity, can have major impacts. These impacts are very visible in the destination region, where tourists interact with local environment, economy, culture and society. Hence, it is conventional to consider the impacts of tourism under the headings of socio-cultural, economic and environmental impacts.

The importance of entrepreneurship education has been realised since the 1970s as a critical intervention to enhance enterprise culture and support entrepreneurship (Sexton & Bowman, 1984). The early pedagogical approach was based on traditional business and management studies which follow a passive educational paradigm. However, entrepreneurship education has evolved into a unique mode of pedagogy that rather than being passive, makes learning a dynamic, active, constructive and goal-orientated process (Béchard & Grégoire, 2005; Fiet, 2000a, 2000b; Kuratko, 2005; Laukkanen, 2000; Lourenço & Jones, 2006; Neck & Greene, 2011; Oosterbeek, Praag, & Ijsselstein, 2010). Apart from stimulating business start-ups via entrepreneurship education, it is also noted that graduates need to have enterprising skills to deal with the fast-changing business environment. It is suggested that graduates with skills to help them act in innovative ways to deal with complex business environment are much appreciated by employers (Gibb, Haskins, & Robertson, 2009; Gibb, 1987, 1993). Entrepreneurship education is therefore an important contributor to facilitate graduates into self-employment as well as to enhance their employability to suit the volatile business environment.

Entrepreneurship education for sustainable development has an important role to play. Educators can therefore inspire new opportunity developments to create new forms of sustainable businesses and innovation to set the right path for tourism development. The shortcomings derived from tourism development can be seen as opportunities instead of a burden or problem (Lourenço, 2013; Lourenço, Jones, & Jayawarna, 2013). The following section aims to showcase entrepreneurship courses integrated in a range of tourism and hospitality degree programmes at the Institute for Tourism Studies, in Macau SAR. Examples are described in order to illuminate ideas where elements of entrepreneurship can be linked to sustainable practice in tourism and hospitality courses.

Case study: education for sustainable entrepreneurship

This case study is situated in Macau SAR, currently known as the gaming capital of the world with its overall revenue generated from the gaming sector larger than Las Vegas in the US. Although during the past few years growth has stopped, the city still tops the revenue for gaming over any other destination in the world. Macau is currently being widely recognised for its burgeoning tourism industry, which has a multi-faceted destination image that incorporates gaming and entertainment, culture and heritage, international festivals and sports events (Choi, Lehto, & Morrison, 2007). Despite the fruitful economic contribution that the gaming and tourism development has made, previous studies found that the local citizens and community have concerns about the industry's negative externalities, particularly environmental pollution (Kwan & Mccartney, 2005; Vong, 2008, 2009; Wan, 2012). Environmental pollution poses a potential threat to Macau as a top tourism destination because poor environmental quality will adversely impact the sustainability of the tourism industry (Choi, Chan, & Wu, 1999; Dymond, 1997). Previous studies have examined environmental quality as a key destination attribute and found that it has the potential to affect the attitudes, intentions and behaviours related to choosing a destination to visit (Chi & Qu, 2008; Nadeau, Heslop, O'Reilly, & Luk, 2008). Therefore, the government realises the importance of promoting sustainability across the board and tourism in particular.

Macao's Institute for Tourism Studies (hereafter called IFT) offers six programmes under the umbrella of tourism and hospitality management. They are: hospitality, tourism, heritage, events, retail and marketing, and culinary arts majors. IFT was established in 1995 and is a higher education institution fully supported by the Macau SAR Government. IFT also offers executive level training programmes in partnership with one of the Ivy League institutions in the US, vocational training programmes to the tourism and hospitality industry, as well as training courses related to creative industries. Aside from training, the faculty of IFT has assisted the Macau SAR Government in research projects related to tourism planning and various development issues in the city. In 2000, IFT earned recognition through the United Nations World Tourism Organization's UNWTO.TedQual award as an institution in tourism education. This confirmed the international standard and quality achieved by IFT in education and training.

In 2016, IFT launched its entrepreneurship course for all of its bachelor degree programme students, namely Culinary Arts Management, Heritage Management, Hotel Management, Tourism Business Management, Tourism Event Management and Tourism Retail and Marketing Management, aiming to stimulate IFT undergraduates' innovation and graduate entrepreneurship. With fast-changing consumer demands and expectations, entrepreneurial thinking and behaviour are critical to meet the rapidly changing needs of consumers and sustain the competitiveness of each firm. This provides an opportunity for the course to integrate and promote sustainability in the direction of entrepreneurial opportunities to nurture positive attitudes towards opportunities in the sustainability arena. The following section provides examples of the specific activities used in the course to stimulate entrepreneurial thinking and motivation towards sustainable entrepreneurship in different degree programmes.

Opportunity identification

This part of the course introduces the concept of where opportunities can be identified, recognised and created via three scopes: future environmental trends, unmet needs or unsolved problems, and gaps in the marketplace (Burns, 2011). Students are taught research methods to help investigate the market as well as the industry. Moreover, design thinking methodology, as proposed by D-School in Stanford University, the US, are taught to facilitate the thinking and concept development process. Via this session, students are encouraged to begin their work by starting with a focus, for example, a particular market segment, industry, sector, problem, product, service or many other starting points where issues of sustainability exist, but the scope has to be related to the focus of their degree programme to bring relevance to their studies. Students then use their research to help the incubation of their ideas. Subsequently, they engage in ideas development leading to conducting more research to assess the feasibility of turning their ideas into viable businesses. In the final part students use business modelling tools (Osterwalder, Pigneur, & Clark, 2010) to develop their ideas with business viability as well as the potential to solve social and environmental issues. This particular part of the course aims to provide students with a methodology whereby ideas can be found by looking into sustainability issues in wide ranging scopes and areas. They are inspired by design thinking where they learn how to design solutions and turn them into businesses. Crucially, the idea of design thinking is there to inform students that nothing is impossible and to stimulate them to identify solutions to key problems.

Triple-bottom-line exercises

This part of the course similarly encourages students to apply various research methods to explore areas such as a particular market segment, industry, sector, problem, product, service, etc. within the area of their degree programme. Subsequently, the focus is directed to assessing and evaluating various forms of economic, social and environmental impacts associated with their focus. There are many sustainability indicators for tourism (Torres-Delgado & Palomeque, 2014; World Tourism Organization, 2004), and for the purpose of the exercise, the European Tourism Indicator System ETIS (European Union, 2016) is adopted to guide students. ETIS aims at helping destinations and the stakeholders to measure their sustainability management processes. It contains four core indicators (destination management, economic value, social and cultural impact, environmental impact) and an indicative set of supplementary indicators (maritime and coastal tourism, accessible tourism, transnational cultural routes).

The tool is given to students to stimulate their thinking when developing new business ideas as well as to evaluate existing business ideas. The focus of this session is to inform students that any industry, sector, product and service will have their impact, either positive or negative. As entrepreneurs, we can develop new businesses and/or new business models by improving our positive impact on the triple bottom line and in balancing these pillars. Nevertheless, the exercise aims to build awareness of the importance of considering the benefits of different stakeholders as well as to look at different bottom lines.

Life-cycle assessment models and stakeholder analysis

To further instil the idea that any business, service and/or goods have multi-level impacts on various stakeholders, there is a session to teach students life-cycle assessment and stakeholder analysis. Firstly, students need to select a focus such as a market segment, industry, sector, problem, product, service, etc. within the area of their degree programme. Secondly, they break down the life-cycle of their chosen focus (Ljungberg, 2005). This aspect of analysis is supported by the identification of individuals or groups (stakeholders) who are likely to be affected by the direct and indirect actions. The final stage of this activity relates to being creative and innovative to propose new business models and/or new designs to reduce the negative impacts and improve the overall quality and positive impacts relating to different aspects in the life-cycle and to different stakeholders. Students are also exposed to sustainability ideals with different philosophical and ethical roots to help them understand the positioning of their ideas in the sustainability spectrum (Macbeth, 2005). The ultimate aim of this activity is not so much about sustainability reporting or incrementally improving an existing business, service and/or product. The idea is about creating, discovering and identifying new opportunities for business start-ups, the development of innovation and competitive advantage for new businesses.

Sustainable innovation models and 4Ps of marketing

This session introduces various innovation models to students and facilitates them to develop new and better ideas to fulfil the core value of sustainability. Students again begin with a focus that could be a market segment, industry, sector, problem, product, service, etc. within the area of their degree programme. Then they evaluate the state of the industry in terms of innovation and propose new ideas where current practices can be pushed to become incremental innovations then radical innovations in the different forms of product, service, process and position, where improvement on the triple bottom line is the primary focus. Their idea is further refined by the development of the 4Ps of marketing strategy (i.e. product, place, price and promotion) to help them see their ideas on a commercial level and as a potential new business.

Guest speakers and video case studies

In order to relate what may be perceived as abstract concepts to real life cases and scenarios, a range of guest speakers are invited to the classroom to share their experience of sustainable practices with the aim of inspiring students to view sustainability as an opportunity to stimulate innovation and to improve business performance. This is very important because students get to see these entrepreneurs in their classroom talking about the application of sustainability practice to help them 'do well by doing good'. In addition, a selection of video case studies is used to inform students on opportunities and best practice, as well as providing crucial advice on starting and running a successful sustainable and profitable business.

Course project and business planning

For each degree programme, the entrepreneurship course requires students to write a business plan. Throughout the course, as described earlier, sessions are designed to help students to identify, recognise and/or create business opportunities where issues of sustainability are informed and used to influence the development of ideas. A sustainability and social responsibility strategy is a prequisite of the plan. Students are also required to discuss how sustainability and their corporate social responsibility strategies are integrated and will assist them in building a profitable, responsible and sustainable business. All of these aspects must be linked to the creation of competitive advantage.

Conclusions and implications

This chapter aimed to showcase entrepreneurship courses integrated in a range of tourism and hospitality degree programmes at IFT, in Macau SAR. Examples were used to illustrate ideas where elements of entrepreneurship can be linked to sustainable practice in tourism and hospitality courses.

Teaching sustainability does not have to follow the incremental path to gain inspiration for sustainable ideas where students are encouraged to 'make things better' due to the negative impact associated with the tourism industry. The integration of entrepreneurial ideals into sustainable development education for sustainable development has the potential to produce much more exciting, opportunistic, positive and forward thinking pedagogical practice leading to the creation of novel, innovative, profitable and sustainable businesses. It is hard to pinpoint where exactly this entrepreneurial approach fits in in the sustainability or ethical value spectrum (Macbeth, 2005) because each entrepreneurial idea or venture can take any position. The best we can do is equip students with the tools to support their thinking and help them understand sustainability and ethical values associated with their ideas. They need to take the journey to develop, test out and further refine their ideas. Moreover, nurturing their personal values as practitioners for the future who are equipped with sustainability tools, skills and ideals.

The entrepreneurship process that they go through should give them enough room to learn, try, make mistakes and develop their own way to lead the future. We hope and believe that this new stream will eventually propagate to replace its outmoded counterpart in order to facilitate the realisation of a sustainable future, supported by multiple stakeholders, and by entrepreneurs in particular. This chapter contributes by sharing best practice with like-minded educationalists on the approaches to instilling positive attitudes that are opportunistic towards issues of sustainability within entrepreneurship courses.

References

Akbaba, A. (2012). Understanding small tourism businesses: a perspective from Turkey. *Journal of Hospitality and Tourism Management, 19*(1), 31–47.

Ball, S. (2005). The importance of entrepreneurship to hospitality, leisure, sport and tourism. *Hospitality, Leisure, Sport and Tourism Network.* Retrieved 30 April 2014, from www-new2.heacademy.ac.uk/assets/hlst/documents/projects/Entrepreneurship/ball.pdf.

Béchard, J.-P., & Grégoire, D. (2005). Entrepreneurship education research revisited: the case of higher education. *Academy of Management Learning & Education, 4*(1), 22–43.

Birnik, A., & Billsberry, J. (2008). Reorienting the business school agenda: the case for relevance, rigor, and righteousness. *Journal of Business Ethics, 82*(4), 985–999.

Bridge, S., O'Neill, K., & Cromie, S. (2003). *Understanding Enterprise, Entrepreneurship and Small Business* (2nd ed.). Basingstoke, UK: Palgrave Macmillan.

Burns, P. (2011). *Entrepreneurship and Small Business.* Basingstoke, UK: Palgrave Macmillan.

Chell, E. (2007). Social enterprise and entrepreneurship: towards a convergent theory of the entrepreneurial process. *International Small Business Journal, 25*(1), 5–26.

Chi, C. G.-Q., & Qu, H. (2008). Examining the structural relationships of destination image, tourist satisfaction and destination loyalty: an integrated approach. *Tourism Management, 29*(4), 624–636.

Choi, S., Lehto, X. Y., & Morrison, A. M. (2007). Destination image representation on the web: content analysis of Macau travel related websites. *Tourism Management, 28*(1), 118–129.

Choi, W. M., Chan, A., & Wu, J. (1999). A qualitative and quantitative assessment of Hong Kong's image as a tourist destination. *Tourism Management, 20*(3), 361–365.

Cohen, B., & Winn, M. I. (2007). Market imperfections, opportunity and sustainable entrepreneurship. *Journal of Business Venturing, 22*(1), 29–49.

Dean, T. J., & McMullen, J. S. (2007). Toward a theory of sustainable entrepreneurship: reducing environmental degradation through entrepreneurial action. *Journal of Business Venturing, 22*(1), 50–76.

Donalson, T., & Preston, L. E. (1995). The stakeholder theory of the corporation: concepts, evidence, and implications. *Academy of Management Review, 20*(1), 65–91.

Dymond, S. J. (1997). Indicators of sustainable tourism in New Zealand: a local government perspective. *Journal of Sustainable Tourism, 5*(4), 279–293.

Elkington, J. (1999). *Cannibals with Forks: The Triple Bottom Line of 21st Century Business.* Chichester, UK: Capstone Publishing Ltd.

European Union. (2016). *The European Tourism Indicator System: ETIS Toolkit for Sustainable Destination Management.* Luxembourg: EU.

Fiet, J. O. (2000a). The pedagogical side of entrepreneurship theory. *Journal of Business Venturing, 16*(2), 101–117.

Fiet, J. O. (2000b). The theoretical side of teaching entrepreneurship. *Journal of Business Venturing, 16*(1), 1–24.

Giacalone, R. A., & Thompson, K. R. (2006). Business ethics and social responsibility education: shifting the worldview. *Academy of Management Learning & Education, 5*(3), 266–277.

Gibb, A., Haskins, G., & Robertson, I. (2009). *Leading the Entrepreneurial University: Meeting the Entrepreneurial Development Needs of Higher Education Institutions.* Coventry, UK: The National Council for Graduate Entrepreneurship.

Gibb, A. A. (1987). Enterprise culture: its meaning and implications for education and training. *Journal of European Industrial Training, 11*(1), 3–38.

Gibb, A. A. (1993). The enterprise culture and education. *international Small Business Journal, 11*(3), 11–34.

Hall, J. K., Daneke, G. A., & Lenox, M. J. (2010). Sustainable development and entrepreneurship: past contributions and future direction. *Journal of Business Venturing, 25*(5), 439–448.

Hartshorn, C., & Hannon, P. D. (2005). Paradoxes in entrepreneurship education: chalk and talk or chalk and cheese? A case approach. *Education + Training, 47*(8/9), 616–627.

Hockerts, K., & Wüstenhagen, R. (2010). Greening Goliaths versus emerging Davids: theorizing about the role of incumbents and new entrants in sustainable entrepreneurship. *Journal of Business Venturing, 25*(5), 481–492.

Jafari, J. (1990). Research and scholarship: the basis of tourism education. *Journal of tourism studies, 1*(1), 33–41.

Koh, K. Y., & Hatten, T. S. (2002). The tourism entrepreneur: the overlooked player in tourism development studies. *International Journal of Hospitality & Tourism Administration, 3*(1), 21–48.

Komppula, R. (2014). The role of individual entrepreneurs in the development of competitiveness for a rural tourism destination: a case study. *Tourism Management, 40*(February), 361–371.

Korsgaard, S., & Anderson, A. R. (2011). Enacting entrepreneurship as social value creation. *International Small Business Journal, 29*(2), 135–151.

Kuratko, D. F. (2005). The emergence of entrepreneurship education: development, trends, and challenges. *Entrepreneurship Theory and Practice, 29*(5), 577–598.

Kwan, A. V. C., & Mccartney, G. (2005). Mapping resident perceptions of gaming impact. *Journal of Travel Research, 44*(2), 177–187.

Laukkanen, M. (2000). Exploring alternative approaches in high-level entrepreneurship education: creating micro mechanisms for endogenous regional growth. *Journal of Entrepreneurship and Regional Development, 12*(1), 25–47.

Ljungberg, L. Y. (2005). Materials selection and design for development of sustainable products. *Materials & Design, 28*(2), 466–479.

Lourenço, F. (2013). To challenge the world view or to flow with it? Teaching sustainable development in business schools. *Business Ethics: A European Review, 22*(3), 292–307.

Lourenço, F., & Jones, O. (2006). Developing entrepreneurship education: comparing traditional and alternative teaching approaches. *International Journal of Entrepreneurship Education, 4*(1), 111–140.

Lourenço, F., Jones, O., & Jayawarna, D. (2013). Promoting sustainable development: the role of entrepreneurship education. *International Small Business Journal, 31*(8), 841–865.

Macbeth, J. (2005). Towards an ethics platform for tourism. *Annals of Tourism Research, 32*(4), 962–984.

Mason, P. (2003). *Tourism Impacts, Planning and Management.* Burlington, MA: Butterworth-Heinemann.

Nadeau, J., Heslop, L., O'Reilly, N., & Luk, P. (2008). Destination in a country image context. *Annals of Tourism Research, 35*(1), 84–106.

Neck, H. M., & Greene, P. G. (2011). Entrepreneurship education: known worlds and new frontiers. *Journal of Small Business Management, 49*(1), 55–70.

Oosterbeek, H., Praag, M. V., & Ijsselstein, A. (2010). The impact of entrepreneurship education on entrepreneurship skills and motivation. *European Economic Review, 54*(3), 442–454.

Osterwalder, A., Pigneur, Y., & Clark, T. (2010). *Business Model Generation: A Handbook for Visionaries, Game Changers, and Challengers.* Hoboken, NJ: John Wiley.

Pacheco, D. F., Dean, T. J., & Payne, D. (2010). Escaping the green prison: entrepreneurship and the creation of opportunities for sustainable development. *Journal of Business Venturing, 25*(5), 464–480.

Patzelt, H., & Shepherd, D. A. (2010). Recognizing opportunities for sustainable development. *Entrepreneurship Theory and Practice, 35*(4), 631–652.

Phillips, R., Freeman, R. E., & Wicks, A. C. (2003). What stakeholder theory is not. *Business Ethics Quarterly, 13*(4), 479–502.

Ritchie, J. R. B., & Crouch, G. I. (2003). *The Competitive Destination. A Sustainable Tourism Perspective.* Oxford, UK: CABI Publishing.

Ryan, T., Mottiar, Z., & Quinn, B. (2012). The dynamic role of entrepreneurs in destination development. *Tourism Planning and Development, 9*(2), 119–131.

Schumpeter, J. A. (1934). *The Theory of Economic Development.* Cambridge, MA.: Harvard University Press.

Sexton, D. L., & Bowman, N. B. (1984). Entrepreneurship education: suggestions for increasing effectiveness. *Journal of Small Business Management, 22*(2), 18–25.

Steurer, R., Langer, M. E., Konrad, A., & Martinuzzi, A. (2005). Corporations, stakeholders and sustainable development: a theoretical exploration of business-society relations. *Journal of Business Ethics, 61*(3), 263–281.

Thomas, R., Shaw, G., & Page, S. J. (2011). Understanding small firms in tourism: a perspective on research trends and challenges. *Tourism Management, 32*(5), 963–976.

Torres-Delgado, A., & Palomeque, F. L. (2014). Measuring sustainable tourism at the municipal level. *Annals of Tourism Research, 49*(November), 122–137.

UN. (2005). *United Nations General Assembly:* 2005 World Summit Outcome (A/RES/60/1). *Retrieved May,* 2007, from http://daccessdds.un.org/doc/UNDOC/GEN/N05/487/60/PDF/N0548760.pdf?OpenElement.

UNEP and WTO. (2005). *Making Tourism More Sustainable: A Guide for Policymakers.* Retrieved November, 2016, from www.unep.fr/shared/publications/pdf/DTIx0592xPA-TourismPolicyEN.pdf.

United Nations World Tourism Organization. (2013). *UNWTO Tourism Highlights 2013 Edition.* Madrid: United Nations World Tourism Organization.

Uriely, N., Yonay, Y., & Simchai, D. (2002). Backpacking and tourist experience: a type and form analysis. *Annals of Tourism Research, 10*(1), 87–107.

Vong, F. (2008). Influence of personal factors on Macau residents' gaming impact perceptions. *UNLV Gaming Research & Review Journal, 12*(1/2), 15–28.

Vong, F. (2009). Changes in residents' gambling attitudes and perceived impacts at the fifth anniversary of Macao's gaming deregulation. *Journal of Travel Research, 47*(3), 388–397.

Waligo, V. M., Clarke, J., & Hawkins, R. (2013). Implementing sustainable tourism: a multi-stakeholder involvement management framework. *Tourism Management, 36*(June), 342–353.

Wan, Y. K. P. (2012). The social, economic and environmental impacts of casino gaming in Macao: the community leader perspective. *Journal of Sustainable Tourism, 20*(5), 737–755.

WCED. (1987). *Our Common Future: The World Commission on Environment and Development* (1st ed.). Oxford, UK: Oxford University Press.

World Tourism Organization. (2004). *Indicators of Sustainable Development for Tourism Destinations: A Guidebook.* Madrid: United Nations World Tourism Organization.

World Travel & Tourism Council. (2017). *Travel & Tourism Economic Impact 2017.* London: World Travel & Tourism Council..

York, J. G., & Venkataramam, S. (2010). The entrepreneur-environment nexus: uncertainty, innovation, and allocation. *Journal of Business Venturing, 25*(5), 449–463.

Part IV

Contextually grounded implications and challenges for sustainable entrepreneurship and blended value generation

4.1 Motivations and barriers to going green amongst Australian businesses

Identifying the on and off switches in small, medium and large firms

Michael T. Schaper

Introduction

Although the concept of "entrepreneurship" is often fiercely debated, and there is as yet no universally agreed common definition of the phenomenon, almost all entrepreneurial behaviour contains a number of common elements: the identification of a business opportunity or challenge which can be converted into wealth-producing activity; marshalling resources to exploit the opportunity; and considered risk-taking behaviour to launch a new business venture. As Shane and Vankataraman (2000) have noted, meaningful entrepreneurship research therefore involves not only understanding the individuals who identify and exploit opportunities but also an examination of the sources of such opportunities and the factors that assist or restrict firms from adopting new innovations.

This is clearly also the case when understanding the phenomenon of sustainable entrepreneurship – or, as it is often referred to, "ecopreneurship" (Schaper 2010). As a relatively recent subset of the broader field of entrepreneurship, there are still large gaps in the body of knowledge, especially at the firm level. What green business practices are actually undertaken by firms, and what factors encourage or discourage them from improving their environmental performance? Do they differ amongst firms of different sizes, especially between large corporations (which tend to be more conservative) and small firms (which are usually more entrepreneurial)?

This chapter seeks to answer some of these questions at the firm level, using data drawn from a recent large-scale quantitative examination of diverse Australian firms. It briefly discusses and summarises some of the existing literature on the phenomenon and explains the methodology used before reporting on the types of environmental practices that businesses currently make. The factors motivating organisations to undertake environmental improvements are also examined, as are the major perceived impediments. It concludes with some suggestions of practical steps that can be taken by policymakers to facilitate the use of more "on" switches and fewer "off" ones.

Ecopreneurship and the Australian context

Since the term first began to adopt wide currency in the early 2000s, the concepts of "ecopreneurship" and "sustainable entrepreneurship" have been examined by a wide variety of researchers, looking into a diverse range of issues (for a review of some recent developments in the field, see Halla, Danekeb & Lenoxc 2010; Shepherd & Patzelt 2011). Whilst most researchers acknowledge that entrepreneurial activities can take place in a variety of different organisational types (including firms of different sizes, in both for-private and not-for-profit ventures, and amongst both the public and private sectors), there is a strong body of thought which argues that small businesses are perhaps the most entrepreneurial of all (Hillary 2000). Small businesses are usually directly managed by the owner-operator, and it is they who typically take on highly risky new business ideas, who survive or fail on the strength of their business idea, who are the most likely to create high-growth ventures and who are most innovative in bringing new ideas and products to market.

A number of barriers and triggers to the uptake of ecopreneurial ideas and ventures have been identified in the literature (see for example Krueger, Schulte & Stamp 2008; Elkington 2012).

However, many of these studies are based on small samples, individual firm case studies, or self-selecting groups with a pre-existing interest or passion for the topic. They are rarely fully representative of the business population at large. Indeed, as Santini (2017) notes, there have been few large-scale empirical measurements of ecopreneurial activities, motivations, barriers and processes.

Amongst Australian firms and the broader community, attitudes to and concerns for the environment are sometimes difficult to clearly discern. The only country to occupy an entire continent, it is often regarded as possessing a relatively healthy ecosystem with a wide diversity of unique endemic flora and fauna. Despite this, the nation has had one of the highest rates of animal species extinction over the last 200 years. Australians overall display a supportive attitude towards environmental issues, but recently this appears to have diminished somewhat (Cubby 2012). Carbon pricing has been a hotly contested political topic in the country, with a short-lived carbon tax at the federal level. There are periodic concerns about the desirable optimum population for the country. Whilst most of the country population is to be found in just five large cities along the coast, and most employment and businesses are found in the services and related sectors, many of the major potential future growth sectors in the economy are dependent upon successful management of the environment: these include agriculture, natural resources management and tourism.

Australia has often been regarded as a nation with a relatively strong entrepreneurial culture. The Global Entrepreneurship Monitor, which assesses levels of enterprising activity worldwide, indicates that Australia regularly appears amongst the top OECD member states in terms of entrepreneurial activities and intentions (Steffens & Davidsson 2014). Small- and medium-sized firms (SMEs) account for more than 99% of the 2.1 million actively trading firms across the country, and more than 300,000 new business ventures commence operations each year (ABS 2015). Given the significance of entrepreneurial activity in the national economy, it seems appropriate to try and determine what factors might encourage (or discourage) businesses from going green.

Methodology

The data discussed in this chapter is based on a 2011–12 study of environmental management practices undertaken by the national census and statistical agency, the Australian Bureau of Statistics (ABS), and made publicly available in 2013. It is the latest iteration of the national Energy, Water and Environment Survey, which is conducted on an irregular basis (the most recent previous results having been those of 2008–9), and collected for the specific objective of helping policymakers "better understand environmental, energy and other related issues . . . across the economy" (ABS 2013).

Under its enabling federal legislation, the ABS is able to compulsorily require individuals and companies to provide information or complete questionnaires and can (on a confidential basis) collect aggregated data from the Australian Taxation Office. The sampling frame for this study was drawn from all private-sector entities in the country which were actively trading (as indicated by regular remittances of goods & services tax to the Tax Office) and selected from the frame of all registered Australian businesses, using stratified random sampling techniques.[1] Only employing businesses were included in the sample, and (for reasons which are not stated) both the agricultural and financial services were excluded.

The national 2011–12 Energy, Water and Environment Survey was a mail-out questionnaire, using a sample of 21,487 businesses; there were no reported non-respondents. Firms were asked to have the survey completed by the most relevant senior officer in the organisation, and the period covered by the collection was the 12 months that ended on 30 June 2012 (that is, the end of the Australian financial reporting year for tax purposes). Respondents were asked to identify whether or not they had undertaken any environmental management activities in the last 12 months before the survey; only those who responded in the affirmative were then included in the subsequent assessment of motivators and barriers to improved environmental performance (ABS 2013).

The study also segmented responses into different categories based on the respondent firms' size. In contrast to definitions of SMEs employed in many other nations, firms in Australia are principally delineated using employment size. Their legal structure, asset base or turnover are not usually taken into account, although firms which are part of a larger corporate body are treated as part of the parent entity, not as an independent enterprise (ABS 2015). Following long-established criteria used extensively by the ABS, government agencies and Australian researchers, firms in this study were categorised using the following approach:

- Small businesses – entities employing fewer than 20 persons
- Medium-sized businesses – those employing 20–199 persons
- Large – organisations with 200 or more employees

It is noteworthy that the final data is subject to a number of significant limitations that reduce the analytical tools which can be applied. Under the relevant taxation and statistics collection legislation, most information can only be presented in a highly generalised form, and typically this takes the form of reports presented only in percentage figures. This precludes the use of many (if not most) statistical procedures, and accordingly the results presented and discussed here are entirely descriptive in nature. Neither can this dataset be compared to previous iterations of the same survey, since the preceding 2008–9 Energy, Water and Environment Management study used a number of different questions, collection methods and form design (ABS 2013).

What sort of environmental improvements do businesses make?

There are potentially a very wide range of activities that any business can undertake to enhance its environmental performance, reduce its impact on the planet and become more sustainable. Some practices are unique to a specific industry, but many others are broadly applicable to most firms.

The results in Table 4.1.1 clearly show that only a minority (about 38%) of enterprises actually undertake any environmental improvement activity. Broadly speaking, these activities seem to fall into three categories. Recycling is clear and away the most popular activity. It is undertaken by about a third of all businesses and is the most prominent single action. A second, broader group of various activities are undertaken by about 9–11% of all businesses. These include purchasing eco-friendly products, staff training, educating the business's customers, and tweaking the operating processes and systems of the firm. These are the relatively easy things to do; more complex, time-consuming and expensive approaches, such as undertaking more R&D, or decreasing the business's physical inputs, are undertaken by only a comparative handful of firms (less than 7%).

The data also indicates a potential size effect in terms of who attempts environmental improvement and the type of activity they undertake. As Table 4.1.1 indicates, small businesses are generally less likely to undertake improvements than their larger counterparts. They score below average on almost all activity indicators, and in some behaviours (such as recycling, R&D and waste audits) lag significantly behind their bigger competitors.

Some of this makes intuitive sense. The extensive use of recycling should not surprise: for many years it has been publicly promoted as one of the simplest and most direct ways individuals can do something for the environment. It is also relatively easy to do for many firms, since recycling facilities are often provided by local governments, waste collectors and many supply chains. Undertaking staff training and deciding to think about environmental issues when purchasing goods, is sometimes also easy to do. But there are also some contradictions. Waste and energy audits are often regarded by many commentators as prime examples of "low hanging fruit" – tasks that can be done relatively easily and yet produce significant cost savings. Such examinations can often identify hidden losses or waste that it is in the company's own best interests to reduce. Despite this, most Australian businesses do not appear to be conducting them. Why this occurs cannot be answered in the current study results, but the results suggest that the path to enhanced environmental performance clearly does not always follow a logical pattern.

Motivators and barriers: the on and off switches of business behaviour

If firms behave differently, is it possible to identify particular causes and obstacles that lead them to act in one way or another? If policymakers can find out what drives particular responses, then perhaps it might be possible to identify ways to encourage more

Table 4.1.1 Businesses undertaking environmental management activities

	Small	*Medium*	*Large*	*All firms*
Total firms undertaking any environmental activity	36.8	61.8	79.3	38.0
Reduce material inputs	4.0	12.4	26.6	4.4
Enhanced research & development	2.5	7.8	20.4	2.8
Changing operating/production processes	9.5	22.3	46.0	10.1
Educating consumers/customers	8.6	17.3	32.9	9.0
Recycling/reuse of materials	32.7	51.7	72.6	33.7
"Green" purchasing	10.7	20.5	39.8	11.2
Staff training on green issues	10.9	27.1	50.2	11.7
Conducting environmental impact assessments	6.1	15.8	43.0	6.7
Waste audits	4.1	11.8	32.7	4.5

Source: ABS (2013) Data provided only in percentiles by ABS.

businesses to adopt eco-friendly practices. As part of its study, the ABS took a subset of its original sample group – namely, the 38% of respondent firms that had implemented actual improvements to their environmental management practices – and asked them to identify the major motivators for them doing what they did (see Table 4.1.2).

Four "Cs" stand out as an obvious impetus to going green: compliance, costs, customers and caution. Obeying laws and regulations were a motivator for a quarter of all firms, and cost savings were important to almost 40%. Effectively managing risk and managing the firm's public reputation were important in about 21% of all cases. None of these, however, comes even close to the single most important driver: ethical and moral reasons (50% of all respondents). It is a major motivator for literally half of all businesses. Clearly personal and organisational values, world views and beliefs count for a lot, even in the supposedly objective world of managerial decision-making.

Once more, there is also a clear and significant difference between small and large firms. Legal compliance, reputational concerns, the desire for cost savings and an attempt to reduce organisational risks are all far more important for large corporations than they are for small-scale enterprises.

A final notable figure is the low number of respondents who identified new market opportunities as a key reason for improving their performance (less than 10%). It is often suggested that ecopreneurs emerge in response to new commercial opportunities or to fill a niche overlooked by large firms, yet these figures suggest otherwise. It appears to be only a relatively minor reason and, in fact, is more likely to be a driving force for large firms than it is for small ones.

The study results also identified some of the barriers ("off" switches) that prevent businesses from being more sustainable and why (see Table 4.1.3). The cost of improving environmental outcomes (30%), a lack of sufficient time or people to do it (23%), and an absence of the necessary in-house technical skills (15%) are the most common barriers that all firms face.

These are common woes. The barriers that firms face do not vary that much by firm size, with small, medium and large organisations all identifying somewhat similar issues. Paradoxically, in the one area where there is a notable size-based differential – the cost and payback time involved – more big businesses than small ones identify this as a problem. It is a curious result, since SMEs are generally more likely to have limited

Table 4.1.2 Major motivating factors for improved environmental management activities

	Small	*Medium*	*Large*	*All firms*
Total firms implementing improvements	13.0	27.0	53.0	13.7
Compliance with laws/regulations	23.5	34.8	51.5	24.8
Government incentives/grants	8.3	10.6	16.3	8.6
Cost savings	37.3	54.2	63.7	39.1
New market opportunities	9.0	16.0	17.0	9.7
Improving customer/shareholder relations	11.0	26.8	33.1	12.6
Improving public relations/reputation	18.6	43.4	52.7	21.2
Risk management/reduction	19.2	29.6	50.0	20.5
Attracting/retaining/motivating staff	9.6	21.9	18.0	10.7
Ethical reasons	48.9	60.0	60.6	50.0
Supply chain issues	6.0	13.3	12.7	6.7

Source: ABS (2013). Data provided only in percentiles by ABS.

Table 4.1.3 Major impediments to improved environmental management activities

	Small	*Medium*	*Large*	*All firms*
Costs involved/payback period too long	28.4	38.8	48.5	29.5
Lack of time or staff resources	22.9	28.3	29.3	23.4
Lack of internal expertise	14.9	16.1	14.8	15.0
Lack of information	9.4	10.4	6.5	9.5
Management resistance	3.5	2.7	3.5	3.4
Employee resistance	3.1	2.2	4.5	3.0
Regulatory barriers	10.8	6.7	10.1	10.5
Lack of market or customer demand	8.7	6.2	5.8	8.4

Source: ABS (2013) Data provided only in percentiles by ABS.

financial resources than their bigger counterparts (Holmes et al. 2003). Once more, it demonstrates that environmental behaviour does not always follow clear cut rules or neat *a priori* assumptions.

Putting the picture together: some tentative conclusions

The results make for some interesting conclusions. First – and perhaps most importantly – is the fact that only a minority of enterprises today are undertaking any environmental activity. With only a 38% participation rate, it is clear that there is major scope for many more businesses to come on board and improve their environmental performance.

Second, size does matter in some cases. As Tables 4.1.1 and 4.1.2 clearly show, small businesses often deal with, and are motivated by, environmental issues in different ways to their larger brethren. Far fewer of them are likely to be going greener than their bigger competitors. And when they do try to improve their performance, they are often driven by different influences and forces. These findings are not new and broadly support the views of researchers such as Hillary (2000), who have long argued that SMEs need to be understood and dealt with differently from bigger firms. As *Harvard Business Review* once memorably put it, a small business is not simply a shrunken-down version of a large corporation (Welsh & White 1981). It is a quite different beast, driven by a different set of objectives, skills and opportunities than those faced by the conventional big firm.

Finally, and despite the above observation about size, there is still a surprisingly high level of uniformity in the perceived barriers that firms face to achieving improved green outcomes. Most businesses seem to face the same sort of difficulties, based around limited financial, organisational or human resources.

The figures do, however, paint a somewhat uncertain picture about the triggers and barriers to sustainable entrepreneurship amongst most responding firms. On the one hand, less than 10% of businesses that adopt environmental improvement practices appear to do so because it provides them with new market opportunities; more prosaic or altruistic reasons appear to be their main motivators. At the same time, insufficient customer or market demand for green practices and products is rarely a barrier to them improving their performance, with less than 9% identifying this as a problematic issue.

Many researchers have tended to use a small, employing business as being an effective proxy indicator of an entrepreneurial firm (Curran & Blackburn 2001). That is not always the case, of course; not every little business has a goal of growing, and many are actually quite comfortable in staying small and settled. But the fact remains that smaller firms do tend to be, overall, more entrepreneurial than their larger counterparts. It is an imperfect measurement, but still a handy one. Using that as a rule of thumb, the data here suggests that small entrepreneurial firms face and deal with environmental issues and practices in different ways from other organisations.

Such a finding should not be a surprise. Small-scale entrepreneurial business ventures are different from large, well-established enterprises in many different ways: how they finance themselves, their goals and objectives, how they recruit and retain staff, their internal governance, management and administration, responses to competitive threats, and so on. In fact, they usually provide a sharp contrast to big business in almost every aspect of what they do – so it stands to reason that their responses to environmental issues will also be different.

Of course, these are only Australian results, and data in other countries may produce different findings. But this is a look into a very large number of enterprises, and Australian firms tend to display many of the same characteristics and face the same issues as their counterparts in other nations. A recent study of UK small firms, for example, also found many of them were actively involved in recycling and motivated by factors such as regulatory compliance, costs and personal environmental concern (Revell, Stokes & Chen 2010). Likewise, Leonidou, Christodoulides and Thwaites (2016) found that many small manufacturing firms in Cyprus were driven to improve their performance by regulations and public concerns, whilst financial cost and internal capabilities can often have an impact on their capacity to go greener. In all probability, then, it appears that the data here may be similar in many other advanced post-industrial economies. It also reinforces earlier findings in previous studies of Australian businesses, which found a strong level of environmental awareness amongst small business owners, but a difficulty in translating that into practical action in many cases (Schaper 2002; Gadenne, Kennedy & McKeiver 2009).

What does it mean in practice?

There is clearly still much more room for more businesses to become greener. The data suggests that most businesses have yet to commit themselves to better environmental performance. Triggering the switches to "go green" is not always easy. It requires a conscious effort, the allocation of often scarce resources, and adopting a number of different business practices compared to business as usual. Researchers do not yet fully understand why some businesses do it and others do not, but as studies like this suggest, it is now possible to identify a few of the "on" and "off" switches which help drive those decisions.

Values matter. Values and ethical considerations are extremely important. The results here suggest that they are the single most important driver for many firms. When 50% or more of respondents indicate that ethical reasons are the major cause behind their business's attempts to go green, it is clear that "feel good" issues are more than just rhetoric.

Key to this is the ability to engage successfully with the key decision-maker of the firm in question. Do they have green values or concerns? In a large corporation, this will typically be the CEO and/or the chairman of the board, but in small firms it can be a slightly more complicated process. Most small and micro-sized enterprises are run by the owner, and so the opportunity to directly influence its environmental performance is high. Sometimes, though, professional managers are appointed who may have different values. Or, in a small workplace of half a dozen individuals, there may be one key employee who sets the tone and culture of the business. As Del Baldo (2012) has noted, it is important to take time to identify the real influencers in the firm, understand their motivations and values, and how this accords with greener business practices.

Simple is best. The responses to this survey also seem to suggest that straight-forward concepts, such as recycling, are more likely to be adopted by businesses than complex or expensive strategies. It seems that it is often easy to recycle or re-use some things, but much more time-consuming to undertake a whole-of-firm environmental impact assessment or the like. Yet the logic of this is not always as obvious as it sounds. As was pointed out earlier, some of the simplest, easiest to perform environmental improvements, such as conducting energy and waste audits (which, coincidentally, also produce some of the quickest and most obvious financial paybacks) are still often disregarded.

Don't overlook the four "Cs". Compliance, costs, customers and caution: each of these will motivate a business in different ways. Managers can be coaxed (or forced) to adopt more eco-friendly practices by the need to comply with legal mandates or the promise of cost savings. Customer demands, firm image and risk control will also play a part.

Small-scale business ventures will typically react to these challenges in different ways than a large corporation might. For example, reducing long-term expenditure matters to many cash-starved small firms, but they will often also lack sufficient immediate access to capital to be able to afford some of the simple measures that can ultimately deliver a significant payback. Instead, they indefinitely defer what seems like an obvious case of "picking the low-hanging fruit." Similarly, some owner-managers, when faced with a new regulatory burden, will often consciously decide to avoid complying and risk the small chance of being caught because of the extra effort and resources that conforming to a new law might impose. It might seem strange to the passing observer but makes perfect sense to those inside the business. Ultimately, every individual business operator deals with environmental issues in his or her own unique way.

Four major barriers or impediments to going green were identified by respondents and paint a picture of the so-called "off switch" that causes firms to ignore environmental issues. These are cost, a lack of staff resources or time, insufficient in-house expertise or knowledge, and (to a lesser extent) regulation. Whilst these can be significant issues for individual firms, it is possible in some cases to develop policies that can remove or reduce those barriers.

Providing for payback. Many small businesses are cash constrained. Some established SMEs operate in industry sectors with very low margins; new businesses often find themselves having to carefully manage their cash flow; and only the most well established, secure businesses tend to have predictable cash and income streams or a discretion in what to do with them. Not surprisingly, then, many respondents in this survey identified the cost of environmental implementation as a block to environmental improvements.

Many enhancements will – as previously discussed – ultimately produce some cost savings for most firms, but it can be a struggle to survive until those paybacks happen. Overcoming this is a more difficult issue than it might seem at first glance. It would be easy to simply suggest that governments might provide loans for such ventures. But this has its own problems. With a limited amount of public funds available, which firms should qualify? Another option might be to encourage banks and other financial institutions to help. But lending to small firms is often risky, and the payback may be hard to quantify – and banks ultimately have an overriding duty to their shareholders to lend prudently.

A smarter approach to delivering information, training and skills. Whether it is categorised as a "lack of time," a "lack of staff resources," a "lack of internal expertise," or a "lack of information," the data clearly shows that (insufficient) knowledge and the ability to apply it is a major impediment. How can this be dealt with? Governments, advocacy groups and educational bodies all have the capacity to enhance the level of environmental knowledge and skills of the business community.

What actually constitutes effective training or skill development has changed dramatically. Until recently, businesses were largely limited to a small number of formal courses that may or may not be developed at a time, place and cost that suited them. Today, the expansion of online and other educational materials means that knowledge can be delivered in convenient loads that best suit most time-constrained business managers and owners. If a business owner does not know how to replace old fluorescent light bulbs with efficient LED models, the information can be found on YouTube. Should a firm want to discuss with a business adviser the pros and cons of obtaining ISO 14000 certification, they can do so on social media. If an entrepreneur cannot attend formal classes, he or she can now enrol in a massive online open course. And so on. Providing such material is not only the province of governments and educational institutions; there is also a significant opportunity for green advocacy groups to also prepare and deliver this information.

The reality of regulation. Regulation can be highly determinative of environmental performance and usually in a positive manner. Compulsory product stewardship of goods, for example, has led many firms to dramatically overhaul and improve their performance.

However, many local, state, national and international regulatory bodies can also create unnecessary obstacles or laws which fail to take environmental issues into account. For example, public health agencies may require safe food products to be repackaged in extra wrapping as a precaution to protect consumers and so adding to waste outputs and landfill. Business records may be required to be kept in hard paper (not electronic) form by a financial services or taxation authority; but this can also confound the objective of reducing waste. And once in place, such rules tend to stay locked in. It is not easy to overcome, reform or remove ineffective legislation. Policymakers need to carefully evaluate the overall impact of all the laws they introduce and how they interact with other existing regulations.

Some limitations and missing pieces

Studies like this are useful, but they have their limitations. Sometimes the omission of certain respondents means that the picture which is being formed is only half-developed.

Whilst this survey examined small, medium and large enterprises, it has missed the biggest group of all firms: non-employing microbusinesses. At first glance, these might seem like an insignificant group, but the reality is quite different. Self-employed owner-managers working on their own account for about 61% of all actively trading businesses in Australia. In contrast, small businesses represent just 27% of all firms, medium-sized businesses only 2%, and large corporations less than 1% (ABS 2015). Globally, too, self-employed microbusinesses represent the majority of all trading enterprises (Schaper, Dana, Anderson & Moroz 2009). Without their inclusion, the picture developed from this survey is extremely limited.

The study also excluded the agriculture sector, an area which contains not only a large number of micro and small businesses but which also has a direct and significant role to play in improving environmental practices. A better understanding of activities, motivations and obstacles in that industry would certainly be helpful.

Finally, the current study only examined motivations and barriers amongst those firms who had already begun to make environmental improvements. Whilst Table 4.1.1

showed what proportion of *all* respondents had undertaken any environmental activities, those firms who did not undertake such tasks were subsequently omitted from the survey (that is, from the results shown in Tables 4.1.2 and 4.1.3).

Yet those firms who do not change are as important as those who do. Policymakers need to understand why such firms have not adopted environmental improvements and what issues might encourage or forestall them from doing so. The current research results discussed in this chapter are skewed towards the cohort of firms who have already decided to adopt sustainable practices; other, less greener, businesses have been omitted. This is a significant omission, especially for advocacy groups, legislatures, public servants, policy agencies and business associations who are trying to understand and compare the two groups. Ideally, any future similar study should also look at the motivators and barriers for those firms who are currently non-participants in environmental improvements.

Conclusions

There is a lot that researchers are beginning to learn about the practices, motivations and barriers to environmental performance by businesses of all sizes. Despite many years of urging firms to "go green," only a minority of enterprises are actually undertaking any type of environmental management activities. As this study reveals, those firms who do try to green their businesses do so for a variety of reasons. Ethical considerations are the single largest motivators, followed by the 4 "Cs": regulatory compliance, cost considerations, customers and cautionary risk management. At the same time, firms are often confronted by obstacles which frequently impede their transition to doing even more. Chief amongst these are cost considerations, insufficient time or staff resources, a lack of internal expertise, and regulatory barriers. Trying to overcome this – to throw the switch from "off" to "on" – may perhaps need to focus on simple, pragmatic suggestions and solutions, which are seemingly more appealing than complex, difficult and time consuming activities.

The results have indicated that there can be significant differences between the most entrepreneurial type of firm, the small business, and the larger corporation. There are some notable variations between small, medium and large firms in terms of who attempts environmental improvement, what activities they actually undertake and what factors motivate them to go green. One of the most significant findings has been that few businesses adopt environmental improvement practices because it provides them with new market opportunities; personal ethical drivers are more important than conventional customer demand.

Rome was not built in a day and neither was any business. We still have a long way to go in terms of the greening of enterprise; but as the results of studies like this suggest, researchers are now beginning to identify a few more potential ways to throw the switch to "on."

Note

1 A full description of the survey design, collection processes and limitations is available online at www.abs.gov.au/AUSSTATS/abs@.nsf/Lookup/4660.0Explanatory%20Notes12011-12?OpenDocument.

References

ABS (2013) *Energy Use, Electricity Generation and Environmental Management, Australia 2011–12* Cat. No. 4660.0, Canberra: ABS.

ABS (2015) *Counts of Australian Businesses, including Entries and Exits, Jun 2010 to Jun 2014* Cat. No. 8165.0, Canberra: ABS.

Cubby, N. (2012) "Nation Now 'Indifferent' To Environment" *Sydney Morning Herald*, April 30 [online] www.smh.com.au/environment/climate-change/nation-now-indifferent-to-environment-20120429–1xt25.html (accessed 16 May 2017).

Curran, J. & Blackburn, R. (2001) *Researching The Small Enterprise*, London: Sage.

Del Baldo, M. (2012) "Family and Territory Values for A Sustainable Entrepreneurship: The Experience of Loccioni Group and Varnelli Distillery in Italy" *Journal of Marketing Development and Competitiveness*, Vol.6 No.3, pp.120–139.

Elkington, J. (2012) *The Zeronauts: Breaking The Sustainability Barrier*, New York: Routledge.

Gadenne, D.L., Kennedy, J. & McKeiver, C. (2009) "An Empirical Study of Environmental Awareness and Practices in SMEs" *Journal of Business Ethics* Vol.84 No.1, pp.45–63.

Halla, J.K., Danekeb, G.A. & Lenoxc, M.J. (2010) "Sustainable Development and Entrepreneurship: Past Contributions and Future Directions" *Journal of Business Venturing*, Vol.25 No.5, pp.439–448.

Hillary, R. (ed.) (2000) *Small and Medium-Sized Enterprises and the Environment: Business Imperatives*, Sheffield, UK: Greenleaf Publishing.

Holmes, S., Hutchinson, P., Forsaith, D., Gibson, B. & McMahon, R. (2003) *Small Enterprise Finance*, Milton, Brisbane: Wiley.

Krueger, N.F., Schulte, W.D. & Stamp, J. (2008) *Beyond Intent: Antecedents of Resilience & Precipitating Events for Social Entrepreneurial Intentions and . . . Action*, January 25 [online] http://dx.doi.org/10.2139/ssrn.1155264 (accessed 16 May 2017).

Leonidou, L.C., Christodoulides, P. & Thwaites, D. (2016) "External Determinants and Financial Outcomes of An Eco-Friendly Orientation In Smaller Manufacturing Firms" *Journal of Small Business Management*, Vol.54 No.1, pp.5–25.

Revell, A., Stokes, D. & Chen, H. (2010) "Small Businesses and the Environment: Turning Over A New Leaf?" *Business Strategy and the Environment*, Vol.19 No.5, pp.273–288.

Santini, C. (2017) "Ecopreneurship and Ecopreneurs: Limits, Trends and Characteristics" *Sustainability*, Vol.9 No.4, pp.492–506.

Schaper, M.T. (2002) "Small Firms and Environmental Management: Predictors of Green Purchasing in Western Australian Pharmacies" *International Small Business Journal*, Vol.20 No.3, pp.235–249.

Schaper, M.T. (ed.) (2010) *Making Ecopreneurs: Developing Sustainable Entrepreneurship* Farnham, UK: Gower. 2nd edition.

Schaper, M.T., Dana, L.P., Anderson, R.B. & Moroz, P.W. (2009) "Distribution of Firms by Size: Observations and Evidence from Selected Countries" *International Journal of Entrepreneurship and Innovation Management*, Vol.10 No.1, pp.88–96.

Shane, S. & Vankataraman, S. (2000) "The Promise Of Entrepreneurship As A Field of Research" *Academy of Management Review*, Vol.25 No.1, pp.217–226.

Shepherd, D.A. & Patzelt, H. (2011) "The New Field of Sustainable Entrepreneurship: Studying Entrepreneurial Action Linking 'What Is to Be Sustained' With 'What Is to Be Developed'" *Entrepreneurship Theory and Practice*, Vol.35 No.1, pp.137–163.

Steffens, P. & Davidsson, P. (2014) *GEM Australia: 2014 National Report*, Brisbane: QUT Business School.

Welsh, J.A. & White, J.F. (1981) "A Small Business Is Not A Big Business" *Harvard Business Review*, Vol.59 No.4, pp.18–32.

4.2 Independent coffee shops in the U.S.

A closer look at sustainable social entrepreneurship

Rob Boyle

Introduction

This chapter serves to examine and review some of the dynamic literature related to sustainable social entrepreneurship. Concepts from the literature are further punctuated and clarified by viewing them through the work of non-profit coffee shops located in three Midwestern American cities. The goal is to help emphasize the notion that sustainability has a broader scope than perhaps many realize. Indeed, sustainable social entrepreneurship can be related to a host of ideas including, but not limited to, the history and structure of buildings, the comfort of gathering places, and the development of safe and inclusive neighborhoods.

Perspectives on social entrepreneurship: from Paris, France to the American Midwest

Famed author Ernest Hemingway seemed to have found solace and inspiration in the cafés of Paris, France, and his classic 1964 novel *A Moveable Feast* brings the reader into these settings to paint a picture of the comfort he discovered there. While writing at a café called the Closerie des Lilas, for example, Hemingway shows appreciation for the pleasant surroundings when he expresses, "It was warm inside in the winter and in the spring and fall it was very fine outside with the tables under the shade of the trees" (Hemingway, 1964, p. 81). In a similar setting later in the book, he fondly comments on the familiar faces he sees: "In the three principal cafés I saw people that I knew by sight and others that I knew to speak to" (Hemingway, 1964, p. 100). He even goes on to acknowledge the strangers that he encounters: "The people that I liked and had not met went into the big cafés because they were lost in them and no one noticed them and they could be alone in them and be together" (Hemingway, 1964, p. 100).

Hemingway seems to unwittingly illuminate an important and perhaps understated angle on sustainable entrepreneurship. The Paris cafés that he enjoyed were safe, diverse, inclusive, and comfortable; elements that evoke a sense of community for him and the people around him. This aligns very well with a perspective on sustainability offered in a book entitled *The Ecology of Place: Planning for Environment, Economy and Community* (Beatley & Manning, 1997). The authors suggest that beyond environmental considerations, sustainable communities are also humane, livable places that offer a high quality of life to the people who live and work there.

It has been argued that this increasingly social perspective on sustainability is often overshadowed by extremely important environmental concerns such as the development of eco-friendly buildings that minimize carbon footprints (Borjesson & Walldin, 2009). More and more, however, there seems to be a strong movement toward balancing both the needs of the environment as well as the psychological needs of people (Wheeler, 2013, p. 13).

The idea that sustainability should focus on the welfare of human beings is further punctuated by the now well-known triple bottom line concept. Through the lens of the triple bottom line, businesses view success from economic, social, and environmental perspectives (Onat, Kucukvar, & Tatari, 2014). It is commonly thought that the notion of triple bottom line is a key component for economic viability because most communities share the goals of a strong economy, a clean environment, healthy people, and livability (Hammer, 2015).

It is, indeed, healthy people and livability that are at the heart of three American non-profit coffeehouses located in the soulful, recovering parts of three Midwestern American cities: Crave Coffeehouse—a social entrepreneurship venture founded in 2005 and housed inside the historic Christ in the City Lutheran Church in St. Louis, Missouri; Urban Abbey—a mission-oriented coffee shop that opened its doors in 2011 inside the 19th-century era, former Windsor Hotel in Omaha, Nebraska; and Rohs Street Café—a community-centered non-profit established in 2003 in the University Christian Church (originally the Clifton Evangelical United Brethren Church built in 1927) in Cincinnati, Ohio.

Lengthy interviews with the visionaries for each of these non-profit coffeehouses helps reveal that social sustainability is at the heart of their day-to-day operations. Donna Green, co-founder and former manager of Crave Coffeehouse, has colorful and important insights about the sophistication involved with running a sustainable social venture. Reverend Debra McKnight, co-founder and pastor at Urban Abbey, clearly sees the peace and spirituality that a well-run coffee shop can provide to patrons. And Keaton Neely, the long-time manager at Rohs Street Café, is a champion for the idea that remaining focused on people and community is paramount for the success of a social venture. Examining each of their approaches helps illuminate the idea that, "sustainable development is a multi-faceted concept, with a variety of meanings used to suit different circumstances and purposes" (Weingaertner & Barber, 2010, p. 1655).

Like the cafés where Hemingway found inspiration and community, Donna Green, Debra McKnight, and Keaton Neely envision coffee shops that bring out the very best in people—lucrative social ventures that are safe, inclusive, and comfortable. By all accounts, Crave Coffeehouse, Urban Abbey, and Rohs Street Café each epitomizes the very best in social sustainability.

History: the rise, the fall, and the rebirth—a new lease on sustainability

In order to fully understand Crave Coffeehouse, Urban Abbey, and Rohs Street Café and their engagement with social sustainability, it is important to know about the history of the buildings where they are housed. It is argued that honoring the past in this way is an important step in developing socially sustainable ventures. As F. Kaid Benfield points out in *25 Ways to Think About Greener, Healthier Cities*:

> [w]hen we consider that nourishing the human spirit is just as important to people habitat as conserving natural resources—we also must consider the past: we must understand what, exactly, we wish to sustain.
>
> (Benfield, 2014, p. 70)

Crave Coffeehouse

In the summer of 1834, a large wave of German immigrants arrived in St. Louis in order to escape government harassment and find better lives in America (Burnett & Luebbering, 1996), and this continual settling of German people led to the development of German communities with German ways of life (Tolzmann, 2004). A natural extension of this influence was the establishment of over 100 German-speaking churches that served the spiritual needs of the changing population (Holl, 2015).

One of the churches established during this era was Christ in the City Lutheran Church, initially known simply as Christ Church. During the seminal years of the church, the members faced a host of challenges that threatened to derail the congregation's efforts. Because of pastor and teacher turnover, population shifts, and financial constraints, parishioners often became discouraged and thought of discontinuing (Christ Lutheran Church, 1958). This came to a head on October 17, 1963 when the church was struck by lightning irreparably destroying the steeple and the original organ which was located directly below. The lighting strike seemed to signify a new challenge-filled era for the church. Not long before this event, a new leader named Reverend Gerecke came to the church. When he arrived, the building was in a weakened condition and there were rumors of rebuilding at a location further to the west (Struck by lightning, 1963).

Also in October 1963, a bulletin celebrating the 95th anniversary of the church offered an unfortunate and foreshadowing statistic. More than two-thirds of Christ Church's former membership had moved to sister churches in outlying areas away from the city (Christ Lutheran Church, 1963). These changes in the congregation were very much in line with broader population shifts in post-World War II American cities. In fact, between 1950 and 2010, the population in St. Louis fell 63% from 856,796 to 319,294 (Taylor, 2013).

It was painfully apparent that the building, the church, and the ministry might no longer be sustainable. Or were they? In recent years, there had been a movement in American cities to repurpose aging buildings to meet the needs of local community members (Beatley & Manning, 1997). Donna Green and a handful of other individuals began brainstorming ways to honor the history of the church and keep the building alive. Inspired by a trend in the development of independent coffeehouses (Putnam, 2000), an idea came to mind. They were convinced that a coffeehouse could be used as a tool for outreach to the community; a small, people-focused business that would support the building and bring their spiritual mission through the doors of the church (D. Green, personal communication, December 18, 2014).

Urban Abbey

In the late 19th century, Omaha was home to two major railway stations serving the Burlington and Union Pacific rail lines (Antiques & Accents, 1989). Because of a demand for lodging among railroad workers and railroad passengers, the Windsor Hotel was built in 1885 at the corner of Tenth and Jackson, just three blocks from the railroad stations. The original owners, an Austrian restaurant owner named Charles Schlank and a City Councilman named Solomon Prince, ran the bustling, low-cost hotel for the next 19 years until its sale in 1914 (Olson, 1985).

For the Windsor Hotel, however, the next 70 years are an unfortunate story of multiple owners, neglect, and decay. By the late 1970s, Omaha had experienced what many other American cities had experienced—a dwindling of the population in the downtown area.

Resource rich business people who worked in the city during the day did not stay in the city at night. The result was dormant buildings that lacked attention from the city and from the real estate community. The once revered Windsor Hotel became infested with rats and cockroaches, and it was riddled with building code violations. Despite still housing tenants at the time, it was finally deemed unlivable in 1979 (Leary, 1979).

Fortunately, the Windsor Hotel building qualified as a certified historic structure, and, as such, it retained a significant amount of value. In 1982, it was purchased by two developers named Emil Vohaska and Pete Drake who renovated the building and renamed it the Windsor Square Apartments (Olson, 1985). The newly renovated building also featured retail space on the ground floor, and it is this space that would eventually catch the eye of Debra McKnight. She and a group of her friends saw the potential for a coffeehouse that could bring community, generosity, and spirituality to a once wounded part of the city (D. McKnight, personal communication, May 8, 2017).

Rohs Street Café

In 1902, Reverend J.E. Yingling sensed a need for spiritual nourishment among members of the Clifton Heights community in Cincinnati, so for the next two years he and other pastors held evangelical meetings in a tent pitched on one of the neighborhood streets. The movement gained momentum, and by the end of 1904 a formal church was organized by 14 charter members and a wooden tabernacle was built on the corner of McMillan Avenue and Rohs Street. By 1907, the tabernacle would be replaced by a brick church and parsonage where the Clifton Evangelical United Brethren Church would serve parishioners for the next 20 years. Despite a heavy debt load and a small congregation, it was decided that in order to firmly establish their presence in the Clifton Heights community, the congregation would build a large, more permanent building. On April 23, 1927, the new sanctuary was dedicated (Hetzler, 1954).

As with other American inner city institutions, however, the church experienced significantly dwindling membership during the latter half of the 20th century. In 1977, 50 years after the sanctuary was opened, the Clifton Evangelical United Brethren Church (which had been renamed Evangelical United Methodist Church in 1969) merged with the Clifton United Methodist Church, and the sanctuary was put up for sale (Smith and Tepe, 1992). In 1979, the building at McMillan Avenue and Rohs Street was purchased by a group of Korean Christians who eventually formalized as the Korean United Methodist Church (Cook, 1992).

Since 1991, the building has served the Clifton Heights community as the University Christian Church, aptly named because of its proximity to the University of Cincinnati. And since 2003, the church has been home to Rohs Street Café, which has been managed by Keaton Neely since 2010. Although Keaton is not an original founder of the café, he continues to lead the non-profit venture with an eye on sustainable practices that respect employees and members of the surrounding community. He views being housed in a historic neighborhood building as a distinct advantage that gives him and his employees the opportunity to be rooted near the people they serve (K. Neely, personal communication, May 18, 2017).

Armed with optimism, work ethic, and a willingness to learn, the visionaries for Crave Coffeehouse, Urban Abbey, and Rohs Street Café all have an eye on developing socially sustainable non-profit ventures that serve their communities and help preserve the buildings that have meant so much to so many people.

The building: old structure, new vision

It is clear that social sustainability is associated with a range of positive outcomes such as community, diversity, cohesion, and equity (Weingaertner & Barber, 2010). Related to this, it is important to understand that the buildings where humans live, play, and work can have a significant impact on attitudes and conduct. "Most introductions to the topic of how physical environments influence behavior begin by noting Winston Churchill's observation that 'we shape our buildings and then they shape us'" (Strange & Banning, 2001, p. 12).

This seems to be in line with the idea that seemingly useless properties and buildings should not be dismissed without considering their capacity to be repurposed in some positive way. "A wasted space may well be an area with problems but should never be pre-judged. An inventory of potential ought to be made . . . before its eventual problem is asserted" (Borjesson & Walldin, 2009, para. 19). Taking this a step further, rough looking buildings can sometimes have an organic appeal for people; seediness can often be associated with authenticity that is accessible and inclusive (Zukin, 2008). These are the types of rough looking buildings that can have a "protective coloration" to ward off pretense and help bring out peoples' true selves (Oldenburg, 1989).

With their image of converting Christ in the City Lutheran Church into a socially sustainable non-profit coffeehouse, Donna Green and the others went to work on renovations to the old church. A cornerstone of sustainability involves recognizing the historic value of old buildings and turning them into businesses that feed the human spirit (Benfield, 2014). Crave clearly had this type of impact. The newly hired staff at Crave found a powerful and meaningful community, and customers found a sanctuary where they could take a break from their lives (D. Green, personal communication, December 18, 2014).

Through a common vision and countless hours of hard work, Donna and the others were able to create a non-profit coffeehouse with physical surroundings that set the stage for social sustainability. At a pivotal moment in their work, for example, they came upon the organ that had been rendered unusable by the lightning strike years earlier, and rather than throwing the organ away, they found an artist in St. Louis who was able to repurpose the parts into decorative sconces and a cross (D. Green, personal communication, December 18, 2014). Their decision about the organ reinforces the notion that respecting the history of existing places is an important part of sustainability (Beatley & Manning, 1997).

A 2008 article in the local St. Louis Post-Dispatch newspaper gushes about the new and inviting environment that was created inside the formerly crumbling building:

> Housed in a former church sanctuary, Crave blends lofty aesthetic details such as vaulted ceilings, gothic supports of gleaming wood and jewel-tone stained glass windows with a modernist red and purple color palette, distressed brick and a high-design, sinuously curving coffee bar.
>
> (Whitlow, 2008, p. G12)

Much like Donna Green, Debra McKnight had a vision of converting an ordinary retail bookstore space on the ground floor of the former Windsor Hotel into a socially sustainable non-profit coffeehouse. Her vision was inspired by a ministry called Wesley Pub that she started in the church where she was an associate pastor. The idea of Wesley

Pub involved creating conversations, asking questions, sharing poetry, and singing songs while sharing fellowship over beer.

In order to make the leap from Wesley Pub to Urban Abbey, she brought together a team of friends with skills ranging from accounting to architecture to human resource management to coffee bean roasting. When their desire to open a coffeehouse was finalized, Debra and the others enlisted the help of volunteers who built and painted most of the coffeehouse. New plumbing was donated, the electrical work was donated, discounted appliances were purchased, homemade chair cushions were donated, and reclaimed barn wood was used to make the tables (D. McKnight, personal communication, May 8, 2017). The space that was once infested with rodents and insects and that had been home to a hotel lounge, a record store, and a book store was now shaping up to be a clean, welcoming, non-profit, mission-centered coffee shop.

It is clear that the original founders of Rohs Street Café were keenly aware of the advantages associated with being housed in an old church nestled in an established neighborhood. In one of their seminal documents they state that "University Christian Church was started and has remained in Clifton Heights for 14 years desiring to be a resource and vital part of this diverse community" (Rohs Street Café, n.d., p. 2). Keaton Neely agrees with the importance of being connected with the old sanctuary. As he becomes more steeped in the coffee industry, he has grown frustrated with coffee shop owners moving into historic areas simply for their "cool factor" rather than being connected to the neighborhood and the building they are occupying.

Punctuating the connection that Rohs Street Café has with the building, Keaton points out that the coffee bar is made out of former wooden joists salvaged from inside the church. The wood was reclaimed, milled, and repurposed without leaving the building that has been its home for the better part of a century. Keaton boasts that this provides a powerful, communal story that he and his staff can share with customers to help them understand the importance of being housed in a historic, neighborhood church (K. Neely, personal communication, May 18, 2017).

None of the visionaries for Crave, Urban Abbey, or Rohs Street Café had worked in a coffeehouse before, much less built a coffeehouse from scratch, yet they were still able to create environments that seemed to bring out the best in people. Related to this, theorists contend that "the layout, location, and arrangement of space and facilities render some behaviors much more likely, and thus more probable, than others" (Strange & Banning, 2001, p. 15). Whether by accident or by design, the public reactions that the visionaries describe make it clear that these three coffeehouses are diverse, cheerful, and uplifting places; inviting and inclusive atmospheres that continually make positive impacts on the people who occupy them.

Beyond wood, brick, and mortar: the value of the place

To appreciate the impact of physical environments on sustainability, it is important to make a distinction between the historical and aesthetic value of the building and the deeper emotional and spiritual value of the place. As such, sustainability should not be limited only to wood, brick, and mortar but should also consider peoples' well-being from the perspective of both their body and their mind (Borjesson, 2006). People value face-to-face interaction with others, and shops, diners, and stores often provide the right kind of community-oriented places for friends and strangers to gather (Beatley & Manning, 1997).

In his enlightening book *The Good Great Place*, Ray Oldenburg (1989) contends that our society sometimes falls short of providing "convenient and open-ended socializing—places where individuals can go without aim or arrangement and be greeted by people who know them and know how to enjoy a little time off" (Oldenburg, 1989, pp. 61–62). Repurposed spaces that are turned into entrepreneurial ventures, like Crave Coffeehouse, Urban Abbey, and Rohs Street Café, have the potential to become important and inviting places with unique physical characteristics, diverse clientele, and rich histories. Providing these types of distinct places where people can gather under positive pretenses has direct implications for social sustainability (Weingaertner & Barber, 2010).

A distinctive place that attracts people because of its unique features is the type of entrepreneurial setting that the three visionaries seemed to consistently have in mind when planning their respective coffeehouses. They knew that after the physical building renovations were complete, they would need to turn their attention toward maintaining what some refer to as a community of place—a locally concentrated, supportive, environment (Fischer, 1982). Specifically, they were creating places where people could rest from the things that weigh them down, discuss the challenges in their lives, and engage in spiritual/meaningful conversations.

In his essay *Sense of Place and Expandable Community Boundaries*, William Forbes says that "defining communities and our attachment to them is a critical component to sustainability" (Williams & Forbes, 2012, p. 159). Unfortunately, modern society and proliferation of suburban life in some cultures has greatly reduced the number of so-called "third places"—locations away from home and work that are social, inclusive, and community-oriented (Oldenburg, 1989). Sociologist Amitai Etzioni advocates for the strengthening of community and encourages the development of what he terms communitarian elements "to provide the social bonds that sustain the moral voice, but at the same time avoid tight networks that suppress pluralism and dissent" (Etzioni, 1993, p. 122). In essence, he seems to be calling for socially sustainable communal spaces that level the playing field and provide opportunities for people to feel interconnected.

Crave, Urban Abbey, and Rohs Street Café all boast many of these positive, socially sustainable characteristics that seem inherent in local coffee shops, and this is in sharp contrast to the settings at more modern chain establishments. Regulars at a local café, for example, may know the names of other patrons, but this is likely not the case for random customers rushing through the line at a fast food restaurant (Putnam, 2000).

As Donna Green puts it, Crave is a healthy place to come and evaluate life and to have an opportunity for meaningful discourse. She goes on to characterize Crave as the kind of accessible space where people should expect to encounter differences—a place that embraces diversity and does not judge human flaws (D. Green, personal communication, December 18, 2014). Debra McKnight adds to this by pointing out that Urban Abbey is a living sanctuary where everyone is relevant; a place where people can come every day, no matter what they need (D. McKnight, personal communication, May 8, 2017). And Keaton Neely further complements these observations by viewing Rohs Street Café as a place for rest and solace, where patrons can feel safe and welcomed regardless of their personal circumstances (K. Neely, personal communication, May 18, 2017).

Coffee shops, it is thought, are not only about the actual coffee that is served but also about the place where the coffee is served. In the well-designed coffee shop, people will feel an attachment to the place; the setting will be predictable, relaxing, social, and will offer patrons a sense of control over their life. It is a place where there is a great deal of trust and where people can feel like genuine versions of themselves (Waxman, 2006).

The notion that people can be genuine versions of themselves is a hallmark of Oldenburg's ideal third place. "The elderly and poor, the ragged and infirm, are interspersed among those looking and doing well. The full spectrum of local humanity is represented" (Oldenburg, 1989, p. 14). And advocates of social sustainability agree—they tout the importance of bringing together people from all socio-economic backgrounds and people of all ages (Williams & Forbes, 2012) in an effort to create warm and welcoming environments.

This celebration of diversity is evident in local coffee shops, like Crave, Urban Abbey, and Rohs Street Café, where there are opportunities to interact with strangers and meet people from many walks of life (Badger, 2014). At Crave, there is a value placed on outreach to people experiencing homelessness. At Urban Abbey, there is an emphasis on the fact that all people are welcomed regardless of their spiritual beliefs or religious affiliation. And at Rohs Street Café, there is a culture coordinator on the staff to help improve diversity in the café through music and art as well as through church and community partnerships.

Both serendipitously and by design, these three coffeehouses have become the types of peaceful, inclusive, and sustainable environments that the visionaries imagined. The buildings were saved, improved, and/or repurposed, the missions are being fulfilled, and revenues from coffee sales are helping to offset the expenses. Adding to all of this is yet another angle on social sustainability—the unforeseen and meaningful impact that these three coffeehouses are having on their surrounding areas.

The neighborhood: stability through coffee

The phrase "life in the canyon" has been used to describe the economic and social demise of many American inner cities in the past 60 years. As viable companies leave urban areas, residents are left with fewer jobs, boarded up buildings, and increased crime (Luria & Rogers, 1999). An unfortunate outcome of city decay is a loss of walk appeal. When locals fear for their personal safety, they are less likely to travel on foot to shop and to socialize (Benfield, 2014). The result can be social detachment where "people are independent of and anonymous to their neighbors—it is all part of the general anomie and isolation of urban life" (Fischer, 1982, p. 129).

Compounding the problem of urban decline is the attitude of newer generations toward city living. Young people in America are encouraged to live highly private lives steeped in personal gain and void of community (Oldenburg, 1989). This represents the very antithesis of socially sustainable settings where community and security needs are met (Borjesson & Walldin, 2009). Often, the products of isolation and declining population are friendless neighborhoods where there are plenty of activities to pass the time but very few opportunities to sustain meaningful relationships with others. As a result, true friendships may be lacking (Fischer, 1982). It does not help that gathering places are limited. A lack of parks and other common spaces can mean that the streets are the only places for people to congregate (MacDonald, 2007); an unpalatable option in unsafe areas.

Historically, addressing the problems of inner city neighborhoods has been a frustrating and often uphill battle. Many efforts to revitalize cities have failed because of the inability to create new, sustainable economic models that bring employment, financial security, improved infrastructure, and other elements that breathe life into forgotten urban areas (Porter, 1995).

Fortunately, more recent attitudes about the potential of the inner city are more favorable and optimistic. In towns and cities, there is a feeling that the right strategic investments can help rebuild a sense of community and mitigate feelings of disconnectedness (Beatley & Manning, 1997). Creating this sort of social sustainability in neighborhoods requires a great deal of foresight by city planners. They need to anticipate the needs of people in an ever-changing urban environment. To achieve this, city planners would do well to listen to the people living in affected neighborhoods—the very people who have the experience and wisdom to guide viable solutions. This type of listening may be the best path to sustainably fulfilling the needs of those living in troubled neighborhoods (Wheeler, 2013):

> Concern with the social dimensions of sustainability suggest that a sustainable community is one that addresses a host of related goals, including adequate and affordable shelter, health care, and other essential services to residents; a safe and crime-free environment; and humane and stimulating work environments.
>
> (Beatley & Manning, 1997, p. 32)

It is evident that fear of physical violence and other types of lawlessness is a major concern that hinders the growth and progress of inner-city neighborhoods (Harvey, 1996). Many contend that the development of local entrepreneurial ventures is one of the keys to creating sustainable communities that mitigate crime and better meet the needs of residents. When a new business is put in an old building, for example, it can inspire everyone in the community to make improvements to their own physical environment which can lead to increased neighborhood pride and reduced petty crime (McDonald, 1986). Because of this, developers should keep in mind the importance of small, local businesses and the impact they can have on both economic and social well-being (Weingaertner & Barber, 2010).

In many ways, Crave Coffeehouse, with its welcoming environment that promotes diversity and discourse, represents the ideal small business to positively influence a struggling neighborhood. Donna Green describes the area surrounding Crave as having been extremely rough prior to the coffeehouse opening in 2005. She recalls the sound of gunshots in the neighborhood and rumors of drug dealing activity not far from the building.

In the years since Crave opened, the neighborhood has improved drastically. Gone are the din of gunshots and the fear of drug activity. While Green admits that Crave is not the only positive influence in the area, she is convinced that the coffeehouse has had a significant impact on safety and appeal of the Tower Grove neighborhood where the coffeehouse resides. Helping to create a better environment outside of Crave was never an intention, but it is a welcome consequence (D. Green, personal communication, December 18, 2014).

Urban Abbey has also had an extremely positive impact on the surrounding neighborhood known as the Old Market. Debra McKnight is on the Board of Directors for the Old Market Business Association and recalls when the air conditioning recently went out at the coffeehouse, other local businesses pitched in to help. A neighboring hair salon opened their space for a worship service that typically takes place in Urban Abbey, and a local hotel opened a meeting room for coffeehouse employees to escape the heat. For their part, Urban Abbey has reached out to a local elementary school where they write cards to teachers, participate in ice cream socials, and conduct macaroni and cheese cook-offs to help them raise money (D. McKnight, personal communication, May 8, 2017).

For Rohs Street Café, much of their connection with the community involves creating positive, sustainable relationships with the students who attend the nearby University of Cincinnati. Beyond this, however, Rohs Street Café aspires to find additional ways to connect with the Clifton Heights neighborhood. Recently, for example, some employees from the café have become involved with a partnership between University Christian Church and a local high school. Together, the organizations are creating a community garden; a partnership that Keaton Neely hopes to see continually grow and flourish (K. Neely, personal communication, May 18, 2017).

Recent social attitudes seem to favor small businesses coming into the neighborhoods where they can become positive influences. Generally speaking, residents tend to welcome independently owned businesses close to or even within their communities (Besel & Nur, 2013). A new venture that utilizes an existing building is an especially welcome addition, because renovating old buildings is an enjoyable and attractive idea for some investors (Montgomery, 2003).

Fortunately for Donna Green, Debra McKnight, and Keaton Neely, coffee shops were and are a highly favored type of small business for neighborhoods to adopt because of their high level of social capital (Badger, 2014). It has been observed that, "'Third places like coffee shops and cafés induce efficacious neighborhood control and social action" (Wo, 2014, p. 1286). More specifically, coffee shops and other local businesses can be the neighborhood eyes and ears that hold all members of the community accountable for their behavior (Papachristos, Smith, Scherer, & Fugiero, 2011).

At the end of the day, socially sustainable neighborhoods benefit from community gathering places (Borjesson & Walldin, 2009), and the impact of such places can help reduce crime and other negative influences. Just as important, coffee shops and other small businesses are the catalysts for building strong social networks, and it is these social networks that lead to an important level of informal social control over their respective neighborhoods (Wo, 2014).

While there is no direct evidence to demonstrate the influence of Crave Coffeehouse, Urban Abbey, and Rohs Street Café on their surrounding communities, it seems reasonable to infer that they have contributed to the sustainability of these areas. As the literature suggests, small businesses (particularly coffeehouses) can have a significantly positive influence on safety and security (Papachristos, Smith, Scherer, & Fugiero, 2011) as well as social capital in neighborhoods (Waxman, 2006). The role that these three coffeehouses have played in their respective communities sets the stage for leaving an indelible mark on the neighborhoods that they call home.

Conclusions: finding capacity where there is seemingly none

Whether it was by accident or by design, the visionaries of Crave, Urban Abbey, and Rohs Street Café seem to understand that "unless you identify a place's inherent capacity you are not able to plan for human/social sustainability" (Borjesson & Walldin, 2009, para. 11). Indeed, they saw the inherent capacity of a 150-year-old, all-but-abandoned, decaying church in the middle of St. Louis, and in the ground-floor retail space of a renovated 19th-century hotel in the Old Market neighborhood of Omaha, and in a 1927 sanctuary built in the Clifton Heights area of Cincinnati.

They understand the historical significance and the legacies of the countless lives that were touched in these places. They understand the potential beauty and draw of buildings that were sold, covered in dust, or left to fall into disrepair. They understand the value of the place and the sense of peace, calm, and safety that they have to offer to those who come through their doors. And they understand the value of the surrounding communities that need positive and productive small businesses to bring hope to challenged neighborhoods. In sum, their views on the value of historic legacies, buildings, places, and neighborhoods help demonstrate that sustainable entrepreneurship is a multi-faceted concept that can flourish under the leadership of competent, conscientious entrepreneurs.

When Ernest Hemingway wrote about the cafés of Paris, France in the middle of the 20th century, he expressed an appreciation for their warmth, their diversity, and their openness to friends and strangers alike. This is what Crave Coffeehouse, Urban Abbey, and Rohs Street Café each have to offer—socially sustainable, pro-community atmospheres that celebrate differences, value safety, and bring out the very best in humanity. It is a long way from Paris, France to the American Midwest. But for an opportunity to experience these three coffeehouses and all they have to offer, perhaps Hemingway would have made the trip.

References

Antiques & Accents. (1989). *Treasures for the accent seeker.*

Badger, E. (2014, April 11). What independent coffee shops say about where we live [Blog post]. Retrieved from www.washingtonpost.com/news/wonk/wp/2014/04/11/what-independent-coffee-shops-say-about-where-we-live/.

Beatley, T. & Manning, K. (1997). *The ecology of place: Planning for environment, economy and community*. Washington, DC: Island Press.

Benfield, F.K. (2014). *25 ways to think about greener, healthier, cities*. Washington, DC: People Habitat Communications.

Besel, K. & Nur, Y.A. (2013). A comparative study of entrepreneurship in new urbanist communities. *Journal of the Indiana Academy of Social Sciences*, 16(2), 35–44.

Borjesson, K. (2006). The affective sustainability of objects: A search for causal connections. Studies of theory, processes and practice related to timelessness as a phenomenon. PhD dissertation, Central Saint Martins College, University of the Arts, London.

Borjesson, K. & Walldin, V. (2009). Sustainable revitalization of places: How to avoid regeneration resulting in degeneration. Paper presented at IAPS-CSBE: Revitalizing Built Environments, Requalifying Old Places for New Uses, Istanbul.

Burnett, R. & Luebbering, K. (1996). *German settlement in Missouri: New land, old ways*. Columbia, MO: University of Missouri Press.

Christ Lutheran Church. (1958). *God's timetable for Christ.*

Christ Lutheran Church. (1963). *Changes at Christ Church.*

Cook, B. (1992). The Korean Church. *Clifton United Methodist Church Bulletin*, 34.

Etzioni, A. (1993). *The spirit of community*. New York: Touchstone.

Fischer, C.S. (1982). *To dwell among friends: Personal networks in town and city*. Chicago, IL: University of Chicago Press.

Hammer, J. (2015). When three equals one. *Economic Development Journal*, 14(3), 5–10.

Harvey, D. (1996). *Readings in urban theory*. Malden, MA: Blackwell Publishers, Inc.

Hemingway, E. (1964). *A moveable feast*. New York: Charles Scribner's Sons.

Hetzler, G.R. (1954). Clifton church: Her past. *Clifton Evangelical United Brethren Church Trumpet*, 20(3), 5–7.

Holl, S. (2015). German churches in St. Louis 1830–1900. *St. Louis County Library Past Ports*, 7(10), 1–12.

Leary, S.P. (1979). Unlamented Windsor Inn. *Omaha Magazine*, 45–50.

Luria, D.D. & Rogers, J. (1999). *Economic solutions for cities and their suburbs*. Boston, MA: Beacon Press.

MacDonald, E. (2007). Wasted space/potential place: Reconsidering urban streets. *Neighborhood Places*, 19(1), 22–27.

McDonald, S.C. (1986). Does gentrification affect crime rates? *Crime and Justice*, 8, 163–201.

Montgomery, D. (2003). Small retail tenacity. *In Business*, 25(4), 30.

Oldenburg, R. (1989). *The great good place.* New York: Paragon House.

Olson, C. (1985). 100-year-old hotel reopens its door to tenants, shops. *World-Herald*, 1.

Onat, N.C., Kucukvar, M., & Tatari, O. (2014). Integrating triple bottom line input-output analysis into life cycle sustainability assessment framework: The case for US buildings. *International Journal of Life Cycle Assessment*, 19, 1488–1505.

Papachristos, A.V., Smith, C.M., Scherer, M.L., & Fugiero, M.A. (2011). More coffee, less crime? The relationship between gentrification and neighborhood crime rates in Chicago, 1991–2005. *City & Community*, 10(3), 215–240.

Porter, M.E. (1995). The competitive advantage of the inner city. *Harvard Business Review*, 73(3), 55–71.

Putnam, R.D. (2000). *Bowling alone.* New York: Simon & Schuster Paperbacks.

Rohs Street Café. (n.d.). *The five purposes of Rohs Street Café.*

Smith, M. & Tepe, G. (1992). History of Clifton Evangelical United Brethren Church. *Clifton United Methodist Church Bulletin*, pp. 11–12.

Strange, C.C. & Banning, J.H. (2001). *Educating by design.* San Francisco, CA: Jossey-Bass.

Struck by lightning (1963). Unidentified newspaper clipping. Lutheran Historical Society, St. Louis, MO.

Taylor, A.N. (2013). Segregation, education, and blurring the lines of division in St. Louis. *Saint Louis University Public Law Review*, 33, 183–190.

Tolzmann, D.H. (2004). *Missouri's German heritage.* Milford, OH: Little Miami Publishing Co.

Waxman, L. (2006). The coffee shop: Social and physical factors influencing place attachment. *Journal of Interior Design*, 31(3), 35–53.

Weingaertner, C. & Barber, A.R.G. (2010). Urban regeneration and socio-economic sustainability: A role for established small food outlets. *European Planning Studies*, 18(10), 1653–1674.

Wheeler, S.M. (2013). *Planning for sustainability.* Oxford, UK: Routledge.

Whitlow, B. (2008). Spirits are lifted at coffeehouse. *St. Louis Post Dispatch*, G12.

Williams, J. & Forbes, W. (2012). *Toward a more livable world: Social dimensions of sustainability.* Nacogdoches, TX: Stephen F. Austin State University Press.

Wo, J.C. (2014). Community context of crime: A longitudinal examination of the effects of local institutions on neighborhood crime. *Crime & Delinquency*, 62(10), 1286–1312.

Zukin, S. (2008). Consuming authenticity: From outposts of difference to means of exclusion. *Cultural Studies*, 22(5), 724–748.

4.3 The SBA 7(a) loan program and the American social entrepreneur

J. Howard Kucher

Introduction

It is almost universal that scholarly articles on social entrepreneurship begin with the acknowledgment that it is an emerging and ill-defined field, with much need for further research (Nicholls, 2010). Within this wide-ranging topic, attention on the specific challenges of funding such a venture is increasing (Grimes, 2010; Van Slyke & Newman, 2006). The ability to access capital is a key element of any entrepreneurial venture (Evans & Leighton, 1989). It is particularly problematic in the sub-sector of social entrepreneurship, where a venture is seeking to balance a broader range of objectives including social and civic as well as economic returns (Grimes, 2010; Lumpkin & Bacq, 2013; Thompson, 2002).

While definitional debates continue within the field (Nicholls, 2010), one important distinction has a significant bearing on the issue of financing. Broad definitions of social entrepreneurship include various forms of enterprise (for-profit, non-profit and hybrid) that seek social objectives. A more narrow definition describes a non-profit entity as one that applies business principles to its operations and seeks to earn revenue from market-based activities as well as from more traditional charitable funding sources (Austin, Stevenson, & Wei-Skillern, 2006). Using this more restrictive definition, I will examine a recent proposal made at a White House conference on the topic of "Building an Impact Economy in America." The participants in this conference proposed the notion of expanding the SBA 7(A) loan program to non-profit social enterprises as one way to improve the ability of social sector enterprises to access capital (Clark, 2011).

While the loan guarantees of the SBA 7(A) loan program have held popular attention as an aid to the growth of new ventures for many years (Craig et al., 2005), the actual effectiveness of the program is a matter of significant debate (Bean, 2001; De Rugy, 2007; Immergluck, 1995). Therefore, a review of the program before any expansion would seem prudent, particularly in times of economic and budgetary challenges such as those currently being experienced in the United States (Clark, 2011).

Funding challenges for social enterprises

Small business lending is inherently problematic. One of the main reasons for this is that the costs involved in reviewing and originating a loan are somewhat fixed but must be allocated over a smaller amount of income, making them less profitable than loans to larger firms. The increased regulatory scrutiny that has developed in the aftermath of the 2007–2008 financial crisis has exacerbated this problem, as banks are being forced to hold higher levels of capital and reduce the risk in their loan portfolios. As a result, the percentage of small business loans in a typical bank's lending portfolio dropped by 20 percentage points over a seven-year period (from 50 percent in 1995 to 30 percent in 2012) (Mills & McCarthy, 2014).

Non-profits have also been subject to difficulty in obtaining loans. Much of this concern comes from a perception that the typical non-profit management team lacks general business expertise (Krishnan, Yetman, & Yetman, 2006). The reliance on donor funding is also often viewed as an indicator that cash flow may not be stable over time, making the surety of loan repayment less certain (Bowman, 2002).

The non-profit social enterprise compounds this problem by sending mixed signals to the potential lender. By seeking to obtain both market-based financial returns and positive social outcomes, these ventures are seen as inherently less profitable (Jensen & Meckling, 1976), further increasing the perceived risk to the lender.

Finally, as the vast majority of social enterprises are small firms (Kickul & Lyons, 2012; Teasdale, Lyon, & Baldock, 2013), the search for capital has all of the challenges normally faced by any small firm (Wiersch & Shane, 2013).

While a for-profit enterprise has a single primary objective of maximizing its return on shareholders' investments, a social enterprise seeks to produce value in social, civic and economic terms (Lumpkin & Bacq, 2013). In seeking to satisfy multiple objectives, the means by which the investor or lender is repaid become harder to quantify (Kickul & Lyons, 2012). Whether organized as a for-profit or non-profit, the social enterprise faces an almost insurmountable challenge in seeking traditional bank financing.

If the SBA 7(A) loan program is to be a potential solution to this problem, then a review of the program may be able to shed some light on its applicability to this complex challenge. Accordingly, I now turn to a brief examination of the SBA in general and the 7(A) loan program in particular.

Politics or purpose? The history of the small business administration

From the various Congressional committees of the Roosevelt administration, through two wars (WWII and the Korean Conflict) and Eisenhower's signing of the Small Business Act of 1953, right up to the present day, the Federal government has attempted to provide support for small businesses. Unfortunately, the ever-changing political fabric of the United States has rendered the various programs ineffective at best and harmful at worst (Blackford, 2003). Despite significant political indifference, The United States Small Business Administration (SBA) was created by the Small Business Act of 1953, which defined a small business as a "business concern that is independently owned and not dominant in its field of operations" (Solomon, 1986). It is interesting to note that the original authorization was intentionally temporary. It granted the SBA the authority to make loans, help small firms secure government contracts, and provide for disaster assistance for small firms, with a total funding of $275 million. It also called for the agency to be abolished within two years unless otherwise extended (Bean, 2001).

Sixty-three years later, the SBA is still alive and well, with an FY2017 budget of $719 million (*SBA Fact Sheet*, 2016). The Office of Capital Access is the largest of the SBA program areas, and within that office, the 7(A) loan program is the most active, with $5.45 billion in loan guarantees in FY2016 (*SBA Gross Loan Approval by Program*, 2016).

The SBA and small business lending

The 7(A) loan program, named for the portion of the Small Business Act that authorized it, does not lend money. Rather, it is a loan guaranty fund that operates through a network of commercial banks. The bank underwrites and administers the loan after undergoing an approval process from the SBA. The SBA then provides a guarantee of 85 percent of the loan value if the borrower defaults on the loan. The theory of this guarantee is that it allows the bank to initiate a loan that it would otherwise decline due to a higher level of risk than the bank would accept without the guarantee (Sherman, 2005). The justification for this policy is that the bias in risk appetite on the part of the lender is in effect unfair and unequal treatment that then becomes the government's responsibility to remedy (Carter & Jones-Evans, 2006). The policy is further rooted in the notion that the ability to access capital is the single largest factor that affects the achievement of business objectives for small firms (Storey, 2002).

Non-profits and the 7(A). While intended to provide support for small firms, non-profit enterprises are excluded from the 7(a) loan program as a matter of policy. The first reason for this exclusion is that SBA was founded as a means to promote economic development, and non-profits were not seen as contributing to economic growth. A second and more practical issue is that non-profits enjoy various tax exemptions. Providing a federally backed loan program to a firm that enjoys such a benefit might be seen as a government intervention to support unfair competition (Blackford, 2003; Craig et al., 2007).

Review of literature on SBA 7(A) program effectiveness

There is a reasonably significant body of literature on the SBA and the 7(A) loan program. One of its strongest critiques comes in the opening pages of Bean's *Big Government and Affirmative Action: The Scandalous History of the Small Business Administration* (2001). Bean observes that the SBA was "created in an interest group vacuum . . . [with] support for the agency [coming] from members of Congress rather than small business owners" (Bean, 2001).

Bean (2001) is extremely skeptical about the entire organization, as can be easily grasped by the use of the word "scandalous" in the title of his book. Bean itemizes a dozen different practices and activities that are, to be generous, questionable. One of the more notable is the designation in 1966 of the American Motors Corporation, a company that at the time had sales of over $1billion and more than 30,000 employees, as a small business. Almost 30 years later, the SBA was deeply involved in a $300,000 loan made to a company named the Whitewater Development Corporation (one of the partners in Whitewater was a young Southern Governor named Clinton). While it is readily apparent that Bean has a significant agenda, his points are not without merit. In fact, one might go so far as to say that trying to manipulate a market, particularly one with so many independent actors, is a fool's errand.

Brock et al. (1986) provide additional insight into this challenge as they review the small business arena from an economist's perspective. They determine that the basic theories of equilibrium so necessary to sound economic theory and the ability to make observations are significantly compromised in this sector as there are limited economies of scale available to the individual firm (Brock et al., 1986). The noted economist Joseph Stiglitz observes that this "disequilibrium" will inevitably result in disruptions in the credit market and an inefficient and inequitable lending process and result in what he calls "credit rationing" (Stiglitz & Weiss, 1981). De Rugy (2007) takes this notion further, arguing that this credit rationing is, in fact, the equilibrium state for the small business market and that there is no point in trying to adjust it. De Rugy goes so far as to say that all SBA loan programs should be eliminated as they are never going to be effective in changing the structure of the lending market for small businesses. Brock et al. (1986) further observe that a large number of firms makes regulation difficult as the ability to gather information reliably is virtually impossible. From this section, one might conclude that the renowned "invisible hand" of Adam Smith (1796) might, in fact, be more effective than a visible hand in the "person" of the SBA.

However, the huge number of actors, each with their issues, objectives, motives, and concerns is only one of the challenges that face the very idea of trying to regulate or affect this market. Bates (1989) proposes that one of the largest impediments to the success of the SBA's initiatives in lending is the breadth of the goals that the policy attempts to address. Bates observes that "because [the] SBA is seeking to accomplish very diverse objectives with its major loan programs, results in terms of loan losses and [the] number of businesses assisted vary dramatically." Van Meter and Van Horn (1975) lend credence to this position in their observation that the ability to achieve goal consensus is critical to the successful implementation of any public policy. It should be clear from this discussion that there is a significant ongoing debate about the effectiveness of the SBA 7(A) loan program.

Evaluation of 7(A) loan program performance

Immergluck (1995) claimed that:

> [t]he only defensible rationale for federal government involvement in the financing of individual small businesses is an economic development rationale. If policies and programs support the creation and retention of jobs and economic activity in places and among communities in real need of economic development they can be justified.

However, the ability of SBA programs to do just that is a matter of open debate. In 2007, the United States Government Accountability Office (GAO) reported that there was a need for significant additional performance measurement of the SBA 7(A) loan program as it was unable to determine if the program had any effect on the reduction of disparity in lending activities (GAO, 2007). This report also indicated that the underlying reasons that a loan may or may not be granted to a particular small business are extremely varied and may in fact not be able to be quantified or affected by the policy. An earlier report by the GAO in 2004 also observed that the true costs to deliver the 7(A) loan program were difficult to measure, due in large part to the difficulties experienced in gathering data from its large network of lenders (GAO, 2004). Both of these reports also indicated a need to expand measurements beyond just approval and default rates and to move toward developing a method for tracking results that take into account a longer-range economic impact assessment. This call for a broader perspective in assessment was not new to the GAO reports and has in fact been coming from other assessors for some time.

Craig et al. (2007) reports that the results of a significant empirical study of the comparison between SBA guaranteed lending activity and regional economic development produced a small but significant positive correlation. However, Craig et al. also note that the results of this study are not able to determine if "SBA loan guarantees are contributing to growth by helping to complete the market or are simply proxying for small business lending in the market." This "proxy" effect is substantiated in part by Glennon and Nigro (2005) in their cumulative analysis of default rates for SBA guaranteed loan rates as compared to a general portfolio of corporate bonds. Stabilizing factors are used to allow for and isolate overall market and economic fluctuations. This study then concludes that it is these market factors, not the presence or absence of an SBA guarantee, which are the primary causes of default in small business lending. Stated another way, the actual probability of a small business being able to repay a loan has much more to do with the market and economic forces than it does with the presence or absence of the guarantee. Two additional studies point out this lack of effective difference in lending behavior.

Petersen and Rajan (1994) review data obtained by the National Survey of Small Business Finances collected under the auspices of the Federal Reserve. They then analyze this data to examine the relationship between borrow and lender regarding how long the relationship has existed, how many products or services provided by the lender are used by the borrower, and what percentage of the borrower's overall financial activity is conducted with the lender. These three metrics attempt to develop length, breadth and depth measurements of the relationship. The study finds that it is these factors and not the presence or absence of an SBA guarantee that has the greatest impact on lending behavior. Stated simply, a strong relationship with your banker gets you the loan, not an SBA guarantee. In a similar vein, Cole, Goldberg, et al. (2004) determine that while larger banks do tend to use more sophisticated metrics for evaluating a borrower, it is the ability to develop knowledge of the character of the individual that most greatly affects the lending. Although not mentioned in this study, it would seem clear that this knowledge is only obtained when there is a relationship of substance between borrower and lender.

One of the more recent and comprehensive studies, undertaken by the Urban Institute in 2008, determines that the outcomes of the SBA 7(A) loan program are mixed at best, and carries forward the argument made by Immergluck (1995). This study finds significant duplication of efforts between SBA and non-SBA lending and a lack of direct correlation between the growth and success of the firm and the presence or absence of an SBA guaranteed loan. This report also brings out the lack of measurement of long-range activity, reporting that despite years of criticism (and significant advancements in public administration), the SBA measures its activity on simple output measures such as the number of loans and dollar amounts guaranteed (Rossman et al., 2008).

The evaluation of program performance would not be complete without consideration of the effects of the banking crisis and federal support for banks and banking that has occurred in recent years. Given the changes in the banking industry that have occurred, one might infer that perhaps SBA's loan guarantees would finally start to meet their purpose. Sadly, despite the massive federal infusions of capital into the lending market and the increase of the SBA guarantee from 85 to 90 percent of the loan amount (Dance, 2009), it seems that the future is more likely to repeat the past. On May 5, 2009 the *Wall Street Journal* reported that SBA 7(A) loan volume had increased in recent months, but concluded that the higher volume of loans might have more to do with historically low interest rates than with the increase in SBA guarantee levels (Flandez, 2009). While it will certainly be some time before recent changes in economic conditions stabilize and the impact of the SBA 7(A) loan program can be assessed in this new context, it seems that early indicators point to more of the same for this program.

Analysis of 7(A) loan program implementation

As we examine the implementation of SBA 7(A), the four-faceted analytical framework developed by Mazmanian and Sabatier (1989) is a useful tool to determine if the outcomes of the 7(A) loan program align with the intent of the SBA.

To begin, we can examine *tractability*—the ability to closely describe, measure, and limit the scope of a problem to be addressed. The SBA 7(A) has clear causal linkages between funding and business activity and direct measurement of lending outcomes in both decision and quantity. However, because "small business" is such a large category (as many as 95 percent of all enterprises in the United States), and because loan decisions have subjective character as well as quantitative analysis, the linkage between 7(A) funding and the larger "small business" category is sometimes imprecise. From the very start of the program, the number of constituencies that the program attempted to address was far too broad in their perspectives and interests to be effectively addressed.

The second facet is *structure*—the clarity and urgency of the underlying policy goals, the sufficiency of program funding, and the autonomy of program decisionmaking. The 7(A) loan program goals are fairly clear; however, there are hundreds of banks making SBA loans, introducing variables in the decision rules of implementing agencies and the commitment levels of the various officials involved.

A third facet is *external conditions*—public and political support for a program and the variations in economic health, technical sophistication, and commitment of its participants. The 7(A) loan program addresses constituencies with diverse needs and capabilities that face discrimination by race, gender, or geography; the waxing and waning of public and political support; and the variability in skill and commitment of SBA political appointees and its partner lenders.

The external conditions for 7(A) have included the politicization of program evaluation. The criteria for evaluation are often set in the establishment of the policy and can be as ambiguous, unclear, and conflicting as the policy itself. In plain English, the methods for keeping score can vary significantly and are often adjusted while the game is underway. These observations certainly have significant relevance to the SBA 7(A) loan program. One aspect that provides the link is the fact that the SBA defines a small firm in many different ways, based on the industry, the type of program, and other internal factors. This "moving definition" causes significant problems in gathering independent data needed to evaluate the success of the program. Another problem in measuring the effectiveness of the 7(A) loan program is that most reporting is done based on the approval or rejection of loans, rather than on the long-term impact of the loan on the business and the economy. This short-term reporting perspective results in a focus on outputs rather than on outcomes.

The final set of issues involve *stages of implementation*—the clarity of regulations, procedures, processes, and enforcement guidelines, and the level of compliance or adherence to the regulation that occurs within the target population. These variables have also been greatly affected by the changes in economic cycles, turnover in the electoral process, and changes in attitudes toward cultural inclusion. Clarity can be affected by the level of information used to develop the policy, the complexity of the issue being addressed, the political utility of ambiguity, and the number and power levels of the stakeholders in the matter. The problems that can be caused by this lack of clarity were certainly evident in the implementation of the 7(A) loan program.

The potential conflicts between the policy at hand and the culture of the lending organization can create significant political challenges in implementation. Further, outside intermediaries can become involved (such as vendors in a privatization program or local state delivery of a federal program) and bring differing views, processes, performance criteria, and compliance issues, as well as immunity from the sanctions that may be imposed on the implementing agency or actor. The impact of intermediaries is one of the major issues in the 7(A) loan program: over 8,633 banks participate in underwriting SBA guaranteed loans (Kobe, 2004). As each of the banks has unique internal guidelines and processes for approving a loan, it becomes clear that it would be extremely difficult for the SBA to ensure consistency in lending practices across all participating institutions.

SBA 7(A) loan program evaluation conclusions

Much needs to be done if the SBA 7(A) program is to serve its intended purpose effectively. However, two studies indicate that the desired goal may in fact not be achievable. The previously cited study completed by Bates (1989) provided us with the observation that the diverse goals and objectives of the SBA produced a wide variety of outcomes regarding loan losses and the number of firms that received SBA assistance. More directly and more currently, the 2007 GAO report cited earlier states quite openly that the issue of improving imperfections in credit markets for small business may, in fact, be something that public policy can achieve (GAO, 2007).

Given the mediocre performance of the program, one would reasonably ask why it remains in effect. Two possible reasons come to mind as to why the 7(A) loan program remains such a large part of the SBA. The first is that the owners of small firms represent a very large proportion of the voting public, with over 27 million firms. Some 99.7 percent of all businesses are small, they create 60 to 80 percent of net job growth, and employ 50 percent of all private sector workers (Kobe, 2004). Accordingly, there is a large political constituency that would be upset if this program were eliminated. The second reason is also a political matter, although more subtle and nuanced. Any politician attempting to dissolve this program would be viewed quite negatively, not just by the small business owner but by the general public. The idea of entrepreneurship, of owning your own business and being your own boss is as much a part of the American dream as owning your own home. Therefore, any attack on this program would be seen as an attempt to tear down the very psychic makeup of the United States and hence be political suicide.

Recommendations

Two significant actions can be taken to improve the level of government support for small enterprises, including those that seek to serve a social purpose. First, the 7(A) loan program could be expanded to include non-profit entities that include earned income in their revenue strategy. This recommendation could be justified by recognizing the effect that continuing budget pressures, combined with increasing concern regarding social inequities, have brought about in shifting the non-profit landscape (Kucher, 2012). During 2002 to 2012, the non-profit sector of the U.S. economy grew by 8.6 percent. As of 2012, non-profits comprised 5.4 percent of the Gross Domestic Product in the United States, contributing over $887.3 billion to the economy. Within the sector, both revenues and assets grew at rates faster than the overall economy. It is particularly interesting to note that 50 percent of the revenue generated by non-profits came not from donations or government grants, but from fees for services rendered. While almost half of those fees (46 percent) were due to government subcontracting, much of the fee-based revenue was generated by income-earning initiatives that look and sound much like the for-profit sector (McKeever & Pettijohn, 2014).

It has been proposed that governmental support of various social enterprise models might serve to reduce public sector deficits. By supporting organizations that produce a social benefit while relying on earned income for at least part of their funding, the need for government subsidies might be reduced (Kucher, 2012). As the 7(A) loan program is a loan guarantee and not an actual loan, extending the program into the non-profit sector for the development of social enterprise could have a significant impact on the growth of these firms. However, the checkered history of the effectiveness of both the SBA in general and the 7(A) in particular might suggest that such an expansion would only spread an existing problem to a broader audience.

The second recommendation is the expansion of other services that the SBA provides. One of them is a program of Small Business Development Centers that provide counseling for small business owners on the many practical challenges of owning and running a small firm. The budget for these programs is tiny compared to the amount of money spent on loan guarantees. There are well-established statistics that indicate that direct technical assistance has a very strong impact on the ability of a small business to grow and thrive (Chilenski et al., 2016; McKenzie & Woodruff, 2014). In fact, there is a marked increase in the success of a new venture when it receives the appropriate coaching, mentoring, and counseling in its early years.

Two recent studies indicate that only 44 percent of small businesses survive for more than four years after start-up (Headd, 2003; Knaup, 2005). However, the National Business Incubation Association (NBIA) reports that 87 percent of companies that receive formal support and coaching can survive this critical hurdle and continue to contribute to the economy (NBIA, 2006). While the NBIA itself cautions that no formal study has been performed to validate this data, it certainly seems like a promising path to pursue (as well as a good topic for additional academic inquiry). Were the SBA to redirect its funding to improving the number of technical assistance programs, there might be a more direct ability to accomplish its stated goals. Given the marked difference in performance of technical assistance programs relative to the checkered history of the 7(A) loan program, such a reallocation might be prudent.

Given the political nature of the SBA, it might be more prudent to propose a change in focus for the SBA rather than simply eliminating or reducing the 7(A) loan program. Moving to a stronger emphasis on technical assistance and expanding 7(A) eligibility to the non-profit social enterprise would have the dual effect of both increasing effective support to fledgling social enterprises and appeasing the various political interests. It might even have a greater ability to continue to move society forward.

References

Austin, J., Stevenson, H., & Wei-Skillern, J. (2006). Social and commercial entrepreneurship: Same, different, or both? *Entrepreneurship Theory and Practice, 30*(1), 1–22.

Bates, T. (1989). The changing nature of minority business: A comparative analysis of asian, nonminority, and black-owned businesses. *The Review of Black Political Economy, 18*(2), 25–42.

Bean, J. J. (2001). *Big government and affirmative action: the scandalous history of the Small Business Administration*. Lexington, KY: University Press of Kentucky.

Blackford, M. G. (2003). *A history of small business in America*. Chapel Hill, NC: University of North Carolina Press.

Bowman, W. (2002). The uniqueness of nonprofit finance and the decision to borrow. *Nonprofit Management and Leadership*, *12*(3), 293–311.

Brock, W. A., Evans, D. S., & Phillips, B. D. (1986). *The economics of small businesses: their role and regulation in the U.S. economy*. New York: Holmes & Meier.

Carter, S., & Jones-Evans, D. (2006). *Enterprise and small business: principles, practice and policy*. Harlow, UK and New York: FT Prentice Hall.

Chilenski, S. M., Perkins, D. F., Olson, J., Hoffman, L., Feinberg, M. E., Greenberg, M., . . . Spoth, R. (2016). The power of a collaborative relationship between technical assistance providers and community prevention teams: A correlational and longitudinal study. *Evaluation and Program Planning*, *54*, 19–29.

Clark, C. (2011). *Building an impact economy*. Retrieved from http://blogs.fuqua.duke.edu/casenotes/2011/08/02/building-an-impact-economy/.

Cole, R. A., Goldberg, L. G., & White, L. J. (2004). Cookie cutter vs. character: The micro structure of small business lending by large and small banks. *The Journal of Financial and Quantitative Analysis*, *39*(2), 227–251.

Craig, B. R., Jackson, W. E., III, & Thomson, J. B. (2005). *SBA guaranteed lending and local economic growth*. Working paper. Retrieved from www.frbatlanta.org/-/media/documents/research/publications/wp/2005/wp0528.pdf.

Craig, B. R., Jackson, W. E., & Thomson, J. B. (2007). Small firm finance, credit rationing, and the impact of SBA-guaranteed lending on local economic growth. *Journal of Small Business Management*, *45*(1), 116–132.

Dance, S. (2009). Stimulus money perks SBA loan demand, but lending still low. *Baltimore Business Journal*, *26*(30), 1.

De Rugy, V. (2007, Spring). The SBA's justification IOU. *Regulation*, pp. 26–34. Retrieved from http://search.ebscohost.com/login.aspx?direct=true&db=buh&AN=25641120&site=ehost-live.

Evans, D. S., & Leighton, L. S. (1989). Some empirical aspects of entrepreneurship. *The American Economic Review*, *79*(3), 519–535.

Flandez, R. (2009). Small-business credit sees thaw: Lenders ease purse strings as more loans sell on secondary market. *Wall Street Journal* May 5. Retrieved from https://ezproxy.stevenson.edu/login?url=https://search.proquest.com/docview/399109031?accountid=36772.

GAO, U.S.G.A.O. (2004). *Small Business Administration: model for 7(a) program subsidy had reasonable equations, but inadequate documentation hampered external reviews*. Washington, DC: U.S. Government Accountability Office.

GAO, U.S.G.A.O. (2007). *Small Business Administration: 7(a) loan program needs additional performance measures*. Washington, DC: U.S. Government Accountability Office.

Glennon, D., & Nigro, P. (2005). An analysis of SBA loan defaults by maturity structure. *Journal of Financial Services Research*, *28*(1–3), 77–111.

Grimes, M. (2010). Strategic sensemaking within funding relationships: The effects of performance measurement on organizational identity in the social sector. *Entrepreneurship Theory and Practice*, *34*(4), 763–783.

Headd, B. (2003). Redefining business success: Distinguishing between closure and failure. *Small Business Economics*, *21*(1), 51–61.

Immergluck, D. (1995). *Moving to economic development: a new goal for SBA Loan Programs—SBA 7(a) lending patterns in San Antonio before and after Lowdoc*. Chicago, IL: Woodstock Institute.

Jensen, M. C., & Meckling, W. H. (1976). Theory of the firm: Managerial behavior, agency costs and ownership structure. *Journal of Financial Economics*, *3*(4), 305–360.

Kickul, J. R., & Lyons, T. S. (2012). *Understanding social entrepreneurship: the relentless pursuit of mission in an ever changing world*. New York: Routledge.

Knaup, A. E. (2005). Survival and longevity in the Business Employment Dynamics data. *Monthly Labor Review*, *128*(5), 50–56.

Kobe, K. (2004). *The Small Business Share of GDP, 1998–2004.* Retrieved from www.sba.gov/advo/research/rs299tot.pdf.

Krishnan, R., Yetman, M. H., & Yetman, R. J. (2006). Expense misreporting in nonprofit organizations. *The Accounting Review, 81*(2), 399–420.

Kucher, J. H. (2012). Social enterprise as a means to reduce public sector deficits. *Journal of Entrepreneurship and Public Policy, 1*(2), 147–158.

Lumpkin, G. T., & Bacq, S. (2013). *Social entrepreneurship and the multiple logics of societal impact.* Paper presented at the 2013 Academy of Management annual meeting, Lake Buena Vista, Florida, USA.

Mazmanian, D. A., & Sabatier, P. A. (1989). *Implementation and public policy: with a new postscript.* Lanham, MD: University Press of America.

McKeever, B. S., & Pettijohn, S. L. (2014). *The nonprofit sector in brief 2014.* Washington, DC: Urban Institute.

McKenzie, D., & Woodruff, C. (2014). What are we learning from business training and entrepreneurship evaluations around the developing world? *The World Bank Research Observer, 29*(1), 48–82.

Mills, K., & McCarthy, B. (2014). The state of small business lending: Credit access during the recovery and how technology may change the game. Harvard Business School General Management Unit Working Paper No. 15-004.

NBIA. (2006). *Business Incubator FAQ.* Retrieved from www.nbia.org/resource_center/bus_inc_facts/index.php.

Nicholls, A. (2010). The legitimacy of social entrepreneurship: Reflexive isomorphism in a pre-paradigmatic field. *Entrepreneurship Theory and Practice, 34*(4), 611–633.

Petersen, M. A., & Rajan, R. G. (1994). The benefits of lending relationships: Evidence from small business data. *The Journal of Finance, 49*(1), 3–37.

Rossman, S. B., Theodos, B., Brash, R., Gallagher, M., Hayes, C., & Temkin, K. (2008). *Key findings from the evaluation of the Small Business Administration's loan and investment programs.* Retrieved from www.urban.org/sites/default/files/publication/31426/411602-Key-Findings-from-the-Evaluation-of-the-Small-Business-Administration-s-Loan-and-Investment-Programs.PDF.

SBA Fact Sheet. (2016). Retrieved from www.sba.gov/sites/default/files/OCPL_SBA_fact_sheet.pdf.

SBA Gross Loan Approval by Program. (2016). Retrieved from www.sba.gov/sites/default/files/WDS_Table2_GrossApproval_Report.pdf.

Sherman, A. J. (2005). *Raising capital: get the money you need to grow your business.* New York: AMACOM.

Smith, A. (1796). *An enquiry into the nature and causes of the wealth of nations.* London: Printed for A. Strahan; and T. Cadell, and W. Davies.

Solomon, S. (1986). *Small business USA: the role of small companies in sparking America's economic transformation.* New York: Crown Publishers.

Stiglitz, J. E., & Weiss, A. (1981). Credit rationing in markets with imperfect information. *The American Economic Review, 71*(3), 393–410.

Storey, D. J. (2002). *Understanding the small business sector.* London: Thomson Learning.

Teasdale, S., Lyon, F., & Baldock, R. (2013). Playing with numbers: A methodological critique of the social enterprise growth myth. *Journal of Social Entrepreneurship, 4*(2), 113–131.

Thompson, J. L. (2002). The world of the social entrepreneur. *International Journal of Public Sector Management, 15*(5), 412–431.

Van Meter, D. S., & Van Horn, C. E. (1975). The policy implementation process: A conceptual framework. *Administration Society, 6*(4), 445–488.

Van Slyke, D. M., & Newman, H. K. (2006). Venture philanthropy and social entrepreneurship in community redevelopment. *Nonprofit Management and Leadership, 16*(3), 345–368.

Wiersch, A. M., & Shane, S. (2013). Why small business lending isn't what it used to be. *Economic Commentary/Cleveland Federal Reserve, 14,* 2013–10. Retrieved from www.clevelandfed.org/newsroom-and-events/publications/economic-commentary/2013-economic-commentaries/ec-201310-why-small-business-lending-isnt-what-it-used-to-be.aspx.

4.4 The corporate social responsibility paradox

Present-day firm challenges in the cacao sector of Indonesia

Edwin B.P. de Jong, Jonas Kolenberg, and Luuk Knippenberg

Introduction

As part of globalization, patterns of production and consumption have changed significantly around the world. Today, most products are no longer consumed solely in the locations where they are produced and processed. Production sites are often located on the other side of the globe and form part of a global value chain with numerous vertical and horizontal links (Boström et al., 2015; Merino and Valor, 2011). Many good examples of the global interlinking of production and consumption can be found in the agro-commodities sectors. One product where this global value chain is particularly evident is cacao.

Cacao beans are produced in the 'Global South', but mainly processed and consumed in the 'Global North', i.e. in the United States, Western Europe, and Japan. The cacao value chain faces many challenges, ranging from achieving stable capital accumulation by the processing industries and wholesalers in the North, to land and soil degradation, crop pests and diseases, and low incomes and sometimes poverty among the producers in the South. For these sorts of reasons, the overall production of cacao in Indonesia, the world's third largest cacao producer, has dropped significantly in recent years. The problems often increase because government interventions to deal with these issues are lacking or ineffective. Other arrangements and efforts, initiated by other stakeholders, are thus becoming vital for the long-term sustainability of the cacao sector, especially for the sustainability and resilience of the base level, i.e. the production of cacao beans.

In Indonesia, one can already observe the emergence of new kinds of multi-stakeholder collaborations and inter-sectoral partnerships in the cacao value chain. These new networks include representatives of civil society, government, and business (Bitzer et al., 2008). Sustainability programs have been designed and implemented as part of these new collaborations. Here, two inter-sectoral partnerships stand out: the Sustainable Cacao Production Programme (SCPP) and the Cacao Sustainability Partnership (CSP). Both have successfully coordinated and aligned the efforts of all the relevant stakeholders. The objectives of these arrangements, and the way they are organized, have much in common with the core objectives underpinning the ideas of corporate social responsibility (CSR).

In this chapter, we examine these two recent collaborations in Indonesia and illustrate how firms are seeking sustainable, long-term solutions and innovations in the cacao sector by adopting a variety of context-specific measurements through dialogue, negotiations, and collaboration with various stakeholders. As such, the findings offer a fresh way to understand and interrogate the challenges confronting present-day firms in implementing and pursuing a sustainability agenda. The argumentation is based on extensive research conducted in Indonesia in 2016 that included field visits, multi-stakeholder meetings, workshops, and 27 in-depth interviews with key representatives of the main stakeholders in the Indonesian cacao value chain.

Overall dynamics in the cacao value chain

Worldwide, cacao, the raw material for chocolate, is a highly valued product. Demand continues to grow, and this trend is expected to continue for the foreseeable future due to the increased demand in growing economies such as China. In 2014, world production was almost 4.9 million tonnes, an increase of 3.2 percent over 2013 (ICCO, 2016). The cacao tree only grows in tropical regions, and the main cacao-bean producers are small-scale farmers in Africa, Asia, and Latin America. The typical size of a cacao farm is two to four hectares (in Indonesia between 0.5 and 1.2 hectares). Each hectare produces about 500 kg of cacao beans in Asia (World Cocoa Foundation, 2014, p. 2).[1]

Cacao is a raw material and needs to be processed (ground) into materials from which other products (primarily chocolate) are made. In the various phases of the cacao value chain, different actors are involved, i.e. farmers, collectors, transporters, grinders, traders, manufacturers (of chocolate), retail outlets, and consumers (see Figure 4.4.1). The manufacturing, and often also the roasting and grinding, is predominantly carried out in those regions where the manufactured chocolate products are consumed. The process of producing, processing, and manufacturing cacao into chocolate is globally dispersed, with the various value-adding activities undertaken in different localities. In effect, the cacao value chain embodies a complex set of steps and interlinkages between a wide variety of actors, all embedded in a globalized system of production, trade, and consumption.

However, in reality, the cacao value chain is financially, and in terms of negotiation power, dominated, by a few multinational firms – those who own the main chocolate brands and produce the chocolate. Table 4.4.1 lists the eight main players, all based in the United States, Japan, or Europe. Together, these eight companies control half of the global market. They own the major chocolate brands and manufacture the end products. Their influence is based on the nature of their value-adding activities, i.e. the manufacturing of the end products, and the scale of their activities.

The large brand-owners, the chocolate and candy manufacturers, keep around 35 percent of the retail price, a substantially higher share than that of, for instance, the cacao-bean producers, the farmers, whose share is 6.6 percent, or the grinders, whose share is 7.6 percent (Fountain and Hütz-Adams, 2015). We also see a large degree of market concentration in the post-processing phase. Just two multinational firms, Barry Callebaut and Cargill, together control 80 percent of the post-processing activities of cacao, while seven trading companies control 75 percent of the international cacao market (Table 4.4.1).

The Indonesian cacao value chain

Historically, Indonesia has a prominent position in the production of cacao. Currently, Indonesia is the world's third largest producer of raw cacao beans. That production is primarily realized by smallholder cacao farmers, with a typical farm size of between 0.5 and 1.2 hectares. The farmers grow, harvest, and dry the cacao beans. The next step, fermentation, is generally done elsewhere, further downstream in the value chain, for example

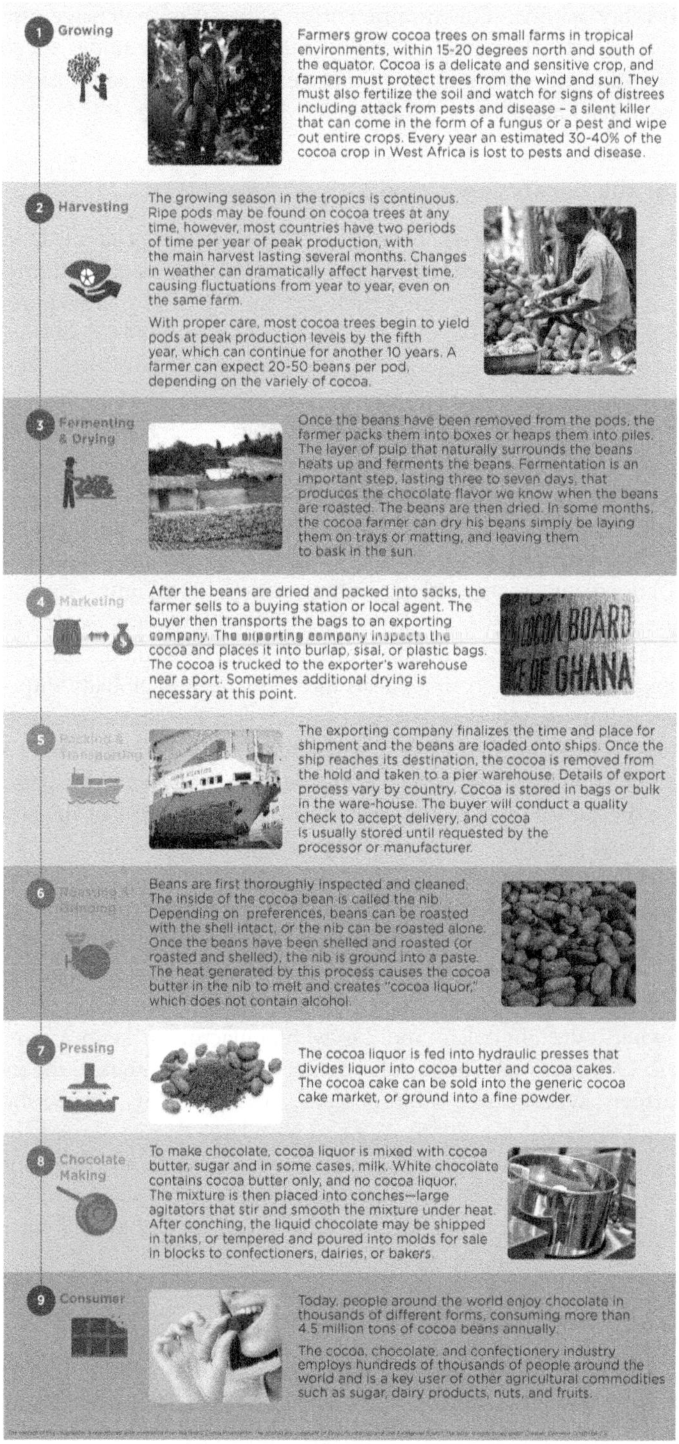

Figure 4.4.1 The cacao value chain[2]

Source: World Cocoa Foundation 2014, pp. 4–5.

Table 4.4.1 Main chocolate producers in 2016

Ranking	*Name*	*Country*	*Net sales in 2016 (in US$)*
1	Mars	USA	18.0 billion
2	Mondelez	USA	12.6 billion
3	Ferrero	Luxembourg	10.6 billion
4	Meiji	Japan	9.6 billion
5	Nestle	Switzerland	9.1 billion
6	Hershey	USA	7.5 billion
7	Pladis	UK	5.2 billion
8	Lindt	Switzerland	3.9 billion

Source: Candy Industry (2017).

by cooperatives and/or in small processing facilities. The fermented beans are then transported from the cacao producing areas, generally situated in isolated rural areas, to the provincial warehouses of trading and processing firms: Makassar in Sulawesi, Lampung in South Sumatra, or Medan in North Sumatra. From these provincial warehouses, the cacao beans are then shipped to the large processing facilities in Indonesia, located in the Jakarta area or in Makassar.

The Indonesian processing capacity increased considerably after 2009 when a new law was issued protecting national processing. As a consequence, the export of unprocessed cacao virtually ceased. Post-processed cacao products, mainly cocoa butter, cocoa liquor, and cocoa powder, are traded and shipped to manufacturing firms located in 'nearby' markets, for example China and the Middle East, or to the large cacao-consuming regions such as the United States, Europe, and Japan. Only a small proportion of Indonesian cacao is used domestically. The Indonesian market is not significant since chocolate is generally seen as a luxury good.

However, there is an expectation that the fast growing Indonesian economy will drive up local demand for chocolate. This would suggest, at first sight, that cacao production in Indonesia will increase. However, the recent reality is the opposite: in recent years, overall cacao production in Indonesia has decreased significantly. Whereas Indonesia produced around 600,000 tonnes of cacao in 2010, the current estimates for 2017 are about half this figure, i.e. around 375,000 tonnes (ICCO, 2016). This is a very sharp decline, so deep that it warrants explanation, if only because if it turns out that the underlying causes of this decline are not temporal or incidental, it suggests that there is something fundamentally wrong with the basis of the cacao value chain.

Looming dangers

A closer look indeed seems to indicate that the underlying problems are structural and potentially damaging to the overall cacao chain, even beyond Indonesia, if they are not adequately addressed. There are several major causes which together threaten to undermine the future of cacao production in Indonesia in the middle to long term. The first factor is the size of the average production plot in Indonesia. These plots are tiny, smaller than the two hectares required to earn a decent income. Another problem is the age of the trees. Most cacao trees were planted in the 1990s, with the help of government funding, and these trees now need replacing, but the farmers lack the capital to do so.

Another problem is the use of outdated agricultural techniques. The small cacao farmers often lack the resources, information, and education needed to innovate. Further, they often also lack the motivation to invest. The average cacao farmer is over 50, and not many have willing successors. Young people do not want to become farmers; they would prefer to go to the city where the opportunities are greater and the wages higher. Another problem is the low return on cacao compared with other cash crops such as palm oil. This induces many cacao farmers to switch to other crops. Then, last but not least, there are growing environmental problems such as changing rainfall patterns, due to climate change, and pests.

This mixture of social, economic, and ecological issues and constraints puts pressure on overall cacao production in Indonesia, a pressure that seems very likely to increase in the near future and could start to endanger the entire cacao value chain if nothing is done.

Potential answers

The dire state of the Indonesian cacao sector, and the possible negative consequences for the sector as a whole, are recognized by the main players in the value chain, in the first place by the brand-owners but also by the grinders and traders. The grinders and traders are indeed the ones who would initially lose the most in absolute money terms and market shares. They are well aware of the fact that, in the middle to long term, 'supply will no longer meet demand', as Soetanto Abdoellah, Chairman of the Indonesian Cacao Board and member of ICCRI, explained. This is all the more so because recent protectionist policies, i.e. taxing the export of raw cacao beans, have drastically increased the processing activities in Indonesia. It is critical for the processing firms, such as Cargill and Barry Callebaut, that they have a guaranteed supply, sufficient to satisfy all their newly built processing capacity. For their factories located in Indonesia, this implies ensuring a guaranteed supply from within Indonesia, since importing large quantities of raw cacao beans from other regions, such as West Africa, is not economically viable.

The position of brand-owning chocolate manufacturers with regard to the Indonesian cacao sector is more diffuse. These firms are mostly located in the northern hemisphere, i.e. in consuming regions, far away from the production areas, and, moreover, they have generally outsourced production. Direct ties between manufacturers and smallholder farmers are scarce or non-existent. These brand-owners were, until recently, completely consumer-focused. Their main goal was to keep their customers satisfied and to protect and increase their market share. They were only inclined to intervene in the upstream process if that was demanded by their customers and then only as far as required by those consumers. Since these consumers, or at least a significant part of those in western countries, indeed started to demand cacao that was more fairly and sustainably produced, these firms started to pay more attention to the upstream processes in the cacao value chain. However, this attention, which could be labelled as a form of CSR, is often limited to expressing good intentions, communication, or planning, precisely because of the great physical distance between the consumer market they serve and the upstream trade and production, and because most of these upstream processes are outsourced.

Nowadays, however, the need to protect their market share requires far deeper interventions in the cacao value chain, precisely because of the above-mentioned developments, which although they are currently most prominent in Indonesia will probably also occur elsewhere. Further, since the demand for cacao is expected to grow in the coming years, certainly in Asia, proactive measures are also required to stimulate production.

New measures, and indeed a completely new approach, are required, an approach that especially needs the far more active involvement of the largest and most wealthy players in the value chain. However, this is easier said than done: identifying the right measures requires a sophisticated approach, fine-tuned to the local circumstances.

Beyond the obvious

The future of the large manufacturers in the Indonesian cacao market depends on whether the arrangements and collaborations present in the cacao value chain are able to generate the right conditions for smallholder farmers to increase their productivity and improve their livelihoods. Private-sector players, and certainly the firms who dominate the value chain, have to play an important role in this. Indeed, we can see, in Indonesia, that these large companies have recognized their responsibilities and are in the middle of upgrading their CSR activities, albeit without labelling them as such, to include far-reaching social-ecological interventions and innovations that are intended to generate far more sustainable production methods and benefit the small-scale farmers and their social-ecological environment.

We can distinguish several policies and interventions that are conventional CSR components that have recently been redesigned by the private-sector actors in the cacao value chain. Existing CSR policies were already focusing on codes of conduct, public commitments, procurement policies, and investment in, or movement toward, certification. Now their approaches have been strengthened and transformed into global *sustainability* frameworks and programs. In parallel to these general sustainability policies and programs, the firms are developing context-specific ones that are aimed at increasing the productivity of smallholder cacao farmers. These are in the form of entrepreneurship training trajectories, certification programs, tree rehabilitation programs (replanting), and farming method optimization, including finance and accounting.

Through multi-stakeholder collaboration, leading firms are investing heavily in the development and wellbeing of their upstream stakeholders by means of so-called sustainability programs that focus on improving productivity combined with – and this is really new – community development to reverse the current decline in overall cacao production.

Measures to improve the sustainable production of cacao

A whole package of measures are being taken with the aim of improving the productivity of the cacao smallholders. One such measure aims to increase the size of the average cacao farm. The typical farm size of the one million Indonesian smallholder families currently growing cacao is between 0.5 and 1.2 hectares, whereas two hectares is the minimum required to make a decent living, i.e. to earn a comparable wage to that earned in the urban industries. The goal is to make cacao farming more attractive for existing and especially for new farmers.

Another, strongly related measure in the program is training in innovative integrative sustainable farming methods, such as agro-forestry, in order to increase the cacao yields per hectare towards the annual two tonnes required for a decent livelihood. The main players in the value chain are very aware of the need to increase the level of professionalism among the smallholder farmers. The idea is to turn them into agricultural entrepreneurs by adopting and copying the approaches previously used to upgrade the agricultural sectors in Western Europe and the United States. Here, the focus is on upscaling, agricultural innovation, improving the 'seed-nursing-harvesting' cycle, including the use of fertilizers and pesticides, and professional managing and accounting. It is accepted that the cacao sector needs a physical, technical, and organizational boost, and a demographic one. For example, Mars, the world's largest chocolate manufacturer, is aiming for a cacao sector in Indonesia that involves only 25 percent of the current number of smallholder farmers and a significant increase in productivity.

The training method that is most commonly applied in the sustainability programs is based on good agricultural practices training modules. The training aims at teaching sustainable and effective farmland practices and farm optimization, and is usually provided by 'field facilitators', usually hired in by the private firms, collaborating NGOs, or certification agencies. In these training sessions, cacao farmers learn how to prune their cacao trees properly for the best yields, how and which pesticides and fertilizers to use, and at what distance trees should be planted (because of shading issues).

Training modules are framed to comply with existing certification criteria, such as the standards set by UTZ or Rainforest Alliance. Generally, cacao farmers get a premium price for certified cacao beans, ensuring the commitment of smallholder farmers to deliver their cacao beans to the private firms who procure most of the certified cacao. The certification criteria stipulate the types of pesticides and fertilizers that can be used and their correct usage and doses.

But private firms clearly express their limited belief in the impact of certification on their sustainability programs. According to Andi Sitti Asmayanti, Southeast Asia sustainability manager of Mondelez International in Indonesia, certification is 'just a tool' and the sustainability program of Mondelez Cacao Life is a quality mark in itself and one 'that goes beyond certification'. Aspects that 'go beyond' regular certification are the premiums paid to the farmers (the whole premium goes directly to the farmers rather than to the certificate holder) and reliable third-party monitoring and verification.

Apart from that there are efforts to strengthen the capacities of farmers' groups and cooperatives to jointly buy pesticides and fertilizers, and there are pilot projects aimed at the production of organic pesticides and fertilizers. In some programs, the role of the supplier of sustainable agro-inputs is centralized around local and district middle men who link the smallholder farmers directly to the major purchasers such as Cargill, Barry Callebaut, BT Cocoa, and Olam.

The training programs are also very much geared towards rehabilitating the cacao farms. Many farms need to be gradually rehabilitated (i.e. replanted), preferably with modern and superior cacao varieties. Gradually, because cacao trees generally only start yielding beans after five years. Rehabilitation is strongly interrelated with the professionalization of cacao farmers. It is a capital intensive and long-term process for which most current farmers do not have the financial means, nor the necessary vision and motivation. Buying new cacao varieties, while at the same time seeing less profit because of smaller productive areas, makes rehabilitation not only costly but also a complex process and difficult to organize. At various moments throughout this process, cacao farmers need to be trained and guided.

The cacao production areas are scattered across Indonesia and are located in different climate zones, with various types of soil, pests, and diseases. Thus, for every region in Indonesia, different varieties of cacao trees need to be cloned. According to the Director Sustainable Agriculture Development and Procurement of Nestlé, the central Indonesian government tried to massively encourage rehabilitation by distributing over 75 million of such new variety trees in a three-year period starting in 2009. However, this policy is generally regarded as a failure because most plantlets were incorrectly planted or not suited to their environment. Nowadays, the Indonesia Coffee and Cacao Research Institute (ICCRI), a government-funded institute, focuses on the development of new tree varieties and new forest-friendly production methods and techniques. ICCRI collaborates with other actors in the cacao sector, including civil society organizations, the Ministry of Agriculture, and the private sector. Recently, they have developed cacao clones for different parts of Indonesia that are expected to produce high yields, even if climate change continues.

Currently, private actors are stimulating the establishment of local cacao nurseries, but their strategies differ. Cargill, for example, focuses on a greater role for middle men, while Mars invests in farmer cooperatives, in collaboration with Swisscontact, a non-profit organization aiming at reducing poverty in developing and transition countries by means of private-sector development.

The whole process of rehabilitation cannot be done without new forms of financing that give small entrepreneurs access to long-term credit on reasonable rent conditions. Most smallholder cacao farmers now lack that access and indeed the knowledge to handle long-term credit. In order to create professional farmers, private-sector actors are increasingly looking at new business models allowing smallholders easier and more manageable access to finance. Nestlé does this, in collaboration with national and international banks, other financial institutions (IFC), and civil society actors (such as IDH in Indonesia). Mars is looking at possibilities of self-financing, an idea that once stood at the basis of the large farmers banks of Germany and the Netherlands, i.e. the *Raiffeisenbank* in Germany and the *Boerenleenbank* (nowadays the RaboBank) in the Netherlands. The general idea is to use E-tools to analyze cacao farms and assess the kinds of changes and investments that have to be made within specific timeframes (medium and long term). Individual smallholder cacao farmers are receiving training on 'good financial practices' and are learning how to manage income and the repayment of loans.

Measure to stimulate community development

The second major category of measures in the sustainability programs of private firms in the Indonesian cacao sector addresses community development. There are very different perspectives and approaches. However, community development is evidently far more complicated to realize than production improvement, certainly for organizations and firms not primarily designed and equipped to do so. Consequently, it is still very problematic for private firms to develop realistic options to address the different needs of the various and diverse cacao-growing communities, and to counterbalance the drivers now pushing young people out of the rural communities towards the towns, leaving their parents without successors for their (cacao) farms.

However, Mars is actively investigating the social-cultural and social-economic dimensions of community life in Indonesia. They are particularly looking for the intrinsic motivation for people to stay in the region and become a cacao farmer. Mondelez has an even more specific and explicit view and policy regarding the development of cacao communities that are part of their sustainability programs. Through a 'community action plan', they are supporting and facilitating local communities to collectively come up with plans to develop their own community. These plans are submitted to local and regional governments to seek funding. The components and outputs of these community action plans vary depending on the specific needs of the community, and range from improved infrastructure and livestock-raising groups to clean sanitation and safe drinking-water schemes, and even plans for protection against flooding. By building the communal capacity to design local plans and policies, and also to assist them in obtaining funding during the implementation process, Mondelez explores the specific needs of their communities and tries to reflect these in their sustainability programs.

All in all, we see surprisingly deep interest and intervention in the local production conditions high up in the cacao value chain by firms themselves that are mainly active at the other end of the chain. This is quite revolutionary and new in fact.

The CSR paradox

This interest in the broader production conditions is even more remarkable when we consider that the main players in the Indonesian cacao chain, the multinationals, with their faraway headquarters, were until recently completely consumer focused, with no or almost no interest in upstream activities, and certainly not in the local production and livelihood conditions of small-scale cacao farmers. This is quite a remarkable development.

As remarkable as this switch towards more social corporate behavior is, the fact is that these firms do not seem to relate their new concerns and quite revolutionary activities to the ideas of CSR. They even refuse to use the notion. This is indeed remarkable given that one would expect the large, consumer-dependent, multinationals that dominate the cacao chain to be very eager to make this link. All the more so given the nature of CSR, which is often more about demonstrating what a firm does or plans to do than about the actual doing. The latter is a far more understandable strategy given the fact that CSR is a rather recent obligation, externally imposed on firms and enforced by consumers and civil society organizations, that requires activities that exceed and may even hinder core business. CSR is a form of self-regulation by business. For a long time, paraphrasing the famous dictum of Friedman (1970), the business of business was only to do business, i.e. to make a profit. That is, CSR has become an additional responsibility and exists because of pressure from consumers and civil society organizations, not governments. If it was government pressure, we would just talk about legislation and doing business within the limits of the existing legislation, which is, to cite Friedman again, as normal as doing business for the sake of business. CSR is, to sum up, a 'voluntary', extra-firm activity, going beyond government prescription and regulation, but, at the same time, an approach that integrates social 'responsibilities' into the firm's core business (see also Knippenberg and de Jong, 2010). It is also an activity that is taken especially seriously by firms that are strongly dependent on western consumers, a category in which the multinationals dominating the cacao value chain clearly fit. This all points towards a discrepancy, or at least a paradox, that deserves an explanation. We see it as a paradox, rather than a contradiction, for the following reasons.

First, as we set out in an earlier article on CSR and the firm (Knippenberg and de Jong, 2010), CSR is too broad and vague a notion and approach to be applied beyond the planning and communication level of a firm, certainly in a large firm. Whether and how CSR-related activities can be applied on the operational level is strongly firm and sector dependent. In practice, CSR has to be tailored to its planned use and the specific needs of specific firms within a given sector (Newell and Frynas, 2007; Van Marrewijk, 2003). As a consequence, the CSR notion can be used to refer to almost anything, from health and safety policy to environmental management, while the position of the firm – as the main implementer of CSR – has often not been adequately addressed (see Knippenberg and de Jong, 2010). These developments have led to firms reducing their interest in the CSR concept: they consider it as too broad with regard to meaning and too narrow in terms of applicability.

Further, and this is our second explanation, globalization, with the accompanying growth of multinational firms and outsourcing, has extended the value chain of almost all products. Most consumer goods contain components produced elsewhere, sometimes on the other side of the world, or require value-adding activities elsewhere. For instance, a considerable volume of cacao is processed in Amsterdam; all cars, wherever they are produced, contain components sourced from all over the world; and even Chinese pork meat might come from Dutch pigs, nourished with cassava originating in, for instance, Vietnam. In practice, CSR is too narrow a concept to encompass this complexity, even for multinational firms, and especially because of the length and complexity of contemporary value chains. In response, other concepts have been developed to analyze the organization of contemporary transnational systems of production and consumption, such as supply chain management, global commodity chains, global production networks, and global value chains. Studying such chains as a whole has become essential, especially since state authorities have increasingly lost the capacity to regulate contemporary developments caused by globalization. This is most evident in developing countries with institutional contexts that are frequently new and fragile (Newell and Frynas, 2007). All kinds of private or hybrid (public-private) governance arrangements have emerged to fill this gap (Boström et al., 2015). The global value chain literature ascribes a key role in the value chain to downstream multinational firm actors because these generally fill a central position in the coordination and governance of the relationships and negotiations regarding sustainability governance between actors in the global value chains, in the design of sustainability governance arrangements, and in their implementation (Bush et al., 2015; Gibbon et al., 2008).

A third explanation can be found in the problems of applying CSR in the context of developing countries, such as institutional weaknesses, the lack of implementation possibilities, limited inclusion and participation, and a lack of willingness of stakeholders to collaborate. Further, CSR is often seen as an imposed activity: imposed from outside the country and as an activity that is not required to do business and may even hamper it. CSR is considered to be inherently political and conflictual, if not paternalistic, as the actors involved have competing priorities, ideas, and motivations in achieving their developmental goals (Newell and Frynas, 2007, p. 676). Moreover, globally formulated CSR promises and policies are, as has been shown for the Indonesian situation, difficult to translate into workable, context-specific policies and programs in practice.

A fourth explanation can be found in the growing awareness among businesses, and certainly the larger ones, that some environmental issues can no longer be ignored without endangering future business prospects, and that environmental, social, political, and economic issues have a growing tendency to merge or at least to contaminate one another. This development has recently been referred to using the term social-ecological transition. This problem is deepened by the fact that governments are often no longer capable of tackling these issues on their own and certainly not in developing countries (see de Jong, Knippenberg, and Bakker, 2017). Sustainability is no longer an empty term for many multinational firms, especially those active in natural resource processing. Here sustainability refers to the broader notion: containing and balancing the social, economic, and ecological pillars or domains (Hermans and Knippenberg, 2006).

The sustainability managers of the leading firms all highlight the importance of a sustainable Indonesian cacao sector. The Director of the Sustainability Department of Nestlé phrased it as follows: 'What all stakeholders need to understand is that helping farmers to be sustainable is a good business'. The Cacao Development Director of Mars pointed out the need for sustainable ways to source raw materials, especially in relation to their long-term availability. The Executive Director of the CSP, also acknowledges this concern:

> [sustainability programs are] more likely to be integrated in a company's strategy . . . It is not really like common CSR in which the corporate social responsibility is just for the people around them [stakeholders] and their consumers. It is integrated into the business: in cacao it is very much related to the sources [of raw materials] in their supply chain. It is not really about being good to the people, but also looking to the business strategy.

Interestingly, leading firms are voluntarily investing considerable resources in specific policies (from procurement policies to codes of conduct), programs, certification procedures, standardization schemes, and so on, all under the banner of sustainability and explicitly not under that of CSR. However, these investments and efforts are clear signs of the leading firms having a sense of responsibility for their impact on society and the natural environment as well as the behavior and wellbeing of their stakeholders, i.e. the smallholder cacao farmers. This is the situation that we call the CSR paradox: one in which firms invest extensively in CSR policies and interventions but fail or refuse to acknowledge that they are doing so.

Most of the leading firms' managers perceive CSR as a notion merely carrying out some small, largely external, activities, more or less as a charity, and not about integrating their social and ecological responsibilities so deeply in the core business of the firm that they become an undistinguishable part of that business. However, although they reject or overlook these 'holistic' aspects of CSR, when asked, in practice more and more act according to them. See, for instance, this quote from Nestlé's Director of Sustainable Agriculture Development and Procurement: 'We don't have CSR; we don't have money that is put aside to help this. We bring [sustainability] into our business model; it is part of the costs of raw materials for us'.

Conclusions

We see that in the cacao value chain a silent revolution is going on, linking the interests of the large multinational downstream players, like Nestlé or Mars, directly with the long-term interests of the small-scale cacao producers and their communities. These major players indeed have started to sustainably upgrade the economic, social, and ecological conditions of the local small-scale cacao production with a special attention for the social conditions of the producers and their communities. That is a development which not that long ago would have been applauded by all advocates of the notion CSR. Considering this, it is even more remarkable that the firms themselves do not regard these activities as CSR, or even reject the notion.

We explained earlier that these developments do not point to a contradiction but rather to a paradox which boils down to the fact that the issues and aspects commonly labelled as CSR are considered less important in the context of the cacao value chain, precisely because those issues and aspects have been internalized and become part of the core business and the value chain as a whole. This is why the head of Barry Callebaut's Sustainability Indonesia Department felt able to clearly state:

> We aim at the ultimate goal: productivity, and then the livelihood of the farmers. We do not call this CSR, it is a bit different from CSR because what we need to do is also to ensure that the sustainability of Barry Callebaut is met. CSR [comes] under a different category, which is more on the community development, we build houses, we also build schools, and we provide clean water.

We think that these developments in the cacao value chain herald a new development and demand a new perspective on CSR, at least with regard to natural resource value chains and the interaction between upstream and downstream activities and priorities.

We argue that apart from paying more attention to the firm level, CSR should focus on the value chain, and within that value chain, shift from an overwhelmingly downstream, consumer-oriented approach towards a more upstream, producer-oriented approach. We indeed strongly plead for a more balanced approach in which sustainability in the broader sense fulfills a pivotal role, i.e. sustainability as the balanced durable improvement of social, economic, and ecological production and consumption conditions within a given value chain, without negative tradeoffs between these three domains of conditions.

Notes

1 In African countries each hectare produces 300 to 400 kg of cacao beans and in the Latin American region it is about 500 to 600 kg (World Cocoa Foundation, 2014, p. 2).

2 Cacao is the name used for the raw material of the cacao beans. The name cocoa refers to the heated form of cacao. In the value chain literature both terms are used interchangeably. We use the notion cacao.

References

Bitzer, V., M. Francken, and P. Glasbergen. (2008). Intersectoral partnerships for a sustainable coffee chain: Really addressing sustainability or just picking (coffee) cherries? *Global Environmental Change*, 18(2), 271–284.

Boström, M., A.M. Jönsson, S. Lockie, A.P.J. Mol, and P. Oosterveer. (2015). Sustainable and responsible supply chain governance: Challenges and opportunities. *Journal of Cleaner Production*, 107, 1–7.

Bush, S.R., P. Oosterveer, M. Bailey, and A.P.J. Mol. (2015). Sustainability governance of chains and networks: A review and future outlook. *Journal of Cleaner Production*, 107, 8–19.

Candy Industry. (2017). *Global Top 100 Confectionery Companies*. Website accessed on 4 April 2017: www.candyindustry.com/articles/87585-the-top-100-candy-companies-in-the-world-in-2017.

Fountain, A.C. and F. Hütz-Adams. (2015). *Cocoa Barometer 2015: USA Edition*. Cocoa Barometer. Website accessed on 15 August 2018. www.cocoabarometer.org/Cocoa_Barometer/About.html.

Friedman, M. (1970). The social responsibility of business is to increase its profits. *The New York Times Magazine*, September 13, 1–5.

Gibbon, P., J. Bair, and S. Ponte. (2008). Governing global value chains: An introduction. *Economy and Society*, 37(3), 315–338.

Hermans, F. and L. Knippenberg. (2006). A principle-based approach for the evaluation of sustainable development. *Journal of Environmental Assessment Policy and Management*, 8(3), 299–319.

ICCO. (2016). Production of Cocoa Beans. *ICCO Quarterly Bulletin of Cocoa Statistics*, 42(1). Website accessed on 15 August 2018. www.marketscreener.com/news/ICCO-International-Cocoa-Organization-Quarterly-Bulletin-of-Cocoa-Statistics-November-2016--23481143/.

Jong, de, E.B.P., L. Knippenberg, and L. Bakker. 2017. New frontiers: An enriched perspective on extraction frontiers in Indonesia. *Critical Asian Studies*, 49(3), 330–348.

Knippenberg, L. and E.B.P. de Jong. (2010). Moralising the market by moralising the firm. *Journal of Business Ethics*, 96(1), 17–31.

Merino, A. and C. Valor. (2011). The potential of corporate social responsibility to eradicate poverty: An ongoing debate. *Development in Practice*, 21(2), 157–167.

Newell, P. and J.G. Frynas. (2007). Beyond CSR? Business, poverty and social justice: An introduction. *Third World Quarterly*, 28(4), 669–681.

Van Marrewijk, M. (2003). Concepts and definitions of CSR and corporate sustainability: Between agency and communion. *Journal of Business Ethics*, 44(2), 95–105.

World Cocoa Foundation. (2014). *Cacao Market Update, 2014*. Washignton, DC: World Cocoa Foundation.

4.5 On the infusion of ethics in entrepreneurial and managerial action

Reconciling actors' CSR-related perceptions in the Malawian tea industry

Introduction

There is little doubt that corporate social responsibility (CSR) remains a contested concept as evidenced to a large degree by a wide variation in the practices companies undertake across different countries (Lindgreen et al., 2009). It tends to be used interchangeably with other concepts such as corporate citizenship (Carroll, 1998, 2015; Matten and Crane, 2005; Moon et al., 2005), corporate social investment (Fig, 2005), corporate social performance and public responsibility (Preston and Post, 1975; Sethi, 1975; Wood, 1991), sustainability (Elkington, 1997) and business ethics (Joyner and Payne, 2002). Among the many reasons for such a contention is that, as many scholars suggest, CSR interpretation is linked to contextual factors within the countries where it is implemented (Brammer et al., 2012; Freeman and Hasnaoui, 2011; Gjølberg, 2009; Kayuni and Tambulasi, 2012; Matten and Moon, 2008). While there is wide agreement that the conceptualisation of CSR and its associated practices tend to vary across different countries, several scholars have pointed out the existence of a gap between globally accepted practices and local priorities especially in the societies of those developing countries where multinational companies are widely considered to be the drivers of the mainstream CSR agenda (Carroll, 2015; Idemudia, 2007, 2011; Muthuri and Gilbert, 2011; Robertson, 2009). However, there is much we still do not know about how the varied understandings of the concept of CSR by various actors in the developing world help such companies reconcile competing demands in foreign countries (Idemudia, 2007; Jamali, 2010; Kolk and Lenfant, 2010).

Over three decades since Carroll developed the model for understanding CSR, CSR and business ethics literature has been inundated not only by studies that have tested the applicability of his model in different contexts but also by the models that have tested and questioned the relevance of Carroll's models beyond North American and Western European regions. A significant majority of these studies, however, tend to be overtly focused on the developed countries and, more recently, on the emerging economies, in particular China, India, South Africa and Nigeria (Amaeshi et al., 2014; Arora and Puranik, 2004; Eweje, 2006; Hamann, 2003; Hamann and Kapelus, 2004; Kolk et al., forthcoming; Okpara and Wynn, 2012). In contrast, there is a shortage of research studies in CSR and business ethics literature which focuses on developing countries especially in Sub-Saharan Africa, although in recent times some efforts have been made to develop an understanding of the CSR agenda in such countries (Amaeshi et al., 2015; Azmat and Samaratunge, 2009; Egri and Ralston, 2008; Kolk and Lenfant, 2010; Lindgreen et al., 2010; Muthuri and Gilbert, 2011; Mutti et al., 2012). Yet, by over-researching the notion of CSR in the developed countries, we are depriving the academic and business community of the insights into different CSR understandings that exist within developing countries where CSR is much needed given the pervasive influence of social, economic and political factors on business–society relations in these areas. Evidence, for example, suggests that firms' managers and stakeholders can have a strong bearing on the moral or ethical direction a firm or company may pursue within society (Maon et al., 2008; Pedersen, 2010). Certainly, alignment of managers' and stakeholders' perceptions about CSR can enhance the likelihood of any CSR programme having a long-lasting impact. It is imperative, therefore, that we understand how managers and stakeholders view the social responsibilities companies may have in developing countries so that we appreciate the challenges the subsidiaries of multinational companies may encounter as they align their CSR agendas with local expectations and priorities (Kolk and Lenfant, 2010).

This chapter explores managerial and stakeholder understanding of the nature of social responsibilities in Malawi, a country that is rapidly integrating into the global economy. In this study, we use Eastern Produce Malawi Limited ('Eastern Produce Malawi'), a tea-producing company that is a subsidiary of a UK-based multinational company, Camellia International plc, as our case study organisation. We selected Eastern Produce Malawi for two major reasons. First, Eastern Produce Malawi – an international CSR related award winner in 2009 – is a leader in the CSR agenda in Malawi – an environment where enabling factors are almost non-existent. Second, by virtue of being a subsidiary of a western-based multinational company, it provides a fertile ground for exploring the reconciliation of the developed countries' understanding of CSR and the local expectations and conceptions of a company's social responsibilities (Amaeshi et al., 2014; Idemudia, 2007; Kolk and Lenfant, 2010).

We review the prominent CSR models by Carroll (1979, 1991) and Visser (2007), but also empirical studies that have tested Carroll's models in different contexts. We argue that while the majority of scholarly contributions have tended to conceptualise CSR in a manner that reflects a leaning towards an instrumental perspective – increasing shareholder value (for example, Aupperle et al., 1985; Kolk et al., forthcoming; Maignan and Ralston, 2002; Pinkston and Carroll, 1994, 1996), in this study we adopt a broader normative approach in understanding the nature of social responsibilities a company can assume in a given society (O'Dwyer, 2003; Okpara and Wynn, 2012). This chapter thus seeks to answer the following question: How do corporate managers and stakeholders based in the developing world interpret the notion of CSR?

The remainder of this chapter is organised as follows. The next section provides a review of the literature that deals with different interpretations of CSR across various contexts, including Carroll's and Visser's models of social responsibilities. We then proceed to describe the study methodology. This is then followed by a presentation and discussion of the research findings. We conclude the chapter with implications for research, practice and policy, but also identify areas for further research.

Literature review

CSR has been the focus of intense academic debates since as early as 1916 (Clark, 1916; see also Carroll, 1979, 1991; Frederick, 1960; Levitt, 1958; McGuire et al., 1988; McWilliams and Siegel, 2001). Over the years, the demands and expectations of society regarding the role of business have evolved, but the consistently contentious issue has been finding a unified definition of the exact social responsibilities of firms (Carroll, 1979, 1991; Dahlsrud, 2008; Wood, 1991). This chapter largely draws on Carroll's models (1979, 1991) and the subsequent perspectives that were either inspired by his framework (Carroll and Shabana, 2010; Maignan and Ralston, 2002; Pinkston and Carroll, 1994; Schwartz and Carroll, 2003; Visser, 2008; Windsor, 2006) or have questioned their universal applicability (Carroll, 2004; Kolk et al., forthcoming; Visser, 2007, 2008).

Carroll's pyramid of corporate social responsibilities

Carroll's (1979) model is considered a solid attempt at understanding the different nature of responsibilities companies can assume in society, integrating the precursor models of social responsibilities (McGuire, 1963; Sethi, 1975). His widely used definition lays out some responsibilities companies might assume in modern society: 'the social responsibility of business that encompasses the economic, legal, ethical, and discretionary categories of the business performance at a given point in time' (Carroll, 1979, p. 499). As a matter of clarity, Carroll organised the four forms of responsibilities into three main groups, and he assigned a non-numerical weighting to each form. The first group – the required responsibilities – comprises the economic and legal obligations which are largely mandatory. The second group – the expected responsibilities – includes ethical responsibilities. The final group – the 'desired' responsibilities – are philanthropic and discretionary in nature and are considered desirable for the wellbeing of society and stakeholders. The expected responsibilities can broadly be regarded as minimalist and essential to the achievement of the company's long-term interests (Windsor, 2006). In this chapter, however, in reviewing Carroll's model, the social responsibilities will be organised into four levels: economic, legal, ethical and philanthropic responsibilities.

Required responsibilities

The first form of required responsibilities of companies in a given society is the economic responsibilities. Companies are seen to undertake their economic responsibilities in society when they are perceived to primarily respond to shareholders' interests by operating profitably (Henderson, 2005). As companies do not operate in a vacuum, their other economic responsibilities include production of goods and services that are desirable by the society in which they operate. Accordingly, economic responsibilities are the most critical responsibilities that a company ought to assume before managers embark on the three remaining responsibilities. While this view is plausible in practice, the only downside is that managers who draw inspiration from the classical school of thought (Henderson, 2005), if left unchecked, could use such a perspective as an excuse to promote their own self-interests and those of their shareholders at the expense of the public good (Wan-Jan, 2006; Windsor, 2006).

Legal responsibilities, a second form of the required social responsibilities, represent those actions undertaken by companies to operate within the rule of law imposed on them by the society in which they perform their economic responsibilities. Carroll (1991) regarded such responsibilities in part as ethical values of a society which are codified to serve as the social contract between businesses and society. Thus, in the event that either party (society or business) contravenes such a contract, the codified terms encompassed in such a contract are much likely to determine the nature of rewards and punishment the contravening or the aggrieved party receives. The critical question is: what really should be considered as the legal responsibilities of the company within the society where they operate, given the divergent positions scholars take with respect to a company's legal obligations (Campbell, 2007; De Schutter, 2008; Maitland, 1985; Shauki, 2011; Vives, 2004). On the one hand, some CSR theorists argue that the legal responsibilities are an end in themselves (Maitland, 1985; Vives, 2004). Thus, by meeting the obligations as enshrined in the legal framework, companies are playing their part in meeting their social responsibilities. This view, however, risks being viewed as minimalist since it assumes that a mere response to legal frameworks could equally be taken as a company's fulfilment of its social responsibilities. Furthermore, this perspective fails to take into account the existence of opportunistic behaviour companies can pursue to take advantage of non-stringent regulations that exist in a particular country (Schwartz and Carroll, 2003).

On the other hand, some theorists in the expansive school of thought consider legal responsibilities as one part of the broader responsibilities companies can assume in society. Given the other group of scholars' views on the existence of market failures and the lack of genuine commitment by companies to social issues, there have been calls for CSR to be regulated to broaden the scope of firms' legal responsibilities within their societies (Deegan and Shelly, 2014; Preston and Post, 1975). The call apparently finds support in Brammer et al. (2012) who argue that in the institutional settings where there is 'implicit' CSR, the social responsibilities of companies are more likely to be influenced by regulations and some quasi arrangements by most powerful stakeholder groups such as the trade unions. However, this view has been criticised for its potential to stifle innovation in CSR but also for its tendency towards the promotion of the erosion of the voluntary spirit of the notion of social obligations (Sethi, 1975; Wood, 1991). Nevertheless, the existence of such contrasting perspectives may be problematic in societies where regulatory regimes for corporate behaviour are less stringent. Free-riding problems are ubiquitous, and the markets do not effectively reward socially responsible behaviour or punish unethical business practices. This underscores the need for a balanced approach in the pursuit of normative objectives and instrumental rationality (Ayres and Braithewaite, 1992; Scherer and Palazzo, 2011).

Expected responsibilities

Ethical responsibilities – the sole form of expected responsibilities – occupy the third level within Carroll's pyramid of CSR. Such responsibilities call for companies to undertake actions that go beyond minimal compliance with regulations. They also reflect what is considered morally right by society. Other scholars consider such responsibilities in terms of corporate commitment to be calls for behaviour that promotes strong moral judgement on issues of social justice and stakeholder rights (Preston and Post, 1975; Windsor, 2006; Wood, 1991). For Carroll (1991), ethical obligations on companies represent standards, norms and expectations which originate from the moral concerns of stakeholder groups. In recent times, companies have commited to meeting such standards and norms by developing and implementing codes of conduct (Kaptein and Schwartz, 2008). The fundamental issue, however, has been the framing of ethical responsibilities in this manner as these appear rather less clear cut with an increasing concern regarding their legitimacy as a form of CSR (Wan-Jan, 2006; Windsor, 2006) because companies may still have a moral obligation to respond to the needs of stakeholders (Donaldson and Preston, 1995). Furthermore, the problem with Carroll (1991)'s conceptualisation of ethical responsibilities is that it does not explicitly tackle the notions of ethical relativism and context and what constitutes 'society'. It is without doubt that the concept of society encompasses a collection of different actors including businesses and their stakeholders, communities and the general citizen (Donaldson and Preston, 1995; Hine and Preuss, 2009). The plurality of the actors within a particular society means that the societal norms and expectations are more likely to be varied depending on the different stakeholder groups, and that ethical responsibilities or what is considered to be 'right or wrong' ought not to be viewed as a 'one size fits all' approach (Maignan and Ralston, 2002; Schwartz and Carroll, 2003).

Desired responsibilities

The desired responsibilities, which include corporate philanthropy, represent actions that a company undertakes to contribute to the general welfare of society. These responsibilities occupy the bottom of Carroll's pyramid and are broadly associated with some form of managerial discretion in the spending of shareholder funds (Carroll and Shabana, 2010; Windsor, 2006). For Carroll, philanthropy is considered a voluntary undertaking that is desirable by society and some stakeholders. Thus, it is not surprising that in his subsequent contribution to the debate – a three-domain approach (Schwartz and Carroll, 2003) – philanthropic responsibilities do not appear as they are not regarded as a 'duty or social responsibility of business, but something that is beyond what duty requires' (2003, p. 506).

Critics argue, however, that corporate engagement in philanthropy is a gross violation of fiduciary duties or responsibility by managers and a distortion of the markets (Henderson, 2005). Others, however, take a limited perspective on the role of business in society but also gravely underestimate the wider contribution philanthropic responsibilities can make to the long-term interests of companies (Lantos, 2001). Corporate philanthropy, if implemented in a strategic manner, can equally enhance the image of the benevolent company in the eyes of stakeholders and help it generate business opportunities (Halme and Laurila, 2009; Windsor, 2006). Nevertheless, by virtue of philanthropic responsibilities being dependent on managerial discretion, in the economic downturn, such responsibilities are much likely to face the 'chop' as managers work towards cost minimisation. Thus, this position is likely to be adopted by managers who are inspired by the 'slack resources or available fund' theory that posits that firms are motivated to invest in social issues only where there is a good indication of a strong financial performance (Cheng and Kenser 1997; Waddock and Graves 1997).

Implications of Carroll's models

Carroll's models have a number of wider implications. First, to meet the key obligations stipulated in these models, it may be imperative for managers to make decisions that not only serve their enlightened self-interests but also enhance the welfare of society in general, such as mitigating or compensating for the harm their company's operations may cause (Richter, 2010). However, in the present form, Carroll's models, in particular the three domain model (Schwartz and Carroll, 2003) in which the philanthropic responsibilities are entirely collapsed, fail to persuade scholars that it is a stark contrast to the classical perspective advanced by scholars such as Henderson (2005).

Second, these models suggest that any decisions managers can make should consider the interests of multiple stakeholders that can affect or are affected by the company's activities (Carroll, 2015; Donaldson and Preston, 1995; Noland and Phillips, 2010). Fundamental to the understanding of social responsibilities a company can assume in a given society is the identification of prominent stakeholder groups at which companies can target specific responsibilities (Maignan and Ralston, 2002). These models are apparently a response to the approach taken by some of the CSR theorists which failed to take into consideration the needs and interests of individual stakeholder groups (Carroll, 2004). To achieve such an alignment, managers would need to draw on the deontological perspective that requires managers to address the claims and moral rights of each stakeholder group. Third, Carroll's models highlight the significance of understanding the contextual factors in determining the direction in which each of the four components can change when it comes to their prioritisation in different countries other than those countries of the North American region where these models originated (Carroll, 2004; Pinkston and Carroll, 1994; Silberhorn and Warren, 2007; Visser, 2007, 2008).

Visser's CSR pyramid for Africa

Visser (2007) reorganised the four levels of CSR in Carroll's pyramid to reflect the priorities of African societies. Like Carroll, the most important responsibilities in Africa are the economic responsibilities. Unlike Carroll (1979, 1991), economic responsibilities are followed by the discretionary responsibilities, legal and ethical responsibilities.

For Visser, the general perception of the stakeholders and businesses in Africa is that a company undertakes its economic responsibilities when it engages in broader economic development activities such as production of goods and services at a profit, payment of taxes, provision of employment, making investment and creation of business opportunities within its host communities. Such an understanding of companies' economic responsibilities, however, seems at odds with Carroll's (1979, 1991) conceptualisation which is based on narrow liberal and western values of increasing shareholder value but which nonetheless resonates well with the perceptions in continental Europe.

Visser suggests that philanthropic responsibilities are ranked second because the poor socio-economic conditions in African countries compel companies and society in general to regard business engagement in corporate donations as a good thing to do. Furthermore, for many companies, taking an active role in such action can be considered to be in their own self-interest as companies would find it extremely difficult to operate in an environment with social malaise (Rosen et al., 2003). The strong and positive perception of philanthropic responsibilities largely reflects the cultural traditions of 'umunthu' or 'ubuntu'[1] and the influence of religion which all encourage charitable actions (Idemudia, 2014; Kayuni and Tambulasi, 2012; Visser, 2005). Because philanthropy is deeply seated in these societies, CSR is usually equated to philanthropy (Muthuri, 2013).

The third most prioritised responsibility in Africa according to Visser's pyramid for Africa are the legal responsibilities. Visser (2007) is quick to point out, however, that a lower ranking does not necessarily suggest that companies do not take their legal responsibilities seriously, but in the African societies legal frameworks or regimes are usually less stringent and are associated with poor enforcement. He further notes that such a lukewarm approach by African governments to strict legal obligations may suggest that wider societies in general do not strongly emphasise the regulation of corporate practices. The low emphasis African societies attach to legal responsibilities is at odds with Carroll's prioritization, which is to a large extent based on the stringent corporate legislative regimes in the liberal and social democratic societies in the western world (Brammer et al., 2012;

Maignan and Ralston, 2002; O'Dwyer, 2003; Silberhorn and Warren, 2007). In part, the quest to attract foreign investors could explain why in most Sub-Saharan African countries, corporate regulations have not featured prominently (Hamann and Kapelus, 2004; Idemudia, 2014; Kamlongera, 2013; Kuada and Hinson, 2012).

Visser (2007) notes that ethical responsibilities are the least prioritised form of social responsibilities in the majority of African countries. Such an assertion is not surprising given the scale of corruption and fraud-related scandals that are widespread in African countries and the annual positions most of the African countries occupy in the global ranking on corruption perception (Idemudia et al., 2010). Nevertheless, in recent years, there has been a realisation of the negative impact of unethical practices on the competitiveness of the continent in attracting much-needed foreign direct investment (GTZ, 2009). Certainly, private companies, the stock markets and a few governments are strongly showing their commitment towards addressing the widespread corruption and bribery practices by, among other things, developing and implementing codes of conduct for employees and suppliers, putting social and environmental performance at the centre of the stock markets' listing requirements and the adoption of the Extractive Industries Transparency Initiative (Sonnenburg and Hamann, 2006). Such a change in orientation is shown in a recent study by Kuada and Hinson (2012) in Ghana where managers of local firms were more likely to implement programmes that addressed ethical dilemmas than those managers in foreign-owned companies. Kuada and Hinson (2012) attribute external factors such as pressure from international markets and international regulations – where most of the local firms market their products – as significant drivers for local firms' orientation to ethical issues.

While conceptualisation of CSR in Africa remains one of the significant contributions to debates about the understanding of the notion of CSR across nations, his pyramid of CSR may be prone to similar accusations to which Carroll's models are subjected. The fundamental weakness is that the model treats African countries as homogenous with similar cultural traditions and similar degrees of exposure to international debates about CSR. However, recent studies show variations exist in the understanding of the notions of CSR across different countries within Africa (Amaeshi et al., 2014, 2015; Kuada and Hinson, 2012), with Lindgreen et al. (2010) for example, showing that in Malawi and Botswana, economic and ethical responsibilities are being prioritised over philanthropic responsibilities. Such an assertion suggests that Visser's model may still not be in a better position to capture the direction of change in CSR orientation in Africa.

Cross-national empirical studies on the relevance of Carroll's and Visser's models of CSR

The early application of Carroll's models was undertaken in the USA in the 1970s, although it gained traction in the 1980s and beyond with a limited number of European countries being regarded as test-beds (Aupperle et al., 1985; Cowton, 1987; Lindgreen et al., 2009; Pinkston and Carroll, 1994, 1996). These studies mainly focused on the investigation of managerial understanding of CSR with respect to the four domains. For example, Aupperle et al. (1985) and Pinkston and Carroll (1996) conducted a study of managers in the USA and confirmed the non-numerical weighting of Carroll's conceptualisation by revealing that managers gave the highest priority to economic responsibilities, followed by legal, ethical and discretionary responsibilities, although Pinkston and Carroll (1996) observed an increasing convergence between economic and legal responsibilities in terms of rankings. Such a convergence was in the later years confirmed by studies on consumer's CSR perceptions, which attributed equal weighting between economic and legal responsibilities to the USA's increased propensity towards litigation for corporate wrong doing.

In Europe, studies which focused on managerial and stakeholders' prioritisation of the four forms of social responsibilities revealed a mixed picture (Brammer et al., 2012; Campbell et al., 2002; Cowton, 1987; Maignan and Ralston, 2002; O'Dwyer, 2003; Silberhorn and Warren, 2007). A significant majority of these studies reported that economic responsibilities continued to dominate in the managerial ranking of social responsibilities in the Republic of Ireland and the UK, although in both these countries, ethical and philanthropic responsibilities appeared to be gaining prominence in the minds of managers (O'Dwyer, 2003; Silberhorn and Warren, 2007). In contrast, in Germany, Sweden and France, consumers ranked legal and ethical responsibilities highly as compared to economic responsibilities (Pinkston and Carroll, 1994). The cross-country variation of CSR conceptions observed in these studies largely reflects the influence of the institutional and contextual factors in the understanding and prioritisation of the different forms of social responsibilities (Brammer et al., 2012; Gjølberg, 2009). For example, in the UK and the USA the influence of liberal and individualistic values means that companies would always view philanthropic and ethical responsibilities as non-legally binding and would always prioritise economic and legal responsibilities because they are instrumental towards satisfying the company's enlightened self-interest (Schwartz and Carroll, 2003). Certainly, in liberal societies, there is a general understanding that companies should have the freedom to pursue their own interests as long as it was within the laws of the land. In contrast, in the more communitarian or social democratic societies such as Germany, France and Sweden, philanthropic and ethical responsibilities are highly prioritised because such societies consider that issues of general societal wellbeing are too precious to be entirely left to the discretion of corporate managers.

While the majority of empirical studies that investigate CSR perceptions may have been limited to developed and western countries, a broadening geographical focus is evident in some recent studies that address emerging and developing economies (e.g. Azmat and Zutshi, 2012; Carroll, 2004; Duarte, 2010; Kolk et al., forthcoming; Lindgreen et al., 2010; Logsdon et al., 2006; Moyeen and West, 2014; Okpara and Wynn, 2012; Vertigans, 2011). Kolk et al. (forthcoming), for example, investigate the influence of culture and values on Chinese consumers' CSR perceptions and find that they generally focus on Carroll (1991)'s two distinct forms of CSR: required and expected. In general, Chinese consumers expect local firms to assume the required form, which encompasses economic and legal responsibilities. These findings are somewhat surprising considering the largely communitarian nature of Chinese culture in which philanthropic responsibilities seemingly should feature prominently in consumers' expectations about local firms' role in society (Kolk et al., 2010).

Azmat and Zutshi (2012) investigate the influence of institutional and country-of-origin factors on the perceptions that Sri Lankan entrepreneurs, based in Australia, hold about CSR. This study finds positive perceptions about CSR in general, though these immigrants ranked philanthropic responsibilities higher than ethical or legal responsibilities, in particular the responsibility to respond appropriately to the needs and interests of host communities. It is interesting to note that although these migrant entrepreneurs have been resident in Australia – a more liberal society where economic and legal responsibilities are highly prioritised – their CSR orientations are still reflective of the communitarian values of their country of origin, which put a primacy on philanthropic responsibilities. Similarly, a recent study among Bangladeshi managers reveals corporate philanthropy, corporate governance, provision of acceptable products and services to consumers and ethical marketing practices as the firm's fundamental responsibilities (Moyeen and West, 2014). The CSR orientations of Bangladeshi managers suggest a strong predisposition towards regarding CSR in a manner that reflects the companies' enlightened self-interest (O'Dwyer, 2003; Windsor, 2006).

Such findings are not limited to South Asian contexts. Okpara and Wynn (2012) find that stakeholders in Nigeria have a relatively broad understanding of the responsibilities businesses might assume in society but strongly view that companies should undertake poverty reduction activities (philanthropy) in their host communities. In Mexico, Logsdon et al. (2006) reveal a CSR orientation that hugely favours philanthropic responsibilities, although other forms such as economic and ethical responsibilities remain central to CSR conceptualisation. The popularity of philanthropic responsibilities could reflect the strong influences of cultural values, political history and religion on these respondents, or it might be a result of their governments' failures to provide basic social rights to their citizens, propelling communities to turn to private businesses for welfare (Visser, 2008).

Fundamentally, the general theme emerging from these studies is that while the dominant CSR models for Africa and developing countries indicate CSR as largely philanthropic in nature (Visser, 2007, 2008), our review of the literature paints a mixed picture. In some respects, managers and stakeholders are now beginning to realise that the notion of CSR represents a fine balance between competing forms of responsibilities and that there is a desire to embrace different perspectives (Logsdon et al., 2006; Muthuri and Gilbert, 2011). For example, separate studies conducted by Lindgreen et al. (2010) in Botswana and Malawi, and Yakovleva and Vazquez-Brust (2012) in Argentina, found managers and stakeholders ranking ethical responsibilities higher than the dominant models by Carroll (1979, 1991) and Visser (2007). As mentioned elsewhere, such a change in perception and understanding may reflect the increased degree of exposure to global standards on CSR and business ethics and the ever-changing institutional factors that impact on managerial and stakeholders' CSR orientation (Amaeshi et al., 2015).

Methodology

Data collection

We report findings drawn from a qualitative case study involving semi-structured interviews with senior managers of Eastern Produce Malawi and external stakeholders, including central and local government officials, inhabitants of host communities, representatives of the NGO community, Western tea packers and members of their representative organisations (see Table 4.5.1 for the list of selected respondents). Prior to undertaking the fieldwork, we drew up a list of potential respondents who could provide insights into the tea supply chain. We also relied on a snowball approach in which the pre-identified interviewees recommended others who might offer insights into the topic of CSR (Table 4.5.1). The interviews lasted between 20 minutes and 2 hours and were recorded, with the consent of respondents (see Table 4.5.3 in the Appendix for the interview schedule).

Table 4.5.1 Interviewed respondents and organisations

Organisation	*Respondent's position*	*Reason for inclusion*	*Number of interviews and length(s)*
Eastern Produce Malawi	Managing Director General Manager	Key decision makers in corporate affairs	Two interviews: one for 2 hours and one for 40 minutes
Tea Association of Malawi Limited	Chief Executive	This association sets industry standards	One interview: 70 minutes
Government of Malawi	Former Deputy Minister of Trade and Industry Principal Secretary of Ministry of Labour Deputy Labour Commissioner District Labour Officer Deputy Director, Environmental Affairs Department Legal Officer, Environmental Affairs Principal Anti-Corruption Officer Chief Executive, Malawi Bureau of Standards	These actors formulate regulations for corporate practices and monitor corporate compliance	Eight interviews; durations varied from 60 to 90 minutes
Suppliers	Sales Executive Chief Executive	They are affected by Eastern Produce Malawi's purchasing policies, and their actions can create significant reputational risks for Eastern Produce Malawi	Two interviews: one for 30 minutes and one for 35 minutes
Professional Associations	Executive Director – Society of Accountants in Malawi Program Officer, Institute of Directors	They set ethical and business integrity standards for members, most of which influence Eastern Produce Malawi's ethical policies.	Two interviews, each for 45 minutes
Tea buyers	Typhoo Technical Manager for Producer Relations	Purchasing practices influence Eastern Produce Malawi's CSR agenda	One interview: 45 minutes
International Certification and Standards Organization	Ethical Tea Partnership Program Manager for Africa and Latin America	Develop standards and codes, and monitor producers' compliance	One interview: 2 hours
Smallholder Outgrowers' Organization	Chairperson Committee member Three smallholder farmers	Smallholder tea producers are affected by the actions of Eastern Produce Malawi	Five interviews: one for 40 minutes, one for 60 minutes and three for 30 minutes
Community (traditional) leaders and members	Two traditional leaders Nine community members	Provide social legitimacy to Eastern Produce Malawi	Two interviews: one for 60 minutes and one for 90 minutes
African Institute of Corporate Citizenship	Project Coordinator – Sustainable Agriculture Business Initiative Technical Advisor	Provides advisory services to Eastern Produce Malawi in the implementation of ethical practices	Two interviews: one for 60 and one for 75 minutes
International Labor Organization	Program Officer	Its conventions and capacity building programs influence corporate practices in Malawi	One interview: 1 hour

We developed the interview questions by drawing insights from prior CSR academic literature. The questions primarily focused on respondents' understanding of the nature of the responsibilities of companies such as Eastern Produce Malawi, as well as how their views have influenced CSR strategies. We provided a brief background and described the aims of the study to facilitate free interactions; the series of open-ended questions also allowed respondents to express their views freely. To gain a broader understanding of both managers' and stakeholders' perceptions of the social responsibilities of companies and the contextual issues, we began by asking them to summarise what they believed CSR meant and what they believed were the responsibilities of Eastern Produce Malawi and of other tea-producing companies, within Malawian society. We also asked Eastern Produce Malawi's management about the kinds of CSR initiatives they had implemented and the antecedents of the company's CSR agenda. We heavily relied on insights provided by the top management, who are the driving force for CSR development and implementation within Eastern Produce Malawi, and perhaps as 'the face' of Camellia International Group plc. This reliance on top management as the source of information is consistent with studies that suggest a significant role of top management in the development of CSR policies and strategies. Managers directly involved in CSR issues should be better able to provide rich descriptions of organisational orientations towards social issues. We also attempted to determine where managers and stakeholder representatives acquired their knowledge about CSR. Consistent with Yin (1999), we conducted three pilot interviews and used the results to revise the interview questions and procedures as necessary.

Data analysis

The recorded interviews and field notes were transcribed and subjected to thematic analyses using open and axial coding to obtain a deeper understanding of the various meanings and interpretations that Eastern Produce Malawi's managers and representatives of various stakeholder groups associate with the notion of CSR (Mzembe and Downs, 2014). We began by evaluating the application of prior CSR literature to our study context. In identifying the major themes, we constructed a primary list of codes, drawing largely from the wider literature on CSR (Carroll, 1991, 2004; Visser, 2008). After identifying these themes *a priori*, we constructed categories within four codes: economic responsibilities, philanthropic responsibilities, legal responsibilities and ethical responsibilities. Because CSR is a social phenomenon, we are aware that various actors tend to exhibit some similarities and differences in the perceptions and expectations of corporate behaviour (Carroll and Shabana, 2010), reflecting not only a fundamentally context specificity of CSR (Brammer et al., 2012; Visser, 2007, 2008) but also the instrumental–normative continuum (O'Dwyer, 2003; Okpara and Wynn, 2012; Windsor, 2006). Therefore, we performed open coding as a starting point, which involved the process of organising the data according to the revealed differences and similarities (Miles and Huberman, 1994). With axial coding, we organised the data into sub-categories and sub-themes plotted onto the *a priori* themes (see Table 4.5.2). The next section deals with the findings from the study.

Findings

In this section, we present the CSR perceptions of Eastern Produce Malawi's management and stakeholders, following Carroll's (1979, 1991) typology. That is, we examine the similarities and differences in the views held by the management and various stakeholder respondents with regard to four key responsibilities.

Table 4.5.2 Analytical dimensions

A priori themes	*Theoretical perspectives*	*Empirically generated subthemes*
Economic responsibilities	Firm's economic responsibility should be viewed in terms of the production of goods and services and profitability (Carroll, 1991; Friedman and Friedman, 1962; Henderson, 2005; Moyeen and West, 2014; Visser, 2008) Payment of taxes (Carroll, 1991; Visser, 2008) Employment opportunities (Visser, 2008)	Making profits for shareholders Contributions to local and national economy Capacity building of smallholder suppliers Payment of corporate taxes Provision of employment to indigenous people
Philanthropic responsibilities	Philanthropic responsibilities can be fulfilled by supporting social and community projects (Carroll, 1991; Visser, 2008) in line with community expectations (Carroll, 1991) Actions that companies implement contribute to societal governance (Visser, 2008)	Giving back to the community through the implementation of community development programmes (construction and renovation of school blocks and health facilities)
Ethical responsibilities	Companies fulfil their ethical responsibilities when their actions are compliant with moral beliefs and societal norms. This occurs when firms go beyond minimum compliance with the laws of the land (Carroll, 1991; Richter, 2010), adopt voluntary codes of conduct, develop and implement business integrity practices (Dahlsrud, 2008; Visser, 2008; Welford and Frost, 2006), avoid harm to humankind and the ecosystem (Carroll, 1991) and ensure fair labour practices and good working conditions	Preservation of the environment Respect for marginalised communities' rights Development of codes of conduct Bribery and corrupt practices prevention Good working conditions for labourers Avoidance of child labour
Legal responsibilities	Companies meet their legal obligations when their actions are in compliance with the laws of the land or produce goods and services that conform to minimal legal requirements (Carroll, 1991) and when they coexist well with regulatory institutions and officials (Visser, 2008); fair trading practices	Compliance with the environmental, anti-bribery and corruption prevention and employment-related regulations

Economic responsibilities

Eastern Produce Malawi's managers overwhelmingly regarded economic responsibilities as part of the company's social responsibilities, in Malawi and beyond. They believe Eastern Produce Malawi's economic responsibility is to increase shareholder value, build the capacity of out-growers, provide employment to Malawians and pay taxes to the government, as illustrated in the following quote:

> Companies would not exist if they didn't make profits. We also have a duty to contribute to the economic development of this country. We have to do our part by paying taxes just like all the companies which operate in Malawi. Since 2005, we have also been assisting our small scale farmers with inputs to increase their productivity.
>
> (Managing Director, Eastern Produce Malawi)

These sentiments suggest that Eastern Produce Malawi's management attaches significant priority to meeting the interests of 'economically crucial' stakeholders, such as suppliers, buyers and shareholders. This view is consistent with Carroll's (1991) argument that the firm's economic responsibilities include the delivery of goods and services and payment of taxes. However, it also contrasts somewhat with Carroll's limited model, which mainly reflects societal expectations in advanced economies, where businesses engage in minimal direct involvement in societal development (Maignan and Ralston, 2002; Matten and Moon, 2008). The views of the Managing Director in the preceding quote appear equally development-oriented in nature, because some of the stated responsibilities reflect the expectations and real developmental needs of wider Malawian society. For example, building capacity among out-growers (i.e. small-scale tea suppliers) is a manifestation of Eastern Produce Malawi's commitment to reduce communities' reliance on philanthropic initiatives and its sustainability agenda. It also indicates Eastern Produce Malawi's drive to integrate a CSR agenda as a core strategy (Porter and Kramer, 2006). These capacity-building initiatives help Eastern Produce Malawi guarantee itself a sustainable source of good quality leaf tea in adequate quantities.

The stakeholders express more divergent impressions about the economic responsibilities of Eastern Produce Malawi, largely depending on whether they represented private-sector or public-interest organisations. The former mainly considered the economic responsibilities of Eastern Produce Malawi in terms of meeting the economic and financial expectations of stakeholders who are crucial to its survival, as the following extract shows:

> I believe the tea companies including Eastern Produce in Malawi have responsibilities to their shareholders, suppliers, consumers in Malawi and abroad. So the economic responsibilities of Eastern Produce are much broader than people may think.
>
> (Chief Executive, Tea Association of Malawi)

These 'economic' stakeholders – shareholders, consumers and suppliers, for example – are powerful and can use their economic strength to threaten or ensure Eastern Produce Malawi's survival. This view reflects an instrumental perspective, entrenched in the private sector, which emphasises the pursuit of economic actions that can enhance shareholders' value while also reducing the company's vulnerability to reputational risks (Roehrich et al., 2014).

These narrow views, however, fail to take societal expectations in general into consideration. The economic challenges that exist in Malawi might compel a private company such as Eastern Produce Malawi to embrace a broader or 'developmental' view of its economic responsibilities (Mzembe and Downs, 2014; Okpara and Wynn, 2012; Visser, 2008). However, the economically oriented perception conforms with a classical view of firms' economic responsibilities, consistent with liberal societies' expectation that companies are private property (Carroll, 1991; Friedman and Friedman, 1962) whose responsibilities are only to serve the interests of shareholders, produce goods and services and pay taxes, leaving the delivery of public good to the state (Henderson, 2005).

In contrast, public interest stakeholders have a broader understanding of the economic responsibilities of Eastern Produce Malawi that encompass contributions to the economic development of Malawi while also meeting the interests of investors, employees and small-scale tea suppliers, as one government stakeholder summarised:

> I think as a private owned company which is getting benefits from this country, they have a big responsibility in assisting the Government of Malawi in its economic development agenda. They are also responsible to their employees and the smallholder farmers who supply them with tea. Above all else, I feel that, as a private company, Eastern Produce needs to make their shareholders happy by making profits.
>
> (District Labour Officer, Government of Malawi)

This broader understanding reflects a general expectation in Malawian society, including within its government, that private companies should take an active role in the economic development of the country, alongside providing goods and services to earn a profit. This finding corresponds with several studies that suggest stakeholders have relatively higher expectations of development-oriented economic responsibilities in developing nations (Mzembe and Downs, 2014; Okpara and Wynn, 2012; Visser, 2008). In our study, it appears that by virtue of working for a public interest organisation, stakeholders' favourable perceptions of development-oriented economic responsibilities have been influenced by personal experiences, values and commitments to delivering public goods. Furthermore, the sentiments in the preceding quote highlight an increased awareness of companies' need to satisfy the economic interests of shareholders, employees and suppliers if they are to operate viably, which contrasts with Mzembe and Downs's (2014) findings in the Malawian mining industry, which indicated that most stakeholders did not perceive the case study company's economic responsibilities towards shareholders and other 'economic' stakeholders positively. This variation may reflect differences in CSR awareness between the sets of stakeholders. For the stakeholders in the tea industry, unlike those of the mining industry, exposures to various international organisations that work with the industry on CSR issues and labour conditions may have heightened their awareness of the triple bottom line and its equivalent emphases on the interests of economic stakeholders.

Philanthropic responsibilities

Philanthropic responsibilities usually refer to the actions companies undertake to pass on to the host societies the benefits that accrue from the companies' operations (Carroll, 1991). Drawing on Carroll's (1991) conceptualisation, we asked the management of Eastern Produce Malawi and various stakeholders about their understanding of philanthropic responsibilities. We found striking similarities. The vast majority of the respondents regarded philanthropic responsibilities as actions undertaken by companies to improve the wellbeing of society, in response to the state's failure to provide social rights, but also to give back some of the proceeds of their economic activities to the host society:

> I have lived in this country for many years, and therefore we have to put back into the communities that surround us. We run seven schools. We support water and road projects for villages surrounding our estates.
>
> (Managing Director, Eastern Produce Malawi)

> I understand philanthropic CSR as businesses being able to plough back part of their profits into the community.
>
> (former Deputy Minister of Trade and Private Sector Development, Malawi Government)

This congruence of understanding and expectations between stakeholders and management about Eastern Produce Malawi's influence on the wellbeing of the host communities may arise because, in Malawi, due to changes in societal governance, societal perceptions about the role of businesses have also changed. The government of Malawi is failing to provide its citizenry with basic social rights, such as clean potable water, education and other social infrastructure elements, so it is not surprising that community expectations have expanded over the years regarding Eastern Produce Malawi's necessary involvement in societal governance. According to the Managing Director, Eastern Produce Malawi is committed to aligning its philanthropic actions with societal expectations, as a good corporate citizen of Malawi. These positive views about philanthropic responsibilities represent a contrast to Pedersen's (2010) findings that managers of western firms perceive that their social responsibilities pertain only to issues closely related to their core business. In contrast, the Managing Director cites responsibilities of Eastern Produce Malawi that are remote from its core business. The difference may arise because, as Matten and Moon (2008) argue, the *former* managers work in societies where public spending on welfare is significant, and firms usually are not expected to undertake philanthropic, social welfare actions.

The perceptions of managers and stakeholders about philanthropic responsibilities are also indicative of the influence of organisational cultures, value systems and personal life experiences (Azmat and Zutshi, 2012). In societies such as Malawi, philanthropic responsibilities are regarded as highly discretionary (Mzembe and Downs, 2014). By virtue of living in Malawi for significant parts of their lives, the stakeholders and the Managing Director of Eastern Produce Malawi may have developed an understanding of their philanthropic responsibilities that has been fundamentally shaped by their direct exposure to Malawian society, with its communitarian value system. Furthermore, the Managing Director's positive views on philanthropic responsibilities appear to derive from the entrenched organisational culture and ethical orientation of the parent company, Camellia Group plc. These sentiments by the Managing Director offer an interesting revelation regarding management's perception of how Eastern Produce Malawi fulfils its philanthropic responsibilities. To some extent, Eastern Produce Malawi regards philanthropy as a discretionary, 'added activity' that might be subject to cutbacks in times of economic turbulence.

Legal responsibilities

Extant studies reveal virtually no disagreements regarding the assertion that firms have legal responsibilities in the societies in which they operate (Carroll, 1991; Carroll and Shabana, 2010; Visser, 2008). However, a contentious issue remains regarding the scope of these legal responsibilities (Carroll and Shabana, 2010; Shauki, 2011; Visser, 2008). Some CSR scholars argue for extensive, firm regulations (Campbell, 2007; De Schutter, 2008); others propose voluntary forms (Maitland, 1985; Vives, 2004).

In light of such contentions, we asked the top management and selected stakeholders of Eastern Produce Malawi about their perceptions of the legal responsibilities of Eastern Produce Limited in Malawian society. These respondents unanimously agreed that Eastern Produce Malawi's legal obligations include complying with the requirements of several legal frameworks: the Employment Act (2000), Occupational Health and Workers Safety Act (1997), Labour Relations Act (1996), Corrupt Practices Act (1995) and the Environmental Management Act (1996). The following extracts are representative:

> As you know, the current government is committed to the fight against corruption; we think as a good corporate citizen, we have to comply with regulations that fight corruption because I have witnessed in this country how corruption can stifle businesses.
>
> (Managing Director, Eastern Produce Malawi)

> I think Eastern Produce has legal responsibilities in Malawi. Although these legal obligations are supposed to ensure that companies do not exploit people like myself, I am concerned that many companies take advantage of the employment and labour laws because they offer a bare minimum requirements while letting these companies make a lot of profits.
>
> (Low skilled worker, Eastern Produce Malawi)

These views highlight the business and normative cases for companies' position to assume legal responsibilities within society (Carroll, 1979, 1991; Carroll and Shabana, 2010). On the one hand, the response from Eastern Produce Malawi's management suggests that within Eastern Produce Malawi there is a strong inclination to meet legal obligations which may have been influenced by their commitment to achieving legitimacy, since operating according to Malawian laws was a prerequisite for obtaining a licence to operate. In addition, compliance with the legal framework that addresses corruption and fraud apparently is in Eastern Produce Malawi's shareholders' interest as their compliance tends to reduce its vulnerability to risks of litigation, reputational and financial loss. On the other hand, for the majority of the stakeholders, it is surprising that their perception of corporate legal responsibilities was rather lukewarm, although it has to be pointed out that the significance they attach to corporate legal responsibilities is in stark contrast to that of management. For these stakeholders in general, as one of the stakeholders' respondents state, there is a general understanding that legal obligations placed on Eastern Produce Malawi are meant to provide a mechanism by which society and stakeholders may be guaranteed protection from corporate abuse and ensure fairness in their relationship with businesses (Carroll, 1979, 1991; Carroll and Shabana, 2010; Deegan and Shelly, 2014). However, as a representative of stakeholders further shows, the scope and effectiveness of the legal obligations Eastern Produce Malawi is expected to comply with remains a major concern, as many companies who fail to comply with their legal responsibilities are often left unpunished. The exception to the general view of these stakeholders unsurprisingly came from stakeholders from the government who had a strong and optimistic view about corporate legal responsibilities.

Considering that noticeable differences arose between management and stakeholders when it specifically came to their perceptions about corporate legal responsibilities, we asked management and stakeholders of Eastern Produce Malawi about the prospect of introducing specific CSR regulations. As expected, we encountered divergent views from the respondents. First, despite the many challenges associated with regulatory oversight that the Government of Malawi faces, stakeholders from the public institutions strongly voiced opinions in favour of CSR regulation. As the following quote reveals, such stakeholders thus believe that it is only if CSR were legislated that the majority of companies in Malawi would produce meaningful CSR agendas:

> I have seen many companies in this country bragging about their CSR activities. But if you closely look at their claims then you quickly realise how insincere these companies are. So, to avoid companies using CSR as a public relation gimmick, we need to have a CSR-specific legislation. Using this legislation, we could also encourage other companies to do their part.
>
> (Senior Official, Department of Environmental Affairs)

As this response suggests, the rationale for CSR regulation largely borders on the fact that the record of many companies' CSR agendas has been associated with piecemeal interventions that have not necessarily translated into societal wellbeing but have only been undertaken to build firm reputations. These views in favour of CSR regulation, however, should be taken with a caveat, as there is an implicit assumption here by the respondent stakeholder that public regulatory institutions are not driven by self-interest – the issue which may run counter to free market principles and eventually interfere with the public interest (Deegan and Shelly, 2014).

The expected exceptions to this view though were mainly stakeholder respondents from the tea industry association and one supplier (private company) and management. Eastern Produce Malawi's management instead believes that CSR regulations run counter to the notions of voluntariness, which are conceptual foundations for the notion of CSR:

> If we start putting in place regulations for CSR, then for sure it will lose its meaning. My understanding is that CSR ought to be morally and ethically driven. Looking it from another angle, regulating would just be costly for businesses and specifically small-scale businesses.
>
> (Managing Director, Eastern Produce Malawi)

From an enlightened, self-interested perspective, their position is that CSR regulation induces additional costs, and such state interference is tantamount to usurping the firm's role in efficiently allocating its resources towards actions to deliver public goods. It would appear Eastern Produce Malawi's management considers that CSR regulation would only promote bare compliance with the minimum requirements, as is the case with any other corporate regulations, rather than going beyond.

For stakeholders who do not work for the regulatory institutions, there were doubts regarding the introduction of a new set of CSR regulations given the poor record of enforcement of the existing legislation that regulates corporate practices:

> I don't think having a separate CSR law will help companies improve their CSR record. As a country, we first need to show that we are capable of enforcing the company regulations we already have. Mind you, we are just quick and good at formulating these laws, but disappointingly poor at implementing them.
>
> (Programme Officer, Non-governmental organisation)

The views from this respondent reveal how corporate legal responsibilities are regarded by the general stakeholdership of businesses in Malawi. It apparently indicates that Malawian society in general does not have sufficient confidence in the existing and any future legal frameworks to protect them and Malawian society from corporate irresponsible practices. It is certain that inadequate institutional capacity within the Government of Malawi and the quest to attract and retain foreign direct investment are the two major factors responsible for the government's failure in addressing companies' socially irresponsible behaviours.

Ethical responsibilities

Ethical responsibilities represent standards, norms and expectations related to issues that society considers fair and just (Carroll, 1991; Carroll and Shabana, 2010). In response to questions about the ethical obligations of Eastern Produce Malawi to Malawi as a country and the wider society, there is a general view that Eastern Produce Malawi should fulfil some ethical obligations within Malawian society. Consistent with other studies conducted elsewhere (e.g. Welford and Frost, 2006), management and some stakeholders understood Eastern Product Malawi's ethical responsibilities as inclusive of environmental preservation; prevention of exploitative labour practices, including any forms of child labour; respect for the rights of the host communities; and prevention of corrupt practices, as summarised in the following quotes:

> I don't believe regulation of companies is working for the good of our society. We expect companies to just develop a sense of duty to the society by doing more even if the law does not require them to do so. I see a lot of child labour for example being used in smallholder farms which sell tea to big tea companies. These are [the] sorts of things tea companies can prevent; they don't require regulation or their buyers to tell them that it is bad for them to stop the practice from happening.
>
> (Advisor, Community (Area) Development Committee)

> My understanding of the company's ethical responsibilities is that the company's actions should be seen to go beyond what is required by the laws of this country. I can proudly say that Eastern Produce Malawi has been a leader in showing the country and stakeholders abroad that we take our ethical responsibilities seriously. We pay our unskilled workers more than what any tea companies in Malawi pay; we have been the pioneer of the fight against corruption in this country; we have an ambitious programme to maintain the integrity of the environment. To further

> show our commitment to ethical practices, we also have a code of conduct for our suppliers; we expect to comply with this code if they want to do business with us.
>
> (General Manager, Tea Division, Eastern Produce Malawi)

> I think companies such as Eastern Produce Malawi should take an active role in embracing ethical issues because they are operating an industry that was in the past well known for unethical behaviour. I think companies such as Eastern Produce Malawi need to address child labour, exploitation of workers, and the damage caused to the environment by deforestation and use of chemicals such as fertiliser and pesticides. Having said that, I think Eastern Produce Malawi is doing well in this respect. Perhaps, it is because they want to please their buyers who frequently visit their estates and factories.
>
> (Official, Government of Malawi)

> Eastern Produce Malawi is already fulfilling some of such responsibilities. Eastern Produce Malawi was a pioneer in the establishment of a coalition against corruption in Malawi; it also has an ethical code of conduct for its suppliers including my company. All these actions are voluntary.
>
> (Sales Director, input supplier to Eastern Produce Malawi)

As these responses show, there is a positive perception among Eastern Produce Malawi's management and stakeholders about the ethical obligations Eastern Produce Malawi is expected to fulfil within Malawi. Such a congruence in perceptions that strongly favour ethical business practices in a society such as Malawi where regulatory regime is weak, is striking and would have been unthinkable to imagine in the period before the late 1990s when such issues were not considered so critical to warrant strong managerial attention. It is apparent after many years of a business culture driven by a 'profit maximisation' agenda, without adequate consideration for and mitigation of the negative impacts of businesses on the wellbeing of Malawian society, that there is now pressure for management and an increased realisation by stakeholders of the need to develop corporate actions that ought to be driven by the desire to consider society in general as an end in itself not as a means to maximise shareholder returns. In addition, the views of managers and stakeholders reflect the changing societal expectations which Carroll (2004, 2015) argues can influence corporate orientations towards moral issues. The growing concerns in the west regarding unethical practices in global supply chains, pressure to align the parent company's policies as well as general concerns about the escalating problem of corruption in Malawi, may have significantly influenced the positive perceptions of both management and stakeholders regarding Eastern Produce Malawi's ethical responsibilities. In line with Kuada and Hinson (2012), the increased exposure by stakeholders to international debates about ethical issues in the global supply chains, regular visits by certification and standards' organisations based in the western countries and the low level of confidence in the regulatory regime may have changed the way these stakeholders view the various ethical dilemmas faced by tea-producing companies such as Eastern Produce Malawi. Fundamentally, stakeholders increasingly are expecting Eastern Produce Malawi to do the 'right thing' as part of its social responsibilities in Malawi. As part of its orientation towards ethical business practices, Eastern Produce Malawi implements voluntary initiatives that could help it not only to exceed the minimum requirements of existing regulatory regimes but also to respond to ethical consumerism in developed countries. In correspondence with Visser (2007, 2008), some of these initiatives include: the development and implementation of a code of conduct for its internal stakeholders and suppliers, and adherence to international codes and standards.

A further example of an area where Eastern Produce Malawi shows its commitment towards its ethical responsibilities relates to its relationship with its small-scale suppliers of green leaf. Interviews with its smallholder out-growers reveal that Eastern Produce Malawi implements a robust capacity building programme for its suppliers, who are usually resource poor, that includes provision of soft loans for farm inputs and also provides them with protection in times of crop losses as a result of natural disasters. Similarly, Eastern Produce Malawi has assisted them to access the lucrative fair trade markets in Western European countries. Eastern Produce Malawi considers such an approach to be fundamental to the recognition of these farmers as an end in themselves and also to the fulfilment of its moral obligation to its host society.

Discussion

With this study, we set out to investigate the perceptions that management and stakeholders have about the social responsibilities in a developing country's context using a case study of Eastern Produce Malawi. We drew insights from Carroll's (1979, 1991) and Visser's (2007) models of CSR in an African context, but also from empirical studies that have tested these models in different national contexts. Two key findings emerge from this study. First, there are similarities and differences between management and stakeholders in their understanding of the social responsibilities companies may assume in Malawi. The findings show management and stakeholders have a broad understanding of CSR, contradicting the popular assertion that CSR in developing countries such as Malawi is primarily regarded as corporate philanthropy (Visser, 2008). There is general awareness across the board that companies such as Eastern Produce Malawi have the four forms of responsibilities proposed by Carroll (1979, 1991) – economic, legal, ethical and philanthropic – within Malawian society. The broader understandings of CSR reflect the increasing exposure in recent years of local stakeholders to global debates about CSR, which in turn could be attributed to the Malawian tea industry's integration into the global tea supply chains.

For the management, their broad perception of Eastern Produce Malawi's nature of its social responsibilities is rather expected given their company's close connection with its parent company, Camellia Group plc, which is based in the UK. Camellia's CSR policy demands its subsidiaries to undertake its business activities while fulfilling their ethical, legal and philanthropic expectations of their host societies. Such a broader conception corresponds with Carroll (1979, 1991, 1998) who calls for businesses to embrace not only synergetic relationships between the four forms of social responsibilities but also the need to undertake such responsibilities simultaneously. Nevertheless, we noted an interesting point of departure from the models of Carroll (1979) and Visser (2007) in that in this study, apart from economic and philanthropic responsibilities, management and stakeholders regarded ethical responsibilities highly as compared to legal responsibilities. On the one hand, the low regard for legal responsibilities highlights the fact that Malawian society is less legalistic as compared to many countries where such studies were conducted (Maignan and Ralston, 2002; Silberhorn and Warren, 2007). Such a state of affairs is asymptomatic of the fact that regulations are usually less stringent and poorly enforced leaving in the process non-compliant companies unsanctioned. On the other hand, the high prioritisation accorded to economic responsibilities, and the growing importance of ethical responsibilities by management and stakeholders, is consistent with studies that have tested Carroll's model in developed countries (Maignan and Ralston, 2002; O'Dwyer, 2003; Pinkston and Carroll, 1994; Silberhorn and Warren, 2007) and in the developing world (Lindgreen et al., 2010; Logsdon et al., 2006; Yakovleva and Vazquez-Brust, 2012). Certainly, the fact that ethical responsibilities are highly regarded in the tea industry in Malawi in comparison with legal responsibilities raises an important question about the universality of Carroll's (1979, 1991) model and Visser's (2007) model of CSR in Africa, which ranks ethical responsibilities below legal responsibilities. As this study shows, it is fundamental that when researching the interpretation of CSR in different countries, contextual features such as the nature of the industry,[2] the institutional settings and value orientations within a given country should be strongly considered (Maignan and Ralston, 2002). The growing importance of ethical responsibilities in the tea industry perhaps suggests not only an increased awareness by stakeholders of the ethical dilemmas companies within the industry are continually confronted with and the influence of communitarian values (Brammer et al., 2012) but also the response to pressure from the parent company and global stakeholders (Carroll, 2015; Kuada and Hinson, 2012). For example, considering the impacts commercial tea production may have on the indigenous communities and ecosystem, the higher prioritisation of ethical responsibilities in this study may not be surprising at all. Consistent with Carroll's (1979, 1991) description of ethical responsibilities, it is apparent that there is a strong realisation by the public interest-oriented stakeholders and management of Eastern Produce Malawi of the need to see Eastern Produce Malawi implementing actions that serve to protect human beings and the ecosystem from harm and also work towards compensating them in the event of damage and loss of livelihood. For Eastern Produce Malawi in particular, its orientation towards ethical issues, such as the fight against corruption and fraud, may not only be normatively fundamental but also guarantees Eastern Produce Malawi's chance of profit maximisation through reduced exposure to financial and reputational loss.

Nevertheless, there were some variations between management and stakeholders with respect to the legal responsibilities of Eastern Produce Malawi, although they all agreed that the company should fulfil such obligations. In correspondence with Carroll and Shabana (2010), fundamental differences between management and certain stakeholders arose when asked about expanding the scope of legal obligations to include CSR regulation. For example, while the management of Eastern Produce Malawi were concerned about CSR regulation, stakeholders who represented the Government of Malawi were supportive of the prospects of introducing such regulation. Management, drawing from an enlightened self-interest perspective, argued against the view of having an additional CSR regulation since they consider additional regulation to be counterproductive and a recipe for unnecessary business cost. In contrast, for stakeholders from the government, their intrinsic goal of protecting the public good may have influenced their positive view regarding additional regulation that specifically deals with CSR issues in the light of market failure that tends to encourage companies to undertake superficial voluntary actions that are beneficial to society (Deegan and Shelly, 2014; Preston and Post, 1975). Their view resonates with the perceptions of stakeholders in the social democratic countries in Western Europe that favour the expansive role of the state in regulating corporate behaviour (Maignan and Ralston, 2002). Such a contrast highlights the tensions between the normative and business cases associated with the legal responsibilities companies such as

Eastern Produce Malawi are expected to assume in a given society (Carroll, 1991; Carroll and Shabana, 2010; Richter, 2010; Scherer and Palazzo, 2011). The non-governmental stakeholders provide an interesting perspective to the debate about the increased scope for corporate legal responsibilities. Unlike the management of Eastern Produce Malawi and their stakeholders who had divergent views about the notion, the non-governmental stakeholders were pessimistic about the prospects of introducing a separate CSR regulation given the Government of Malawi's poor record of enforcing laws that regulate corporate practices. For these stakeholders, the introduction of separate CSR regulation without addressing the existing institutional challenges that hamper the enforcement of existing legislation may not necessarily lead to the delivery of the desired social outcomes. Hence, it appears that these stakeholders hold less legalistic views in comparison with the stakeholders who are based in the social democratic countries of Western Europe, despite having similar communitarian views that support increased regulation of business practices (Maignan and Ralston, 2002).

Finally, in line with arguments advanced by CSR theorists (Carroll, 2004, 2015; Visser, 2007, 2008) and studies conducted in Latin America (Logsdon et al., 2006; Yakovleva and Vazquez-Brust, 2012), evidence suggests that management's understanding of CSR to a large extent is consistent with the desire to reconcile global expectations of being a subsidiary of a UK-based multinational company with the ever changing expectations of Malawian society. Fundamentally, the management of Eastern Produce Malawi is consistently under intense pressure to develop a narrative that shows their company's alignment with the expectations of its host society and the local stakeholders, particularly when it comes to the domains of economic and philanthropic responsibilities. Moreover, Visser (2007) argues that the conceptualisation of different forms of social responsibilities in Africa is to a great extent influenced by cultural and other socio-economic factors. For example, it has been demonstrated in this study that while economic responsibilities of companies such as Eastern Produce Malawi and its parent company in the UK are narrowly constructed in terms of meeting the interests of its shareholders and the provision of goods and services, management exhibits a broader understanding of the economic responsibilities their company is required to assume within Malawian society. It is certain that by operating in Malawi – a host country where socio-economic indicators are dangerously worrisome – it has become imperative for the management of Eastern Produce Malawi to consider their economic responsibilities beyond serving their shareholders by including actions that can stimulate local and national economic development. The positive aspect of such a perspective for Eastern Produce Malawi is that undertaking development leaning towards economic responsibilities may be a critical part of its value proposition in Malawi and indirectly contributes to the creation of an enabling environment for its survival (Pedersen, 2010; Visser, 2007).

Despite the fact that such a developmental-oriented conception of economic responsibilities is not common and that philanthropic responsibilities are ranked low in liberal societies such as the UK (Aupperle et al., 1985; Pinkston and Carroll, 1996), it seems that management's dynamic interaction with local stakeholders and their understanding of the social responsibilities of companies within the tea industry and the country as a whole may have been sufficient to influence managerial perceptions on these key social responsibilities. This argument is supported by the work by Carroll (2015) which highlights the significance of the dynamic interaction between the country of origin and the host country factors in influencing the understanding of different forms of CSR. In particular, the interactions between insights gained from Malawi and the global expectations of its parent company to conceptualise such responsibilities in line with Carroll (1979, 1991), may have served as a learning ground that has introduced a different and new perspective regarding certain aspects of the social responsibilities Eastern Produce Malawi is required to undertake and which are desirable within a Malawian context (Logsdon et al., 2006).

Conclusions

This exploratory research study responded to calls for a nuanced understanding of social responsibilities in a developing country context (Blowfield and Frynas, 2005; Jamali, 2010). The findings from our study raise an important question regarding the universal application of both Carroll's (1979, 1991) model and Visser's (2007) model of CSR in Africa and highlights the significance of considering contextual factors in comprehensively understanding managerial and stakeholders' conceptions of the notion of CSR.

Implications for policy and practice

This study brings to light several important practical and research implications. First, though the notion of CSR remains embryonic, we uncover a broad understanding of what constitutes the social responsibilities of Eastern Produce Malawi and other companies in similar settings. This finding indicates the increased exposure of management and stakeholders to current CSR developments, likely due to the industry's connections to international markets that emphasise the integration of CSR or ethical practices with supply chain management. Accordingly, public policy should focus on facilitating learning and the exchange of information between those that currently possess knowledge about CSR (e.g. actors in the tea industry) and those that have yet to adopt CSR. For example, the government of Malawi might help disseminate national and international best practices to stakeholders and the business community; work with stakeholders such as Chambers of Commerce and Industry to develop a broad-based CSR framework to guide companies (foreign or local) in implementing CSR initiatives that are responsive to changing societal expectations; and spearhead the introduction of CSR and business ethics into tertiary-level curricula to help future businesses and leaders of public-interest organisations to develop a better understanding of CSR. Second, this study finds that there is a dynamic interaction between the home country and host country expectations regarding the different forms of social responsibilities. In view of this, managers of companies should take advantage of such positive, broad-based perceptions of CSR to influence the debate about CSR in developing country contexts. Such debates can provide opportunities to make stakeholders' expectations known to managers. In turn, managers can develop CSR initiatives that not only meet the concerns of their stakeholders but also help their companies achieve their economic objectives.

Limitations and implications for research

Our study is exploratory and based on a single company operating in the tea industry in Malawi. In no way is our case study company representative of all companies operating in Malawi or any other developing country. We do not intend to assert that the views obtained from this study are generalisable to all companies operating in the tea industry or Malawi. The purpose of case study research is never to generalise the findings beyond the case (Silverman, 2005). Instead, our study has achieved its objective to investigate the perceptions that managers and stakeholders of Eastern Produce Malawi hold about CSR. In light of this, further studies are necessary to reveal the perceptions of stakeholders in different industries and countries of the developing world. Such studies, while showing increased sensitivity to contextual factors such as the nature of the industry and specific national issues, should adopt a mixed methods design (qualitative and quantitative) involving multiple cases. These studies could take a comparative approach in which managerial and stakeholders' perceptions of national and subsidiaries of multinational companies could be explored. Furthermore, a Likert-type scale could produce a ranking of each component of CSR, which might enhance tests of the applicability of Visser's (2007) and Carroll's (1991) models in different geographical regions, including the developing world.

Although our study reveals that values have profound influences on perceptions of CSR, this concept cannot be neatly depicted in a single case study that involves only top managers and influential stakeholders, as was the case in our study. Different sets of actors within the company or society – some of whom were not included in this study – might exhibit different values with alternative, strong bearings on their understanding of CSR. Therefore, we call for studies that investigate the relationship between the values of other groups, such as middle managers, and their understanding of CSR. In addition to values, such studies might explore in greater depth the influence of culture on the ethical decision making of leaders who are based in developing countries.

Appendix

Table 4.5.3 Interview schedule

1.0 Eastern Produce Malawi management

- What do you understand by the concept of corporate social responsibility?
- What is your previous experience with CSR implementation in a company?
- What do you think are the roles of businesses in the wider Malawian society?
- Archie B. Carroll, an academic in the USA, in 1979 developed a framework for understanding the social responsibilities of businesses in the society. He categorised these responsibilities into four: a) economic responsibilities; b) legal responsibilities; c) ethical responsibilities; and d) philanthropic responsibilities. Given this categorisation, what would you consider as the social responsibilities of Eastern Produce Malawi in Malawi?
- How would you prioritise these responsibilities?
- What motivates you to drive your company towards engagement in CSR or any other ethical initiatives?
- What CSR initiatives is Eastern Produce Malawi engaged in?
- What is your opinion on calls by stakeholders that Eastern Produce Malawi should engage in social projects such as education and health services programmes?

2.0 Institutional stakeholders and experts or opinion former

- What do you understand by the concept of corporate social responsibility?
- Where did you learn about corporate social responsibility?
- What do you think are the roles of businesses in the wider Malawian society?
- Archie B. Carroll, an academic in the US, in 1979 developed a framework for understanding the social responsibilities of businesses in the society. He categorised these responsibilities into four: a) economic responsibilities; b) legal responsibilities; c) ethical responsibilities; and d) philanthropic responsibilities. Given this categorisation, what do you consider as the social responsibilities of companies such as Eastern Produce Malawi which are operating in Malawi?
- How would you prioritise these responsibilities?

3.0 Community stakeholders

- What do you think are the roles of businesses in the wider Malawian society?
- Archie B. Carroll, an academic in the US, in 1979 developed a framework for understanding the social responsibilities of businesses in the society. He categorised these responsibilities into four: a) economic responsibilities; b) legal responsibilities; c) ethical responsibilities; and d) philanthropic responsibilities. Given this categorisation, what do you consider as the social responsibilities of companies operating in Malawi?
- How would you prioritise these responsibilities?
- What is your opinion on calls that Eastern Produce Malawi should engage in social projects such as education and health services programmes?

Notes

1 These terms are commonly used in the Southern African region (Ubunthu in South Africa and Umunthu in Malawi, for example) to denote a belief in humanity and in some cases in sharing.
2 This should also include consideration of factors such as the degree of threat and opportunities to which the industry players are exposed.

References

Amaeshi, K., Adegbite, E., Ogbechie, C., Idemudia, U., Kan, K.A.S., Issa, M. and Anakwue, O.I.J. (2015). Corporate social responsibility in SMEs: A shift from philanthropy to institutional works? *Journal of Business Ethics*, 138(2), 385–400.

Amaeshi, K., Adegbite, E. and Rajwani, T. (2014). Corporate social responsibility in challenging and non-enabling institutional contexts: Do institutional voids matter? *Journal of Business Ethics*, 134(1), 135–153.

Arora, B. and Puranik, R. (2004). A review of corporate social responsibility in India. *Development*, 47, 93–100.

Aupperle, K.E., Carroll, A.B. and Hatfield, J.D. (1985). An empirical examination of the relationship between corporate social responsibility and profitability. *Academy of Management Journal*, 28, 446–463.

Ayres, I. and Braithewaite, J. (1992). *Transcending the Deregulation Debate*. New York: Oxford University Press, chapter 1.

Azmat, F. and Samaratunge, R. (2009). Responsible entrepreneurship in developing countries: Understanding the realities and complexities. *Journal of Business Ethics*, 90, 437–452.

Azmat, F. and Zutshi, A. (2012). Influence of home country culture and regulatory environment on corporate social responsibility perceptions: The case of Sri-Lankan immigrant entrepreneurs. *Thunderbird International Business Review*, 54, 15–27.

Blowfield, M. and Frynas, J. G. (2005). Setting new agendas: Critical perspectives on corporate social responsibility in the developing world. *International Affairs*, 81, 499–513.

Brammer, S., Jackson, G. and Matten, D. (2012). Corporate social responsibility and institutional theory: New perspectives on private governance. *Socio-Economic Review*, 10, 3–28.

Campbell, D., Moore, G. and Metzger, M. (2002). Corporate philanthropy in the UK 1985–2000: Some empirical findings. *Journal of Business Ethics*, 39, 29–41.

Campbell, J.L. (2007). Why would corporations behave in socially responsible ways? An institutional theory of corporate social responsibility. *Academy of Management Journal*, 32, 946–967.

Carroll, A. (1979). A three dimensional conceptual model of corporate social performance. *Academy of Management Review*, 4, 497–505.

Carroll, A.B. (1991). The pyramid of corporate social responsibility: Towards the moral management of organisational stakeholders. *Business Horizons*, 34, 39–48.

Carroll, A.B. (1998). The four faces of corporate citizenship. *Business and Society Review*, 100/101, 1–7.

Carroll, A.B. (2004). Managing ethically with global stakeholders: A present and future challenge. *Academy of Management Executive*, 18, 114–120.

Carroll, A.B. (2015). Corporate social responsibility: The centrepiece of competing and complimentary frameworks. *Organisational Dynamics*, 44, 87–96.

Carroll, A.B. and Shabana, K.M. (2010). The business case for corporate social responsibility: A review of concepts, research and practice. *International Journal of Management Reviews*, 12, 85–105.

Cheng, J. and Kenser, I. (1997). Organisational slack and response to environmental shifts: The impact of resource allocation patterns. *Journal of Management*, 23, 1–18.

Clark, J.M. (1916). The changing basis of economic responsibility. *Journal of Political Economy*, 24, 209–229.

Cowton, C.J. (1987). Corporate philanthropy in the United Kingdom. *Journal of Business Ethics*, 6, 553–558.

Dahlsrud, A. (2008). How corporate social responsibility is defined: An analysis of 37 definitions. *Corporate Social Responsibility and Environmental Management*, 15, 1–13.

Deegan, C. and Shelly, M. (2014). Corporate social responsibilities: Alternative perspectives about the need to legislate. *Journal of Business Ethics*, 121, 499–526.

De Schutter, O. (2008). Corporate social responsibility European style. *European Law Journal*, 14, 203–236.

Donaldson, T. and Preston, L.E. (1995). The stakeholder theory of the corporation: Concepts, evidence, and implications. *Academy of Management Review*, 20, 65–91.

Duarte, F. (2010). Working with corporate social responsibility in Brazilian companies: The role of managers' values in the maintenance of CSR cultures. *Journal of Business Ethics*, 96, 355–368.

Egri, C.P. and Ralston, D.A. (2008). Corporate responsibility: A review of international management research from 1998 to 2007. *Journal of International Management*, 14, 319–339.

Elkington, J. (1997). *Cannibals with Forks: The Triple Bottom Line of 21st Century Business*. Gabriola Island, BC: New Society Publishers.

Eweje, G. (2006). The role of MNEs in community development initiative in developing countries: Corporate social responsibility at work in Nigeria and South Africa. *Business and Society*, 45, 93–129.

Fig, D. (2005). Manufacturing amnesia: Corporate social responsibility in South Africa. *International Affairs*, 81, 599–617.

Frederick, W.C. (1960). The growing concern over business responsibility. *California Management Review*, 2, 54–61.

Freeman, I. and Hasnaoui, A. (2011). The meaning of corporate social responsibility: The vision of four nations. *Journal of Business Ethics*, 100, 419–443.

Friedman, M. and Friedman, R. (1962). *Capitalism and Freedom*. Chicago, IL: University of Chicago Press, chapter 1.

Gjølberg, M. (2009). The origin of corporate social responsibility: Global forces or national legacies? *Socio-Economic Review*, 7, 605–637.

GTZ. (2009). *Corporate Social Responsibility in the Sub-Saharan Africa*. Retrieved from www.csr-weltweit.de/uploads/tx_jpdownloads/GTZ_2009_built_in_or_bolt_on_Ghana_01.pdf.

Halme, M. and Laurila, J. (2009). Philanthropy, integration or innovation? Exploring the financial and societal outcomes of different types of corporate responsibility. *Journal of Business Ethics*, 84, 325–339.

Hamann, R. (2003). Mining companies' role in sustainable development: The 'why' and 'how' of corporate social responsibility from a business perspective. *Development Southern Africa*, 20, 237–254.

Hamann, R. and Kapelus, P. (2004). Corporate social responsibility in mining in Southern Africa: Fair accountability or just greenwash? *Development*, 47(3), 85–92.

Henderson, D. (2005). The role of business in the world of today. *Journal of Corporate Citizenship*, 17, 30–32.

Hine, J.A.H.S. and Preuss, L. (2009). Society is out there, organisation is in here: On the perceptions of corporate social responsibility held by different managerial groups. *Journal of Business Ethics*, 88(2), 381–393

Idemudia, U. (2007). Community perceptions and expectations: Reinventing the wheels of corporate social responsibility practices in the Nigerian oil industry. *Business and Society Review*, 112, 369–405.

Idemudia, U. (2011). Corporate social responsibility and developing countries: Moving the critical CSR research agenda in Africa forward. *Progress in Development Studies*, 11, 1–18.

Idemudia, U. (2014). Corporate social responsibility and development in Africa: Issues and possibilities. *Geography Compass*, 8, 421–435.

Idemudia, U., Cragg, W. and Best, B. (2010). The challenges and opportunities of implementing the integrity pact as a strategy for combating corruption in Nigeria's oil rich Niger Delta region. *Public Administration and Development*, 30, 277–290.

Jamali, D. (2010). The CSR of MNC subsidiaries in developing countries: Global, local, substantive or diluted? *Journal of Business Ethics*, 93, 181–200.

Joyner, B.E. and Payne, D. (2002). Evolution and implementation: A study of values, business ethics and corporate social responsibility. *Journal of Business Ethics*, 41, 297–311.

Kamlongera, P.J. (2013). The mining boom in Malawi: Implications for community development. *Community Development Journal*, 48, 377–390.

Kaptein, M. and Schwartz, M.S. (2008). The effectiveness of business codes: A critical examination of existing studies and the development of an integrated research model. *Journal of Business Ethics*, 77, 111–127.

Kayuni, H.M. and Tambulasi, R.I.H. (2012). Ubuntu and corporate social responsibility: The case of selected Malawian organisations. *African Journal of Economic and Management Studies*, 3, 64–76.

Kolk A., Hong, P. and Van Dolen, W. (2010). Corporate social responsibility in China: An analysis of domestic and foreign retailers' sustainability dimensions. *Business Strategy and the Environment*, 19, 289–303.

Kolk, A. and Lenfant, F. (2010). MNC reporting on CSR and conflict in Central Africa. *Journal of Business Ethics*, 93, 241–255.

Kolk, A., Van Dolen, W. and Ma, L. (Forthcoming). Consumer perceptions of CSR: (How) is China different? *International Marketing Review*.

Kuada, J. and Hinson, R.E. (2012). Corporate social responsibility (CSR) practices of foreign and local companies in Ghana. *Thunderbird International Business Review*, 54, 521–536.

Lantos, G.P. (2001). The boundaries of strategic corporate social responsibility. *Journal of Consumer Marketing*, 18, 595–632.

Levitt, T. (1958). The dangers of social responsibility. *Harvard Business Review*, (September-October), 41–50.

Lindgreen, A., Swaen, V. and Campbell, T.T. (2010). Corporate social responsibility practices in developing and transnational countries: Botswana and Malawi. *Journal of Business Ethics*, 90, 429–440.

Lindgreen, A., Swaen, V. and Johnston, W. (2009). Corporate social responsibility: An empirical investigation of U.S. organizations. *Journal of Business Ethics*, 85, 303–323.

Logsdon, J.M., Thomas, D.E. and Van Buren, H.J. (2006). Corporate social responsibility in large Mexican firms. *Journal of Corporate Citizenship*, 21, 51–60.

Maignan, I. and Ralston, D.A. (2002). Corporate social responsibility in Europe and the U.S.: Insights from businesses' self-presentations. *Journal of International Business Studies*, 33, 497–514.

Maitland, I. (1985). The limits of business self-regulation. *California Management Review*, 27, 132–146.

Maon, F., Lindgreen, A. and Swaen, V. (2008). Thinking of the organization as a system: The role of managerial perceptions in developing a corporate social responsibility strategic agenda. *Systems Research and Behavioral Science*, 25, 413–426.

Matten, D. and Crane, A. (2005). Corporate citizenship: Towards an extended theoretical conceptualisation. *Academy of Management Review*, 30, 166–179.

Matten, D. and Moon, J. (2008). Implicit and explicit CSR: A conceptual framework for a comparative understanding of corporate social responsibility. *Academy of Management Review*, 33, 404–424.

McGuire, J. (1963). *Business and Society*. New York: McGraw-Hill.

McGuire, J., Sundgren, A. and Schneewiss, T. (1988). Corporate social responsibility and firm financial performance. *Academy of Management Journal*, 31, 854–872.

McWilliams, A. and Siegel, D. (2001). Corporate social responsibility: A theory of firm perspective. *Academy of Management Review*, 26, 117–127.

Miles, M.B. and Huberman, A.M. (1994). *Qualitative Data Analysis*. Thousand Oaks, CA: Sage, chapter 3–5.

Moon, J., Crane, A. and Matten, D. (2005). Can corporations be citizens? Corporate citizenship as a metaphor for business participation in society. *Business Ethics Quarterly*, 15, 429–453.

Moyeen, A. and West, B. (2014). Promoting CSR to foster sustainable development. *Asia–Pacific Journal of Business Administration*, 6, 97–115.

Muthuri, J. and Gilbert, V. (2011). An institutional analysis of corporate social responsibility in Kenya. *Journal of Business Ethics*, 98, 467–483.

Muthuri, J.N. (2013). Corporate social responsibility in Africa: Definition, issues and process. In T.R. Lituchy, B.J. Punnett and B.B. Puplampu (eds) *Management in Africa: Macro and Micro Perspective* (pp. 90–111). New York and London: Routledge.

Mutti, D., Yakovleva, N., Vazquez-Brust, D. and DiMarco, M.H. (2012). Corporate social responsibility in the mining industry: Perspectives from stakeholder groups in Argentina. *Resources Policy*, 37, 212–222.

Mzembe, A.N. and Downs, Y. (2014). Managerial and stakeholder perceptions of an Africa-based multinational mining company's corporate social responsibility (CSR). *The Extractive Industries and Society*, 1, 225–236.

Noland, J. and Phillips, R.A. (2010). Stakeholder engagement, discourse ethics and strategic management. *International Journal of Management Review*, 12(1), 39–49.

O'Dwyer, B. (2003). Conceptions of corporate social responsibility: The nature of managerial capture. *Accounting, Auditing & Accountability Journal*, 16, 523–557.

Okpara, J.O. and Wynn, P.M. (2012). Stakeholders' perceptions about corporate social responsibility: Implications for poverty alleviation. *Thunderbird International Business Review*, 54, 91–103.

Pedersen, E.R. (2010). Modelling CSR: How managers understand the responsibilities of business towards society. *Journal of Business Ethics*, 91, 155–166.

Pinkston, T.S. and Carroll, A.B. (1994). Corporate citizenship perpectives and foreign direct investment in the US. *Journal of Business Ethics*, 13, 157–169.

Pinkston, T.S. and Carroll, A.B. (1996). A retrospective examination of CSR orientations: Have they changed? *Journal of Business Ethics*, 15, 199–206.

Porter, M.E. and Kramer, M.R. (2006). Strategy and society: The link between competitive advantage and corporate social responsibility. *Harvard Business Review*, December, 78–92.

Preston, L. and Post, J. (1975). *Private Management and Public Policy*. Englewood Cliffs, NJ: Prentice-Hall.

Richter, U.H. (2010). Liberal thought in reasoning on CSR. *Journal of Business Ethics*, 97, 625–649.

Robertson, D.C. (2009). Corporate social responsibility and different stages of economic development: Singapore, Turkey and Ethiopia. *Journal of Business Ethics*, 88, 617–633.

Roehrich, J.K., Grosvold, J. and Hoejmose, S.U. (2014). Reputational risks and sustainable supply chain management: Decision making under bounded rationality. *International Journal of Operations & Production Management*, 34, 695–719.

Rosen, S., Simon, J., Vincent, J., MacLeod, W., Fox, M. and Donald, T. (2003). AIDS is your business. *Harvard Business Review*, February, 81–87.

Scherer, A.G. and Palazzo, G. (2011). The new political role of business in a globalised world: A review of a new perspective on CSR and its implications for the firm, governance and democracy. *Journal of Management Studies*, 48, 899–931.

Schwartz, M. and Carroll, A. (2003). Corporate social responsibility: A three-domain approach. *Business Ethics Quarterly*, 13, 503–530.

Sethi, S.P. (1975). Dimensions of corporate social performance: An analytical framework. *California Management Review*, 17(3), 58–64.

Shauki, E. (2011). Perceptions on corporate social responsibility: A study in capturing public confidence. *Corporate Social Responsibility and Environmental Management*, 18, 200–208.

Silberhorn, D. and Warren, R.C. (2007). Defining corporate social responsibility: A view from big companies in Germany and the UK. *European Business Review*, 19, 352–372.

Silverman, D. (2005). *Doing Qualitative Research*. London: Sage, chapter 2.

Sonnenburg, D. and Hamann, R. (2006). The JSE socially responsible investment index and the state of sustainability reporting in South Africa. *Development Southern Africa*, 23, 305–320.

Vertigans, S. (2011). CSR as corporate social responsibility or colonial structures return? A Nigerian case study. *International Journal of Sociology and Anthropology*, 3, 159–162.

Visser, W. (2005). Is South Africa World class in corporate citizenship? How do South African companies measure up? In Freemantle, A. (ed.) *The Good Corporate Citizen* (pp. 118–123). Johannesburg, South Africa: Trialogue.

Visser, W. (2007) Revisiting Carroll's CSR pyramid: An African perspective. In A. Crane (ed.) *Corporate Social Responsibility in the Global Context* (pp. 195–212). Los Angeles, CA: Sage.

Visser, W. (2008). Corporate social responsibility in developing countries. In A. Crane, A. McWilliams, D. Matten, J. Moon and D. Siegel (eds) *The Oxford Handbook of Corporate Social Responsibility* (pp. 473–479). Oxford, UK: Oxford University Press.

Vives, A. (2004). The role of multilateral development institutions in fostering corporate social responsibility. *Development*, 47, 45–52.

Waddock, S. and Graves, S. (1997). Corporate social performance: Financial performance link. *Strategic Management Journal*, 18(4), 303–319.

Wan-Jan, W.S. (2006). Defining corporate social responsibility. *Journal of Public Affairs*, 6, 176–184.

Welford, R. and Frost, S. (2006). Corporate social responsibility in Asian supply chains. *Corporate Social Responsibility and Environmental Management*, 13, 166–176.

Windsor, D. (2006). Corporate social responsibility: Three key approaches. *Journal of Management Studies*, 43, 93–114.

Wood, D. (1991). Corporate social performance revisited. *Academy of Management Review*, 16, 691–718.

Yakovleva, N. and Vazquez-Brust, D. (2012). Stakeholder perspectives on CSR of mining MNCs in Argentina. *Journal of Business Ethics*, 106, 191–211.

Yin, R.K. (1999). Enhancing the quality of case studies in health services research. *Health Services Research*, 34, 1209–1224.

4.6 The value of public data for assessing sustainability

The case of Mexican entrepreneurs and the rural census

Rosario Michel-Villarreal, Eliseo Vilalta-Perdomo, and Martin Hingley

Introduction

Nowadays, multiple environmental and socio-economic changes are increasing the pressure on the sustainability and vulnerability of agri-food systems. Environmental changes result mainly from climate change and soil degradation (Alrøe et al., 2016; Hubeau et al., 2017; Tendall et al., 2015), while socio-economic changes arise from globalization, population growth, political and economic crises, asymmetric price transmission, changing customer demands (Hubeau et al., 2017; Tendall et al., 2015) and changes in market and supply channel relations (Hingley, 2005). Concurrently, unsustainable food systems have severe impacts on ecological and social systems (Carlsson et al., 2017) and result in climate change and the loss of biodiversity and environmental resources such as water, soil and air (Alrøe et al., 2016; Foley et al., 2011; Schader et al., 2014). In response to this, significant efforts have been made since the late 1990s towards defining sustainability in the context of food systems. Furthermore, a range of approaches and frameworks for the assessment of what is understood as a sustainable food system have been developed (Alrøe and Noe, 2016; Schader et al., 2014).

The necessity to assess sustainability of food systems worldwide is accentuated as countries start working towards the achievement of the UN Sustainable Development Goals (SDG), and many of them appear to struggle with implementing the full range of official SDG indicators (Sachs et al., 2017). The importance of developing sustainable food systems is stressed in the SDG 2 (SDG 2) and its associated target 2.4. This target aims at ensuring sustainable food production systems and implementation of resilient agricultural practices to "increase productivity and production, that help maintain ecosystems that strengthen capacity for adaptation to climate change, extreme weather, drought, flooding, and other disasters and that progressively improve land and soil quality" (UN, 2017, p.5). For the assessment of this target, the UN identifies the indicator of the "proportion of agricultural area under productive and sustainable agriculture" (UN, 2017, p.5). However, the definitions of such a target and associated indicator are aspirational rather than operational, as there is no clear indication regarding what qualifies as 'sustainable agriculture' or how to assess it.

In this context, the choice and use of a framework for the assessment of sustainability within food systems, at a national level, is not straightforward and can lead to results that are not comparable. In the quest for facilitating the global assessment of sustainability in agriculture through a common language, FAO (2014a) created the Sustainability Assessment of Food and Agriculture Systems (SAFA); which build on and acknowledge existing sustainability tools. SAFA strives to be a holistic and universal framework by measuring four main overarching dimensions of sustainability at the business level: good governance, environmental integrity, economic resilience and social well-being. According to FAO (2014a), the SAFA framework is adaptable to all contexts and can be used by small-, medium- and large-scale enterprises that participate in crop, livestock, forestry, aquaculture and fishery value chains, and could also be relevant to governments' strategies, policy and planning. As SAFA already incorporates many of the aspects of other sustainability assessment approaches, its implementation may be less disruptive and users can make use of existing data. Overall, SAFA has been recognized as a step towards making sustainability assessment results more comparable (Alrøe and Noe, 2016; Schader et al., 2014). To evaluate such judgements, this chapter explores if SAFA is a useful tool for the assessment of sustainability in enterprises participating in a real food system. The research problem concerns how to avoid 'response fatigue' among the entrepreneurs surveyed, because "the more times a person reports requests for survey cooperation, the more unfavorable is his or her attitude toward the method" (Goyder, 1986, p.38). Therefore, the rationale behind this research is to reduce negative reactions from agri-food entrepreneurs, who may consider SAFA a repetition of the rural census they are compelled to answer by government officials. Accordingly, this chapter focuses on substituting data that would be collected from SAFA applications to individual entrepreneurs, with data collected from a national rural census. For this purpose, this exercise is contextualized in a country that runs periodical national rural censuses, rather than using samples or integrating information from different databases; specifically Mexico.

Therefore, by using the SAFA framework, this study aims to determine to what extent sustainability of Mexican rural entrepreneurs can be assessed using publicly available data from the Mexican Agriculture, Livestock and Forestry Census 2007 (CAGF-2007). This rural census constitutes the most significant and recent source of data for assessing the structure and functioning of the Mexican agricultural sector and its sustainable development (INEGI, 2017).

Research background

The definition of 'sustainability', accepted and used worldwide, was first proposed by the World Commission on Environment and Development (WCED). According to the WCED, sustainable development is "development that meets the needs of the present without compromising the ability of future generations to meet their own needs" (United Nations, 1987). This vague definition of sustainability has led to debate over the past few decades due to the difficulty of putting this theory into practice. For instance, Giddings et al. (2002) suggest that sustainable development is a contested concept, with theories shaped by people's and organizations' different worldviews, which in turn influence how issues are formulated and actions proposed. Furthermore, Peano et al. (2015) suggest that the difficulty of interpreting sustainability is accentuated when speaking of its evaluation based on externally defined indicators and their application to varying and complex entrepreneurial contexts.

The most common framework for the conceptualization of sustainability consists of three dimensions: environmental, social and economic sustainability (Figure 4.6.1), generally known as the triple-bottom line (Elkington, 1997). These dimensions have been represented in a variety of ways, from pillars (United Nations, 2005) to interlocking circles (Adams, 2006). However, this framework of sustainability appears to be flawed as it allows for trade-offs among its dimensions. For instance, trade-offs between environmental and social issues could suggest that some pollution is acceptable to increase growth (Hopwood et al., 2005). This suggest that elements inside each sustainability dimension interact through different protocols. Westernized societies claim to strive for consensus to achieve coordinated collective actions. As such, capitalist economies establish decision-making by means of optimizing economic-based approaches, and the environment cannot communicate in the same way humans do, even though some (e.g. environmentalists, politicians or scientists) take the flag to fight under its name for its protection. In a nutshell, to decipher *a priori* if a particular human action is sustainable seems an impossible task (Vilalta-Perdomo et al., 2017), as intervening simultaneously in such different dimensions demands a more comprehensive approach.

Overall, there is no unified notion of sustainability as new challenges in relation to its three main dimensions arise continuously. Furthermore, due to its vagueness, the concept is open to a wide range of interpretations, and its conceptualization can be influenced by the pre-conceived ideas and needs of individuals. From environmentalists to business people, a wide variety of actors use 'sustainability' or 'sustainable development' to express sometimes very diverse visions of how the economy and environment should be managed (Adams, 2006). Even though the concept is ambiguous, it provides a framework in which to debate choices against global issues such as eradicating poverty (meeting our needs) and stopping environmental degradation (ensuring needs of future generations are met). Proponents of sustainable development agree that a change in society is needed, though there are debates as to the changes necessary and the tools/frameworks and actors for these changes (Hopwood et al., 2005). Actors are seen as crucial leverage points for sustainability transitions, because transitions will be brought forward by actors and their

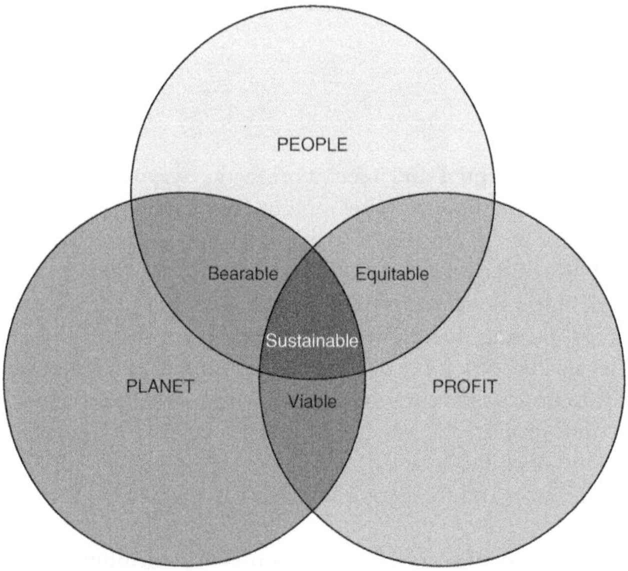

Figure 4.6.1 Triple-bottom line
Source: Elkington, 1997.

interactions (Hörisch, 2016). Here, sustainable entrepreneurship is proposed as a rather new concept which aims to link sustainable development to business activities and entrepreneurs (Koe et al., 2015; Schaltegger and Wagner, 2008).

Sustainable entrepreneurship underlines enterprise development with a main focus on transformative ideas related to the triple-bottom line dimensions, such as the reduction in environmental degradation, social equity and economic stability (Juma et al., 2017). Richomme-Huet and De Freyman (2011) recognize that, through the blend of values related to the classical three dimensions of sustainability, sustainable entrepreneurship is focused on the preservation of natural and community-related resources in the pursuit of opportunities to create future products, processes and services for economic and non-economic gains for individuals, the economy and society. The overall concept of sustainable entrepreneurship is incipient, and mechanisms or ways for entrepreneurs to become more sustainable have not been greatly explored yet. Therefore, one of the aims of this study is to reduce this gap by discussing whether agri-food entrepreneurs' sustainability can be evaluated using publicly available data (i.e. CAGF-2007) and a holistic framework for sustainability assessment (i.e. SAFA).

Tools and approaches for the assessment of sustainability in food systems

In a context where global food systems are dominated by processes that constantly undermine the environmental and social systems, while failing to effectively meet human nutritional needs (Alrøe and Noe, 2016), significant efforts have been made towards a better understanding, measuring and improvement of sustainability. This has led to the development of a wealth of tools, frameworks and approaches for 'sustainability assessment' (Alrøe et al., 2016; Schader et al., 2014; Singh et al., 2009), which is viewed as a significant aid in the transition towards sustainable development (Triste et al., 2014). Just as with the notion of sustainability, *sustainability assessment* is also open to different interpretations, and extensive research has been carried out to compare and classify existing sustainability assessment approaches.

For instance, De Ridder et al. (2007) propose a framework for tool selection in sustainability assessment and divide sustainability assessment tools into eight types with similar characteristics: *assessment frameworks, participatory tools, scenario analysis tools, multi-criteria analysis tools, cost-benefit tools, accounting tools, physical analysis tools and indicator sets, and model tools.* Peano et al. (2015) divide the most used approaches in sustainability into three principal groups: approaches that use indicator checklists, approaches that use composite indicators and approaches that apply a framework. De Olde et al. (2016) analyze four farm-level indicator-based sustainability assessment tools and conclude that they vary widely in their scoring and aggregation method, time requirement and data input. Similarly, Schader et al. (2014) discern considerable differences amongst thirty-five existing sustainability assessment approaches used in food systems in terms of scope, level of assessment and the precision of indicators used for impact assessment. However, only seven of these sustainability assessment approaches included in the study are seen as globally applicable. In terms of scope, all the approaches consider the environmental dimension of sustainability, whereas only nineteen approaches cover the social dimension. Overall, seventeen approaches cover the three dimensions of sustainability, economic, environmental and social (see Figure 4.6.2).

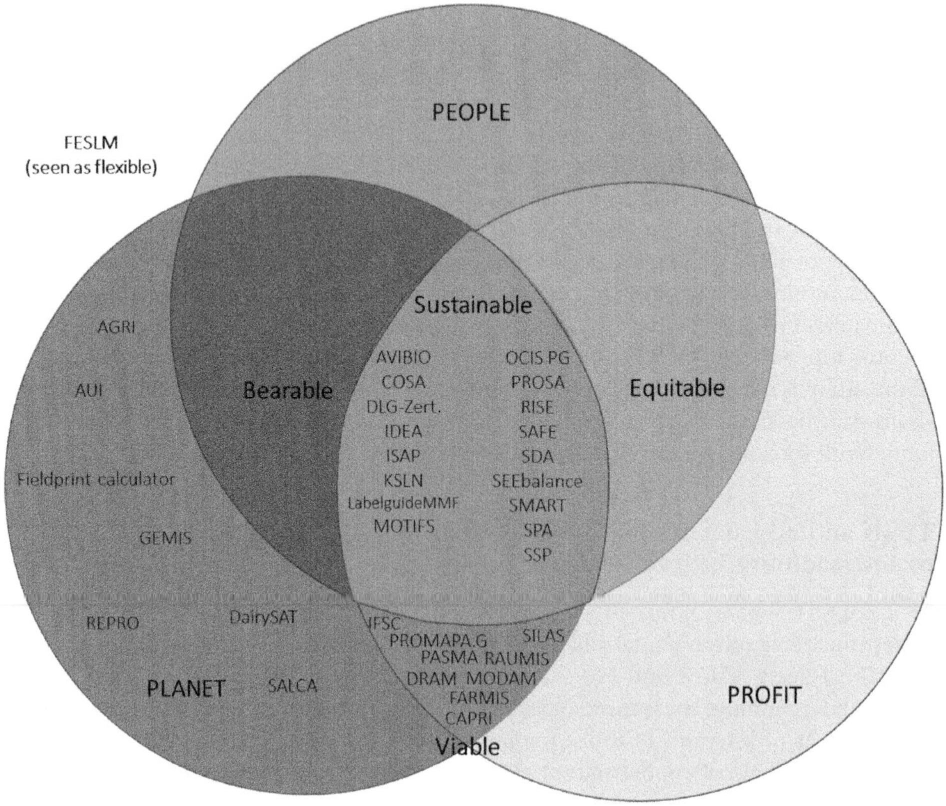

Figure 4.6.2 Sustainability assessment approaches and their coverage of the triple-bottom line
Source: Own production based on Elkington (1997) and Schader et al. (2014).

Conclusions from previous studies suggest that sustainability assessment approaches need to be chosen in considering the task for which they will be applied (De Ridder et al., 2007) and their geographical coverage (Schader et al., 2014). However, the use of different tools produces different assessments, which creates a difficulty in determining the best answer (Alrøe and Noe, 2016). In food systems, this could create barriers for the comparison of the sustainable development performance of farms that use different sustainability assessment approaches and provides no sustainability benchmarking to entrepreneurs at the individual level. Thus, it has been suggested that there is a need for harmonizing existing assessment approaches in order to facilitate the comparison of sustainability performance of enterprises (Alrøe and Noe, 2016; Schader et al., 2014). Additionally, FAO (2014a) suggests that in existing sustainability frameworks, stakeholders and small- and medium-sized enterprises, particularly from developing and emerging countries, are less represented. As a response to these challenges, FAO (2014a) proposes the SAFA framework. SAFA builds on and acknowledges existing sustainability tools and is said to be adaptable to all contexts within food and agriculture systems regardless of size, geography or role, thus providing a common language for the assessment of sustainability. This, in principle, suggests that SAFA may play an important role for the assessment of sustainability at the individual level and become an effective informative tool for entrepreneurs.

SAFA's guiding vision is that four overarching dimensions characterize all food systems: *good governance, environmental integrity, economic resilience and social well-being* (FAO, 2014a). Thus, SAFA considers the classical three dimensions of sustainability but adds a fourth dimension related to governance of enterprises. The rationale for including this additional dimension is that for sustainability not to remain an illusion, enterprises need to develop sustainability-oriented governance structures. SAFA's four dimensions are translated into twenty-one themes that represent universal sustainability themes (as depicted in Figure 4.6.3). Each of the themes is in turn divided into sub-themes that relate to specific objectives. Furthermore, a set of 116 default indicators are suggested for the evaluation of performance and to measure progress towards the achievement of objectives.

Even though the indicators are applicable to all enterprise sizes and types and to all contexts, FAO (2014a) recognizes that a default indicator set is not sufficient; accordingly, customized indicators related to SAFA's sub-themes (objectives) should be developed depending on context. In particular, it acknowledges that small-scale producers encounter specific challenges regarding sustainability assessment; for example, limited existing data or lack of resources for conducting the assessment or collecting primary data, and the relevance of global indicators. To facilitate the use of SAFA guidelines in this context,

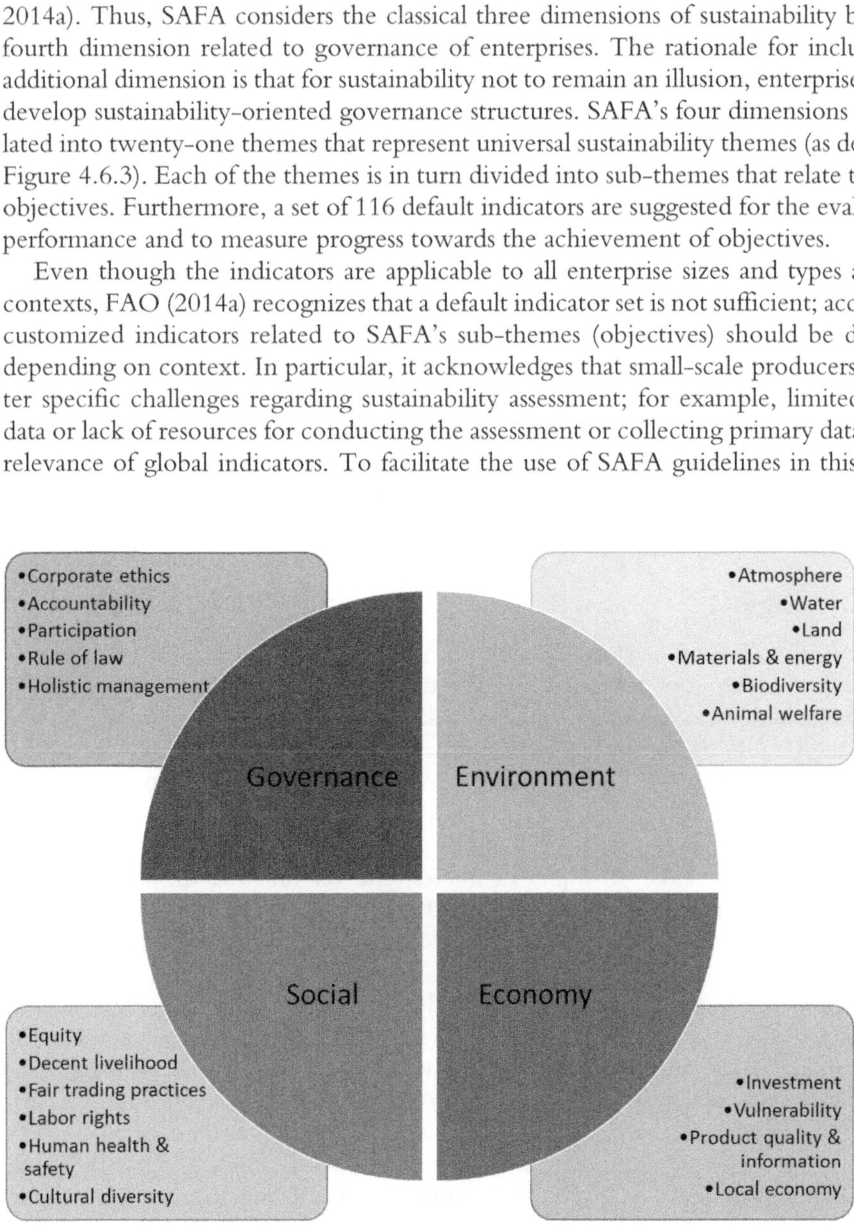

Figure 4.6.3 SAFA framework

Source: Adapted from FAO, 2014a.

FAO (2014a) developed a dedicated SAFA Smallholder APP, which includes indicators that address some of the concerns specific to small enterprises. For instance, in terms of the sub-theme 'soil quality', SAFA Smallholder APP only evaluates the indicator related to 'soil improvement practices' as, for technical and financial reasons, small enterprises struggle to measure all the parameters related to the indicators 'soil chemical quality' and 'soil biological quality'. Thus, the SAFA Smallholder App assesses sustainability based on a questionnaire comprised of 100 questions[1] related to 44 indicators of the 116 default indicators of the SAFA framework.

SAFA acknowledges that there is similarity in some existing approaches and schemes (for example, certifications) for sustainability assessment in food systems and therefore recognizes their importance for conducting SAFA. It also highlights the importance of norms and standards currently used within enterprises in expediting the adoption of SAFA and avoiding duplication by integrating existing data (FAO, 2014a). Overall, SAFA builds on existing sustainability efforts and provides a framework that aims at harmonizing the assessment and reporting of sustainability at the enterprise level (not products or processes). Nevertheless, the global applicability of the framework is yet to be tested within different contexts and under different conditions (Schader et al., 2014). This study is an effort to fill that gap; the aim is to investigate whether the sustainability of rural enterprises can be assessed using SAFA and existing data collected through CAGF-2007. CAGF-2007 is an effort by the Mexican government to assess the structure and functioning of the Mexican rural economy and its sustainable development (INEGI, 2017). Any areas of improvement regarding the assessment of SAFA's sustainability dimensions through the CAGF-2007 will be identified.

Research design

Like SAFA, CAGF-2007 evaluates a series of indicators at the enterprise level using a questionnaire consisting of 160 questions.[2] To determine to what extent CAGF-2007's data can be used to assess SAFA's sustainability dimensions, a comparison was conducted between the CAGF-2007 questionnaire and the SAFA Smallholder App questionnaire. The latter seems appropriate for this study as 73% of Mexican rural enterprises are small and up to 50% are subsistence enterprises (FAO, 2014b).

CAGF-2007 was conducted in 2007 and its structure was developed in accordance with the following criteria: (a) topics of interest and relevance at the national level, (b) compatible with previous censuses, (c) able to fill information gaps and (d) attentive to different users' needs. Questions are grouped in eighteen main sections as depicted in Table 4.6.1.

CAGF-2007 collects data from all the 'production units' in Mexico. A production unit is defined as a set of land properties located in the same municipality and owned by the same individual(s) with farming activities (INEGI, 2017). The concept is similar to what is known as a rural enterprise.

This study identifies which of the SAFA Smallholder App questions are also assessed via the CAGF-2007 questionnaire. When SAFA Smallholder App questions could not be identified in the CAGF-2007 questionnaire, it also investigated whether the indicators were assessed in an alternative way (different questions related to the same indicators), or that the indicators were only partially assessed. Therefore, SAFA indicators that were not included in CAGF-2007 were identified, and the coverage of SAFA themes was also evaluated.

Table 4.6.1 Structure of the CAGF-2007 questionnaire

Sections (18)	*Questions (160)*
General characteristics of the production unit	6
Agriculture	24
Destination of agriculture production	9
Pasture and uncultivated land	2
Forest utilization	15
Destination of wood production	6
Destination of non-wood production	2
Animals' breeding and exploitation	37
Destination of livestock production	3
Verification questions	5
Tractors, vehicles and machinery	4
Credit, insurance, supports and savings	7
Organization for the unit of production and labor management	5
Producers' organization	5
Technical training and assistance	6
Activity and main problems	6
Socio-demographic characteristics of the producer	12
Identification data of the producer	6

Source: INEGI (2017).

Results

Overlaps and differences between the SAFA Smallholder App dimensions and those of CAGF-2007 are depicted in Figure 4.6.4. The largest crossover (47%) exists between the SAFA's dimension of Environmental Integrity and CAGF-2007, as seventeen questions of the census questionnaire were found to be similar to questions in the SAFA Smallholder App. In decreasing order, there was also an overlap of 33% with the dimension of Economic Resilience, 18% with the dimension of Good Governance and 7% with the dimension of Social Well-being. The following sections offer a detailed description of the results obtained from the comparison of the CAGF-2007 questionnaire and SAFA's themes, indicators and questions.

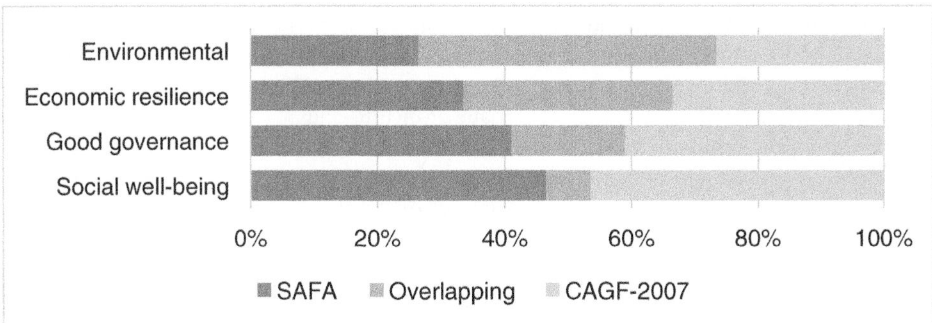

Figure 4.6.4 Overlap between SAFA and CAGF-2007

Source: Authors.

Good governance

SAFA describes governance as the process of making and implementing decisions related to social, economic and environmental dimensions (FAO, 2014a). For assessment of Good Governance, the SAFA Smallholder App considers themes and indicators as depicted in Table 4.6.2.

Overall, CAGF-2007 questions relate to only two of the five themes of *Good Governance*; these are *Participation* and *Rule of Law*. *Participation*'s goal is that all stakeholders affected by enterprises' activities are identified and part of the decision-making process related to activities impacting their lives and the environment (FAO, 2015). *Participation* is evaluated according to three questions related to *Organizational Membership, Value Membership* and *Conflict Resolution*. CAGF-2007 only evaluates *Organizational Membership* with question CQ127, which investigates whether the producer belongs to an organization. *Rule of Law*'s goal is to ensure that the enterprise is committed to fairness, legitimacy and protection of the rule of law (FAO, 2015). This is evaluated based on three questions related to *Tenure Security, Tenure Constraints* and *Compliance*. Of these questions, only SQ96: *Tenure Security* has some overlap with CAGF-2007. SQ96 investigates whether the smallholder feels secure with his tenure, whereas CAGF-2007 investigates the matter in a different way; in this, CQ139 provides a list with the most common problems affecting their agricultural activities and asks them to check those who apply to them. One of the problems listed is 'disputes over land'.

Corporate Ethics' goal is that enterprises have publicly available sustainability objectives, as well as effective means for implementation and validation (FAO, 2015). This theme is evaluated based on the indicator *Mission Explicitness* in the SAFA Smallholder App and is not considered in CAGF-2007. In the same way, *Accountability*, which is evaluated based on whether enterprises keep accurate records of their production processes, is not investigated in CAGF-2007. Lastly, the theme *Holistic Management* is assessed based on whether the enterprise has a plan to minimize risk and improve its sustainable management. This is not evaluated through the CAGF-2007 questionnaire.

Table 4.6.2 Good governance themes, indicators, and questions vs CAGF-2007 questions

Themes	*Indicators*	*Topic*	*SAFA questions*	*CAGF-2007 questions*
Corporate ethics	Mission explicitness	Farm values	SQ1	None
Accountability	Accountability	Accuracy of records	SQ2	None
Participation	Participation	Organizational membership	SQ3	CQ127
		Value of membership	SQ4	None
	Conflict resolution	Conflict resolution	SQ5	None
Rule of law	Tenure rights	Tenure security	SQ95	CQ139
		Tenure constraints	SQ96	None
	Legitimacy	Compliance	SQ32	None
Holistic management	Sustainability management plan	Management plan	SQ6	None
		Plan success	SQ7	None
		Elements of plan	SQ8	None

Source: Authors.

Environmental integrity

The dimension *Environmental Integrity* relates to the protection of Earth's life support systems essential for human survival (FAO, 2014a). This overarching dimension of SAFA is assessed based on the following themes: *Atmosphere, Water, Land, Biodiversity, Materials and Energy* and *Animal Welfare. Environmental Integrity* is the dimension that shows the largest overlap with CAGF-2007, as 47% of its indicators are also evaluated in CAGF-2007 (see Table 4.6.3). Overall, five themes of *Environmental Integrity* are evaluated in CAGF-2007 to different extents, while one theme, *Materials and Energy*, is not addressed.

Atmosphere's goal is that enterprises' activities should not have a negative impact on the health of ecosystems, plants, animals or humans, through the excessive emission of greenhouse gases (GHG) and air pollution (FAO, 2015). For the assessment of this theme, the SAFA Smallholder App focuses on two main indicators: *GHG Mitigation Practices* and *Air Pollution Prevention*. Three of six questions related to *GHG Mitigation Practices* are investigated in CAGF-2007: *Tillage Method, Ruminant Production* and *Fertilizer Type*, whereas CAGF-2007 does not collect information regarding *Tree Coverage, Change in Tree Cover* and *Manure Management. Air Pollution Prevention* is evaluated based on two questions related to *Indoor Air Pollution* and *Burning Fields*. CAGF-2007 only addresses issues related to *Burning Fields*.

Water's goal is that enterprises' activities do not contaminate water, which could have an impact on the health of humans, plants and animals (FAO, 2015). This theme evaluates two indicators, *Water Conservation* and *Water Pollution Prevention Practices*, based on five questions related to *Water Use Reduction, Irrigation, Type of Irrigation, Use of Synthetic Pesticides* and *Water Pollution*. CAGF-2007 partially addresses *Water*'s two indicators as it collects data regarding *Irrigation, Type of Irrigation and Use of Synthetic Pesticides*. On the other hand, it does not investigate *Water Use Reduction* or *Water Pollution*.

Land's goal is that no land is lost and soil fertility is preserved and enhanced (FAO, 2015). This theme is evaluated based on two indicators: *Soil Improvement Practices* and *Land Conservation and Rehabilitation Practices*. This theme is addressed more comprehensively in CAGF-2007 as four of the five questions that are used to evaluate this theme are also included in CAGF-2007's questionnaire. Only *Soil Management* is not investigated in CAGF-2007.

Biodiversity's goal is that enterprises ensure conservation of all forms of biodiversity in all areas under agricultural activities (FAO, 2015). This theme is evaluated based on three indicators: *Ecosystem Diversity, Species Conservation Practices* and *Saving Seeds and Breeds*. All three indicators are addressed in CAGF-2007 although it does not investigate topics related to species conservation or sourcing seeds and breeds. Regarding the topic *Locally Adapted Varieties*, CAGF-2007 investigates a related issue by asking producers if they use improved or genetically modified seeds.

Materials and Energy's goal is to minimize damage to ecosystems through efficient use of non-renewable material and energy, recycling and safe disposal (FAO, 2015). The following indicators are assessed in this theme: *Nutrient Balance, Renewable and Recycled Materials, Energy Use* and *Food Loss and Waste Reduction*. None of these indicators or topics related to them is assessed in CAGF-2007.

Animal welfare's goal is that animals are kept in such conditions that they are free from disease and distress (FAO, 2015). This theme is evaluated through the following indicators: *Access to Veterinary Care, Livestock Disease* and *Animal Well-Being. Animal Well-Being* is thoroughly investigated by CAGF-2007 through questions related to

Table 4.6.3 Environmental integrity themes, indicators, and questions vs CAGF-2007 questions

Theme	*Indicators*	*Topic*	*SAFA questions*	*CAGF-2007 questions*
Atmosphere	GHG mitigation practices	Tree coverage	SQ33	None
		Change in tree cover	SQ34	None
		Tillage method	SQ36	CQ21, CQ22
		Ruminant production	SQ37	CQ71
		Manure management	SQ38	None
		Fertilizer type	SQ41	CQ23
	Air pollution prevention practices	Indoor air pollution	SQ39	None
		Burning fields	SQ40	CQ23
Water	Water conservation practices	Water use reduction	SQ55	None
		Irrigation	SQ56	CQ17
		Type of irrigation	SQ57	CQ18
	Water pollution prevention practices	Synthetic pesticides	SQ45	CQ23
		Water pollution	SQ58	None
Land	Soil improvement practices	Fertilizer type	SQ41	CQ23
		Soil fertility	SQ42	CQ23
	Land conservation and rehabilitation practices	Tillage method	SQ36	CQ21, CQ22
		Soil management	SQ44	None
		Land use and land cover change	SQ49	CQ40
Biodiversity	Ecosystem diversity	Land use and land cover change	SQ49	CQ40
	Species conservation practices	Burning fields	SQ40	CQ23
		Species conservation	SQ50	None
		Crops disease management	SQ51	CQ23
		Diversity of production	SQ52	CQ8, CQ10, CQ12, CQ27, CQ30
	Saving seeds and breeds	Locally adapted varieties	SQ53	CQ23
		Sourcing seeds and breeds	SQ54	None
Materials and energy	Nutrient balance	Fertilizer application	SQ43	None
	Renewable and recycled materials	Biomass management	SQ59	None
		Materials recycling	SQ60	None
	Energy use	Energy efficiency	SQ61	None
		Renewable energy source	SQ62	None
		Renewable energy type	SQ63	None
	Food loss and waste reduction	Pre- and post-harvest food losses	SQ64	None
		Food loss reduction	SQ65	None
Animal welfare	Animal health and welfare	Access to veterinary care	SQ66	None
		Livestock disease	SQ67	None
		Animal well-being	SQ68	CQ71, CQ72, CQ73, CQ79, CQ80, CQ86, CQ87, CQ92, CQ96

Source: Authors.

methods of farming husbandry, breeding technology, application of vaccines, balanced feed, deworming, genetic improvement techniques, farming equipment and technology. *Access to Veterinary Care* and *Livestock Disease* are not addressed in CAGF-2007 with precision.

Economic resilience

Economic Resilience relates to the ability of enterprises to pay all their debts, generate positive cash flow and set up buffer mechanisms to cope with external shocks (FAO, 2014a). This is evaluated based on the following themes: *Investment, Vulnerability, Product Quality and Information* and *Local Economy*. All four themes of *Economic Resilience* are partially evaluated in CAGF-2007. Overall, an overlap of 33% was identified between the SAFA Smallholder App and CAGF-2007's questionnaires (see Table 4.6.4).

Investment's goal is that enterprises improve their sustainability performance and the sustainable development at all levels, through investments (FAO, 2015). This theme evaluates the following indicators: *Community Investment* and *Profitability*. *Community Investment* is not addressed by CAGF-2007. On the other hand, only one aspect of *Profitability*, commercial production, is evaluated in CAGF-2007, and it does not investigate issues related to revenue knowledge, labor cost, production cost, animal cost or positive revenues.

Vulnerability's goal is that enterprises' production, supply and marketing are resilient in the face of environmental, economic and social change (FAO, 2015). *Vulnerability*'s four indicators are addressed in CAGF-2007 even though some are investigated to a greater extent. For instance, the two indicators related to *Product Diversification* are comprehensively addressed in CAGF-2007. *Stability of Market* is investigated in terms of *Buyers' Diversification* (i.e. range and number of buyers), but CAGF-2007 does not explore the nature of relationships with buyers or market choice. *Liquidity* is investigated in CAGF-2007 in terms of loan sources and savings. However, it does not investigate whether enterprises actually received a loan and, if so, the amount they received. Regarding *Safety Nets*, CAGF-2007 investigates whether enterprises have access to insurance but does not explore issues related to risk management or on-farm measures to reduce environmental risks.

Product Quality and Information's goal is to avoid any produce contamination and ensure nutritional quality and traceability (FAO, 2015). This theme is assessed based on the following indicators: *Food Quality, Certified Products* and *Hazardous Pesticides*. Surprisingly, indicators *Food Quality* and *Certified Products* are not addressed in CAGF-2007. Furthermore, CAGF-2007 only investigates one of the four indicators of *Hazardous Pesticides*, which is *Crop Disease*.

Local Economy's goal is that enterprises contribute to sustainable local value creation (FAO, 2015). This theme is evaluated based on the indicator *Regional Workforce* and is also addressed in the CAGF-2007 questionnaire.

Social well-being

Social Well-Being relates to the contribution of enterprises towards the fulfillment of human needs/rights (FAO, 2014a). This overarching dimension is evaluated based on indicators related to six main themes: *Decent Livelihood, Fair Trading Practices, Labor Rights, Equity, Human Health and Safety* and *Cultural Diversity* (see Table 4.6.5). *Social Well-Being*

Table 4.6.4 Economic resilience themes, indicators, and questions vs CAGF-2007 questions

Themes	*Indicators*	*Topic*	*SAFA questions*	*CAGF-2007 questions*
Investment	Community investment	Participation	SQ97	None
	Profitability	Commercial production	SQ9	CQ27, CQ30, CQ35, CQ57, CQ62, CQ79, CQ81, CQ88, CQ93, CQ95, CQ97, CQ99, CQ100 and CQ102
		Revenue knowledge	SQ10	None
		Labor cost	SQ11	None
		Production cost	SQ12	None
		Animal cost	SQ13	None
		Positive revenues	SQ14	None
Vulnerability	Product diversification	Products and services on sale	SQ15	CQ8, CQ10, CQ12, CQ27, CQ30, CQ58, CQ59 and CQ62
		Added-value	SQ16	CQ24, CQ37 and CQ60
	Stability of market	Buyers' diversification	SQ17	CQ35, CQ58 and CQ102
		Relationships	SQ18	None
		Market choice	SQ19	None
	Liquidity	Loan source	SQ22	CQ114
		Loan received	SQ23	None
		Savings	SQ24	CQ119
	Safety nets	Insurance	SQ25	CQ117
		Risk management	SQ26	None
		On-farm Measures	SQ27	None
Product quality and information	Food quality	Product quality	SQ28	None
		Assessment	SQ29	None
	Certified products	Certification	SQ30	None
		Certified ratio	SQ31	None
	Hazardous pesticides	Crop disease	SQ45	CQ23 and CQ52
		Pesticides	SQ46	None
		Label	SQ47	None
		Mixing	SQ48	None
Local economy	Regional force	Workforce	SQ89	CQ123

Source: Authors.

is not investigated to a great extent in CAGF-2007 as only two of the twenty-seven questions (7%) related to this dimension overlap with questions in CAGF-2007.

The overlap is observed among CAGF-2007 and themes *Decent Livelihood* and *Human Health and Safety*. Nevertheless, these themes are not evaluated in a comprehensive way, as only some of the indicators of such themes are evaluated via the CAGF-2007

Table 4.6.5 Social well-being themes, indicators, and questions vs CAGF-2007 questions

Theme	*Indicators*	*Topic*	*SAFA questions*	*CAGF-2007 questions*
Decent livelihood	Quality of life	Quality of life	SQ98	None
	Wage level	Producer's living wage	SQ99	None
		Worker's living wage	SQ100	None
	Capacity development	Training	SQ77	CQ23, CQ131, CQ135, CQ136
Fair trading practices	Fair pricing	Understanding buyer prices	SQ20	None
		Knowledge of market prices	SQ21	None
Labor rights	Employment relations	Equal pay	SQ79	None
	Freedom of association and right to bargaining	Freedom to associate and bargain	SQ80	None
	Forced labor	Forced labor	SQ81	None
	Child labor	School attendance	SQ82	None
Equity	Non-discrimination	Non-discrimination	SQ83	None
	Gender equality	Men's decisions	SQ85	None
		Women's decisions	SQ86	None
		Girls' and boys' education	SQ87	None
		Men's and women's training	SQ88	None
Human health and safety	Workplace and health provisions	Distance of medical care	SQ69	None
		Affordability of medical care	SQ70	None
		Distance of safe drinking water	SQ71	None
		Access to sufficient and adequate water	SQ72	CQ154
		Pesticide application	SQ73	None
		Pesticide protective gear	SQ74	None
		Farm injuries	SQ75	None
		Risk avoidance	SQ76	None
Cultural diversity	Food sovereignty	Right to choose production type	SQ90	None
		Access to culturally appropriate food	SQ91	None
		Meal availability	SQ92	None
	Indigenous knowledge	Link with indigenous community	SQ94	None

Source: Authors.

questionnaire. *Decent Livelihood*'s goal is that enterprises increase the livelihood security of their personnel and their local community (FAO, 2015). This is evaluated based on four questions related to *Quality of Life, Producer's Living Wage, Worker's Living Wage* and *Training*. Only *Training* is evaluated in CAGF-2007 through four questions that investigate the type of training received by producers. *Human Health and Safety*'s goal is that work environments are safe, hygienic and healthy (FAO, 2015). This theme is assessed based on eight questions related to access to and affordability of medical care, access to safe drinking water, pesticide application and protective gear, farm injuries and risk avoidance. Of these topics, CAGF-2007 only investigates whether producers have access to tap water in their homes, which relates to SQ74 (see Table 4.6.5).

Fair Trading Practices' goal is that sustainable trading practices provide suppliers and buyers with prices that reflect the true cost of the entire production processes (FAO, 2015). This theme is evaluated based on two questions related to *Understanding Buyer Prices* and *Knowledge of Market Prices*. None of these topics is evaluated in CAGF-2007. The theme *Labor Rights*' goal is that enterprises provide employment that is compliant with national law and international agreements (FAO, 2015). This theme is evaluated based on four indicators: *Employment Relations, Freedom of Association and Right to Bargaining, Forced Labor* and *Child Labor*. CAGF-2007 partially evaluates the indicator *Child Labor* as it only investigates whether producers employ children but does not explore whether they get the opportunity to attend school. All other indicators related to *Labor Rights* are not evaluated though CAGF-2007.

Equity's goal is that enterprises have non-discrimination policies and support vulnerable groups (FAO, 2015). For the assessment of this theme, SAFA investigates the indicators *Non-Discrimination* and *Gender Equality* through four questions, whereas CAGF-2007 does not addresses these issues. Similarly, *Cultural Diversity*, related to respecting food sovereignty and cultural knowledge, is not explored through the CAGF-2007 questionnaire.

Discussion and conclusions

Comparisons from the previous section confirm that the SAFA Smallholder App cannot be applied in Mexican rural enterprises by using only information from CAGF-2007 as it does not comprehensively cover all dimensions, themes and indicators. Overall, thirteen of the twenty-one themes (62%) of the SAFA Smallholder App are addressed in CAGF-2007. The eight themes that are not investigated in CAGF-2007 relate mainly to the *Good Governance* and *Social Well-being* dimensions. This indicates that CAGF-2007 has a special focus on the environmental and economic dimensions of sustainability. Furthermore, the depth of analysis of the twenty-one themes varies widely and is limited in some instances, as 52% of the indicators used to evaluate SAFA's themes are not addressed in the CAGF-2007 questionnaire. Even though there are limitations in scope, the CAGF-2007 questionnaire and the SAFA Smallholder App show an overall overlap of 48% in their indicators, which suggests that publicly available data can be an important source for sustainability assessment. Furthermore, as expected by FAO (2014a), the use of data collected through the CAGF-2007 questionnaire, and possibly future versions of the rural census, could expedite the adoption of SAFA by rural enterprises.

To obtain a more comprehensive and comparable sustainable development assessment through the CAGF-2007 questionnaire, we identified some general recommendations:

- *Good Governance* shows a very limited depth of analysis and is virtually overlooked by CAGF-2007. Thus, an effort is needed to incorporate more indicators related to corporate ethics, accountability, rule of law and holistic management. The importance of evaluating this overarching dimension relies on the notion that enterprises that ignore sustainability principles will likely not achieve a sustainable operation in the long run (FAO, 2014a).

- *Social Well-Being* is the dimension that shows the smallest overlap with CAGF-2007 (7%). This is not surprising, as findings from Schader et al. (2014) showed that only 54% of the thirty-five sustainability approaches they compared address the social dimension of sustainability. SAFA (FAO, 2014a) recognizes the importance of this dimension as it is closely related to the satisfaction of basic human needs and protection of human rights. Therefore, a bigger effort is required for the assessment of decent livelihoods, fair trading prices, labor rights, equity, human health and cultural diversity.
- One-third of the *Economic Resilience*'s indicators are addressed in CAGF-2007. Even though all main themes of this dimension are evaluated to some extent, some gaps where identified. For instance, CAGF-2007 evaluates agricultural production but not productivity. CAGF-2007 does not collect information regarding food quality or certified products. Concerning hazardous pesticides, CAGF-2007 only evaluates the use of synthetic pesticides but not safe practices. Similarly, safety nets and stability of markets are only partially assessed in CAGF-2007.
- *Environmental Integrity* shows the largest crossover with CAGF-2007, with only one theme, *Materials and Energy*, not being evaluated at all. Further efforts could be made to evaluate topics such as: species conservation, water pollution, nutrient balance, renewable and recycled materials, energy use, food loss and waste reduction, and animal health.

In conclusion, with respect to public data, although it currently does not seem to be able to fully support entrepreneurs in assessing sustainability in their practices, it may become an important source in informing them about how to develop sustainable businesses. The Mexican case illustrates that to achieve this, current governmental ways of collecting data on entrepreneurial activities, like the CAGF-2007 questionnaire, require adjustments. One practical way, suggested in this chapter, involves introducing additional questions developed by sustainability assessment tools, such as SAFA.

This study recommends the use of the SAFA framework because it was developed as a set of guidelines that would provide practical orientation to enterprises striving to achieve sustainable practices. The main attributes of SAFA are (a) its universal application, (b) its capability to support benchmarking practices and (c) its simplicity to constitute an informative tool that is simultaneously effective at the individual and the collective level. In this context, it is important to notice that SAFA is a generalizable procedure and, in this sense, it may be considered a knowledge-building tool. Such knowledge is not limited to solely assisting policy-makers to measure a nation's progress towards the fulfillment of SDG 2. It is also able to better inform entrepreneurs and their collectives (for example, marketing associations, supply chains or unions) about the sustainability level achieved in their current practices. This is fundamental to provide a sense of future direction for rural entrepreneurs striving towards more sustainable practices.

Notes

1 The complete SAFA smallholders App questionnaire can be accessed on this link: www.fao.org/fileadmin/user_upload/suistainability/docs/SAFASmallApp_Manual-final.pdf.

2 The CAGF-2007 questionnaire can be accessed in the following link: www.inegi.org.mx/est/contenidos/proyectos/agro/ca2007/resultados_agricola/doc/cuestionario_viii_censo_agricola_ganadero_y_forestal.pdf.

References

Adams, W.M. (2006) *The Future of Sustainability Re-thinking Environment and Development in the Twenty-first Century*. Available from: http://cmsdata.iucn.org/downloads/iucn_future_of_sus tanability.pdf (accessed 22 August 2017).

Alrøe, H.F., Moller, H., Læssøe, J. and Noe, E. (2016) Opportunities and challenges for multicriteria assessment of food system sustainability. *Ecology and Society*, 21(1), 38–45.

Alrøe, H.F. and Noe, E. (2016) Sustainability assessment and complementarity. *Ecology and Society*, 21(1), 30. Available from: http://dx.doi.org/10.5751/ES-08220-210130 (accessed 15 August 2018).

Carlsson, L., Callaghan, E., Morley, A. and Broman, G. (2017) Food system sustainability across scales: A proposed local-to-global approach to community planning and assessment. *Sustainability*, 9, 1061–1074.

De Olde, E.M., Oudshoorna, F.W., Sørensena, C.A.G., Bokkersc, E.A.M. and De Boer, I.J.M. (2016) Assessing sustainability at farm-level: Lessons learned from a comparison of tools in practice. *Ecological Indicators*, 66, 391–404.

De Ridder, W., Turnpenny, J., Nilsson, M. and Von Raggamby, A. (2007) A framework for tool selection and use in integrated assessment for sustainable development. *Journal of Environmental Assessment Policy and Management*, 9(4), 423–441.

Elkington, J. (1997/1999) *Cannibals with Forks: The Triple Bottom Line of 21st Century Business*. Oxford, UK: Capstone Publishing Ltd.

FAO (2014a) *SAFA Guidelines Version 3.0, Rome*. Available from: www.fao.org/3/a-i3957e.pdf (accessed 25 June 2017).

FAO (2014b) *Gestión Pública con base en resultados: Herramientas para el diseño e instrumentación de programas públicos de desarrollo rural mediante el enfoque del ciclo del proyecto*. Santiago, Chile. Available from: www.fao.org/3/a-i4013s.pdf (accessed 10 July 2017).

FAO (2015) *SAFA smallholders APP version, Rome*. Available from: www.fao.org/fileadmin/user_upload/suistainability/docs/SAFASmallApp_Manual-final.pdf (accessed 26 June 2017).

Foley, J.A., Ramankutty, N., Brauman, K.A., Cassidy, E.S., Gerber, J.S., Johnston, M., Mueller, N.D., O'Connell, C., Ray, D.K. and West, P.C. (2011) Solutions for a cultivated planet. *Nature*, 478, 337–342.

Giddings, B., Hopwood, B. and O'Brien, G. (2002) Environment, economy and society: Fitting them together into sustainable development. *Sustainable Development*, 10, 187–196.

Goyder, J. (1986) Surveys on surveys: Limitations and potentialities. *Public Opinion Quarterly*, 50(1), 27–41.

Hingley, M.K. (2005) Power imbalanced relationships: Cases from UK fresh food supply. *International Journal of Retail and Distribution Management*, 33(8), 551–564.

Hopwood, B., Mellor, M. and O'Brien, G. (2005) Sustainable development: Mapping different approaches. *Sustainable Development*, 13, 38–52.

Hörisch, J. (2016) Entrepreneurship as facilitator for sustainable development? Editorial for the Special Issue *Advances in Sustainable Entrepreneurship*". *Administrative Sciences*, 6(1), 4. Available from: https://doi.org/10.3390/admsci6010004 (accessed 15 August 2018).

Hubeau, M., Marchand, F., Coteur, I., Mondelaers, K., Debruyne, L. and Van Huylenbroeck, G. (2017) A new agri-food systems sustainability approach to identify transformation pathways towards sustainability. *Ecological Economics*, 131, 52–63.

INEGI (2017) *Censo Agropecuario 2007*. Presentación. Instituto Nacional de Estadística y Geografía. (online) Available from www.inegi.org.mx/est/contenidos/proyectos/agro/ca2007/resulta dos_agricola/presentacion.aspx?p=21 (accessed 10 August 2017).

Juma, N.A., James, C.D. and Kwesiga, E. (2017) Sustainable entrepreneurship in Sub-Saharan Africa: The collaborative multi-system model. *Journal of Small Business & Entrepreneurship*, 29(3), 211–235.

Koe, W., Omar, R. and Sa'ari, J.R. (2015) Factors influencing propensity to sustainable entrepreneurship of SMEs in Malaysia. *Procedia: Social and Behavioral Sciences*, 172, 570–577.

Peano,C., Tecco, N., Dansero, E., Girgenti, V. and Sottile, F. (2015) Evaluating the sustainability in complex agri-food systems: The SAEMETH Framework. *Sustainability*, 7, 6721–6741.

Richomme-Huet, K. and De Freyman, J. (2011) What sustainable entrepreneurship looks like: An exploratory study from a student perspective. In: A. Lundström, C. Zhou, Y. von Friedrichs and E. Sundin (eds.) *Social Entrepreneurship Leveraging Economic, Political, and Cultural Dimensions*. Berlin: Springer, 155–178.

Sachs, J., Schmidt-Traub, G., Kroll, C., Durand-Delacre, D. and Teksoz, K. (2017) *SDG Index and Dashboards Report 2017*. New York: Bertelsmann Stiftung and Sustainable Development Solutions Network (SDSN).

Schader, C., Grenz, J., Meier, M.S. and Stolze, M. (2014) Scope and precision of sustainability assessment approaches to food systems. *Ecology and Society*, 19(3), 42. Available from: http://dx.doi.org/10.5751/ES-06866-190342 (accessed 15 August 2018).

Schaltegger, S. and Wagner, T. (2008) Types of sustainable entrepreneurship and conditions for sustainability innovation: From the administration of a technical challenge to the management of an entrepreneurial opportunity. In: R. Wüstenhagen, J. Hamschmidt, S. Sharma and M. Starik (eds.) *Sustainable Innovation and Entrepreneurship*. Cheltenham, UK: Edward Elgar, 27–48.

Singh, R.K., Murty, H.R., Gupta, S.K. and Dikshit, A.K. (2009) An overview of sustainability assessment methodologies. *Ecological Indicators*, 9(2) 189–212.

Tendall, D.M., Joerin, J., Kopainsky, B., Edwards, P., Shreck, A., Le, Q.B., Kruetli, P., Grant, M. and Six, J. (2015) Food system resilience: Defining the concept. *Global Food Security*, 6, 17–23.

Triste, L., Marchand, F., Debruyne, L., Meul, M. and Lauwers, L. (2014) Reflection on the development process of a sustainability assessment tool: Learning from a Flemish case. *Ecology and Society*, 19(3), 47. Available from: http://dx.doi.org/10.5751/ES-06789-190347 (accessed 15 August 2018).

United Nations (1987) *Our Common Future*. Available from: www.un-documents.net/our-common-future.pdf (accessed 4 June 2017).

United Nations (2005) Resolution adopted by the General Assembly. Available from: http://data.unaids.org/topics/universalaccess/worldsummitoutcome_resolution_24oct2005_en.pdf (accessed 12 July 2017).

United Nations (2017) Resolution adopted by the General Assembly on 6 July 2017. Available from: https://undocs.org/A/RES/71/313 (accessed 12 July 2017).

Vilalta-Perdomo, E.L., Michel-Villarreal, R. and Corliss, J. (2017) On defining "sustainability". An impossible task? In: K. Coperich, H. Nembhard and E. Cudney (eds.) *Proceedings of the 2017 Industrial and Systems Engineering Conference*. Institute for Industrial and Systems Engineering (IISE) Annual Conference and Expo, 20–23 May Pittsburgh, USA. Available from: http://eprints.lincoln.ac.uk/28079/ (accessed 15 August 2017).

Index

Locators in **bold** refer to tables and those in *italics* to figures.